Complete Curriculum

Grade 6

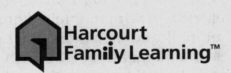

Harcourt Family Learning™

© 2006 by Flash Kids
Adapted from *Steck-Vaughn Spelling: Linking Words to Meaning, Level 6* by John R. Pescosolido;
© 2002 by Harcourt Achieve • Adapted from *Steck-Vaughn Spelling: Linking Words to Meaning, Level 6* by John R. Pescosolido;
© 2002 by Harcourt Achieve. • Adapted from Steck-Vaughn Working with Numbers, Level F; © 2001
by Harcourt Achieve. • Adapted from *Language Arts, Grade 6*; © 2003 by Harcourt Achieve. • Adapted from
Experiences with Writing Styles Grade 6; © 1998 by Steck-Vaughn Company and *Writing Skills Grade 6*; © 2003
by Steck-Vaughn Company. • Adapted from *Test Best for Test Prep, Level F*; © 1999 by Harcourt Achieve.
Licensed under special arrangement with Harcourt Achieve.

For more information, please visit *www.flashkidsbooks.com*
Please submit all inquiries to FlashKids@bn.com

ISBN: 978-1-4114-9879-2

Printed and bound in Canada

Lot #:
17 19 20 18 16
05/15

Flash Kids
A Division of Barnes & Noble
122 Fifth Avenue
New York, NY 10011

Dear Parent,

Beginning a new grade is a milestone for your child, and each new subject is bound to present some challenges that may require some attention out of the classroom. With this comprehensive sixth-grade book at hand, you and your child can work together on any skill that he or she is finding difficult to master.
Here to help are hundreds of fun, colorful pages for learning and practicing reading, spelling, math, language arts, writing, and test preparation.

In the reading section, the wide range of high-interest stories will hold your child's attention and help develop his or her proficiency in reading. Each of the six units focuses on a different reading comprehension skill: finding facts, detecting a sequence, learning new vocabulary through context, identifying the main idea, drawing conclusions, and making inferences. Mastering these skills will ensure that your child has the necessary tools for a lifetime love of reading.

Lessons in the spelling section present sixth-grade words in lists grouped by vowel sound, suffix, or related forms, like plurals and contractions. This order will clearly show your child the different ways that similar sounds can be spelled. Your child will learn to sort words, recognize definitions, synonyms, and base words, as well as use capitalization and punctuation. Each lesson also features a short passage containing spelling and grammar mistakes that your child will proofread and correct.

The math section starts with basics like place value and number comparison, followed by addition and subtraction with multiple digits and regrouping. Next your child is introduced to multiplication, division, and simple fractions, as well as units reviewing geometry, time, and measurement. Each section begins with clear examples that illustrate new skills, and then practice drills, problem-solving lessons, and unit reviews encourage your child to master each new technique.

More than 100 lessons in the language arts section provide clear examples of and exercises in language skills such as parts of speech, sentences, mechanics, vocabulary and usage, writing, and research skills. Grammar lessons range from using nouns and verbs to constructing better sentences. Writing exercises include the friendly letter and the book report. These skills will help your child improve his or her communication abilities, excel in all academic areas, and increase his or her scores on standardized tests.

Each of the six units in the writing section focuses on a unique type of writing: personal narrative, informative writing, descriptive writing, opinion and comparative writing, story, and short report. The first half of each unit reinforces writing aspects such as putting ideas in a sequence and using descriptive details, in addition to providing fun, inspirational writing ideas for your child to explore alone or with a friend. In the second half of each unit, your child will read a practice paragraph, analyze it, prepare a writing plan for his or her own paper or paragraph, and then write and revise.

Lastly, the test prep section employs your child's knowledge in reading, math, and language to the basic standardized test formats that your child will encounter throughout his or her school career. Each unit in the first half of this section teaches specific test strategies for areas such as word study skills, reading comprehension, and mathematics. The second half of the section allows your child to apply these test-taking skills in a realistic testing environment. By simulating the experience of taking standardized tests, these practice tests can lessen feelings of intimidation during school tests.

As your child works through the test prep section, help him or her keep in mind these four important principles of test-taking:

1. *Using Time Wisely*

All standardized tests are timed, so your child should learn to work rapidly but comfortably. He or she should not spend too much time on any one question, and mark items to return to if possible. Use any remaining time to review answers. Most importantly, use a watch to keep on track!

2. *Avoiding Errors*

When choosing the correct answers on standardized tests, your child should pay careful attention to directions, determine what is being asked, and mark answers in the appropriate place. He or she should then check all answers and not make stray marks on the answer sheet.

3. *Reasoning*

To think logically toward each answer, your child should read the entire question or passage and all the answer choices before answering a question. It may be helpful to restate questions or answer choices in his or her own words.

4. *Guessing*

When the correct answer is not clear right away, your child should eliminate answers that he or she knows are incorrect. If that is not possible, skip the question. Then your child should compare the remaining answers, restate the question, and then choose the answer that seems most correct.

An answer key at the back of this workbook allows you and your child to check his or her work in any of the subject sections. Remember to give praise and support for each effort. Also, learning at home can be accomplished at any moment—you can ask your child to read aloud to you, write grocery lists, keep a journal, or measure the ingredients for a recipe. Use your imagination! With help from you and this workbook, your child is well on the way to completing the sixth grade with flying colors!

TABLE OF CONTENTS

Reading Skills

Spelling Skills

Math Skills

Language Arts

Writing Skills

Test Prep

Answer Key

Reading
Skills

unit 1

What Are Facts?

Facts are sometimes called details. They are small pieces of information. Facts can appear in true stories, such as those in the newspaper. They can also appear in legends and other stories that people make up.

How to Read for Facts

You can find facts by asking yourself questions. Ask *who*, and your answer will be a fact about a person. Ask *what*, and your answer will be a fact about a thing. Ask *where*, and your answer will be a fact about a place. Ask *when*, and your answer will be a fact about a time. Ask *how many* or *how much*, and your answer will be a fact about a number or an amount.

Try It!

Read this story and look for facts as you read. Ask yourself *when* and *who*.

The First Airplane Flight

Wilbur and Orville Wright read everything they could find about flying machines. They began building their own airplane in 1900. They carefully tested every part of the airplane. Finally on a cold, windy day in December 1903, they flew their plane for the first time. Orville was the pilot as the plane lifted into the air. It stayed in the air for only 12 seconds and traveled just 120 feet the first time. After three more tries that same day, the plane's longest trip was almost a full minute and more than 850 feet.

Did you find these facts when you read the paragraph? Write the facts on the lines below.

◆ When did the Wrights fly for the first time?

Fact: _December 1903_

◆ Who was the pilot?

Fact: _Orville_

7/13

Practice Finding Facts

Below are some practice questions. The first two are already answered. Answer the third one on your own.

 1. How long was the plane's longest trip?
    A. 120 feet   **C.** 850 feet
    B. 85 feet   **D.** 12 feet

Look at the question and answers again. *How long* is asking for a number. There are many numbers in the paragraph, but you are looking for one that describes the plane's longest trip. Read the paragraph until you find the words *longest trip.* You should find this sentence: "After three more tries that same day, the plane's longest trip was almost a full minute and more than 850 feet." So **C** is the correct answer. Answer **A** is also a fact from the story, but it describes the first trip, not the longest one.

 2. The Wright brothers first flew their plane in
    A. summer   **C.** fall
    B. spring   **D.** winter

Look at the question. The first answer you might think of is a place, but the possible answers are seasons. Search the story for words about seasons or time of year. You should find this sentence: "Finally on a cold, windy day in December 1903, they flew their plane for the first time." The correct answer is *winter.* The answer uses different words, but the fact is the same.

Now it's your turn to practice. Answer the next question by writing the letter of the correct answer on the line.

3. The Wrights first started working on their airplane in
    A. 1903   **C.** 1908
    B. 1900   **D.** 1809

7|13

Read each story. After each story you will answer questions about the facts in the story. Remember, a fact is something that you know is true.

Scarecrows Then and Now

Birds have always been a problem for farmers. They like to eat the seeds in farmers' fields. As soon as a farmer plants seeds, the birds arrive for dinner. Often these birds are crows.

Farmers try to get rid of their unwanted visitors by making scarecrows. A scarecrow is supposed to scare away crows and other birds. The first scarecrows were made hundreds of years ago. They were sticks stuck in the ground with big rags tied to the top. When the wind blew, the rags flapped and frightened the birds.

As time went on, farmers began making better scarecrows. They nailed a second stick across the top of the one in the ground. Now the scarecrows had arms and could wear old shirts. When farmers stuffed the shirts with straw, the scarecrows began to look like real people. Some even had faces.

_____ **1.** Birds like to eat
      A. fields   **C.** rags
      B. seeds   **D.** sticks

_____ **2.** A scarecrow is supposed to scare away
      A. gardens   **C.** birds
      B. seeds   **D.** sticks

_____ **3.** The first scarecrows were made from sticks and
      A. rags   **C.** rugs
      B. plants   **D.** hats

_____ **4.** Later, farmers filled scarecrows with
      A. cotton   **C.** straw
      B. air   **D.** string

_____ **5.** Scarecrows flapped because of the
      A. arms   **C.** birds
      B. noise   **D.** wind

When farmers began using modern machines, they didn't need scarecrows anymore. The new farm machines were big and made a lot of noise. They scared the birds away quite well.

In the 1960s people became interested in folk art such as scarecrows. Suddenly scarecrows were popular again. People wanted them for their yards and vegetable gardens. Even people in cities bought scarecrows for their porches.

Today some artists make scarecrows to sell. They use natural materials such as sticks and straw for the bodies. However, these new scarecrows are often dressed in fancy clothes. Some wear sunglasses, belts, or scarves. Some scarecrows may have beads, flowers, and purses.

_____ **6.** People didn't need scarecrows because they had
    A. clothes   **C.** workers
    B. machines   **D.** crows

_____ **7.** In the 1960s people thought that scarecrows were
    A. folk art   **C.** farm workers
    B. sunglasses   **D.** fine art

_____ **8.** People put scarecrows on porches and in
    A. machines   **C.** yards
    B. cities   **D.** parks

_____ **9.** Today some artists make scarecrows for
    A. sale   **C.** sail
    B. beads   **D.** style

_____ **10.** Scarecrows sometimes have beads, flowers, and
    A. ties   **C.** pins
    B. shoes   **D.** purses

7/13

Merry-Go-Rounds

The organ starts, and its music fills the air. The horses slowly begin to move. Riders hold tightly as their colorful horses go up and down and around and around. These riders are on a carousel. *Carousel* is another word for *merry-go-round*.

Carousels have a long history. In the 1400s soldiers in France liked to play a ball game on horseback. The soldiers had to throw and catch while their horses were moving. The French invented a way to help the soldiers practice for the game.

This invention was the first carousel. It was different from modern carousels. The biggest difference was that the horses were real! They turned the carousel as they moved in a circle. Years later, people began using carousels for fun. By the 1800s carousel horses were no longer real. Carousels were run by motors.

D **1.** *Merry-go-round* is another word for
   A. ferris wheel   **C.** roller coaster
   B. moving horse   **D.** carousel

B **2.** The music for carousels comes from
   A. riders   **C.** pianos
   B. organs   **D.** radios

D **3.** The first carousel was made to help players
   A. fight wars   **C.** ride horses
   B. invent tricks   **D.** practice skills

A **4.** The horses on the first carousels were
   A. real   **C.** painted
   B. wood   **D.** motors

C **5.** The first people to use a carousel were
   A. inventors   **C.** soldiers
   B. sailors   **D.** children

Once there were 10,000 merry-go-rounds in the United States. Most were made in Pennsylvania and New York. Workers carved and painted the carousel horses. Some horses had fine saddles and roses around their necks. Others had a wild look in their shiny glass eyes. No two horses were the same.

Today there are fewer than 300 merry-go-rounds in North America. Some of these rides are now treasured as historic places.

One of the nation's oldest merry-go-rounds is in Oak Bluffs, Massachusetts. This carousel is called the Flying Horses. It was built around 1880. Riders on the Flying Horses can have some extra fun. As the merry-go-round spins, riders try to grab rings from a post on the wall. The person who gets the most rings is the winner. The reward is a free ride.

_____ **6.** No two carousel horses were
      A. bright   **C.** carved
      B. wild   **D.** alike

_____ **7.** One state where carousels were made was
      A. Massachusetts   **C.** France
      B. Pennsylvania   **D.** Oak Bluffs

_____ **8.** Some carousels are now considered to be
      A. too fast   **C.** historic
      B. dangerous   **D.** too small

_____ **9.** One of America's oldest carousels is called the
      A. Oak Bluffs   **C.** Fighting Horses
      B. Flying Horses   **D.** New York

_____ **10.** A free ride on this merry-go-round is given as a
      A. prize   **C.** ring
      B. horse   **D.** win

7/14

How to Win a Prize

There are all kinds of contests. Have you ever heard of the Apple Seed Popping Contest? It's held on the first weekend in October in Lincoln, Nebraska. How does it work? Line up with everybody else. Take a fresh apple, and squeeze it hard in your fist. If your apple seeds pop the farthest, you're a winner!

Do you like food contests? Every August in Fulton, Kentucky, there's a banana contest. If you eat the most bananas within a set time, you win some more bananas. If you like milk, go to Los Angeles, California, in September. Sign up for the Milk Drinking Contest. If you win, you get a ribbon.

In Albany, Oregon, anyone between the ages of 5 and 12 can enter the Bubble Gum Blowing Contest. You'll win some books if you blow the first bubble, the biggest bubble, or the bubble that lasts the longest.

_B_ 1. The Apple Seed Popping Contest is held in
   A. California   C. August
   B. October   D. Albany

_D_ 2. To win the Apple Seed Popping Contest, you must
   A. be under 16   C. pop seeds the farthest
   B. line up the seeds D. squeeze the fresh apple

_C_ 3. The winner of the banana contest gets
   A. a set time   C. more bananas
   B. a ribbon   D. a trip to Fulton

_A_ 4. People who like milk could sign up for a contest in
   A. Los Angeles   C. Oregon
   B. Nebraska   D. Kentucky

_C_ 5. The person who blows the biggest bubble wins
   A. gum   C. books
   B. food   D. bikes

7/14

Some contests require a special animal. In May bring your chicken to the Chicken Flying Meet in Rio Grande, Ohio. Put your chicken on the launchpad. At the signal, give it a little push. If your chicken flies the farthest, you win a cash prize.

People 14 and under can enter the Greasy Pig Scramble in Dothan, Alabama. The pigs are greased with peanut oil. You have to catch the greasy pig and hold on to it until it crosses the finish line. If you win, you get the pig.

If you have a pet crab, you can enter it in the World Championship Crab Race in California. The International Frog Jumping and Racing Contest is held in Louisiana. Winners of both contests get medals. Petaluma, California, holds an Ugly Dog Contest. The winners receive medals and are invited to come back next year for the Ugliest Dog Contest.

_____ **6.** In some contests, you need a pet that is
- **A.** slow
- **B.** prized
- **C.** afraid
- **D.** unusual

_A_ **7.** The Chicken Flying Meet is in
- **A.** Ohio
- **B.** Alabama
- **C.** California
- **D.** Louisiana

_B_ **8.** In the Dothan, Alabama, contest you have to
- **A.** use peanuts
- **B.** hold on
- **C.** count pigs
- **D.** push chickens

_A_ **9.** Louisiana has a special contest for
- **A.** frogs
- **B.** dogs
- **C.** crabs
- **D.** pigs

_____ **10.** The Ugliest Dog Contest is for dogs that
- **A.** are not strange
- **B.** live in Ohio
- **C.** won the year before
- **D.** like to get medals

7/14

Lesson 4

The Birth of an Island

It was a gray November day in 1963. A fishing boat rocked in the Atlantic Ocean off the southern coast of Iceland. Suddenly a great black cloud burst from the water. Loud noises rumbled from the ocean. The ship's captain sent out a radio call. Something very unusual was happening!

In the next three hours, scientists and reporters arrived at the scene. By now the cloud was 12,000 feet high. Huge explosions sent ash, dust, and hot rocks into the air. The watchers could see something just under the water's surface.

By that night a new mountain had pushed itself up from the boiling sea. The mountain continued to rise during the next days. It also grew wider. A fiery island was growing in the Atlantic. It was caused by a volcano in the ocean.

_C_ **1.** The fishing boat was off the coast of
  A. Ireland   **C.** Iceland
  B. Greenland   **D.** November

_A_ **2.** The ship's captain used a
  A. radio   **C.** telephone
  B. light   **D.** surface

_B_ **3.** The explosions sent up ash, dust, and hot
  A. food   **C.** ice
  B. rocks   **D.** fish

_A_ **4.** The mountain grew into
  A. an island   **C.** a valley
  B. a nation   **D.** an iceberg

_B_ **5.** The explosion came from
  A. an island   **C.** an earthquake
  B. a volcano   **D.** a fishing boat

The new island continued to grow for two years. It finally stopped in August of 1965. It was 550 feet high. It was more than 1 mile long and about 6 miles around.

The people of Iceland named the new island Surtsey. This name comes from an old myth. In the story Surtur was a mighty fire giant. People thought that Surtsey was also a giant by the time it stopped growing.

Scientists are very interested in Surtsey. It is the first new island to appear in the North Atlantic in 200 years. Scientists want to learn more about how this happened. They are also studying how plant life begins on a new island. Another thing scientists want to know is how long Surtsey will last. They wonder whether the island will be destroyed by the same volcano that created it.

_____ **6.** The new island became quiet in

       A. 1956   **C.** the old story

       B. 1963   **D.** 1965

_____ **7.** Surtur was a fire giant in an old

       A. tale   **C.** snow

       B. island   **D.** volcano

_____ **8.** In the myth Surtur was

       A. cloudy   **C.** powerful

       B. weak   **D.** peaceful

_____ **9.** Scientists are studying

       A. plant life   **C.** people

       B. dead fish   **D.** animal life

_____ **10.** Scientists also want to know how long Surtsey will

       A. return   **C.** burn

       B. remain   **D.** flood

7/25

How to Box the Gnat

All over the country, many Americans are learning to "dip for the oyster," "box the gnat," and "wring the dishrag." These are special names for different movements in square dances.

A square-dance party may be called by many names. Such a party may be called a hog wrassle, a hoedown, a barndance, or a shindig. All square dances are alike in certain ways. Four couples line up and face each other. A caller chants or sings directions. The dancers shuffle, glide, or run while people clap.

Pioneers in New England started these dances. As people moved westward and southward, new movements were added. In the Midwest, dancers created the "grand right and left." In the far West, cowboys lifted their partners off the ground during "the swing."

_____ **1.** The dance movements have special
      A. squares   **C.** shindigs
      B. names   **D.** boxes

_____ **2.** A hoedown is a kind of
      A. party   **C.** step
      B. sport   **D.** tool

_____ **3.** The caller gives
      A. parties   **C.** squares
      B. directions   **D.** barndances

_____ **4.** Square dancing started in
      A. the Far West   **C.** New England
      B. the South   **D.** the Midwest

_____ **5.** In "the swing," men lifted their partners
      A. to the right   **C.** off the ground
      B. to the left   **D.** grand right and left

Square dancing comes from dances done long ago in England. People there did *country dances.* In one country dance, dancers formed a circle. This dance was called a round. Another country dance was the longways. In this one, two long lines of dancers faced one another. A popular longways is called the Virginia reel.

Around the year 1900, square dancing was dying out. Dancers liked the new *couple dancing* better. In the 1940s, people became interested in the songs and dances the pioneers enjoyed. Square dancing became popular again. The interest in square dancing is still growing, but it's not easy to learn some of those movements! Square-dance contests award ribbons or badges to the winners. If you're invited to a hog wrassle, get ready for music, action, and fun.

_A___ **6.** In a round
  A. a circle is formed   **C.** people wrestled
  B. a longways is danced   **D.** people dance in Virginia

_A___ **7.** The Virginia reel is a
  A. longways   **C.** couple dance
  B. square   **D.** new name

_D___ **8.** Between 1900 and 1940, couple dancing became
  A. impossible   **C.** a round
  B. popular   **D.** a longways

_____ **9.** Square dancing started again when people became
  A. interested in history   **C.** tired of couples
  B. better Americans   **D.** buyers of clothing

_D__ **10.** In a square-dance contest, people earn
  A. boots   **C.** difficult movements
  B. music   **D.** ribbons or badges

7/25

Home Sweet Home

How would you like to come home after a long day, open the door, and walk into an elephant? That's what you would do if you lived in Elephant House in Margate, New Jersey. The elephant-shaped house was built in 1881 by James Lafferty. In 1962, Herbert Green built a chicken-shaped house.

Sarah Winchester tried to build a ghost-proof house in San Jose, California. Workers built fake chimneys, doors that open onto blank walls, and stairs that lead nowhere. Many rooms were torn down and then rebuilt in a new way to confuse the ghosts. It took 38 years to complete the house!

Some houses are built of strange materials. A house in Pigeon Cove, Massachusetts, is built from more than 100,000 newspapers. In Canada, George Plumb built a house entirely out of bottles.

_A_ **1.** The elephant-shaped house was built in
  A. 1881   **C.** 1922
  B. 1884   **D.** 1962

_A_ **2.** Herbert Green's house is shaped like
  A. a chicken   **C.** an elephant
  B. a door   **D.** a pigeon

_B_ **3.** Sarah Winchester built a house in
  A. Massachusetts   **C.** New Jersey
  B. California   **D.** Oklahoma

_D_ **4.** Winchester tried to build a house that was
  A. a castle   **C.** rebuilt
  B. fool-proof   **D.** ghost-proof

_D_ **5.** George Plumb's house is built of
  A. newspapers   **C.** chimneys
  B. aluminum cans   **D.** bottles

Some homes stand for great wealth and power. The Palace of Alhambra in Spain is one of the most beautiful homes in the world. The man who built it loved water. A stream runs through all 9 acres of the palace. In each room there is a small pool of sparkling water.

Wealthy Americans design dream houses too. In 1895, Cornelius Vanderbilt moved into a house named the Breakers. He called it his summer cottage. It cost $10 million to build and has walls trimmed with gold. This "summer cottage" could hold 60 guests comfortably.

Dream houses don't have to be expensive. A man named Baldasera built a house with 90 rooms for about $300 by digging under the earth. Baldasera worked alone. He spent about 40 years completing his underground house.

___B___ 6. The Palace of Alhambra covers
    A. 40 years   **C.** $10 million
    B. 9 acres   **D.** 90 rooms

___A___ 7. The builder of the Palace of Alhambra loved
    A. water   **C.** wealth and power
    B. chances to swim   **D.** pools with lights

___C___ 8. Vanderbilt designed the Breakers to be his summer
    A. museum   **C.** home
    B. camp   **D.** dream

___C___ 9. Baldasera built his home
    A. in Spain   **C.** without much money
    B. at the Breakers   **D.** in a mountain

___C___ 10. To build his house, Baldasera needed much
    A. help   **C.** time
    B. water   **D.** money

Nature Paints a Turtle

A dozen small turtles slide off a rock and slip into the pond. These turtles look as if an artist had painted them. Pale yellow stripes cross their upper shells, and a red border circles the edge. More red and yellow stripes are on the turtles' heads, and just behind each eye is another yellow spot.

These eastern painted turtles live in slow-moving rivers, marshy areas, and ponds. They like to be in places where rocks and fallen trees project from the water. The turtles like to climb out onto the rocks or dead trees to sleep in the warm sunlight. If something frightens them, they slide quickly into the water.

Eastern painted turtles keep regular schedules. They nap at certain times, and they eat at certain times. In the late morning and the late afternoon, the turtles search for food.

_D_ **1.** Eastern painted turtles are mainly red and
    A. green   **C.** blue
    B. orange   **D.** yellow

_C_ **2.** These turtles live near rivers that are
    A. deep   **C.** slow
    B. warm   **D.** fast

_A_ **3.** The turtles like to sleep
    A. in the sunlight   **C.** inside trees
    B. under the water   **D.** while eating

_D_ **4.** The turtles move quickly when they are
    A. hungry   **C.** sleepy
    B. certain   **D.** frightened

_B_ **5.** In the late afternoon, the turtles
    A. climb on rocks   **C.** slide into the water
    B. search for food   **D.** go swimming

Painted turtles eat almost anything they can find in their water homes. They feed on plants, insects, crayfish, and snails. Since young turtles need to grow fast, they usually eat more animal food than older turtles do. When winter comes, the turtles dig into the underwater mud and sleep there until warm weather returns.

Once a year, in the early summer, the females crawl to dry land. There they dig nests and lay their eggs. In about 10 weeks, the young turtles hatch, and the real battle for life begins. As the turtles creep toward the water, many of them are caught and eaten by hungry raccoons, snakes, and bullfrogs.

Some varieties of young eastern painted turtles stay in their nests all through their first summer, fall, and winter. When they come out the following spring, they are larger, stronger, and quicker. Then they have a better chance of escaping their enemies.

_____B___ **6.** To turtles, crayfish and snails are
  A. insects   **C.** enemies
  B. food   **D.** friends

_____A___ **7.** Animal food helps turtles
  A. grow quickly   **C.** eat more
  B. swim faster   **D.** sleep longer

_____C___ **8.** In the winter the turtles live
  A. close to water   **C.** under the mud
  B. on dry land   **D.** in warm homes

_____C___ **9.** Little turtles can be caught as they
  A. dig their nests   **C.** crawl toward water
  B. lay their eggs   **D.** hunt snakes

_____B__ **10.** Some varieties of turtles remain in their nests
  A. until they lay eggs   **C.** for about 10 weeks
  B. for almost a year   **D.** to hide from raccoons

7/26

Hunter in the Sky

Stargazing takes imagination. People who love stargazing see the stars as shining spots in a dot-to-dot drawing game. They imagine lines that connect groups of stars called constellations. A constellation is a group of stars that looks like a person, an animal, or an object.

The constellation Orion is known as the hunter, after a hero from ancient Greek myths. To find Orion, first find the Big Dipper. The Big Dipper looks like a huge cup with a long handle. After you find the Big Dipper, turn around. There's Orion! He is outlined by four bright stars that form two triangles. The tips of the triangles seem to come together. Where they meet, there are three more bright stars. These form Orion's belt. Some fainter stars appear to hang from the belt. These are Orion's sword.

_____ A **1.** When looking at a constellation, people try to imagine
      A. lines   **C.** spots
      B. games   **D.** groups

_____ C **2.** Groups of stars are called
      A. stargazers   **C.** constellations
      B. ancient myths   **D.** connections

_____ D **3.** Orion is named after a Greek
      A. object   **C.** animal
      B. story   **D.** hero

_____ B **4.** The four bright stars in Orion form
      A. a big cup   **C.** a long handle
      B. two triangles   **D.** an animal

_____ **5.** Three bright stars form Orion's
      A. shoulder   **C.** belt
      B. sword   **D.** spear

Different kinds of stars are in the constellation Orion. The star Betelgeuse makes Orion's right shoulder. *Betelgeuse* is an Arabic word that means "shoulder of the giant." The star itself is so huge that it is called a supergiant. Its diameter is 400 times greater than that of our Sun. Betelgeuse is considered a cool star. It is probably not as hot as our Sun.

Rigel is the star that makes Orion's left foot. *Rigel* is the Arabic word for *foot*. Rigel is much brighter than Betelgeuse because it is much hotter. It's more than three times as hot as our Sun. However, Rigel is just a baby in size compared to Betelgeuse.

A large, misty area near Orion's sword is called a nebula. It is a mass of shining gas and dust. The gases whirl together and may form new stars. As the new stars begin to shine, Orion will be brighter than ever.

___B___ **6.** Betelgeuse makes
- **A.** Arabic words
- **B.** Orion's shoulder
- **C.** different stars
- **D.** huge sizes

___A___ **7.** Betelgeuse is much larger than
- **A.** our Sun
- **B.** a supergiant
- **C.** a diameter
- **D.** any nebula

___C___ **8.** Rigel is brighter than Betelgeuse because it is
- **A.** bigger
- **B.** smaller
- **C.** hotter
- **D.** cooler

___D___ **9.** Near Orion's sword is
- **A.** a cool star
- **B.** strange material
- **C.** a new star
- **D.** a nebula

___B___ **10.** Orion may shine brighter
- **A.** when Rigel explodes
- **B.** as new stars shine
- **C.** as dust shines
- **D.** as dust forms

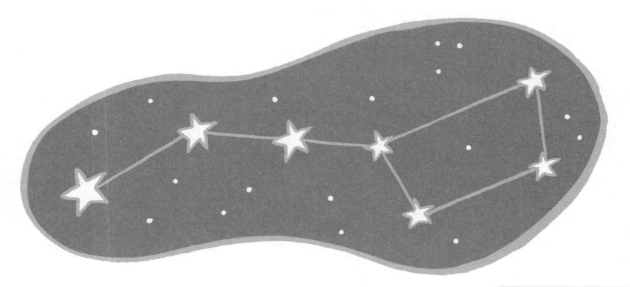

Writing Roundup

Read the story below. Think about the facts. Then answer the questions in complete sentences.

Have you ever seen the Statue of Liberty? It is a tall figure of a robed woman holding a torch. She stands proudly on Liberty Island in New York Harbor. The statue is a symbol of freedom for the United States. It was given as a gift to the United States by France in 1884.

The statue is one of the largest ever built. It stands 151 feet high from its base to the top of the torch. When the statue was shipped to America, it could not be sent in one piece. Instead it was taken apart and packed in 214 separate crates.

1. What is the Statue of Liberty?

it's a tall figure of a robed woman holding a torch this symbol is freedom for unied states.

2. Who gave the statue to the United States?

France

3. How tall is the statue?

151 feet

1. Put these events in the order that they happened. What happened first? Write the number **1** on the line by that sentence. Then write the number **2** by the sentence that tells what happened next. Write the number **3** by the sentence that tells what happened last.

_____ The sailors saw signs of land.

_____ The sailors heard the blast of a cannon.

_____ The sailors cheered.

_____ **2.** When did the sailors notice signs of land?
- **A.** before they left Spain
- **B.** before October 11
- **C.** after they heard a cannon blast

_____ **3.** When did sailors see reeds in the water?
- **A.** after a whale swam by
- **B.** after birds flew by
- **C.** after everyone cheered

_____ **4.** When did Columbus see a light?
- **A.** at ten o'clock at night
- **B.** at midnight
- **C.** at dawn

_____ **5.** When did everyone hear the sound of the cannon blast?
- **A.** before Columbus saw land
- **B.** before the *Pinta* sank
- **C.** after the *Pinta* crew saw land

Disappearing Dinosaurs

For more than 160 million years, dinosaurs ruled Earth. Some were no larger than chickens. Others were more than 100 feet long and may have weighed 100 tons. Some dinosaurs ate plants. Others ate other dinosaurs! The last of these reptiles vanished about 65 million years ago.

Until recently scientists have thought that dinosaurs disappeared slowly. They thought that the temperature on Earth cooled. Plants and dinosaurs that were used to warm weather couldn't survive the cold climate. Also, early mammals might have eaten dinosaur eggs. Over many years, all the dinosaurs finally died.

In 1980, two scientists came up with a new idea about how the dinosaurs vanished. Luis Alvarez and his son Walter studied a layer of clay. In this clay the two men found iridium. This substance is rarely found in Earth's crust. It is found in meteors that fall to Earth from outer space. The two men now think that dinosaurs might have died quickly.

The Alvarezes think that millions of years ago a huge meteorite might have slammed into warm, sunny Earth. The impact sent a huge cloud of dust into the air. For months the dust cloud shut out the light of the Sun. With no sunlight all plants on Earth died. The plant-eating dinosaurs had no food, so they died too. The meat-eating dinosaurs then died quickly, because their food source was gone.

Today not all scientists agree with the idea of "quick death." Some think the idea should be studied. As time goes by, scientists will continue to study how the dinosaurs disappeared.

1. Put these events in the order that they happened. What happened first? Write the number **1** on the line by that sentence. Then write the number **2** by the sentence that tells what happened next. Write the number **3** by the sentence that tells what happened last.

_____ The Alvarezes found iridium.

_____ The Alvarezes developed a new idea.

_____ The Alvarezes studied the clay.

_____ **2.** When did dinosaurs vanish from Earth?
   A. about 65 million years ago
   B. more than 100 million years ago
   C. before a meteorite landed

_____ **3.** What happened as Earth grew colder?
   A. The mammals disappeared.
   B. The dinosaurs died.
   C. Meteorites fell.

_____ **4.** When did the huge dust cloud fill the air?
   A. after the plants died
   B. when the meteorite fell
   C. after the dinosaurs died

_____ **5.** According to the Alvarezes, when did the dinosaurs die?
   A. while Earth was sunny
   B. thousands of years ago
   C. after sunlight was shut out

Skywriting began in England during World War I. The Royal Air Force made signals with smoke from airplanes. The signals could be seen from great distances. In 1922, the first words written in the sky over America were "Hello USA." That year skywriting began to be used for advertising. It stayed popular until the 1950s when more ads began appearing on television.

Here's how one pilot makes letters ¼ mile tall. First he writes the letters backward on a piece of paper and tapes that in his plane. Next he walks through turns and loops he'll have to fly. Then, in a plane that used to be a crop duster, he takes off and rises about 9,000 feet. He locates landmarks on the ground that will help him keep his lines straight. At last he flips a switch and smoke blasts out of the exhaust pipes.

It's challenging to put a message in the sky. The pilot counts seconds to know when to turn the smoke on and off. He has to concentrate to write backward, especially the numbers *2* and *5*. Wind moves the letters, so the pilot watches their shadows on the ground or their pattern in the sky. If it's a snowy day, the pilot in the plane won't see the white letters over the white land, but observers on the ground will see them in the sky. The view is awesome.

1. Put these events in the order that they happened. What happened first? Write the number **1** on the line by that sentence. Then write the number **2** by the sentence that tells what happened next. Write the number **3** by the sentence that tells what happened last.

_____ The television was used more for advertising.

_____ Skywriting was used to send signals in the war.

_____ Skywriting was used for advertising.

_____ **2.** When did skywriting begin?
   A. during World War I
   B. during the 1950s
   C. during the Great Depression

_____ **3.** When does the pilot walk through the turns and loops he will fly?
   A. after he writes the letters on paper
   B. after he rises to 9,000 feet
   C. after he releases smoke from the plane

_____ **4.** When does the pilot write letters in the sky?
   A. before takeoff
   B. after he jumps from a plane
   C. after he locates landmarks

_____ **5.** When are letters in the sky invisible to the pilot?
   A. when the pilot lands
   B. when the Sun is out
   C. when snow covers the ground

Lesson 5 Ready! Get Set! Pedal!

Some people put their bicycles away once they learn how to drive a car. For many people, bicycling is not just an easy way of getting around town. It is also an exciting sport. Serious cyclists often enter races.

One kind of race is the time trial. Each racer leaves the starting line at a different time and pedals hard toward the finish line. The cyclist who covers the distance in the shortest amount of time wins the race. A time trial is a safe race for beginners because the bicycles are spread out and are not as likely to run into each other.

Another kind of race is more difficult. A few city blocks are closed to traffic. Then all the racers line up in a tight pack and begin racing at the same time. They cover many laps, going around and around the city blocks. The race requires more than speed. It also requires skillful handling of the bicycle as it darts around other bicycles. The racer who completes all the laps first is the winner.

Road races are usually the longest cycling contests. Racers have to cover anywhere from 35 miles to almost 3,000 miles. The race course may be a straight stretch of road or a long series of roads across the country. The prize goes to the first person who crosses the finish line.

Between races cyclists stay in condition by doing exercises that build their strength so they can keep riding for long periods of time. Some cyclists ride on a special raceway called a velodrome. It's a safe place to practice because there is no automobile traffic.

As cyclists become more experienced, they often join bicycling groups and become licensed racers. Then they can enter special races all over the country. Coaches watch the cyclists in these special races. The coaches are always looking for winners to join national teams. If you're a cyclist, keep pedaling! You could become a star!

1. Put these events in the order that they happened. What happened first? Write the number **1** on the line by that sentence. Then write the number **2** by the sentence that tells what happened next. Write the number **3** by the sentence that tells what happened last.

_____ The cyclists cover many laps.

_____ The winner crosses the finish line.

_____ The racers wait at the starting line.

_____ **2.** When does a cyclist finish the time trial?
     A. after the racer has covered the distance
     B. before the cyclist begins racing
     C. when the racer goes around the city blocks

_____ **3.** When do some cyclists build their strength?
     A. in between races
     B. right before a race is over
     C. during a race

_____ **4.** What happens after cyclists become more experienced?
     A. They enter time trials.
     B. They ride around town.
     C. They often become licensed racers.

_____ **5.** When do coaches of national teams watch cyclists?
     A. after a cyclist enters special races
     B. before a racer enters time trials
     C. during regular road races

Lesson 6 Umbrellas

Umbrellas are useful, rain or shine. They have been used for both kinds of weather for more than 3,000 years. You might say that umbrellas are dripping with history.

Early Egyptian rulers used them in ceremonies. Leaders of old Japan walked under red umbrellas. They were a sign of power. The kings of Burma rode on white elephants under white umbrellas. People in Greece and Rome also used umbrellas long ago. The umbrellas of early times were used in warm lands as protection against the Sun.

By the 1600s umbrellas had appeared in northern Europe. In these countries they were used on rainy days, too. The umbrellas were thought to be big and clumsy. They were used only by people who didn't have carriages.

By the 1700s umbrellas had become more popular in countries such as England. During this time many umbrellas had jewels and fancy handles made of rare wood. Some umbrellas had hollow handles. Perfume, knives, and even pens and paper were kept in these handles.

Umbrellas were improved in the 1800s. Before that time most were made with whalebone spokes. They weighed 10 pounds! By 1826, their weight was down to 1 ½ pounds. Steel frames were first used in 1852. Covers for these umbrellas were made of waxed silk or oiled paper.

Today's umbrellas are very light. Some people think they turn inside out too easily, but modern umbrellas do have some good points. For example, they fold up into smaller packages. Some have plastic windows in them so people can see where they're walking. When the rain comes down, people can pop open their umbrellas quickly and be on their way.

1. Put these events in the order that they happened. What happened first? Write the number **1** on the line by that sentence. Then write the number **2** by the sentence that tells what happened next. Write the number **3** by the sentence that tells what happened last.

_____ Umbrellas weighed 10 pounds.

_____ Umbrellas folded up into smaller packages.

_____ Umbrellas weighed 1 ¹/₂ pounds.

_____ **2.** When were umbrellas used mainly to protect against the sun?
   A. before the 1600s
   B. by the 1700s
   C. during modern times

_____ **3.** When were umbrellas first used in northern Europe?
   A. before the 1500s
   B. during the 600s
   C. by the 1600s

_____ **4.** When were umbrellas used to protect against rain?
   A. before they were used in Burma
   B. during early times in Egypt
   C. after they appeared in northern Europe

_____ **5.** When were umbrellas decorated with jewels?
   A. before they first appeared in northern Europe
   B. when they were first used in Greece and Rome
   C. after they had become more popular in England

Lesson 7 Toy on a String

Long ago in the jungles of the Philippine Islands, soldiers developed a powerful weapon. They took heavy stones and carved a ridge around the outside of each one. Next they wrapped a thick rope about 20 feet long around the ridge. The stone could be thrown out quickly with tremendous force and then pulled back. Enemies had a hard time fighting these weapons. The Filipino soldiers named them *yo-yos*, a word that means "to return."

In the early 1900s, a man named Pedro Flores made a toy out of the yo-yo. He carved small yo-yos out of wood and put strings around them. Then he gave them to children. The toys could be moved up and down by handling the string just right. When Flores moved to California in the 1920s, he started his own yo-yo factory. Children loved yo-yos, and so did many adults.

Then Donald F. Duncan saw the yo-yos. He thought he could make them even more popular all across the country. He bought Flores's company. Then he developed a stronger string, which he called a slip-string. The slip-string helped children perform all sorts of tricks with a yo-yo. To help sell the toy, Duncan sent yo-yo experts all over the United States. These experts taught the tricks to children and their parents.

Playing with yo-yos soon became a national sport. For a while the Duncan factory in Luck, Wisconsin, was turning out 3,600 yo-yos per hour. Luck was called the "Yo-Yo Capital of the World." During World War II, yo-yo production slowed. Materials were hard to get during that time.

After the war the yo-yo business picked up again. Plastic yo-yos were developed. They lasted longer, and it was easier to do tricks with them. In one yo-yo contest, a man named John Winslow won a special prize. He played with a yo-yo for 120 hours without stopping.

1. Put these events in the order that they happened. What happened first? Write the number **1** on the line by that sentence. Then write the number **2** by the sentence that tells what happened next. Write the number **3** by the sentence that tells what happened last.

_____ Flores moved to California.

_____ Soldiers developed yo-yos.

_____ Flores carved yo-yos out of wood.

_____ **2.** When were yo-yos first made as toys?
    A. in the early 1900s
    B. 20 years ago
    C. after Flores moved to California

_____ **3.** When were yo-yos first given to children?
    A. after experts taught them
    B. when yo-yos were made of plastic
    C. after Flores made wooden yo-yos

_____ **4.** When was material for yo-yos hard to find?
    A. before 1920
    B. when Filipinos used yo-yos as weapons
    C. during World War II

_____ **5.** What happened after plastic yo-yos were developed?
    A. Nobody liked them.
    B. A man won a special prize.
    C. Each hour 3,600 were made.

Lesson 8 Windsurfing

Have you ever seen someone glide across a lake on what looks like a surfboard with a sail? That's a windsurfer.

Windsurfers use a sailboard. It is a board much like a surfboard. It is made of plastic or fiberglass. A mast, or vertical pole, stands in the center of the board. The sail is hooked to the mast. There is a plastic window in the sail so that the surfer can see where the board is going. The surfer keeps his or her balance and steers by holding onto a boom. The boom is a horizontal bar that is attached to the sail. The surfer lifts the sail out of the water with a rope that is attached to the boom.

There have been many arguments over who first invented the sailboard. In 1982, a court ruled that a 12-year-old British boy had made the first sailboard in 1958. This sport first became popular in Europe in the 1970s.

In 1968 two Americans, Jim Drake and Hoyle Schweitzer, designed a flat-bottomed sailboard. It became very popular. It is easiest to learn how to windsurf on flat-bottomed sailboards. Learning this sport is not hard, but it takes practice. First you must be able to stand on the sailboard and pull the sail up out of the water. This takes a great amount of strength and balance. Then you must learn how to turn the sail to make the best use of the wind.

Funboarding is a special kind of windsurfing. Funboards were designed to be used in strong winds. In 1977, Larry Stanley added footstraps to a funboard. This let surfers ride big waves and jump out of the water with their boards. Funboarding is a popular sport in Hawaii.

1. Put these events in the order that they happened. What happened first? Write the number **1** on the line by that sentence. Then write the number **2** by the sentence that tells what happened next. Write the number **3** by the sentence that tells what happened last.

_____ Footstraps were added to funboards.

_____ Drake and Schweitzer designed a board with a flat bottom.

_____ A court decided who had invented the sailboard.

_____ **2.** When was the sailboard invented?
    A. during 1958
    B. after 1982
    C. during the 1984 Olympics

_____ **3.** When did windsurfing first become popular?
    A. before World War II
    B. during the 1970s
    C. at the same time that surfing became popular

_____ **4.** When do you pull the sail out of the water?
    A. while you are sailing
    B. before you turn the sail in the wind
    C. after you learn to ride big ocean waves

_____ **5.** When were footstraps added to funboards?
    A. just before strong winds rose
    B. after the 1982 trial
    C. during 1977

Writing Roundup

Read the paragraph below. Think about the sequence, or time order. Answer the questions in complete sentences.

Janet places bands on baby bald eagles' legs to help study the birds. First Janet straps spurs onto her shoes and loops a rope around a tree. Next she climbs up to the eagles' nest and ties herself to the tree. Then she slowly pulls a baby close with her hooked stick. The babies can't fly, but they might jump from the nest if frightened. Finally Janet attaches a metal band to each bird's leg.

1. What is the first thing Janet does?

_____

_____

2. When does Janet tie herself to the tree?

_____

_____

3. When does Janet clamp the band on one of the eagle's legs?

_____

_____

4. When might a baby jump from the nest?

_____

_____

Prewriting

Think about something that you have done, such as doing your laundry, training to improve your fitness, or tie-dyeing a T-shirt. Write the events in sequence below.

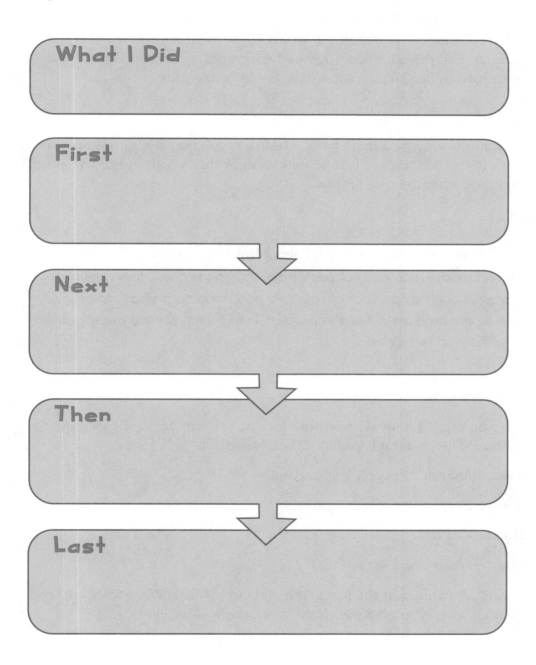

What I Did

First

Next

Then

Last

On Your Own

Now use another sheet of paper to write a paragraph about what you have done. Write the events in the order that they happened. Use time order words.

unit 3

What Is Context?

Context means all the words in a sentence or all the sentences in a paragraph. In a sentence all the words together make up the context. In a paragraph all the sentences together make up the context. You can use the context to figure out the meaning of unknown words.

Try It!

The following paragraph has a word that you may not know. See whether you can use the context (the sentences and other words in the paragraph) to decide what the word means.

Scientists are very concerned about **famine** in many parts of the world today. Thousands of people are starving because they cannot grow enough crops. Lack of rain and poor farming methods sometimes cause the problem. Often the problem is that there are too many people for the land to support.

If you don't know what **famine** means, you can decide by using the context. The paragraph contains these words:

Clue: thousands of people are starving

Clue: cannot grow enough crops

Clue: lack of rain

Clue: too many people

Find these clues in the paragraph and circle them. What words do you think of when you read the clues? Write the words below:

_____

Did you write *hunger* or a similar word? The context clue words tell you that **famine** is a lack of food.

Working with Context

This unit asks questions that you can answer by using context clues in paragraphs. There are two kinds of paragraphs. The paragraphs in the first part of this unit have blank spaces in them. You can use the context clues in the paragraphs to decide which words should go in each space. Here is an example:

Baboons live in groups. Usually there are about 60 ___1___ in the group, but there may be as many as 200 or as few as 10. Living in a tribe ___2___ the baboons from their enemies.

___C___ 1. **A.** jars   **B.** museums   **C.** individuals   **D.** patients

_____ 2. **A.** hides   **B.** safeguards   **C.** leads   **D.** grazes

Look at the answer choices for question 1. Try putting each choice in the paragraph to see which one makes the most sense. Treat the paragraph as a puzzle. Determine which pieces don't fit and which piece fits best. The paragraph tells about baboons living in groups. It doesn't make sense to say that there are 60 *jars*, *museums*, or *patients*. *Individuals* (answer **C**) is the only choice that makes sense in this paragraph. Now try to answer question 2 on your own.

The paragraphs in the second part of this unit are different. For these you figure out the meaning of a word that is printed in **dark letters** in the paragraph. Here is an example:

Many vines have long **clusters** of sweet-smelling flowers. Vines will climb posts and other objects. They are often planted for their beauty and shade.

In this paragraph, the word in dark type is **clusters**. Find the context clues, and treat the paragraph as a puzzle. Then choose a word that means the same as **clusters**.

_____ 3. In this paragraph, the word **clusters** means
      A. animals   **C.** drinks
      B. stems   **D.** bunches

Lesson 1

Read the passages and answer the questions about context. Remember, context is a way to learn new words by thinking about the other words used in a story.

Saudi Arabia is a desert country where ___**1**___ is always a problem. Some years ago the king planned to tow a huge ___**2**___ from the South Pole to supply his country with water.

_____ **1.** **A.** chocolate   **B.** drought   **C.** camel   **D.** fashion

_____ **2.** **A.** fish   **B.** fountain   **C.** leaf   **D.** iceberg

More than 100 years ago, Charles Babbage drew a ___**3**___ for a machine that could calculate. If built, the ___**4**___ would have been the first computer.

_____ **3.** **A.** diagram   **B.** bet   **C.** cake   **D.** problem

_____ **4.** **A.** water   **B.** device   **C.** book   **D.** game

Watching television can be ___**5**___. After a while, you may feel bored. That's the time to come up with your own ___**6**___. Make a new friend, start a hobby, or learn a skill.

_____ **5.** **A.** general   **B.** housework   **C.** usual   **D.** relaxing

_____ **6.** **A.** elevator   **B.** sunshine   **C.** recreation   **D.** recipes

Some lawmakers think there should be laws about false teeth. They want these ___**7**___ teeth to have a special ___**8**___ to identify the owner in case of accident.

_____ **7.** **A.** clean   **B.** sharp   **C.** open   **D.** artificial

_____ **8.** **A.** numeral   **B.** river   **C.** tooth   **D.** brush

In ancient times ___9___ in different parts of the world named the stars. In almost every ___10___, stars were named for animals.

_____ 9. A. seas   B. astronomers   C. stars   D. meters

_____10. A. student   B. civilization   C. third   D. time

The first movie with a ___11___ about traveling to the Moon was made in 1902 in France. In the film, moon walkers put up umbrellas to avoid the ___12___ of the Sun.

_____11. A. check   B. camera   C. producer   D. plot

_____12. A. hobbies   B. rain   C. movie   D. rays

The continents are slowly drifting apart. Since they are not ___13___, North and South America will one day ___14___ entirely. Then the ocean will flow between them.

_____13. A. clean   B. stationary   C. moving   D. land

_____14. A. name   B. reverse   C. separate   D. lock

Deer know each other from the scent on the ___15___ of their hind legs. Each deer has a different scent. A ___16___ knows its mother by sniffing her hind legs.

_____15. A. shoes   B. trim   C. ankles   D. head

_____16. A. monkey   B. fawn   C. father   D. turn

The kangaroo and the wombat keep their newborns very close after birth. Many of them raise their young in their ___**1**___ until the babies have ___**2**___ strength to leave.

_____ **1.** **A.** farm   **B.** tree   **C.** steady   **D.** pouch

_____ **2.** **A.** no   **B.** sufficient   **C.** many   **D.** national

A man named Richebourg was a spy in France nearly 300 years ago. He was only 23 inches tall. He was most ___**3**___ when he was disguised as an ___**4**___ being carried by his nurse.

_____ **3.** **A.** modern   **B.** friendly   **C.** successful   **D.** French

_____ **4.** **A.** infant   **B.** extra   **C.** armor   **D.** owl

Many people have an ___**5**___ of bats as bloodthirsty animals. This is not a true picture. Most bats live on a ___**6**___ of insects, flowers, or fruit.

_____ **5.** **A.** answer   **B.** action   **C.** elevator   **D.** image

_____ **6.** **A.** diet   **B.** plate   **C.** tree   **D.** bush

Cheese factories ___**7**___ many health inspections. Some people feel that the taste of cheese has gotten worse. It has been ___**8**___ by processes designed to make it safe.

_____ **7.** **A.** remind   **B.** require
        C. read   **D.** milk

_____ **8.** **A.** altered   **B.** helped
        C. freed   **D.** risen

Many movies show deserts as hot areas covered with sand ____9____ . In real life the typical desert does look ____10____ , but it is covered with rocks, not sand.

_____ 9. **A.** lakes   **B.** castles   **C.** sneezes   **D.** dunes

_____10. **A.** watery   **B.** cool   **C.** harsh   **D.** carpeted

Laws about using water to ____11____ crops go back to ancient times. Thousands of years ago, the Babylonians had many laws and ____12____ for the use of water.

_____11. **A.** irrigate   **B.** burn   **C.** park   **D.** destroy

_____12. **A.** rulers   **B.** regulations   **C.** families   **D.** phones

The coconut got its name from the Portuguese word *coco*. This word describes the ____13____ on the face of someone who is in pain. The "face" of the coconut seems to have this same ____14____ look.

_____13. **A.** scars   **B.** expression   **C.** love   **D.** teeth

_____14. **A.** smiling   **B.** partly   **C.** miserable   **D.** watch

The fruit of the banana plant takes from three to five months to ____15____ completely. Bananas don't ripen ____16____ unless picked. This is why they are picked when they are still green.

_____15. **A.** talk   **B.** care   **C.** mature   **D.** cease

_____16. **A.** properly   **B.** tomorrow   **C.** bubbly   **D.** madly

William Enos did not have a driver's ___1___. He could not operate a car, but he invented stop signs and one-way streets. He also wrote the first ___2___ of traffic regulations.

_____ 1. **A.** job   **B.** speed   **C.** license   **D.** ticket

_____ 2. **A.** play   **B.** song   **C.** manual   **D.** street

One kind of caterpillar can ___3___ itself. It puffs up its head and part of its body into a triangle that looks like a snake's head. When it ___4___ a snake, it may scare away enemies.

_____ 3. **A.** wrap   **B.** feed   **C.** disguise   **D.** climb

_____ 4. **A.** mimics   **B.** sees   **C.** follows   **D.** chases

Rachel Jackson did not want her husband Andrew to be a ___5___ for president. She ___6___ his decision to run for office, but she did not try to stop him.

_____ 5. **A.** candidate   **B.** senator   **C.** voter   **D.** failure

_____ 6. **A.** liked   **B.** regretted   **C.** halted   **D.** wished

Ida Lewis, a light keeper's daughter, kept the light burning in the lighthouse at Lime Rock Light in Rhode Island. She was only 15 when she rescued four men from the sea. Their boat had ___7___. This ___8___ and others like it made her famous. She is credited with saving lives.

_____ 7. **A.** sailed
         B. won
         C. capsized
         D. floated

_____ 8. **A.** woman
         B. light
         C. fiction
         D. incident

The bagpipe is a musical instrument played in Scotland. It makes a lonely, __9__ sound. One pipe plays the melody while the other three play low __10__ notes.

_____ 9. **A.** moist   **B.** angry   **C.** forlorn   **D.** misty

_____ 10. **A.** sick   **B.** narrow   **C.** argue   **D.** bass

---

In 1908, the president of an automobile company put on an exciting demonstration. He __11__ the parts of three different cars. Then the cars were put back together. This showed that cars could be built with parts that were interchangeable. __12__ each part could fit only the car it was made for.

_____ 11. **A.** melted   **B.** jumbled   **C.** waited   **D.** froze

_____ 12. **A.** Previously   **B.** Above   **C.** Beneath   **D.** Beside

---

In the Middle Ages, a __13__ did more than just cut hair. This person would often act as a doctor and perform __14__ on sick people.

_____ 13. **A.** man   **B.** writer   **C.** barber   **D.** wife

_____ 14. **A.** operations   **B.** jokes   **C.** weddings   **D.** lights

---

People who can't use their arms or legs the way most others do are called __15__. They learn to do things new ways. Adults who can't use their leg muscles might learn to drive a car using hand switches. Some people may learn how to cook while standing with __16__.

_____ 15. **A.** tired   **B.** disabled   **C.** young   **D.** sir

_____ 16. **A.** tables   **B.** elevators   **C.** curbs   **D.** crutches

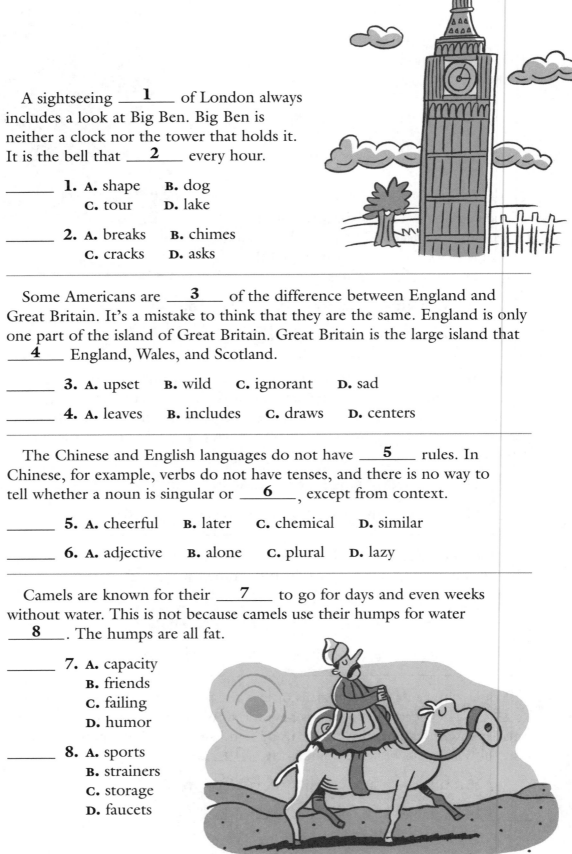

A sightseeing __1__ of London always includes a look at Big Ben. Big Ben is neither a clock nor the tower that holds it. It is the bell that __2__ every hour.

_____ 1. **A.** shape   **B.** dog
        C. tour   **D.** lake

_____ 2. **A.** breaks   **B.** chimes
        C. cracks   **D.** asks

Some Americans are __3__ of the difference between England and Great Britain. It's a mistake to think that they are the same. England is only one part of the island of Great Britain. Great Britain is the large island that __4__ England, Wales, and Scotland.

_____ 3. **A.** upset   **B.** wild   **C.** ignorant   **D.** sad

_____ 4. **A.** leaves   **B.** includes   **C.** draws   **D.** centers

The Chinese and English languages do not have __5__ rules. In Chinese, for example, verbs do not have tenses, and there is no way to tell whether a noun is singular or __6__, except from context.

_____ 5. **A.** cheerful   **B.** later   **C.** chemical   **D.** similar

_____ 6. **A.** adjective   **B.** alone   **C.** plural   **D.** lazy

Camels are known for their __7__ to go for days and even weeks without water. This is not because camels use their humps for water __8__. The humps are all fat.

_____ 7. **A.** capacity
        B. friends
        C. failing
        D. humor

_____ 8. **A.** sports
        B. strainers
        C. storage
        D. faucets

The deepest ___9___ in the United States is not the Grand Canyon. It is Hells Canyon. The ___10___ at Hells Canyon is greater than the one at the Grand Canyon by half a mile.

_____ 9. **A.** water   **B.** pond   **C.** thinker   **D.** gorge

_____10. **A.** flyer   **B.** animal   **C.** chasm   **D.** hill

---

A small, seaside ___11___ had a terrible problem. It had too many ___12___. These bloodsucking insects bit the tourists. The town solved its problem. It brought in hundreds of dragonflies, which feed on the pests.

_____11. **A.** community   **B.** boat   **C.** anchor   **D.** tree

_____12. **A.** frogs   **B.** mosquitoes   **C.** woodpeckers   **D.** things

---

Peter Stuyvesant was one of the most disliked governors in the New World, but he also began the first American fire ___13___ system. He had people ___14___ chimneys for possible fire dangers.

_____13. **A.** prevention   **B.** starting   **C.** average   **D.** inning

_____14. **A.** launch   **B.** welcome   **C.** inspect   **D.** punch

---

Helicopters are lifted into the air by one or two ___15___ wings. These fast-turning wings whirl through the air. They work against gravity to produce lift. Lift keeps the helicopter ___16___.

_____15. **A.** rotating   **B.** slow   **C.** serious   **D.** fixed

_____16. **A.** engine   **B.** heavy   **C.** pilot   **D.** aloft

The king cobra is a very dangerous snake. Its bite can kill an elephant in three hours. Most animals attack only when threatened, but the king cobra will attack without being **provoked**.

_____ **1.** In this paragraph, the word **provoked** means
    A. rescued   **C.** affected
    B. given a reason   **D.** poisoned

The tall buildings called skyscrapers might not have been built without the Chicago Fire of 1871. The fire **devastated** the wooden buildings of the city. The first skyscraper was built on the ruins of the fire.

_____ **2.** In this paragraph, the word **devastated** means
    A. built   **C.** destroyed
    B. designed   **D.** sold

Scientists have wondered how the Moon came to be. More and more facts **reinforce** the idea that the Moon was probably created by a tremendous crash. A planet the size of Mars hit Earth, and the Moon broke off from Earth.

_____ **3.** In this paragraph, the word **reinforce** means
    A. plan   **C.** trim
    B. send   **D.** support

On the ocean, distance is measured in **nautical** miles. This kind of mile is about 800 feet longer than the mile used for measuring land.

_____ **4.** In this paragraph, the word **nautical** means
    A. sea   **C.** shorter
    B. whale   **D.** probably untrue

How would you like a soup made from a bird's nest? Diners in China **consider** bird's nest soup delicious. The right kind of bird's nests for this soup are found in caves.

_____ **5.** In this paragraph, the word **consider** means
- **A.** make
- **B.** think
- **C.** take
- **D.** sell

Roberto Clemente was the first Hispanic player to be admitted into the Baseball Hall of Fame. He won many awards for his **superb** hitting and fielding skills.

_____ **6.** In this paragraph, the word **superb** means
- **A.** poor
- **B.** quick
- **C.** outstanding
- **D.** outdoor

The Trail of Tears was a journey that took place in the United States. White settlers wanted the land where some Native Americans lived. The government forced these native people to move away from their homes. Thousands of them died on the **tragic** trip.

_____ **7.** In this paragraph, the word **tragic** means
- **A.** sad
- **B.** happy
- **C.** rude
- **D.** brief

Many things we use every day were **invented** in the 1800s. Someone from England gave us the bicycle. An American designed the safety pin.

_____ **8.** In this paragraph, the word **invented** means
- **A.** first made
- **B.** finally broken
- **C.** fixed
- **D.** always needed

Divers uncover many **underwater** secrets. Ancient ships, old cities, and works of art have been found. The sea has hidden some of its treasures for thousands of years.

_____ **1.** In this paragraph, the word **underwater** means
- **A.** on a mountain
- **B.** in the sea
- **C.** near
- **D.** blue

Yellowstone is the oldest national park in the United States. Congress **established** it as a national park in 1872.

_____ **2.** In this paragraph, the word **established** means
- **A.** cut
- **B.** crowded
- **C.** loved
- **D.** started

Some batters think that a curve ball drops 5 feet from home plate. Some have the **view** that it falls 10 feet. Some say that a certain star pitcher's curve ball looked as if it were rolling off a table.

_____ **3.** In this paragraph, the word **view** means
- **A.** bat
- **B.** opinion
- **C.** fly
- **D.** eyes

Popcorn is different from other kinds of corn. The **kernels** have hard shells. The water inside each piece of corn turns to steam. The steam makes the pieces of corn swell and pop.

_____ **4.** In this paragraph, the word **kernels** means
- **A.** soldiers
- **B.** cobs
- **C.** flavors
- **D.** seeds

The mummies of Egypt are very old, so people assume the Egyptians had special ways of **embalming**. Actually it was the dry air that helped preserve their dead.

_____ 5. In this paragraph, the word **embalming** means
    A. making pyramids   **C.** keeping things alive
    B. preventing decay   **D.** dealing with heat

Modern **appliances** make our lives much easier. Washing machines, dryers, and dishwashers make completing household chores much faster than in the old days. The "good old days" meant hard work!

_____ 6. In this paragraph, the word **appliances** means
    A. movies   **C.** machines
    B. people   **D.** apples

Lincoln's **proclamation** ending slavery had no immediate effect. His announcement was made in the middle of the Civil War. The South ignored the order.

_____ 7. In this paragraph, the word **proclamation** means
    A. secret message   **C.** review of the war
    B. official, public order **D.** loud voice

Across deserts and mountains, Pony Express riders on horseback carried the mail in the Old West. Most riders were young boys. They needed great courage and skill. **Incompetent** riders couldn't do the job!

_____ 8. In this paragraph, the word **incompetent** means
    A. genuine   **C.** independent
    B. poorly skilled   **D.** experienced

Lions are not as **noble** as people think. For instance, lions sometimes kill for no reason. They do not kill only to get food.

_____ **1.** In this paragraph, the word **noble** means
    A. strong   **C.** good
    B. mean   **D.** fierce

Some people think that W. C. Fields's **epitaph** reads: "I would rather be in Philadelphia." This is not true. The funny actor's tombstone says: "W. C. Fields, 1880–1946."

_____ **2.** In this paragraph, the word **epitaph** means
    A. dying words   **C.** most famous joke
    B. last telegram   **D.** words on a grave marker

A farmer can't build a new barn alone. To get help, farmers in the 1800s held barn raisings. The neighbors would **congregate** and work all day to complete the barn.

_____ **3.** In this paragraph, the word **congregate** means
    A. complain   **C.** come together
    B. work alone   **D.** leave

The Constitution does not say that a jury's **verdict** has to be agreed upon by all members. The idea of a jury trial is older than United States laws. It came to the United States from England.

_____ **4.** In this paragraph, the word **verdict** means
    A. dinner   **C.** invitation
    B. chamber   **D.** decision

At first the meaning of the word *nice* wasn't nice at all. *Nice* once meant "ignorant." It began to **imply** a more pleasant meaning after the sixteenth century.

_____ **5.** In this paragraph, the word **imply** means
- **A.** reply
- **B.** suggest
- **C.** understand
- **D.** remove

Many people believe that Rome is the oldest **metropolis** in use, but other cities are much older. Rome was founded in 753 B.C. Damascus, Syria, was founded in 3000 B.C.

_____ **6.** In this paragraph, the word **metropolis** means
- **A.** ruins
- **B.** government
- **C.** river
- **D.** city

The killer whale deserves its name in the wild. There it destroys dolphins, birds, and fish. However, a captured killer whale is **meek** and friendly to people.

_____ **7.** In this paragraph, the word **meek** means
- **A.** necessary
- **B.** mean
- **C.** quietly obedient
- **D.** easily discouraged

The opossum **utilizes** its tail for grasping. But baby opossums do not use their tails to hold onto the mother while riding on her back. They use their paws.

_____ **8.** In this paragraph, the word **utilizes** means
- **A.** uses
- **B.** holds
- **C.** exercises
- **D.** stretches

Lesson 8

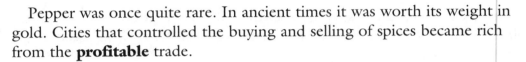

There's a house in Massachusetts **fashioned** entirely from newspapers. The walls and roof are pages glued together to form thick boards. The curtains are woven from the funny pages.

_____ **1.** In this paragraph, the word **fashioned** means
- **A.** printed
- **B.** built
- **C.** read
- **D.** clothed

Pepper was once quite rare. In ancient times it was worth its weight in gold. Cities that controlled the buying and selling of spices became rich from the **profitable** trade.

_____ **2.** In this paragraph, the word **profitable** means
- **A.** cheap
- **B.** slow
- **C.** well-paying
- **D.** confusing

In 1980, someone threw a grape more than 300 feet. A man caught the grape in his mouth. The **site** of this event was a football field in Louisiana.

_____ **3.** In this paragraph, the word **site** means
- **A.** toss
- **B.** place
- **C.** time
- **D.** game

In 1902, a man asked a woman to marry him. She said yes. They decided to wait a few years before they got married. They finally got around to **matrimony** in 1969.

_____ **4.** In this paragraph, the word **matrimony** means
- **A.** talking
- **B.** trying
- **C.** marrying
- **D.** dying

Animals that live in the desert are well protected. Their small bodies help them escape the heat that **scorches** the ground. Some animals stay in tunnels when the hot sun beats down.

_____ **5.** In this paragraph, the word **scorches** means
A. buries
B. waters
C. burns
D. digs

A woman in Australia and a woman in England were pen pals. Their **correspondence** lasted 75 years.

_____ **6.** In this paragraph, the word **correspondence** means
A. letter writing
B. friends
C. phone calls
D. mailbox

At many beaches people enter contests for building castles from sand. Some of the castles are very **elaborate**. They have towers, windows, and even bridges.

_____ **7.** In this paragraph, the word **elaborate** means
A. sandy
B. short
C. plain
D. fancy

Spanish explorers took gold from the New World aboard their ships. They tried to carry it to Europe. However, many of the ships sank before they reached their **destination**. The old ships still lie beneath the sea. The treasure awaits inside them.

_____ **8.** In this paragraph, the word **destination** means
A. silver
B. goal
C. surface
D. mountain

Writing Roundup

Read each paragraph. Write a word that makes sense on each line.

What a terrible day Nick had! Because of a sore throat,

he had to stay at home and miss the **(1)**_____.

To make matters worse, he couldn't even eat his favorite food,

(2)_____.

I'm sure Mrs. Soliz is the friendliest person in the whole

(3)_____. Whenever new families move into

our apartment building, she's the first one to greet them.

She always makes them feel **(4)**_____.

Jill is a pilot. She loves to fly high above the

(5)_____. From the air, cars look as

tiny as **(6)**_____.

Read each paragraph. Write a sentence that makes sense on each line.

Eric lives on a wildlife preserve where animals roam freely. Each day he wonders what wild animal might come into his front yard. **(1)** _____

_____ .

One morning Eric looked out his window. What a sight! **(2)** _____ .

Quickly he got his camera. **(3)** _____

_____ .

The citizens planned to celebrate the one hundredth anniversary of Springfield. One committee discussed how to decorate the city hall. **(4)** _____

_____ .

The program committee couldn't decide what type of program to have. **(5)** _____

_____ .

Then the mayor, Ms. Carter, had a suggestion. **(6)** _____ .

What Is a Main Idea?

The main idea sentence of a paragraph tells what the paragraph is about. The other sentences are details or small parts. They add up to the main idea. The main idea sentence is often the first or last sentence in a paragraph, but you may find it in the middle of a paragraph too.

This example may help you think of main ideas:

$$8 \quad + \quad 9 \quad + \quad 7 \quad = \quad 24$$

detail + detail + detail = main idea

The *8*, *9*, and *7* are like details. They are smaller than their sum, *24*. The *24*, like the main idea, is bigger. It is made up of several smaller parts.

Try It!

Read the following story. Then underline the main idea sentence.

Ostriches will eat anything. These birds eat grass, but they also eat wood, stones, bones, and gold. In South Africa, ostriches are hunted for the diamonds that they may swallow. Ostriches in zoos have been known to eat wallets, watches, keys, and coins.

The main idea sentence is the first sentence about ostriches. The other sentences are details. They give examples of what the main idea sentence states.

The main idea could come at the end of the paragraph:

Ostriches eat grass, but they also eat wood, stones, bones, and gold. In South Africa, ostriches are hunted for the diamonds they may swallow. Ostriches in zoos have been known to eat wallets, watches, keys, and coins. Ostriches will eat anything.

Practice Finding the Main Idea

This unit asks you to find the main ideas of paragraphs. For example, read the paragraph and answer the question below.

The people of ancient Egypt created an advanced civilization. More than 6,000 years ago, they developed a calendar with 360 days divided into 12 months. The people made paper and learned to write. They built huge monuments with machines they invented.

_B_ **1.** The story mainly tells
   A. how people made paper
   B. about the creation of Egyptian civilization
   C. where an ancient calendar was invented
   D. how the people built monuments

The correct answer is **B**. The first sentence says, "The people of ancient Egypt created an advanced civilization." This is the main idea sentence. It tells what the people did. The other sentences are details. They tell how the Egyptians were an advanced society.

Sometimes a story does not have a main idea sentence. It is made up only of details. You put all the details together to find the main idea. Read the story below and answer the question. Write the letter of your answer on the blank line.

Microchips provide the power for wristwatches. They are also the brains in our computers, and they control robots. These chips are used in video games and space shuttles. They make our cameras, radios, and televisions small and light.

_____ **2.** The story mainly tells
   A. how computers work
   B. why televisions are small
   C. how microchips are used
   D. how cameras are made

Lesson 1

Read each passage. After each passage you will answer a question about the main idea of the passage. Remember, the main idea is the main point in a story.

1. Imagine testing glass by throwing chickens at it! Sometimes fast-moving airplanes fly through flocks of birds. If the birds hit the windshield of a plane, the glass could shatter and cause a crash. Airplane manufacturers have made a chicken cannon that fires rubber chickens at glass windshields. If the windshield doesn't break when the rubber chicken hits it, the designers know that the glass can withstand the force of a real crash.

_____ **1.** The story mainly tells
    A. why birds can be dangerous to airplanes
    B. how a chicken cannon tests glass
    C. how big a bird has to be to damage an airplane
    D. how the chicken cannon works

---

2. The harmless hognose snake is a champion bluffer. When this snake is threatened, it hisses and acts as if it will bite. If you don't run away, the hognose snake "plays dead." It rolls over on its back, wiggling around as if it's in distress. Then it "dies" with its mouth open and tongue hanging out. If you turn it on its stomach, the snake will roll over on its back again.

_____ **2.** The story mainly tells
    A. where the hognose snake is found
    B. what things frighten the hognose snake
    C. how dangerous the hognose snake is
    D. how the hognose snake bluffs

3. Doctors think that wearing red-tinted glasses can relieve sadness. Some people get very moody and sad in the winter. They may be affected by the brief days. Bright lights help some people but not everyone. The reddish light coming through rose-colored glasses seems to make people feel happy.

_____ **3.** The story mainly tells
 A. why happy people wear rose-colored glasses
 B. when some people get sad
 C. how short the daylight is in winter
 D. how colored glasses may help people feel better

---

4. The Marines had a problem in World War II. Orders were sent in code, but the enemy kept learning the code. Nothing could be kept secret. Then someone thought that Navajo soldiers could help the Marines. Since very few other people could speak Navajo, this language was used as a code. No one on the enemy side knew Navajo, so the messages stayed secret.

_____ **4.** The story mainly tells
 A. how Navajo people kept secrets
 B. when the secret code was used
 C. how the Marines used Navajo as a code
 D. why the original code had to be changed

---

5. Dogs have been called our best friends, but they are also good helpers. They can be used in many ways. Some dogs hunt while others guard animals and property. Boxers and German shepherds are trained to lead people who are blind. A dog named Laika was the first animal in space.

_____ **5.** The story mainly tells
 A. how many types of dogs there are
 B. what the name of the space dog was
 C. what kind of dogs can lead people who are blind
 D. how dogs are useful

1. Tap dancing started in America. It began as folk dancing that had much kicking and stamping. Over time two kinds of dancing developed. In one kind the dancers wore hard shoes and danced very fast. In the other they wore soft shoes and danced slowly and easily. There wasn't really any *tap* in tap dancing until 1925. That's when someone put metal pieces on the toes and heels of tap shoes.

_____ **1.** The story mainly tells
  A. how there are two kinds of tap dancing
  B. how tap shoes are made
  C. where some folk dances came from
  D. how tap dancing developed

---

2. Trousers are a recent style in the history of fashion. Men wore tights under short, loose pants until the early 1800s when the first real pants for men appeared. Until the 1940s few women wore long pants. During World War II, women factory workers started wearing long pants. The fashion caught on.

_____ **2.** The story mainly tells
  A. that long pants are a somewhat new fashion
  B. when men stopped wearing pantaloons
  C. who wore tights
  D. why women don't wear trousers

---

3. When you take a multiple-choice test, do you ever change your answers? Some scientists think that it is a smart thing to do. They found out that most students who change their answers make the right decision and make better scores on their tests.

_____ **3.** The story mainly tells
  A. how to study for tests
  B. what scientists think about answers
  C. how to score better on a multiple-choice test
  D. which answers to change on tests

4. It takes more than food to make babies grow up to be healthy and happy. If babies are not patted and hugged, they grow more slowly and are less healthy. Also they will not be as smart or as happy when they become adults. Many studies show that love is the most important thing in children's lives.

_____ **4.** The story mainly tells
- **A.** why good food is important to babies
- **B.** what makes babies grow up
- **C.** that children need love to grow up healthy
- **D.** how to have smart children

---

5. Probably the best-known rodeo cowboy in the world is Larry Mahan. Mahan was the national champion six times before he was 30. He was good at every event and was so successful that he had his own plane. When he got too old to be in the rodeo, he didn't stop doing rodeo work. He started a rodeo school.

_____ **5.** The story mainly tells
- **A.** where to ride bulls and rope calves
- **B.** about the most famous rodeo cowboy in the world
- **C.** how to get rich in the rodeo
- **D.** where to go to rodeo school

1. The lack of gravity in space makes even simple tasks a challenge. Astronauts have to wear boots that hold their feet to the floor so that they can walk around. Eating is a real chore. Dried and frozen foods are stored in plastic bags. To eat chicken soup, the astronauts cut a hole in one end of the bag and squeeze the soup into their mouths.

_____ **1.** The story mainly tells
- **A.** why there is little gravity in space
- **B.** why easy tasks are challenging in space
- **C.** why space food is stored in plastic bags
- **D.** how to eat chicken soup

2. "The War of the Worlds," a radio story, once started a panic. Because many people didn't hear that it was just a story about monsters from space, they thought the fake news bulletins were true. People were frantic. It took hours to calm them down and convince them that it was only a radio play.

_____ **2.** The story mainly tells
- **A.** what people thought about news stories
- **B.** why people were afraid of the monsters
- **C.** how a radio play fooled many people
- **D.** where the monsters in the story came from

3. Can fish climb trees? It sounds like a fishy story, but mudskippers living in the swamps of Asia really can climb trees. After filling their gills with air and water, they climb onto land. Mudskippers use their front fins to move along the ground. Suckers on their fins help them climb trees.

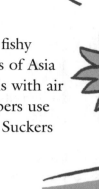

_____ **3.** The story mainly tells
    A. where mudskippers live
    B. how they fill their gills
    C. how mudskippers can climb trees
    D. where mudskippers have suckers

---

4. The peanut is a humble plant with hundreds of functions. Most peanuts are roasted in their shells and lightly salted. About half the peanuts eaten in the United States are ground into a thick paste called peanut butter. The rich oil made from peanuts is good for frying foods and is used for oiling machines and making soaps and paint. Even peanut shells are used to make plastics and to fertilize soil.

_____ **4.** The story mainly tells
    A. why peanut oil is used for frying
    B. how much peanut butter is eaten in the United States
    C. about the many uses of the peanut
    D. why peanut shells make good fertilizer

---

5. Some college teachers in Michigan have made a small computer that looks like an orange. It will be picked and handled like real fruit. Since much fruit is damaged on its way to market, this machine will measure shaking and temperature changes. The computerized orange will help people find ways to avoid damaging fruits during shipping.

_____ **5.** The story mainly tells
    A. where the computerized orange was created
    B. how the computer company helped make the machine
    C. what the computerized orange looks like
    D. about the purpose of the computerized orange

1. There are many ways to learn about people. You can learn a lot about people by simply watching or talking to them. Looking at the floor can also give you information about people. You can tell where people walk most frequently because of the worn carpet. The next time you're riding in someone else's car, notice the music on the radio. The type of music played on the station can tell a lot about the person!

_____ **1.** The story mainly tells
   A. how to guess where people walk
   B. how to learn about people
   C. how to listen to the radio
   D. how to watch people

2. A scientist believes that millions of animals have died every 26 million years. He thinks that comets are responsible for those deaths. Comets would explode on impact as they slammed into Earth. Dust from the explosions blocked light and heat from the Sun. Plants and animals on Earth could not withstand such conditions, so they died.

_____ **2.** The story mainly tells
   A. how often animals died
   B. why comets may come near Earth
   C. where the dust comes from
   D. about a possible cause of animal deaths in the past

3. The diamond is a hard element that can cut through almost any metal. That is why it is often used for industrial purposes. Whole diamond stones are set into tools. Dust from crushed diamond stones is used for coating the edges of tools. Care must be taken when exposing diamonds to extreme heat because heat can turn them into graphite. Graphite is the soft material used in the manufacture of lead for pencils.

_____ **3.** The story mainly tells
   A. how to turn a diamond into graphite
   B. how diamonds are used in industry
   C. how diamond dust coats tool edges
   D. when diamonds are used in pencils

4. Many people in India don't eat beef, but they still find many uses for cattle. Cows provide milk for drinking and for other dairy products. Young cattle are used for plowing fields and carrying big loads.

_____ **4.** The story mainly tells
- **A.** how cows are used in India
- **B.** where some people do not eat beef
- **C.** which cows plow fields
- **D.** what milk is used for

---

5. Fabergé, a jeweler, made eggs from rare metals and jewels. A Russian emperor liked them so much that he often gave them away as gifts. The elaborate eggs are only a few inches high. Some have tiny clocks inside them. Others hold small pictures or toys. The highest price ever paid for a Fabergé egg was more than $5.5 million!

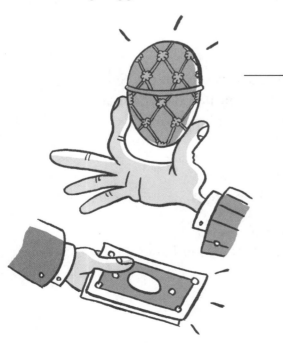

_____ **5.** The story mainly tells
- **A.** what Fabergé eggs are like
- **B.** who bought and gave the eggs as gifts
- **C.** what Fabergé eggs have in them
- **D.** how Fabergé made the eggs

1. Computers have changed quite a bit through the years. An early model could add 18 million numbers per hour. One person would have needed many years to do the same job. A modern computer can add 1 ½ trillion numbers in less than three hours.

_____ **1.** The story mainly tells
   A. who uses computers
   B. how long one person takes to do a job
   C. how computers have gotten faster over time
   D. how fast modern computers can add

2. Dolley Madison was the wife of President James Madison. She was quite a brave First Lady. When the White House burned down, Dolley rescued important government papers. She also saved the portrait of George Washington that hangs in the East Room today.

_____ **2.** The story mainly tells
   A. who Dolley Madison's husband was
   B. how the White House burned down
   C. about Dolley Madison's courageous acts
   D. where the portrait of George Washington hangs

3. Ages ago living things like bugs and leaves got trapped in soft tree resin. The resin hardened into what we know as amber. It kept the trapped bugs and leaves in perfect shape. Now scientists are learning much about the distant past from amber samples. Some scientists say they are more useful than fossils.

_____ **3.** The story mainly tells
- **A.** where bugs and leaves got trapped
- **B.** what hard resin is called
- **C.** why amber samples are important to scientists
- **D.** what scientists think of fossils

4. The beaver's front teeth have a hard, bright-orange covering. These teeth are used to cut and tear the bark off trees. The back teeth are flat and rough and are used for chewing. There are two flaps of skin between the front and back teeth. These flaps keep water and splinters from entering the beaver's mouth.

_____ **4.** The story mainly tells
- **A.** about the color of the front teeth
- **B.** how the two flaps of skin are used
- **C.** about the specially designed mouth of the beaver
- **D.** how splinters get into the beaver's mouth

5. Product codes on items consist of bars and numbers on the product label. The first numbers tell which company made the item. The last numbers identify the product and size. A laser reads the bars at the checkout. A computer finds the price for that product and prints the price on the cash-register slip. Store owners can change prices of items by changing the computer. The records in the computer help the owners learn which goods sell well.

_____ **5.** The story mainly tells
- **A.** how the product codes are developed
- **B.** how the product-code system is effective
- **C.** how one machine reads the numbers and bars
- **D.** how the numbers are assigned to companies

1. Native Americans dried strips of meat, pounded it into a paste, and then mixed it with fat. Sometimes they added berries and sugar. Then they pressed it into small cakes. They called these cakes pemmican. Pemmican didn't spoil, and it provided lots of energy for people traveling or going hunting. Today explorers still carry and eat this food.

_____ **1.** The story mainly tells
- **A.** who uses pemmican today
- **B.** what can be put into pemmican
- **C.** how pemmican was prepared by Native Americans
- **D.** why people eat pemmican today

2. Because lambs are sometimes eaten by coyotes, ranchers may hunt or trap the coyotes. However, killing coyotes may upset nature's balance. Scientists have found a way to protect sheep without killing coyotes. Coyotes are fed lamb meat treated with a drug. When they eat the meat, they get sick. Later, coyotes won't even go near lambs. They'll hunt rabbits instead.

_____ **2.** The story mainly tells
- **A.** why coyotes prefer rabbits to lambs
- **B.** why killing coyotes upsets nature's balance
- **C.** how scientists protect sheep and coyotes
- **D.** what kind of people do not like coyotes

3. The spots on a fawn's coat let it hide in shady areas without being seen. The viceroy butterfly looks like the bad-tasting monarch, so birds avoid both. The hognose snake hisses and rolls on its back when it fears another animal. When the opossum is attacked, it plays dead. Distressed turtles hide in their shells until they're sure it's safe to come out again.

_____ **3.** The story mainly tells
- **A.** how some animals protect themselves
- **B.** why some harmless animals look dangerous
- **C.** why spots or stripes make animals less visible
- **D.** why birds don't like monarch butterflies

4. For years food chemists have tasted hot peppers used for chili sauce, catsup, and pizza, but people had a hard time figuring out the spiciness of the peppers. After eating two or three, their taste buds were burning. Now a machine can test different kinds of hot peppers. It measures the chemicals that provide the spicy taste of the peppers.

_____ **4.** The story mainly tells
  A. how scientists measure chemicals
  B. how hot and spicy peppers are used
  C. why people have trouble tasting hot peppers
  D. how a machine helps the hot-pepper industry

---

5. The temperature in Antarctica once fell to 128 degrees below zero Fahrenheit. In the summertime, temperatures average well below freezing. Most of the land is covered with ice that is up to 2 miles thick. Only a few strong mosses and sturdy spiders can live on this big block of ice. Since very little snow or rain falls there, Antarctica is a desert.

_____ **5.** The story mainly tells
  A. about a desert with extremely cold temperatures
  B. which plants and insects live in Antarctica
  C. how much snow and rain fall there
  D. how low the temperature once fell

1. The rare Chinese panda lives on tender, young bamboo shoots. Most bamboo plants die right after flowering. Without the bamboo the pandas starve. Because some people fear that the rare pandas may die out, in some places food is given to the hungry animals. Some pandas are airlifted to places where bamboo is still plentiful.

_____ **1.** The story mainly tells
- **A.** what the Chinese pandas usually eat
- **B.** how the bamboo plants flower
- **C.** how people are keeping pandas alive
- **D.** why pandas sometimes starve to death

2. Air plants, such as mosses and lichens, grow on buildings and stones and get their food and water from the air around them. Other plants such as mistletoe get their food and water from the trees they live on. Sometimes these trees die if the plants take away too much food or water.

_____ **2.** The story mainly tells
- **A.** what kinds of plants grow on buildings
- **B.** why mistletoe sometimes kills trees
- **C.** how some plants don't live in soil
- **D.** how mosses and lichens get food and water

3. Alfred Nobel invented dynamite to help builders, but it was used for war, which made him feel very guilty about the misuse of his invention. He was a rich man, so he set up a $9 million fund. Today the fund is used to reward people who have improved human life. Nobel Prizes are awarded in six fields, including peace, medicine, and chemistry.

_____ **3.** The story mainly tells
  A. what the Nobel Prizes are awarded for
  B. why Nobel founded the Nobel Prize fund
  C. how much money was set aside for rewards
  D. what invention Alfred Nobel created

---

4. Bob Geldof talked to the top musical talents of the world and asked them to sing at a concert to raise money. The stars agreed. Geldof found a stadium, arranged for TV coverage, and set up a trust fund. He said that none of the stars would get special treatment. Everyone would work together. In 1985, the Live Aid concert raised more than $100 million for starving children.

_____ **4.** The story mainly tells
  A. how Geldof found a stadium
  B. how many musical stars agreed to sing
  C. why people are hungry in Africa
  D. how a concert benefited starving children

---

5. In real life, rattlesnakes try to avoid people and seldom attack. Most people are bitten only after they step on these snakes. A rattlesnake may not even inject its poison when it bites. In fact, more Americans die from insect stings than from snakebites!

_____ **5.** The story mainly tells
  A. how rattlesnakes aren't as dangerous as everyone believes
  B. why insects kill people
  C. when rattlesnakes use their poison
  D. how snakes bite

1. Every year hungry deer do millions of dollars' worth of damage to young pine trees. Scientists in Washington have found a way to protect the trees. They use a substance called selenium. Selenium produces a bad smell when dissolved. A bit of this element is put in the ground near trees. Rain dissolves the selenium, and the trees absorb it. The bad smell keeps the deer away until the trees are fully grown.

_____ **1.** The story mainly tells
    A. how much damage deer do to trees
    B. how trees can be protected from deer
    C. what selenium is
    D. why deer eat pine trees

2. Kitty O'Neil wanted to become a stunt person. She performed incredible stunts, such as 100-foot falls. O'Neil has been deaf since birth. She says she can concentrate better than most people who can hear. She is not bothered by the sounds around her.

_____ **2.** The story mainly tells
    A. when O'Neil fell 100 feet
    B. how long O'Neil has been deaf
    C. how O'Neil's disability has helped her career
    D. how to become a stunt person

3. Virginia Hamilton started writing at a young age. People in her family were great storytellers. She loved to listen to their tales about her African American heritage. When she grew up, Hamilton brought the tales to life in stories. Now she is a famous writer of books for children.

_____ **3.** The story mainly tells
    A. when Virginia Hamilton started writing
    B. how Hamilton's family told stories
    C. how family stories led to a writing career
    D. what kind of tales Hamilton's family told

4. Sharks have a keen sense of hearing and can smell blood from almost 2,000 yards away. Sharks also have a special system of channels in their skin that helps them feel the vibrations of a splashing swimmer. We know that in clear water, sharks can see dinner from about 50 feet away. If you ever spot a shark, always swim away smoothly!

_____ **4.** The story mainly tells
  A. how well sharks hear
  B. why sharks have poor vision
  C. how sharks sense food
  D. when to swim away smoothly

---

5. Garlic is one of the ingredients that makes pasta sauce taste so good. Now doctors think garlic has healing powers, too. Early tests show that it can kill harmful germs. Garlic also has been found to have a good effect on the blood. Doctors think it can help protect people against heart disease.

_____ **5.** The story mainly tells
  A. how garlic can help keep people healthy
  B. what goes into pasta sauce
  C. how garlic kills harmful bacteria
  D. how garlic affects the blood

Writing Roundup

Read each paragraph. Think about the main idea. Write the main idea in your own words.

1. In France, people like to eat a mushroomlike food called truffles. Truffles are not easy to find because they grow underground. Some people in France train pigs to find the right place to dig. The pigs can smell the truffles even though they are deep in the soil.

What is main idea of this paragraph?

_____

_____

2. A ballet that tells a story was not always performed the way we see such ballets now. Long ago only men were in the dance groups, and they wore masks when they danced the women's parts. The audiences were not fooled by these men playing women's parts.

What is the main idea of this paragraph?

_____

_____

_____

_____

3. Jan Matzeliger came to the United States from Africa. He worked as a shoemaker. This gave him the idea for a shoe-shaping machine. He sold the idea to others. The machine greatly increased shoe production. Matzeliger died in 1889. Sadly, few people knew that he had invented the machine until later.

What is the main idea of this paragraph?

_____

_____

Prewriting

Think of a main idea that you would like to write about, such as a great invention, a country you'd like to visit, or something you might train your pet to do. Fill in the chart below.

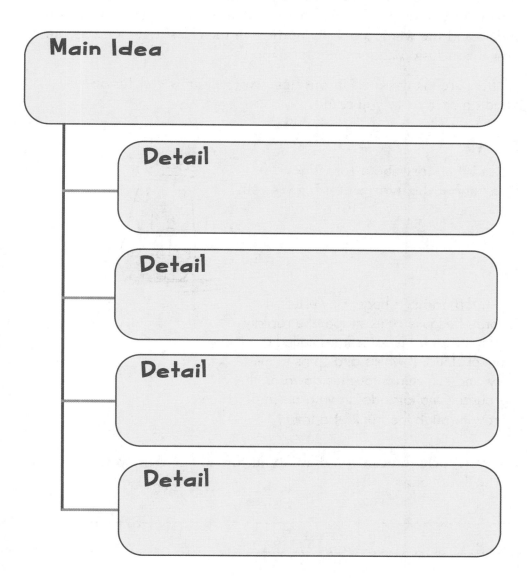

Main Idea

Detail

Detail

Detail

Detail

On Your Own

Now use another sheet of paper to write your paragraph. Underline the sentence that tells the main idea.

unit
5

What Is a Conclusion?

A conclusion is a decision you make after thinking about all the information you have. The writer may not state his or her conclusions in a story. As you read, you often have to hunt for clues. These help you understand the whole story. By putting all the clues together, you can draw a conclusion about the information.

There are many stories in this unit. You will draw conclusions based on each story you read.

Try It!

Read this story about tornadoes. Think about the information it gives you.

A tornado is a huge, powerful storm. Because of its shape, the rapidly spinning cloud is sometimes called a funnel cloud. It whirls and spins in the sky and sometimes touches down on the ground. One tornado drove a piece of straw through the trunk of a tree!

What conclusion can you draw about tornadoes? Write your conclusion on the lines below.

_____

_____

You might have written something such as, "Tornadoes can cause much destruction," or "Tornadoes can be very dangerous." You can draw these conclusions from the story. The first sentence says that a tornado is a very powerful storm. This conclusion is supported by the example in the last sentence. The third sentence tells you that these dangerous storms sometimes touch the ground. From these clues you can draw the conclusions above.

Using What You Know

Read each story on this page. Hunt for clues that will help you draw a conclusion about the location of the person telling each story.

1. I'm wearing a new suit. My hair is nicely combed. I got lost on my way here, but I drove around until I found it. I tucked a few papers into my briefcase. I took a few deep breaths, put on my best smile, and opened the office door. I really hope to get this job.

Where am I? _____

2. The first thing I do is drop some coins into a slot. Then I hold and point a hose at the car. The water comes out in a powerful spray, so I have to be careful not to put my hand in it. I can choose from cycles such as soap, rinse, and wax.

Where am I? _____

3. A few cars zoom by. Then a noisy bus passes. If only the light would hurry up and change. I must return the books before the library closes.

Where am I? _____

4. All I can hear is the wind. There isn't any traffic here. The air is very thin at this altitude. I try to take deep breaths. I think I'll have a snack before I climb any higher. I'm near the top, and I can see down into the valley, but I won't make it to the peak before lunchtime.

Where am I? _____

Read each passage. After each passage you will answer a question that will require you to draw a conclusion about the story. Remember, a conclusion is a decision you make after putting together all the clues you are given.

1. Doug Seuss trains bears to wreck cabins and chase actors in the movies. The animal trainer believes that the beasts are affectionate and smart. He romps in the creek with his 1,300-pound friend, Bart. Bart rides in the back of Doug's pickup truck to the car wash. That's where Bart takes a bath.

_____ **1.** From this story you can tell that
   A. bears don't take baths often
   B. Bart doesn't like pickups
   C. Doug is probably a good animal trainer
   D. Bart weighs less than Doug

2. The abacus is an ancient device made of beads that slide on sticks. It is widely thought that the abacus was used by storekeepers and money changers only in Asia. In fact, the abacus was also used in ancient Rome and Greece. The Russian scientists who launched the spacecraft *Sputnik* also used an abacus to do their calculations.

_____ **2.** From the story you can tell that an abacus
   A. is used to print money
   B. is used to do math
   C. is an invention of the Greeks
   D. is no longer used today

3. In the 1800s two brothers were traveling west in a covered wagon. They grew to detest each other so much that one brother sawed the wagon in half and drove away. He left his brother stranded on the prairie with the back half of the wagon and one set of oxen.

_____ **3.** The stranded brother probably
   A. was angry
   B. bought a car
   C. read some books
   D. was sleepy

4. A gorilla named Koko learned sign language. One day Koko pulled two fingers across her cheeks to indicate whiskers. She wanted a kitten. She was given one that she named All Ball. Koko cuddled and stroked All Ball just as a mother gorilla would stroke a baby gorilla. She dressed All Ball in linen napkins and hats. Koko and All Ball also tickled each other. How did Koko feel about All Ball? "Soft, good cat cat," she said in sign language.

_____ **4.** You can tell from the story that
   A. kittens like to wear hats
   B. Koko hates to tickle animals
   C. gorillas can be loving and intelligent
   D. baby gorillas have whiskers

5. Thomas Jefferson's home, Monticello, is famous. Many people visited the president there and Jefferson could not turn guests away. He had another home near Lynchburg, Virginia. It was called Poplar Forest, and Jefferson went there when Monticello got too crowded.

_____ **5.** For Jefferson, Poplar Forest was a place
   A. to get away from the heat at Monticello
   B. where he could be a real farmer
   C. he liked better than Monticello
   D. to be alone

1. The planet Saturn is famous for the rings around it. The rings are made of tiny pieces of matter floating around the planet. The space ship *Voyager 2* has shown that gravity pulls the pieces away from the ring. They fall toward Saturn. As more pieces fall, there appears to be less of a ring.

_____ 1. This story suggests that
      A. Saturn may not always have its rings
      B. Saturn is the only planet to have rings
      C. *Voyager 2* changed the rings of Saturn
      D. gravity keeps the rings in place

2. Weather experts can predict rain, snow, and sunshine fairly well. Now scientists can predict where lightning will strike. They can warn airplane pilots to change their routes. Also, people in charge of golf tournaments can adjust the playing schedule.

_____ 2. From this story you can tell that
      A. experts can predict when lightning will strike
      B. airplanes aren't affected by lightning
      C. experts are usually in charge of tournaments
      D. lightning is a common danger at golf tournaments

3. The American tarantula is a large, hairy spider. It scares most people when they see it. Fortunately, the spider's bite is harmless, but it can be painful.

_____ 3. From this story you can tell that
      A. tarantulas move fast
      B. all people are afraid of tarantulas
      C. tarantulas sting many people
      D. most people try to avoid tarantulas

4. In 1791, surgeon George Hamilton went down with a ship off the coast of Australia. Years later when divers examined the wreck, they found the doctor's silver pocket watch stopped at 12 minutes past 11. They also found a small bottle with an oily liquid in it. It contained oil of cloves used by the doctor. The liquid was still fragrant after almost 200 years in the ocean.

_____ **4.** From the story you can conclude that
    A. glass helps preserve liquids under water
    B. surgeon Hamilton had many children
    C. the divers found the wreck at 11:12 P.M.
    D. small bottles hold liquids better than big bottles

5. The male bowerbird of Australia courts his mate inside a colorful bower, or playhouse. First the bird builds a kind of castle made of towers, huts, and pathways. He decorates this den with butterfly wings, flowers, shells, and stones. Then he waits for the female bowerbird to admire his work.

_____ **5.** You can tell that the male bowerbird
    A. cannot fly very far
    B. builds its bower to keep out the rain and heat
    C. is a coastal bird that eats fish
    D. builds its bower to attract a mate

1. Tomatoes used to be considered poisonous, perhaps because of their bright color. In 1820, a man in Salem, New Jersey, proved that they weren't harmful. Robert Johnson ate an entire basket of tomatoes in front of the whole town. His doctor was there and was sure that Johnson would die.

_____ **1.** From this story you can tell that
- **A.** some brightly colored plants are poisonous
- **B.** tomatoes are usually dull looking
- **C.** Johnson was afraid he would die
- **D.** Johnson's doctor liked tomatoes

2. Only one president has been stopped for speeding while holding office. A police officer stopped Ulysses S. Grant when he was driving a horse and buggy too fast. This was not even Grant's first offense. He was fined $5 twice before for breaking the speed limit.

_____ **2.** From this story you can tell that
- **A.** Grant was stopped for speeding five times
- **B.** speed limits were in use before cars were invented
- **C.** Grant had a special reason for speeding
- **D.** the speed limit was 5 miles per hour then

3. There is actually a summer camp for dogs in New York. The counselors hold treasure hunts for dogs by hiding dog biscuits. The camp sends regular reports about the dogs to their owners. Each report is signed with the dog's paw print.

_____ **3.** You can conclude that the dogs probably
- **A.** learn weaving and crafts on rainy days
- **B.** get homesick often
- **C.** are owned by people who treat their dogs like children
- **D.** are taught tricks by the counselors

---

4. Mechanical clocks are about 700 years old, but daily time was measured as many as 3,000 years ago. The ancient Egyptians measured time with a shadow stick. It cast a shadow across markers as the sun moved. Another "clock" was a candle marked with numbers.

_____ **4.** You can tell from the story that
- **A.** you can use a shadow stick at night
- **B.** the Egyptians were interested in mechanical clocks
- **C.** measuring time has interested people for ages
- **D.** people have always measured time with candles

---

5. Many people believe that margarine was invented during World War II. This substitute for butter was actually made by the French in 1869. It wasn't used widely in the United States because dairy farmers were against its sale. Wisconsin had the last law against it. That law ended in 1967.

_____ **5.** You can tell from the story that
- **A.** dairy farmers approved of the use of margarine
- **B.** Wisconsin probably had many dairy farmers
- **C.** French dairy farmers opposed the use of margarine
- **D.** margarine was widely used in America before 1967

1. Most people are afraid of something. A study was conducted to determine the things that people fear most. The research found that men and women tend to have the same fears. The basic difference is the order in which they rate these fears. For example, men fear bats and speaking in public the most. Women fear fire, dead people, and rats the most.

_____ **1.** From the story you can tell that
- **A.** male and female fears are alike and yet different
- **B.** everyone likes rats
- **C.** women fear bats more than men do
- **D.** everyone is afraid of chickens

2. Sarah Winnemucca worked to protect Native American rights. Her father was a chief of the Paiute tribe in Nevada. As a child she moved to California, where she lived with a white family. She attended school and learned to speak English. As an adult she became a teacher and tried to make peace between the white settlers and her native tribe. She even met to discuss the situation with President Hayes.

_____ **2.** From the story you <u>cannot</u> tell
- **A.** where Winnemucca's tribe lived
- **B.** that Winnemucca spoke English
- **C.** the name of Winnemucca's father
- **D.** what Winnemucca did as an adult

3. Man o' War was a wonderful racehorse. He won 20 of 21 races and set five world records. When Man o' War died in 1947, his owner Samuel Riddle had him buried. Riddle, who died in 1963, remembered the horse in his last will and testament. He left $4,000,000 to maintain Man o' War's grave.

_____ **3.** From the story you <u>cannot</u> tell
- **A.** when Man o' War died
- **B.** how many races Man o' War won
- **C.** when Samuel Riddle died
- **D.** where Man o' War is buried

4. William Pace was a pig farmer in Mississippi. He didn't raise his pigs in the ordinary way. Instead of letting the pigs wallow in the mud and heat, he fattened the creatures in the barn by using a giant fan and a TV set. Pace believed that the pigs were happier if they could watch television. The pigs' favorite show seemed to be wrestling!

_____ **4.** You can conclude that William Pace
    A. thought happy pigs grew fatter
    B. used regular ways to raise pigs
    C. lived in Missouri
    D. trained his pigs to wrestle

---

5. In the 1800s miners carried canaries into the mines with them. The canaries not only provided music but also served an important purpose. If the birds stopped singing, it was a signal to the miners that there was little oxygen left in the mine.

_____ **5.** The story suggests that canaries
    A. were good miners
    B. needed enough air to sing
    C. were useless to the miners
    D. needed darkness to sing

1. Restaurants come in many shapes in Los Angeles, California. One building looks like a large chili bowl. Another one is shaped like a hot dog. For a fast snack, you can drive through a building that looks like two doughnuts.

_____ **1.** You can conclude that
  A. these restaurants serve the best food
  B. all the restaurants serve doughnuts
  C. these buildings were designed by cooks
  D. the shapes tell about the main food served

2. Travelers often stop to wonder at unusual buildings. There's a house made of salt in Grand Saline, Texas. Both Kentucky and Tennessee have houses built from coal. In a town in Maine, visitors gape at a building made from paper. A tour of a house in Florida tells how this house was carved from coral.

_____ **2.** You can tell that unusual houses are
  A. tourist attractions
  B. pleasant to live in
  C. not very popular
  D. usually built of wood

3. One of the deadliest fish in the world is the puffer. In Japan this fish is called fugu. Some people in Japan like to eat fugu. Cooks have been trained to remove the poisonous parts from the fish. Then they arrange the raw fish into beautiful designs and serve it. Even so, as many as 50 Japanese die from fugu poison each year.

_____ **3.** From this story you can tell that
    A. eating fugu is safe
    B. most Japanese eat fugu
    C. eating fugu is a daring deed
    D. puffers are found only in Japan

4. Scientists are working to make computers think more like people. People say things such as "add a little more." Today's computers cannot understand "little." *Little* is not a real amount. They can only understand terms such as *5 ounces*.

_____ **4.** From this story you can tell that
    A. computers will think like people in 20 years
    B. computers would not understand *a bunch*
    C. people think like machines
    D. computers give the wrong information

5. Alice Childress wrote *A Hero Ain't Nothin' but a Sandwich.* The novel tells the story of Benjie Johnson. Benjie is a 13-year-old boy. His life becomes difficult when he gets involved with the wrong people.

_____ **5.** This story does <u>not</u> tell
    A. who the author of the book is
    B. what the title of the book is
    C. how old Benjie is
    D. how Benjie solves his problems

1. Longfellow wrote a poem that made Paul Revere famous for his ride to Concord to warn that the British were coming. Actually, Revere never made it to Concord, and he did not ride alone. Two other riders, William Dawes and Dr. Samuel Prescott, went with him. It was Dr. Prescott who warned Concord about the British.

_____ **1.** From this story you <u>cannot</u> tell
    A. whether the people of Concord were warned
    B. how the people of Concord got the warning
    C. that Revere never made it to Concord
    D. whether or not Longfellow wrote a good poem

2. The United States is full of small, special museums. There is a Sport Fishing Museum in New York, a museum of locks in Connecticut, and the Maple Museum in Vermont. The Lumberman's Museum is located in Maine, and the Petrified Creatures Museum is found in New York.

_____ **2.** In the Vermont museum, you could probably find
    A. a sport fish caught by a lumberman
    B. a petrified fish
    C. maple syrup buckets
    D. a petrified lumberman

3. The parasol ant of South America gets its name from the way it carries a bit of leaf over its head. Native Brazilians call them doctor ants. They use the ants' strong jaws to clamp down on deep cuts and keep them closed. Once the jaws clamp, the Brazilians pinch off the ants' bodies to keep the wound sealed.

_____ **3.** From the story you can tell that
    A. parasol ants haven't been named correctly
    B. the ants' jaws stay closed after the ants die
    C. native Brazilians named the ants "parasol ants"
    D. the ants like sunshine

4. In 1883, a California postal carrier named Jim Stacy found a stray dog, whom he called Dorsey. Dorsey accompanied Stacy on his mail route. Stacy got sick shortly after finding Dorsey, so he tied the mail along with a note to the dog's back and sent him out alone. Dorsey delivered the mail in this fashion until 1886.

_____ **4.** From this story you can conclude that
   A. Stacy was sick for a long time
   B. Dorsey would never leave Stacy's side
   C. the note told people what to feed Dorsey
   D. Dorsey received a medal from the post office

5. The odd-looking dodo bird became extinct shortly after it was discovered. In 1598, it was found on an island by a Dutch admiral. The admiral took some birds back with him to Europe. Pictures of the dodo were painted and appeared everywhere. But by 1681, every dodo in the world had died.

_____ **5.** The story suggests that
   A. the discovery of the dodo led to its disappearance
   B. the birds were painted for their great beauty
   C. the Dutch were good painters
   D. the dodo came from Europe originally

1. Working at home sounds like fun. You can work in your pajamas, or you can play the radio as loud as you want. You can even sleep an extra hour in the morning. However, making money at home takes drive and dedication. To be successful you must use basic business practices. You must make yourself work rather than play.

_____ **1.** To be successful you would probably need to
   A. stock the refrigerator with plenty of food
   B. make a schedule and stick to it
   C. plan when to take naps
   D. work as little as possible

2. In the seventeenth century, the Incan people of South America had an empire that stretched more than 2,500 miles. They built highways throughout their empire. One of their tunnels extended 750 feet through a mountain cliff. One of their rope suspension bridges is still used today.

_____ **2.** From this story you <u>cannot</u> tell
   A. the size of the Inca Empire
   B. in what period the Inca lived
   C. if the Inca were skilled in engineering
   D. why the roads were important to the Inca

3. When the Tacoma Narrows Bridge was built in 1940, it was the world's third-largest suspension bridge. Large suspension bridges had been built before, but the builders didn't count on the winds near Tacoma, Washington. Four months after its opening, the bridge was blown down.

_____ **3.** From this story you can conclude that
  A. earlier bridges weren't in high-wind areas
  B. the Tacoma Narrows Bridge was too large
  C. high winds have little effect on suspension bridges
  D. the two larger bridges had similar problems

4. From news reports about Russia, you may think that the Kremlin is a large building in Moscow. Actually, there are many kremlins in Russia. _Kremlin_ means "fortress" in Russian. In Moscow the Kremlin is not one building but many buildings inside a walled yard.

_____ **4.** You can tell that Moscow's Kremlin probably
  A. is the only one in Russia
  B. is a large building in Russia
  C. was originally a fortress
  D. is never visited by news reporters

5. The Egyptian pyramids were built from stones weighing about 2 ½ tons each. The structures are 40 stories high. The number of stones used in each pyramid could build a wall around France. Yet the Egyptians used no animals. They had no cranes at that time. The wheel wasn't even in use.

_____ **5.** You can tell from this story that
  A. the Egyptians built a wall around France
  B. the work must have been done by many people
  C. the pyramids were 2 ½ stories high
  D. each pyramid weighed about 2 ½ tons

1. Ana carefully filled the bird feeders in her backyard. The many trees that grew on her property were home to various kinds of birds. Ana enjoyed watching the birds and listening to them as they came to eat the seeds she provided for them.

_____ **1.** This story does <u>not</u> tell
   A. what kind of food Ana gives the birds
   B. what kinds of birds come to the bird feeders
   C. where the bird feeders are located
   D. where the birds lived

2. The special material in our body that makes us who we are is called DNA. Except for identical twins, everybody has different DNA. Since DNA is everywhere in the body, DNA patterns are generally better than fingerprints for identifying people. Police sometimes use DNA patterns to identify suspects.

_____ **2.** From this story you can tell that
   A. some people have no DNA
   B. DNA is not found in hair
   C. fingerprints are the only way to identify people
   D. DNA patterns can help solve crimes

3. Wind does not push sailboats forward. Instead, the sailboats *fall*. The sails on the boat form a curve when the wind passes across them. The curve creates an empty space behind the sail. The boat goes forward by falling into the empty space.

_____ **3.** From this story you <u>cannot</u> tell
   A. why the sails on a sailboat form a curve
   B. how the sailboat moves forward
   C. how an empty space is created
   D. how the sails are attached to the boat

4. In a radio interview, Albert Einstein was once asked whether he got his great thoughts while relaxing in the bathtub, walking, or sitting in his office. Einstein replied, "I don't really know. I've only had one or maybe two."

_____ **4.** From this story you can tell that Einstein
  A. thought much like the interviewer
  B. enjoyed radio interviews
  C. thought too much value was placed on his ideas
  D. thought best while walking

5. A comet is like a dirty ball of snow. It is made of frozen gases, frozen water, and dust. As a comet approaches the sun, the icy center gets hot and evaporates. The gases made by the evaporation form the tail of the comet. The dust left behind in the process forms meteor showers.

_____ **5.** You can conclude from the story that
  A. comets are made of snow
  B. throwing a ball of snow can turn it into a comet
  C. the sun helps create the tail of the comet
  D. meteor showers are visible with a telescope

Writing Roundup

Read each paragraph. Think about a conclusion you can draw. Write your conclusion in a complete sentence.

1. Polo is a game played on horseback. Each team has four players who attempt to hit a ball with their sticks. Each player has to handle the stick with his or her right hand and control the horse with the left hand. The team that scores more goals wins. Goals are scored by hitting the ball inside the other team's goalposts.

What conclusion can you draw from this paragraph?

_____

_____

2. Phillis Wheatley was born in Africa. At the age of eight, she was brought to America as a slave. There she learned English and Latin, and she managed to gain her freedom. In 1770, she published her first poem. After that she gained fame as a poet. She even shared her poetry with others when she made a trip to England in 1773.

What conclusion can you draw from this paragraph?

_____

_____

3. Alonso is building a weather station. He wants to record details about the weather in his town. So far he has a thermometer to measure air temperature, a gauge to measure rainfall, and a windsock to check wind direction. He still needs something to measure snowfall.

What conclusion can you draw from this paragraph?

_____

_____

Read the paragraph below. What conclusions can you draw? Use the clues in the paragraph to answer the questions in complete sentences.

Juneteenth is a holiday in Texas. It's also celebrated by some people in California and other western states. It can be traced back to the time Union troops arrived in Texas on June 19, 1865. They brought news that the Civil War had ended and that all the slaves were free. This put an end to slavery in Texas. Juneteenth got its name from some people in Texas who had their own way to say "June 19th." Their way stuck!

1. Is Juneteenth a holiday in all states? How do you know?

_____

_____

2. Was there slavery in Texas? How do you know?

_____

_____

3. Before the Union troops arrived, did Texans know the Civil War was over? How do you know?

_____

_____

4. Did Californians coin the word *Juneteenth*? How do you know?

_____

_____

What Is an Inference?

An inference is a guess you make after thinking about what you already know. For example, suppose you plan to go to the beach. From what you know about beaches, you might infer that the beach is covered with sand and the sun is shining.

An author does not write every detail in a story. If every detail were included, stories would be long and boring, and the main point would be lost. As you read, the writer expects you to fill in missing details from your own experiences. Suppose you read, "Sabrina went to the library." The writer does not have to tell you the specifics about what a library is. You already know it is a place where people go when they want to borrow books. You might infer that there are tables and chairs where people can sit and read books and magazines. People who have library cards may check out books and other materials and take them home. By filling in these missing details, you can infer that Sabrina went to the library to check out books. You can make this inference based on what you know.

Try It!

Read this story about blacksmiths, and then think about the facts.

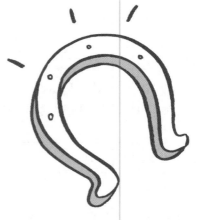

There were many blacksmiths in colonial America. Blacksmiths spent long hours hammering the hot iron used to make tools. They made horseshoes, axes, hoes, plow blades, kettles, and pots for the townspeople. Blacksmiths who lived near shipyards made anchors, rudder irons, and tools for ships.

What inference can you make about blacksmiths? Write an inference on the line below.

_____

You might have written something such as, "Blacksmiths made most of the important tools in colonial America." You can make these inferences by putting together the facts in the story and what you already know.

Practice Making Inferences

Read each story, and then read the statements that follow. Some of the statements are facts. They can be found in the story. Other statements are inferences. Decide whether each statement is a fact or an inference. The first one has been done for you.

Rebecca's mother woke her up at 6:30. "I have to leave early for work this morning," she said. "Please get up and start dressing so you'll be ready when the bus comes." Rebecca turned over and pulled the pillow over her head.

Fact	Inference		
○	●	**1.** **A.**	Rebecca went back to sleep.
●	○	**B.**	Rebecca's mother woke her up.
○	●	**C.**	Rebecca missed the bus.
○	●	**D.**	Rebecca wasn't ready to get up.

The first sentence of the story says that Rebecca's mother woke her, so we know that **B** is a fact. You can guess that Rebecca went back to sleep, but it isn't stated in the story, so **A** is an inference. You can also guess that Rebecca missed the bus and that she wasn't ready to get up, but neither of these is stated in the story. Therefore, **C** and **D** are also inferences.

Every summer sea turtles come to the remote beaches near Boca Raton, Florida. With their large front flippers, the female turtles dig large pits in the sand and then deposit perfectly round, white eggs. The eggs have leathery shells. The female turtle pushes sand over the eggs, and then she crawls back into the ocean. Scientists take many groups of people to see the sea turtles laying their eggs.

Fact	Inference		
○	○	**2.** **A.**	Sea turtles dig large pits in the sand.
○	○	**B.**	Many people are interested in the sea turtles.
○	○	**C.**	The mother turtle does not stay with the eggs.
○	○	**D.**	The eggs have leathery shells.

Read the passages. Use what you know about inference to answer the questions. Remember, an inference is a guess you make by putting together what you know and what you read or see in the stories.

1. The construction of the Tower of Pisa began in 1174. The builders made a big mistake. They built the foundation in sand, and sand shifts frequently. Over the years the tower started to lean. It now is more than 16 feet out of line.

Fact	Inference		
○	○	**1. A.**	Modern builders don't build on sand.
○	○	**B.**	The shifting sand caused the tower to lean.
○	○	**C.**	Construction of the tower began in 1174.
○	○	**D.**	The tower now leans more than 16 feet.

---

2. Men and women button their clothes differently. There is a good reason for this difference. Buttons were first used to fasten clothes more than 700 years ago. Buttons were expensive then, and only rich people could buy them. Most men are right-handed, so men's clothes were made to be buttoned easily by right-handed men. In those days most rich women were dressed by their right-handed servants. The servants faced the women to button their clothes. Women's clothes had buttons on the left so they could be buttoned easily by the servants.

Fact	Inference		
○	○	**2. A.**	Buttons were first used more than 700 years ago.
○	○	**B.**	At first buttons were expensive.
○	○	**C.**	Rich men dressed themselves.
○	○	**D.**	Most rich women were dressed by servants.

3. Scientists measure the distances in space in light-years. A light-year is the distance that light travels in 365 days. A light-year is about 5,880 billion miles. The closest star to Earth is about 4.3 light-years away. That means that the light from the star took 4.3 years to reach Earth.

Fact   Inference

○   ○   **3.** **A.** Distance in space is measured in light-years.

○   ○   **B.** The light we see from stars has traveled through space for many years.

○   ○   **C.** Light from different stars travels through space at the same speed.

○   ○   **D.** The farther away a star is, the longer it takes the light to reach Earth.

---

4. Rodney bragged to his friends that he could find his way around anywhere. One day, though, Rodney was delivering pizza in a strange part of town. Though he searched for half an hour, he could not locate the address. Finally he had to stop to ask for directions. His face turned red, and he stuttered as he asked how to find the place.

Fact   Inference

○   ○   **4.** **A.** Rodney didn't have a city map.

○   ○   **B.** Asking for directions embarrassed Rodney.

○   ○   **C.** Rodney delivered pizzas.

○   ○   **D.** Rodney searched for half an hour.

---

5. The Civil War ended in 1865. The two opposing generals, Ulysses S. Grant and Robert E. Lee, met to discuss the terms of surrender. The site was a small town in Virginia called Appomattox Courthouse. The meeting was quiet and short, and they soon agreed to the terms. Afterward Grant said he was not overjoyed by the end of the war. Instead Grant felt sad Lee had lost. Grant respected Lee as a man who fought bravely for a cause he believed in.

Fact   Inference

○   ○   **5.** **A.** The Civil War ended in 1865.

○   ○   **B.** Lee felt the terms were fair.

○   ○   **C.** Lee and Grant met in Virginia.

○   ○   **D.** Grant felt sad that Lee had lost.

1. John Milton was one of England's greatest poets, but at the age of 44 he went blind. Since Milton could no longer write, he had to tell his poems to his daughter, who wrote them down. This method was slow and tiring. Milton's greatest poem, *Paradise Lost*, was long and took many months to complete.

Fact	Inference		
○	○	**1. A.**	John Milton was a poet.
○	○	**B.**	Milton's daughter was very helpful.
○	○	**C.**	John Milton went blind.
○	○	**D.**	Milton's greatest poem was *Paradise Lost*.

2. Mary worked as a cook in a cafe. One day she got the great idea to cook the world's largest pancake. For days she worked to build a giant frying pan. Then she mixed pancake batter all night long. When she poured the batter in the pan and heard the familiar sizzle, she knew her idea had worked.

Fact	Inference		
○	○	**2. A.**	Mary worked in a cafe.
○	○	**B.**	Mary wanted to do something unusual.
○	○	**C.**	She cooked the world's largest pancake.
○	○	**D.**	The large pancake made Mary famous.

3. Roy Campanella was a baseball catcher for the Brooklyn Dodgers. He was named the best player in the National League three times. His career came to a halt suddenly in 1958 when he was paralyzed in a car wreck.

Fact	Inference		
○	○	**3. A.**	Roy Campanella was a catcher.
○	○	**B.**	The Dodgers played in Brooklyn.
○	○	**C.**	Campanella was in a car wreck in 1958.
○	○	**D.**	His injuries were very serious.

4. The hare thought he was a pretty fast fellow. One day he thought he would have some fun, so he challenged the tortoise to a race. Much to the hare's delight, the tortoise accepted the challenge. When the day of the race arrived, the hare quickly got ahead and decided to take a nap. The tortoise kept up a slow, steady pace and soon passed the sleeping hare. By the time the hare woke up, it was too late, for the steady tortoise had won the race.

Fact	Inference	
○	○	**4. A.** The hare thought he could beat the tortoise.
○	○	**B.** The race was between the hare and tortoise.
○	○	**C.** The hare underestimated the tortoise.
○	○	**D.** The tortoise won the race.

5. John Wesley Powell loved the American West. He liked to study its different rocks and their forms. In 1871, when he was exploring the Colorado River, he found an enormous canyon. It was later named the Grand Canyon. Powell and his group then followed the river through the canyon. Theirs was the first recorded boat trip through the Grand Canyon.

Fact	Inference	
○	○	**5. A.** Powell explored the Colorado River.
○	○	**B.** Powell found the Grand Canyon.
○	○	**C.** The boat ride in the canyon was exciting.
○	○	**D.** Powell studied rocks and their forms.

1. Janna liked to jog every day. One day as she was jogging, she spotted something in the grass, so she decided to investigate. It was a wallet full of money. Janna knew she could just keep the money and no one would ever find out about it. Janna also knew that the person who lost the wallet probably needed the money. Janna took the wallet to the police station.

Fact	Inference	
○	○	**1. A.** Janna was an honest person.
○	○	**B.** A wallet was lying in the grass.
○	○	**C.** The police looked for the owner of the wallet.
○	○	**D.** Jogging was one of Janna's favorite activities.

2. In Greek legends King Midas loved gold and wealth. For an act of friendship, Midas received a wish. Midas wished that everything he touched would turn to gold. The king was granted his wish, but he soon realized he had made a serious mistake when even his food and drink turned to gold.

Fact	Inference	
○	○	**2. A.** King Midas loved gold.
○	○	**B.** Everything Midas touched turned to gold.
○	○	**C.** King Midas was greedy.
○	○	**D.** The king didn't like his golden touch.

3. When Jim Abbott was born, part of his arm had not formed completely. He had only one working hand, but Jim made the most of his situation. In college Jim became the star pitcher of the baseball team. He played so well that he was later signed by a professional team. Jim Abbott became a major-league pitcher.

Fact	Inference		
○	○	**3. A.**	Abbott overcame his disability.
○	○	**B.**	People were impressed by Abbott's skill.
○	○	**C.**	In college Abbott was a pitcher.
○	○	**D.**	Abbott was signed by a professional team.

4. Mosquitoes are a tremendous problem in the summer. Mosquitoes love the hot weather. Then they can fly around and bite as many people as they want. Mosquitoes can't beat their wings in cool weather. The temperature must be more than 60 degrees for mosquitoes to fly.

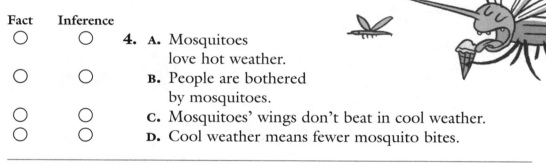

Fact	Inference		
○	○	**4. A.**	Mosquitoes love hot weather.
○	○	**B.**	People are bothered by mosquitoes.
○	○	**C.**	Mosquitoes' wings don't beat in cool weather.
○	○	**D.**	Cool weather means fewer mosquito bites.

5. Janet was waiting in line at the supermarket. The line at the checkout counter was long, and some of the customers were getting angry. The clerk was having trouble with the cash register. Janet could see that the clerk was about to cry. Finally Janet's turn came to check out. Janet paid for her purchase and smiled as the clerk returned her change. After counting the change, Janet realized the clerk had given her too much money. Janet informed the clerk, and the clerk smiled in appreciation.

Fact	Inference		
○	○	**5. A.**	The customers didn't like waiting in line.
○	○	**B.**	Janet was a good person.
○	○	**C.**	The clerk was having a bad day.
○	○	**D.**	Janet received too much change.

1. The Pig War took place in the 1880s between Great Britain and the United States. It was not really a war, just a big argument. The dispute happened on an island off the state of Washington. An American man shot a pig owned by a British man. Because of this event, the two nations were willing to go to war. In the end, the problem was solved without fighting.

Fact	Inference		
○	○	**1.** **A.**	The Pig War took place on an island.
○	○	**B.**	The man was upset that his pig was shot.
○	○	**C.**	An American man shot the pig.
○	○	**D.**	The two governments met to discuss the problem.

2. As the ants worked to gather food for the winter, the grasshopper enjoyed himself. He played the fiddle and took long naps. The ants warned him that he should get busy, but he ignored them. Soon winter arrived, and the grasshopper found himself hungry and miserable out in the cold.

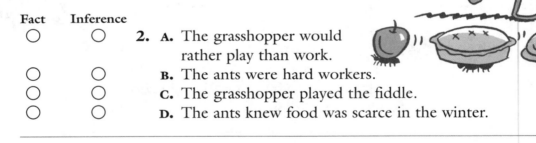

Fact	Inference		
○	○	**2.** **A.**	The grasshopper would rather play than work.
○	○	**B.**	The ants were hard workers.
○	○	**C.**	The grasshopper played the fiddle.
○	○	**D.**	The ants knew food was scarce in the winter.

3. Richard Byrd was a famous American explorer. In 1930, he was in Antarctica. His party had to leave suddenly because of illness. Byrd returned to his base there three years later. Though the buildings they had used earlier were covered with ice, things inside were exactly as they had left them. A mess on a dining table remained. Food they had left was still good. Even the lights sprang to life after being off for so long.

Fact	Inference		
○	○	**3.** **A.**	Antarctica is cold and icy.
○	○	**B.**	Richard Byrd was an American explorer.
○	○	**C.**	Richard Byrd was in Antarctica in 1930.
○	○	**D.**	The explorers were in a hurry when they left.

4. Thaddeus Cahill knew from an early age that he wanted to invent things. He loved studying the way musical sounds are made. In 1906, he created the largest and most expensive musical instrument ever made. He gave it a long name—the Telharmonium. It was 60 feet long and weighed 200 tons. This instrument could generate many sounds that no one had ever heard before.

Fact   **Inference**

○   ○   **4. A.** The instrument was the largest ever made.
○   ○   **B.** Cahill wanted to invent things.
○   ○   **C.** The instrument weighed 200 tons.
○   ○   **D.** Cahill knew a lot about instrument sounds.

---

5. As a child Jane Goodall loved to study animals and insects. She took notes on birds and bugs. She even opened a small museum for her friends. She hoped to travel to Africa when she grew up. At age 26 she got her wish and went to Kenya. She stayed in Africa and has become a famous scientist. Her field of study is the behavior of chimpanzees. Goodall has claimed her success is due to patience, courage, observation, and will power.

Fact   **Inference**

○   ○   **5. A.** Jane Goodall studies chimpanzees.
○   ○   **B.** Her friends liked Goodall's museum.
○   ○   **C.** Jane Goodall enjoys her work.
○   ○   **D.** Goodall went to Kenya at age 26.

1. Tulips were first grown in Turkey. The word *tulip* comes from a Turkish word meaning *turban*. A turban is a type of scarf worn wrapped around the head. In the 1600s tulips became very popular in Holland. Single tulip bulbs were bought and sold for incredibly high prices.

Fact	Inference		
○	○	**1. A.**	Tulips were popular in Holland.
○	○	**B.**	Only wealthy people could buy tulips.
○	○	**C.**	The word *tulip* comes from a Turkish word.
○	○	**D.**	Tulips look similar to turbans.

2. Kristin and her younger brother Andrew were planning to surprise their parents for their anniversary. They wanted to take them out to a nice French restaurant. After considering several ways to earn money, Kristin had an idea. The next Saturday Kristin and Andrew set up a soft-pretzel and lemonade stand in the park. They sold 57 soft pretzels and 83 cups of lemonade. The money they made was more than enough for their parents' anniversary surprise.

Fact	Inference		
○	○	**2. A.**	Andrew is younger than Kristin.
○	○	**B.**	Kristin and Andrew like French food.
○	○	**C.**	The people at the park were thirsty.
○	○	**D.**	Kristin and Andrew sold pretzels.

3. Have you ever wondered how a remote control unit can communicate with your TV set? It looks like magic, but it can be easily explained. The remote control unit sends a signal to the television as an invisible light. Humans cannot see it, but the television can. When the television senses the light, it responds by changing the channel or adjusting the volume.

Fact	Inference		
○	○	**3.** **A.**	Remote controls make changing channels easy.
○	○	**B.**	Remote controls send an invisible light.
○	○	**C.**	Remote controls send different signals for different channels.
○	○	**D.**	Televisions can see the invisible light.

4. In 1826, a French inventor named Joseph Niepce made the first photograph. He coated a metal plate with a special chemical. Then he exposed the plate to light for about eight hours. British inventor William Fox Talbot introduced the use of negatives 13 years later. This process allowed many photos to be made from one negative.

Fact	Inference		
○	○	**4.** **A.**	Niepce made the first photograph.
○	○	**B.**	It was easier to make photos from negatives.
○	○	**C.**	Niepce did not use negatives.
○	○	**D.**	The metal plate was exposed for eight hours.

5. Many breeds of dogs are used for work. In some cultures dogs are used to herd sheep. The dogs keep the flock from being attacked by animals such as wolves. They also keep sheep from wandering off. Sheepdogs are known for their loyalty and gentleness.

Fact	Inference		
○	○	**5.** **A.**	Wolves are afraid of sheepdogs.
○	○	**B.**	Sheepdogs are gentle and loyal.
○	○	**C.**	There are many breeds of dogs.
○	○	**D.**	Sheepdogs are intelligent.

1. Sundials are an ancient way of measuring time. Experts believe they were used by the Babylonians in 2000 B.C. A sundial measures the angle of a shadow cast by the Sun. As the Sun moves from east to west during the day, so does the shadow. The shadow is cast by a flat piece of metal in the center of the dial. In the Northern Hemisphere, the metal piece must point toward the North Pole.

Fact	Inference	
◯	◯	**1. A.** Sundials measure time.
◯	◯	**B.** The Sun moves from east to west.
◯	◯	**C.** Sundials are useless at night.
◯	◯	**D.** Time was important to the Babylonians.

2. Allison was upset over a difficult homework problem. She had been working on it for a while, but she still couldn't get the answer. "Why don't we go outside for a walk?" her dad suggested. Allison looked up at the stars as they walked. Her dad pointed out the planet Venus. When they returned home, Allison felt ready to tackle the homework problem. "Thanks for the walk, Dad," she said.

Fact	Inference	
◯	◯	**2. A.** The walk helped Allison calm down.
◯	◯	**B.** Allison's father wanted to help her.
◯	◯	**C.** Allison was doing her homework at night.
◯	◯	**D.** Allison was upset over her homework.

3. Scott was tired from jogging, so he sat down on a park bench. He noticed a pair of glasses on the bench. When he asked several people sitting nearby whether the glasses belonged to them, they all said no. Since he couldn't find the owner, Scott decided he would take the glasses home. He put an ad in the lost and found section of the local newspaper.

Fact	Inference	
◯	◯	**3. A.** Scott was tired from jogging.
◯	◯	**B.** Scott is a responsible person.
◯	◯	**C.** The glasses were on the bench.
◯	◯	**D.** Scott placed an ad in the paper.

4. The first band-aid was created in 1921 by Earle Dickson. He was a cotton buyer for a drug company. The bandage was designed for Dickson's wife, who frequently cut herself while cooking.

Fact	Inference		
○	○	**4.** **A.**	Dickson's wife frequently cut herself.
○	○	**B.**	Band-aids were created in 1921.
○	○	**C.**	Dickson worked for a drug company.
○	○	**D.**	Dickson was concerned about his wife.

---

5. The average weight for male cats is 8.6 pounds. The average for females is 7.2 pounds. The heaviest recorded weight for a cat is nearly 47 pounds. This cat lived in Cairns, Australia, and was named Himmy. Himmy lived to be 10 years old. The average male cat that is well fed and receives good medical care lives about 15 years.

Fact	Inference		
○	○	**5.** **A.**	Male cats are usually bigger than females.
○	○	**B.**	Himmy weighed nearly 47 pounds.
○	○	**C.**	An average male cat weighs 8.6 pounds.
○	○	**D.**	Himmy lived to be 10 years old.

1. The sun was just beginning to peek through the pine trees when Marisa opened her eyes. She had slept soundly in her sleeping bag all through the night. The birds sang as she got up, packed her heavy backpack, and continued the hike with the rest of her family. After two hours of steep, uphill hiking, they reached the top of the mountain. Marisa took off her backpack and sat down to smell the clean air and enjoy the view.

Fact	Inference		
○	○	**1. A.**	Marisa slept soundly.
○	○	**B.**	Marisa's family was on vacation.
○	○	**C.**	Marisa's backpack was heavy.
○	○	**D.**	Marisa enjoys hiking.

2. Stonehenge is a circle of huge stones on the Salisbury Plain in England. The average weight of each stone is 28 tons. The monument was probably built between 2800 and 2000 B.C., but no one knows who placed the stones there or what their exact purpose was. Placement of the stones made it possible to predict sunrises and sunsets, changes in the seasons, and even eclipses of the Sun and Moon.

Fact	Inference		
○	○	**2. A.**	Stonehenge is in England.
○	○	**B.**	No one is sure of Stonehenge's purpose.
○	○	**C.**	Each stone weighs about 28 tons.
○	○	**D.**	Eclipses were important to ancient people.

3. Every May across the United States, Asian Americans celebrate their cultures. May is called Asian Pacific American Heritage Month. President Bush made it official in 1990. Since then, it has grown in popularity. Today, there are parades, festivals, art shows, and workshops.

Fact	Inference	
○	○	**3. A.** Many Americans enjoy learning about different cultures.
○	○	**B.** The president of the United States can declare special celebrations.
○	○	**C.** Asian Americans are proud of their heritage.
○	○	**D.** Asian Americans celebrate in May.

4. The big homecoming dance was Friday night, and Suzanne needed a dress to wear. As she was sorting through her closet, her older sister Jean tapped her on the shoulder. She knew that Suzanne had always liked her blue dress. "How would you like to wear this?" she asked. Suzanne's eyes lit up. She hugged Jean and ran to try on the dress.

Fact	Inference	
○	○	**4. A.** Jean was kind to her sister.
○	○	**B.** Suzanne was excited about wearing the dress.
○	○	**C.** The dance was Friday night.
○	○	**D.** Jean is older than Suzanne.

5. Dragons aren't just creatures found in fairy tales. Komodo dragons are 10-foot-long lizards. They are found on the island of Komodo and other small islands in Indonesia. They have long tails and are covered with small scales. The open mouth of a Komodo dragon reveals rows of teeth that look like the edge of a saw.

Fact	Inference	
○	○	**5. A.** Komodo dragons don't live in the United States.
○	○	**B.** Komodo dragons have scales.
○	○	**C.** Komodo dragons live on islands.
○	○	**D.** Komodo dragons look very scary.

1. A limousine is a large luxury car. Most limousines are custom made. One special limousine is called "The American Dream." It is 60 feet long, has two engines, and needs two people to drive it. One person drives from the front, and the other drives from the back. The two drivers use headphones to communicate with each other.

Fact	Inference		
○	○	**1. A.**	A limousine is a car.
○	○	**B.**	"The American Dream" needs two drivers.
○	○	**C.**	It is difficult to drive "The American Dream."
○	○	**D.**	"The American Dream" has two engines.

2. Mount Vesuvius erupted in A.D. 79. The ancient city of Pompeii was buried for hundreds of years. Pompeii was a Roman port that was also an important center of business. Wealthy landowners, shopkeepers, merchants, manufacturers, and slaves lived in Pompeii. Today more than half of Pompeii has been uncovered, and visitors can get a glimpse of what life was like in the ancient Roman Empire.

Fact	Inference		
○	○	**2. A.**	Mount Vesuvius erupted in A.D. 79.
○	○	**B.**	Pompeii was buried for hundreds of years.
○	○	**C.**	Slavery was allowed in Pompeii.
○	○	**D.**	Pompeii was a large city.

3. Bill loved to explore the forest near his house. He stopped for a while to throw stones into the lake. Then he decided to hike deeper into the woods. After more than an hour of hiking, he stopped to rest. When it was time to go home, he realized he was unsure of which direction to go.

Fact	Inference		
○	○	**3. A.**	Bill is adventurous.
○	○	**B.**	The forest is near Bill's house.
○	○	**C.**	Bill threw stones into the lake.
○	○	**D.**	Bill was tired after hiking.

4. Anna had stayed up late on Thursday night to finish her model of a volcano for the science fair at school. The next morning she was late for school and did not have time to carefully pack her science project. As she started to dash across the crosswalk in front of the school, she had to stop suddenly to avoid a car she had not seen. "Oh, no!" cried Anna. "Look at my science project!"

Fact   Inference
○   ○   **4. A.** Anna made a model volcano.
○   ○   **B.** On Friday Anna overslept.
○   ○   **C.** Anna dropped her science project.
○   ○   **D.** Anna was late for school.

---

5. Ramón smelled the flowers he had brought with him to the tutoring session. He quickly hid them behind his back when Mrs. Jenkins came into the room. Mrs. Jenkins had been tutoring him in English for the past year, and today was the last session. As Mrs. Jenkins sat down, Ramón surprised her with the bouquet.

Fact   Inference
○   ○   **5. A.** Ramón wanted to thank Mrs. Jenkins.
○   ○   **B.** Mrs. Jenkins was Ramón's tutor.
○   ○   **C.** Ramón is thoughtful.
○   ○   **D.** Mrs. Jenkins did not expect the flowers.

Writing Roundup

Read each story. Then read the question that follows it. Write your answer on the lines below each question.

1. Juanita copied the exact way Sammy Sosa positioned his feet. She had examined pictures of him standing by the plate for the Chicago Cubs. She also copied the exact way he positioned his powerful hands on a bat. Standing there and looking out toward the mound, she knew she was ready.

What is Juanita doing?

_____

_____

2. Nicholas congratulated himself. He kept his old aid for a spare in case of an emergency. Now his new aid wasn't working. He quickly removed it. Then he fixed his spare aid in place in his ear. It worked perfectly. He hadn't missed much of the movie.

What was Nicholas doing?

_____

_____

3. Moving rapidly through aisle 1, Keisha sees soups in packages and in many different size cans. In aisle 2, she sees frozen foods, including vegetables and fruits. Upon reaching aisle 3, she sees envelopes, magazines, and many greeting cards.

Where is Keisha?

_____

_____

Read the paragraph below. Then answer the questions.

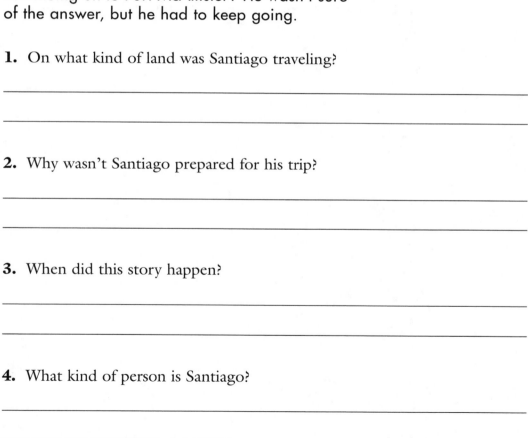

Santiago had been riding for six hours. He guessed it would still be a few hours before the blazing sun went down. His faithful horse was thirsty. He could tell by the way the horse's breathing sounded. Along the way, Santiago hadn't noticed any signs of water. There weren't even many cactuses. There was what seemed like an ocean of sand and an occasional rock. He was thirsty too, and he suspected he was beginning to sound like his poor horse. Was he capable of continuing on to Fort McAllister? He wasn't sure of the answer, but he had to keep going.

1. On what kind of land was Santiago traveling?

_____

_____

2. Why wasn't Santiago prepared for his trip?

_____

_____

3. When did this story happen?

_____

_____

4. What kind of person is Santiago?

_____

_____

Spelling Skills

spelling strategies

What can you do when you aren't sure how to spell a word?

Say the word aloud. Make sure you say it correctly. Listen to the sounds in the word. Think about letters and patterns that might spell the sounds.

Look in the Spelling Table on page 265 to find common spellings for sounds in the word.

Think about related words. They may help you spell the word you're not sure of.

departure—depart

Guess the spelling of the word and check it in a dictionary.

Write the word in different ways. Compare the spellings and choose the one that looks correct.

explane   explayn   expleyn   (explain)

Think about any spelling rules you know that can help you spell the word.

To form the plural of some singular words ending in f or fe, change f to v and add -s or -es.

knife—knives   wolf—wolves

Listen for a common word part, such as a prefix, suffix, or ending.

pass<u>age</u>

com<u>fort</u>able

Break the word into syllables and think about how each syllable might be spelled.

at-mos-phere
in-cor-rect

Create a memory clue to help you remember the spelling of the word.

<u>We</u> told <u>her</u> about the <u>wea</u>ther.

Dictionary Skills

Guide Words

The guide words at the top of a dictionary page are the first and last entry words on the page. When you look for a word in a dictionary, look for the two guide words between which the word falls, according to alphabetical order.

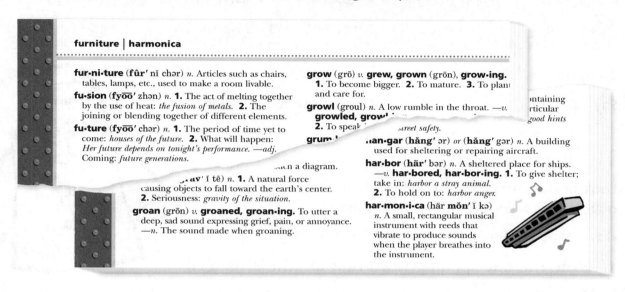

furniture | harmonica

fur·ni·ture (fûr′ nĭ chər) *n.* Articles such as chairs, tables, lamps, etc., used to make a room livable.

fu·sion (fyōō′ zhən) *n.* **1.** The act of melting together by the use of heat: *the fusion of metals.* **2.** The joining or blending together of different elements.

fu·ture (fyōō′ chər) *n.* **1.** The period of time yet to come: *houses of the future.* **2.** What will happen: *Her future depends on tonight's performance.* —*adj.* Coming: *future generations.*

...on a diagram.

...av′ ĭ tē) *n.* **1.** A natural force causing objects to fall toward the earth's center. **2.** Seriousness: *gravity of the situation.*

groan (grōn) *v.* **groaned, groan·ing.** To utter a deep, sad sound expressing grief, pain, or annoyance. —*n.* The sound made when groaning.

grow (grō) *v.* **grew, grown** (grōn), **grow·ing. 1.** To become bigger. **2.** To mature. **3.** To plant and care for.

growl (groul) *n.* A low rumble in the throat. —*v.* **growled, grow... 2.** To speak... ...street safety.

grum...

...ontaining ...rticular ...good hints

...an·gar (hăng′ ər) *or* (hăng′ gər) *n.* A building used for sheltering or repairing aircraft.

har·bor (här′ bər) *n.* A sheltered place for ships. —*v.* **har·bored, har·bor·ing. 1.** To give shelter; take in: *harbor a stray animal.* **2.** To hold on to: *harbor anger.*

har·mon·i·ca (här mŏn′ ĭ kə) *n.* A small, rectangular musical instrument with reeds that vibrate to produce sounds when the player breathes into the instrument.

Each pair of guide words below is followed by a list of entry words.
Write the entry words that are on the same dictionary page as the guide words.

1. about/animal   accent   attract   alphabet   August

_____   _____

2. cabin/cause   cavity   catalog   camera   cabbage

_____   _____

3. search/secret   scramble   season   sandwich   second

_____   _____

4. paragraph/photograph   Pacific   pass   people   pigeon

_____   _____

Words with /ā/

trace	invade	raincoat	entertain	congratulate
mayor	complain	remain	hesitate	straight
parade	misplace	safety	explain	weighted
escape	stain	neighborhood	agent	disobey

Say and Listen

Say each spelling word. Listen for the /ā/ sound you hear in *trace*.

Think and Sort

Look at the letters in each word. Think about how /ā/ is spelled. Spell each word aloud.

How many spelling patterns for /ā/ do you see?

raincoat

1. Write the **one** spelling word that has the *a* pattern.

2. Write the **two** spelling words that have the *ay* or *ey* pattern, like *mayor*.

3. Write the **eight** spelling words that have the *a*-consonant-*e* pattern, like *trace*. Circle the *a*-consonant-*e* pattern in each word.

4. Write the **six** spelling words that have the *ai* pattern, like *stain*.

5. Write the **three** spelling words that have the *aigh* or *eigh* pattern, like *straight*.

1. a Word

_____

2. ay, ey Words

_____ _____

3. a-consonant-e Words

_____ _____ _____

_____ _____ _____

_____ _____

4. ai Words

_____ _____ _____

_____ _____ _____

5. aigh, eigh Words

_____ _____

Antonyms

Antonyms are words that have opposite meanings.
Write the spelling word that is an antonym of each word.

1. danger _____

2. retreat _____

3. obey _____

4. crooked _____

5. find _____

6. bore _____

7. leave _____

Definitions

Write the spelling word for each definition. Use a dictionary if you need to.

8. to pause before acting _____

9. loaded down _____

10. to discolor, spot, or soil _____

11. to get away or get free _____

12. to say something is wrong or annoying _____

13. an area within a larger town or city _____

14. a waterproof coat worn for protection from rain _____

15. the highest official in city or town government _____

16. to make plain or clear _____

17. a small quantity or amount _____

18. to praise someone for success or achievement _____

19. to pass by in a large group _____

trace	invade	raincoat	entertain	congratulate
mayor	complain	remain	hesitate	straight
parade	misplace	safety	explain	weighted
escape	stain	neighborhood	agent	disobey

Proofreading

Proofread the following paragraphs from a newspaper article. Use proofreading marks to correct five spelling mistakes, three capitalization mistakes, and two punctuation mistakes.

Proofreading Marks

◯ spell correctly

／ make lowercase

⊙ add period

Parade to Begin Fourth of July Events

Evanston's Fourth of July celebration will begin in a special way this year. Early in the day, the mayer will lead a parade strate down Main Street Marching Bands and colorful floats from each neighborhood will pass by for the crowd to enjoy.

For the safty of everyone, police will stop all traffic No cars will be allowed to remane on the Road.

Everyone is invited to attend. The Parade starts at 10 A.M. Parade organizers promise to entertan all the citizens of Evanston.

Language Connection

Capitalization and Punctuation

A sentence begins with a capital letter. Names of people and pets also begin with a capital letter.

A sentence ends with a period, a question mark, or an exclamation point.

> Jeffrey **W**atkins came to visit**.**
> **W**ould **M**ax be a good name for my new puppy**?**
> **R**ocky and **D**an walked ten miles yesterday afternoon**!**

The sentences below contain errors in spelling, capitalization, and punctuation. Write each sentence correctly.

1. may our dog sunny march in the neihborhood parade with us

_____

_____

2. even rhonda and eric did not hesitat to jump in the river for a swim

_____

_____

3. watch out for that spider on the ranecoat next to taylor

_____

_____

4. when kelly leaves, tiger and fluffy compleyn with loud meows

_____

_____

Words with /ĕ/

length	envelope	echo	guest	treasure
tennis	pleasant	excellent	measure	metric
instead	energy	breakfast	restaurant	separate
guessed	headache	insects	against	success

Say and Listen

Say each spelling word. Listen for the /ĕ/ sound you hear in *length*.

tennis

Think and Sort

Some of the spelling words have more than one e, but only one has the /ĕ/ sound. Look at the letters in each word. Think about how /ĕ/ is spelled. Spell each word aloud.

How many spelling patterns for /ĕ/ do you see?

1. Write the **eleven** spelling words that have the *e* pattern, like *length*. Circle each *e* that has the /ĕ/ sound.

2. Write the **six** spelling words that have the *ea* pattern, like *instead*.

3. Write the **two** spelling words that have the *ue* pattern, like *guest*.

4. Write the **one** spelling word that has the *ai* pattern.

1. e Words

2. ea Words

3. ue Words

4. ai Word

Classifying

Write the spelling word that belongs in each group.

1. snails, worms, _____
2. volleyball, soccer, _____
3. width, height, _____
4. stomachache, earache, _____
5. company, visitor, _____
6. stamp, letter, _____
7. dinner, lunch, _____
8. great, wonderful, _____
9. riches, wealth, _____
10. supposed, suspected, _____
11. divide, set apart, _____
12. in place of, rather than, _____

Clues

Write the spelling word for each clue.

13. This is the opposite of *for*. _____
14. This word describes a warm, calm day. _____
15. Solar power and electricity are types of this. _____
16. If you hear a repeated sound, it might be this. _____
17. This word names a system of measurement. _____
18. People use rulers and yardsticks to do this. _____
19. This is the opposite of *failure*. _____

length	envelope	echo	guest	treasure
tennis	pleasant	excellent	measure	metric
instead	energy	breakfast	restaurant	separate
guessed	headache	insects	against	success

Proofreading

Proofread the following paragraphs from a story. Use proofreading marks to correct five spelling mistakes, two punctuation mistakes, and three missing words.

Proofreading Marks

◯ spell correctly

? add question mark

⋏ add

Marian edged along the lenth of the hallway. Where was echo coming from Someone else in the tower behind her was shouting. This was exellent timing. Perhaps the noise would keep any other guests from discovering her. She needed to get into the room with red door.

Marian leaned against the wall for a moment. Her hedache was getting worse. She took a deep breath and tried concentrate. This was her final chance to get the tresure back! Would it be a sucess

The door to the room with the red door opened. Marian gasped in surprise to see Robin smiling down at her.

Language Connection

Punctuation

A series is a list that contains three or more single words or groups of words. A comma is used to separate the parts of a series. Notice that the final comma is placed before *and* or *or*.

> Jake needed crayons, paint, and cardboard to make a poster.
> My glasses weren't on my desk, in the car, or at the library.

The following sentences contain spelling errors and errors in the use of commas. Write each sentence correctly.

1. Mother served our guest a plesant breakfast of eggs bacon, and toast.

   _____

2. We all played, tennis, softball, and tag to use up our extra enegry.

   _____

3. Extreme heat biting insecks, and pouring rain ruined our camping trip.

   _____

4. At the restraunt we talked about hitting a home run, scoring a touchdown, and, catching a high fly.

   _____

   _____

5. Our guest left behind, a sealed invelope, a metric converter, and a tape measure.

   _____

   _____

Words with /ə/

darken	lessen	prison	lesson	captain
person	onion	strengthen	fasten	mountains
weaken	listen	lemonade	kitchen	soften
often	quicken	seldom	ransom	custom

Say and Listen

Say each spelling word. Listen for the vowel sound in the syllable that is not stressed.

Think and Sort

lemonade

The weak vowel sound that you hear in unstressed syllables is called a **schwa**. It is shown as /ə/. Look at the letters in each word. Think about how /ə/ is spelled. Spell each word aloud.

How many spelling patterns for /ə/ do you see?

1. Write the **ten** spelling words that have /ə/ spelled *e*, like *fasten*.

2. Write the **eight** spelling words that have /ə/ spelled *o*, like *lesson*.

3. Write the **two** spelling words that have /ə/ spelled *ai*, like *captain*.

---

1. e Words

_____   _____   _____

_____   _____   _____

_____   _____   _____

_____

2. o Words

_____   _____   _____

_____   _____   _____

_____   _____

3. ai Words

_____   _____

Antonyms

Write the spelling word that is an antonym of each word.

1. valleys _____

2. harden _____

3. lighten _____

4. strengthen _____

5. rarely _____

6. frequently _____

7. increase _____

8. unfasten _____

Analogies

An analogy states that two words go together in the same way as two others. Write the spelling word that completes each analogy.

9. *Eye* is to *see* as *ear* is to _____.

10. *Energize* is to _____ as *construct* is to *build*.

11. *Sleeping* is to *bedroom* as *cooking* is to _____.

12. *Kidnapper* is to _____ as *burglar* is to *jewelry*.

13. *Clinic* is to *hospital* as *jail* is to _____.

14. *Learn* is to _____ as *draw* is to *picture*.

15. *Lettuce* is to *cabbage* as _____ is to *garlic*.

16. *Men* is to *man* as *people* is to _____.

17. *Practice* is to _____ as *rule* is to *law*.

18. *Lemon* is to _____ as *egg* is to *omelet*.

19. *Length* is to *lengthen* as *quick* is to _____.

darken	lessen	prison	lesson	captain
person	onion	strengthen	fasten	mountains
weaken	listen	lemonade	kitchen	soften
often	quicken	seldom	ransom	custom

Proofreading

Proofread the e-mail below. Use proofreading marks to correct five spelling mistakes, three capitalization mistakes, and two unnecessary words.

Proofreading Marks

◯ spell correctly
≡ capitalize
ℓ take out

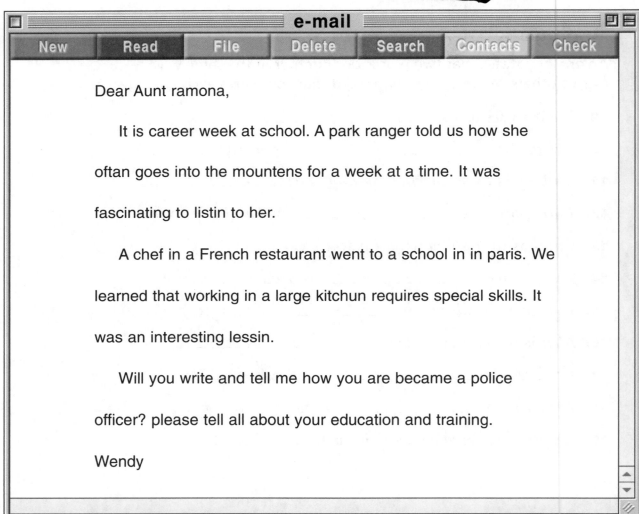

---

e-mail

New	Read	File	Delete	Search	Contacts	Check

Dear Aunt ramona,

It is career week at school. A park ranger told us how she oftan goes into the mountens for a week at a time. It was fascinating to listin to her.

A chef in a French restaurant went to a school in in paris. We learned that working in a large kitchun requires special skills. It was an interesting lessin.

Will you write and tell me how you are became a police officer? please tell all about your education and training.

Wendy

Common Nouns

A common noun names any person, place, thing, or idea. A common noun is not capitalized. The common nouns in the sentence below appear in dark type.

> The **couple** arranged **flowers** in a **vase**. Their **shop** in the **market** attracted many **customers**. **Work** was an enjoyable **part** of their **life**.

Unscramble the words in the following sentences to write sensible sentences. Circle the common nouns.

1. often My television watches movies on father.

_____

2. the was about One an West old outlaw film in.

_____

3. was hiding He in a canyon mountains in the.

_____

4. seldom He had enough to eat food.

_____

5. custom It was his with open one eye to sleep.

_____

6. never found out I of the story end the.

_____

7. to the kitchen I to make went lemonade.

_____

Geography Words

Caribbean Sea	Atlantic Ocean	Africa	Andes
Himalayas	Asia	Rocky Mountains	Europe
North America	Pacific Ocean	Central America	Mississippi River
Indian Ocean	Alps	Mediterranean Sea	South America
Australia	Nile River	Appalachian Mountains	Amazon River

Say and Listen

Say the spelling words. Listen for the number of syllables in each word.

Think and Sort

All of the spelling words name places around the world. Some of the place names, such as North America, contain two words.

Rocky Mountains

1. Write the **thirteen** two-word place names, like *Caribbean Sea*.

2. A **syllable** is a word or a word part with one vowel sound. Sort the remaining **seven** spelling words by number of syllables and write them under the correct headings.

---

1. Two-word Names

_____   _____   _____

_____   _____   _____

_____   _____   _____

_____   _____   _____

_____

2. One-syllable Name   Two-syllable Names   Three-syllable Names

_____   _____   _____

_____   _____

Four-syllable Name   _____

_____

What's the Answer?

Write the spelling word that answers each question.

1. What mountain range is found in south-central Europe? _____

2. What is the longest river in Africa? _____

3. What body of water is found in the central United States? _____

4. What continent extends from the Atlantic Ocean to Asia? _____

Clues

Write the spelling word for each clue.

5. chief mountain range in North America _____

6. mountains in South America _____

7. highest mountains in the world _____

8. ocean between Africa and Australia _____

9. area between Mexico and South America _____

10. body of water that is part of the Atlantic Ocean _____

11. sea between Africa and Europe _____

12. largest continent _____

13. longest river in South America _____

14. continent southeast of North America _____

15. continent between Atlantic and Indian oceans _____

16. mountains found in eastern North America _____

17. continent on which Canada is located _____

18. continent between Indian and Pacific oceans _____

19. ocean just east of North America _____

Caribbean Sea	Atlantic Ocean	Africa	Andes
Himalayas	Asia	Rocky Mountains	Europe
North America	Pacific Ocean	Central America	Mississippi River
Indian Ocean	Alps	Mediterranean Sea	South America
Australia	Nile River	Appalachian Mountains	Amazon River

Proofreading

Proofread the following part of an essay. Use proofreading marks to correct five spelling mistakes, three capitalization mistakes, and two mistakes in word order.

Proofreading Marks

⬯ spell correctly

☰ capitalize

∿ trade places

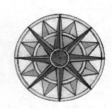

A Trip to Remember

by Rachel Block

First Period Language Arts

last summer my friend Akiko and her family traveled

from one coast of Narth America to the other. They

began at the New Jersey shore of the Atlantic Ocean.

Then they drove south along the Apallaichan Mountains

on their way to alabama. From they there headed

west and crossed the Missisipi River and the

Rockey Mountains. Two weeks after they started, they

ended in up Oxnard, california, at the Pacifc Ocean.

Here is the story of their trip.

Language Connection

Proper Nouns

Proper nouns are names of specific persons, places, or things. Each important word in a proper noun should begin with a capital letter. Notice the proper nouns in the sentences below.

> Last **August, Joanne** moved from **New Mexico** to **New York City**. She visited the **Statue of Liberty** and the **Empire State Building**.

The following sentences contain errors in capitalization. Write each sentence correctly.

1. Today my teacher, mrs. ward, talked about the climate in europe and asia.

_____

2. Then gayle pointed out the atlantic ocean, the pacific ocean, and the indian ocean.

_____

_____

3. Last month I did a report on the nile river in africa.

_____

4. I hope billy spinney will tell us about his trip to the andes.

_____

5. Last year he actually traveled down the amazon river in south america!

_____

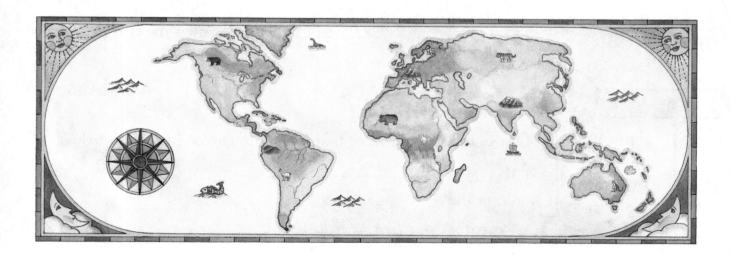

unit 1 Review
Lessons 1-5

accent
imagine
paragraph
salmon
laughed

Words with /ă/

Write the spelling word for each definition.

1. to form a mental picture _____

2. a manner of speech typical of a region _____

3. a fish common to northern waters _____

4. to show amusement through repeated sounds

_____

5. a part of a piece of writing _____

agent
congratulate
mayor
disobey
straight
weighted

Words with /ā/

Write the spelling word that completes each sentence.

6. Did the naughty puppy _____ you?

7. Our picnic basket was _____ down with lots of food.

8. We wanted to _____ Max on his good work.

9. The sides of a square are four _____ lines of th same length.

10. Our travel _____ planned a good trip for us.

11. The _____ called a town meeting yesterday.

separate
measure
guessed
against

Words with /ĕ/

Write the spelling word that is an antonym of each word below.

12. estimate _____

13. join _____

14. for _____

15. knew _____

strengthen
person
seldom
captain

Words with /ə/

Write the spelling word that belongs in each group.

16. sailor, mate, _____

17. _____, place, thing

18. toughen, improve, _____

19. rarely, _____, sometimes

Central America
Pacific Ocean
Mediterranean Sea
Mississippi River
Appalachian Mountains
Europe

Geography Words

Write the spelling word that identifies the place where each person is.

20. a traveler driving somewhere between Mexico and South America _____

21. a tourist visiting England, France, and Italy _____

22. a hiker on the Appalachian Trail in eastern North America _____

23. a tugboat captain along the west coast of North America _____

24. a steamboat captain docking in St. Louis, Missouri _____

25. a sailor off the coast of Greece, between Europe and Africa _____

Words with /ē/

breeze	breathing	piano	piece	liter
complete	meter	memory	speaker	library
brief	ceiling	scene	repeat	extremely
degrees	gasoline	succeed	receive	increase

Say and Listen

Say each spelling word. Listen for the /ē/ sound you hear in *breeze*.

gasoline

Think and Sort

Look at the letters in each word. Think about how /ē/ is spelled.
Spell each word aloud. How many spelling patterns for /ē/ do you see?

1. Write the **five** spelling words that have the *e, y,* or *i* pattern,
    like *meter*. Circle the letter that spells /ē/ in each word.

2. Write the **eleven** spelling words that have the *ea, ee, ie,* or *ei* pattern,
    like *repeat*. Circle the letters that spell /ē/ in each word.

3. Write the **two** spelling words that have the *e*-consonant-*e* pattern, like *complete*.

4. Write the **one** spelling word that has both the *e*-consonant-*e* and the *y* pattern.

5. Write the **one** spelling word that has the *i*-consonant-*e* pattern.

1. e, y, i Words

_____   _____   _____

_____   _____

2. ea, ee, ie, ei Words

_____   _____   _____

_____   _____   _____

_____   _____   _____

_____   _____

3. e-consonant-**e** Words

_____   _____

4. e-consonant-**e** and **y** Word   **5. i**-consonant-**e** Word

_____   _____

Classifying

Write the spelling word that belongs in each group.

1. inches, ounces, _____

2. accomplish, achieve, _____

3. add, expand, _____

4. retell, echo, _____

5. short, condensed, _____

6. thought, remembrance, _____

7. entire, whole, _____

8. accept, acquire, _____

9. very, greatly, _____

10. announcer, presenter, _____

11. eating, sleeping, _____

12. part, segment, _____

13. puff, gust, _____

14. play, act, _____

15. meter, kilogram, _____

Making Connections

Complete each sentence by writing the spelling word that goes with the person.

16. A gas station attendant pumps _____.

17. A city employee reads a parking _____.

18. A pianist plays the _____.

19. A librarian helps people find books in the _____.

breeze	breathing	piano	piece	liter
complete	meter	memory	speaker	library
brief	ceiling	scene	repeat	extremely
degrees	gasoline	succeed	receive	increase

Proofreading

Proofread the part of a history report below. Use proofreading marks to correct five spelling mistakes, three capitalization mistakes, and two punctuation mistakes.

Proofreading Marks

◯ spell correctly
≡ capitalize
⊙ add period

Explorers are often the first people to travel to little-known places. many early explorers kept logs, or records, of their journeys. they knew it was extremly important to preserve the memry of each seene and event that they observed

Some explorers wrote down a compleet record of their experiences. other explorers just jotted down breif notes Their records give us important clues to life in the past. They also reveal the explorers' feelings and attitudes about the places and people they saw along the way.

Using the Spelling Table

If you need to look up a word in a dictionary but aren't sure how to spell it, a spelling table can help. A spelling table lists common spellings for sounds. Suppose you are not sure how the vowel sound in *brief* is spelled. First, find the pronunciation symbol for the sound. Then read the first spelling listed for /ē/ and look up *bref* in a dictionary. Look for each spelling in the dictionary until you find the correct one.

Sound	Spellings	Examples
/ē/	e e_e ea ee ei eo ey i i_e ie y	meter, scene, speaker, degrees, receive, people, monkey, piano, gasoline, brief, memory

Write each of the following words, spelling the sound in dark type correctly. Use the Spelling Table on page 265 and a dictionary.

1. lăgh _____
2. trāc _____
3. gĕss _____
4. tŭch _____
5. mĭth _____
6. appēr _____
7. knŏledge _____
8. hesitāt _____
9. althō _____
10. chōs _____

Words with /ŭ/

thumb	touch	double	enough	tough
struggle	government	justice	crumb	discuss
umbrella	tongue	difficult	among	plumber
flood	trouble	compass	cousin	result

Say and Listen

Say each spelling word. Listen for the /ŭ/ sound you hear in *thumb*.

Think and Sort

Look at the letters in each word. Think about how /ŭ/ is spelled.
Spell each word aloud.

How many spelling patterns for /ŭ/ do you see?

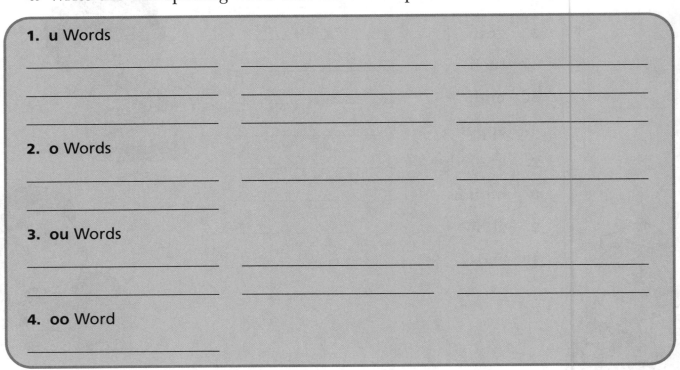

umbrella

1. Write the **nine** spelling words that have the *u* pattern, like *thumb*.

2. Write the **four** spelling words that have the *o* pattern, like *among*.

3. Write the **six** spelling words that have the *ou* pattern, like *touch*.

4. Write the **one** spelling word that has the *oo* pattern.

1. u Words

_____ _____ _____

_____ _____ _____

_____ _____ _____

2. o Words

_____ _____ _____

_____

3. ou Words

_____ _____ _____

_____ _____ _____

4. oo Word

_____

Clues

Write the spelling word for each clue.

1. This helps people to find their way. _____
2. This is very useful in rainy weather. _____
3. Congress is part of this. _____
4. This word means *sufficient*. _____
5. This word names a relative. _____
6. This word means the opposite of *easy*. _____
7. People do this when they share ideas. _____
8. This word means the same as *outcome*. _____
9. This can be the remains of a piece of toast. _____
10. People want this in a court of law. _____
11. A frog catches flies with this. _____

Rhymes

Write the spelling word that completes each sentence and rhymes with the underlined word.

12. The lights were <u>strung</u> _____ the trees in the back yard.
13. The _____ left a lot of <u>mud</u> in the cellar.
14. I'll blow a <u>bubble</u> that is _____ the size of yours!
15. It's a _____ to <u>juggle</u> four balls at once.
16. My _____ was <u>numb</u> from the cold.
17. The man's <u>gruff</u> voice makes him seem _____.
18. <u>Double</u> vision is _____ for a driver.
19. Do not _____ my <u>crutch</u> when I am walking.

thumb	touch	double	enough	tough
struggle	government	justice	crumb	discuss
umbrella	tongue	difficult	among	plumber
flood	trouble	compass	cousin	result

Proofreading

Proofread the letter below. Use proofreading marks to correct five spelling mistakes, three punctuation mistakes, and two unnecessary words.

Proofreading Marks

○ spell correctly
∧ add comma
℘ take out

4100 Wilmette Lane

Chicago IL 60660

June 10 2003

Dear Captain Murphy

My cuzin is a police officer in your squad. She said to

ask you about my being a police detective. I like solving

dificult problems, and I like to help people in in truble. I

think I'll be good enouf for the the job when I grow up.

Could you discous this with me next week? I will call you

and make an appointment to see you.

Sincerely,

Cameron Burns

Subject of a Sentence

The simple subject of a sentence tells who or what is doing the action or is being talked about. It is usually one word. The complete subject of a sentence includes the simple subject and all the words that modify, or describe, it. In the example sentence below, the complete subject appears in dark type. The simple subject is underlined.

> **Several <u>members</u> of the crew** were sewing costumes for the play.

Write each of the following sentences. Circle the simple subjects and underline the complete subjects.

1. My favorite cousin lives in a small southern town.

_____

2. A major flood badly damaged the area.

_____

3. The federal government soon moved in to help the people.

_____

4. The difficult struggle to survive was over.

_____

5. My cousin's old compass was ruined in the flood.

_____

6. His family had to hire a plumber to repair the damaged pipes.

_____

Words with /yōo/ or /ōo/

refuse	coupon	improvement	juice	humor
glue	renew	smooth	through	ruin
student	human	beautiful	threw	pollute
nuisance	canoe	rude	clue	cruel

Say and Listen

Say each spelling word. Listen for the /ōo/ sound you hear in *refuse* and *glue*.

Think and Sort

All of the spelling words have the /ōo/ sound. In *refuse* and some other /ōo/ words, /y/ is pronounced before the /ōo/.

Look at the letters in each spelling word. Think about how /ōo/ or /yōo/ is spelled. Spell each word aloud.

1. Write the **six** words that have the *oo* or *u* pattern, like *smooth*.

2. Write the **seven** words that have the *ew, ue,* or *u*-consonant-*e* pattern, like *threw*.

3. Write the **four** words that have the *ou, oe,* or *o*-consonant-*e* pattern, like *through*.

4. Write the **three** words that have the *ui* or *eau* pattern, like *juice*.

glue

1. oo, u Words

_____   _____   _____
_____   _____   _____

2. ew, ue, u-consonant-**e** Words

_____   _____   _____
_____   _____   _____
_____

3. ou, oe, o-consonant-**e** Words

_____   _____   _____
_____

4. ui, eau Words

_____   _____   _____

Analogies

Write the spelling word that completes each analogy.

1. *Bicycle* is to *motorcycle* as _____ is to *motorboat*.

2. *Potato* is to *chip* as *apple* is to _____.

3. *Tremble* is to *anger* as *laugh* is to _____.

4. *Automobile* is to *car* as _____ is to *person*.

5. *Melt* is to *freeze* as *clean* is to _____.

6. *Destruction* is to *crush* as _____ is to *bother*.

7. *Unsightly* is to *ugly* as *gorgeous* is to _____.

8. *Bridge* is to *over* as *tunnel* is to _____.

9. *Improve* is to _____ as *manage* is to *management*.

10. *Discount* is to _____ as *admittance* is to *ticket*.

Synonyms

Complete each sentence with the spelling word that is a synonym of the underlined word.

11. Cold lemonade will <u>refresh</u> you and _____ your energy.

12. Marissa's skin is as _____ and <u>silky</u> as a baby's.

13. That _____ is a very strong <u>adhesive</u>.

14. Sara <u>tossed</u> the ball to Ling, who _____ it to Miguel.

15. Although he was _____ to us, we were not <u>impolite</u> to him.

16. We <u>decline</u> your offer and _____ to play.

17. His _____ actions were met with a <u>vicious</u> growl.

18. Ann's <u>hint</u> was the _____ that solved the mystery.

19. A bad fire can <u>destroy</u> property and _____ lives.

refuse	coupon	improvement	juice	humor
glue	renew	smooth	through	ruin
student	human	beautiful	threw	pollute
nuisance	canoe	rude	clue	cruel

Proofreading

Proofread the following section from a safety booklet. Use proofreading marks to correct five spelling mistakes, three capitalization mistakes, and two punctuation mistakes.

Proofreading Marks

○ spell correctly

/ make lowercase

⊙ add period

Life Jackets may seem like a nusanse, but they are very important safety equipment. Make sure that life jackets fit the Wearers properly. A life jacket that is too big is dangerous Always remember that the belt must be securely fastened around the waist. You and your fellow boaters may not look buitiful, but you'll be safe If some of your boaters refuze to wear life jackets, do not let them remain on your Boat. You are responsible for your safety and theirs. Over time, regular use will rouin life jackets, so remember to replace them. If your life jackets are in good shape and everyone wears them properly, you'll have smyooth sailing!

Multiple Pronunciations

Some words may be pronounced in more than one way. A dictionary gives all the acceptable pronunciations for these words, but the one listed first is generally preferred.

> **strength·en** (strĕngk' thən) *or* (strĕng'-) *or* (strĕn'-) *v.* **strength·ened, strength·en·ing.** To make or become stronger: *Exercise helps strengthen muscles.*

Look at the pronunciations for *strengthen* given in the entry above. Notice that only the syllable that is pronounced in different ways is given in the second and third pronunciations. Study the differences in the pronunciations. Then say *strengthen* to yourself and see which pronunciation you use.

Write the spelling word for each pair of pronunciations below. Then write the pronunciation that you use. Include all of the syllables.

	Word	Pronunciation I Use
1. (sto͞od' nt) or (styo͞od'-)	_____	_____
2. (no͞o' səns) or (nyo͞o'-)	_____	_____
3. (tə mā' tō) or (-mä'-)	_____	_____
4. (ko͞o' pŏn) or (kyo͞o'-)	_____	_____
5. (frăj' əl) or (-īl')	_____	_____
6. (rĭ no͞o') or (-nyo͞o')	_____	_____
7. (ro͞om' māt') or (ro͝om'-)	_____	_____
8. (no͞o' trəl) or (nyo͞o'-)	_____	_____

Plural Words

knives	canoes	holidays	voyages	pianos
loaves	memories	industries	countries	factories
tomatoes	halves	wolves	bakeries	echoes
mysteries	mosquitoes	heroes	potatoes	libraries

Say and Listen

Say the spelling words. Listen to the ending sounds.

mosquitoes

Think and Sort

All of the spelling words are plurals. A **base word** is a word to which prefixes, suffixes, and word endings can be added to form new words. Most plurals are formed by adding -s to the base word. Other plurals are formed by adding -es. The spelling of some base words changes when -es is added.

bakery + es = baker**ies**   wolf + es = wol**ves**

Look at the letters in each word. Think about how each plural is formed. Spell each word aloud.

1. Write the **four** spelling words formed by adding -s to the base word, like *canoes.*

2. Write the **five** -es spelling words with no changes in the base word, like *echoes.*

3. Write the **eleven** -es spelling words with changes in the base word, like *wolves.*

1. -s Plurals

_____ _____ _____

_____

2. -es Plurals with No Base Word Changes

_____ _____ _____

_____ _____

3. -es Plurals with Base Word Changes

_____ _____ _____

_____ _____ _____

_____ _____ _____

_____ _____

Definitions

Write the spelling word for each definition.

1. repeated sounds bouncing off something _____

2. things that cannot be explained _____

3. people known for courage _____

4. nations or states _____

5. things that are remembered _____

6. bread baked in large pieces _____

7. groups of businesses _____

8. underground stems eaten as vegetables _____

9. two equal parts of a whole _____

Clues

Write the spelling word for each clue.

10. This vegetable is often eaten in salads. _____

11. Another word for this is *journeys*. _____

12. These are places where cars are manufactured. _____

13. Pianists play these. _____

14. These flying insects can be annoying. _____

15. People use paddles to move these. _____

16. These places sell pastries. _____

17. People borrow books at these places. _____

18. People use these to cut bread. _____

19. These animals are related to dogs. _____

knives	canoes	holidays	voyages	pianos
loaves	memories	industries	countries	factories
tomatoes	halves	wolves	bakeries	echoes
mysteries	mosquitoes	heroes	potatoes	libraries

Proofreading

Proofread the following part of a book review. Use proofreading marks to correct five spelling mistakes, three capitalization mistakes, and two unnecessary words.

Proofreading Marks

◯ spell correctly

≡ capitalize

ℓ take out

Book Review: *Everyday Heroes*

this nonfiction book deserves a shelf of its own in the libarys of countrees around the world. The people featured in the book have not sailed on dangerous voyags or or wrestled with wolffs or other wild animals. instead, they work at regular jobs in factories and bakreys. Thomas Metcalf, a steel worker from Texas, saved the lives of five people when molten steel spilled out of its vat. He is just one of the the real people in this book about unremarkable people who do remarkable things. they're all everyday heroes.

Titles of Works

Titles of long works such as books and movies appear in italic type in printed books. Because people cannot write in italics, underlining is used for these titles in handwritten materials. Quotation marks are used around the titles of short works such as poems, short stories, and songs.

> Olivia read <u>Little Women</u> for her last book report.
>
> Today her class read a sad poem called "Losing."

The following sentences contain misspelled words and titles that are not written correctly. Write each sentence correctly.

1. One of my heros is Julie, the main character in the book Julie of the Wolves.

   _____

2. I'm writing a poem called Holidayes of the Year.

   _____

3. I like the song Whippoorwills because of the echoze in it.

   _____

4. The movie The Red-Headed League is one of my favorite misteries.

   _____

5. My father likes the book Where the Red Fern Grows because it brings back childhood memorys.

   _____

   _____

Words with /əl/

nickel	muscle	castle	example	novel
several	vegetable	carnival	whistle	label
wrestle	hospital	bicycle	principal	tunnel
natural	grumble	general	principle	usually

Say and Listen

Say each spelling word. Listen for the /əl/ sounds you hear at the end of *nickel*.

castle

Think and Sort

Look at the letters in each word. Think about how /əl/ is spelled. Spell each word aloud.

How many spelling patterns for /əl/ do you see?

1. Write the **seven** spelling words that have the *al* pattern, like *general.*

2. Write the **four** spelling words that have the *el* pattern, like *nickel.*

3. Write the **nine** spelling words that have the *le* pattern, like *muscle.*

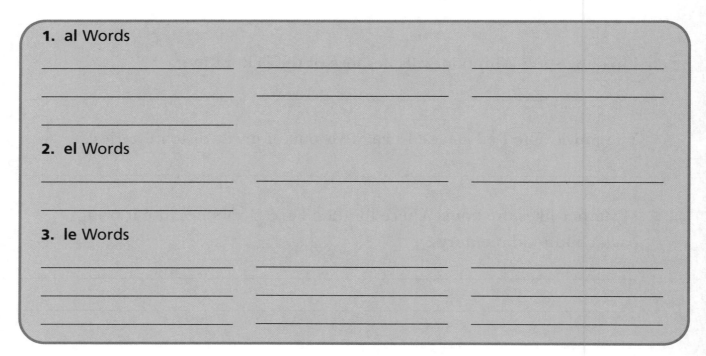

1. al Words

_____   _____   _____

_____   _____   _____

_____

2. el Words

_____   _____   _____

_____

3. le Words

_____   _____   _____

_____   _____   _____

_____   _____   _____

Classifying

Write the spelling word that belongs in each group.

1. circus, fair, _____

2. sample, model, _____

3. tag, sticker, _____

4. penny, _____, dime

5. complain, mutter, _____

6. lieutenant, captain, _____

7. few, some, _____

8. seldom, sometimes, _____

9. mansion, palace, _____

10. meat, grain, _____

11. student, teacher, _____

12. real, pure, _____

Making Connections

Complete each sentence by writing the spelling word that goes with the person or persons.

13. The coach showed his team the correct way to _____.

14. The famous author wrote a new _____.

15. The body builder developed his _____ tone.

16. Doctors and nurses often work in a _____.

17. The miners worked all day in the dark _____.

18. A cyclist rides a _____.

19. The referee blew her _____ at the end of the game.

nickel	muscle	castle	example	novel
several	vegetable	carnival	whistle	label
wrestle	hospital	bicycle	principal	tunnel
natural	grumble	general	principle	usually

Proofreading

Proofread the e-mail below. Use proofreading marks to correct five spelling mistakes, three capitalization mistakes, and two punctuation mistakes.

Proofreading Marks

◯ spell correctly
≡ capitalize
⊙ add period

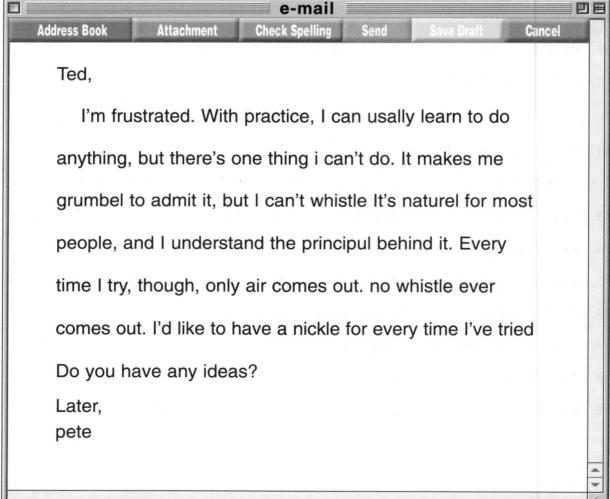

e-mail
Address Book	**Attachment**	**Check Spelling**	**Send**	**Save Draft**	**Cancel**

Ted,

I'm frustrated. With practice, I can usally learn to do anything, but there's one thing i can't do. It makes me grumbel to admit it, but I can't whistle It's naturel for most people, and I understand the principul behind it. Every time I try, though, only air comes out. no whistle ever comes out. I'd like to have a nickle for every time I've tried

Do you have any ideas?

Later,
pete

Multiple Meanings

Many words have more than one definition. Some definitions may surprise you. Look at the dictionary entry for *nickel* below.

nick·el (nĭk′əl) *n.* **1.** A hard, silvery-white metal. **2.** A coin in the United States and Canada worth five cents.

1. Write the entry word. _____

2. In which definition is *nickel* a coin? _____

3. In which definition is *nickel* a metal? _____

When the meaning of a word changes, the part of speech sometimes changes. Look at the entries below.

grum·ble (grŭm′ bəl) *v.* **grum·bled, grum·bling.** To complain in a low, angry voice. — *n.* A muttered complaint.

tun·nel (tŭn′ əl) *n.* An underground passageway, as for trains or cars. —*v.* **tun·neled** or **tun·nelled, tun·nel·ing** or **tun·nel·ling.** To make or dig a tunnel: *Moles have tunneled under the lawn.*

4. Write the entry words. _____   _____

5. What two parts of speech are given for each word? _____

_____

Write a sentence using *tunnel* as a noun and a sentence using *grumble* as a verb.

6. _____

7. _____

unit 2 review
LESSONS 6-10

meter
liter
library
succeed
piece
breathing
receive
extremely
gasoline

Words with /ē/

Write the spelling word for each clue.

1. People use this to run a car. _____

2. If it's not the whole thing, it's this. _____

3. This is a liquid measurement. _____

4. This place is full of books. _____

5. People work very hard in an effort to do this.
_____

6. Our lungs help us with this. _____

7. This is a measurement of distance. _____

8. This word is the opposite of *give*. _____

9. This is another word for *very*. _____

justice
government
enough
flood

Words with /ŭ/

Write the spelling word that is a synonym for each word.

10. administration _____

11. deluge _____

12. fairness _____

13. plenty _____

LESSON 8

human
cruel
coupon
canoe
threw
nuisance

Words with /yōō/ or /ōō/

Write the spelling word for each definition.

14. a long, narrow boat with pointed ends _____

15. flung with an arm motion _____

16. of the species to which people belong _____

17. a bother _____

18. a ticket that can be redeemed for something

_____

19. mean or unkind _____

LESSON 9

pianos
tomatoes
memories
knives

Plural Words

Write the spelling word that belongs in each group.

20. thoughts, remembrances, _____

21. forks, spoons, _____

22. accordions, organs, _____

23. cucumbers, carrots, _____

LESSON 10

principal
several

Words with /əl/

Write the spelling word that completes each analogy.

24. *No one* is to *everyone* as *few* is to _____.

25. *Town* is to *mayor* as *school* is to _____.

Words with /ĭ/

million	margarine	spinach	select	detective
business	opinion	equipment	system	experiment
electric	myth	gymnastic	relative	scissors
rhythm	brilliant	definite	witness	liquid

Say and Listen

Say each spelling word. Listen for the /ĭ/ sound you hear in *million*.

liquid

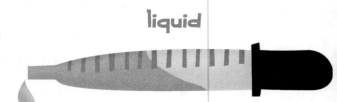

Think and Sort

Look at the letters in each word. Think about how /ĭ/ is spelled. Spell each word aloud.

How many spelling patterns for /ĭ/ do you see? Which words contain more than one spelling pattern for /ĭ/?

1. Write the **eight** spelling words with only the *i* pattern, like *million*.

2. Write the **three** spelling words with only the *y* pattern, like *myth*.

3. Write the **two** spelling words with only the *e* pattern, like *select*.

4. Write the **seven** spelling words with more than one spelling pattern for /ĭ/, like *spinach*. Circle the letters that spell /ĭ/ in each word.

1. i Words

_____   _____   _____

_____   _____   _____

_____   _____

2. y Words

_____   _____   _____

3. e Words

_____   _____

4. Words with More Than One Pattern

_____   _____   _____

_____   _____   _____

_____

Analogies

Write the spelling word that completes each analogy.

1. *Cut* is to _____ as *write* is to *pencil*.

2. *Magenta* is to *color* as _____ is to *number*.

3. *Rock* is to a *solid* as *water* is to _____.

4. *Vegetable* is to _____ as *fruit* is to *apple*.

5. *Jam* is to *jelly* as *butter* is to _____.

6. *Choose* is to _____ as *purchase* is to *buy*.

7. *Parent* is to *mother* as _____ is to *cousin*.

8. *Mend* is to *repair* as *smart* is to _____.

9. *Beat* is to _____ as *tune* is to *melody*.

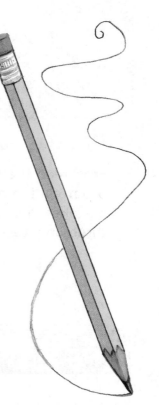

Clues

Write the spelling word for each clue.

10. This is a method of doing something. _____

11. This person sees a crime take place. _____

12. This story tries to explain something in nature. _____

13. This word describes exercises involving stunts on mats and bars.

_____

14. This person investigates crimes. _____

15. This is the making, buying, and selling of goods. _____

16. You might perform this in science class. _____

17. This is the opposite of *fact*. _____

18. *Specific* and *sure* are synonyms for this word. _____

19. These are all the things that help you do a specific job. _____

million	margarine	spinach	select	detective
business	opinion	equipment	system	experiment
electric	myth	gymnastic	relative	scissors
rhythm	brilliant	definite	witness	liquid

Proofreading

Proofread the following e-mail. Use proofreading marks to correct five spelling mistakes, two punctuation mistakes, and three unnecessary words.

Proofreading Marks

◯ spell correctly
⊙ add period
ℓ take out

e-mail

New	Read	File	Delete	Search	Contacts	Check

Hi, Lane!

Ruth just called me. Her brilyent idea is to to start a detectave agency called "Ruth's Sleuths." In her appinion it won't take a million dollars to and open her bisness. She'll need her brain and some basic eqwipment, such as a note pad, a the pen, and a phone Ruth wants us to join her. I'm not sure it's such a great idea. I don't know many adults who would select a twelve-year-old to solve an important case. What do you think? Write me soon to let me know

Adele

Time Expressions

When time is written in numerals, a colon is used to separate the hour from the minutes. The use of the colon makes reading the numbers easier.

hour ⟶ 8:10 ⟵ minutes   hour ⟶ 1:15 ⟵ minutes

The abbreviation A.M. is used to indicate the time period between 12:00 midnight and 12:00 noon. The abbreviation P.M. is used to indicate the time period between 12:00 noon and 12:00 midnight. The abbreviation A.M. or P.M. is not repeated if the time period does not change.

> Caroline will pick me up at **7:30** P.M. and take me to the movies. The movie begins at **8:15** and ends at **10:00**.

The following sentences contain spelling errors and time expressions written as words. Write the sentences, using numerals and colons for time expressions and spelling all words correctly.

1. At five forty-five A.M. on April Fool's Day, my electrik alarm clock rang.

_____

2. Then I decided to conduct a brilent experiment.

_____

3. I switched the margerine and the butter at six fifteen.

_____

4. "This isn't margarine," my sister said at six forty-five.

_____

5. She was a good detectiv and no April Fool!

_____

More Words with /ĭ/

luggage	sausage	message	desperate	pirate
cabbage	advantage	immediate	courage	accurate
private	beverage	storage	average	language
percentage	passage	image	chocolate	fortunate

Say and Listen

Say each spelling word. Listen for the /ĭ/ sound you hear in *luggage*.

Think and Sort

Look at the letters in each word. Think about how /ĭ/ is spelled. Spell each word aloud.

How many spelling patterns for /ĭ/ do you see? Which words contain more than one spelling pattern for /ĭ/?

chocolate

1. Write the **eighteen** spelling words that have only the *a*-consonant-*e* pattern, like *luggage*.

2. Write the **two** spelling words that have the *i* and *a*-consonant-*e* patterns, like *image*. Circle the letters that spell /ĭ/ in each word.

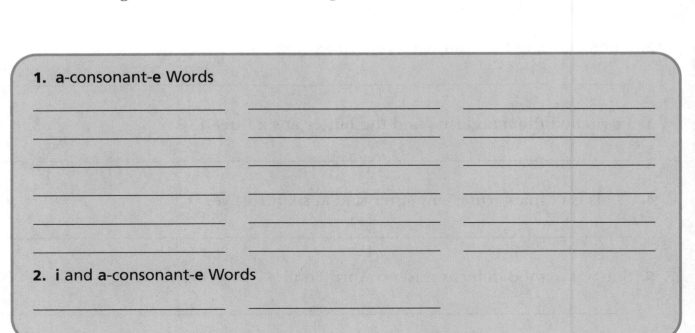

1. a-consonant-e Words

_____   _____   _____

_____   _____   _____

_____   _____   _____

_____   _____   _____

_____   _____   _____

_____   _____   _____

2. i and a-consonant-e Words

_____   _____

Synonyms

Write the spelling word that is a synonym for each word below.

1. suitcases _____

2. drink _____

3. lucky _____

4. correct _____

5. personal _____

6. typical _____

7. statement _____

Definitions

Write the spelling word for each definition.

8. words spoken and understood by a group of people _____

9. a narrow path _____

10. a place for keeping things _____

11. a leafy light-green vegetable _____

12. a mental picture _____

13. taking place at once _____

14. someone who lives by robbing ships _____

15. a better position _____

16. a food made from cacao seeds _____

17. a spicy meat mixture shaped like a frankfurter _____

18. in an almost hopeless situation _____

19. portion of a whole _____

luggage	sausage	message	desperate	pirate
cabbage	advantage	immediate	courage	accurate
private	beverage	storage	average	language
percentage	passage	image	chocolate	fortunate

Proofreading

Proofread the following paragraphs from a story. Use proofreading marks to correct five spelling mistakes, three capitalization mistakes, and two punctuation mistakes.

Proofreading Marks

◯ spell correctly
≡ capitalize
⊙ add period

Vera was fortunit to live on an island in the Gulf of mexico. According to legend, a well-known pyret called Raven had once lived there, and a secret passege in his home led to his treasure—a million dollars in gold Vera wasn't sure if the story was acurrate, but she decided to hunt for Raven's gold.

Her first task was to find out whether Raven's home was still standing. Early friday morning Vera headed to the pelican Island city library On a dusty stack of shelves by a storige room, she found a history of the town and began to read.

Hyphenation

Sometimes we cannot fit a whole word at the end of a line and must break it into parts. A word should only be broken between syllables. A hyphen is placed at the end of the line, and the rest of the word is written on the next line. To break a word correctly, look it up in a dictionary and check the syllable breaks in the entry word.

The owner of the missing car began to grow **des-perate** as the night grew darker.

The following sentences contain errors in hyphenation. Write each sentence, using a dictionary to hyphenate words correctly.

1. For dinner tomorrow we will have chicken pot pie, corn salad, and chocol-ate pudding.

   _____

   _____

2. The awards dinner at the middle school last night honored a large perc-entage of the students.

   _____

   _____

3. Many of my friends and classmates won ribbons and trophies for perfo-rmances that were clearly above average.

   _____

   _____

Words with /ī/

strike	violin	notify	deny	silence
surprise	survive	appetite	advertise	design
style	realize	sigh	recognize	apply
science	violet	describe	choir	assign

Say and Listen

Say each spelling word. Listen for the /ī/ sound you hear in *strike*.

surprise

Think and Sort

Look at the letters in each word. Think about how /ī/ is spelled. Spell each word aloud.

How many spelling patterns for /ī/ do you see?

1. Write the **eight** spelling words with the *i*-consonant-*e* pattern, like *strike*.

2. Write the **three** spelling words with the *y* pattern, like *deny*.

3. Write the **seven** spelling words with the *i* pattern, like *science*.

4. Write the **one** spelling word with the *igh* pattern.

5. Write the **one** spelling word with the *y*-consonant-*e* pattern.

1. i-consonant-e Words

_____ _____ _____

_____ _____ _____

_____ _____

2. y Words

_____ _____ _____

3. i Words

_____ _____ _____

_____ _____ _____

_____

4. igh Word   **5. y-consonant-e Word**

_____ _____

Classifying

Write the spelling word that belongs in each group.

1. guitar, cello, _____

2. hunger, craving, _____

3. history, math, _____

4. tell, inform, _____

5. purple, blue, _____

6. understand, discover, _____

7. quiet, hush, _____

8. plan, create, _____

9. appoint, designate, _____

10. shock, astonish, _____

11. remain, outlast, _____

12. identify, recall, _____

Rhymes

Write the spelling word that completes each sentence and rhymes with the underlined word.

13. Pilots must _____ for a license to <u>fly</u>.

14. The miners would <u>like</u> to _____ gold.

15. Can you _____ how that ancient <u>tribe</u> lived?

16. Can we <u>hire</u> a _____ to sing at the assembly?

17. I like that _____ of floor <u>tile</u>.

18. Julia looked up at the <u>sky</u> with a wishful _____.

19. Don't <u>try</u> to _____ that it was your idea.

strike	violin	notify	deny	silence
surprise	survive	appetite	advertise	design
style	realize	sigh	recognize	apply
science	violet	describe	choir	assign

Proofreading

Proofread the following journal entry. Use proofreading marks to correct five spelling mistakes, two punctuation mistakes, and three mistakes in word order.

Proofreading Marks

◯ spell correctly
≡ capitalize
∿ trade places

April 7

Today I got a big suprise. Dr. Kenneth Brill, the conductor of the Tipton Falls Symphony Orchestra, invited me play to my vilin at a concert. He called this afternoon, and I can't discribe how proud I was when he asked me to join the orchestra for an evening. I was so excited that I could hardly eat dinner tonight, even though Dad my made favorite, meat loaf. Later, Keesha said that our chior will perform, too, and she'll sing a solo I asked her if she's excited, she and didn't deny it. We both realyze how lucky we are

Verbs

A verb is a word that shows action or a state of being. Sometimes a verb includes an auxiliary, or helping, verb such as *is, are, was, will, could,* or *have.* Study the verbs in the following sentences.

Watch out when you **are swimming** in this pond. It **is** quite deep.

Unscramble each group of words below to make a sensible sentence. Write the sentence and circle the verbs.

1. we a Here suggestions are some TV sent to that station.

_____

2. us Always notify future programs of.

_____

3. intelligent we are that viewers Realize.

_____

4. at all talent recognize ages should You.

_____

5. products Advertise that offer services us good.

_____

6. false advertising Deny time to have companies that.

_____

7. turn you off Remember we can that turn us off, if you!

_____

Science Words

merge	spiral	clockwise	foreground	concentrate
distort	illusion	revolve	profiles	constantly
appear	incorrect	parallel	slanting	continue
unusual	background	equal	square	object

Say and Listen

Say the spelling words. Listen for the number of syllables in each word.

square

Think and Sort

Look at the letters in each word. Think about the number of syllables in the word. Spell each word aloud.

1. Write the **two** spelling words that have one syllable, like *merge*.

2. Write the **eleven** spelling words that have two syllables, like *distort*. Draw dashes between the syllables, like dis-tort.

3. Write the **six** spelling words that have three syllables, like *continue*. Draw dashes between the syllables.

4. Write the **one** spelling word that has four syllables. Draw dashes between the syllables.

1. One-syllable Words

_____   _____

2. Two-syllable Words

_____   _____   _____

_____   _____   _____

_____   _____   _____

_____   _____

3. Three-syllable Words

_____   _____   _____

_____   _____   _____

4. Four-syllable Word

_____

Antonyms

Complete each sentence by writing the spelling word that is an antonym of the underlined word.

1. The pasta tasted quite _____. <u>ordinary</u>

2. We watched the image _____ in the distance. <u>vanish</u>

3. Was your answer _____? <u>correct</u>

4. The lanes of this road _____ just outside of the city. <u>separate</u>

5. After people get off, the train will _____ its journey. <u>stop</u>

6. Did you cut the cake into _____ pieces? <u>unequal</u>

Clues

Write the spelling word for each clue.

7. A circular staircase is this. _____

8. This word means "to do something nonstop." _____

9. The hands on a watch turn in this direction. _____

10. This geometric figure has four equal sides. _____

11. Magicians are known for creating this. _____

12. These lines are the same distance apart. _____

13. This word is the opposite of *background*. _____

14. If things rotate, they do this. _____

15. This is the scene behind the main object of a painting. _____

16. These are side views of faces. _____

17. This word means "something that can be seen." _____

18. If something is sloping, it is this. _____

19. You do this when you fix your attention on one thing. _____

merge	spiral	clockwise	foreground	concentrate
distort	illusion	revolve	profiles	constantly
appear	incorrect	parallel	slanting	continue
unusual	background	equal	square	object

Proofreading

Proofread the diary entry below. Use proofreading marks to correct five spelling mistakes, two punctuation mistakes, and three missing words.

Proofreading Marks

◯ spell correctly

? add question mark

∧ add

Dear Diary,

It had be an alusion, didn't it There I was in the art museum, sketching a painting of some pink roses in a vase, when I noticed a skware object in the painting. It hadn't been there before that moment. For more than an hour, it would suddenly apear in the fourground of painting and spiral downward. Then just as suddenly it would gone. I blinked my eyes really hard and tried to concintrait. Was I seeing things I must have been dreaming.

Commas

Words such as *yes, no, well,* and *okay* should be followed by a comma when they begin a sentence.

> **Yes,** I'd like to go for a drive.
> **No,** we don't need the map.

The following sentences lack commas after introductory words. They also contain spelling errors. Write each sentence correctly.

1. Yes the bright light looked unusuall against the dark night sky.

_____

_____

2. No it didn't continyew to shine past midnight.

_____

_____

3. Okay it did seem to ravolve around a smaller light.

_____

_____

4. Well it could have been one airplane moving clokwize around another one.

_____

_____

Social Studies Words

society	woven	culture	scientists	primitive
excavation	resources	ceremonies	identify	environment
influence	behavior	fragile	region	adapted
nature	skeletons	artifacts	climate	evidence

Say and Listen

Say each spelling word. Listen for the number of syllables.

nature

Think and Sort

Look at the letters in each word. Think about the number of syllables in the word. Spell each word aloud.

1. Write the **six** spelling words that have two syllables, like *woven*. Draw dashes between the syllables, like wo-ven.

2. Write the **nine** spelling words that have three syllables, like *evidence*. Draw dashes between the syllables.

3. Write the **five** spelling words that have four syllables, like *environment*. Draw dashes between the syllables.

---

1. Two-syllable Words

_____   _____   _____

_____   _____   _____

2. Three-syllable Words

_____   _____   _____

_____   _____   _____

_____   _____   _____

3. Four-syllable Words

_____   _____   _____

_____   _____

Definitions

Write the spelling word for each definition.

1. remnants of ancient civilizations   _____
2. the world of living things and the outdoors   _____
3. things used to make other things   _____
4. the way in which people or animals act   _____
5. people who work in any of the sciences   _____
6. a part of the earth's surface   _____
7. the power to cause a change   _____
8. a community that lives and works together   _____
9. original, earliest   _____
10. the natural conditions of a place   _____

Synonyms

Complete each sentence by writing the spelling word that is a synonym for the underlined word.

11. We studied the _____ of the ancient Aztecs.   <u>customs</u>
12. The _____ of several buffalo were uncovered near the river.   <u>bones</u>
13. Europeans _____ to life in the New World.   <u>adjusted</u>
14. Scientists found _____ of dinosaurs in fossils.   <u>proof</u>
15. The ancient clay vase was very _____.   <u>delicate</u>
16. The _____ uncovered an ancient Roman city.   <u>dig</u>
17. Can you _____ the seven continents?   <u>name</u>
18. Many Native American _____ involved dance.   <u>rituals</u>
19. Cloth was _____ to create large mats.   <u>interlocked</u>

society   *woven*   *culture*   *scientists*   *primitive*

excavation   *resources*   *ceremonies*   *identify*   *environment*

influence   *behavior*   *fragile*   *region*   *adapted*

nature   *skeletons*   *artifacts*   *climate*   *evidence*

Proofreading

Proofread the following part of a newspaper article. Use proofreading marks to correct five spelling mistakes, three capitalization mistakes, and two punctuation mistakes.

Proofreading Marks

◯ spell correctly

⹀ capitalize

⊙ add period

Sixth Grade Visits Southwest Dig

last month the sixth grade classes visited an exscevation site in new Mexico Students toured a cave filled with ancient artifacts. these objects once belonged to a primative society that lived in the regin more than a thousand years ago. The classes also saw two ancient turkey skelatins that sientists had found. After touring the digging site, students visited a nearby museum collection that featured prehistoric sandals, stone and bone tools, and shell jewelry

Direct Quotations

Use a comma to set off a speaker's words from the rest of the sentence. Enclose the exact words in quotation marks. If the quotation ends the sentence, place the sentence end mark inside the final quotation mark. Study the following examples.

> "It's starting to rain," Courtney said.
> Her mother asked, "Do you have your umbrella?"

Write the following sentences, punctuating them correctly.

1. I read articles about scientists digging in excavation sites said Matthew.

_____

_____

2. I have pictures of beautiful Pueblo artifacts exclaimed Victoria.

_____

_____

3. Mr. Fine said We are going to discuss the behavior of the Pueblo people.

_____

_____

4. Mr. Fine asked How did the environment influence their society?

_____

_____

LESSON 11

million
opinion
scissors
definite
rhythm
electric
spinach

Words with /ĭ/

Write the spelling word for each definition. Use a dictionary if you need to.

1. specific or sure _____

2. a leafy green vegetable _____

3. one thousand thousands _____

4. what someone thinks about something _____

5. operated by electrical energy _____

6. a regular beat in music _____

7. a tool used for cutting _____

LESSON 12

private
message
desperate
average

More Words with /ĭ/

Write the spelling word that belongs in each group.

8. information, note, _____

9. typical, common, _____

10. urgent, pressing, _____

11. personal, secret, _____

LESSON 13 — Words with /ī/

surprise
realize
describe
deny
science
choir
design
sigh
style

Write the spelling word that completes each sentence.

12. The _____ sang many well-known holiday songs.

13. I enjoy his _____ of singing.

14. My birthday party was a complete _____.

15. The tired worker let out a long, deep _____.

16. The pattern on your shirt is a nice _____.

17. It was difficult to _____ my feelings in words.

18. Do you _____ that you're an hour early?

19. Many criminals _____ that they did anything wrong.

20. We studied how the earth was formed in _____ class.

LESSON 14 — Science Words

revolve
parallel

Write the spelling word that completes each analogy.

21. *Railroad track* is to _____ as *intersection* is to *perpendicular*.

22. *Motionless* is to *still* as *turn* is to _____.

LESSON 15 — Social Studies Words

fragile
climate
environment

Write the spelling word for each clue.

23. This word describes something that breaks easily.

_____

24. This is another word for *surroundings*. _____

25. This word names the average weather conditions over time. _____

Words with /ŏ/

closet	astonish	equality	moccasins	tonsils
ecology	knowledge	molecule	proper	operate
comic	opposite	impossible	honor	honesty
probably	omelet	forgotten	octopus	demolish

Say and Listen

Say each spelling word. Listen for the /ŏ/ sound you hear in *closet.*

octopus

Think and Sort

Look at the letters in each word. Think about how /ŏ/ is spelled. Spell each word aloud.

How many spelling patterns for /ŏ/ do you see?

1. Write the **eighteen** spelling words that have the *o* pattern, like *closet.*

2. Write the **one** spelling word that has the *a* pattern.

3. Write the **one** spelling word that has the *ow* pattern.

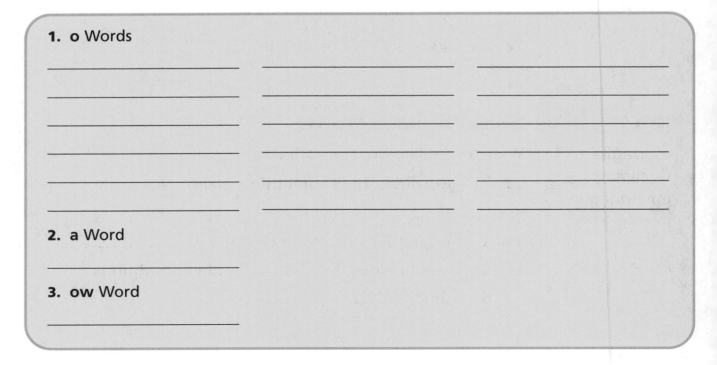

1. o Words

_____   _____   _____

_____   _____   _____

_____   _____   _____

_____   _____   _____

_____   _____   _____

2. a Word

_____

3. ow Word

_____

Antonyms

Write the spelling word that is an antonym of each word below.

1. ignorance   _____

2. remembered   _____

3. disgrace   _____

4. improper   _____

5. possible   _____

Analogies

Write the spelling word that completes each analogy.

6. *Legality* is to *legal* as _____ is to *equal*.

7. *Lettuce* is to *salad* as *egg* is to _____.

8. *Cupboard* is to *dish* as _____ is to *coat*.

9. *Jungle* is to *tiger* as *ocean* is to _____.

10. *Lie* is to *dishonesty* as *truth* is to _____.

11. *Science* is to _____ as *mathematics* is to *geometry*.

12. *Mouth* is to *tongue* as *throat* is to _____.

13. *Alike* is to _____ as *early* is to *late*.

14. *Delicious* is to *flavorful* as *funny* is to _____.

15. *Build* is to *make* as _____ is to *wreck*.

16. *Huge* is to *mountain* as *tiny* is to _____.

17. *Surprise* is to _____ as *scare* is to *terrify*.

18. *Often* is to *sometimes* as *certainly* is to _____.

19. *Write* is to *author* as _____ is to *surgeon*.

closet	astonish	equality	moccasins	tonsils
ecology	knowledge	molecule	proper	operate
comic	opposite	impossible	honor	honesty
probably	omelet	forgotten	octopus	demolish

Proofreading

Proofread the letter below. Use proofreading marks to correct five spelling mistakes, three capitalization mistakes, and two punctuation mistakes.

Proofreading Marks

◯ spell correctly

/ make lowercase

⊙ add period

612 Taylor Road

Appleton, WI 54911

February 16, 2003

Dear Ms. Lin:

Thank You for writing the excellent article, "Save the North Woods!" I admire your honnesty and your knoledge of our local ecalogy

It's imposible to please everyone, But people should remember that trees keep the air clean. If our trees are cut down, many Animals will prabably lose their homes, too

Sincerely,

Isabel Rollo

Dictionary Skills

Multiple Spellings

Some words have two correct spellings. Even though a dictionary gives both spellings, the first is more common.

Study the two dictionary entries below. Notice that each entry includes two spellings.

---

cat·a·log or **cat·a·logue** (kăt′ l ôg′) *or* (-ŏg′) *n.* A booklet that lists items, giving a description of each one: *Dad ordered a parka from a sportswear catalog.*

---

om·e·let, also **om·e·lette** (ŏm′ ə lĭt) *or* (ŏm′ lĭt) *n.* Beaten eggs cooked into a flat pancake that can be folded over a filling.

1. Write the more common spelling included in the first entry. _____

2. Write the more common spelling included in the second entry. _____

Sometimes spelling variations are listed as separate entries in a dictionary. Study the following entries for *honor* and *practice.* Notice the notes that explain where two of the spelling variations come from.

---

hon·or (ŏn′ ər) *n.* **1.** Special respect or high regard: *displaying the flag to show honor to the United States.* **2.** A special privilege or mark of distinction: *Election to baseball's hall of fame is an honor that comes to few players.*

hon·our (ŏn′ ər) Chiefly British form of the word **honor.**

---

prac·tice (prăk′ tĭs) *v.* To do or work on over and over in order to learn or master: *practiced a jump shot; practice the piano.*

prac·tise (prăk′ tĭs) Chiefly British form of the word **practice.**

---

3. Write the American spelling for *honour.* _____

4. Write the British spelling for *practice.* _____

Words with /ō/

noble	grown	propose	plateau	telephone
loan	poetry	lone	suppose	bureau
throne	telescope	groan	solar	although
approach	thrown	microphone	snowy	blown

Say and Listen

Say each spelling word. Listen for the /ō/ sound you hear in *noble*.

telescope

Think and Sort

Look at the letters in each word. Think about how /ō/ is spelled. Spell each word aloud. How many spelling patterns for /ō/ do you see?

1. Write the **three** spelling words that have the *o* pattern, like *noble*.
2. Write the **seven** spelling words that have the *o-consonant-e* pattern, like *lone*.
3. Write the **three** spelling words that have the *oa* pattern, like *loan*.
4. Write the **four** spelling words that have the *ow* pattern, like *blown*.
5. Write the **two** spelling words that have the *eau* pattern, like *bureau*.
6. Write the **one** spelling word that has the *ough* pattern.

1. o Words

_____   _____   _____

2. o-consonant-e Words

_____   _____   _____

_____   _____   _____

_____

3. oa Words

_____   _____

4. ow Words

_____   _____

_____

5. eau Words   **6. ough Word**

_____   _____

Making Connections

Write the spelling word that completes each sentence and goes with the person.

1. The queen sat on her _____.

2. An officer at the bank gave the man a _____.

3. The writer created beautiful rhyming _____.

4. The singer used a wireless _____.

5. An astronomer uses a _____ to look at the stars.

Clues

Write the spelling word for each clue.

6. People do this when they make a sad sound. _____

7. Winter weather is this in some places. _____

8. The sun creates this type of energy. _____

9. People do this when they walk toward something. _____

10. This piece of furniture has drawers. _____

11. The wind has done this. _____

12. This is another word for *guess*. _____

13. This word is a synonym for *single*. _____

14. A duke belongs to this kind of family. _____

15. This is a word like *however*. _____

16. If something has been tossed, it has been this. _____

17. This word is a homophone of *groan*. _____

18. If you make a suggestion, you do this. _____

19. This is a high, flat area of land. _____

noble	grown	propose	plateau	telephone
loan	poetry	lone	suppose	bureau
throne	telescope	groan	solar	although
approach	thrown	microphone	snowy	blown

Proofreading

Proofread the article below. Use proofreading marks to correct five spelling mistakes, two missing commas, and three unnecessary words.

Proofreading Marks

◯ spell correctly
⌃, add comma
◯ take out

Science Department to Return Telescope

Our school teliscope has been on lown from the San Francisco Academy of Sciences since January 25 1995. We have grone to like having it it around our science lab. Now the museum wants it back. Fifth graders, sixth graders and seventh graders all let out a growne when they heard the the news. So did our science teacher, Mr. Comini.

We are glad that we have had the opportunity to use the telescope for several years. Now that we must return it, the Student Post would like to prepose that all classes write letters to to the museum to thank them for their generosity.

Dictionary Skills

Parts of a Dictionary Entry

A dictionary entry has several parts. Study the following dictionary entry for *bureau*.

bu·reau (**byŏŏr′** ō) *n.*, *pl.* **bu·reaus** or **bu·reaux** (**byŏŏr′** ōz). **1.** A chest of drawers. **2.** An office for special business: *travel bureau.* **3.** A department of a government.

tel·e·phone (**tĕl′** ə fōn′) *n.* An instrument for sending and receiving speech and other sounds over electric wires. —*v.* **tel·e·phoned, tel·e·phon·ing.** To use this instrument to speak to someone; call: *Please telephone me tomorrow.*

The entry word is divided into syllables, and its pronunciation is listed in parentheses. Then the abbreviation for the part of speech is given. If the plural is formed in an irregular way, the plural is given, along with the abbreviation *pl.*

Bureau has two acceptable plural forms, so both are listed. The definitions of the word follow. A sample sentence or phrase sometimes accompanies a definition.

1. Write the pronunciation for *bureau.* _____

2. Write the part of speech for *bureau.* _____

3. Write the plural forms of *bureau.* _____

Some words can be used as more than one part of speech. Definitions for these words are organized according to the different parts of speech.

In the entry for *telephone* above, its noun definition is given first. Then its verb definition is listed, preceded by the principal parts of the verb: the past (-ed form), past participle, and present participle (-ing) forms. Because the past and past participle of telephone are the same, telephoned appears only once.

4. Write the sample sentence given for *telephone* when it is used as a verb.

_____

5. Write a sample sentence of your own in which you use *telephone* as a noun.

_____

Words with /ô/

crawl	support	formal	chalk	autumn
sword	audience	course	chorus	coarse
ordinary	awful	saucers	forward	auditorium
laundry	perform	daughter	wharf	orchestra

Say and Listen

Say each spelling word. Listen for the /ô/
sound you hear in *crawl* and *sword*.

Think and Sort

 orchestra

Look at the letters in each word. Think about how /ô/ is spelled. Spell each word aloud.

How many spelling patterns for /ô/ do you see?

1. Write the **two** spelling words that have the *aw* pattern, like *crawl*.
2. Write the **six** spelling words that have the *au* or *augh* pattern, like *laundry*.
3. Write the **eight** spelling words that have the *o* pattern, like *sword*.
4. Write the **two** spelling words that have the *a* pattern, like *wharf*.
5. Write the **two** spelling words that have the *oa* or *ou* pattern, like *coarse*.

---

1. aw Words

_____   _____

2. au, augh Words

_____   _____   _____

_____   _____   _____

3. o Words

_____   _____   _____

_____   _____   _____

_____   _____

4. a Words

_____   _____

5. oa, ou Words

_____   _____

Classifying

Write the spelling word that belongs in each group.

1. cups   plates   _____

2. dock   pier   _____

3. rough   bristly   _____

4. run   walk   _____

5. shield   helmet   _____

6. eraser   blackboard   _____

7. sideways   backward   _____

8. horrible   terrible   _____

9. spring   summer   _____

Clues

Write the spelling word for each clue.

10. People use a compass to help them stay on this. _____

11. Musicians do this. _____

12. You need a washer and a dryer to do this. _____

13. A tuxedo is an example of this type of clothing. _____

14. This contains many musicians and instruments. _____

15. This word is the opposite of *unusual*. _____

16. Walls do this to a roof. _____

17. This child is not a son. _____

18. A group of people sing together in this. _____

19. This is where singers may perform. _____

crawl	support	formal	chalk	autumn
sword	audience	course	chorus	coarse
ordinary	awful	saucers	forward	auditorium
laundry	perform	daughter	wharf	orchestra

Proofreading

Proofread the invitation below. Use proofreading marks to correct five spelling mistakes, three capitalization mistakes, and two punctuation mistakes.

Proofreading Marks

◯ spell correctly
≡ capitalize
∧, add comma

You're Invited

To: Aunt Jo, Uncle elmer and Cousin Renae

From: Rudy and Jennie

What: Jennie will preform in a play, and i will play
         in the orchestrer.

When: march 1 2006

Where: Cook School auditaurium

Time: 7:00 P.M.

Dress: casual for you but formel for me

RSVP: Rudy — 555-8955

We hope to see you in the audiance!

Language Connection

Adjectives

An adjective is a word that modifies, or describes, a noun or a pronoun by telling what kind, how many, or which one.

Several skunks just walked by **that red** barn.

Write the sentences below, correcting the misspelled words. Then circle the adjectives.

1. She sewed a (blue) (silk) gown for her (dawhter.) daughter

_____

2. The ancient whorf was covered with (pink) starfish.

_____

3. The choris sang our new school song.

_____

4. The (handsome) knight carried a massive bronze sord. sword

_____

5. I put my (dirty green) shirt in the laundery. laundery

_____

6. That tiny baby will soon learn to crawel.

_____

Compound Words

bathrobe	farewell	chessboard	tablecloth	old-fashioned
passport	backpack	thunderstorm	throughout	eavesdrop
weekday	waterproof	flashlight	weekend	cross-country
brand-new	proofread	roommate	self-confidence	applesauce

Say and Listen

chessboard

Each of the spelling words is a compound word. Say each word. Listen for the two words that make up each compound word.

Think and Sort

The compound words in this lesson are written in two ways. Some are written as one word. Others are **hyphenated**—that is, they are written with a hyphen between them.
Look at each spelling word. Think about how it is written. Spell each word aloud.

1. Write the **sixteen** compound words that are written as one word, like *applesauce*.

2. Write the **four** compound words that are hyphenated, like *old-fashioned*.

1. One-word Compounds

_____   _____   _____

_____   _____   _____

_____   _____   _____

_____   _____   _____

_____   _____   _____

_____

2. Hyphenated Compounds

_____   _____   _____

_____

Making Connections

Complete each sentence by writing the spelling word that goes with the person.

1. A chess player needs chess pieces and a _____.

2. A spy must sometimes _____ to get information.

3. A waiter will replace a _____ if it is soiled.

4. A world traveler needs a _____ to go from country to country.

5. A mountain climber needs a _____ for carrying things.

Analogies

Write the spelling word that completes each analogy.

6. *Wick* is to *candle* as *bulb* is to _____.

7. *Water* is to _____ as *fire* is to *fireproof*.

8. *Long* is to *short* as _____ is to *local*.

9. *Fear* is to *terror* as *self-assurance* is to _____.

10. *Work* is to *weekday* as *play* is to _____.

11. *Computer* is to *modern* as *typewriter* is to _____.

12. *Prior* is to *before* as _____ is to *during*.

13. *Author* is to *write* as *editor* is to _____.

14. *Strawberry* is to *jam* as *apple* is to _____.

15. *Saturday* is to *weekend* as *Thursday* is to _____.

16. *Blizzard* is to *snow* as _____ is to *rain*.

17. *Class* is to *classmate* as *room* is to _____.

18. *Hello* is to *welcome* as *good-bye* is to _____.

19. *Bathe* is to _____ as *swim* is to *swimsuit*.

bathrobe	farewell	chessboard	tablecloth	old-fashioned
passport	backpack	thunderstorm	throughout	eavesdrop
weekday	waterproof	flashlight	weekend	cross-country
brand-new	proofread	roommate	self-confidence	applesauce

Proofreading

Proofread the e-mail below. Use proofreading marks to correct five spelling mistakes, two capitalization mistakes, and three unnecessary words.

Proofreading Marks

◯ spell correctly
≡ capitalize
℘ take out

---

e-mail

New	Read	File	Delete	Search	Contacts	Check

Hi, brandon!

I entered the the cross-contry bicycle race today! I think the race will have more than thirty kids from our school and some from lincoln High, too. Even my brother's roomate from college is going to ride! That's a lot of competition, but I have a lot of self-confadence. I'm strong and at in good shape. And of course, I have an my awesome, brand-neu bike. See you next weekind!

Speedy

Language Connection

Adverbs

An adverb is a word that modifies, or describes, a verb, an adjective, or another adverb by telling how, when, where, how often, or to what degree.

> Jane skated **powerfully** but **gracefully**.
> Then she **quickly** ran **inside**.

Write the sentences below, correcting the misspelled words. Then circle the adverbs.

1. I wore my batherobe and slept deeply.

_____

2. The thundersturm started suddenly.

_____

3. Our waterpruff rain gear covered us completely.

_____

4. My flashligt shone brightly.

_____

5. We hungrily ate some apelsauce.

_____

6. Finally Dad and I said farewele to camping.

_____

Words Often Confused

breath	choose	lose	accept	desert
breathe	chose	loose	except	dessert
all ready	dairy	quiet	weather	cloths
already	diary	quite	whether	clothes

Say and Listen

Say each pair of spelling words. Listen to the pronunciation of each word in the pair.

dessert

Think and Sort

The pairs of spelling words in this lesson are often confused because they have similar spellings. The words in most pairs are pronounced differently and have different meanings. The words in some pairs are pronounced the same but have different meanings. Look at each pair of words. Think about how each word is pronounced and spelled. Spell each word aloud.

1. Write the **eight** word pairs in which the words are pronounced differently, like *breath* and *breathe.*

2. Write the **two** word pairs in which the words are pronounced in the same way, like *weather* and *whether.*

1. Different Pronunciations

_____   _____

_____   _____

_____   _____

_____   _____

_____   _____

_____   _____

_____   _____

_____   _____

2. Same Pronunciations

_____   _____

_____   _____

Classifying

Write the spelling word that belongs in each group.

1. outfits   costumes   _____

2. eat   sleep   _____

3. forest   tundra   _____

4. salad   soup   _____

5. before   formerly   _____

6. still   silent   _____

7. journal   log   _____

8. sports   news   _____

Definitions

Write the spelling word for each definition. Use a dictionary if you need to.

9. to fail to win   _____

10. pieces of material woven or knitted from fibers   _____

11. the air drawn into and exhaled from the lungs   _____

12. to select   _____

13. not securely fastened   _____

14. more than usual   _____

15. to take what is offered   _____

16. other than   _____

17. no matter if   _____

18. to be fully prepared to do something   _____

19. selected   _____

breath	choose	lose	accept	desert
breathe	chose	loose	except	dessert
all ready	dairy	quiet	weather	cloths
already	diary	quite	whether	clothes

Proofreading

Proofread the report below. Use proofreading marks to correct five spelling mistakes, two punctuation mistakes, and three unnecessary words.

Proofreading Marks

◯ spell correctly

⋏ add comma

℧ take out

Fables

Fables are in told in many countries around the world. They are stories that teach lessons about life. In on some fables, the characters looze something, such as a contest. The loss is sometimes hard to acept, but it often happens because the characters chuse to be selfish lazy or mean.

Wether or not you've read many fables, you alredy know many of their lessons. For example, you know that a truly brave person is brave in deeds as well as deeds words. That is the moral of Aesop's fable "The Hunter and the Woodsman."

Language Connection

Punctuation

When two or more simple sentences are joined by a connecting word, the result is a compound sentence. The connecting words are generally *and, but, or, nor,* and *for.* Use a comma before the connecting word in a compound sentence.

My cousin wants to be a veterinarian, and I hope she'll work here in town. We already have one vet in town, but we can always use another.

Choose the correct word from each pair in parentheses to complete each sentence. Then use commas to write the sentences correctly.

1. Either Audrey is very shy or she is just extremely (quite, quiet).

_____

_____

2. Her family (chose, choose) to move here for it's a good place to start a (diary, dairy) business.

_____

_____

3. They used to live in the (desert, dessert) and it was terribly hot.

_____

_____

4. Audrey told us she wore (loose, lose) (cloths, clothes) but she was still (quite, quiet) uncomfortable.

_____

_____

unit 4 review
Lessons 16-20

Lesson 16

probably
opposite
impossible
forgotten
honesty
equality
knowledge

Words with /ŏ/

Write the spelling word for each clue.

1. This is the opposite of *possible*. _____

2. The brain contains a lot of this. _____

3. People use this word if something is
likely to happen. _____

4. This is the opposite of *have remembered*.

_____

5. This is a good quality to have. _____

6. People should be treated with this. _____

7. This is what an antonym is. _____

Lesson 17

solar
telephone
groan
thrown
although
plateau

Words with /ō/

Write the spelling word that belongs in each group.

8. because   however   _____

9. lunar   planetary   _____

10. television   telegram   _____

11. mountain   prairie   _____

12. moan   sigh   _____

13. tossed   flung   _____

LESSON **18**

awful
daughter
chalk
ordinary
course
coarse

Words with /ô/

Write the spelling word for each definition.

14. a soft, white writing material _____

15. a female offspring _____

16. horrible or unpleasant _____

17. rough _____

18. route or travel direction _____

19. usual; common _____

LESSON **19**

roommate
old-fashioned

Compound Words

Find the two words in each sentence that make up a spelling word.

20. Marie fashioned a handkerchief out of some old cloth.

_____

21. The ship's first mate had a very pleasant

room. _____

LESSON **20**

lose
loose
quiet
quite

Words Often Confused

Write the spelling word that completes each analogy.

22. *Snug* is to _____ as *tight* is to *baggy*.

23. *Peach* is to *teach* as *right* is to _____.

24. *Noisy* is to *stadium* as _____ is to *library*.

25. *Happiness* is to *sadness* as *find* is to _____.

Words with /ou/

howl	doubt	mound	surround	proudly
crowded	couch	allowance	coward	scout
prowl	cloudy	ouch	growled	snowplow
blouse	eyebrow	wound	pronounce	thousand

Say and Listen

Say each spelling word. Listen for the /ou/ sound you hear in *howl*.

howl

Think and Sort

Look at the letters in each word. Think about how /ou/ is spelled. Spell each word aloud.

How many spelling patterns for /ou/ do you see?

1. Write the **twelve** spelling words that have the *ou* pattern, like *mound*.

2. Write the **eight** spelling words that have the *ow* pattern, like *howl*.

1. ou Words

_____   _____   _____

_____   _____   _____

_____   _____   _____

_____

2. ow Words

_____   _____   _____

_____   _____   _____

_____

Classifying

Write the spelling word that belongs in each group.

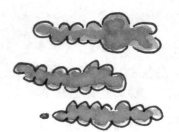

1. bulldozer, steamroller, _____

2. wail, whine, _____

3. snarled, howled, _____

4. hundred, _____, million

5. _____, foggy, rainy

6. jammed, packed, _____

7. eyelash, eyelid, _____

8. speak, say, _____

9. salary, _____, payment

10. happily, _____, grandly

Rhymes

Write the spelling word that completes each sentence and rhymes with the underlined word.

11. Howard was no _____, but he was afraid of heights.

12. There was no _____ that we took the wrong route.

13. Miguel cried, "_____" when he dropped the heavy mail pouch on his foot.

14. We found a _____ of stones in the middle of the field.

15. We watched the bear _____ for trout in the stream.

16. My stuffed mouse wears a little white _____.

17. The fox on the _____ looked for chickens and other fowl.

18. I'm a real grouch when I have to sleep on a lumpy old _____.

19. I _____ the yarn around my knitting needles.

howl	doubt	mound	surround	proudly
crowded	couch	allowance	coward	scout
prowl	cloudy	ouch	growled	snowplow
blouse	eyebrow	wound	pronounce	thousand

Proofreading

Proofread the following paragraph from a report. Use proofreading marks to correct five spelling mistakes, three capitalization mistakes, and two unnecessary words.

Proofreading Marks

◯ spell correctly

≡ capitalize

𝓵 take out

The Iditarod Race

Every year in March, people and dogs compete in the Iditarod Sled Dog Race, which covers about 1,100 miles of snow and ice. The course crosses mountain ranges and frozen waterways. The Iditarod is not a race for a coword. it is a test of bravery and stamina. Of that there is a little doutbe. wolves have been known to prowel near the racers and howll along the way. the first race in 1973 took the winning team about 20 days, but the winning time has been reduced by almost half. The dogs proudley run run until they can run no more.

Dictionary Skills

Homographs

A homograph is a word spelled like another word but different in meaning. Homographs appear in the dictionary as separate, numbered entries.

Some homographs are not pronounced alike and are used as different parts of speech. Notice the different pronunciations and parts of speech for *desert* and *wound* in the entries below. In addition, many homographs have different origins. *Desert 1* comes from the Latin word *desertum,* meaning "wasteland." *Desert 2* comes from the Latin word *desertus,* meaning "abandon."

---

des·ert¹ (**dĕz′** ərt) *n.* A dry land covered with sand and having very little plant life.

de·sert² (dĭ **zûrt′**) *v.* **de·sert·ed, de·sert·ing.** To forsake or leave someone or something needing you: *The mother lion deserted her cubs.*

---

wound¹ (wo͞ond) *n.* A physical injury in which the skin is cut. —*v.* To hurt either a part of the body or the feelings: *The rabbit was wounded by the trap. His sharp words wound me deeply.*

wound² Look up **wind.**
wind (wīnd) *v.* **wound** (wound), **wind·ing.** **1.** To twist or wrap (something) around or on top: *She wound a string around her finger.* **2.** To turn or tighten a crank or propelling spring: *to wind a watch.*

Write the number of the *desert* or *wound* homograph that is used in each sentence below.

1. Mother lions almost never desert their cubs. _____

2. I set the time and wound my wristwatch. _____

3. Camels live in the desert. _____

4. The soldier's wound required immediate care. _____

Words with /ûr/

curly	purchase	worry	emergency	prefer
refer	furniture	disturb	curtains	service
personal	thirsty	current	observe	urgent
worst	merchant	squirrel	murmur	occurred

Say and Listen

Say each spelling word. Listen for the /ûr/ sound you hear in *curly*.

squirrel

Think and Sort

Look at the letters in each word. Think about how /ûr/ is spelled. Spell each word aloud.

How many spelling patterns for /ûr/ do you see?

1. Write the **seven** spelling words that have the *er* pattern, like *refer*.

2. Write the **two** spelling words that have the *ir* pattern, like *thirsty*.

3. Write the **nine** spelling words that have the *ur* pattern, like *curly*.

4. Write the **two** spelling words that have the *or* pattern, like *worst*.

1. er Words

_____   _____   _____

_____

_____

2. ir Words

_____   _____

3. ur Words

_____   _____   _____

_____   _____   _____

_____   _____   _____

4. or Words

_____   _____

Synonyms

Write the spelling word that is a synonym for each word.

1. wavy   _____

2. buy   _____

3. important   _____

4. happened   _____

5. bother   _____

6. mumble   _____

7. fret   _____

8. assistance   _____

9. shopkeeper   _____

10. watch   _____

Clues

Write the spelling word for each clue.

11. This is what you do when you look at your notes when making a speech.   _____

12. This word is the opposite of *best*.   _____

13. These cover windows.   _____

14. This is how people who need water feel.   _____

15. This word means "up to date."   _____

16. An ambulance is often needed for this.   _____

17. This word describes a person's diary.   _____

18. This word means "to like better."   _____

19. A table and chairs are pieces of this.   _____

curly	purchase	worry	emergency	prefer
refer	furniture	disturb	curtains	service
personal	thirsty	current	observe	urgent
worst	merchant	squirrel	murmur	occurred

Proofreading

Proofread the following part of a newspaper article. Use proofreading marks to correct five spelling mistakes, three capitalization mistakes, and two unnecessary words.

Proofreading Marks

○ spell correctly

╱ make lowercase

℩ take out

A new the pet store opened in our area today. The owner, J. P. Byrd, says that her store is a great place to to perchase all kinds of Pet items. She also says that her staff will help pet owners who obsurve Strange pet behavior. If your cat is always thrsty, or if your Dog chews your farniture, they will be able to help. Ms. Byrd also has ideas for you if your neighbor's pets disterb you!

Dictionary Skills

Combined Entries

Some words can be used as more than one part of speech. In such cases the different parts of speech are defined in a single dictionary entry called a combined entry. The following entries for *current* and *worry* are combined entries.

cur·rent (kûr′ ənt) *or* (kŭr′-) *adj.* **1.** Taking place during present time or now: *the current movie; current events.* **2.** Done or used by everyone: *High-button shoes are no longer current.* —*n.* **1.** A flow of air or water: *The current washed the boat ashore.* **2.** A flow of electricity.

wor·ry (wûr′ ē) *or* (wŭr′-) *v.* **wor·ried, wor·ry·ing.** To have or to cause a feeling of concern or anxiety: *His bad health worried his mother.* —*n.* A cause for anxiety or concern: *The chance of fire in this wooden house is a worry to me.*

Answer the following questions.

1. What two parts of speech are given for *current*? _____

2. Write a sentence using *current* as an adjective.

_____

3. Write a sentence using *current* as a noun.

_____

4. Write a sentence using *worry* as a noun.

_____

5. Write a sentence using *worry* as a verb.

_____

Words with /ä/

carve	guard	apartment	arch	guitar
salami	armor	marble	harbor	departure
barber	marvelous	marvel	regard	harmony
partner	argument	scarlet	carpenter	harmonica

Say and Listen

Say each spelling word. Listen for the /ä/ sound you hear in *carve*.

Think and Sort

Look at the letters in each word. Think about how /ä/ is spelled. Spell each word aloud.

How many spelling patterns for /ä/ do you see?

1. Write the **nineteen** spelling words that have the *a* pattern, like *carve*.

2. Write the **one** spelling word that has the *ua* pattern.

barber

1. a Words

_____   _____   _____

_____   _____   _____

_____   _____   _____

_____   _____   _____

_____   _____   _____

_____

2. ua Word

_____

Definitions

Write the spelling word for each definition.

1. a curved structure over an open space _____

2. a fight with words; a disagreement _____

3. a small, rectangular wind instrument _____

4. something amazing _____

5. a person in business with another person _____

6. excellent _____

7. the act of going away _____

8. to look at closely _____

9. to watch over _____

10. someone who builds or works with wood _____

11. someone who cuts hair _____

12. to cut a piece of meat _____

13. a pleasing mix of musical sounds _____

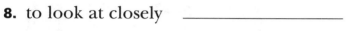

Making Connections

Complete each sentence by writing the spelling word that goes with the person.

14. A ship's captain docks her vessel in a _____.

15. Sculptors carve _____ statues.

16. A renter pays money to live in a house or an _____.

17. A sausage maker makes _____.

18. A folk singer plucks the strings on a _____.

19. A knight wears metal _____.

carve	guard	apartment	arch	guitar
salami	armor	marble	harbor	departure
barber	marvelous	marvel	regard	harmony
partner	argument	scarlet	carpenter	harmonica

Proofreading

Proofread the e-mail below. Use proofreading marks to correct five spelling mistakes, three capitalization mistakes, and two missing words.

Proofreading Marks

◯ spell correctly

≡ capitalize

⋀ add

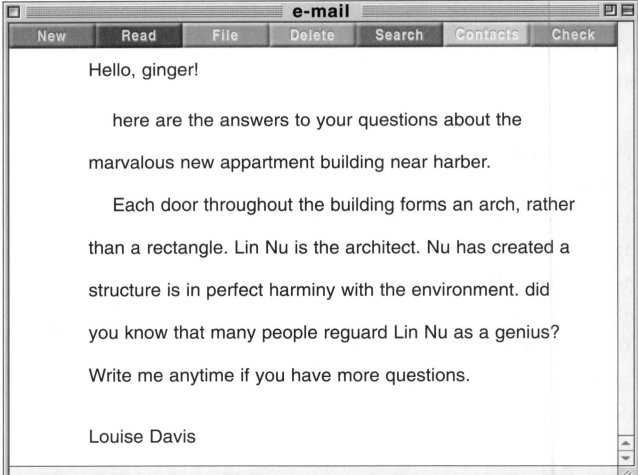

e-mail

| New | Read | File | Delete | Search | Contacts | Check |

Hello, ginger!

here are the answers to your questions about the marvalous new appartment building near harber.

Each door throughout the building forms an arch, rather than a rectangle. Lin Nu is the architect. Nu has created a structure is in perfect harminy with the environment. did you know that many people reguard Lin Nu as a genius? Write me anytime if you have more questions.

Louise Davis

Capitalization

Important words in names of companies are capitalized.

> That magazine is published by **Three Winds Press**.
> I bought a storage cabinet at **Box and Crate**.

Read the following letter. Find the three incorrectly written company names and the three misspelled words. Write them correctly below.

25 Apple Drive
Dearborn, ME 04622
November 11, 2003

Marvelous music company
14 Harbor Drive
Oakdale, ME 04962

To Whom It May Concern:

   I have no problem with the gittar that I just bought from you, but I must complain about the harmonnica. Half of the holes are closed! I held your products in high ragard, but now I'll take my business to your competitor, Notes and strings, inc.

   Since I am returning the instrument, I expect a full refund. If it is not received, I will contact the consumer Complaint bureau in Augusta.

Sincerely,
I.M. Feddup

Correct Spellings

1. _____

2. _____

3. _____

Correct Company Names

4. _____

5. _____

6. _____

Words with Suffixes

terrible	available	flexible	possible	reasonable
responsible	invisible	comfortable	remarkable	lovable
enjoyable	flammable	breakable	valuable	honorable
disagreeable	divisible	usable	sensible	probable

Say and Listen

Say each spelling word. Listen for the ending sounds.

Think and Sort

The endings *-able* and *-ible* are called suffixes. A **suffix** is a word part added to a base word that changes the base word's meaning. The suffixes *-able* and *-ible* mean "capable of" or "tending to be." Look at each spelling word. Think about what the word means and how it is spelled. Spell each word aloud.

valuable

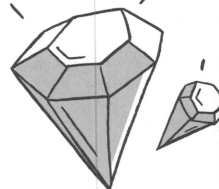

1. Write the **thirteen** spelling words that end with *-able,* like *usable.*

2. Write the **seven** spelling words that end with *-ible,* like *terrible.*

1. -able Words

_____   _____   _____

_____   _____   _____

_____   _____   _____

_____   _____   _____

_____

2. -ible Words

_____   _____   _____

_____   _____   _____

_____

Clues

Write the spelling word that describes the person or the object named in each clue.

1. an object that will shatter when dropped _____

2. someone who is sensible and fair _____

3. something that is fit for use _____

4. someone who does the right thing _____

5. a person who has good sense _____

6. something that can be divided _____

7. an activity that is fun _____

8. a person who is reliable and trustworthy _____

9. something that is likely to happen _____

10. something that can really happen _____

11. a person who is easily loved _____

12. something that is worthy of notice _____

13. a person who is never happy _____

Antonyms

Complete each sentence by writing the spelling word that is an antonym of the underlined word.

14. Luís said the play was <u>wonderful</u>, but I said it was _____.

15. The thieves took some <u>worthless</u> items and some _____ ones.

16. This amazing new substance can be both <u>stiff</u> and _____.

17. Do you know if Sheila is _____ or <u>unavailable</u> for the meeting?

18. The flickering light was <u>visible</u>, then _____.

19. The <u>fireproof</u> items survived the fire, but the _____ ones did not.

terrible	available	flexible	possible	reasonable
responsible	invisible	comfortable	remarkable	lovable
enjoyable	flammable	breakable	valuable	honorable
disagreeable	divisible	usable	sensible	probable

Proofreading

Proofread the following message from a bulletin board. Use proofreading marks to correct five spelling mistakes, three capitalization mistakes, and two punctuation mistakes.

Proofreading Marks

⬭ spell correctly

≡ capitalize

⊙ add period

Free Puppy

we have a lovible puppy that needs a home His name is max, and he's avalable for adoption. He needs a comfterble home and a risponsable, sensible, loving person to take care of him He'd be a valuble addition to any family. can you help?

Language Connection

Adjectives

An adjective is a word that modifies, or tells more about, a noun or pronoun. Many words that end in *-able* or *-ible* are adjectives. These words are often the result of adding *-able* or *-ible* to a noun. In the second example sentence below, the word *reasonable* modifies the noun *answer*.

> There is no **reason** to be upset. (noun)
> That is a **reasonable** answer. (adjective)

Unscramble the following groups of words to write sensible sentences. Then circle the adjectives.

1. terrible me from My puppy, Bongo, saved problem a.

_____

2. curtains Flammable were burning kitchen in the.

_____

3. knocked The pup breakable lamp over a.

_____

4. valuable lamp The crash me awakened of the.

_____

5. jumped comfortable I bed out of my and help got.

_____

Weather Words

nimbus	windchill	pollution	cirrus	thermometer
humidity	forecast	Celsius	Fahrenheit	thunderhead
temperature	long-range	cumulus	meteorologist	precipitation
flurries	atmosphere	velocity	prediction	overcast

Say and Listen

Say each spelling word. Listen for the syllables in the word.

windchill

Think and Sort

Look at the letters in each word. Think about how each syllable is spelled. Spell each word aloud.

1. Write the **six** spelling words that have two syllables, like *nimbus*. Circle the compound words.

2. Write the **eight** spelling words that have three syllables, like *atmosphere*. Circle the compound words.

3. Write the **four** spelling words that have four syllables, like *thermometer*.

4. Write the **one** spelling word that has five syllables.

5. Write the **one** spelling word that has six syllables.

1. Two-syllable Words

_____ _____ _____

_____ _____ _____

2. Three-syllable Words

_____ _____ _____

_____ _____ _____

_____ _____

3. Four-syllable Words

_____ _____ _____

_____

4. Five-syllable Word   5. Six-syllable Word

_____   _____

Compound Words

Write the spelling word that is made from the two underlined words in each sentence.

1. The fisherman <u>cast</u> his line <u>over</u> the bridge. _____

2. Every <u>cast</u> member in the golfing movie cried, "<u>Fore</u>!" _____

3. The climbers felt the cold <u>chill</u> of the howling <u>wind</u>. _____

4. We rode our horses on the <u>range</u> for a <u>long</u> time. _____

5. Alicia turned her <u>head</u> when she heard the <u>thunder</u>. _____

Clues

Write the spelling word for each clue.

6. light snow showers _____

7. a temperature scale on which water freezes at 0° _____

8. damage caused by chemicals and trash _____

9. made up of the gases surrounding the Earth _____

10. what a thermometer measures _____

11. the amount of moisture in the air _____

12. someone who forecasts weather _____

13. a word that describes high, thin, wispy clouds _____

14. a temperature scale on which water freezes at 32° _____

15. what people make when they guess what will happen next

_____

16. moisture that falls from the sky _____

17. a word that describes dark, low clouds _____

18. a word that describes big, white, fluffy clouds _____

19. the speed of the wind _____

nimbus	windchill	pollution	cirrus	thermometer
humidity	forecast	Celsius	Fahrenheit	thunderhead
temperature	long-range	cumulus	meteorologist	precipitation
flurries	atmosphere	velocity	prediction	overcast

Proofreading

Proofread the journal entry below. Use proofreading marks to correct five spelling mistakes, three capitalization mistakes, and two punctuation mistakes.

Proofreading Marks

◯ spell correctly

／ make lowercase

⌃, add comma

January 12 2005

    I just finished watching the weather forcast on television, and the meteorologist says there will be no change from last week. We'll have freezing winds more snow, and more ice. The weather for our area never changes much from day to day in Winter. The predicshun almost always includes some type of pricipatation, such as Snow flurrys, rain, or icy sleet. The sky is usually overcast, and the tempirture falls far below zero. It's difficult to imagine warm Spring days when the weather is so nasty.

Language Connection

Capitalization

The names of holidays and temperature scales are capitalized.

> **Valentine's Day** comes before **Mother's Day**.
> Water freezes at 32 degrees **Fahrenheit** or 0 degrees **Celsius**.

The following sentences contain spelling and capitalization errors. Write each sentence correctly.

1. We had some snow flerries a few weeks ago on thanksgiving.

   _____

2. The sky was overkast, and the temperature was only 30 degrees fahrenheit.

   _____

3. The long-rainge prediction is that we will have a white new year's Day.

   _____

4. The meteorlogist on TV gave the temperature tonight as 0 degrees celsius.

   _____

5. I don't care if we have presipitation on memorial day, the fourth of july, or even labor day.

   _____

   _____

LESSON 21

doubt
pronounce
proudly
crowded
allowance

Words with /ou/

Write the spelling word for each clue.

1. People do this when they say a word. _____

2. This can help you buy things you want.

   _____

3. This word describes a highway at rush hour.

   _____

4. When people do this, they are not sure
   of something. _____

5. A runner might walk this way after winning
   a race. _____

LESSON 22

emergency
squirrel
furniture
occurred
curtains
worst

Words with /ûr/

Write the spelling word that belongs in each group.

6. chipmunk, woodchuck, _____

7. bad, worse, _____

8. blinds, drapes, _____

9. furnishing, fixture, _____

10. took place, happened, _____

11. disaster, accident, _____

marvelous
argument
departure
guitar
guard

Words with /ä/

Write the spelling word that is a synonym for the underlined word.

12. The male bird will <u>protect</u> the nest. _____

13. Gail plays the <u>lute</u> and other musical instruments.

_____

14. Tim and Fred had a <u>quarrel</u> yesterday.

_____

15. Everyone agreed that the movie was <u>wonderful</u>.

_____

16. The thief made a quick <u>exit</u> when he heard the

sirens. _____

usable
comfortable
disagreeable
terrible
possible

Words with Suffixes

Write the spelling word that completes each sentence.

17. Because I am confident, I believe it is _____
to achieve my goals.

18. My new bed is soft and _____.

19. When Lea is in a bad mood, she is very _____.

20. A broken TV is not _____ anymore.

21. Our vacation was _____ because everything
went wrong.

atmosphere
temperature
velocity
precipitation

Weather Words

Write the spelling word for each definition.

22. any form of water that falls to the ground _____

23. speed in a given direction _____

24. hotness or coldness of something _____

25. the air around the Earth _____

More Words with /ə/

pencil	legend	item	balcony	cabinet
triumph	injury	amount	husband	multiply
history	atlas	balloon	focus	engine
pajamas	fortune	circus	celebrate	purpose

Say and Listen

The weak vowel sound in unstressed syllables is called **schwa** and is written as /ə/. Say each spelling word. Listen for the /ə/ sound.

balloon

Think and Sort

Look at the letters in each word. Think about how /ə/ is spelled. Spell each word aloud.

How many spelling patterns for /ə/ do you see?

1. Write the **five** spelling words that have /ə/ spelled *a*, like *balloon.*

2. Write the **three** spelling words that have /ə/ spelled *e*, like *item.*

3. Write the **four** spelling words that have /ə/ spelled *i*, like *pencil.*

4. Write the **three** spelling words that have /ə/ spelled *o*, like *history.*

5. Write the **five** spelling words that have /ə/ spelled *u*, like *circus.*

1. /ə/ Words with **a**

_____   _____   _____

_____   _____

2. /ə/ Words with **e**

_____   _____   _____

3. /ə/ Words with **i**

_____   _____   _____

_____

4. /ə/ Words with **o**

_____   _____   _____

5. /ə/ Words with **u**

_____   _____   _____

_____   _____

Clues

Write the spelling word for each clue.

1. a place to sit in a theater _____

2. what a bruise or a cut is _____

3. what people do at a birthday party _____

4. what sometimes floats high in the sky _____

5. chance or luck _____

6. what people do when they adjust a lens to get a clear image _____

7. the car part that runs _____

8. the opposite of *divide* _____

9. the story of the past _____

10. a book of maps _____

11. a synonym for *goal* _____

Classifying

Write the spelling word that belongs in each group.

12. success, victory, _____

13. myth, tale, _____

14. thing, object, _____

15. closet, cupboard, _____

16. quantity, total, _____

17. pen, marker, _____

18. carnival, fair, _____

19. father, uncle, _____

pencil	legend	item	balcony	cabinet
triumph	injury	amount	husband	multiply
history	atlas	balloon	focus	engine
pajamas	fortune	circus	celebrate	purpose

Proofreading

Proofread the diary entry below. Use proofreading marks to correct five spelling mistakes, three capitalization mistakes, and two punctuation mistakes.

Proofreading Marks

◯ spell correctly

≡ capitalize

⊙ add period

dear Diary,

Last night a loud whooshing sound woke me I thought it was an enjen. i stepped out onto my balcany to see what it was. At first my vision was very blurry, but after I rubbed my tired eyes, I was able to focus on a huge hot-air baloon right in front of me. It had a silver top and a purple basket. A woman and her huzbind were in the balloon's basket and were waving at me. they wore a look of triumf on their faces I'm sure I wore a look of amazement on mine. It took quite a while for me to get back to sleep!

Apostrophes

A contraction is a shortened form of two words in which the words are joined, but one or more letters are left out. An apostrophe is used in place of the missing letter or letters.

> Do not pick the flowers.   Don't pick the flowers.
>
> They are here for display.   They're here for display.

Apostrophes are also used in the possessive form of nouns. The possessive form indicates ownership. An apostrophe and -s are added to singular nouns. Only an apostrophe is added to plural nouns that end in s. For other plurals that do not end in s, such as *children,* an apostrophe and -s are added.

> **Possessive Singular Noun**   **Sally's** hat is in her room.
>
> **Possessive Plural Noun**   The **girls'** clothes are in their closet.
>
> **Possessive Plural Noun**   The **mice's** home is an old tree trunk.

Write the following sentences, adding apostrophes wherever necessary.

1. Henry and his brother went to the circus to celebrate Henrys birthday.

_____

2. The boys father wanted to take them up in a hot-air balloon.

_____

3. Henry also received a set of colored pencils and a childrens atlas.

_____

4. Dads plan was for Henry to draw what he saw.

_____

Words with /ər/

cellar	modern	favorite	bother	lunar
fever	soccer	discover	similar	answer
director	vinegar	customer	governor	effort
cheeseburger	hamburger	calendar	computer	consumer

Say and Listen

computer

Say each spelling word. Listen for the /ər/ sounds you hear in *cellar*.

Think and Sort

Look at the letters in each word. Think about how /ər/ is spelled. Spell each word aloud.

How many spelling patterns for /ər/ do you see?

1. Write the **five** spelling words that have /ər/ spelled *ar,* like *cellar.*

2. Write the **eleven** spelling words that have /ər/ spelled *er,* like *answer.*

3. Write the **four** spelling words that have /ər/ spelled *or,* like *effort.*

---

1. /ər/ Words with ar

_____ _____ _____

_____ _____

2. /ər/ Words with er

_____ _____ _____

_____ _____ _____

_____ _____ _____

_____ _____

3. /ər/ Words with or

_____ _____ _____

_____

Analogies

Write the spelling word that completes each analogy.

1. *Court* is to *basketball* as *field* is to _____.

2. *State* is to _____ as *country* is to *president*.

3. *Clock* is to *day* as _____ is to *year*.

4. *Up* is to *down* as *old-fashioned* is to _____.

5. *Chills* is to *cold* as _____ is to *hot*.

6. *Movie* is to _____ as *orchestra* is to *conductor*.

7. *Attic* is to *high* as _____ is to *low*.

8. *Moon* is to _____ as *sun* is to *solar*.

9. *Push* is to *shove* as _____ is to *annoy*.

10. *Clerk* is to _____ as *waiter* is to *diner*.

Definitions

Write the spelling word for each definition. Use a dictionary if you need to.

11. a piece of cooked ground beef served on a bun   _____

12. a hamburger with cheese   _____

13. an electronic machine used at home and at work   _____

14. someone who buys and uses goods or services   _____

15. something that is liked the most   _____

16. a reply to a question   _____

17. an attempt to do something   _____

18. almost the same as   _____

19. to find out   _____

cellar	modern	favorite	bother	lunar
fever	soccer	discover	similar	answer
director	vinegar	customer	governor	effort
cheeseburger	hamburger	calendar	computer	consumer

Proofreading

Proofread the e-mail below. Use proofreading marks to correct five spelling mistakes, two punctuation mistakes, and three misplaced words.

Proofreading Marks

⬭ spell correctly

⊙ add period

∿ trade places

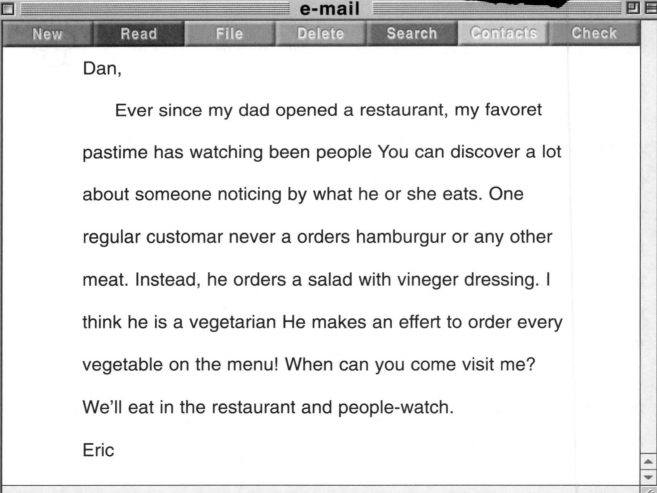

---

e-mail

New	Read	File	Delete	Search	Contacts	Check

Dan,

Ever since my dad opened a restaurant, my favoret pastime has watching been people You can discover a lot about someone noticing by what he or she eats. One regular customar never a orders hamburgur or any other meat. Instead, he orders a salad with vineger dressing. I think he is a vegetarian He makes an effert to order every vegetable on the menu! When can you come visit me? We'll eat in the restaurant and people-watch.

Eric

Language Connection

Predicates

The predicate is the part of a sentence that tells what the subject of the sentence does or did, or is or was. It includes all the words that modify, or tell more about, the verb. The words of some predicates do not appear together. Study the predicates in the example sentences below.

> Today the Alleycats play a professional team.
> The game is a sellout!

Write each of the following sentences. Circle all parts of the predicate.

1. Soccer fever hit Alleyville this year.

_____

2. My sister and I rode a city bus to the stadium.

_____

3. On the way we bought a hamburger and a cheeseburger.

_____

4. With much effort the Alleycats won by three goals.

_____

5. The governor of the state congratulated the players.

_____

6. Everyone in town marked the next game on their calendar.

_____

More Words with /ə/

special	spacious	social	commercial	tremendous
courageous	generous	mysterious	various	official
jealous	delicious	efficient	nervous	dangerous
serious	genius	curious	ancient	conscious

Say and Listen

Say each spelling word. Listen for the /ə/ sound you hear in *special*.

delicious

Think and Sort

Look at the letters in each word. Think about how /ə/ is spelled. Spell each word aloud.

How many spelling patterns for /ə/ do you see?

1. Write the **thirteen** spelling words that have /ə/ spelled *ou*, like *nervous*.

2. Write the **four** spelling words that have /ə/ spelled *a*, like *special*.

3. Write the **two** spelling words that have /ə/ spelled *e*, like *ancient*.

4. Write the **one** spelling word that has /ə/ spelled *u*.

1. /ə/ Words with **ou**

_____   _____   _____

_____   _____   _____

_____   _____   _____

_____   _____   _____

_____

2. /ə/ Words with **a**

_____   _____   _____

_____

3. /ə/ Words with **e**

_____   _____

4. /ə/ Word with **u**

_____

Analogies

Write the spelling word that completes each analogy.

1. *Nature* is to *natural* as *office* is to _____.

2. *Plain* is to *homely* as _____ is to *nosy*.

3. *Thoughtful* is to _____ as *jump* is to *leap*.

4. *Skyscraper* is to *modern* as *pyramid* is to _____.

5. *Courtesy* is to *courteous* as *mystery* is to _____.

6. *Unique* is to _____ as *happy* is to *joyful*.

7. *Brilliant* is to _____ as *brave* is to *hero*.

8. *Advertisement* is to *magazine* as _____ is to *television*.

9. *Tiny* is to *petite* as _____ is to *enormous*.

10. *Unproductive* is to _____ as *empty* is to *full*.

11. *Real* is to *reality* as _____ is to *society*.

Synonyms

Complete each sentence by writing the
spelling word that is a synonym for the underlined word.

12. Our ten-room apartment is very _____.   roomy

13. Fighting a forest fire is a _____ thing to do.   brave

14. Sometimes Theo was a bit _____ of his best friend.   envious

15. I get _____ when I have to make a speech.   worried

16. The students thought of _____ ways to
solve the problem.   different

17. The restaurant serves _____ food.   tasty

18. Are you _____ of the fact that your shoelaces are untied?   aware

19. Volunteer workers are _____ people.   unselfish

special	spacious	social	commercial	tremendous
courageous	generous	mysterious	various	official
jealous	delicious	efficient	nervous	dangerous
serious	genius	curious	ancient	conscious

Proofreading

Proofread the book review below. Use proofreading marks to correct five spelling mistakes, three capitalization mistakes, and two unnecessary words.

Proofreading Marks

◯ spell correctly

≡ capitalize

℺ take out

Book Review

The Outer Space Adventure Club is a science fiction novel full of action-packed adventures. The main character, rosa, is very nervous when she becomes an offishul member of the club. This isn't just a soshil group. The members are are serious and corajuss. they travel a tramendis number of miles to various planets and stars in our spasciuos universe. Rosa has scary experiences, but she discovers that some some very curious-looking creatures can become good friends. young adults are sure to enjoy this exciting book.

Adverbs

An adverb modifies a verb, an adjective, or another adverb by telling how, when, where, how often, or to what degree. Many adverbs end in *-ly.*

> Marco wore a brightly colored shirt.
>
> Tomorrow I will get there quickly.
>
> Deirdre skated quite beautifully.
>
> She seldom becomes angry.

Unscramble the following groups of words to write sensible sentences. Circle the adverbs.

1. woman yesterday mysterious A visited me.

_____

2. drove up a spacious car slowly in She.

_____

3. was nervous I extremely and curious.

_____

4. she was politely said official a special She that.

_____

5. questions quickly some Then she serious asked.

_____

6. send me She highly dangerous wanted to mission on a.

_____

More Words with Suffixes

attendance	sentence	constant	apparent	difference
assistant	intelligent	different	vacant	entrance
incident	performance	experience	distance	absent
assignment	instrument	ignorance	instant	distant

Say and Listen

Say each spelling word. Listen for the ending sounds.

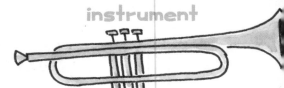

instrument

Think and Sort

Each of the spelling words in this lesson contains a suffix. A **suffix** is a word part added to the end of a base word. A suffix changes the meaning of a base word.

Look at the letters in each word. Think about how the suffix is spelled. Spell each word alou

How many suffixes do you see?

1. Write the **five** spelling words with the -*ance* suffix, like *attendance*.

2. Write the **three** spelling words with the -*ence* suffix, like *sentence*.

3. Write the **five** spelling words with the -*ant* suffix, like *instant*.

4. Write the **five** spelling words with the -*ent* suffix, like *absent*.

5. Write the **two** spelling words with the -*ment* suffix, like *instrument*.

1. -ance Words

_____   _____   _____

_____   _____

2. -ence Words

_____   _____   _____

3. -ant Words

_____   _____   _____

_____   _____

4. -ent Words

_____   _____   _____

_____   _____

5. -ment Words

_____   _____

Classifying

Write the spelling word that belongs in each group.

1. door, gate, _____

2. smart, brilliant, _____

3. helper, aide, _____

4. clear, obvious, _____

5. word, phrase, _____

6. empty, unoccupied, _____

7. event, instance, _____

8. unusual, dissimilar, _____

What's the Answer?

Write the spelling word that answers each question.

9. What does an actor in a play give? _____

10. What do you have when you have lived through an event?

_____

11. A clarinet is an example of what? _____

12. What is a lack of knowledge called? _____

13. When you aren't present, what are you? _____

14. What is the amount of space between two places? _____

15. What is a very short length of time? _____

16. The number of people who are present is called what?

_____

17. What do you call the amount of being different? _____

18. Homework is an example of what? _____

19. What word is a synonym for *continuous*? _____

attendance	sentence	constant	apparent	difference
assistant	intelligent	different	vacant	entrance
incident	performance	experience	distance	absent
assignment	instrument	ignorance	instant	distant

Proofreading

Proofread the news article below. Use proofreading marks to correct five spelling mistakes, three capitalization mistakes, and two punctuation mistakes.

Proofreading Marks

◯ spell correctly

╱ make lowercase

⊙ add period

Disappointing describes last week's performance of the eagerly awaited special effects generator that has taken more than ten years to develop It soon became aparent that the new Instrument did not work. One assisstant claimed that the three-dimensional image should have appeared in an instint. The Scientists in attendance waited anxiously. Was the problem a result of the Inventor's ignorence? No one could ask its creator. The inventor was abzint from the presentation and did not return our calls

Idioms

Sometimes a group of words does not mean exactly what it says. In the first sentence of the pair below, the tree strikes the roof when it falls. In the second sentence, however, "hit the roof" is an idiom meaning that Dad is angry; he does not actually hit the roof.

> The oak tree fell over and **hit the roof**.
> When I was late for dinner, Dad **hit the roof.**

Some dictionary entries include common idioms containing the entry word or a form of it. Study the following entry for *distance*.

> **dis·tance** (dĭs′ təns) *n.* **1.** The length of a path, especially a straight line segment, that joins two points. **2.** A stretch of space without definite limits: *a plane flying some distance off its course.* **3.** The condition of being apart in space or time.
>
> **in the distance.** In a space far removed: *Ocean Park seemed small in the distance.*
>
> **keep (one's) distance. 1.** To remain apart from; stay away from. **2.** To be aloof or unfriendly.

1. Write the two idioms given for the word *distance*.

_____

_____

Look up the following words in a dictionary. Write an idiom given for each one.

2. advantage _____

3. breath _____

4. double _____

Words with -tion or -ture

collection	attention	transportation	information	conversation
fixture	future	station	direction	invention
fraction	agriculture	election	education	lecture
correction	feature	signature	population	selection

Say and Listen

Say the spelling words. Listen for the ending sounds.

collection

Think and Sort

Each spelling word ends in *-tion* or *-ture*. Look at the letters in each word. Think about how each word is spelled. Spell each word aloud.

1. Write the **fourteen** spelling words that have *-tion*, like *fraction*.

2. Write the **six** spelling words that have *-ture*, like *feature*.

1. -tion Words

_____ _____ _____

_____ _____ _____

_____ _____ _____

_____ _____ _____

_____ _____

2. -ture Words

_____ _____ _____

_____ _____ _____

Word Forms

Complete each sentence by writing the spelling word that is a form of the underlined word.

1. The telephone is an exciting _____. <u>invent</u>

2. Buses are one form of _____. <u>transport</u>

3. A college _____ can be very useful. <u>educate</u>

4. Our candidate won after an exciting _____. <u>elect</u>

5. The city's _____ grew to more than a million. <u>populate</u>

6. My mother and I had a great _____. <u>converse</u>

7. I made the _____ in my report. <u>correct</u>

Definitions

Write the spelling word for each definition. Use a dictionary if you need to.

8. the act of watching and listening _____

9. things brought together for a purpose _____

10. a prepared talk given on one or more topics _____

11. a part of something that stands out _____

12. the period of time that will come _____

13. something you put in place to stay _____

14. data or facts _____

15. guidance, assistance, or supervision _____

16. the business of farming _____

17. a person's handwritten name _____

18. a regular stopping place _____

19. a choice _____

collection	attention	station	information	conversation
fixture	future	transportation	direction	invention
fraction	agriculture	election	education	lecture
correction	feature	signature	population	selection

Proofreading

Proofread the diary entry below. Use proofreading marks to correct five spelling mistakes, three capitalization mistakes, and two punctuation mistakes.

Proofreading Marks

⬭ spell correctly

☰ capitalize

⊙ add period

Dear Diary,

If i had a convasashun with sojourner Truth, I would give her infamasion about the dyrekshun that women's rights have taken in the past hundred years She would probably be thrilled that women now vote in each elekshun. she always hoped that women of the futer would be able to vote Would she be surprised that many women are judges, mayors, and presidents of big companies? I wonder what she would say if I told her women now run for senator, governor, and even president of the United States of America!

Dictionary Skills

Using the Spelling Table

A spelling table can help you find the spelling of a word in a dictionary. Suppose you are not sure how the vowel sound in *brief* is spelled. You can use a spelling table to find the different spellings for the sound. First, find the pronunciation symbol for the sound. Then read the first spelling listed for /ē/ and look up *bref* in a dictionary. Look for each spelling in the dictionary until you find the correct one.

Sound	Spellings	Example
/ē/	e e_e ea ee ei eo ey i i_e ie y	meter, scene, speaker, degrees, receive, people, monkey, piano, gasoline, brief, memory

Write each of the following words, spelling the sound in dark type correctly. Use the Spelling Table on page 265 and a dictionary.

1. māor _____

2. plĕsant _____

3. agĕnst _____

4. lōves _____

5. carnivəl _____

6. sĭstem _____

7. privĭt _____

8. sī _____

9. burō _____

10. lôndry _____

11. thûrsty _____

12. invisəble _____

13. balcəny _____

14. differənt _____

15. lectəre _____

16. correcshən _____

unit 6 Review
Lessons 26-30

LESSON 26

balloon
celebrate
pencil
purpose
injury

More Words with /ə/

Write the spelling word that completes each sentence.

1. I like to sketch with a colored pen and _____.

2. My arm hurt, but the _____ was just a sprain.

3. The red _____ popped loudly!

4. Every year we _____ the holidays with my aunt.

5. My _____ for studying is to raise my grades.

LESSON 27

calendar
answer
favorite

Words with /ər/

Write the spelling word that answers each question.

6. What do people expect when they ask a question? _____

7. What word names something you like best? _____

8. What helps people keep track of the date? _____

LESSON 28

special
ancient
efficient
conscious
mysterious
courageous

More Words with /ə/

Write the spelling word for each clue.

9. This word describes very old ruins. _____

10. If something is unusual, it is this. _____

11. This word is an antonym of *cowardly*. _____

12. This word describes something that is unknown.

_____

13. This word means "aware and awake." _____

14. This is what you are when you work without wasting time.

_____

LESSON **29**

distance
experience
sentence
assistant
different
assignment

More Words with Suffixes

Write the spelling word for each definition. Use a dictionary
if you need to.

15. a group of words that expresses a complete thought

_____

16. not like any other _____

17. a helper or an aide _____

18. the amount of space between two points

_____

19. work given for a specific purpose _____

20. to live through or witness _____

LESSON **30**

collection
attention
direction
future
signature

Words with -tion or -ture

Write the spelling word that completes each analogy.

21. *Yesterday* is to *tomorrow* as *past* is to _____.

22. *Selection* is to *select* as _____ is to *collect*.

23. *Write* is to _____ as *draw* is to *picture*.

24. *Love* is to *affection* as *care* is to _____.

25. *Compass* is to _____ as *watch* is to *time*.

commonly misspelled words

address	enough	many	they're
again	environment	might	though
a lot	especially	morning	threw
always	every	myself	through
another	everyone	once	today
anything	except	other	together
anyway	exciting	outside	tomorrow
around	family	people	too
beautiful	favorite	piece	tried
because	finally	probably	until
before	first	really	usually
beginning	friend	right	vacation
believe	friends	said	want
birthday	getting	scared	weird
bought	goes	school	were
business	guess	sent	we're
buy	happened	should	when
children	heard	since	where
clothes	himself	some	which
college	hospital	sometimes	whole
cousin	house	started	would
decided	into	surprise	write
different	it's	their	writing
doesn't	know	there	wrote
eighth	little	they	you're

spelling table

Sound	Spellings	Examples
/ă/	a ai au	catalog, plaid, laughed
/ā/	a a_e ai aigh ay ea eigh ey	agent, invade, stain, straight, mayor, break, weighted, surveyor
/ä/	a ea ua	salami, heart, guard
/âr/	are air ere eir	aware, dairy, there, their
/b/	b bb	barber, cabbage
/ch/	ch tch t	sandwich, kitchen, amateur
/d/	d dd	dawn, meddle
/ĕ/	e ea a ai ay ie ue	length, instead, many, against, says, friend, guest
/ē/	e e_e ea ee ei eo ey i i_e ie y	meter, scene, speaker, degrees, receive, people, monkey, piano, gasoline, brief, memory
/f/	f ff gh ph	fever, different, laugh, graph
/g/	g gg	glue, struggle
/h/	h wh	half, whole
/ĭ/	a a_e e ee ei i u ui y	spinach, luggage, select, been, forfeit, million, business, build, myth
/ī/	i i_e ie igh uy y y_e eye	science, strike, die, sigh, buy, deny, style, eye
/îr/	er ear eer eir ere yr	periodical, hear, cheer, weird, here, lyrics
/j/	j g dg	justice, voyages, pledge
/k/	k c cc ck ch	kitchen, cabinet, soccer, clockwise, choir
/ks/	x	excavation
/kw/	qu	quiet
/l/	l ll	label, umbrella
/m/	m mb mm mn	meter, thumb, mammal, condemn
/n/	n kn nn	novel, knife, tunnel
/ng/	n ng	thank, strengthen
/ŏ/	o ow a	ecology, knowledge, equality

Sound	Spellings	Examples
/ō/	o o_e oa oe ou ough ow eau ew	noble, throne, loan, toe, poultry, although, grown, plateau, sew
/oi/	oi oy	coin, enjoyable
/ô/	a au augh aw o oa ou ough	chalk, laundry, daughter, awful, often, coarse, course, thought
/o͝o/	oo o ou u	book, wolf, could, education
/o͞o/	oo eu ew u u_e ue o o_e oe ou ui	smooth, neutral, threw, truth, refuse, clue, whom, improve, canoe, coupon, juice
/ou/	ou ow	couch, howl
/p/	p pp	pass, apply
/r/	r rh rr wr	ring, rhythm, worry, wrong
/s/	s sc ss c	slant, scene, dress, justice
/sh/	sh s ce ci	flashlight, sugar, ocean, special
/shən/	tion	station
/t/	t tt ed	tennis, attention, thanked
/th/	th	whether
/th/	th	throw
/ŭ/	u o oe oo ou	result, among, does, flood, touch
/ûr/	ear er ere ir or our ur	earn, personal, were, thirsty, worst, flourish, curly
/v/	v f	violin, of
/w/	w wh o	wind, wharf, once
/y/	y	yolk
/yo͞o/	eau eu u u_e	beautiful, feud, human, use
/z/	z zz s ss x	zone, quizzical, wise, dessert, xylophone
/zh/	s	treasure
/ə/	a e i o u ai ou	hospital, weaken, principle, person, circus, captain, various

Math
Skills

Place Value

A **place-value chart** can help you understand **whole numbers**. Each **digit** in a number has a value based on its place in the number.

The digit 6 means 6 ten thousands, or 60,000.
The digit 2 means 2 thousands, or 2,000.
The digit 0 means 0 hundreds, or 0.
The digit 4 means 4 tens, or 40.
The digit 0 means 0 ones, or 0.

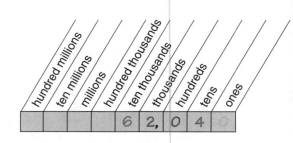

We read the number as sixty-two thousand, forty. Notice that commas are used to separate the digits into groups of three, called *periods*. This helps make larger numbers easier to read.

Write each number in the place-value chart.

1. 468,937,574

2. 5,910,382,654

3. 8,342,384

4. 76,098

	billions	hundred millions	ten millions	millions	hundred thousands	ten thousands	thousands	hundreds	tens	ones
1.		4	6	8,	9	3	7,	5	7	4
2.	5	9	1	0	3	8	2	6	5	4
3.			8	3	4	2	3	8	4	
4.					7	6	0	9	8	

Write the place name for the digit 3 in each number.

	a		*b*
5.	56,837,784	ten thousands	887,654,321	hundreds
6.	90,543	ones	675,345,242	hundred thousands
7.	898,865,436	tens	3,876,544,098	billions
8.	3,565	thousands	24,356,540,912	ten billions

Write each number in words. Insert commas where needed.

9. 132,342 _____ one hundred thirty-two thousand, three hundred forty-two

10. 7,642,353 _____ Seven million six hundred forty two thousands three hundred fifty three

2/14

Comparing and Ordering Numbers

To compare two numbers, begin with the highest place value.
Compare the digits in each place.

The symbol < means **is less than.**   **23 < 57**
The symbol > means **is greater than.**   **3 > 1**
The symbol = means **is equal to.**   **234 = 234**

Compare 354 and 57.

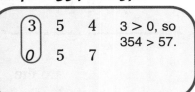

3 > 0, so
354 > 57.

Compare 2,243 and 1,542.

2 > 1, so
2,243 > 1,542.

Compare 134 and 187.

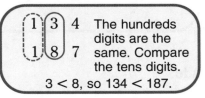

The hundreds digits are the same. Compare the tens digits.
3 < 8, so 134 < 187.

Compare. Write < , > , or = .

	a		b	
1.	45 __<__ 67		165 __>__ 85	
2.	23 __>__ 57		34 __<__ 598	
3.	675 __<__ 765		654 __=__ 654	
4.	4,554 __<__ 6,368		4,342 __<__ 4,367	
5.	653 __<__ 785		4,321 __>__ 824	
6.	65,342 __<__ 85,542		4,575 __<__ 39,864	
7.	973,765 __<__ 1,000,000		453,643 __>__ 255,764	

Write in order from least to greatest.

8. 54 96 21 _____ 21 54 96 _____

9. 468 532 487 _____ 468 532 487 _____

10. 322 231 632 _____ 231 632 322 _____

11. 94,234 45,875 67,956 _____ 45,875 67,956 94,234 _____

12. 765,645 543,865 565,978 _____ 543,865 565,978 765,645 _____

13. 16,576 13,764 432,877 _____ 13,764 16,576 432,877 _____

7/25

Addition of Whole Numbers

To add, start with the digits in the ones place.
Regroup as needed.

Find: 322 + 699

Add the ones. Regroup.	Add the tens.	Add the hundreds.

Th	H	T	O
		1	
	3	2	**2**
+	6	9	**9**
			1

Th	H	T	O
	1	1	
	3	**2**	2
+	6	**9**	9
		2	1

Th	H	T	O
	1	1	1
	3	2	2
+	**6**	9	9
1,	0	2	1

Add.

1.

a
Th	H	T	O
1	1	1	
	4	5	2
+	5	5	9
1,	0	1	1

b
Th	H	T	O
	1		
	6	4	4
+	4	8	4
1	1	2	8

c
Th	H	T	O
		1	
	5	1	7
+	5	6	3
1	0	8	0

d
Th	H	T	O
		1	1
	2	0	9
+	9	5	0
1	1	5	9

2.

a
```
  5,3 4 7
+9,5 2 0
 14867
```

b
```
 1 5,0 4 2
+8 6,9 9 6
 102038
```

c
```
 3 4,8 5 3
+4 7,5 3 2
  82385
```

d
```
 5 4 7,0 8 4
+7 4 3,7 5 4
 1290838
```

3.

a
```
 3 4 2,5 3 5
+7 5 7,6 4 3
 1100178
```

b
```
 7 4,5 7 4
+9 3,7 4 3
 168417
```

c
```
 3 5 5,6 8 4
+8 9 5,4 4 5
 1251129
```

d
```
 5 4 6,7 8 3
+3 5 6,5 3 7
  903326
```

Line up the digits. Then find the sums.

4.

a
6,535 + 5,764 = __12,309__
```
 6,535
+5,764
 12309
```

b
543 + 528 = __1071__
```
 43
+28
1071
```

5.

a
231,456 + 76,421 = __307,877__
```
 231,456
+ 76,421
 307,877
```

b
341 + 4,352 = __4,693__
```
 4,352
+ 341
 4693
```

7/25

Addition of Three or More Numbers

To add three or more numbers, use the same steps as when adding two numbers. Regroup as needed.

Find: 36 + 358 + 296

Add the ones. Regroup.	Add the tens.	Add the hundreds.

H T O
  2
  3 6
3 5 8
+2 9 6
    0
	H T O
	1 2
	  3 6
	3 5 8
	+2 9 6
	  9 0
		H T O
		1 2
		  3 6
		3 5 8
		+2 9 6
		6 9 0

Add.

        a   b   c   d

1.

a)
```
Th H T O
   1 1 1
     4 2 7
       7 8
 +   8 4 3
   1,3 4 8
```

b)
```
Th H T O
       1
     1 2 0
     6 5 9
 +   9 3 2
   1 7 1 1
```

c)
```
Th H T O
         7
     6 4 3
       6 7
 +     
   7 1 7
```

d)
```
Th H T O
     3 2 5
     8 9 6
 +       4
   1 2 3 5
```

2.

a)
```
     3 9
   3 4 2
 +6 9 0
   1 0 7 1
```

b)
```
   1 2
   4 7 9
   7 5 6
 +   5 7
   1 2 9 2
```

c)
```
     8 7 9
   3,9 5 0
 +     4 3
   4 8 7 2
```

d)
```
   3,4 0 4
     8 6 5
 +7,4 3 6
   1 1 7 0 5
```

3.

a)
```
   9 3 9,8 4 2
   8 7 4,8 9 0
     4 5,3 7 6
 +4 3 2,9 8 6
   2 2 9 3 1 0 4
```

b)
```
   6 3,9 2 8
   3 2,7 4 0
     5,3 2 1
 +6 0,4 5 3
   1 6 3 4 4 2
```

c)
```
   8 4 9,9 0 4
   4 3 2,8 4 0
   5 0 8,3 4 6
 +5 6 7,7 8 5
   2 3 5 8 8 7 5
```

d)
```
   5 8 9,4 9 3
   7 4 3,9 0 7
   9 0 8,3 5 4
 +5 6 7,8 6 9
   2 8 0 9 6 2 3
```

Line up the digits. Then find the sums.

               a   b

4. 554 + 860 + 64 = __1,478__

```
  1
  554
  860
 + 64
 1478
```

```
 22
 + 9
  31
```

379 + 940 + 390 = __1,709__

```
  3
  379
 +940
  390
 1709
```

```
 7 26
```

Subtraction of Whole Numbers

To subtract, start with the digits in the ones place.
Regroup as needed.

Find: 715 − 239

Regroup. Subtract the ones.	Regroup. Subtract the tens.	Subtract the hundreds.

Regroup. Subtract the ones.

$$\begin{array}{c|c|c} H & T & O \\ & 0 & 15 \\ 7 & \cancel{1} & \cancel{5} \\ -2 & 3 & 9 \\ \hline & & 6 \end{array}$$

Regroup. Subtract the tens.

$$\begin{array}{c|c|c} H & T & O \\ 6 & 10 & 15 \\ \cancel{7} & \cancel{1} & \cancel{5} \\ -2 & 3 & 9 \\ \hline & 7 & 6 \end{array}$$

Subtract the hundreds.

$$\begin{array}{c|c|c} H & T & O \\ 6 & 10 & 15 \\ \cancel{7} & \cancel{1} & \cancel{5} \\ -2 & 3 & 9 \\ \hline 4 & 7 & 6 \end{array}$$

Subtract.

	a	*b*	*c*	*d*

1.

a
$$\begin{array}{c|c|c} H & T & O \\ & 11 & \\ 7 & \cancel{1} & 17 \\ \cancel{8} & \cancel{2} & \cancel{7} \\ -5 & 3 & 8 \\ \hline 2 & 8 & 9 \end{array}$$

b
$$\begin{array}{c|c|c} H & T & O \\ \cancel{7} & \cancel{4} & \cancel{2} \\ -5 & 4 & 4 \\ \hline 1 & 9 & 8 \end{array}$$

c
$$\begin{array}{c|c|c} H & T & O \\ 1 & \cancel{3} & \cancel{5} \\ -1 & 2 & 9 \\ \hline 0 & 0 & 6 \end{array}$$

d
$$\begin{array}{c|c|c} H & T & O \\ 6 & \cancel{5} & \cancel{6} \\ -5 & 0 & 7 \\ \hline 1 & 4 & 9 \end{array}$$

2.

a $\begin{array}{r} \cancel{5}\,\cancel{4}\,3 \\ -1\,8\,9 \\ \hline 3\,5\,4 \end{array}$

b $\begin{array}{r} \cancel{7}\,0\,0 \\ -5\,4\,6 \\ \hline 6\,4 \end{array}$

c $\begin{array}{r} 5{,}0\,0\,0 \\ -\ \ \ 8\,9\,9 \\ \hline 2\,2\,1\,1 \end{array}$

d $\begin{array}{r} 7{,}6\,\cancel{4}\,3 \\ -4{,}9\,0\,8 \\ \hline 2\,7\,3\,5 \end{array}$

3.

a $\begin{array}{r} 5{,}7\,6\,4 \\ -\ \ \ 2\,0\,0 \\ \hline 5\,5\,6\,4 \end{array}$

b $\begin{array}{r} 4\,3{,}6\,\cancel{7}\,5 \\ -2\,3{,}5\,0\,7 \\ \hline 2\,0\,1\,6\,8 \end{array}$

c $\begin{array}{r} 4\,3\,9{,}\cancel{7}\,0\,9 \\ -2\,3\,4{,}5\,6\,4 \\ \hline 2\,0\,5\,1\,4\,5 \end{array}$

d $\begin{array}{r} 7\,4\,2{,}4\,5\,7 \\ -\ \ \ 6\,5{,}3\,4\,5 \\ \hline 7\,7\,7\,1\,2 \end{array}$

Line up the digits. Then find the differences.

	a	*b*

4. 543 − 32 = __511__

$$\begin{array}{r} 543 \\ -\ \ 32 \\ \hline 511 \end{array}$$

726 − 549 = __177__

$$\begin{array}{r} \cancel{7}\cancel{2}6 \\ -549 \\ \hline 177 \end{array}$$

5. 34,565 − 23,597 = __10,968__

$$\begin{array}{r} 34{,}565 \\ -23{,}597 \\ \hline 10968 \end{array}$$

9,000 − 6,533 = __2,467__

Estimation of Sums and Differences

To estimate a sum or difference, first round each number to the same place value. Then add or subtract the rounded numbers.

Estimate: 56,493 + 255

> Round each number to the same place value. Add.
>
> $$\begin{array}{r} 5\ 6,4\ 9\ 3 \rightarrow\ 56{,}500 \\ +\quad 2\ 5\ 5 \rightarrow +\quad 300 \\ \hline 56{,}800 \end{array}$$
>
> Each number is rounded to the hundreds place.

Estimate: 39,465 − 442

> Round each number to the same place value. Subtract.
>
> $$\begin{array}{r} 3\ 9,4\ 6\ 5 \rightarrow\ 39{,}500 \\ -\quad 4\ 4\ 2 \rightarrow -\quad 400 \\ \hline 39{,}100 \end{array}$$
>
> Each number is rounded to the hundreds place.

Estimate the sums.

	a	b	c	d
1.	516 → 500 +6,724 → +6,700	4,332 → 4,000 + 789 → 800 4,800	53,500 → 53,000 300 + 284 → 53,300	4,325 → 4,000 +534,643 → ~~53~~ 500,000 504,000
2.	8,583 → 9,000 ~~000~~ +2,393 → 3,000 14,000	4,325 → 4,000 +7,543 → 8,000 12,000	6,436 → 6,000 +8,964 → ~~9,000~~ 15,000 9,000	8,975 → +9,633 → 19,000

Estimate the differences.

	a	b	c	d
3.	563 → 600 −265 → − 300	895 → 900 −435 → 400 500	865 → 900 −657 → 700 200	975 → 1,000 −864 → 900 100
4.	53,864 → 54,000 900 − 896 → 53,100	14,535 → −2,356 →	74,543 → 75,000 − 4,864 → 5,000 70,000	49,564 → 50,000 − 7,534 → 8,000 42,000

Problem-Solving Method: Guess and Check

Thomas Jefferson was the sixth youngest person to sign the Declaration of Independence in 1776. Benjamin Franklin was 37 years older than Jefferson. The sum of their ages was 103. How old was Jefferson when he signed the Declaration of Independence?

Understand the problem.

- **What do you want to know?**
  Jefferson's age when he signed the Declaration of Independence

- **What information is given?**
  Clue 1: Jefferson's age + 37 = Franklin's age
  Clue 2: Jefferson's age + Franklin's age = 103

Plan how to solve it.

- **What method can you use?**
  You can guess an answer that satisfies the first clue.
  Then check to see if your answer satisfies the second clue.

Solve it.

- **How can you use this method to solve the problem?**
  Try to guess in an organized way so that each of your guesses gets closer to the exact answer. Use a table.

Guess Jefferson's Age	Check Clue 1	Check Clue 2	Evaluate the Guess
30	30+37=67	30+67=97	too low
40	40+37=77	40+77=117	too high
35	35+37=72	35+72=107	too high
34	34+37=71	34+71=105	too high
33	33+37=70	33+70=103	satisfies both clues

- **What is the answer?**
  Thomas Jefferson was 33 years old when he signed the Declaration of Independence.

Look back and check your answer.

- **Is your answer reasonable?**
  You can check addition with subtraction.
  70 − 37 = 33
  103 − 70 = 33

  The addition checks and the age satisfies both clues.
  The answer is reasonable.

Use guess and check to solve each problem.

1. Aaron is 1 year younger than Laura. The sum of their ages is 23 years. How old is each of them?

Answer ___Aaron= 22 laura=23___

2. Combined, the movies *Titanic* and *Gone with the Wind* won 19 Academy Awards. *Titanic* won 3 more awards than *Gone with the Wind*. How many awards did each movie win?

Answer ___22___

3. A millipede has 14 more legs than a caterpillar. Together they have 46 legs. How many legs does a caterpillar have?

Answer ___32 legs___

4. Nicole did an aerobics class and a yoga class for a total of 1 hour and 10 minutes. The yoga class was 30 minutes longer than the aerobics class. How long was each class?

Answer _____

5. Alan has seven United States coins. Their total value is 61 cents. What coins and how many of each does he have?

Answer _____

Multiplication of One-digit and Two-digit Numbers

To multiply by one-digit numbers, use basic multiplication facts.
To multiply by two-digit numbers, multiply by the ones first. Then multiply by the tens.
Then add these two **partial products**.

Find: 38 × 42

Multiply by 2 ones. Regroup.	Write a zero place holder. Multiply by 4 tens.	Add the partial products.
Th|H|T|O 1 3 8 × 4 2 7 6	Th|H|T|O 3 3 8 × 4 2 7 6 1,5 2 0	Th|H|T|O 3 8 × 4 2 7 6 + 1,5 2 0 1,5 9 6

Multiply.

   a   b   c   d

1.
H|T|O   H|T|O   H|T|O   H|T|O
3 4   2   2
   4 5   1 3   2 4   3 5
×   8   ×   3   ×   9   ×   5
3 6 0   3 9   2 1 6   1 7 5

2.
7 3   4 2   3 1
1 4 5   6 0 1   7 6 4   9 4 2
×   6   ×   3   ×   7   ×   8
3 7 0   1 8 0 4   5 3 4 8   7 5 3 6

3.
2 2   1 6 0 0   1 2 3
5 6 7   + 2 4 0 0   3 2 0   8 1 6   9 2 6
×   3 4   2 4 0 0 0   ×   7 5   ×   3 9   ×   4 5
1 9 2 7 8   4,0 0 0   2 4 9 0 2 4   4 3 0 7 0
2 2 1 0   2 3
7 1 1   3 1

4.
1, 5 4 3   2, 6 5 0   2, 5 0 1   3 4, 6 0 3
×   5 3   ×   9 7   ×   2 8   ×   3 5
4 6 2 9   1 8 5 5 0   2 0 0 0 8   1 7 3 0 1 5
+ 7 7 1 5 0   + 1 3 8 5 0 0 + 5 0 0 3 0   + 1 7 1 8 0 9 0

Line up the digits. Then find the products.
8 1, 7 7 9   1 5 7, 0 5 0   1 0 0, 0 3 8   1 8 9, 1 1 0 5

        a   b
5. 573 × 3 = __1,719__   2,506 × 94 = __33064__   20,463 × 83 = _____

2
573
×   3
1 7 1 9

+ 1 0 0 2 4
2 3 0 4 0
3 3 0 6 4

2 5 2 5 0 6
× 9 4

1 0 0 2 4
2 3 0 4 0

Estimation of Products

To estimate products, round each **factor**.
Then multiply the rounded factors.

Estimate: 72 × 35

Round each factor to the greatest place value.
Multiply.

$$
\begin{array}{r}
72 \rightarrow \quad 70 \\
\times 35 \rightarrow \times \quad 40 \\
\hline
2,800
\end{array}
$$

Estimate: 369 × 21

Round each factor to the greatest place value.
Multiply.

$$
\begin{array}{r}
369 \rightarrow \quad 400 \\
\times \quad 21 \rightarrow \times \quad 20 \\
\hline
8,000
\end{array}
$$

Estimate the products.

	a	b	c	d

1.
$$
\begin{array}{r}
31 \rightarrow \quad 30 \\
\times 46 \rightarrow \times \quad 50 \\
\hline
1,500
\end{array}
$$
  $\begin{array}{r} 22 \rightarrow \\ \times 53 \rightarrow \\ \hline \end{array}$
  $\begin{array}{r} 74 \rightarrow \\ \times 55 \rightarrow \\ \hline \end{array}$
  $\begin{array}{r} 86 \rightarrow \\ \times 91 \rightarrow \\ \hline \end{array}$

2.
$\begin{array}{r} 65 \rightarrow \\ \times 21 \rightarrow \\ \hline \end{array}$
  $\begin{array}{r} 47 \rightarrow \\ \times 32 \rightarrow \\ \hline \end{array}$
  $\begin{array}{r} 39 \rightarrow \\ \times 63 \rightarrow \\ \hline \end{array}$
  $\begin{array}{r} 59 \rightarrow \\ \times 77 \rightarrow \\ \hline \end{array}$

3.
$\begin{array}{r} 276 \rightarrow \\ \times \quad 45 \rightarrow \\ \hline \end{array}$
  $\begin{array}{r} 671 \rightarrow \\ \times \quad 93 \rightarrow \\ \hline \end{array}$
  $\begin{array}{r} 253 \rightarrow \\ \times \quad 85 \rightarrow \\ \hline \end{array}$
  $\begin{array}{r} 712 \rightarrow \\ \times \quad 97 \rightarrow \\ \hline \end{array}$

Line up the digits. Then estimate the products.

	a	b	c

4. 67 × 23 _____   94 × 52 _____   749 × 28 _____

$$
\begin{array}{r}
67 \rightarrow \quad 70 \\
\times 23 \rightarrow \times \quad 20 \\
\hline
\end{array}
$$

One-digit and Two-digit Divisors with Remainders

To divide by a one-digit divisor, first choose a **trial quotient.** Then multiply and subtract. Remember, if your trial quotient is too large or too small, try another number.

To divide by a two-digit divisor, first choose a trial quotient. Multiply and subtract. Then write the remainder in the quotient.

Find: 739 ÷ 22

Divide.	Multiply and subtract.	Multiply and subtract.	Check:
H T O 22)7 3 9 7 < 22 22 does not go into 7.	H T O 3 22)7 3 9 − 6 6 ↓ 7 9 2)7 is about 3. So, 22)73 is about 3.	H T O 3 3 R 13 22)7 3 9 − 6 6 7 9 − 6 6 1 3 2)7 is about 3. So, 22)79 is about 3.	33 ×22 726 + 13 739

Divide.

	a	b	c	d
1.	3 4 R1 2)6 9 −6 ↓ 0 9 − 8 1	6)5 6 8	3)2 8 9	5)2 7 4
2.	27)4,5 2 1	84)5,9 3 4	41)5,2 1 9	62)8,6 9 4

Set up the problems. Then find the quotients.

	a	b	c
3.	461 ÷ 3 = _____ 3)461	784 ÷ 5 = _____	32,692 ÷ 12 = _____

Dividing by Multiples of 10

To divide by multiples of ten, choose a trial quotient.
Then multiply and subtract.

Find: 570 ÷ 40

Divide.	Multiply and subtract.	Multiply and subtract.	Check:

H T O
40)5 7 0
 	
5 < 40
 	
40 does not
go into 5.
	H T O
	  1
	40)5 7 0
	− 4 0 ↓
	  1 7 0
	
	Think: 4)5 is about 1.
	So, 40)57 is about 1.
	Put the 1 above the 7.
		H T O
		  1 4 R 10
		40)5 7 0
		− 4 0
		  1 7 0
		− 1 6 0
		    1 0
		
		Think: 4)17 is about 4.
		So, 40)170 is about 4.
			14
			×40
			560
			+ 10
			570

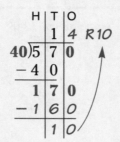

Divide.

       a   *b*   *c*   *d*

1.
        1 1 R 39
   40)4 7 9
    − 4 0 ↓
       7 9
     − 4 0
       3 9

         80)4 3 0   20)3 6 8   10)4 9 7

2.
    50)6, 3 6 0   20)3, 8 5 6   40)5, 9 0 0   80)7, 8 5 0

Set up the problems. Then find the quotients.

                a   *b*

3. 3,875 ÷ 70 = _____   5,183 ÷ 20 = _____

   70)3,875

Trial Quotient: Too Large or Too Small

When you divide, you may have to try several quotients.
Use rounding to choose a trial quotient. Then multiply and subtract.
If it is too large or too small, try again.

Find: 672 ÷ 24

Use rounding to choose a trial quotient.	Multiply and subtract.	Try a smaller number. Multiply and subtract.	Finish the problem.
$24\overline{)6\ 7\ 2}$	$\begin{array}{r} 3 \\ 24\overline{)6\ 7\ 2} \\ -7\ 2 \end{array}$	$\begin{array}{r} 2 \\ 24\overline{)6\ 7\ 2} \\ -4\ 8 \\ \hline 1\ 9 \end{array}$	$\begin{array}{r} 2\ 8 \\ 24\overline{)6\ 7\ 2} \\ -4\ 8\downarrow \\ \hline 1\ 9\ 2 \\ -1\ 9\ 2 \\ \hline 0 \end{array}$
Think: 24 rounds to 20. $\begin{array}{r}3\\2\overline{)6}\end{array}$ So, $24\overline{)67}$ is about 3.	Since 72 > 67, 3 is too large.	Since 19 < 24, 2 is correct.	

Find: 675 ÷ 15

$15\overline{)6\ 7\ 5}$	$\begin{array}{r} 3 \\ 15\overline{)6\ 7\ 5} \\ -4\ 5 \\ \hline 2\ 2 \end{array}$	$\begin{array}{r} 4 \\ 15\overline{)6\ 7\ 5} \\ -6\ 0 \\ \hline 7 \end{array}$	$\begin{array}{r} 4\ 5 \\ 15\overline{)6\ 7\ 5} \\ -6\ 0\downarrow \\ \hline 7\ 5 \\ -7\ 5 \\ \hline 0 \end{array}$
Think: 15 rounds to 20. $\begin{array}{r}3\\2\overline{)6}\end{array}$ So, $15\overline{)67}$ is about 3.	Since 22 > 15, 3 is too small.	Since 7 < 15, 4 is correct.	

Write *too large, too small,* or *correct* for each trial quotient.
Then write the correct trial quotient.

a   b

1. $\begin{array}{r}2\\25\overline{)4\ 7\ 5}\end{array}$ ____too large____ $\begin{array}{r}3\\15\overline{)6\ 8\ 2}\end{array}$ _____

____1____   _____

2. $\begin{array}{r}4\\61\overline{)2,4\ 1\ 9}\end{array}$ _____ $\begin{array}{r}3\\42\overline{)1,2\ 5\ 3}\end{array}$ _____

_____   _____

3. $\begin{array}{r}8\\54\overline{)4\ 1,2\ 4\ 9}\end{array}$ $\begin{array}{r}3\\27\overline{)6\ 5,4\ 8\ 7}\end{array}$

Zeros in Quotients

When you cannot divide, write a zero in the quotient as a place holder.

Find: 2,430 ÷ 4

Divide.

Th	H	T	O
4)2,	4	3	0

2 < 4

4 does not go into 2.

Multiply and subtract.

Th	H	T	O
	6		
4)2,	4	3	0
− 2	4	↓	
	0	3	

$$4\overline{)24} \quad 6$$

Multiply and subtract.

Th	H	T	O
	6	0	
4)2,	4	3	0
− 2	4	↓	
	0	3	
		0	
		3	0

← Write a zero in the quotient as a place holder.

$$4\overline{)3} \quad 0$$

Multiply and subtract.

Th	H	T	O
	6	0	7	R 2
4)2,	4	3	0
− 2	4	↓	
	0	3	
		0	
		3	0
	− 2	8	
		2	

Divide.

　　　　　　　　a　　　　　　　　　　*b*　　　　　　　　　　*c*　　　　　　　　　　*d*

1.
```
    3 0 4
2)6 0 8
 −6 ↓
   0 0
 −  0 ↓
     0 8
 −   8
     0
```

b. 4)4 2 8

c. 9)1, 8 4 5

d. 7)1, 4 6 3

2.
81)4 1, 0 6 7

97)5 8, 3 9 4

89)1 8, 5 1 2

Estimation of Quotients

To estimate quotients, round the numbers to use basic division facts.

Estimate: 243 ÷ 5

Round the dividend until you can use a basic fact. Divide.

$5\overline{)243}$ $243 ÷ 5$

Think: $25 ÷ 5 = 5$

$250 ÷ 5 = 50$

Estimate: 424 ÷ 61

Round the dividend and the divisor until you can use a basic fact. Divide.

$61\overline{)424}$ $424 ÷ 61$

Think: $42 ÷ 6 = 7$

$420 ÷ 60 = 7$

Round the dividends to estimate the quotients.

a	b	c
1. $3\overline{)121} \rightarrow 3\overline{)120}$ with 40	$4\overline{)284} \rightarrow$	$8\overline{)712} \rightarrow$
2. $8\overline{)5,747} \rightarrow$	$7\overline{)2,312} \rightarrow$	$5\overline{)2,934} \rightarrow$

Round the dividends and the divisors to estimate the quotients.

a	b	c
3. $23\overline{)783} \rightarrow$	$35\overline{)805} \rightarrow$	$29\overline{)597} \rightarrow$
4. $42\overline{)807} \rightarrow$	$53\overline{)754} \rightarrow$	$84\overline{)644} \rightarrow$

Improper Fractions and Mixed Numbers

An **improper** fraction is a fraction with a numerator that is greater than or equal to the denominator.

$\frac{6}{6}$, $\frac{12}{3}$, and $\frac{8}{5}$ are improper fractions.

An improper fraction can be written as a whole or mixed number.

A **mixed number** is a whole number and a fraction.

$$1\frac{3}{4} \text{ is a mixed number.}$$

A mixed number can be written as an improper fraction.

Write $\frac{6}{6}$ and $\frac{12}{3}$ as whole numbers.

Write $\frac{8}{5}$ as a mixed number.

Write $1\frac{3}{4}$ as an improper fraction.

Divide the numerator by the denominator.

$$\begin{array}{r} 1 \\ 6{\overline{)6}} \end{array} \qquad \frac{6}{6} = 1$$

$$\begin{array}{r} 4 \\ 3{\overline{)12}} \end{array} \qquad \frac{12}{3} = 4$$

Divide the numerator by the denominator. Write the remainder as a fraction by writing the remainder over the divisor.

$$\begin{array}{r} 1\frac{3}{5} \\ 5{\overline{)8}} \\ -5 \end{array} \qquad \frac{8}{5} = 1\frac{3}{5}$$

Multiply the whole number by the denominator. Add this product to the numerator. Then write the sum over the denominator.

$$1\frac{3}{4} = \frac{1 \times 4 + 3}{4} = \frac{4 + 3}{4} = \frac{7}{4}$$

$$1\frac{3}{4} = \frac{7}{4}$$

Write as a whole number.

	a	b	c	d
1.	$\frac{16}{4} = $ ___4___	$\frac{15}{5} = $ ___3___	$\frac{28}{4} = $ ___7___	$\frac{48}{6} = $ ___8___

Write as a mixed number.

	a	b	c	d
2.	$\frac{15}{4} = $ ___$3\frac{3}{4}$___	$\frac{21}{5} = $ ___$4\frac{1}{5}$___	$\frac{23}{6} = $ ___$3\frac{5}{6}$___	$\frac{7}{2} = $ ___$3\frac{1}{2}$___

Write as an improper fraction.

	a	b	c	d
3.	$2\frac{7}{10} = $ ___$\frac{27}{10}$___	$8\frac{1}{3} = $ ___$\frac{25}{3}$___	$5\frac{1}{6} = $ ___$\frac{31}{6}$___	$3\frac{2}{5} = $ ___$\frac{15}{2}$___

 24   30

Equivalent Fractions

To add or subtract fractions, you might need to use **equivalent fractions**, or fractions that have the same value.

To change a fraction to an equivalent fraction in **higher terms,** multiply the numerator and the denominator by the same number.

Rewrite $\frac{3}{4}$ with 8 as the denominator.

Compare the denominators.	Multiply both the numerator and the denominator by 2.
$\frac{3}{4} = \frac{}{8}$ Think: $4 \times 2 = 8$	$\frac{3}{4} = \frac{3 \times 2}{4 \times 2} = \frac{6}{8}$

You can also use the **lowest common denominator (LCD)** to write equivalent fractions.

Use the LCD to write equivalent fractions for $\frac{1}{2}$ and $\frac{2}{5}$.

List several multiples for each denominator.	Find the LCD. It is the smallest number that appears on both lists.	Write equivalent fractions.
Multiples of 2: 2 4 6 8 10 12 **Multiples of 5:** 5 10 15 20 25	The LCD of $\frac{1}{2}$ and $\frac{2}{5}$ is 10.	$\frac{1}{2} = \frac{1 \times 5}{2 \times 5} = \frac{5}{10}$ $\frac{2}{5} = \frac{2 \times 2}{5 \times 2} = \frac{4}{10}$

Rewrite each fraction as an equivalent fraction in higher terms.

    a   *b*   *c*   *d*

1. $\frac{5}{8} = \frac{5 \times 2}{8 \times 2} = \frac{10}{16}$ $\frac{3}{4} = \frac{3 \times 4}{4 \times 4} = \frac{12}{16}$ $\frac{2}{3} = \frac{2 \times 4}{3 \times 4} = \frac{8}{12}$ $\frac{2}{5} = \frac{2 \times 2}{5 \times 2} = \frac{4}{10}$

2. $\frac{3}{5} = \frac{3 \times 5}{5 \times 5} = \frac{15}{25}$ $\frac{2}{5} = \frac{2 \times 3}{5 \times 3} = \frac{6}{15}$ $\frac{5}{6} = \frac{5 \times 4}{6 \times 4} = \frac{20}{24}$ $\frac{7}{8} = \frac{7 \times 4}{8 \times 2} = \frac{1}{16}$

Use the LCD to write equivalent fractions.

    a   *b*   *c*   *d*

3. $\frac{1}{3} = \frac{1 \times 2}{3 \times 2} = \frac{2}{6}$ $\frac{1}{2} = \frac{1 \times 2}{2 \times 2} = \frac{2}{4}$ $\frac{7}{10} = \frac{7 \times 2}{10 \times 2} = \frac{14}{20}$ $\frac{2}{3} = \frac{2 \times 3}{3 \times 3} = \frac{6}{9}$

$\frac{1}{2} = \frac{1 \times 3}{2 \times 3} = \frac{3}{6}$ $\frac{3}{5} = \frac{3 \times 12}{5 \times 12} = \frac{36}{12}$ $\frac{3}{4} = \frac{3 \times 4}{4 \times 4} = \frac{12}{16}$ $\frac{5}{7} = \frac{5 \times 7}{7 \times 9} = \frac{1}{4}$

Simplifying Fractions

When you find the answer to a problem with fractions, you might need to change the fraction to an equivalent fraction in simplest terms. To **simplify** a fraction, divide both the numerator and the denominator by the same greatest number possible.

Simplify: $\frac{8}{14}$

$\frac{8}{14} =$ **Consider the numerator and denominator.**

Think: 14 can be divided by 7 but 8 cannot.
8 can be divided by 4 but 14 cannot.
Both 14 and 8 can be divided by 2.

Divide the numerator and the denominator by 2.

$\frac{8}{14} = \frac{8 \div 2}{14 \div 2} = \frac{4}{7}$

A fraction is in simplest terms when 1 is the only number that divides both the numerator and the denominator evenly.

The fraction $\frac{4}{7}$ is in simplest terms.

Simplify.

	a	b	c	d
1.	$\frac{9}{21} = \frac{9 \div 3}{21 \div 3} = \frac{3}{7}$	$\frac{2}{10} = \frac{1}{5}$	$\frac{4}{12} = \frac{2}{6} = \frac{1}{3}$	$\frac{12}{18} = \frac{2}{3}$
2.	$\frac{4}{6} = $	$\frac{2}{8} = $	$\frac{8}{20} = $	$\frac{10}{12} = $
3.	$\frac{45}{45} = \frac{1}{1}$	$\frac{9}{15} = $	$\frac{2}{12} = \frac{1}{2}$	$\frac{6}{14} = \frac{6}{14} 2$
4.	$\frac{9}{12} = $	$\frac{3}{9} = $	$\frac{10}{20} = $	$\frac{6}{8} = $
5.	$\frac{9}{21} = \frac{3}{3} \frac{3}{7}$	$\frac{2}{20} = \frac{1}{10}$	$\frac{4}{36} = \frac{1}{4}$	$\frac{12}{24} = \frac{2}{4} = \frac{1}{2}$

Addition and Subtraction of Fractions with Like Denominators

To add or subtract fractions with like denominators, add or subtract the numerators. Use the same denominator. Simplify the answer.

Remember,

- **to simplify an improper fraction, write it as a whole number or a mixed number.**

- **to simplify a proper fraction, write it in simplest terms.**

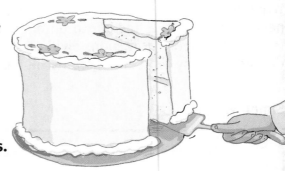

Find: $\frac{9}{10} + \frac{8}{10}$

Add the numerators.	Use the same denominator.
$\frac{9}{10}$ $+\frac{8}{10}$ $\overline{17}$	$\frac{9}{10}$ $+\frac{8}{10}$ $\overline{\frac{17}{10}} = 1\frac{7}{10}$ Simplify the answer.

Find: $\frac{11}{12} - \frac{7}{12}$

Subtract the numerators.	Use the same denominator.
$\frac{11}{12}$ $-\frac{7}{12}$ $\overline{4}$	$\frac{11}{12}$ $-\frac{7}{12}$ $\overline{\frac{4}{12}} = \frac{1}{3}$ Simplify the answer.

Add. Simplify.

	a	b	c	d	e
1.	$\frac{3}{8}$ $+\frac{1}{8}$ $\overline{\frac{4}{8}} = \frac{1}{2}$	$\frac{3}{10}$ $+\frac{1}{10}$	$\frac{2}{6}$ $+\frac{1}{6}$	$\frac{5}{16}$ $+\frac{1}{16}$	$\frac{7}{16}$ $+\frac{3}{16}$
2.	$\frac{5}{6}$ $+\frac{2}{6}$	$\frac{7}{8}$ $+\frac{5}{8}$	$\frac{8}{10}$ $+\frac{5}{10}$	$\frac{4}{5}$ $+\frac{3}{5}$	$\frac{11}{12}$ $+\frac{6}{12}$

Subtract. Simplify.

	a	b	c	d	e
3.	$\frac{5}{8}$ $-\frac{3}{8}$ $\overline{\frac{2}{8}} = \frac{1}{4}$	$\frac{7}{10}$ $-\frac{3}{10}$	$\frac{7}{12}$ $-\frac{5}{12}$	$\frac{5}{8}$ $-\frac{1}{8}$	$\frac{15}{16}$ $-\frac{3}{16}$

Addition of Fractions with Different Denominators

To add fractions with different denominators, first rewrite the fractions as equivalent fractions with like denominators. Then add the numerators and simplify the answer.

Find: $\frac{1}{6} + \frac{1}{3}$

Write equivalent fractions with like denominators.

$$\frac{1}{6} = \frac{1}{6}$$
$$+\frac{1}{3} = \frac{2}{6}$$

Remember,

$$\frac{1}{3} = \frac{1 \times 2}{3 \times 2} = \frac{2}{6}$$

Add the numerators. Use the same denominator.

$$\frac{1}{6} = \frac{1}{6}$$
$$+\frac{1}{3} = \frac{2}{6}$$
$$\frac{3}{6} = \frac{1}{2} \quad \text{Simplify the answer.}$$

Add. Simplify.

	a	b	c	d
1.	$\frac{1}{5} = \frac{2}{10}$ $+\frac{1}{10} = \frac{1}{10}$ $\frac{3}{10}$	$\frac{1}{4}$ $+\frac{1}{2}$	$\frac{1}{2}$ $+\frac{3}{8}$	$\frac{3}{4}$ $+\frac{1}{8}$
2.	$\frac{3}{4}$ $+\frac{1}{12}$	$\frac{1}{2}$ $+\frac{1}{6}$	$\frac{1}{10}$ $+\frac{1}{2}$	$\frac{5}{12}$ $+\frac{1}{4}$
3.	$\frac{1}{2}$ $+\frac{3}{10}$	$\frac{5}{16}$ $+\frac{1}{4}$	$\frac{1}{2}$ $+\frac{5}{12}$	$\frac{4}{9}$ $+\frac{1}{3}$

Set up the problems. Then find the sums. Simplify.

a	b	c

4. $\frac{1}{3} + \frac{2}{9} =$ _____ $\frac{2}{8} + \frac{1}{24} =$ _____ $\frac{3}{6} + \frac{2}{18} =$ _____

$\frac{1}{3}$
$+\frac{2}{9}$

Addition of Fractions Using the Least Common Denominator

Find: $\frac{1}{2} + \frac{3}{5}$

Write equivalent fractions with like denominators. Use the LCD.

$$\frac{1}{2} = \frac{1 \times 5}{2 \times 5} = \frac{5}{10}$$
$$+ \frac{3}{5} = \frac{3 \times 2}{5 \times 2} = \frac{6}{10}$$

Add the numerators. Use the same denominator.

$$\frac{1}{2} = \frac{5}{10}$$
$$+ \frac{3}{5} = \frac{6}{10}$$
$$\frac{11}{10} = 1\frac{1}{10} \quad \text{Simplify the answer.}$$

Add. Simplify.

a	b	c	d

1.
$\frac{1}{2} = \frac{3}{6}$
$+ \frac{2}{3} = \frac{4}{6}$
$\frac{7}{6} = 1\frac{1}{6}$

$\frac{3}{7}$
$+ \frac{1}{2}$

$\frac{2}{3}$
$+ \frac{3}{4}$

$\frac{2}{5}$
$+ \frac{7}{9}$

2.
$\frac{2}{3}$
$+ \frac{7}{8}$

$\frac{3}{8}$
$+ \frac{5}{6}$

$\frac{4}{5}$
$+ \frac{2}{3}$

$\frac{2}{7}$
$+ \frac{2}{3}$

3.
$\frac{5}{6}$
$+ \frac{3}{4}$

$\frac{1}{3}$
$+ \frac{3}{10}$

$\frac{5}{6}$
$+ \frac{3}{5}$

$\frac{1}{2}$
$+ \frac{5}{9}$

Set up the problems. Then find the sums. Simplify.

a	b	c

4. $\frac{3}{7} + \frac{1}{4} =$ _____

$\frac{4}{5} + \frac{7}{11} =$ _____

$\frac{1}{7} + \frac{2}{8} =$ _____

$\frac{3}{7}$
$+ \frac{1}{4}$

Problem-Solving Method: Make a Graph

Coach Esteves took a survey to choose the team's mascot. Of the 24 players, $\frac{1}{3}$ chose Bulldogs, $\frac{1}{2}$ chose Bears, and $\frac{1}{6}$ chose Lions. How can he present the results of the survey to the team?

Understand the problem.

- **What do you want to know?**
  how to present the results of the survey

- **What information is given?**
  24 people voted: $\frac{1}{3}$ for Bulldogs, $\frac{1}{2}$ for Bears, and $\frac{1}{6}$ for Lions.

Plan how to solve it.

- **What method can you use?**
  You can make a circle graph to show the data as parts of a whole.

Solve it.

- **How can you use this method to solve the problem?**
  Use a circle divided into 24 equal parts to represent the whole team. Then shade and label the number of votes for each mascot.
  (Remember, to find $\frac{1}{2}$ of 8, divide 8 by 2. $\frac{1}{2}$ of 8 = 8 ÷ 2 = 4)

TEAM MASCOT VOTE

Mascot	Fraction of All the Votes	Number of Votes
Bulldogs	$\frac{1}{3}$ of 24 =	8
Bears	$\frac{1}{2}$ of 24 =	12
Lions	$\frac{1}{6}$ of 24 =	4

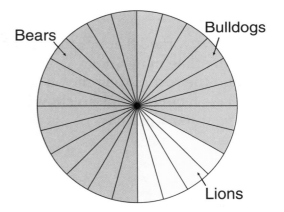

- **What is the answer?**
  The results of the survey can be presented in a circle graph.

Look back and check your answer.

- **Is your answer reasonable?**
  The whole circle represents the whole survey—24 votes.
  The sum of the number of votes in each section should be 24.

  8 + 12 + 4 = 24

  The answer is reasonable.

Make a graph to solve each problem.

1. Jamal has 28 CDs in his collection. $\frac{1}{4}$ of the CDs are Rock, $\frac{1}{2}$ are R&B, and $\frac{1}{4}$ are Jazz. Make a circle graph to show Jamal's CD collection.

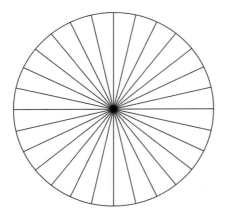

2. Twelve students voted for their favorite ice cream. Vanilla got $\frac{1}{6}$ of the votes, chocolate got $\frac{2}{3}$, and strawberry got $\frac{1}{6}$. Make a circle graph to show how many students voted for each flavor.

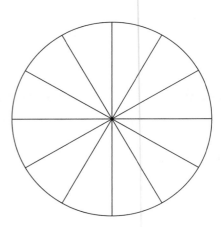

3. Laura worked 8 hours today. She spent $\frac{1}{2}$ the time in meetings, $\frac{1}{8}$ on the phone, and the rest of the time on the computer. Make a circle graph to show how Laura spent her work day.

4. In the United States, $\frac{7}{10}$ of the population has brown hair, $\frac{3}{20}$ has blonde hair, $\frac{1}{10}$ has black hair, and $\frac{1}{20}$ are redheads. Make a circle graph to show the hair color of an average group of 20 people in the United States.

Adding Mixed Numbers, Whole Numbers, and Fractions

To add mixed numbers, whole numbers, and fractions, first check for unlike denominators. Write mixed numbers and fractions as equivalent fractions with like denominators. Add the fractions. Then add the whole numbers and simplify.

Find: $2\frac{7}{12} + \frac{1}{4}$

Write the fractions with like denominators.	Add the fractions.	Add the whole numbers.	Simplify.
$2\frac{7}{12} = 2\frac{7}{12}$ $+\ \frac{1}{4} = \ \frac{3}{12}$	$2\frac{7}{12} = 2\frac{7}{12}$ $+\ \frac{1}{4} = \ \frac{3}{12}$ $\frac{10}{12}$	$2\frac{7}{12} = 2\frac{7}{12}$ $+\ \frac{1}{4} = \ \frac{3}{12}$ $2\frac{10}{12}$	$2\frac{10}{12} = 2\frac{5}{6}$

Remember, $\frac{1}{4} = \frac{3}{12}$.
They are equivalent fractions.

Add. Simplify.

	a	b	c	d
1.	$4\frac{1}{2} = 4\frac{2}{4}$ $+\ \ \frac{1}{4} = \ \frac{1}{4}$ $4\frac{3}{4}$	$\frac{1}{2}$ $+\ 8\frac{1}{8}$	$6\frac{1}{4}$ $+\ \ \frac{1}{8}$	$\frac{1}{2}$ $+\ 9\frac{3}{8}$
2.	$1\ 2\frac{1}{3}$ $+\ \ \ 9\frac{1}{6}$	$8\frac{1}{2}$ $+\ 9\frac{1}{10}$	$1\ 2\frac{1}{5}$ $+\ \ \ 7\frac{1}{10}$	$6\frac{1}{3}$ $+\ 8\frac{1}{9}$
3.	$\frac{1}{3}$ $+\ 2\frac{1}{4}$	$3\frac{1}{4}$ $+\ \ \ \frac{2}{3}$	$7\frac{1}{2}$ $+\ \ \ \frac{1}{3}$	$\frac{3}{8}$ $+\ 1\frac{1}{7}$
4.	$5\frac{1}{8}$ $+\ 6\frac{1}{6}$	$8\frac{1}{4}$ $+\ 9\frac{1}{3}$	$4\frac{2}{5}$ $+\ 7\frac{1}{2}$	$7\frac{1}{2}$ $+\ 8\frac{3}{10}$

Adding Mixed Numbers with Large Sums

When adding mixed numbers, whole numbers, and fractions, your sum might contain an improper fraction. To regroup a sum that contains an improper fraction, first write the improper fraction as a mixed number. Then add and simplify.

Find: $5\frac{1}{3} + \frac{5}{7}$

Write the fractions with like denominators. Add.

$$5\frac{1}{3} = 5\frac{7}{21}$$
$$+ \quad \frac{5}{7} = \quad \frac{15}{21}$$
$$\overline{\qquad 5\frac{22}{21}}$$

The sum $5\frac{22}{21}$ contains an improper fraction. To regroup, write the improper fraction as a mixed number.

$$\frac{22}{21} = 1\frac{1}{21}$$

Then add.

$$5\frac{22}{21} = 5 + 1\frac{1}{21} = 6\frac{1}{21}$$

Add. Simplify.

	a	b	c	d
1.	$4\frac{1}{2} = 4\frac{3}{6}$ $+ \quad \frac{5}{6} = \quad \frac{5}{6}$ $4\frac{8}{6} = 5\frac{1}{3}$	$9\frac{2}{5}$ $+ \quad \frac{5}{6}$	$3\frac{2}{3}$ $+ \quad \frac{8}{9}$	$\frac{3}{7}$ $+ 6\frac{7}{8}$
2.	$2\frac{3}{4}$ $+ 7\frac{5}{6}$	$9\frac{1}{3}$ $+ 4\frac{7}{9}$	$10\frac{5}{7}$ $+ \quad 7\frac{9}{11}$	$1\frac{1}{2}$ $+ 9\frac{11}{12}$
3.	$9\frac{2}{3}$ $+ \quad \frac{3}{4}$	$7\frac{3}{9}$ $+ \quad \frac{1}{2}$	$10\frac{9}{10}$ $+ \quad \frac{2}{5}$	$8\frac{1}{2}$ $+ \quad \frac{2}{3}$
4.	$\frac{1}{3}$ $3\frac{2}{3}$ $+ 9\frac{7}{12}$	$2\frac{3}{10}$ $15\frac{3}{5}$ $+ \quad \frac{7}{10}$	$1\frac{1}{2}$ $17\frac{1}{2}$ $+ \quad \frac{7}{10}$	$2\frac{3}{8}$ $\frac{5}{8}$ $+ 7\frac{1}{2}$

Subtraction of Fractions with Different Denominators

To subtract fractions with different denominators, first rewrite the fractions as equivalent fractions with like denominators. Then subtract and simplify the answer.

Find: $\frac{4}{5} - \frac{3}{4}$

Write equivalent fractions with like denominators. Use the LCD.

$$\frac{4}{5} = \frac{4 \times 4}{5 \times 4} = \frac{16}{20}$$
$$-\frac{3}{4} = \frac{3 \times 5}{4 \times 5} = \frac{15}{20}$$

Subtract the numerators. Use the same denominators.

$$\frac{4}{5} = \frac{16}{20}$$
$$-\frac{3}{4} = \frac{15}{20}$$
$$\frac{1}{20}$$

Subtract. Simplify.

	a	b	c	d

1.
a)
$$\frac{1}{3} = \frac{4}{12}$$
$$-\frac{1}{4} = \frac{3}{12}$$
$$\frac{1}{12}$$

b)
$$\frac{1}{4} = \frac{}{20}$$
$$-\frac{1}{5} = \frac{}{20}$$

c)
$$\frac{3}{5} = \frac{}{10}$$
$$-\frac{1}{2} = \frac{}{10}$$

d)
$$\frac{2}{3} = \frac{}{6}$$
$$-\frac{1}{2} = \frac{}{6}$$

2.
a)
$$\frac{5}{6}$$
$$-\frac{1}{4}$$

b)
$$\frac{5}{6}$$
$$-\frac{3}{8}$$

c)
$$\frac{4}{5}$$
$$-\frac{1}{2}$$

d)
$$\frac{1}{2}$$
$$-\frac{1}{5}$$

3.
a)
$$\frac{4}{5}$$
$$-\frac{3}{10}$$

b)
$$\frac{5}{6}$$
$$-\frac{5}{9}$$

c)
$$\frac{3}{4}$$
$$-\frac{3}{8}$$

d)
$$\frac{7}{9}$$
$$-\frac{1}{4}$$

Set up the problems. Then find the differences. Simplify.

a) **4.** $\frac{14}{15} - \frac{1}{3} =$ _____

$$\frac{14}{15}$$
$$-\frac{1}{3}$$

b) $\frac{8}{9} - \frac{3}{8} =$ _____

c) $\frac{11}{12} - \frac{3}{8} =$ _____

Subtraction of Fractions and Mixed Numbers from Whole Numbers

Sometimes you will need to subtract a fraction from a whole number.
Write the whole number as a mixed number with a like denominator.
Subtract the fractions. Subtract the whole numbers.

Find: $7 - 2\frac{5}{8}$

To subtract, you need two fractions with like denominators.	Write 7 as a mixed number with 8 as the denominator.	Subtract the fractions.	Subtract the whole numbers.
$\begin{array}{r} 7 \\ -2\frac{5}{8} \\ \hline \end{array}$	$7 = 6 + \frac{8}{8} = 6\frac{8}{8}$ Remember, $\frac{8}{8} = 1$	$\begin{array}{r} 7 = 6\frac{8}{8} \\ -2\frac{5}{8} = 2\frac{5}{8} \\ \hline \frac{3}{8} \end{array}$	$\begin{array}{r} 7 = 6\frac{8}{8} \\ -2\frac{5}{8} = 2\frac{5}{8} \\ \hline 4\frac{3}{8} \end{array}$

Write each whole number as a mixed number.

	a	*b*	*c*	*d*
1.	$8 = 7 + \frac{4}{4} = 7\frac{4}{4}$	$12 = 11 + \frac{3}{} =$	$18 = 17 + \frac{}{8} =$	$28 = 27 + \frac{12}{} =$

Subtract. Simplify.

	a	*b*	*c*	*d*
2.	$\begin{array}{r} 8 = 7\frac{3}{3} \\ -4\frac{2}{3} = 4\frac{2}{3} \\ \hline 3\frac{1}{3} \end{array}$	$\begin{array}{r} 4 = 3\frac{}{4} \\ -2\frac{3}{4} = 2\frac{3}{4} \\ \hline \end{array}$	$\begin{array}{r} 6 = 5\frac{}{8} \\ -2\frac{5}{8} = 2\frac{5}{8} \\ \hline \end{array}$	$\begin{array}{r} 14 = 13\frac{}{6} \\ -9\frac{5}{6} = 9\frac{5}{6} \\ \hline \end{array}$
3.	$\begin{array}{r} 15 \\ -12\frac{1}{2} \\ \hline \end{array}$	$\begin{array}{r} 19 \\ -14\frac{5}{8} \\ \hline \end{array}$	$\begin{array}{r} 12 \\ -8\frac{1}{5} \\ \hline \end{array}$	$\begin{array}{r} 15 \\ -\frac{3}{10} \\ \hline \end{array}$
4.	$\begin{array}{r} 12 \\ -9\frac{1}{6} \\ \hline \end{array}$	$\begin{array}{r} 16 \\ -\frac{3}{4} \\ \hline \end{array}$	$\begin{array}{r} 13 \\ -10\frac{5}{9} \\ \hline \end{array}$	$\begin{array}{r} 9 \\ -\frac{3}{5} \\ \hline \end{array}$

Subtraction of Mixed Numbers with Regrouping

To subtract mixed numbers, it may be necessary to regroup first. Write the whole number part as a mixed number. Add the mixed number and the fraction. Then subtract and simplify.

Find: $8\frac{7}{12} - 2\frac{3}{4}$

Write the fractions with like denominators. Compare the numerators.

$$8\frac{7}{12} = 8\frac{7}{12}$$
$$-2\frac{3}{4} = 2\frac{9}{12}$$

$\frac{9}{12}$ is greater than $\frac{7}{12}$. You can't subtract the fractions.

To regroup, write **8** as a mixed number.

$$8 = 7\frac{12}{12}$$

Add the mixed number and the fraction.

$$8\frac{7}{12} = 7\frac{12}{12} + \frac{7}{12} = 7\frac{19}{12}$$

Remember, $\frac{19}{12}$ is an improper fraction.

Now you can subtract and simplify.

$$8\frac{7}{12} = 7\frac{19}{12}$$
$$-2\frac{9}{12} = 2\frac{9}{12}$$
$$5\frac{10}{12} = 5\frac{5}{6}$$

Subtract. Simplify.

a

1. $8\frac{1}{5} = 7\frac{6}{5}$
$-2\frac{4}{5} = 2\frac{4}{5}$
$5\frac{2}{5}$

b

$7\frac{1}{4} = 6\frac{}{4}$
$-\frac{3}{4} = \frac{3}{4}$

c

$8\frac{7}{12} = 7\frac{}{12}$
$-4\frac{11}{12} = 4\frac{11}{12}$

2. $9\frac{3}{8}$
$-\frac{1}{2}$

$10\frac{1}{3}$
$-8\frac{2}{3}$

$7\frac{1}{5}$
$-4\frac{5}{8}$

3. $16\frac{1}{12}$
$-9\frac{11}{12}$

$12\frac{1}{10}$
$-\frac{1}{5}$

$16\frac{1}{2}$
$-8\frac{4}{9}$

Set up the problems. Then find the differences. Simplify.

a

4. $6\frac{3}{5} - 4\frac{9}{10} = $ _____

$6\frac{3}{5}$
$-4\frac{9}{10}$

b

$9\frac{1}{4} - 7\frac{3}{7} = $ _____

c

$15\frac{1}{3} - \frac{2}{3} = $ _____

Problem-Solving Method: Use Estimation

Stacey's bowl holds 15 cups of punch. Her recipe for punch is $9\frac{1}{3}$ cups of juice mixed with $6\frac{3}{4}$ cups of ginger ale. Does she need a bigger bowl?

Understand the problem.
- **What do you want to know?**
  if the punch will fit in the bowl

- **What information is given?**
  The bowl holds 15 cups.
  The punch is made with $9\frac{1}{3}$ cups of juice and $6\frac{3}{4}$ cups of ginger ale.

Plan how to solve it.
- **What method can you use?**
  Since the problem is not asking for an exact answer, you can use estimation to find the sum of the punch ingredients.

Solve it.
- **How can you use this method to solve the problem?**
  Round the mixed numbers to whole numbers. If the fractional part is less than $\frac{1}{2}$, drop the fraction and leave the whole number unchanged. If it is greater than or equal to $\frac{1}{2}$, round up to the next whole number.

$$
\begin{array}{lllll}
9\frac{1}{3} & \textbf{Think: } \frac{1}{3} < \frac{1}{2} & \text{Round down.} & & 9 \\
+6\frac{3}{4} & \textbf{Think: } \frac{3}{4} > \frac{1}{2} & \text{Round up.} & + & 7 \\
\hline
& & & & \textbf{16 cups of punch}
\end{array}
$$

- **What is the answer?**
  Stacey needs a bigger bowl.

Look back and check your answer.
- **Is your answer reasonable?**
  You can check your estimate by finding the exact answer.

$$
\begin{aligned}
9\frac{1}{3} &= 9\frac{4}{12} \\
+6\frac{3}{4} &= 6\frac{9}{12} \\
\hline
15\frac{13}{12} &= 16\frac{1}{12}
\end{aligned}
$$

The exact answer shows that the 15-cup bowl is not large enough to hold all the punch.
The estimate is reasonable.

Use estimation to solve each problem.

1. Kim leaves her house at 10:00 A.M. It takes $1\frac{1}{2}$ hours to drive to the airport and $\frac{3}{4}$ hour to check in. Will she make her 12:00 P.M. flight?

Answer _____

2. Tom planned to sell his stock when it reached $25 per share. In the morning, the stock was $19\frac{1}{5}$ per share. It went up $6\frac{2}{9}$ by the afternoon. Did he sell his stock?

Answer _____

3. Maya hiked $15\frac{3}{8}$ miles on Saturday and $13\frac{1}{2}$ miles on Sunday. Her 2-day goal was to hike 30 miles. Did she reach her goal?

Answer _____

4. It snowed $2\frac{1}{4}$ inches on Monday, 3 inches on Tuesday, and $\frac{5}{8}$ inch on Wednesday. About how many inches did it snow in the three days altogether?

Answer _____

5. Ellen has 4 cups of sugar. She needs $3\frac{2}{3}$ cups to make a cake and $1\frac{1}{4}$ cups to make the icing. Does she have enough sugar?

Answer _____

UNIT 2 Review

Write the fraction and the word name for the part that is shaded.

a	*b*	*c*

1.

 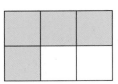 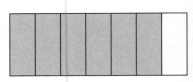

_____ or _____   _____ or _____   _____ or _____

Write as a whole or mixed number. Simplify.

a	*b*	*c*	*d*
2. $\frac{35}{5} =$ _____	$\frac{26}{3} =$ _____	$\frac{15}{3} =$ _____	$\frac{21}{6} =$ _____

Write as an improper fraction.

a	*b*	*c*	*d*
3. $3\frac{1}{4} =$ _____	$2\frac{7}{8} =$ _____	$4\frac{3}{5} =$ _____	$1\frac{7}{10} =$ _____

Rewrite each fraction as an equivalent fraction in higher terms.

a	*b*	*c*	*d*
4. $\frac{4}{7} = \frac{}{21}$	$\frac{1}{9} = \frac{}{45}$	$\frac{2}{3} = \frac{}{24}$	$\frac{5}{6} = \frac{}{18}$

Use the LCD to write equivalent fractions.

a	*b*	*c*	*d*
5. $\frac{1}{4} =$	$\frac{1}{5} =$	$\frac{3}{8} =$	$\frac{1}{2} =$
$\frac{1}{3} =$	$\frac{3}{4} =$	$\frac{2}{3} =$	$\frac{4}{11} =$

Simplify.

a	*b*	*c*	*d*
6. $\frac{4}{24} =$	$\frac{3}{9} =$	$\frac{2}{30} =$	$\frac{15}{45} =$
7. $\frac{6}{42} =$	$\frac{12}{20} =$	$\frac{3}{27} =$	$\frac{16}{32} =$

UNIT 2 Review

Add. Simplify.

	a	b	c	d
8.	$\frac{2}{7}$ $+ \frac{6}{7}$	$\frac{2}{3}$ $+ \frac{1}{9}$	1 $+ 2\frac{3}{11}$	$3\frac{3}{8}$ $+ 2\frac{1}{5}$
9.	$3\frac{8}{9}$ $+ 5$	$2\frac{5}{12}$ $+ 4\frac{7}{8}$	$1\frac{9}{10}$ $+ 3\frac{4}{5}$	$\frac{1}{6}$ $+ \frac{2}{7}$
10.	$\frac{3}{4}$ $+ \frac{5}{6}$	$\frac{4}{7}$ $+ 15\frac{1}{3}$	$\frac{6}{11}$ $+ 5\frac{9}{11}$	4 $+ \frac{9}{16}$
11.	$1\frac{5}{6}$ $\frac{2}{3}$ $+ 4$	$9\frac{2}{3}$ $\frac{1}{9}$ $+ 12$	$\frac{5}{6}$ $9\frac{1}{4}$ $+ 18$	$6\frac{7}{8}$ $3\frac{4}{5}$ $+ 2$

Subtract. Simplify.

	a	b	c	d
12.	$\frac{5}{8}$ $- \frac{1}{3}$	8 $- 2\frac{2}{5}$	3 $- \frac{3}{7}$	$5\frac{11}{12}$ $- 3\frac{1}{6}$
13.	4 $- 3\frac{1}{2}$	2 $- \frac{11}{12}$	$\frac{5}{8}$ $- \frac{3}{8}$	$\frac{5}{6}$ $- \frac{1}{4}$
14.	$7\frac{1}{4}$ $- 2\frac{5}{9}$	$\frac{4}{5}$ $- \frac{1}{2}$	$9\frac{1}{12}$ $- 2\frac{5}{8}$	$2\frac{1}{4}$ $- \frac{3}{4}$
15.	$10\frac{3}{5}$ $- 8\frac{1}{4}$	$4\frac{1}{7}$ $- \frac{2}{7}$	$5\frac{6}{9}$ $- 1\frac{4}{5}$	$\frac{7}{11}$ $- \frac{5}{9}$

unit 3
Multiplication and Division of Fractions

Multiplication of Fractions

To multiply fractions, multiply the numerators and multiply the denominators. Simplify the product.

Find: $\frac{1}{2} \times \frac{3}{4}$

Multiply the numerators.

$$\frac{1}{2} \times \frac{3}{4} = \frac{1 \times 3}{} = \frac{3}{}$$

Multiply the denominators.

$$\frac{1}{2} \times \frac{3}{4} = \frac{1 \times 3}{2 \times 4} = \frac{3}{8}$$

Find: $\frac{3}{4} \times \frac{2}{6}$

Multiply the numerators.

$$\frac{3}{4} \times \frac{2}{6} = \frac{3 \times 2}{} = \frac{6}{}$$

Multiply the denominators. Simplify.

$$\frac{3}{4} \times \frac{2}{6} = \frac{3 \times 2}{4 \times 6} = \frac{6}{24} = \frac{1}{4}$$

Multiply. Simplify.

a

b

1. $\frac{2}{5} \times \frac{1}{3} = \frac{2 \times 1}{5 \times 3} = \frac{2}{15}$

$\frac{3}{10} \times \frac{1}{5} =$

2. $\frac{4}{7} \times \frac{3}{5} =$

$\frac{5}{6} \times \frac{7}{8} =$

3. $\frac{1}{2} \times \frac{4}{7} =$

$\frac{1}{3} \times \frac{6}{11} =$

4. $\frac{3}{4} \times \frac{1}{3} =$

$\frac{5}{8} \times \frac{3}{10} =$

5. $\frac{4}{10} \times \frac{5}{16} =$

$\frac{3}{12} \times \frac{1}{3} =$

Multiplication of Fractions Using Cancellation

Instead of simplifying fractions after they have been multiplied,
it may be possible to use **cancellation** before multiplying.
To cancel, find a common factor of a numerator and a denominator.
Divide the numerator and the denominator by the common
factor. Then multiply, using the new numerator and denominator.

Find: $\frac{3}{4} \times \frac{2}{5}$ **using cancellation.**

Find the common factor.	Cancel.	Multiply the new numerators and denominators. Simplify.
$\frac{3}{4} \times \frac{2}{5}$	$\frac{3}{\overset{}{4}} \times \frac{\overset{1}{2}}{5}$ $\quad 2$	$\frac{3 \times 1}{2 \times 5} = \frac{3}{10}$
The common factor of 4 and 2 is 2.	Divide both the 4 and the 2 by 2.	

Multiply using cancellation.

a

1. $\frac{3}{4} \times \frac{1}{3} = \frac{\overset{1}{3}}{4} \times \frac{1}{\underset{1}{3}} = \frac{1 \times 1}{4 \times 1} = \frac{1}{4}$

b

$\frac{7}{8} \times \frac{4}{9} =$

2. $\frac{4}{7} \times \frac{3}{8} =$

$\frac{5}{16} \times \frac{1}{5} =$

3. $\frac{2}{3} \times \frac{1}{8} =$

$\frac{3}{4} \times \frac{1}{9} =$

4. $\frac{7}{10} \times \frac{5}{6} =$

$\frac{3}{4} \times \frac{13}{15} =$

5. $\frac{5}{6} \times \frac{3}{10} =$

$\frac{4}{9} \times \frac{3}{8} =$

6. $\frac{2}{3} \times \frac{3}{4} =$

$\frac{4}{5} \times \frac{5}{8} =$

Multiplication of Whole Numbers by Fractions

To multiply a whole number by a fraction, first write the whole number as an improper fraction. Use cancellation if possible. Multiply the numerators and the denominators. Simplify.

Find: $8 \times \frac{5}{16}$

Write the whole number as an improper fraction.	Cancel.	Multiply using the new numbers. Simplify.
$8 \times \frac{5}{16} = \frac{8}{1} \times \frac{5}{16}$	$\overset{1}{\cancel{8}} \times \frac{5}{\underset{2}{\cancel{16}}}$	$\frac{1 \times 5}{1 \times 2} = \frac{5}{2} = 2\frac{1}{2}$
	Divide 8 and 16 by 8.	

Write each whole number as a fraction.

	a	b	c	d	e
1.	$7 = \frac{7}{1}$	$18 =$	$20 =$	$4 =$	$12 =$

Multiply using cancellation. Simplify.

	a	b	c
2.	$10 \times \frac{1}{5} = \frac{\overset{2}{\cancel{10}}}{1} \times \frac{1}{\underset{1}{\cancel{5}}} = \frac{2 \times 1}{1 \times 1} = 2$	$14 \times \frac{2}{7} =$	$15 \times \frac{3}{10} =$
3.	$9 \times \frac{1}{6} =$	$12 \times \frac{3}{4} =$	$8 \times \frac{5}{6} =$
4.	$\frac{2}{3} \times 9 =$	$\frac{3}{10} \times 25 =$	$\frac{4}{5} \times 25 =$
5.	$\frac{8}{9} \times 27 =$	$\frac{11}{16} \times 24 =$	$\frac{5}{8} \times 32 =$

Multiplication of Mixed Numbers by Whole Numbers

To multiply a mixed number by a whole number, first write the mixed number and the whole number as improper fractions. Use cancellation if possible. Multiply the new numerators and denominators. Simplify the answer.

Find: $4\frac{1}{2} \times 6$

Write the whole number and the mixed number as improper fractions.	Cancel.	Multiply the new numerators and denominators. Simplify.
$4\frac{1}{2} \times 6 = \frac{9}{2} \times \frac{6}{1}$	$\frac{9}{\underset{1}{2}} \times \frac{\overset{3}{6}}{1}$	$\frac{9 \times 3}{1 \times 1} = \frac{27}{1} = 27$

Multiply. Simplify. Use cancellation if possible.

	a	b	c
1.	$2\frac{1}{2} \times 6 =$ $\frac{5}{\underset{1}{2}} \times \frac{\overset{3}{6}}{1} = \frac{15}{1} = 15$	$2\frac{1}{3} \times 3 =$	$4\frac{1}{2} \times 8 =$
2.	$4 \times 2\frac{1}{2} =$	$6 \times 2\frac{1}{3} =$	$1\frac{3}{4} \times 8 =$
3.	$6 \times 2\frac{1}{6} =$	$9 \times 2\frac{1}{3} =$	$4 \times 12\frac{1}{2} =$
4.	$3\frac{1}{3} \times 20 =$	$2 \times 5\frac{3}{4} =$	$4 \times 3\frac{1}{5} =$
5.	$4 \times 2\frac{1}{10} =$	$5 \times 2\frac{1}{15} =$	$11 \times 7\frac{4}{22} =$
6.	$8\frac{4}{15} \times 5 =$	$4\frac{1}{9} \times 30 =$	$2\frac{4}{9} \times 2 =$

Multiplication of Mixed Numbers by Fractions

To multiply a mixed number by a fraction, first write the mixed number as an improper fraction. Use cancellation if possible. Multiply the new numerators and denominators. Simplify.

Find: $2\frac{1}{4} \times \frac{1}{3}$

Write the mixed number as an improper fraction.	Cancel.	Multiply the new numerators and denominators.
$2\frac{1}{4} \times \frac{1}{3} = \frac{9}{4} \times \frac{1}{3}$	$\frac{\overset{3}{\cancel{9}}}{4} \times \frac{1}{\underset{1}{\cancel{3}}}$	$\frac{3 \times 1}{4 \times 1} = \frac{3}{4}$

Multiply. Simplify. Use cancellation if possible.

a	*b*	*c*
1. $\frac{2}{5} \times 1\frac{1}{2} =$ $\frac{\overset{1}{\cancel{2}}}{5} \times \frac{3}{\underset{1}{\cancel{2}}} = \frac{3}{5}$	$\frac{3}{8} \times 1\frac{3}{5} =$	$\frac{1}{5} \times 4\frac{1}{6} =$
2. $\frac{7}{8} \times 2\frac{2}{5} =$	$1\frac{1}{4} \times \frac{3}{5} =$	$\frac{7}{10} \times 1\frac{3}{14} =$
3. $\frac{7}{10} \times 1\frac{1}{3} =$	$\frac{2}{3} \times 5\frac{7}{8} =$	$\frac{4}{5} \times 6\frac{3}{4} =$
4. $4\frac{1}{2} \times \frac{2}{3} =$	$5\frac{1}{4} \times \frac{2}{3} =$	$8\frac{3}{4} \times \frac{2}{5} =$
5. $12\frac{1}{2} \times \frac{4}{5} =$	$2\frac{3}{4} \times \frac{4}{22} =$	$3\frac{3}{4} \times \frac{16}{20} =$

Multiplication of Mixed Numbers by Mixed Numbers

To multiply a mixed number by a mixed number, write both mixed numbers as improper fractions. Use cancellation if possible. Then multiply the new numerators and denominators. Simplify.

Find: $3\frac{2}{3} \times 4\frac{1}{2}$

Write the mixed numbers as improper fractions.	Cancel.	Multiply the new numerators and denominators. Simplify.
$3\frac{2}{3} \times 4\frac{1}{2} = \frac{11}{3} \times \frac{9}{2}$	$\frac{11}{\cancel{3}_1} \times \frac{\cancel{9}^3}{2}$	$\frac{11 \times 3}{1 \times 2} = \frac{33}{2} = 16\frac{1}{2}$

Multiply. Simplify. Use cancellation if possible.

	a	b	c
1.	$3\frac{1}{5} \times 2\frac{1}{4} =$ $\frac{\cancel{16}^4}{5} \times \frac{9}{\cancel{4}_1} = \frac{36}{5} = 7\frac{1}{5}$	$1\frac{1}{2} \times 1\frac{1}{2} =$	$1\frac{2}{3} \times 1\frac{3}{5} =$
2.	$2\frac{1}{2} \times 3\frac{1}{3} =$	$4\frac{1}{3} \times 3\frac{3}{4} =$	$2\frac{3}{4} \times 2\frac{2}{3} =$
3.	$5\frac{1}{4} \times 3\frac{1}{2} =$	$4\frac{1}{2} \times 3\frac{1}{5} =$	$6\frac{3}{4} \times 8\frac{1}{3} =$
4.	$4\frac{4}{5} \times 3\frac{1}{8} =$	$4\frac{2}{7} \times 2\frac{1}{10} =$	$5\frac{5}{8} \times 2\frac{2}{3} =$
5.	$3\frac{3}{5} \times 3\frac{1}{3} =$	$2\frac{4}{10} \times 3\frac{1}{3} =$	$4\frac{4}{5} \times 1\frac{7}{8} =$

Problem-Solving Method: Solve Multi-step Problems

Babies gain an average of $2\frac{1}{5}$ pounds each month for the first three months after they are born. Matt weighs $7\frac{1}{2}$ pounds at birth. How much will he probably weigh in 3 months?

Understand the problem.

- **What do you want to know?**
  Matt's weight after 3 months

- **What information is given?**
  He weighs $7\frac{1}{2}$ pounds at birth.
  He gains about $2\frac{1}{5}$ pounds each of the 3 months.

Plan how to solve it.

- **What method can you use?**
  You can separate the problem into steps.

Solve it.

- **How can you use this method to solve the problem?**
  First find the total weight Matt will gain in the 3 months.
  Then add that total to his birth weight.

Step 1	Step 2
$2\frac{1}{5} \times 3 = \frac{11}{5} \times \frac{3}{1} = \frac{33}{5} = 6\frac{3}{5}$ **Total weight gain = $6\frac{3}{5}$ pounds**	$\begin{aligned} 7\frac{1}{2} &= \ 7\frac{5}{10} \\ + \ 6\frac{3}{5} &= \ 6\frac{6}{10} \\ \hline &= 13\frac{11}{10} = 14\frac{1}{10} \text{ pounds} \end{aligned}$

- **What is the answer?**
  Matt will probably weigh $14\frac{1}{10}$ pounds in 3 months.

Look back and check your answer.

- **Is your answer reasonable?**
  You can add to check your multiplication.
  The answer matches the sum.

$$7\frac{1}{2} + 2\frac{1}{5} + 2\frac{1}{5} + 2\frac{1}{5} = 14\frac{1}{10}$$

The answer matches the sum.
The answer is reasonable.

Separate each problem into steps to solve.

1. On average, a baby's head grows $\frac{1}{2}$ inch every month for the first 4 months after birth. Then, from 4 months old to 1 year old, it grows another 2 inches. How many inches does a baby's head grow the first year after it is born?
(1 year = 12 months)

Answer _____

2. Mei earns $8 an hour at the coffee shop. She worked $7\frac{1}{2}$ hours on Saturday and $5\frac{1}{4}$ hours on Sunday. How much money did she earn for the 2 days altogether?

Answer _____

3. The average person dreams for $\frac{1}{4}$ of the time he or she sleeps. If Anna sleeps for 8 hours, and Brian sleeps for 9 hours, how much longer does Brian dream?

Answer _____

4. Antoine mixed $1\frac{1}{4}$ gallons of blue paint with $\frac{4}{5}$ gallon of yellow paint to make green. Then he mixed $1\frac{3}{4}$ gallons of red paint with $\frac{1}{2}$ gallon of white paint to make pink. Which color did Antoine mix the most of, green or pink?

Answer _____

5. United States athletes set some top records for long jumps. The third longest was $29\frac{1}{12}$ feet. The second longest was $\frac{2}{3}$ foot longer than the third. The world's longest jump was $\frac{2}{3}$ foot longer than the second. Which of these jumps was the longest?

Answer _____

6. A recipe for 1 batch of sugar cookies needs $\frac{3}{4}$ tablespoon of vanilla. One batch of lemon cookies needs $\frac{1}{2}$ tablespoon of vanilla. If Ken makes 2 batches of sugar cookies and $\frac{1}{2}$ a batch of lemon cookies, how much vanilla does he need in all?

Answer _____

Finding Reciprocals

Dorren 2/22/19

To divide by a fraction, you need to know how to find reciprocals.
Reciprocals are numbers whose numerators and denominators have been inverted, or switched. The product of two reciprocals is 1.

$\frac{13}{+8}$

Write the reciprocals.

$\frac{3}{4}$ reciprocal $= \frac{4}{3}$	$\frac{1}{5}$ reciprocal $= \frac{5}{1} = 5$	$7 = \frac{7}{1}$ reciprocal $= \frac{1}{7}$

Write the reciprocal.

	a		b		c		d		e
1. $\frac{2}{3}$	$\frac{3}{2}$	$\frac{1}{6}$	$\frac{6}{1}$	$\frac{7}{8}$	$\frac{8}{7}$	$\frac{5}{9}$	$\frac{9}{5}$	8	$\frac{8}{1}$
2. $\frac{3}{5}$	$\frac{5}{3}$	$\frac{9}{13}$	$\frac{13}{9}$	$\frac{7}{4}$	$\frac{4}{7}$	25	$\frac{25}{1}$	$\frac{1}{4}$	$\frac{4}{1}$

Write as an improper fraction. Then write the reciprocal. *reciprille*

	a		b		c		d	
3. $4\frac{1}{3} =$	$\frac{13}{3}$	$\frac{3}{13}$	$2\frac{4}{5}$	$\frac{15}{5}$ $\frac{5}{9}$	$1\frac{7}{9}$	$\frac{16}{9}$ $\frac{9}{16}$	$5\frac{1}{4}$	$\frac{21}{4}$ $\frac{4}{21}$
4. $5\frac{1}{11}$	$\frac{56}{11}$	$\frac{11}{56}$	$1\frac{8}{13}$	$\frac{21}{13}$ $\frac{13}{21}$	$6\frac{1}{8}$	$\frac{49}{8}$ $\frac{8}{49}$	$3\frac{5}{6}$	$\frac{23}{6}$ $\frac{6}{2}$

Write the missing factor.

	a	b	c	d
5.	$\frac{7}{9} \times \frac{9}{7} = 1$	$\frac{1}{5} \times \frac{5}{1} = 1$	$9 \times \frac{9}{1} = 1$	$3\frac{1}{2} \times 3\frac{2}{1} =$

Division of Fractions by Fractions

Darren 2/2 4/19

To divide a fraction by a fraction, multiply by the reciprocal of the second fraction. Simplify the answer if needed. Remember, only the second fraction is inverted.

Find: $\frac{5}{8} \div \frac{3}{4}$

Multiply by the reciprocal of the second fraction.	Cancel.	Multiply the new numerators and denominators.
$\frac{5}{8} \div \frac{3}{4} = \frac{5}{8} \times \frac{4}{3}$	$\frac{5}{\underset{2}{8}} \times \frac{\overset{1}{4}}{3}$	$\frac{5 \times 1}{2 \times 3} = \frac{5}{6}$

Divide. Simplify.

             a   *b*

1. $\frac{2}{3} \div \frac{5}{7} = \frac{2}{3} \times \frac{7}{5} = \frac{2 \times 7}{3 \times 5} = \frac{14}{15}$ $\frac{3}{8} \div \frac{1}{3} = \frac{3}{8} \times \frac{3}{1} = \frac{3 \times 3}{8 \times 1} = \frac{9}{8}$

$\frac{\times \frac{5}{2}}{75}$

2. $\frac{8}{15} \div \frac{16}{45} = \frac{8}{15} \times$ ~~$\frac{7}{5}$~~ $= \frac{56}{75}$ $\frac{9}{16} \div \frac{3}{8} = \frac{9}{16} \times \frac{8}{3} = \frac{9 \times 8}{16 \times 3} = \frac{72}{48}$ $\frac{\overset{16}{y}\ \overset{1}{3}}{48}$

     a   *b*   *c*

3. $\frac{4}{5} \div \frac{1}{10} =$ $\frac{5}{12} \div \frac{3}{4} =$ $\frac{1}{5} \div \frac{1}{20} =$

4. $\frac{1}{4} \div \frac{4}{9} =$ $\frac{5}{8} \div \frac{5}{8} =$ $\frac{5}{12} \div \frac{3}{2} =$

5. $\frac{3}{10} \div \frac{1}{10} =$ $\frac{7}{12} \div \frac{3}{8} =$ $\frac{11}{32} \div \frac{5}{16} =$

6. $\frac{15}{16} \div \frac{3}{5} =$ $\frac{17}{18} \div \frac{2}{3} =$ $\frac{11}{12} \div \frac{1}{6} =$

Division of Fractions by Whole Numbers

To divide a fraction by a whole number, multiply by the reciprocal of the whole number. Simplify the quotient. Remember, the reciprocal of a whole number is 1 divided by that number.

Find: $\frac{3}{4} \div 12$

Multiply by the reciprocal of the whole number.	Cancel.	Multiply.
$\frac{3}{4} \times \frac{1}{12}$	$\frac{\cancel{3}^{1}}{4} \times \frac{1}{\cancel{12}_{4}}$	$\frac{1 \times 1}{4 \times 4} = \frac{1}{16}$

Divide. Simplify.

        a   *b*

1. $\frac{5}{8} \div 10 = \frac{\cancel{5}^{1}}{8} \times \frac{1}{\cancel{10}_{2}} = \frac{1 \times 1}{8 \times 2} = \frac{1}{16}$ $\frac{3}{4} \div 6 = \frac{3}{4} \times \frac{1}{6} =$

2. $\frac{3}{4} \div 2 = \frac{3}{4} \times \underline{\hspace{2cm}} = \underline{\hspace{2cm}}$ $\frac{7}{15} \div 7 = \frac{7}{15} \times \underline{\hspace{2cm}} = \underline{\hspace{2cm}}$

        a   *b*   *c*

3. $\frac{6}{7} \div 18 =$ $\frac{7}{10} \div 21 =$ $\frac{5}{12} \div 20 =$

4. $\frac{7}{8} \div 28 =$ $\frac{5}{6} \div 30 =$ $\frac{8}{15} \div 16 =$

5. $\frac{15}{16} \div 5 =$ $\frac{2}{15} \div 8 =$ $\frac{4}{13} \div 20 =$

6. $\frac{7}{10} \div 35 =$ $\frac{11}{12} \div 33 =$ $\frac{21}{25} \div 14 =$

Division of Whole Numbers by Fractions

To divide a whole number by a fraction, write the whole number as an improper fraction. Multiply by the reciprocal of the second fraction. Simplify the answer.

Find: $12 \div \frac{3}{4}$

Write the whole number as an improper fraction.	Multiply by the reciprocal of the second fraction.	Cancel.	Multiply and simplify.
$12 \div \frac{3}{4} = \frac{12}{1} \div \frac{3}{4}$	$\frac{12}{1} \times \frac{4}{3}$	$\overset{4}{\cancel{12}} \over 1} \times \frac{4}{\underset{1}{\cancel{3}}}$	$\frac{4 \times 4}{1 \times 1} = \frac{16}{1} = 16$

Divide. Simplify.

a

1. $10 \div \frac{4}{5} = \frac{10}{1} \div \frac{4}{5} = \frac{\overset{5}{\cancel{10}}}{1} \times \frac{5}{\underset{2}{\cancel{4}}} = \frac{25}{2} = 12\frac{1}{2}$

b

$5 \div \frac{2}{3} =$

2. $3 \div \frac{3}{4} =$ $3 \div \frac{6}{7} =$

3. $4 \div \frac{2}{7} =$ $6 \div \frac{2}{5} =$

4. $3 \div \frac{15}{16} =$ $27 \div \frac{9}{10} =$

5. $4 \div \frac{1}{2} =$ $2 \div \frac{2}{9} =$

6. $14 \div \frac{3}{7} =$ $8 \div \frac{2}{3} =$

Division of Mixed Numbers by Whole Numbers

To divide a mixed number by a whole number, write the mixed number as an improper fraction. Multiply by the reciprocal of the whole number. Simplify the answer.

Find: $2\frac{1}{3} \div 7$

Write the mixed number as an improper fraction.	Multiply by the reciprocal of the whole number.	Cancel.	Multiply and simplify.
$2\frac{1}{3} \div 7 = \frac{7}{3} \div \frac{7}{1}$	$\frac{7}{3} \times \frac{1}{7}$	$\overset{1}{\cancel{\frac{7}{3}}} \times \frac{1}{\cancel{7}}_{1}$	$\frac{1 \times 1}{3 \times 1} = \frac{1}{3}$

Divide. Simplify.

        a   *b*   *c*

1. $3\frac{1}{3} \div 5 =$ $2\frac{1}{2} \div 5 =$ $7\frac{1}{2} \div 3 =$

$\frac{\overset{2}{\cancel{10}}}{3} \div \frac{5}{1} = \frac{\cancel{10}}{3} \times \frac{1}{\cancel{5}}_{1} = \frac{2}{3}$

2. $6\frac{2}{3} \div 10 =$ $4\frac{1}{5} \div 3 =$ $5\frac{1}{4} \div 7 =$

3. $6\frac{2}{3} \div 5 =$ $4\frac{1}{6} \div 10 =$ $1\frac{7}{8} \div 5 =$

4. $7\frac{1}{5} \div 6 =$ $2\frac{1}{12} \div 15 =$ $8\frac{2}{3} \div 39 =$

5. $3\frac{4}{7} \div 10 =$ $4\frac{1}{8} \div 11 =$ $5\frac{1}{3} \div 24 =$

Division of Mixed Numbers by Fractions

To divide a mixed number by a fraction, write the mixed number as an improper fraction. Multiply by the reciprocal of the second fraction. Simplify the answer.

Find: $1\frac{3}{4} \div \frac{3}{8}$

Write the mixed number as an improper fraction.	Multiply by the reciprocal of the second fraction.	Cancel.	Multiply and simplify.
$1\frac{3}{4} \div \frac{3}{8} = \frac{7}{4} \div \frac{3}{8}$	$\frac{7}{4} \times \frac{8}{3}$	$\frac{7}{\underset{1}{4}} \times \frac{\overset{2}{8}}{3}$	$\frac{7 \times 2}{1 \times 3} = \frac{14}{3} = 4\frac{2}{3}$

Divide. Simplify.

	a	b	c
1.	$2\frac{1}{3} \div \frac{1}{3} =$	$4\frac{1}{2} \div \frac{1}{2} =$	$3\frac{1}{9} \div \frac{2}{9} =$

$$\frac{7}{3} \div \frac{1}{3} = \frac{7}{\underset{1}{3}} \times \frac{\overset{1}{3}}{1} = \frac{7}{1} = 7$$

2.	$6\frac{5}{8} \div \frac{3}{4} =$	$3\frac{5}{8} \div \frac{1}{4} =$	$1\frac{7}{12} \div \frac{5}{6} =$
3.	$5\frac{3}{4} \div \frac{1}{8} =$	$10\frac{4}{5} \div \frac{7}{10} =$	$2\frac{3}{8} \div \frac{19}{21} =$
4.	$3\frac{1}{7} \div \frac{4}{11} =$	$2\frac{3}{10} \div \frac{4}{5} =$	$5\frac{1}{7} \div \frac{5}{14} =$
5.	$2\frac{3}{4} \div \frac{8}{9} =$	$4\frac{7}{8} \div \frac{7}{8} =$	$4\frac{3}{5} \div \frac{7}{10} =$

Division of Mixed Numbers by Mixed Numbers

To divide a mixed number by a mixed number, write both mixed numbers as improper fractions. Multiply by the reciprocal of the second fraction. Simplify the answer.

Find: $4\frac{3}{4} \div 1\frac{1}{8}$

Write the mixed numbers as improper fractions.	Multiply by the reciprocal of the second fraction.	Cancel.	Multiply and simplify.
$4\frac{3}{4} \div 1\frac{1}{8} = \frac{19}{4} \div \frac{9}{8}$	$\frac{19}{4} \times \frac{8}{9}$	$\frac{19}{\overset{}{\underset{1}{4}}} \times \frac{\overset{2}{8}}{9}$	$\frac{19 \times 2}{1 \times 9} = \frac{38}{9} = 4\frac{2}{9}$

Divide. Simplify.

                   a   *b*

1. $4\frac{2}{3} \div 3\frac{1}{2} = \frac{14}{3} \div \frac{7}{2} = \frac{\overset{2}{14}}{3} \times \frac{2}{\underset{1}{7}} = \frac{4}{3} = 1\frac{1}{3}$ $16\frac{2}{3} \div 2\frac{1}{2} =$

2. $6\frac{2}{3} \div 6\frac{1}{4} =$ $6\frac{2}{3} \div 1\frac{1}{4} =$

3. $6\frac{2}{5} \div 5\frac{1}{3} =$ $1\frac{1}{5} \div 2\frac{1}{6} =$

4. $6\frac{2}{3} \div 2\frac{1}{8} =$ $3\frac{1}{10} \div 10\frac{1}{3} =$

5. $2\frac{1}{4} \div 3\frac{3}{8} =$ $2\frac{4}{5} \div 1\frac{2}{5} =$

6. $4\frac{2}{3} \div 5\frac{3}{5} =$ $1\frac{1}{9} \div 2\frac{2}{3} =$

Problem-Solving Method: Write a Number Sentence

Some people measure the height of a horse in hands. One inch equals $\frac{1}{4}$ hand. An average Clydesdale horse is 16 hands high. How tall is a Clydesdale in inches?

Understand the problem.

- **What do you want to know?**
  the height of a Clydesdale in inches

- **What information is given?**
  An average Clydesdale horse is 16 hands high.
  1 inch $= \frac{1}{4}$ hand

Plan how to solve it.

- **What method can you use?**
  You can write a number sentence to model the problem.

- **How can you use this method to solve the problem?**
  You want to know how many groups of $\frac{1}{4}$ hand can be divided into the total 16 hands. Write a division number sentence.

$$16 \quad \div \quad \frac{1}{4} \quad = \quad \underline{\hspace{2cm}}$$

total height   number of hands   total height
in hands   in 1 inch   in inches

- **What is the answer?**

$$16 \div \frac{1}{4} = \frac{16}{1} \times \frac{4}{1} = 64$$

An average Clydesdale horse is 64 inches tall.

Look back and check your answer.

- **Is your answer reasonable?**
  You can check division with multiplication.

$$64 \text{ inches} \times \frac{1}{4} = \frac{64}{1} \times \frac{1}{4} = \frac{64}{4} = 16 \text{ hands}$$

The product matches the dividend.
The answer is reasonable.

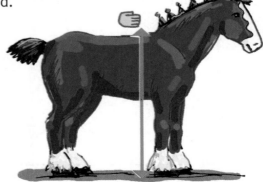

Write a number sentence to solve each problem.

1. Sam had $1\frac{3}{16}$ yards of ribbon. He cut it into pieces $\frac{1}{8}$ of a yard long. How many pieces did he cut?

   Answer _____

2. Fresh apples float because $\frac{1}{4}$ of their weight is air. If a bag of apples weighs $2\frac{1}{2}$ pounds, how many pounds is air?

   Answer _____

3. During its lifetime, one honeybee makes $\frac{1}{12}$ teaspoon of honey. How many honeybees are needed to make $\frac{1}{2}$ teaspoon of honey?

   Answer _____

4. Cheryl has 30 pounds of clay. Each of the refrigerator magnets she is making uses $\frac{3}{4}$ pound of clay. How many magnets can she make?

   Answer _____

5. Yuma, Arizona, and Las Vegas, Nevada, are the two driest cities in the United States. Yuma gets an average of $2\frac{2}{3}$ inches of rain each year. Las Vegas gets about $4\frac{1}{5}$ inches. How many inches does it rain each year in the two cities combined?

   Answer _____

6. The world's tallest dog was a Great Dane that was $3\frac{5}{11}$ feet tall. The world's smallest dog was a Yorkshire terrier. It was only $\frac{2}{9}$ foot tall. What was the difference between the heights of the two dogs?

   Answer _____

UNIT 3 Review

Write each whole number as a fraction.

	a	b	c	d	e
1.	$19 =$	$3 =$	$25 =$	$16 =$	$17 =$

Multiply. Use cancellation if possible. Simplify.

	a	b	c
2.	$\frac{2}{5} \times \frac{2}{3} =$	$\frac{2}{3} \times \frac{1}{7} =$	$\frac{1}{2} \times \frac{5}{8} =$
3.	$\frac{1}{2} \times \frac{3}{4} =$	$\frac{5}{6} \times \frac{3}{4} =$	$\frac{2}{8} \times \frac{1}{4} =$
4.	$\frac{15}{16} \times 4 =$	$12 \times \frac{3}{4} =$	$\frac{1}{6} \times 26 =$
5.	$20 \times \frac{2}{5} =$	$24 \times \frac{7}{10} =$	$\frac{2}{3} \times 15 =$
6.	$3\frac{1}{3} \times 4 =$	$9 \times 4\frac{2}{3} =$	$10\frac{1}{5} \times 4 =$
7.	$6\frac{1}{4} \times \frac{3}{5} =$	$\frac{3}{8} \times 4\frac{4}{5} =$	$\frac{1}{6} \times 2\frac{3}{8} =$
8.	$5\frac{1}{3} \times 3\frac{3}{8} =$	$4\frac{3}{5} \times 2\frac{3}{7} =$	$1\frac{1}{2} \times 8\frac{3}{4} =$
9.	$1\frac{4}{7} \times 4\frac{1}{2} =$	$3\frac{2}{3} \times 3\frac{1}{5} =$	$4\frac{1}{4} \times 6\frac{2}{3} =$

Write the reciprocal.

	a	b	c	d	e
10.	$\frac{1}{7}$ _____	$\frac{5}{12}$ _____	$\frac{4}{9}$ _____	$2\frac{3}{7}$ _____	$\frac{2}{15}$ _____

Divide. Use cancellation if possible. Simplify.

	a	b	c
11.	$\frac{1}{4} \div \frac{1}{8} =$	$\frac{3}{5} \div \frac{1}{5} =$	$\frac{3}{10} \div \frac{2}{7} =$
12.	$\frac{2}{3} \div \frac{3}{7} =$	$\frac{1}{9} \div \frac{4}{5} =$	$\frac{4}{11} \div \frac{1}{8} =$
13.	$\frac{13}{24} \div 6 =$	$\frac{5}{9} \div 18 =$	$\frac{6}{15} \div 5 =$
14.	$\frac{3}{4} \div 12 =$	$\frac{3}{25} \div 9 =$	$\frac{5}{6} \div 10 =$
15.	$15 \div \frac{3}{7} =$	$2 \div \frac{1}{12} =$	$7 \div \frac{4}{11} =$
16.	$7\frac{1}{5} \div 15 =$	$5\frac{3}{4} \div 12 =$	$2\frac{7}{8} \div 20 =$
17.	$12\frac{1}{2} \div 2\frac{3}{4} =$	$6\frac{2}{5} \div 5\frac{1}{3} =$	$4\frac{5}{6} \div 3\frac{4}{7} =$
18.	$2\frac{1}{9} \div 7\frac{3}{8} =$	$8\frac{1}{3} \div 1\frac{3}{5} =$	$9\frac{4}{6} \div 3\frac{3}{9} =$

UNIT 3 Review

Separate each problem into steps to solve.

19. Sara made hot chocolate mix to give to her neighbors. She mixed $4\frac{1}{4}$ cups of sugar with $2\frac{1}{4}$ cups of cocoa. Then she poured $1\frac{1}{2}$ cups of the mix in each jar. How many jars did she fill?

Answer _____

20. The eucalyptus is the world's fastest growing tree. It grows an average of $2\frac{1}{2}$ centimeters every day. If a eucalyptus tree is 50 centimeters tall when it is planted, how tall will it be in 5 days?

Answer _____

Write a number sentence to solve each problem.

21. Maya runs $3\frac{1}{2}$ miles around the track every morning. One lap around the track is $\frac{1}{8}$ mile. How many times does she run around the track every morning?

Answer _____

22. In the frog-jumping contest, the winner jumped $10\frac{4}{5}$ feet. The second-placed frog jumped $9\frac{3}{4}$ feet. What was the difference in the length of their jumps?

Answer _____

23. Will completed $\frac{1}{3}$ of his passes during the football season. If he threw 90 passes, how many did he complete?

Answer _____

Reading and Writing Decimals

To read a **decimal**, read it as a whole number.
Then name the place value of the last digit.

Read and write 0.246 as two hundred forty-six thousandths.

To read a decimal that has a whole number part,
- read the whole number part.
- read the **decimal point** as *and*.
- read the decimal part as a whole number then name the place value of the last digit.

Read and write 37.05 as thirty-seven and five hundredths.

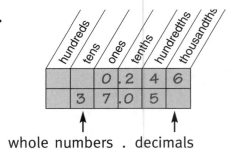

whole numbers . decimals

Write as a decimal.

          a   *b*

1. two tenths _____ *0.2* _____   two hundredths _____

2. two thousandths _____   six and two hundredths _____

3. twenty-one thousandths _____   one and one thousandths _____

Write each decimal in words.

4. 8.07 _____ *eight and seven hundredths* _____

5. 53.009 _____

6. 76.12 _____

Write each money amount with a dollar sign and a decimal point.

       a   *b*   *c*

7. six dollars _____ *$6.00* _____   sixty cents _____   six cents _____

8. ninety-nine cents _____   twelve cents _____   thirty-one dollars _____

9. four hundred twenty dollars and five cents _____

10. three thousand dollars and ninety-eight cents _____

Comparing and Ordering Decimals

To compare two decimal numbers, begin at the left.
Compare the digits in each place.

The symbol > means **is greater than.** $0.54 > $0.37

The symbol < means **is less than.**   0.829 < 0.84

The symbol = means **is equal to.**   0.23 = 0.230

Compare: 4.1 and 4.3

4 . 1
4 . 3

The ones digits
are the same.
Compare
the tenths.

1 < 3, so 4.1 < 4.3

Compare: $0.52 and $0.09

$ 0 . 5 2
$ 0 . 0 9

The ones
digits are
the same.
Compare
the tenths.

5 > 0, so $0.52 > $0.09

Compare: 7.5 and 7.52

7 . 5 0
7 . 5 2

The ones and
tenths digits
are the same.
Write a zero.
Compare the
hundredths.

0 < 2, so 7.5 < 7.52

Compare. Write <, >, or =. Write in zeros as needed.

	a	b	c

1. 0.6 ___<___ 0.8   0.4 _____ 0.44   0.061 _____ 0.16

2. $5.25 _____ $5.50 $4.99 _____ $4.98 $0.83 _____ $0.65

3. 8.9 _____ 8.90   1.36 _____ 1.365   0.921 _____ 0.29

Write in order from least to greatest.

a   b

4. 0.42   0.4   0.2 ___0.2   0.4   0.42___   0.31   0.13   0.031 _____

0 . 4 2
0 . 4
0 . 2

5. 8.1   0.081   0.18 _____   275   2.75   27.5 _____

Fraction and Decimal Equivalents

Sometimes you will need to either change a decimal to a fraction or a fraction to a decimal.

To write a decimal as a fraction, identify the value of the last place in the decimal. Use this place value to write the denominator.

Decimal		Fraction or Mixed Number
0.3	=	$\frac{3}{10}$
0.05	=	$\frac{5}{100}$
0.036	=	$\frac{36}{1,000}$
1.98	=	$\frac{198}{100}$ or $1\frac{98}{100}$

To write a fraction that has a denominator of 10, 100, or 1,000 as a decimal, write the digits from the numerator. Then write the decimal point.

Fraction or Mixed Number		Decimal
$\frac{7}{10}$	=	0.7
$\frac{82}{100}$	=	0.82
$\frac{125}{1,000}$	=	0.125
$\frac{805}{100}$ or $8\frac{05}{100}$	=	8.05

Write each decimal as a fraction.

	a	b	c	d
1.	0.5 $\frac{5}{10}$	0.4 _____	0.2 _____	0.6 _____
2.	0.05 _____	0.04 _____	0.02 _____	0.06 _____

Write each decimal as a mixed number.

	a	b	c	d
3.	2.1 $2\frac{1}{10}$	45.9 _____	31.6 _____	99.9 _____
4.	3.94 _____	6.25 _____	12.54 _____	10.01 _____

Write each fraction as a decimal.

	a	b	c	d
5.	$\frac{9}{10}$ 0.9	$\frac{3}{10}$ _____	$\frac{1}{10}$ _____	$\frac{8}{10}$ _____
6.	$\frac{7}{100}$ _____	$\frac{91}{100}$ _____	$\frac{63}{1,000}$ _____	$\frac{527}{1,000}$ _____
7.	$\frac{67}{10}$ _____	$\frac{42}{10}$ _____	$\frac{87}{10}$ _____	$\frac{76}{10}$ _____
8.	$\frac{204}{100}$ _____	$\frac{610}{100}$ _____	$\frac{1,754}{1,000}$ _____	$\frac{3,062}{1,000}$ _____

Fraction and Decimal Equivalents

Not all fractions can be changed to **decimal form** easily. To write fractions that have denominators other than 10, 100, or 1,000 as decimals, first write an equivalent fraction that has a denominator of 10, 100, or 1,000. Then write the equivalent fraction as a decimal.

Remember, not all fractions have simple decimal equivalents.

Examples: $\frac{2}{11} = 0.1818\ldots$ and $\frac{2}{3} = 0.666\ldots$

Write $\frac{3}{4}$ as a decimal.

Write $\frac{3}{4}$ with 100 as the denominator.	Write the fraction as a decimal.
$\frac{3}{4} = \frac{3 \times 25}{4 \times 25} = \frac{75}{100}$	$= 0.75$

Write $2\frac{1}{2}$ as a decimal.

Write $2\frac{1}{2}$ as an improper fraction.	Write the new fraction with 10 as the denominator.	Write the fraction as a decimal.
$2\frac{1}{2} = \frac{5}{2}$	$\frac{5}{2} = \frac{5 \times 5}{2 \times 5} = \frac{25}{10}$	$= 2.5$

Write each fraction as a decimal.

	a	b	c
1.	$\frac{2}{5} = \frac{2 \times 2}{5 \times 2} = \frac{4}{10} = 0.4$	$\frac{1}{4} =$ _____	$\frac{1}{2} =$ _____
2.	$\frac{5}{20} =$ _____	$\frac{5}{25} =$ _____	$\frac{7}{20} =$ _____
3.	$\frac{17}{4} =$ _____	$\frac{7}{2} =$ _____	$\frac{13}{5} =$ _____
4.	$\frac{37}{25} =$ _____	$\frac{43}{20} =$ _____	$\frac{79}{25} =$ _____

Write each mixed number as a decimal.

	a	b
5.	$6\frac{1}{5} = \frac{31}{5} = \frac{31 \times 2}{5 \times 2} = \frac{62}{10} = 6.2$	$10\frac{3}{4} =$ _____
6.	$3\frac{5}{25} =$ _____	$4\frac{7}{25} =$ _____
7.	$13\frac{1}{2} =$ _____	$7\frac{2}{5} =$ _____

Problem-Solving Method: Use Logic

Christine Arron, Florence Griffith-Joyner, and Marion Jones are three of the fastest-running women on Earth. Their times for the 100-meter dash are 10.73 seconds, $10\frac{13}{20}$ seconds, and 10.49 seconds. Jones' time has a 6 in the tenths place. Griffith-Joyner is faster than Arron. Who is the fastest-running woman on Earth?

Understand the problem.

- **What do you want to know?**
  who the fastest-running woman on Earth is

- **What information do you know?**
  Their times are 10.73 seconds, $10\frac{13}{20}$ seconds, and 10.49 seconds.
  The fastest time is the smallest number.
  Clue 1: Jones' time has a 6 in the tenths place.
  Clue 2: Griffith-Joyner is faster than Arron.

Plan how to solve it.

- **What method can you use?**
  You can organize all the possibilities in a table.
  Then you can use logic to match the clues to the possibilities.

Solve it.

- **How can you use this method to solve the problem?**
  First, change all the times to decimals so they can be compared.
  Since each of the runners has one time, there can only be one **YES** in each row and column.

	10.73	$10\frac{13}{20} = 10.65$	10.49
Arron	**YES**	no	no
Griffith-Joyner	no	no	**YES**
Jones	no	**YES**	no

- **What is the answer?**
  Florence Griffith-Joyner is the fastest-running woman on Earth.

Look back and check your answer.

- **Is your answer reasonable?**
  Clue 1: Jones' time has a 6 in the tenths place.
  Clue 2: Griffith-Joyner is faster than Arron.

  Check:
  10.**6**5
  $10.49 < 10.73$

  The answer matches the clues.
  The answer is reasonable.

Use logic to solve each problem.

1. Three of the largest earthquakes ever recorded took place in Chile, Russia, and Alaska. They measured $9\frac{1}{10}$, 9.5, and $9\frac{1}{5}$ on the Richter scale. The largest earthquake was in Chile. The earthquake in Russia was smaller than the one in Alaska. What did the three earthquakes measure on the Richter scale?

Chile _____

Russia _____

Alaska _____

2. The National Park Service has measured the Statue of Liberty's hand, face, and the tablet she holds. Their lengths are 16.42 feet, $17\frac{1}{4}$ feet, and 25.58 feet. Her hand is the shortest of the three. The length of her face has a 5 in the hundredths place. What are the lengths of the Statue of Liberty's hand, face, and tablet?

hand _____

face _____

tablet _____

3. Alpha Centauri, Barnard's Star, and Proxima Centauri are the three closest stars to Earth. Their distances from Earth are 5.98 light years, $4\frac{7}{20}$ light years, and $4\frac{11}{50}$ light years. Barnard's Star is farthest from Earth. Alpha Centauri's distance from Earth has a 3 in the tenths place. What is the closest star to Earth?

Answer _____

Rounding Decimals

Round decimals to estimate how many. You can use a number line to round decimals.

Remember, when a number is halfway, always round up.

Round 31.2 to the nearest one.

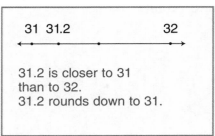

31.2 is closer to 31 than to 32.
31.2 rounds down to 31.

Round $4.67 to the nearest dollar.

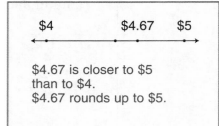

$4.67 is closer to $5 than to $4.
$4.67 rounds up to $5.

Round 6.15 to the nearest tenth.

6.1   6.15   6.2

6.15 is halfway between 6.1 and 6.2.
6.15 rounds up to 6.2.

Round to the nearest one.

	a	b	c	d
1.	4.4 ___4___	3.6 _____	2.5 _____	8.4 _____
2.	43.7 _____	51.5 _____	44.6 _____	73.1 _____
3.	6.39 _____	8.76 _____	5.02 _____	9.93 _____

Round each amount to the nearest dollar.

	a	b	c	d
4.	$3.92 ___$4___	$25.47 _____	$7.92 _____	$6.35 _____
5.	$8.04 _____	$2.56 _____	$9.53 _____	$62.06 _____
6.	$1.21 _____	$6.49 _____	$2.95 _____	$8.50 _____

Round to the nearest tenth.

	a	b	c	d
7.	0.58 ___0.6___	0.91 _____	0.64 _____	0.79 _____
8.	4.08 _____	8.67 _____	2.34 _____	9.33 _____
9.	39.96 _____	25.81 _____	72.02 _____	21.63 _____

Addition and Subtraction of Decimals

To add or subtract decimals, line up the decimal points. Write zeros as needed. Then add or subtract the same way as whole numbers.

Find: 8.3 + 5.96

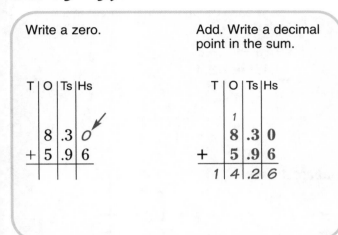

Write a zero.	Add. Write a decimal point in the sum.

T	O	Ts	Hs
	8	.3	0
+ 5	.9	6	

T	O	Ts	Hs
	1		
	8	.3	0
+	5	.9	6
1	4	.2	6

Find: 39.2 − 26.71

Write a zero.	Regroup. Subtract. Write a decimal point in the difference.

T	O	Ts	Hs
3	9	.2	0
− 2	6	.7	1

T	O	Ts	Hs
		11	
	8	X	10
3	9	.2	0
− 2	6	.7	1
1	2	.4	9

Add or subtract. Write zeros as needed.

          a   *b*   *c*   *d*

1.

a)
T	O	Ts
1	1	
1	6	.2
+2	4	.9
4	1	.1

b)
T	O	Ts
5	0	.6
+3	8	.4

c)
T	O	Ts
	12	
6	2	11
7	3	X
−2	5	.3
4	7	.8

d)
T	O	Ts	Hs
$4	8	.5	0
− 3	0	.6	3

2.

a) 2.3 5 6
  +8.6 7 9

b) 4.6 2 9
  +3.4 7 5

c) 2 4.6 1
  −   2.8

d) 8 7.5 9
  −4 9

3.

a) $ 4 5.8 5
  +   3 2.1 4

b) $ 2 6.1 8
  +   1 3.7 5

c) 3.7 5 7
  −0.5 0 9

d) 6 1.0 0 5
  −5 7.3 7 6

4.

a) 2 8.2 4
  1 6.4 5
  +1 4.2 3

b) 7 8.0 9
  2 5.1 0
  +2 1 8.4 5

c) 8
  −0.5 2 9

d) 9 6
  −   4.0 0 1

Estimation of Decimal Sums and Differences

To estimate a decimal sum or difference, first round the decimals to the same place value. Then add or subtract the rounded numbers.

Estimate: 7.13 + 2.89

Round each decimal to the nearest one. Add.

$$7.13 \rightarrow 7$$
$$+2.89 \rightarrow +3$$
$$\overline{10}$$

Estimate: 9.26 − 3.42

Round each decimal to the nearest tenth. Subtract.

$$9.76 \rightarrow 9.8$$
$$-3.42 \rightarrow -3.4$$
$$\overline{6.4}$$

Estimate each sum or difference by rounding to the nearest one.

	a	*b*	*c*
1.	$7.3 \rightarrow 7$ $+0.6 \rightarrow +1$ $\overline{8}$	$\$\ 2.5\ 6 \rightarrow$ $+\ \ 3.8\ 9 \rightarrow$	$\$\ 1\ 3.8\ 4 \rightarrow$ $+\ \ \ \ \ \ 7.6\ 3 \rightarrow$
2.	$5.4 \rightarrow$ $-4.6 \rightarrow$	$\$\ 6.1\ 8 \rightarrow$ $-\ \ \ 2.5\ 9 \rightarrow$	$\$\ 8\ 2.6\ 4 \rightarrow$ $-\ \ \ \ 3\ 3.2\ 1 \rightarrow$
3.	$2.9\ 4 \rightarrow$ $+3.8 \rightarrow$	$7.6 \rightarrow$ $+5.2\ 7 \rightarrow$	$5\ 3.8\ 7 \rightarrow$ $+1\ 2.9 \rightarrow$

Estimate each sum or difference by rounding to the nearest tenth.

	a	*b*	*c*
4.	$3.6\ 4 \rightarrow 3.6$ $+2.7\ 8 \rightarrow +2.8$	$5.4\ 5 \rightarrow$ $+1.7\ 4 \rightarrow$	$2\ 7.2\ 6 \rightarrow$ $+1\ 4.3\ 5 \rightarrow$
5.	$5\ 3.8\ 7 \rightarrow$ $+\ \ 6\ 2.6 \rightarrow$	$4\ 8.6 \rightarrow$ $-1\ 2.2\ 3 \rightarrow$	$2.6 \rightarrow$ $-0.5\ 9\ 4 \rightarrow$

Problem-Solving Method: Work Backwards

Jerome has $646.15 in his bank account. During the last two weeks, he withdrew $115.28, deposited $83.30, and withdrew $62.97. How much did Jerome have in his account two weeks ago?

Understand the problem.

- **What do you want to know?**
  How much money was in Jerome's account two weeks ago?

- **What information is given?**
  There is $646.15 in the account now.
  He withdrew $115.28, deposited $83.30, and withdrew $62.97.

Plan how to solve it.

- **What method can you use?**
  You can work backwards. Work from the money in the account now to find the money in the account two weeks ago.

Solve it.

- **How can you use this method to solve the problem?**
  Addition and subtraction are opposite operations. So, add the amounts withdrawn and subtract the amount deposited.

$$
\begin{array}{rl}
\$646.15 & \rightarrow \text{ amount in bank now} \\
+\ 115.28 & \rightarrow \text{ amount withdrawn} \\
\hline
\$761.43 & \\
-\ \ \ 83.30 & \rightarrow \text{ amount deposited} \\
\hline
\$678.13 & \\
+\ \ \ 62.97 & \rightarrow \text{ amount withdrawn} \\
\hline
\$741.10 &
\end{array}
$$

- **What is the answer?**
  Two weeks ago, Jerome had $741.10 in his account.

Look back and check your answer.

- **Is your answer reasonable?**
  You can check by working forwards from the amount of money in the account two weeks ago.

$$
\begin{array}{r}
\$741.10 \\
-\ 115.28 \\
\hline
\$625.82 \\
+\ \ \ 83.30 \\
\hline
\$709.12 \\
-\ \ \ 62.97 \\
\hline
\$646.15
\end{array}
$$

The amount in his account and the answer match.
The answer is reasonable.

Work backwards to solve each problem.

1. Anne has $85.97 left over from her paycheck. She spent $117.43 for insurance and $49.05 for her phone bill. Then she spent $37.28 for groceries. How much was Anne's paycheck?

Answer_____

2. Sue is guessing her grandfather's age. He tells her that when you divide his age by 3 and then subtract 7, the result is 13. How old is Sue's grandfather?

Answer_____

3. Half of the students in Linda's class are girls. Half of the girls have blue eyes. Seven girls have blue eyes. How many students are in Linda's class?

Answer_____

4. Gabrielle used 18.5 centimeters of wire to make a bracelet. Then she made 2 earrings using 4.75 centimeters of wire for each one. She had 26.38 centimeters of wire left over. How much wire did Gabrielle start with?

Answer_____

5. The park cleanup started at 9:00 A.M. By noon, there were three times more people than had started. At 12:30, another 12 people arrived. Now there are 42 people in all. How many people started at 9:00 A.M.?

Answer_____

Write as a decimal.

a   b

1. sixty-seven thousandths _____   seventy-six hundredths _____

Write each decimal in words.

2. 42.615 _____

3. 0.078 _____

Write each money amount with a dollar sign and a decimal point.

4. sixty-eight dollars and twenty-seven cents _____

5. four hundred five dollars and three cents _____

Compare. Write <, >, or =. Write in zeros as needed.

a   b   c

6. 0.52 _____ 0.25   0.213 _____ 0.123   1.806 _____ 1.860

Write in order from least to greatest.

a   b

7. 0.5   0.052   0.25 _____   0.19   0.91   0.019 _____

Write each decimal as a fraction.

a   b   c   d

8. 0.3 _____   0.25 _____   0.07 _____   0.8 _____

Write each decimal as a mixed number.

a   b   c   d

9. 1.75 _____   5.2 _____   24.06 _____   16.75 _____

Write each fraction as a decimal.

a   b   c   d

10. $\frac{108}{100}$ _____ $\frac{7}{10}$ _____ $\frac{3}{5}$ _____ $\frac{11}{25}$ _____

Write each mixed number as a decimal.

a   b   c   d

11. $2\frac{7}{10}$ _____ $5\frac{3}{5}$ _____ $10\frac{1}{4}$ _____ $8\frac{3}{4}$ _____

Round to the nearest one.

	a	b	c	d
12.	7.6 _____	2.2 _____	3.8 _____	0.5 _____

Round each amount to the nearest dollar.

	a	b	c	d
13.	$7.95 _____	$4.27 _____	$9.03 _____	$15.49 _____

Round to the nearest tenth.

	a	b	c	d
14.	0.38 _____	0.19 _____	5.12 _____	72.09 _____

Add or subtract. Write zeros as needed.

	a	b	c	d
15.	4 2.7 +6 8.9	3.0 0 1 +0.9 5 7	$ 2 9.9 5 + 5 6.4 9	6 8.5 + 0.8 1 4

	a	b	c	d
16.	$ 1 6.1 5 3 9.0 6 + 3 4.7 9	1 −0.8 1	4 0 − 0.3 6 1	1 1 3.5 3 6.9 +2 0 7.4 6

Estimate each sum or difference by rounding to the nearest one.

	a	b	c	d
17.	4.1 → +9.8 →	6.5 → +3.7 →	9 4.7 → −1 6.4 →	1 1.3 2 → − 8.2 →

Estimate each sum or difference by rounding to the nearest tenth.

	a	b	c	d
18.	1.3 6 → +8.2 5 →	5.6 4 → +7.0 2 →	6.7 9 → −4.1 4 →	2 5.6 8 → −1 2.4 9 →

Use logic to solve each problem.

19. Donovan Bailey, Leroy Burrell, and Carl Lewis are among the fastest-running men on Earth. Their times for the 100-meter dash are 9.86 seconds, $10\frac{17}{20}$ seconds, and 9.84 seconds. Burrell's time has a 5 in the hundredths place. Bailey is faster than Lewis. Whose time is the fastest?

Answer _____

20. The three tallest trees in the United States measure 100.3 meters, 95.4 meters, and $83\frac{22}{25}$ meters. One of the trees is a Douglas fir. The other two trees are a redwood and a giant sequoia. The sequoia has a 4 in the tenths place. The redwood is not the tallest. What are the heights of the three trees?

Douglas fir _____

Redwood _____

Giant sequoia _____

Work backwards to solve each problem.

21. Celia's model train set now has 68.3 feet of tracks. After she bought it, she added 24.65 feet of tracks. But it was too long for the room. She then took off 9.7 feet. How many feet of tracks came with Celia's train set when she bought it?

Answer _____

22. Sean spent a total of $106.43 for the team party. He paid $6.98 for invitations and $74.25 for food and drinks. He spent the rest of the money on decorations. How much did Sean pay for the decorations?

Answer _____

unit 5
multiplication and division of decimals

Multiplying by Powers of 10

To multiply decimals by **powers of ten,** move the decimal point in the product to the right as many places as there are zeros in the multiplier.

Remember, sometimes you might need to write zeros in the product in order to move the decimal point the correct number of places.

Study these examples.

$10 \times 0.24 = 2.4$	$100 \times 0.54 = 54$	$1{,}000 \times 0.36 = 360$
$10 \times 0.245 = 2.45$	$100 \times 0.545 = 54.5$	$1{,}000 \times 0.367 = 367$
$10 \times 2.4 = 24$	$100 \times 5.4 = 540$	$1{,}000 \times 3.670 = 3{,}670$
$10 \times 2.04 = 20.4$	$100 \times 5.04 = 504$	$1{,}000 \times 3.067 = 3{,}067$

Multiply. Write zeros as needed.

	a	b	c
1.	$0.58 \times 10 = \underline{\quad 5.8 \quad}$	$5.8 \times 10 = \underline{\qquad}$	$0.058 \times 10 = \underline{\qquad}$
2.	$7.5 \times 10 = \underline{\qquad}$	$0.83 \times 10 = \underline{\qquad}$	$4.6 \times 10 = \underline{\qquad}$
3.	$2.8 \times 100 = \underline{\qquad}$	$0.7 \times 100 = \underline{\qquad}$	$0.07 \times 100 = \underline{\qquad}$
4.	$4.6 \times 1{,}000 = \underline{\qquad}$	$6.2 \times 1{,}000 = \underline{\qquad}$	$0.075 \times 1{,}000 = \underline{\qquad}$
5.	$3.1 \times 10 = \underline{\qquad}$	$3.1 \times 100 = \underline{\qquad}$	$3.15 \times 1{,}000 = \underline{\qquad}$

Multiplying Decimals by Whole Numbers

To multiply decimals by whole numbers, multiply the same way as whole numbers.
Place the decimal point in the product by counting the numbers of decimal places in each factor.
The product will have the same number of decimal places.

Find: 18 × 2.3

Multiply. Write the decimal point in the product.

```
      2.3          1 decimal place
  ×   18         +0 decimal places
    184
     23
    41.4           1 decimal place
```

Find: 63 × 0.128

Multiply. Write the decimal point in the product.

```
    0.128          3 decimal places
  ×    63        +0 decimal places
    384
    768
   8.064           3 decimal places
```

Multiply. Write zeros as needed.

a	b	c	d

1.

```
a            b            c            d
  0.2          0.2 4        4.7          3.0 9 2
×   8        ×     4      ×   5        ×       6
  1.6
```

2.

```
    3 2        4 0 7        0.2 3 1        4 3 7
× 0.0 4      ×   2.8      ×     4 7      × 0.0 0 2
```

3.

```
  3.0 0 2      0.2 0 5        3 6 8        1.1 0 1
×     2 6      ×   3 5      × 0.0 3 2      ×   8 0 9
```

Line up the digits. Then find the products. Write zeros as needed.

       a   *b*   *c*

4. 41 × 15.4 = _____   16 × 4.3 = _____   112 × 448.5 = _____

```
   1 5.4
×    4 1
```

Multiplying Decimals by Decimals

To multiply decimals by decimals, multiply the same way as whole numbers. Place the decimal point in the product by counting the number of decimal places in each factor. The product will have the same number of decimal places.

Remember, sometimes you might need to write a zero in the product in order to place the decimal point correctly.

Find: 0.92×15.4

Multiply. Write the decimal point in the product.

```
   0.92          2 places
 ×15.4          +1 place
  368
  460
  092
 14.168          3 places
```

Find: 0.49×0.05

Multiply. Write the decimal point in the product.

```
   0.49          2 places
 × 0.05         +2 places
   245
   000
 0.0245          4 places
```
└─ Write a zero.

Multiply. Write zeros as needed.

a	b	c	d

1.
```
   0.5          0.6          5.2          9.6
  ×0.8         ×0.9         ×0.7         ×0.4
  0.4 0
```

2.
```
  0.6 2        0.1 2        0.0 5        0.1 6
  × 0.5        ×  0.3       ×  0.6       ×  0.2
```

3.
```
  0.4 8        0.7 6        0.5 6        0.2 4
  ×6.9 5       ×4 3.5       ×9.1 2       ×1 8.7
```

Line up the digits. Then find the products. Write zeros as needed.

a	b	c

4. $0.137 \times 0.06 =$ _____ $1.284 \times 0.48 =$ _____ $4.507 \times 0.52 =$ _____

```
   0.137
  ×0.06
```

Problem-Solving Method: Identify Extra Information

The planet Mercury is 36,000,000 miles from the sun. It orbits, or circles, the sun faster than any other planet. At a speed of 29.76 miles per second, it only takes Mercury 87.969 days to orbit the sun. How far does Mercury travel in 1 minute?

Understand the problem.

- **What do you want to know?**
  how far Mercury travels in 1 minute (60 seconds)

- **What information is given?**
  Mercury's distance from the sun, the miles per second, and the days to complete a full orbit

Plan how to solve it.

- **What method can you use?**
  You can identify extra information that is not needed to solve the problem.

Solve it.

- **How can you use this method to solve the problem?**
  Reread the problem. Cross out any unnecessary facts. Then you can focus on the needed facts to solve the problem.

  > ~~The planet Mercury is 36,000,000 miles from the sun. It orbits, or circles, the sun faster than any other planet.~~ At a speed of 29.76 miles per second, ~~it only takes Mercury 87.969 days to orbit the sun.~~ How far does Mercury travel in 1 minute?

- **What is the answer?**

  $29.76 \times 60 = 1{,}785.6$

  In 1 minute, Mercury travels 1,785.6 miles.

Look back and check your answer.

- **Is your answer reasonable?**
  You can estimate to check your answer.

  $30 \times 60 = 1{,}800$

  The estimate is close to the answer.
  The answer is reasonable.

In each problem, cross out the extra information. Then solve the problem.

1. Earth is 92.96 million miles from the sun. It orbits the sun in about 365.26 days, traveling at an average speed of 18.51 miles per second. How far does Earth travel in 1 minute? (60 seconds)

   Answer _____

2. Fleas can jump up to 150 times the length of their bodies. This is equivalent to a person jumping nearly 1,000 feet. The average flea is about 0.2 inch long. How high can it jump?

   Answer _____

3. Fingernails grow about 0.004 inch a day. After not cutting his nails for 44 years, a man in India has the world's longest nails. His thumbnail is 4.67 feet long. How many inches do fingernails grow in 1 week? (7 days)

   Answer _____

4. Every day, 274,000 carats of diamonds are mined. One carat is 0.02 grams. The Cullinan Diamond is the largest diamond ever discovered. It is 3,106 carats. How many grams does the Cullinan Diamond weigh?

   Answer _____

5. The movie *Forrest Gump* earned a total of $679.7 million worldwide. $329.7 million of that total was made in the United States. *Forrest Gump* was nominated for 13 Academy Awards and won 6. How much of its total earnings were made outside the U.S.?

   Answer _____

6. At 179.6 feet, the "Rattler" is one of the world's tallest wooden roller coasters. Each ride is 2.25 minutes long. "Superman the Escape" is one of the world's tallest steel roller coasters, at 415 feet. Its ride lasts 0.467 minutes. How much longer is a ride on the "Rattler" than on "Superman"?

   Answer _____

Dividing by Powers of 10

To divide a decimal by a power of ten, move the decimal point in the dividend to the left as many places as there are zeros in the divisor.

Remember, sometimes you might need to write zeros in the quotient in order to correctly insert the decimal point.

Study these examples.

$0.75 \div 10 = 0.075$

$0.715 \div 10 = 0.0715$

$7.5 \div 10 = 0.75$

$7.05 \div 10 = 0.705$

$0.35 \div 100 = 0.0035$

$0.315 \div 100 = 0.00315$

$3.5 \div 100 = 0.035$

$3.05 \div 100 = 0.0305$

$0.91 \div 1,000 = 0.00091$

$0.315 \div 1,000 = 0.000315$

$3.5 \div 1,000 = 0.0035$

$3.05 \div 1,000 = 0.00305$

Divide. Write zeros as needed.

	a	b	c
1.	$6.89 \div 10 = \underline{\quad 0.689 \quad}$	$0.7 \div 10 = \underline{\qquad}$	$0.56 \div 10 = \underline{\qquad}$
2.	$12.3 \div 10 = \underline{\qquad}$	$0.49 \div 10 = \underline{\qquad}$	$8.1 \div 10 = \underline{\qquad}$
3.	$14.11 \div 100 = \underline{\qquad}$	$0.03 \div 100 = \underline{\qquad}$	$2.89 \div 100 = \underline{\qquad}$
4.	$37.737 \div 1,000 = \underline{\qquad}$	$9.91 \div 1,000 = \underline{\qquad}$	$134.2 \div 1,000 = \underline{\qquad}$
5.	$0.039 \div 10 = \underline{\qquad}$	$\div 100 = \underline{\qquad}$	$7.15 \div 1,000 = \underline{\qquad}$

Dividing Decimals by Whole Numbers

To divide a decimal by a whole number, write the decimal
point in the quotient directly above the decimal in the dividend.
Then divide the same way as you divide whole numbers.

Find: $11.88 ÷ 12

Write a decimal
point in the quotient.

$$12\overline{)\$11.88}$$

Divide.

$$\begin{array}{r} \$0.99 \\ 12\overline{)\$11.88} \\ -\ \ 0 \\ \hline 118 \\ -\ 108 \\ \hline 108 \\ -108 \\ \hline 0 \end{array}$$

Divide.

a
1.
$$\begin{array}{r} 2.2 \\ 3\overline{)6.6} \\ -6 \\ \hline 0\ 6 \\ -0\ 6 \\ \hline 0 \end{array}$$

b
$$4\overline{)18.4}$$
2.6
16
2.4
24

c $64
6.4
$$9\overline{)\$5.76}$$
54
36
36

d
1.6
$$8\overline{)12.8}$$
8
48
$26

2.
r 2
1.2
$$22\overline{)26.4}$$
22
4 4
4 4
0

b 2
$$19\overline{)96.9}$$

c
$$45\overline{)234.0}$$

d
.26
$$25\overline{)\$6.50}$$
2 66   50
3 75
4 100   150
5   125 150
6   150

Set up the problems. Then find the quotients.

a
3. 37.68 ÷ 60 = _____

$$60\overline{)37.68}$$

b
543.20 ÷ 10 = _____

c
31.35 ÷ 57 = _____

Dividing Decimals by Decimals

To divide a decimal by a decimal, change the divisor to a whole number by moving the decimal point. Move the decimal point in the dividend the same number of places. Then divide.

Remember, write a decimal point in the quotient directly above the position of the *new* decimal point in the dividend.

Find: 8.64 ÷ 0.6

Move each decimal point 1 place.   Divide.

$$0.6\overline{)8.6\,4}$$

$$\begin{array}{r} 1\ 4.4 \\ 6\overline{)8\ 6.4} \\ -6 \\ \hline 2\ 6 \\ -2\ 4 \\ \hline 2\ 4 \\ -2\ 4 \\ \hline 0 \end{array}$$

Find: 0.5280 ÷ 0.96

Move each decimal point 2 places.   Divide.

$$0.9\,6\overline{)0.5\,2\,8\,0}$$

$$\begin{array}{r} 0.5\ 5 \\ 9\ 6\overline{)5\ 2.8\ 0} \\ -4\ 8\ 0 \\ \hline 4\ 8\ 0 \\ -4\ 8\ 0 \\ \hline 0 \end{array}$$

Divide.

	a	*b*	*c*	*d*
1.	$$\begin{array}{r} 2.6 \\ 3.4\overline{)8.8\ 4} \\ -6\ 8 \\ \hline 2\ 0\ 4 \\ -2\ 0\ 4 \\ \hline 0 \end{array}$$	$0.9\overline{)1\ 5.3}$	$0.7\overline{)4.0\ 6}$	$1.5\overline{)4.9\ 5}$

2.

$6.1\overline{)3\ 2.9\ 4}$	$3.9\overline{)2\ 9.6\ 4}$	$8.4\overline{)1\ 0\ 5.8\ 4}$	$7.3\overline{)5\ 7\ 0.1\ 3}$

Set up the problems. Then find the quotients.

	a	*b*	*c*
3.	6.12 ÷ 3.4 = _____	1.328 ÷ 0.8 = _____	333.32 ÷ 5.2 = _____

Dividing Whole Numbers by Decimals

To divide a whole number by a decimal, change the divisor
to a whole number by moving the decimal point. To move the decimal
point in the dividend the same number of places, you will need to add
one or more zeros. Then divide.

Find: 48 ÷ 3.2

Move each decimal point 1 place.	Divide.
$3.2\overline{)4\,8.0}$	$\begin{array}{r} 1\,5 \\ 3\,2\overline{)4\,8\,0} \\ -3\,2 \\ \hline 1\,6\,0 \\ -1\,6\,0 \\ \hline 0 \end{array}$

Find: 39 ÷ 0.13

Move each decimal point 2 places.	Divide.
$0.13\overline{)3\,9.00}$	$\begin{array}{r} 3\,0\,0 \\ 1\,3\overline{)3,9\,0\,0} \\ -3\,9 \\ \hline 0\,0 \\ -0 \\ \hline 0\,0 \\ -0 \\ \hline 0 \end{array}$

Divide. Write zeros as needed.

	a	b	c	d
1.	$\begin{array}{r} 4 \\ 0.5\overline{)2.0} \\ -2\,0 \\ \hline 0 \end{array}$	$0.6\overline{)5\,4}$	$1.3\overline{)7\,8}$	$4.5\overline{)6\,7\,5}$
2.	$0.14\overline{)8\,4}$	$0.36\overline{)9\,7\,2}$	$0.99\overline{)3,4\,6\,5}$	$7.2\overline{)1\,3,1\,7\,6}$

Set up the problems. Then find the quotients.

a

3. 288 ÷ 0.8 = _____

b

636 ÷ 1.2 = _____

c

4,698 ÷ 0.54 = _____

Decimal Quotients

Often when you divide, your answer will have a remainder.
You can add zeros in the dividend and continue to divide until the
remainder is zero. If the dividend is a whole number, add a decimal
point and add zeros as needed.

Remember, zeros also may be needed in the quotient.

Find: 26.7 ÷ 4

Divide until you have a remainder.	Add zeros.
6.6 4)2 6.7 −2 4↓ 2 7 −2 4 3	6.6 7 5 4)2 6.7 0 0 −2 4↓ 2 7 −2 4↓ 3 0 −2 8↓ 2 0 −2 0 0

Find: 802 ÷ 4

Divide until you have a remainder	Add a decimal point and a zero.
2 0 0 4)8 0 2 −8↓ 0 0 − 0↓ 0 2	2 0 0.5 4)8 0 2.0 −8↓ 0 0 − 0↓ 0 2 − 0↓ 2 0 −2 0 0

Divide. Write zeros as needed.

	a	b	c	d
1.	2.0 7 5 4)8.3 0 0 −8↓ 0 3 − 0↓ 3 0 −2 8↓ 2 0 −2 0 0	5)5 7.1	9)1 8.6 3	6)0.6 5 7 0
2.	1.7 5 3 2)5 6.0 0 −3 2↓ 2 4 0 −2 2 4↓ 1 6 0 −1 6 0 0	4 0)8 5 0	1 8)4 5	8 5)8,7 0 4

Rounding Quotients

Sometimes when you have a remainder, adding zeros to the dividend and continuing to divide will result in a remainder of zero. Sometimes the remainder will never be zero, or may take too many steps. You may need to round the quotient. You may also need to round the quotient when you are dividing money.

Find: 23 ÷ 7.1

Find: $1.85 ÷ 10

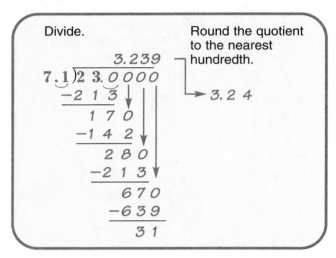

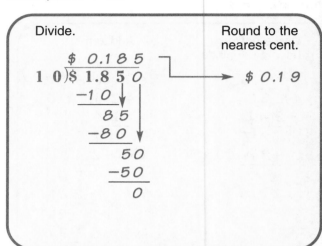

Divide. Round to the place named.

	a	*b*	*c*
	nearest tenth	nearest hundredth	nearest tenth

1.

$$\begin{array}{r} 6.27 \rightarrow 6.3 \\ 5.1\overline{)3\ 2.0\ 0\ 0} \\ -3\ 0\ 6 \downarrow \\ \hline 1\ 4\ 0 \\ -1\ 0\ 2 \downarrow \\ \hline 3\ 8\ 0 \\ -3\ 5\ 7 \\ \hline 2\ 3 \end{array}$$

$3\overline{)2\ 2}$

$8\overline{)6.4\ 8}$

	nearest cent	nearest cent	nearest dollar

2.

$$\begin{array}{r} \$\ 0.3\ 2\ 5 \rightarrow \$\ 0.3\ 3 \\ 6\overline{)\$\ 1.9\ 5\ 0} \\ -1\ 8 \downarrow \\ \hline 1\ 5 \\ -1\ 2 \downarrow \\ \hline 3\ 0 \end{array}$$

$1\ 0\overline{)\$\ 4\ 0\ 5.7\ 5}$

$2\ 9\overline{)\$\ 6\ 0\ 8}$

Problem-Solving Method: Complete a Pattern

Earth's oldest living organisms are bristlecone pine trees. One found in California is almost 5,000 years old. Bristlecones are also one of Earth's slowest growers, at only 0.0003 inch a day. How many days does it take the tree to grow 12 inches (1 foot)?

Understand the problem.

- **What do you want to know?**
  how many days it takes a bristlecone to grow 12 inches

- **What information is given?**
  They grow 0.0003 inch a day.

Plan how to solve it.

- **What method can you use?**
  You can find and complete a pattern.

Solve it.

- **How can you use this method to solve the problem?**
  Start with a basic division fact. Then follow the pattern in the decimal points to find 12 ÷ 0.0003.

12	÷	3	=	4	← Basic Fact
12	÷	0.3	=	40	
12	÷	0.03	=	400	
12	÷	0.003	=	4,000	
12	÷	0.0003	=	40,000	

Decimal point moves **4** places to the **left.** Decimal point moves **4** places to the **right.**

- **What is the answer?**
  It takes 40,000 days for a bristlecone pine tree to grow 12 inches.

Look back and check your answer.

- **Is your answer reasonable?**
  You can check your division with multiplication.

$$
\begin{array}{r}
40,000 \\
\times\ \ 0.0003 \\
\hline
12.0000
\end{array}
$$

The product matches the dividend.
The answer is reasonable.

Complete a pattern to solve each problem.

1. Human hair grows about 0.02 inch a day. How many days does it take hair to grow 6 inches?

6	÷	2	=	3
6	÷	0.2	=	30
6	÷	0.02	=	

   Answer _____

2. A garden snail moves only 0.03 miles per hour. How far can a snail move in 8 hours?

8	×	3	=	
8	×	0.3	=	
8	×	0.03	=	

   Answer _____

3. One milliliter is equal to 0.001 of a liter. How many milliliters are in a 2-liter bottle of soda?

2	÷	1	=	
2	÷	0.1	=	
2	÷	0.01	=	
2	÷	0.001	=	

   Answer _____

4. In a certain week, one Japanese yen was worth 0.008 United States dollars. How many United States dollars could you get for 10 yen?

10	×	8	=	
10	×	0.8	=	
10	×	0.08	=	
10	×	0.008	=	

   Answer _____

5. One nickel is worth 0.05 of a dollar. How many nickels do you need to have $15.00?

15	÷	5	=	
15	÷	0.5	=	
15	÷	0.05	=	

   Answer _____

6. In some places, sales tax is 0.05 times the price of an item. If a hat costs $9.00, how much sales tax will be charged?

9	×	5	=	
9	×	0.5	=	
9	×	0.05	=	

   Answer _____

UNIT 5 Review

Multiply. Write zeros as needed.

a	b	c
1. $2.31 \times 10 =$ _____	$0.56 \times 100 =$ _____	$7.8 \times 1,000 =$ _____
2. $0.83 \times 10 =$ _____	$6.4 \times 100 =$ _____	$0.38 \times 1,000 =$ _____

Multiply. Write zeros as needed.

	a	b	c	d
3.	$\begin{array}{r} 7.2\ 3 \\ \times\quad 2 \\ \hline \end{array}$	$\begin{array}{r} 6 \\ \times 5.0\ 1\ 4 \\ \hline \end{array}$	$\begin{array}{r} \$\ 0.6\ 7 \\ \times\qquad 3 \\ \hline \end{array}$	$\begin{array}{r} 8 \\ \times 0.9\ 1 \\ \hline \end{array}$
4.	$\begin{array}{r} 6\ 8 \\ \times\ \ 0.0\ 5 \\ \hline \end{array}$	$\begin{array}{r} 5\ 7\ 4 \\ \times\qquad 3.7 \\ \hline \end{array}$	$\begin{array}{r} 0.9\ 3\ 1 \\ \times\qquad 7\ 5 \\ \hline \end{array}$	$\begin{array}{r} \$\ 1\ 6.9\ 9 \\ \times\qquad 1\ 2 \\ \hline \end{array}$
5.	$\begin{array}{r} 0.9 \\ \times 0.5 \\ \hline \end{array}$	$\begin{array}{r} 3.6 \\ \times 0.7 \\ \hline \end{array}$	$\begin{array}{r} 1.6 \\ \times 8.4 \\ \hline \end{array}$	$\begin{array}{r} 1\ 2.7 \\ \times\ \ 6.3 \\ \hline \end{array}$
6.	$\begin{array}{r} 4.2\ 7 \\ \times 0.0\ 2 \\ \hline \end{array}$	$\begin{array}{r} 0.0\ 5\ 5 \\ \times\ \ 1.0\ 8 \\ \hline \end{array}$	$\begin{array}{r} 6.\ 7 \\ \times 9.3 \\ \hline \end{array}$	$\begin{array}{r} 0.9\ 3\ 1 \\ \times\qquad 5.8 \\ \hline \end{array}$

Line up the digits. Then find the products. Write zeros as needed.

a	b	c
7. $17 \times 2.5 =$ _____	$25 \times 7.3 =$ _____	$32 \times 41.5 =$ _____
8. $0.63 \times 0.5 =$ _____	$0.29 \times 1.84 =$ _____	$3.18 \times 1.54 =$ _____

Darren 2/2211

Divide. Write zeros as needed.

	a	b	c
9.	$0.34 \div 10 =$ _____	$0.92 \div 100 =$ _____	$1.58 \div 1{,}000 =$ _____
10.	$0.05 \div 10 =$ _____	$1.9 \div 100 =$ _____	$6.495 \div 1{,}000 =$ _____

Divide.

	a	b	c	d
11.	$7\overline{)9.1}$	$5\overline{)3\ 1.5}$	$4\overline{)\$\ 3\ 0.4\ 0}$	$8\overline{)1\ 6.8}$
12.	$2.6\overline{)3.9}$	$0.9\overline{)1\ 9.8}$	$0.1\ 6\overline{)3.0\ 4}$	$8.2\overline{)2\ 1\ 7.3}$
13.	$5.6\overline{)1{,}6\ 8\ 0}$	$0.8\overline{)1\ 6}$	$2.5\overline{)2{,}8\ 2\ 0}$	$3.4\overline{)1{,}5\ 9\ 8}$

Divide. Round to the value named.

	a	b	c
	nearest tenth	nearest cent	nearest hundredth
14.	$2.\ 3\overline{)2.8\ 7\ 5}$	$7\overline{)\$\ 1\ 5.0\ 2}$	$5\overline{)1.7\ 3\ 2}$

UNIT 5 Review

In each problem, cross out the extra information. Then solve the problem.

15. Pluto is the farthest planet from the sun, at 5.9 billion kilometers. It takes Pluto 90.950 days to orbit the sun at a speed of 4.74 kilometers per second. How far does Pluto travel in 30 seconds?

Answer_____

16. In 1996, 31.9% of students in the United States had access to a computer. The average student that year used a computer 5.3 hours a week. How many hours did the average student use a computer each day in 1996? Round the answer to the nearest tenth. (1 week = 7 days)

Answer_____

---

17. In-line skates were introduced to the United States in the late 1970s. In 1998, the record for the highest speed on in-line skates was set at 64.02 miles per hour. How far could a person skate in 2 hours at this speed?

Answer_____

18. On December 17, 1903, Orville Wright became the first man to fly an engine-powered airplane. His flight took place near Kitty Hawk, North Carolina, and covered 120 feet in 0.2 minutes. On average, how many feet per minute did the plane fly?

Answer_____

Find and complete a pattern to solve each problem.

19. One cup is about 0.06 of a gallon. How many cups of water do you need to fill a 54-gallon fish tank?

54	÷	6	=	_____
54	÷	0.6	=	_____
54	÷	0.06	=	_____

Answer_____

20. A lamp with one bulb costs an average of $0.02 per hour for electricity. If you leave a lamp turned on for 12 hours, how much will it cost?

12	×	2	=	_____
12	×	0.2	=	_____
12	×	0.02	=	_____

Answer_____

unit 6
measurement

Customary Length

The customary units that are used to measure length are **inch, foot, yard,** and **mile.** The chart gives the relationship of one unit to another.

You can multiply or divide to change units of measurement.

To compare two measurements, first change them to the same unit.

1 foot (ft.)	=	12 inches (in.)
1 yard (yd.)	=	3 ft.
	=	36 in.
1 mile (mi.)	=	1,760 yd.
	=	5,280 ft.

Find: $3\frac{1}{2}$ ft. = _____ in.

To change larger units to smaller units, multiply.

$$1 \text{ ft.} = 12 \text{ in.}$$

$$3\frac{1}{2} \times 12 = \frac{7}{2} \times 12 = 42$$

$$3\frac{1}{2} \text{ ft.} = 42 \text{ in.}$$

Find: 10 ft. = _____ yd.

To change smaller units to larger units, divide.

$$3 \text{ ft.} = 1 \text{ yd.}$$

$$10 \div 3 = 3\frac{1}{3}$$

$$10 \text{ ft.} = 3\frac{1}{3} \text{ yd.}$$

Change each measurement to the smaller unit.

        a   *b*   *c*

1. $5\frac{1}{6}$ yd. = _____ ft. $1\frac{1}{2}$ mi. = _____ ft. $7\frac{1}{3}$ ft. = _____ in.

2. $1\frac{1}{4}$ yd. = _____ in.   21 yd. = _____ ft.   4 mi. = _____ yd

Change each measurement to the larger unit.

        a   *b*   *c*

3. 51 in. = _____ ft.   38 ft. = _____ yd.   60 in. = _____ ft.

4. 4,400 yd. = _____ mi.   222 in. = _____ ft.   15,840 ft. = _____ mi

Compare. Write <, >, or =.

        a   *b*

5. 24 in. _____<_____ 4 ft.   3 mi. _____ 10,000 ft
     1 ft. = 12 in.
     4 ft. = 4 × 12 = 48 in.

6. 12 ft. _____ 4 yd.   3,600 yd. _____ 2 mi

Customary Weight

The customary units that are used to measure weight are **ounce, pound,** and **ton**. The chart shows the relationship of one unit to another.

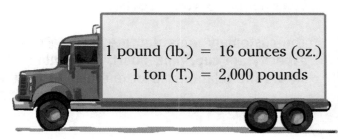

1 pound (lb.) = 16 ounces (oz.)
1 ton (T.) = 2,000 pounds

Find: $5\frac{1}{2}$ lb. = _____ oz.

To change larger units to smaller units, multiply.

$$1 \text{ lb.} = 16 \text{ oz.}$$
$$5\frac{1}{2} \times 16 = \frac{11}{2} \times 16 = 88$$
$$5\frac{1}{2} \text{ lb.} = 88 \text{ oz.}$$

Find: 6,500 lb. = _____ T.

To change smaller units to larger units, divide.

$$2,000 \text{ lb.} = 1 \text{ T.}$$
$$6,500 \div 2,000 = 3\frac{1}{4}$$
$$6,500 \text{ lb} = 3\frac{1}{4} \text{ T.}$$

Change each measurement to the smaller unit.

	a	b	c
1.	$3\frac{1}{4}$ lb. = _____ oz.	$2\frac{1}{2}$ T. = _____ lb.	6 lb. = _____ oz.
2.	4 T. = _____ lb.	$1\frac{3}{8}$ lb. = _____ oz.	$4\frac{3}{16}$ lb. = _____ oz.

Change each measurement to the larger unit.

	a	b	c
3.	53 oz. = _____ lb.	7,000 lb. = _____ T.	80 oz. = _____ lb.
4.	72 oz. = _____ lb.	36 oz. = _____ lb.	2,400 lb. = _____ T.

Compare. Write $<$, $>$, or $=$.

	a	b
5.	40 lb. _____ 640 oz.	10,000 lb. _____ 4 T.

$$1 \text{ lb.} = 16 \text{ oz.}$$
$$40 \text{ lb.} = 40 \times 16 = 640 \text{ oz.}$$

	a	b
6.	$6\frac{1}{2}$ lb. _____ 100 oz.	$\frac{1}{8}$ T. _____ 300 lb.

Customary Capacity

The customary units that are used to measure **capacity** are **cup, pint, quart,** and **gallon**. The chart shows the relationship of one unit to another.

1 pint (pt.)	=2 cups (c.)
1 quart (qt.)	=2 pt.
	=4 c.
1 gallon (gal.)	=4 qt.
	=8 pt.
	=16 c.

Find: $3\frac{3}{4}$ **qt. =** _____ **c.**

To change larger units to smaller units, multiply.

$$1 \text{ qt.} = 4 \text{ c.}$$
$$3\frac{3}{4} \times 4 = \frac{15}{4} \times 4 = 15$$
$$3\frac{3}{4} \text{ qt.} = 15 \text{ c.}$$

Find: **21 qt. =** _____ **gal.**

To change smaller units to larger units, divide.

$$4 \text{ qt.} = 1 \text{ gal.}$$
$$21 \div 4 = 5\frac{1}{4}$$
$$21 \text{ qt.} = 5\frac{1}{4} \text{ gal.}$$

Change each measurement to the smaller unit.

	a	b	c
1.	$8\frac{1}{2}$ pt. = _____ c.	$2\frac{1}{4}$ gal. = _____ qt.	13 qt. = _____ pt.
2.	$4\frac{1}{8}$ gal. = _____ pt.	9 qt. = _____ c.	$1\frac{1}{2}$ gal. = _____ c

Change each measurement to the larger unit.

	a	b	c
3.	7 c. = _____ qt.	21 pt. = _____ gal.	11 c. = _____ pt.
4.	24 qt. = _____ gal.	14 pt. = _____ qt.	54 c. = _____ gal.

Compare. Write <, >, or =.

	a	b
5.	12 c. ____>____ 5 pt.	50 gal. _____ 2,000 qt.
	1 pt. = 2 c	
	5 pt. = 5 × 2 = 10 c.	
6.	$5\frac{1}{2}$ qt. _____ 22 c.	15.6 pt. _____ 2 gal.

Computing Measures

You can add, subtract, multiply, and divide measures that are given in two units. For example, 1 yd. 5 in. uses 2 units to measure one length.

Find: 1 lb. 14 oz. + 6 lb. 10 oz.

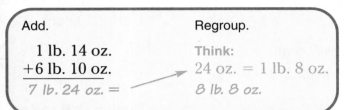

Add.	Regroup.
1 lb. 14 oz.	Think:
+6 lb. 10 oz.	24 oz. = 1 lb. 8 oz.
7 lb. 24 oz. =	8 lb. 8 oz.

Find: 5 × 4 gal. 3 qt.

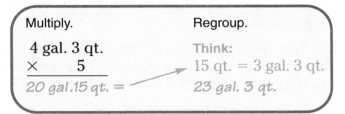

Multiply.	Regroup.
4 gal. 3 qt.	Think:
× 5	15 qt. = 3 gal. 3 qt.
20 gal.15 qt. =	23 gal. 3 qt.

Find: 12 ft. 4 in. − 6 ft. 9 in.

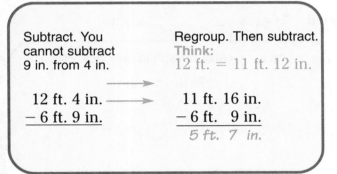

Subtract. You cannot subtract 9 in. from 4 in.	Regroup. Then subtract. Think: 12 ft. = 11 ft. 12 in.
12 ft. 4 in.	11 ft. 16 in.
− 6 ft. 9 in.	− 6 ft. 9 in.
	5 ft. 7 in.

Find: 8 T. 200 lb. ÷ 6

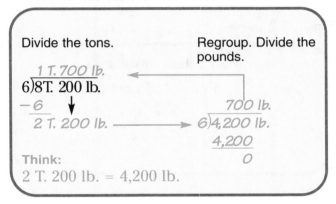

Divide the tons.

$$6)\overline{8\text{ T. }200\text{ lb.}}$$
1 T. 700 lb.
−6
2 T. 200 lb.

Think:
2 T. 200 lb. = 4,200 lb.

Regroup. Divide the pounds.

700 lb.
$$6)\overline{4,200\text{ lb.}}$$
4,200
0

Find each answer.

	a	b	c
1.	5 gal. 2 qt. +2 gal. 3 qt. 7gal. 5 qt. = 8 gal. 1 qt.	9 ft. 6 in. +4 ft. 8 in.	7 yd. 1 ft. +3 yd. 2 ft.
2.	8 yd. 1 ft. −6 yd. 2 ft.	5 gal. 2 qt. −3 gal. 3 qt.	18 lb. 6 oz. × 4 oz.
3.	5 ft. 8 in. × 7 in.	8)10 lb. 8 oz.	7)9 yd. 1 ft.

Metric Length

The **meter** (m) is the basic metric unit of length. A meter can be measured with a meter stick. The length of your arm is about 0.7 m.

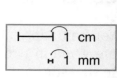

A **centimeter** (cm) is one hundredth of a meter. (*Centi* means 0.01.) The centimeter is used to measure small lengths. The width of a paper clip is about 1 cm.

A **millimeter** (mm) is one thousandth of a meter. (*Milli* means 0.001.) The millimeter is used to measure very small lengths. The thickness of a nickel is about 2 mm.

A **kilometer** (km) is one thousand meters. (*Kilo* means 1,000.) The kilometer is used to measure long distances. The distance between two cities can be measured in kilometers.

1 km = 1,000 m
1 m = 100 cm
1 cm = 10 mm

1 m = 0.001 km
1 cm = 0.01 m
1 mm = 0.1 cm

Find: 8.2 m = _____ cm

> To change larger units to smaller units, multiply.
> 1 m = 100 cm
> 8.2 × 100 = 820
> 8.2 m = 820 cm

Find: 63 m = _____ km

> To change smaller units to larger units, divide.
> 1,000 m = 1 km
> 63 ÷ 1,000 = 0.063
> 63 m = 0.063 km

Circle the best measurement.

a

1. length of a snail
  2 cm   2 m

2. width of a paper clip
  8 mm   8 cm

b

distance from Boston to New York
300 m   300 km

length of a car
5 cm   5 m

Change each measurement to the smaller unit.

a

3. 14.5 km = _____ m

4. 3.4 m = _____ cm

b

7.25 m = _____ cm

21 m = _____ mm

c

18 cm = _____ mm

0.9 km = _____ m

Change each measurement to the larger unit.

a

5. 48 mm = _____ cm

6. 8,542 m = _____ km

b

79.6 cm = _____ m

3,128 mm = _____ m

c

61 m = _____ km

930 cm = _____ m

Metric Mass

The **gram** (g) is the basic unit of mass. The gram is used to measure very light objects. A dime equals about 2 grams.

The **kilogram** (kg) is one thousand grams. It is used to measure heavier objects. Use kg to measure a bicycle. Remember, *kilo* means 1,000.

1 kg = 1,000 g
1 g = 0.001 kg

Find: 8.4 kg = _____ g

To change larger units to smaller units, multiply.

1 kg = 1,000 g

8.4 × 1,000 = 8,400

8.4 kg = 8,400 g

Find: 24.7 g = _____ kg

To change smaller units to larger units, divide.

1,000 g = 1 kg

24.7 ÷ 1,000 = 0.0247

24.7 g = 0.0247 kg

Circle the best measurement.

a

1. mass of a large dog

27 g   27 kg

b

mass of a package of frozen vegetables

283 g   28.3 kg

2. mass of a bagel

70 g   7 kg

mass of a television

450 g   45 kg

Change each measurement to the smaller unit.

a

3. 32 kg = _____ g

4. 0.49 kg = _____ g

b

0.007 kg = _____ g

825 kg = _____ g

c

1.8 kg = _____ g

6.783 kg = _____ g

Change each measurement to the larger unit.

a

5. 12.8 g = _____ kg

6. 5,268 g = _____ kg

b

9 g = _____ kg

25 g = _____ kg

c

137 g = _____ kg

4.9 g = _____ kg

Metric Capacity

The **liter** (L) is the basic metric unit of capacity. A liter of liquid will fill a box 10 centimeters on each side. A large jug of apple cider holds about 4 L.

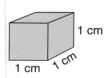

A **milliliter** (mL) is one thousandth of a liter. It is used to measure very small amounts of liquid. A milliliter of liquid will fill a box 1 centimeter on each side. A small carton of milk holds about 250 mL.

Remember, *milli* **means 0.001.**

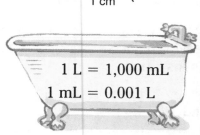

1 L = 1,000 mL
1 mL = 0.001 L

Find: 2.5 L = _____ mL

To change larger units to smaller units, multiply.

$$1 \text{ L} = 1,000 \text{ mL}$$
$$2.5 \times 1,000 = 2,500$$
$$2.5 \text{ L} = 2,500 \text{ mL}$$

Find: 5,672 mL = _____ L

To change smaller units to larger units, divide.

$$1,000 \text{ mL} = 1 \text{ L}$$
$$5,672 \div 1,000 = 5.672$$
$$5,672 \text{ mL} = 5.672 \text{ L}$$

Circle the best measurement.

           a   *b*

1. capacity of a container of yogurt

    200 mL   200 L

  capacity of a can of tomato juice

    450 mL   450 L

2. capacity of a bathtub

    50 mL   50 L

  capacity of a large carton of juice

    2.84 mL   2.84 L

Change each measurement to the smaller unit.

        a   *b*   *c*

3. 27 L = _____ mL   5.3 L = _____ mL   7.45 L = _____ mL

4. 0.825 L = _____ mL   2 L = _____ mL   39.6 L = _____ mL

Change each measurement to the larger unit.

        a   *b*   *c*

5. 3,096 mL = _____ L   6,000 mL = _____ L   412.5 mL = _____ L

6. 58 mL = _____ L   798 mL = _____ L   19.2 mL = _____ L

Computing Metric Measures

You can add, subtract, multiply, and divide measures that are given in two units.
For example, 2 m 26 cm uses 2 units to measure one length.

Find: 2 km 750 m + 1 km 300 m

Add.	Regroup.
2 km 750 m	*Think:*
+1 km 300 m	*1,050 m = 1 km 50 m*
3 km 1,050 m =	*4 km 50 m*

Find: 3 × 2 L 425 mL

Multiply.	Regroup.
2 L 425 mL	*Think:*
× 3	*1,275 mL = 1 L 275 mL*
6 L 1,275 mL =	*7 L 275 mL*

Find: 4 kg 200 g − 1 kg 900 g

Subtract. You cannot subtract 900 g from 200 g.	Regroup. Then subtract.
	Think:
	4 kg = 3 kg 1,000 g
4 kg 200 g →	*3 kg 1,200 g*
−1 kg 900 g →	*−1 kg 900*
	2 kg 300 g

Find: 6 L 500 mL ÷ 5

Divide the liters.	Regroup. Divide the milliliters.
1 L 300 mL	
5)6 L 500 mL	*300 mL*
−5 ↓	*5)1,500 mL*
1 L 500 mL →	*1,500*
Think:	*0*
1 L 500 mL = 1,500 mL	

Find each answer. Simplify.

	a	b	c
1.	19 cm 2 mm +15 cm 29 mm *34 cm 31 mm = 37 cm 1*	3 kg 750 g +4 kg 375 g	8 L 125 mL +3 L 650 mL
2.	8 kg 150 g −6 kg 200 g	5 L 425 mL −2 L 300 mL	33 m 65 cm −10 m 70 cm
3.	9 km 375 m × 3	5 kg 30 g × 7	7 L 750 mL × 6
4.	4)5 kg 100 g	5)19 L 200 mL	2)4 km 500 m

Problem-Solving Method: Make an Organized List

Every metric measurement has a **prefix** and a **base unit**. The prefix deca means 10. The prefix mega means 1,000,000. A **decagon** is a polygon with 10 sides, and a **megaton** is 1,000,000 tons. How many different metric measurements can you write with these two prefixes and the base units meter, liter, and gram?

Understand the problem.

- **What do you want to know?**
  how many different metric measurements you can write with those prefixes and base units

- **What information is given?**
  Prefixes: deca and mega
  Base Units: meter, liter, and gram

Plan how to solve it.

- **What method can you use?**
  You can make a list of the different prefix–base unit combinations. Then count the combinations.

Solve it.

- **How can you use this method to solve the problem?**
  Start with the first prefix and list all of its bases. Then do the same thing for the other prefix.

Prefix	Base	Measurement
deca-	meter	decameter
	liter	decaliter
	gram	decagram
mega-	meter	megameter
	liter	megaliter
	gram	megagram

- **What is the answer?**
  You can write 6 different metric measurements.

Look back and check your answer.

- **Is your answer reasonable?**
  You can multiply to check your answer.

  number of prefixes × number of bases = number of combinations

  $2 \times 3 = 6$

  The product matches the count.
  The answer is reasonable.

Make an organized list to solve each problem.

1. The prefix *hecto* means 100. The prefix *deci* means $\frac{1}{10}$. What are the possible measurements with these prefixes and the base units meter and gram?

   Answer _____

   _____

   _____

   _____

2. There are three main trails at the park. One is 1.2 km, one is 2.5 km, and the third is 4 km long. You can hike, bike, or ride a horse. How many different ways can you explore the trails?

   Answer _____

3. Sam, Tim, and Chantall all want to sit next to each other at the movies. In how many different ways can they do this?

   Answer _____

Change each measurement to the smaller unit.

       a   *b*   *c*

1. $4\frac{1}{3}$ yd. = _____ ft.   21 cm = _____ mm $2\frac{1}{6}$ yd. = _____ in.

2. $1\frac{1}{5}$ T. = _____ lb. $4\frac{1}{2}$ kg = _____ g $2\frac{1}{2}$ lb. = _____ oz.

3. $5\frac{1}{4}$ gal. = _____ pt.   21 L = _____ mL   7 qt. = _____ c.

Circle the best measurement.

       a   *b*

4. distance from Miami to Atlanta   length of a desk
    30 m   300 km   2.5 m   250 mm

5. mass of a pencil   capacity of a bottle
    2 kg   2 g   3 L   3 mL

Change each measurement to the larger unit.

       a   *b*   *c*

6. 168 oz. = _____ lb.   3,520 yd. = _____ mi.   1,123 m = _____ km

7. 5.9 g = _____ kg   4,000 lb. = _____ T.   2,102 g = _____ kg

8. 2,500 mL = _____ L   56 c. = _____ gal.   21.5 mL = _____ L

Compare. Write <, >, or =.

       a   *b*

9. 36 in. _____ 4 ft.   3 km _____ 30,000 m

10. 128 oz. _____ 10 lb.   12 gal. _____ 40 c.

Find each answer.

       a   *b*   *c*   *d*

11.   7 gal. 3 qt. $3\overline{)5\,\text{cm}\,7\,\text{mm}}$ 3 L 6 mL   16 gal. 5 pt.
     −4 gal. 2 qt.   − 2 L 2 mL   ×   6

Make an organized list to solve each problem.

12. Matt has $0.75 in United States coins. He has exactly 1 half-dollar and no pennies. What are all the possible coin combinations Matt could have?

13. There are four marbles in a bag. One is black, one is silver, one is clear, and one is blue. You reach inside without looking and choose 2 marbles. What are all the possible marble pairs you could pick?

Answer

_____

Answer

_____

14. Sam packed black pants, jeans, and khaki pants for his vacation. He packed three different T-shirts: blue, white, and black. How many different outfits can he wear?

Answer

_____

Points, Lines, and Planes

A **point** is an exact location in space.	P •	point *P* or *P*
A **plane** is a flat surface that extends forever in all directions. It is named by any three points.	*L* *M* *N* *O*	plane *LMN*
A **line** is an endless straight path.	←•——•→ *A* *B*	line *AB* or line *BA* ↔ ↔ *AB* or *BA*
A **line segment** is a straight path between two points.	•——• *R* *S*	line segment *RS* or line segment *SR* ‾‾ ‾‾ *RS* or *SR*
A **ray** is an endless straight path starting at one point.	•——•→ *B* *G*	ray *BG* → *BG*

Within a plane, lines can have different relationships.

Lines that cross at one point are **intersecting lines.**

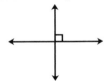

Lines that intersect to form four 90° angles are **perpendicular lines.**

Lines that never intersect are **parallel lines.** They are always the same distance apart.

Use the drawing at right for Exercises 1–8.

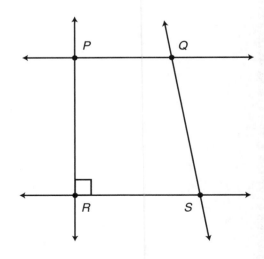

1. Name a plane. _____ *plane PQR* _____

2. Name a line. _____

3. Name a line segment. _____

4. Name a ray. _____

5. Name a point. _____

6. Name 2 parallel lines. _____

7. Name 2 intersecting lines. _____

8. Name 2 perpendicular lines. _____

Name each figure. Write *point, plane, line, line segment,* or *ray.*

a b c d

9.

 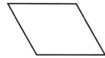 

_____line_____ _____ _____ _____

Name each figure using symbols.

a b c d

10.

B L R

M S

___*AB̅ or BA̅*___ _____ _____ _____

Describe the lines. Write *intersecting, perpendicular,* or *parallel.*

a b c d

11.

___*intersecting*___ _____ _____ _____

Angles

An **angle** is two rays with a common endpoint called a **vertex**.

Angles are measured in **degrees** (°).

Angles are classified by their size.

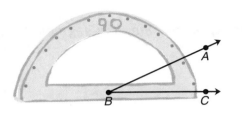

angle *ABC* or angle *CBA* or angle *B*

∠ *ABC* or ∠*CBA* or ∠*B*

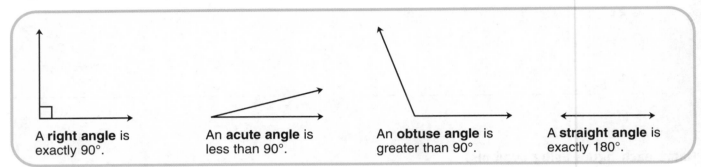

A **right angle** is exactly 90°.

An **acute angle** is less than 90°.

An **obtuse angle** is greater than 90°.

A **straight angle** is exactly 180°.

Name each angle using symbols.

	a	b	c	d

1.
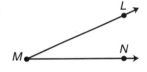

∠LMN or ∠NML _____ _____ _____

Classify each angle. Write *right, acute, obtuse,* or *straight*.

	a	b	c	d

2.

obtuse _____ _____ _____

Congruent Segments and Angles

Congruent line segments and angles have the same measure. The symbol for congruent is ≅.

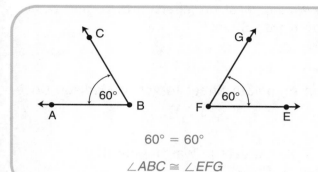 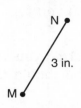 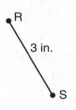

$$60° = 60°$$

$$\angle ABC \cong \angle EFG$$

$$3 \text{ in.} = 3 \text{ in.}$$

$$\overline{MN} \cong \overline{RS}$$

Write whether the angles are _congruent_ or _not congruent_.

               _a_   _b_

1.

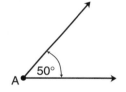 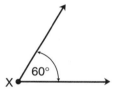   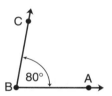

_____ _not congruent_ _____   _____

Write whether the line segments are _congruent_ or _not congruent_.

               _a_   _b_

2.

 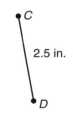   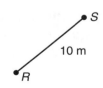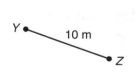

_____   _____

Problem-Solving Method: Make a Drawing

Madison Drive and Jefferson Drive are parallel streets in Washington, D.C. Madison runs along the north side of the park and Jefferson runs along the south of the park. 14th Street intersects both streets and is perpendicular to both streets. If you are walking west on Jefferson Drive and want to get to Madison Drive, should you turn right or left onto 14th Street?

Understand the problem.

- **What do you want to know?**
  if you should turn right or left onto 14th Street to get to Madison Drive

- **What information is given?**
  the description and directions of 3 streets in Washington, D.C.
  You are walking west on Jefferson Drive.

Plan how to solve it.

- **What method can you use?**
  You can make a drawing of the streets.

Solve it.

- **How can you use this method to solve the problem?**
  Draw and label the streets. Then follow the information in the problem to find Madison Drive from 14th Street.

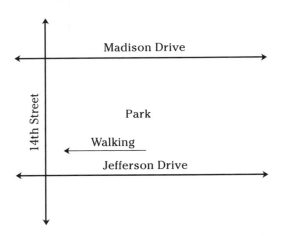

- **What is the answer?**
  You should turn right onto 14th Street.

Look back and check your answer.

- **Is your answer reasonable?**
  Reread the descriptions in the problem and check that they match your drawing.

  The answer matches the descriptions.
  It is reasonable.

Make a drawing to solve each problem.

1. Main Street runs east to west. Elm Street is perpendicular to and intersects Main Street. Taylor Avenue intersects both Main and Elm Streets at different points. What shape do the three streets form?

2. The town square has a statue at each corner. A bricked sidewalk starts at each statue and runs diagonally across the square. What kind of angles are formed by the intersection of the 4 sidewalks?

Answer _____

Answer _____

3. Peter and Marcia are building a stone wall that will be 38 feet long. Peter starts from one end and builds 9 feet of the wall. Marcia starts at the other end and builds 7 feet of the wall. How much of the wall is not built?

Answer _____

Perimeter of a Rectangle

Perimeter is the distance around a figure. To find the perimeter of a rectangle, count the number of units around the rectangle.

Find the perimeter of this rectangle by counting units.

Start at point *A*. Move clockwise and count the units from *A* to *B* (8), to *C* (13), to *D* (21), to *A* (26).

The perimeter of this rectangle is 26 units.

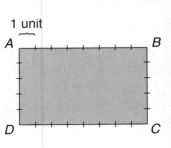
1 unit

Find the perimeter of each rectangle.

	a	b	c

1.

_____
16 units

_____   _____

2.

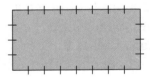   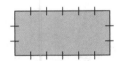

_____   _____   _____

3.

    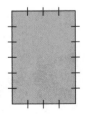   

_____   _____   _____

4.

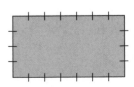   

_____   _____   _____

Formula for Perimeter of a Rectangle

To find the perimeter of a rectangle, you can also use a **formula**.

Notice that the opposite sides of a rectangle are equal.

The formula, $P = 2l + 2w$, means the perimeter of a rectangle equals 2 times the length (l) plus 2 times the width (w).

Find the perimeter of this chalkboard by using the formula.

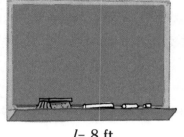

Write the formula.	$P = 2l + 2w$
Substitute the data.	$P = (2 \times 8) + (2 \times 5)$
Solve the problem.	$P = 16 + 10$
	$P = 26$

w= 5 ft.

l= 8 ft.

The perimeter of this chalkboard is 26 feet.

Find the perimeter of each rectangle by using the formula.

a	b	c
1. length = 15 in. width = 12 in. $P = 2l + 2w$ $P = (2 \times 15) + (2 \times 12)$ $P = 30 + 24$ $P = 54$ in.	length = 32 cm width = 27 cm	width = 2 m length = 2.5 m
2. width = 29 yd. length = 33 yd.	length = 24 in. width = 18 in.	length = $6\frac{1}{4}$ ft. width = $4\frac{1}{2}$ ft.
3. length = 12.4 m width = 10.5 m	width = 46 mm length = 54 mm	length = 22 yd. width = 18 yd.
4. length = 92 cm width = 75 cm	width = 15.2 m length = 18.6 m	length = 29 ft. width = 27 ft.

Area of a Rectangle

Area is the number of **square units** needed to cover a figure. To find the area of a rectangle, count the number of square units covering the rectangle.

1 square unit

Find the area of this window by counting all the square units covering it.

The area of this window is 40 square units.

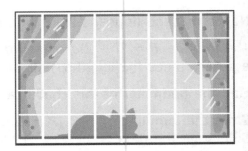

Find the area of each rectangle by counting the square units.

| | a | b | c |

1.

 12 square units   _____   _____

2.

      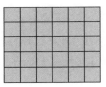

_____   _____   _____

3.

   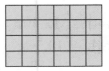

_____   _____   _____

4.

_____   _____   _____

Formula for Area of a Rectangle

To find the area of a rectangle, you can also use a formula.

The formula, $A = lw$, means the area of a rectangle equals the length times the width.

Find the area of the side of the doghouse by using the formula.

Write the formula. $A = l \times w$
Substitute the data. $A = 8 \times 5$
Solve the problem. $A = 40$

The area of the side of the doghouse is 40 square feet.

Remember, write your answer in *square* units.

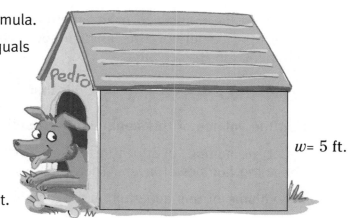

$w = 5$ ft.

$l = 8$ ft.

Find the area of each rectangle by using the formula.

a	b	c
1. length = 18 cm	length = 78 mm	length = $7\frac{1}{2}$ ft.
width = 15 cm	width = 42 mm	width = $1\frac{1}{2}$ ft.

$A = l \times w$
$A = 18 \times 15$
$A = 270$ square centimeters

a	b	c
2. width = 3.8 m	length = 19 yd.	width = 8 ft.
length = 6.5 m	width = 4 yd.	length = 20 ft.

a	b	c
3. length = 85 in.	width = 1.8 m	length = 17.5 cm
width = 37 in.	length = 2.2 m	width = 4.3 cm

a	b	c
4. length = $4\frac{1}{2}$ yd.	width = 9 m	length = 8 in.
width = $2\frac{1}{4}$ yd.	length = 13 m	width = $3\frac{1}{2}$ in.

Volume of a Rectangular Solid

Volume is the number of **cubic units** needed to fill a solid figure. To find the volume of a rectangular solid, count the number of cubic units in the rectangular box.

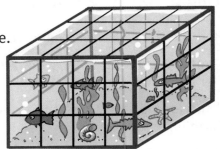

1 cubic unit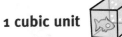

Find the volume of this aquarium by counting cubic units.

Count the number of cubes in the top layer.
Count the number of layers. Then multiply.

$$\begin{array}{r} 12 \\ \times\ 3 \\ \hline 36 \end{array}$$

The volume of this aquarium is 36 cubic units.

Find the volume of each rectangular solid by counting the cubic units.

	a	b	c

1.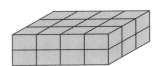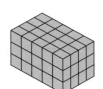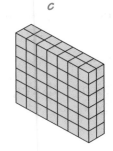

_____24 cubic units_____   _____   _____

2.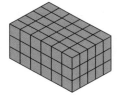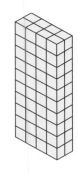

_____   _____   _____

3.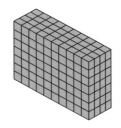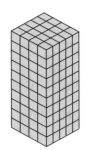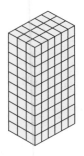

_____   _____   _____

Formula for Volume of a Rectangular Solid

To find the volume of a rectangular solid, you can also use a formula.

The formula, $V = lwh$, means the volume of a rectangular solid equals the length times the width times the height.

Find the volume of this gift box.

Write the formula. $V = l \times w \times h$
Substitute the data. $V = 4 \times 3 \times 3$
Solve the problem. $V = 36$

The volume of this gift box is 36 cubic centimeters.

Remember, write your answer in *cubic* units.

$h = 3$ cm

$w = 3$ cm

$l = 4$ cm

Find the volume of each rectangular solid. Use the formula.

| a | b | c |

1. length = 20 ft.
   width = 10 ft.
   height = 7 ft.

$V = l \times w \times h$
$V = 20 \times 10 \times 7$
$V = 1,400$ cubic ft.

length = 25 mm
width = 24 mm
height = 10 mm

length = 34 in.
width = 28 in.
height = 16 in.

2. length = 4 cm
   width = 1.5 cm
   height = 2.6 cm

length = $12\frac{1}{2}$ in.
width = 5 in.
height = 20 in.

length = 15 ft.
width = 12 ft.
height = 8 ft.

3. length = 20 yd.
   width = 16 yd.
   height = 6 yd.

length = 8 m
width = 5.5 m
height = 6.4 m

length = 12 yd.
width = $8\frac{1}{4}$ yd.
height = 10 yd.

Problem-Solving Method: Use a Formula

One of the world's largest chocolate candy bars was made in England. It was 12.9 feet long, 4.9 feet wide, and 1 foot tall. How many cubic feet of chocolate were used to make the bar?

Understand the problem.

- **What do you want to know?**
  how much chocolate was in the candy bar

- **What information is given?**
  The bar was 12.9 feet long, 4.9 feet wide, and 1 foot tall.

Plan how to solve it.

- **What method can you use?**
  You can use a formula.

Solve it.

- **How can you use this method to solve the problem?**
  Since a bar is a rectangular solid, you can use the formula for the volume of a rectangular solid.

$$V = l \times w \times h$$

$$V = 12.9 \times 4.9 \times 1$$

$$V = 63.21$$

- **What is the answer?**
  The bar had 63.21 cubic feet of chocolate.

Look back and check your answer.

- **Is your answer reasonable?**
  You can estimate to check your answer.

  $$10 \times 5 \times 1 = 50$$

  The estimate is close to the answer.
  The answer is reasonable.

Use a formula to solve each problem.

1. The total capacity of your lungs is about the same as the volume of a 12 in. × 8 in. × 5 in. shoe box. About how many cubic inches of air can your lungs hold?

Answer _____

2. A regulation football field is 100 yards long and $53\frac{1}{3}$ yards wide. How many square yards of grass would you need to cover the whole field?

Answer _____

3. Greg's rectangular fish tank is 30.5 cm long, 18.6 cm wide, and 12 cm tall. How many cubic centimeters of water will fill Greg's fish tank?

Answer _____

4. A twin bed is 39 inches wide and 72 inches long. How long is a dust ruffle that goes around the bottom of a twin bed?

Answer _____

5. A professional soccer field is 75 meters wide and 110 meters long. Linda ran around the soccer field three times after practice. How far did she run?

Answer _____

6. Each can of paint covers 40 square feet. Each wall in Charlene's bedroom is 10 feet tall and 8 feet wide. How many cans does she need to paint the 4 walls?

Answer _____

Use the drawing at right for Exercises 1–7.

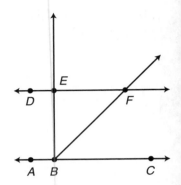

1. Name a point. _____

2. Name a line. _____

3. Name an acute angle. _____

4. Name a ray. _____

5. Name a pair of parallel lines. _____

6. Name a line segment. _____

7. Name two congruent angles. _____

Count the units to find the following.

a

b

c

8.

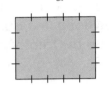

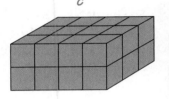

Perimeter _____   Area _____   Volume _____

Find the perimeter of each rectangle. Use the formula $P = 2l + 2w$.

a	b	c
9. length = 2.7 m	length = 90 cm	length = $11\frac{2}{3}$ yd.
width = 1.4 m	width = 80 cm	width = $5\frac{2}{3}$ yd.

_____   _____   _____

Find the area of each rectangle. Use the formula $A = l \times w$.

a	b	c
10. length = 21 mm	length = $42\frac{1}{2}$ in.	length = 3.9 cm
width = 8 mm	width = $30\frac{1}{2}$ in.	width = 1.7 cm

_____   _____   _____

Find the volume of each rectangle. Use the formula $V = l \times w \times h$.

a	b	c
11. length = 8 yd.	length = 10 m	length = 25 ft.
width = 6 yd.	width = 3.4 m	width = $2\frac{1}{4}$ ft.
height = 9 yd.	height = 5 m	height = 4 ft.

_____   _____   _____

Make a drawing to solve each problem.

12. Lombard and Pratt Streets both run east to west and are parallel to each other. Charles and Franklin Streets both run north to south and are parallel to each other. Describe the shape that is formed where the four streets meet.

Answer

_____

13. Karen, Tremont, Joe, and Anita sat on the same side of the picnic table. Karen sat between Joe and Tremont. Joe sat between Anita and Karen. Which two people sat at the ends of the table?

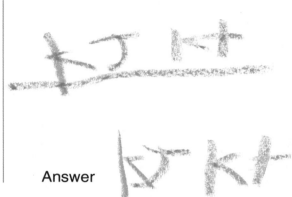

Answer

_____

Use a formula to solve each problem.

14. In 1506, Leonardo da Vinci painted the *Mona Lisa* on a piece of pinewood, 30 in. by $20\frac{7}{8}$ in. How much wood was needed to frame the *Mona Lisa?*

Answer

_____

15. A compact disc case is 14 cm long, 12.5 cm wide, and 1 cm tall. What is the area of the case's top cover? What is the volume of the case?

Answer

_____

Language Arts

Nouns

A **noun** is a word that names a person, place, thing, or an idea.
Examples:
boy, Juan, river, Texas, house, beach, joy

DIRECTIONS → List the nouns from the sentences. Label each noun *person, place, thing,* or *idea.*

1. Carlos spent a week visiting his aunt and uncle.

   _____

2. Their daughter, Mary, is his favorite cousin.

   _____

3. The two children had long discussions about happiness.

   _____

4. The family lives on a ranch in Montana.

   _____

5. On Saturday my neighbor cooked a delicious meal.

   _____

6. Grandma helped clear the dishes from the table.

   _____

7. Sam did not leave the kitchen until the dishes were clean.

   _____

8. This month we will honor the memory of veterans of our town.

   _____

9. Volunteers will paint a mural at our school.

   _____

10. Dr. García, the mayor, will lead a parade with marching bands.

    _____

11. The lifeguard works two days a week.

    _____

12. Lightning struck the new barn.

    _____

Common Nouns and Proper Nouns

There are two main types of nouns: **common nouns** and **proper nouns**.
A **common noun** names any person, place, thing, or idea.
Examples:
    pilot, city, park
A **proper noun** names a particular person, place, or thing.
A proper noun begins with a capital letter.
Examples:
    Amelia Earhart, Chicago, Katmai National Park

DIRECTIONS ▸ **Rewrite the sentences correctly. Capitalize each proper noun and underline each common noun.**

1. Harriet tubman was born as a slave in the state of maryland.

_____

2. Her husband, john tubman, was free.

_____

3. Harriet fled from the plantation of her master.

_____

4. The former slave found freedom in philadelphia.

_____

5. Her family and friends were still enslaved.

_____

6. This courageous woman returned for her sister, mary ann.

_____

7. Her brother, james, escaped later with his family.

_____

8. During her life, harriet led many other escapes.

_____

Common and Proper Nouns, page 2

DIRECTIONS > Underline each common noun.

1. Monet was the first painter of the school of painting called Impressionism.

2. The name of this new style came from a painting by Monet called *Impression: Sunrise*.

3. The movement began in nineteenth-century France.

4. Monet was joined by thirty-nine other artists.

5. Those painters included Pierre-Auguste Renoir, Edgar Degas, and Paul Cézanne.

6. The first exhibit of paintings by this group was in Paris in April 1874.

7. The Impressionists wanted to capture on canvas how the eye saw light.

8. These painters were concerned with the way objects reflect light.

9. Monet often painted from a boat on the Seine River.

10. The painter died on December 5, 1926.

11. Children around the world play hopscotch.

12. There are many versions of the game.

13. In my town, Plainview, New York, children draw a board with eight squares.

14. They throw a stone or a coin into a square, hop on one foot into each square, and then return.

15. Can you write a paragraph about a sport that you like to play?

DIRECTIONS > Underline each proper noun.

16. Diego Rivera was one of the greatest painters and muralists of Mexico.

17. Because he loved Mexico, his works often portray the culture and history of that country.

18. One of his paintings reflects the time before the Spanish conquered Mexico.

19. That painting shows the Zapotec Indians making gold jewelry.

20. Although Rivera did some of his most famous murals in Mexico City, several of his works were painted in the United States.

21. Visit the Detroit Institute of Arts in Michigan to see some of the best works by Diego Rivera.

22. The Constitution of the United States was drafted at the Constitutional Convention.

23. Leaders from around the country met in Philadelphia, Pennsylvania.

24. The Bill of Rights was written by James Madison.

25. On April 30, 1789, George Washington took office as the leader of the country.

Common and Proper Nouns, page 3

DIRECTIONS Read the following sentences. Draw one line under each common noun. Circle each proper noun.

The four generals met beside the river. General Tang raised his violin and began playing a sad tune.

"Oh, I cannot bear to feel such sorrow," said General Wang. So Tang played a bright, happy song.

"How wonderful!" exclaimed General Lang. "That melody fills me with joy!"

"Yes," agreed General Mang. "But we have not come to this place to hear songs. We have come to discuss the future of our country. How can we be certain that this peace will last?"

DIRECTIONS Write common or proper nouns to complete the webs below. Use nouns from the paragraphs above. Then add two more nouns to each web.

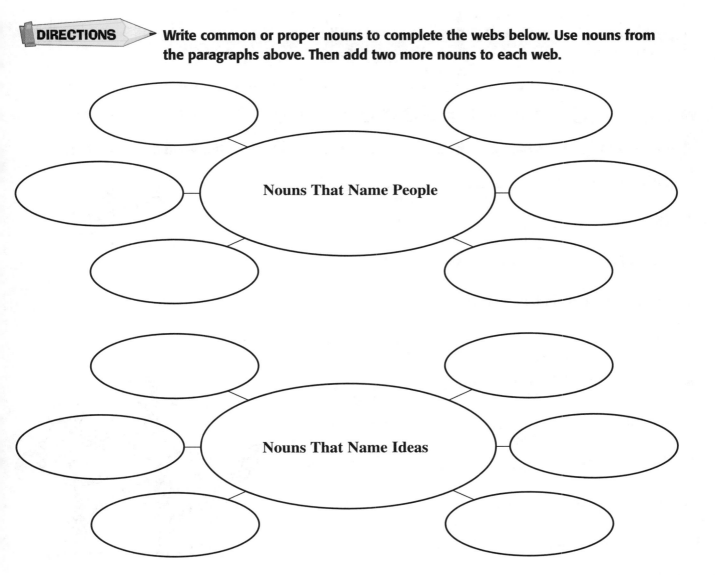

Nouns That Name People

Nouns That Name Ideas

Singular and Plural Nouns

A **singular noun** names one person, place, or thing.
Examples:
   principal, cafeteria, stereo
A **plural noun** names more than one person, place, or thing.
Examples:
   principals, cafeterias, stereos
Add *s* to most nouns to make them plural.
Examples:
   principal, principals   building, buildings
Add *es* to most nouns ending in *ch, sh, s,* or *x* to make them plural.
Examples:
   switch, switches   wish, wishes   box, boxes
If a noun ends in a consonant and *y*, change the *y* to *i* and add *es*.
Examples:
   community, communities   party, parties
If a noun ends in a vowel and *y*, add *s* to make it plural.
Examples:
   toy, toys   play, plays

DIRECTIONS ▷ **Complete each sentence, using the plural form of the noun in parentheses.**

1. Sally's family has _____.
   (horse)

2. They have _____, too.
   (donkey)

3. Sally's favorite horse is white with _____ of brown.
   (patch)

4. She always goes riding on clear _____.
   (day)

5. Her _____ like to trot along behind the horse.
   (puppy)

6. She waves to neighbors on their _____.
   (porch)

7. Several _____ like to ride with her.
   (lady)

8. They never wear _____ for riding.
   (dress)

9. Sally likes to ride over the _____.
   (hill)

10. She gallops on the _____.
    (trail)

Singular and Plural Nouns, page 2

Some nouns ending in *f* or *fe* are made plural by changing the *f* or *fe* to *ves*.
Examples:
     leaf, leaves   wife, wives
Some nouns ending in *f* are made plural by adding *s*.
Examples:
     roof, roofs   chief, chiefs
Most nouns ending in *o* that have a vowel just before the *o* are made plural by adding *s*.
Examples:
     radio, radios   stereo, stereos
Some nouns ending in *o* preceded by a consonant are made plural by adding *es*, but others are made plural by adding only *s*.
Examples:
     potato, potatoes   piano, pianos
A few nouns have irregular plural forms.
Examples:
     foot, feet   mouse, mice
A few nouns have the same form for both the singular and the plural.
Examples:
     sheep, sheep   trout, trout

DIRECTIONS ▷ **Complete each sentence, using the plural form of the noun in parentheses.**

1. Two _____ live on a farm in Alaska.
             (woman)

2. _____ cannot drive on the road by themselves.
      (Car)

3. The _____ on the farm have had _____.
          (ox)   (calf)

4. The farmers also raise _____.
                      (sheep)

5. _____ sometimes try to attack them.
        (Wolf)

6. A wolf's _____ are as sharp as _____.
            (tooth)   (knife)

7. Some of the land is used to grow _____.
                       (potato)

8. The farmers grow _____ during the summer.
            (tomato)

9. _____ eat the _____ of the plants.
   (Deer)   (leaf)

Singular and Plural Nouns, page 3

DIRECTIONS ▸ Write the plural form for each singular noun and the singular form for each plural noun.

1. brush

2. lice

3. butterflies

4. man

5. suitcases

6. turkey

7. watches

8. melody

9. cheeses

10. gases

11. cranberry

12. scarf

13. hero

14. ax

15. blueberries

16. geese

17. mouth

18. reef

19. canary

20. glitches

21. umbrellas

22. wells

23. vase

24. mosses

25. lance

26. mass

27. patch

28. video

29. baby

30. gulch

31. cello

32. sash

Possessive Nouns

A **possessive noun** shows ownership or possession.

A **singular possessive noun** shows ownership by one person or thing. To form the possessive of most singular nouns, add an apostrophe (') and *s*.

Examples:

> my aunt's house   the tree's limbs

A **plural possessive noun** shows ownership by more than one person or thing. To form the possessive of a plural noun that ends in *s*, add an apostrophe (').

Examples:

> my friends' parents   the teachers' classes

To form the possessive of a plural noun that does not end in *s*, add an apostrophe (') and *s*.

Examples:

> the men's shoes   the mice's cheese

DIRECTIONS ▷ Rewrite each phrase using a possessive noun.

1. the book by Lewis Carroll _____

2. the edge of the knife _____

3. the cover of the book _____

4. the speech given by Mayor Sanita _____

5. the aroma of the flowers _____

6. the bicycle that belongs to the children _____

7. the roar of the sirens _____

8. the colors of the rainbow _____

9. the shoes that Chris owns _____

10. the purses that belong to the women _____

DIRECTIONS ▷ Write a possessive noun to complete each sentence.

11. I saw the _____ smile.

12. The _____ spots will not come off.

13. My _____ stories always make me laugh.

14. At midnight, you can see the _____ glow.

15. _____ illustrations are amazing.

Possessive Nouns, page 2

DIRECTIONS ⟩ Write the singular possessive form of each noun.

1. sculptor _____
2. artist _____
3. hour _____
4. country _____
5. thief _____
6. Robert Frost _____
7. week _____
8. minute _____

9. weaver _____
10. Samuel Clemens _____
11. wolf _____
12. nurse _____
13. King Henry _____
14. moment _____
15. secretary _____
16. Mr. Jones _____

DIRECTIONS ⟩ Write the plural possessive form of each noun.

17. hostesses _____
18. teachers _____
19. women _____
20. masters _____
21. workers _____
22. hours _____

23. oxen _____
24. spies _____
25. buffaloes _____
26. surgeons _____
27. sheep _____
28. secretaries _____

DIRECTIONS ⟩ Rewrite each sentence. Use a possessive noun for part of the underlined phrase.

29. Charles Green was <u>the worst balloonist in Britain</u>.

   _____

30. With <u>the help of a colleague</u>, he prepared for flight.

   _____

31. Suddenly, <u>the ropes of the balloon</u> slipped off.

   _____

32. How surprised the onlookers must have been to hear <u>the calls for help from the flyers</u>!

   _____

Possessive Nouns, page 3

DIRECTIONS ▸ Write the possessive form of each noun in parentheses. Then label the possessive noun *singular* or *plural*.

1. (Luis) family celebrated Christmas together.

   _____

2. The (children) grandmother had the celebration at her ranch.

   _____

3. Their (parents) car was loaded with gifts.

   _____

4. They drove past the (sheep) pens on the way to the house.

   _____

5. They saw that the lettuce had become two (deer) dinner.

   _____

6. They could see their (cousins) faces through the window.

   _____

7. Each (person) gift from Grandmother was a sweater.

   _____

8. The (adults) sweaters were larger than the (children).

   _____

9. A turkey from the (Wilsons) ranch was the main course.

   _____

10. (Uncle Bernie) stuffing was a success as usual.

    _____

11. That night we went to the (neighbor) house to sing Christmas carols.

    _____

12. This was our (families) best Christmas ever!

    _____

Pronouns

A **pronoun** takes the place of one or more than one noun.
Examples:

I, you, he, she, it, we, they

◎ ◎◎ ◎◎ ◎◎◎◎◎◎◎ ◎◎ ◎ ◎◎◎ ◎◎◎◎◎◎◎◎ ◎◎◎◎◎ ◎◎◎ ◎◎ ◎

DIRECTIONS ▷ Write the pronoun from each sentence. Then write the noun that each pronoun refers to.

1. Some stories are designed to teach lessons; they are called fables.

   _____

2. Aesop, a Greek slave, died more than two thousand years ago, but his fables are still famous.

   _____

3. The slave told stories because he wanted to teach lessons.

   _____

4. A story about a discontented donkey was first told by Aesop; it is one of Aesop's best fables.

   _____

5. This fable is about a donkey and its owner.

   _____

6. The owner had a dog she treated well.

   _____

   _____

DIRECTIONS ▷ Rewrite each sentence, replacing appropriate nouns with pronouns.

7. The owner gave the dog a soft bed and fed the dog well.

   _____

8. The donkey tried to make the donkey's owner treat the donkey well.

   _____

9. The donkey learned that the donkey should not try to be something else.

   _____

10. Can you write two fables and illustrate the fables?

    _____

11. The chief engineer and the chief engineer's team watched.

    _____

12. Moses took a kite and attached a rope to the kite.

    _____

Agreement of Pronouns with Antecedents

When using a pronoun, make sure its **antecedent**, the noun to which it refers, is clear.
Example:

Nicolás heard. He heard.

Pronouns should agree with their antecedents in **number** and **gender**. Number tells whether a pronoun is singular or plural. Gender tells whether a pronoun is masculine, feminine, or neutral.
Example:

Nicolás heard *a librarian* tell *stories.*
He heard *her* tell *them.*

In the above example, *He* is singular and masculine, *her* is singular and feminine, and *them* is plural and neutral.

DIRECTIONS ➤ **Write each pronoun. Then write its antecedent.**

1. Thurgood Marshall was born in Maryland; his grandfather had been taken to Maryland as a slave.

   _____

2. Marshall's parents wanted to give their son a good education.

   _____

3. Marshall's mother was a teacher in the school her son attended.

   _____

4. Marshall decided that he wanted to be a lawyer.

   _____

5. Marshall attended Howard University Law School. It accepted black students when many other schools did not.

   _____

DIRECTIONS ➤ **Write the pronoun in parentheses that correctly completes each sentence.**

6. Marshall's mother sold _____ engagement ring to help pay for law school.
   (his, her)

7. Marshall was grateful to _____.
   (him, her)

8. Marshall later graduated first in _____ class.
   (his, their)

9. President Johnson appointed _____ to the Supreme Court.
   (him, them)

10. When people disagree with a court decision, _____ appeal to the Supreme Court.
    (they, it)

Subject and Object Pronouns

A **subject pronoun** is used as the subject or as part of the subject of a sentence. The subject pronouns are *I, you, he, she, it, we,* and *they.*
Example:
    We are ready to go.
An **object pronoun** is used as a direct or indirect object in a sentence. It can also be used after a preposition. The object pronouns are *me, you, him, her, it, us,* and *them.*
Example:
    Rebecca gave *me* a gift.   Rebecca gave the gift to *him.*

DIRECTIONS ▶ Complete each sentence by circling the correct pronoun in parentheses. Then write *subject pronoun* or *object pronoun* to identify the form you used.

1. Aunt Alicia gave (we, us) a book about Elizabeth Blackwell.

   _____

2. Elizabeth Blackwell's life story was fascinating to Lisa and (I, me).

   _____

3. (She, Her) and her sister became doctors.

   _____

4. (She, Her) was the first woman in the United States to enter medical school.

   _____

5. Other people disapproved of (she, her).

   _____

6. According to Daniel, (we, us) have many more opportunities than the girls did in Blackwell's day.

   _____

7. (He, Him) and his brother will have the same opportunities that women have.

   _____

8. Women like Elizabeth Blackwell have helped (we, us) by their example.

   _____

9. I admire (she, her) and her sister.

   _____

10. My father always tells (I, me) that I can become anything I want to be if I work hard.

    _____

11. I believe (he, him).

    _____

12. Can (you, him) reach for the stars?

    _____

13. Patricia and (I, me) will sing for you.

    _____

14. (They, Them) are ready to play soccer.

    _____

15. Bring (he, him) some paper and a pencil.

    _____

Subject and Object Pronouns, page 2

> **DIRECTIONS** > Write the pronoun in parentheses that correctly completes each sentence.

1. My friends and _____ wish Anna Pavlova were still alive and dancing.
   (I, me)

2. _____ ballet fans consider her one of the greatest dancers of all time.
   (We, Us)

3. Anna's parents took _____ to a ballet.
   (she, her)

4. _____ encouraged their daughter to dance.
   (They, Them)

5. Anna later made _____ very proud.
   (they, them)

6. Anna met the great dancer Vaslav Nijinsky and danced with _____.
   (he, him)

7. I am sure _____ made a wonderful dancing couple.
   (they, them)

8. I wish I could have seen _____ dance.
   (they, them)

9. Perhaps _____ too will become a great dancer someday.
   (I, me)

10. _____ had a strange experience.
    (We, Us)

11. How did _____ get here?
    (I, me)

12. _____ were staring at the television.
    (They, Them)

13. Tell _____ what that is.
    (he, him)

14. People sang and danced for _____ all the time.
    (she, her)

15. Everyone was staring at _____.
    (they, them)

> **DIRECTIONS** > Find two pronouns you did not use in the exercise above. Use each pronoun in a sentence.

_____

_____

_____

_____

Possessive Pronouns

A **possessive pronoun** shows ownership or possession of something.
The possessive pronouns *my, your, his, her, its, our,* and *their* are used before nouns.
Example:
    Jerome is learning about *his* ancestors.
The possessive pronouns *mine, yours, his, hers, ours,* and *theirs* stand alone.
Example:
    The picture is *his.*   The books are *mine.*

DIRECTIONS ➤ Rewrite each sentence. Use possessive pronouns to make the sentence less wordy.

1. Annie Oakley was famous for the shooting ability of Annie Oakley.

    _____

2. Mr. Oakley let her use the gun that he owned.

    _____

3. Buffalo Bill made Annie a star in the show that he had.

    _____

4. Annie never missed the target for which she aimed.

    _____

5. Audiences could hardly believe the eyes that belonged to them.

    _____

6. Jeremy wants to use the stereo that belongs to you.

    _____

7. The dog devoured the food that it had.

    _____

8. The Reynas had the couch that they owned reupholstered.

    _____

9. I want to change the schedule that belongs to me.

    _____

10. The animals ran for the lives of the animals.

    _____

Possessive Pronouns, page 2

DIRECTIONS ▷ Complete each sentence with a possessive pronoun.

1. Residents of St. Petersburg, Russia, are proud of _____ city.

2. We traveled to St. Petersburg to visit _____ friends.

3. Boris took us to see some of the most beautiful sights in _____ native city.

4. Marie and I, together with _____ friends, took a boat down the canals of the city.

5. Boris pointed out palaces where some of Russia's great rulers had made _____ homes.

6. At night the sun still shed _____ light on the city.

7. On nights at home, Russians love to make tea; it is _____ favorite beverage.

8. Tea and apple cake is a favorite late-night snack of _____.

9. St. Petersburg is full of flea markets where merchants show off _____ wares.

10. The traders set up _____ stalls along Nevsky Prospekt.

11. Marie invited us on a trip to one of _____ favorite places, the Kirov Islands.

12. This place has a charm all _____ own.

13. During World War II, the citizens of St. Petersburg endured a 900-day siege of _____ city by the Germans.

14. We saw a man with a ribbon on _____ coat, showing that he was a veteran of that siege.

15. People who suffered through that period wear _____ ribbons proudly.

16. Snow, ice, hunger, and disease took _____ toll among the brave residents of St. Petersburg.

17. _____ name at the time was Leningrad, in honor of Lenin, a leader of the revolution of 1917.

Reflexive Pronouns

A **reflexive pronoun** usually refers to the subject of a sentence.
The reflexive pronouns are *myself, yourself, himself, herself, itself, ourselves, yourselves,* and *themselves.*
Example:
    Marie found *herself* alone in the quiet forest.

DIRECTIONS > Underline each reflexive pronoun. Write the subject to which it refers.

1. Diane shook the sand off herself.

   _____

2. Ben dried himself with a towel.

   _____

3. The members of the other team warmed themselves up by swimming laps.

   _____

4. We discussed the race among ourselves.

   _____

5. I needed to be by myself for a few minutes.

   _____

6. Do you ever need to be by yourself?

   _____

7. The dog dried itself off by rolling in the grass.

   _____

8. Ed and Beverly made themselves a mushroom and sausage pizza.

   _____

9. I chopped the bell peppers and the onions myself.

   _____

10. Estella and I won a prize for ourselves.

   _____

DIRECTIONS > Complete each sentence with a reflexive pronoun that agrees with its subject.

11. Elaine's towel was not in the pile when she went to dry _____.

12. It was at the end of the bench by _____.

13. For a moment, Ben found _____ without a towel.

14. Be sure you dry _____ well.

15. We must protect _____ from the cold.

16. I suggest that all swimmers dress _____ quickly.

17. I know that I have to keep _____ warm.

18. We also have to keep _____ covered.

19. Try not to allow _____ to get a cold.

20. The girls scared _____ by telling scary stories.

Indefinite Pronouns

An **indefinite pronoun** is a pronoun that does not refer to a specific person, place, thing, or idea.

The indefinite pronouns are *everyone, everything, everybody, anybody, many, most, few, each, some, someone, all, nothing, nobody,* and *no one*.

Example:

     Someone is knocking at the door.

An indefinite pronoun can be singular or plural. Follow the rules for subject-verb agreement when using indefinite pronouns as subjects.

Examples:

     Some of the girls are absent.   *Everyone* is sick.

DIRECTIONS ▷ Write the indefinite pronoun from each sentence. Then write *singular* or *plural* to identify the indefinite pronoun.

1. Everyone seems to be leaving.

_____

2. Some have to stay.

_____

3. Everything needs to be picked up.

_____

4. Is anybody volunteering?

_____

5. I see that many of you want to leave.

_____

DIRECTIONS ▷ Write the verb form in parentheses that correctly completes each sentence.

6. Most of you _____ been fairly neat.
        (has, have)

7. A few _____ problems for the rest.
     (creates, create)

8. If each of you _____, it will not take long to clean up the mess.
     (helps, help)

9. Someone _____ to carry the trash to the bins.
     (needs, need)

10. All of us _____ to go home.
     (want, wants)

11. Now, nothing _____ out of place.
     (is, are)

Who, Whom, Whose

Use **who** as a subject pronoun and **whom** as an object pronoun.
Example:
   Who is not going?   To whom am I speaking?
Do not confuse the possessive pronoun *whose* with the contraction *who's.*
Example:
   Whose books are these?   Who's that at the door?

DIRECTIONS > Write *who* or *whom* to complete each sentence.

1. _____ will help decorate the gym for the costume party?

2. _____ did you call?

3. Do you know _____ is planning to attend?

4. With _____ are you going?

5. _____ are you going to pretend to be?

6. From _____ did you get that idea?

7. Do you think the others will know _____ you are?

8. _____ can pick up the refreshments?

9. From _____ do we get the money to pay for them?

10. _____ is going to be the costume judge?

DIRECTIONS > Write *whose* or *who's* to complete each sentence.

11. _____ going to drive everyone?

12. _____ parents have a van?

13. _____ your favorite cartoon character?

14. _____ the boy in the Napoleon costume?

15. This mask is mine, but _____ mask is that?

16. _____ costume did you borrow?

17. _____ Bradley supposed to be?

18. _____ selecting the best costume?

19. I can't decide _____ costume should win.

20. The person _____ the winner will get a prize.

Using Pronouns

DIRECTIONS ▸ Underline the pronouns in each sentence.

1. Leon asked Anne to tell him about some of her favorite books.
2. "Okay," Anne told him.
3. She chose two books and opened them.
4. Here are a few of the biographies about women pioneers.
5. I could talk about one of them.
6. Leon told her to pick one.
7. He enjoyed it.
8. I have been reading about Marie Dorion.
9. When Marie accompanied the trappers to Oregon, they showed her great respect.
10. Marie loved Pierre Dorion and traveled with him.
11. One day Marie found herself alone in the quiet forest.
12. Marie Dorion untied the horse and loaded it with supplies.
13. As the three of them left, Marie Dorion made herself a promise—that she and her children would survive.
14. Nine days later, a snowstorm trapped her and the boys.
15. The Dorions kept themselves alive for 53 days.
16. The Walla Walla Indians found Marie Dorion; they rescued her and the boys.
17. Anna Taylor went to Niagara Falls, but she crossed it differently.
18. Witnesses watched with their mouths open.
19. Taylor squeezed herself into a barrel.
20. Was she the first person to survive a trip over Niagara Falls?
21. The Kung people use eggshells to store their water supply.
22. A Ndaka bride is carried to her wedding on a shaded platform; indeed, the day is almost entirely hers.
23. Monica told herself that she must drive slowly.
24. Monica's younger sister and brother were with her.
25. Bob said that he was hungry.
26. The children amused themselves by singing.
27. Cars pulled off the highway because it was icy.
28. Monica drove slowly, but she still lost control.
29. For a moment she found herself helpless.
30. Then she maneuvered the car and stopped it.
31. Marla and Darnell both told me the news, but I didn't believe them at first.
32. I asked Mr. O'Reilly, but he hadn't heard anything about it.
33. Then Trina ran in and said that she had seen the whole thing.
34. After Trina explained just what had happened, I thanked her as politely as I could.
35. Then I smiled secretly, just to myself, and hurried away.

Adjectives

An **adjective** is a word that modifies, or describes, a noun or a pronoun.
Example:

We saw *lazy* lions beneath a *shady* tree.

Adjectives tell *what kind, how many,* or *which one.*
Examples:

lazy lions, *three* adults, *that* tree

The adjectives *a, an,* and *the* are called **articles**.
Use *a* before a word that begins with a consonant sound.
Examples:

a lion, *a* tree

Use *an* before a word that begins with a vowel sound.
Examples:

an adventure, *an* older lioness

DIRECTIONS ➤ Write each adjective. Label it *article* or *describing*.

1. Russia is an enormous country.

   _____

2. It has long, cold winters.

   _____

3. Rich crops are grown in the black, fertile earth.

   _____

4. Many of the farms have early harvests.

   _____

5. The lion is a sociable creature.

   _____

6. A lioness, calm but alert, watches over her smallest cub.

   _____

7. Cubs learn important skills at an early age.

   _____

8. Nightly hunts may provide rich feasts.

   _____

Adjectives, page 2

DIRECTIONS > **Change the meaning and tone of each sentence by replacing the adjectives. Write each new sentence.**

1. The empty countryside has a lonely feeling.

   _____

2. We had a dull, boring visit in the dreary forests of Russia.

   _____

3. We then returned to the lively, bustling cities of the United States.

   _____

DIRECTIONS > **Use adjectives and articles to complete these sentences.**

4. When the _____ lion is on the prowl, other _____

   animals must be cautious.

5. _____ wildebeest or _____ antelope could become a

   _____ lion's dinner.

6. Then the pride of lions, _____ and _____, might settle

   in for a _____ nap.

DIRECTIONS > **Imagine that you are an archaeologist being interviewed about the ancient Egyptians and their way of life. Use adjectives to answer the reporter's questions.**

7. What words describe their kingdoms?

   _____

8. What type of person do you think a king or queen had to be in ancient Egypt?

   _____

9. What words describe their clothing and jewelry?

   _____

10. How do you feel about your most recent discovery?

   _____

Proper Adjectives

A **proper adjective** is an adjective that is formed from a proper noun. A proper adjective always begins with a capital letter.

Examples:

Proper Noun	Proper Adjective
Africa	African
Scotland	Scottish

DIRECTIONS ▸ Write the proper adjective from each sentence. Then write the proper noun from which the proper adjective was formed.

1. The African nations were especially interesting.

   _____

2. We bought some beautiful Hungarian crystal.

   _____

3. The English language was spoken there.

   _____

4. Our Yugoslavian friend came with us on our trip around the world.

   _____

5. Joyce enjoyed the Italian paintings.

   _____

6. Ralph liked the visit to a Tibetan monastery.

   _____

7. I studied Islamic law at the university.

   _____

8. Ron purchased a postcard with a picture of Nefertiti, a beautiful Egyptian queen.

   _____

9. We purchased Japanese paper for origami.

   _____

10. The Mexican pottery was less expensive at the market.

    _____

DIRECTIONS ▸ Write a sentence using the proper adjective formed from each proper noun.

11. China (Chinese)

    _____

12. Spain (Spanish)

    _____

13. Armenia (Armenian)

    _____

14. Britain (British)

    _____

15. Texas (Texan)

    _____

This, That, These, Those

A **demonstrative adjective** tells which one. The words *this, that, these,* and *those* are demonstrative adjectives.
Example:
> *This* book has more illustrations than *those* magazines.

DIRECTIONS ▶ Write the demonstrative adjective from each sentence. Label the demonstrative adjective *singular* or *plural*.

1. This open house is going to be a real success.

   _____

2. Ask those students to come and help.

   _____

3. These science projects need to be arranged.

   _____

4. Where shall we display these drawings?

   _____

5. Put them on that bulletin board.

   _____

6. You must seize this opportunity.

   _____

DIRECTIONS ▶ Label each underlined word *adjective* or *pronoun*. Rewrite each sentence in which *this, that, these,* or *those* is used as a pronoun. Change the pronoun into a demonstrative adjective.

7. What shall I do with <u>these</u>?

   _____

8. Arrange them on <u>that</u> table.

   _____

9. Do we have any more of <u>those</u>?

   _____

10. Look in <u>this</u> drawer.

    _____

11. Did you draw <u>that</u>?

    _____

12. Are <u>those</u> maps clear?

    _____

13. Shall I look in <u>these</u>?

    _____

14. <u>That</u> table is covered with books and maps.

    _____

Predicate Adjectives

A **predicate adjective** is an adjective that follows a linking verb and describes the subject of a sentence. Forms of *be* are the most common linking verbs. Other linking verbs include forms of *taste, look, smell, feel, appear, seem*, and *become*.
Example: I look *tired*, but I feel *fine*.

DIRECTIONS ▷ Write the predicate adjective from each sentence. Then write the word it modifies.

1. The air feels warm today. _____

2. The flowers smell unusually sweet. _____

3. High in the sky is the sun. _____

4. The horses look peaceful in the meadow. _____

5. Sharon feels happy outside. _____

6. She is eager for a ride on her horse. _____

7. Her horse appears ready to go. _____

8. How beautiful is the day! _____

9. The surgeon was skillful in the operating room. _____

10. The mango tastes bitter, but I will eat it anyway. _____

11. That horse at the far end of the meadow is fast. _____

12. Its coat appears gray in the shade. _____

13. However, it becomes silver in the bright sun. _____

14. Horses like that are unusual. _____

15. They are usually well-trained. _____

16. Rin Tin Tin and Lassie seem brave in their movies. _____

17. When audiences watched, they felt good. _____

18. Rin Tin Tin looked fearless. _____

DIRECTIONS ▷ Use the linking verb to write a sentence containing a predicate adjective.

19. feel _____

20. taste _____

Comparison with Adjectives: *er, est*

An adjective has three degrees of comparison: **positive**, **comparative**, and **superlative**.
The *positive degree* of an adjective is used when no comparison is being made.
Example:
> This is a *hot* day.

The *comparative degree* of an adjective is used to compare two items. Form the comparative of most one-syllable adjectives by adding *er*. For some words that end in consonants, double the consonant before you add *er*.
Example:
> Today is *hotter* than yesterday.

The *superlative degree* of an adjective is used to compare three or more items. Form the superlative of most one-syllable adjectives by adding *est*. For some words that end in consonants, double the consonant before you add *est*.
Example:
> This is the *hottest* day of the year.

DIRECTIONS ➤ Write the comparative form and the superlative form of each adjective.

Positive	Comparative	Superlative
1. cold	_____	_____
2. safe	_____	_____
3. funny	_____	_____
4. flat	_____	_____
5. shiny	_____	_____
6. tall	_____	_____
7. white	_____	_____
8. sweet	_____	_____
9. sad	_____	_____
10. young	_____	_____

DIRECTIONS ➤ Choose the form of the adjective in parentheses that correctly completes the sentence.

11. France is _____ than Luxembourg.
(large)

12. Austria is _____ than France.
(small)

13. Luxembourg is the _____ of the three countries.
(small)

Other Comparisons

Use **more** or **less** and **most** or **least** to form the comparative and the superlative of most adjectives with two or more syllables.
Examples:

wonderful, more wonderful, most wonderful

wonderful, less wonderful, least wonderful

Some adjectives have special forms for comparing. Memorize adjectives that change spelling completely in the comparative and the superlative degrees.
Examples:

good, better, best

DIRECTIONS ▶ Write the comparative form and the superlative form of each adjective.

Positive	Comparative	Superlative
1. energetic		
2. difficult		
3. generous		
4. affectionate		
5. active		
6. bad		
7. much		
8. likely		
9. expensive		
10. crowded		

DIRECTIONS ▶ Rewrite each sentence. Use the form of the adjective in parentheses that correctly completes the sentence.

11. Ruffles is the (beautiful) puppy of the litter.

_____

12. Sport is (intelligent) than Ruffles.

_____

13. Of all the puppies, Tuffy is the (much) fun.

_____

Using Adjectives

DIRECTIONS Write the correct degree of comparison for the adjective in parentheses.

1. The stone houses of wealthy Mayas looked _____ (strong) and

   _____ (impressive) than those of their poorer neighbors.

2. The clothing of Mayan priests was the _____ (elaborate) of all.

3. The _____ (beautiful) city of Tenochtitlán may have been the Aztecs'

   _____ (great) achievement.

4. The Incas, who seem to have been _____ (aggressive) than the Aztecs or

   the Mayas, ruled the _____ (large) empire in the hemisphere.

5. We were all competing to see who could create the _____ (good) poster

   about an ancient civilization.

6. The Great Wall of China wasn't a _____ (bad) idea at all!

7. This poster is definitely _____ (good) than last year's winner.

8. Ms. Mata is feeling _____ (good) than she did yesterday, rather than

   _____ (bad), so she'll judge the posters this afternoon.

9. This contest has been _____ (much) fun than last year's contest.

10. In fact, it may be the _____ (good) activity of the year.

DIRECTIONS Underline the adjectives in each sentence below.

11. The fierce battle at Gettysburg took place in 1863.

12. This battle was not the first conflict of the Civil War.

13. Few Southerners reached Union lines.

14. A general named Robert E. Lee led the Confederate army.

15. The Confederates approached under heavy gunfire.

16. That army would not turn back during an attack.

17. Many soldiers on both sides were killed.

18. Gettysburg is a pivotal battle in American history.

19. President Lincoln visited the site several months later.

20. He read a memorable speech, now known as the Gettysburg Address.

Action Verbs

DIRECTIONS ▸ Underline the action verb in each sentence.

1. Dr. James Naismith originated the game of basketball.

2. The Hillside team and the Seaside team compete every year.

3. The two centers leaped for the ball.

4. They stretched their arms high into the air.

5. A Hillside forward grabbed the ball.

6. The forward dribbled the ball to the end of the court.

7. She aimed for the basket.

8. The ball flew through the air.

9. The ball bounced off the backboard.

10. Several players jumped for the ball.

DIRECTIONS ▸ Rewrite each sentence. Use a strong action verb to make the sentence more vivid.

11. A Seaside forward got the ball.

_____

12. Her teammate went to the other end of the court.

_____

13. The forward sent the ball the length of the court.

_____

14. Romelia put the ball into the basket.

_____

15. The Seaside fans and players yelled excitedly.

_____

Linking Verbs

A **linking verb** connects the subject of a sentence to a noun that renames the subject or to an adjective that describes it.

The most common linking verb is *be*. Some forms of *be* are *am, is, are, was,* and *were*.

Example:

Carolyn *is* tired.

DIRECTIONS ▷ Write the verb from each sentence. Label it *action* or *linking*.

1. The family celebrated Thanksgiving at Uncle Tómas's house.

   _____

2. His house is large enough for us all.

   _____

3. His table reaches from one end of the dining room to the other.

   _____

4. Uncle Tómas cooked the whole dinner by himself.

   _____

5. He appeared tired.

   _____

6. However, he greeted everyone with warmth and enthusiasm.

   _____

7. The turkey smelled wonderful.

   _____

8. Everyone became impatient.

   _____

9. The dinner table looked beautiful.

   _____

10. The greenhouse effect is a danger to our environment.

    _____

11. Heat rises.

    _____

12. Some heat energy escapes Earth's atmosphere.

    _____

13. Many gases are colorless and odorless.

    _____

14. High levels of carbon dioxide were present.

    _____

15. The Industrial Revolution was a turning point for the environment.

    _____

16. Many researchers study global warming.

    _____

17. Our community recycles glass, newspaper, and aluminum.

    _____

18. It was a terrific place.

    _____

19. Connie opened the big umbrella.

    _____

20. The king and queen were quite argumentative.

    _____

Action Verbs and Linking Verbs

DIRECTIONS > Read the following passage. Then underline the action verbs and circle the linking verbs.

Marathoners are amazing athletes. They compete in races more than 26 miles long. The best marathoners are usually small and slight. They need very strong legs and powerful lungs, too. Youth, however, is not necessarily an advantage in a marathon.

This long race carries the name of an ancient battlefield. In 490 B.C., the Greeks defeated the Persians at Marathon. According to legend, a Greek soldier ran all the way from Marathon to Athens with news of the victory. He ran more than 20 miles. Now a marathon is a regular part of the Olympic Games. The official distance for an Olympic marathon is 42,195 meters, or 26 miles and 385 yards.

DIRECTIONS > Complete the following sentences. Add the kind of verb identified in parentheses.

1. The team members _____ every day.
   (action)

2. Their coach _____ them.
   (action)

3. The day of the big race _____ .
   (action)

4. The athletes _____ enthusiastic.
   (linking)

5. They _____ .
   (action)

6. Coal, oil, and natural gas _____ fossil fuels.
   (linking)

7. Dr. Huong _____ global warming.
   (action)

8. Some students _____ a model of our planet.
   (action)

9. Wood _____ a renewable resource.
   (linking)

10. Technology _____ problems as well as solutions.
    (action)

Main Verbs and Helping Verbs

A verb phrase is made up of two or more verbs. The **main verb** is the most important verb in a verb phrase.
Example:
> My teacher <u>was *born*</u> in Venezuela.

The last word of a verb phrase is the main verb. The other words are **helping verbs**.
Example:
> My teacher <u>*was* born</u> in Venezuela.

DIRECTIONS ▷ Underline the verb phrase in each sentence, and circle the main verb.

1. The Powells are moving.

2. They have lived next door for ten years.

3. I am missing them already.

4. Their son has been my best friend for a long time.

5. The family had moved here from California.

6. Why do they want a different house?

7. Mrs. Powell has accepted a job in New York.

8. Her sister is living in New York.

9. She was working for a large publishing company.

10. The same company did offer Mrs. Powell a job.

11. Does she like big cities?

12. She was not complaining in her last letter.

13. She had lived in Chicago at one time.

14. She is enjoying the museums.

15. Mr. Powell will find a good job.

16. Their son has entered school.

17. He might meet many new friends.

18. A tai chi master may visit our school.

19. His daughter is living in the United States.

20. She could give us a lesson in tai chi.

Main Verbs and Helping Verbs, page 2

DIRECTIONS > Write *main verb* or *helping verb* to identify the underlined verb in each sentence.

1. The tiny curtain <u>will</u> slowly open. _____

2. Two figures <u>are</u> dancing into view. _____

3. The figures are <u>called</u> puppets. _____

4. Puppets can be <u>made</u> out of cloth and wood. _____

5. Our puppet theater may <u>give</u> three shows a year. _____

6. Each show <u>is</u> performed for four weekends. _____

7. New plays are <u>rehearsed</u> carefully. _____

8. I <u>have</u> become a puppeteer with the company. _____

9. I <u>am</u> memorizing lines and movements. _____

10. The new play was <u>written</u> in Spanish and English. _____

11. Sometimes our lines are <u>spoken</u> in English. _____

12. Sometimes audiences <u>have</u> asked for Spanish. _____

13. All the puppeteers <u>can</u> speak both languages. _____

14. We <u>should</u> do this for several years. _____

15. <u>Do</u> the audiences enjoy the shows? _____

DIRECTIONS > Complete these sentences with a main verb and a helping verb from the box.

are	were	does	need	should
will	be	blooming	picked	visit

16. The roses _____ _____ today.

17. The garden _____ _____ beautiful next year.

18. Everyone _____ _____ during the summer.

19. A sturdy sunflower _____ not _____ support.

20. The apples _____ already _____ .

420 LANGUAGE ARTS

Principal Parts of Verbs

The **principal parts** of verbs are the **present, present participle, past,** and **past participle**.

For regular verbs, the present participle is formed by adding *ing* to the present. It is used with a form of the helping verb *be*.

The past and the past participle of regular verbs are formed by adding *ed* or *d* to the present. The past participle uses a form of the helping verb *have*.

Examples:

Present	Present Participle	Past	Past Participle
play	(is, are, am) playing	played	(have, has, had) played
move	(is, are, am) moving	moved	(have, has, had) moved

An irregular verb forms its past and past participle in other ways. A dictionary shows the principal parts of these verbs.

DIRECTIONS Underline the main verb in each sentence. Write *present, present participle, past,* or *past participle* to label the main verbs.

1. Randy's class studies world history. _____

2. The students are reading about the Renaissance. _____

3. The teacher has taught them about the art of that time. _____

4. They have learned much about Renaissance painting. _____

5. Yesterday they visited an art museum. _____

6. They had always gone to a different museum before. _____

7. They had seen a display of Egyptian art at the Egyptian Museum. _____

8. The English teachers had read two new novels. _____

9. The band director is planning the fall musical. _____

10. The cafeteria monitor talks to the children. _____

DIRECTIONS Write the correct form of the verb in parentheses in each sentence. At the end of each sentence, label the verb *present, present participle, past,* or *past participle*.

11. These days the class _____ something about history every week. (learn)

_____

12. Today the students are _____ a movie about Leonardo da Vinci. (watch)

_____

Principal Parts of Verbs, page 2

DIRECTIONS Write the present participle, past, and past participle of each verb.

Present	Present Participle (with *is, are, am*)	Past	Past Participle (with *have, has, had*)
1. hike	hiking	hiked	hiked
2. try			
3. show			
4. talk			
5. bring			
6. ring			
7. create			
8. fly			
9. drink			
10. witness			
11. wear			
12. catch			
13. grow			
14. begin			
15. go			
16. sit			
17. think			
18. see			
19. teach			
20. understand			
21. forget			
22. splash			
23. eat			
24. watch			
25. arrive			

Present, Past, and Future Tenses

The **tense** of a verb tells the time of the action or being.
Present tense tells that something is happening now.
Examples:

Dena *laughs* at the jokes.   Jon *walks* home.

Past tense tells that something happened in the past. The action is over.
Examples:

Dena *laughed* at the jokes.   Jon *walked* home.

Future tense tells that something will happen in the future. Use *will* with the verb.
Examples:

Dena *will laugh* at the jokes.   Jon *will walk* home.

DIRECTIONS ➤ Write the verb from each sentence and label it *present, past,* or *future*.

1. Marlene works in her garden every day.

   _____

2. Yesterday she prepared the ground for the tomatoes.

   _____

3. Tomorrow she will set the plants in the ground.

   _____

4. She planted carrots last week.

   _____

5. Leaves will appear in a few days.

   _____

6. Marlene will pick radishes tomorrow.

   _____

7. She pulls weeds every day.

   _____

8. The garden will soon be full of vegetables.

   _____

9. Teddy's team will bat first.

   _____

10. The visiting team always bats first.

    _____

11. In the last game, she played first base.

    _____

12. Sometimes a player changes positions.

    _____

13. The coach gives everyone a chance to play.

    _____

DIRECTIONS ➤ Write a sentence with each verb, using the tense in parentheses.

14. water (present) _____

15. dig (future) _____

16. grow (future) _____

17. help (past) _____

Perfect Tenses

There are three **perfect tenses: present perfect, past perfect**, and **future perfect**.
Form the perfect tenses with the past participle and the helping verbs *have, has, had,*
or *will have*.
Examples:
> Mr. Lee *has arranged* a comedy show for us. (present perfect)
> Mr. Lee *had arranged* a comedy show for us. (past perfect)
> Mr. Lee *will have arranged* a comedy show for us. (future perfect)

DIRECTIONS ▸ Underline the verb in each sentence and label it *present perfect, past perfect,*
or *future perfect*.

1. We have started a reading club.
   _____

2. By next year, we will have discussed eight
   books.
   _____

3. Susan often had suggested the book *Little
   Women* to the club members.
   _____

4. I have always enjoyed books by Louisa May
   Alcott.
   _____

5. I will have finished the book before the next
   meeting.
   _____

6. The school newspaper has written about our
   group.
   _____

7. The reporter had interviewed us last year.
   _____

8. We have chosen the book *The Secret Garden*
   as our next selection.
   _____

DIRECTIONS ▸ Complete each sentence, using the correct perfect tense of the verb in
parentheses.

9. Tom _____ sitting next to Francie this year. (enjoy)

10. He _____ not _____ her before September. (meet)

11. Next week they _____ each other for six months. (know)

12. They _____ often _____ their favorite books this
    year. (share)

13. Francie read a novel because Tom _____ it. (recommend)

Irregular Verbs

An **irregular verb** does not end with *ed* to form the past and the past participle. Verbs such as *be, have*, and *do* form the past and the past participle in other ways.
Examples:

Present	Past	Past Participle
is, are, am	was	were
has, have	had	had
do, does	did	done

DIRECTIONS ▷ **Complete each sentence with the correct form of the verb in parentheses.**

1. I _____ excited about our camping trip.
   (am, is)

2. I _____ wanted to visit Yosemite for years.
   (has, have)

3. _____ you looking forward to it, too?
   (Is, Are)

4. _____ your family go camping often?
   (Does, Do)

5. Last year we _____ going camping once each month.
   (was, were)

6. We _____ planning to go camping every year.
   (is, are)

7. Jason _____ going to come camping with us.
   (was, were)

8. His parents _____ not letting him go camping.
   (is, are)

9. I _____ not think that is fair.
   (does, do)

10. We _____ purchased a lot of camping equipment.
    (has, have)

DIRECTIONS ▷ **Use a form of *be, have*, or *do* to complete each sentence.**

11. Yosemite Valley _____ carved by glaciers.

12. Glaciers _____ cut a mountain in half.

13. The mountain _____ called Half Dome.

14. _____ anyone ever climb Half Dome?

More Irregular Verbs

Remember that an **irregular verb** is a verb that does not end with *ed* to show the past and the past participle.
Examples:

      I *ate* at home.   I *have eaten* at home.

DIRECTIONS   Complete each sentence. Write the past or the past participle form of the verb in parentheses.

1. Nancy's peach tree has _____ several feet.
                                    (grow)

2. She _____ it five years ago.
                (buy)

3. Another gardener had _____ it to her.
                            (sell)

4. Since then, she has _____ hours caring for it.
                          (spend)

5. She has _____ very good care of it.
                    (take)

6. It has _____ a very large tree.
                (become)

7. Her friends have never _____ such beautiful peaches.
                        (see)

8. Nancy has _____ some peaches to them.
                  (give)

9. Her family has already _____ a few this summer.
                      (eat)

10. Last year she _____ several pounds of peaches.
                (freeze)

11. She _____ dozens of pies.
          (make)

12. This year she has _____ the bruised peaches for jam.
              (choose)

13. The neighbors have _____ Nancy how to make jam.
              (tell)

14. They also _____ a variety of vegetables in their garden.
             (grow)

15. Sarah and María have _____ fresh produce at the market.
            (buy)

Direct Objects

A **direct object** is the noun or pronoun that receives the action of the verb. A direct object tells who or what receives the action.
Example:
> Bobby loved his *parents*.

DIRECTIONS ▸ Underline the direct object in each sentence.

1. A narrow strip of land once connected North America with South America.

2. The strip of land blocked ocean travel between the Atlantic Ocean and the Pacific Ocean.

3. The Panama Canal now divides the two continents.

4. It provides a short route from the Atlantic Ocean to the Pacific Ocean.

5. The United States operated the canal after building it.

6. Before the eruption of Mount St. Helens, people heard a deep rumble.

7. People more than 200 miles away noticed the noise.

8. Hot gas and ash burned entire forests.

9. The eruption killed more than 60 people.

10. Many residents lost their homes.

11. My dog Chester eats tomatoes.

12. He devours potatoes.

13. My dog wrinkles the covers on the bed.

14. I flatten the pillows on the sofa.

15. Silvia takes a nap every afternoon.

DIRECTIONS ▸ Rewrite each incomplete sentence, adding a direct object.

16. Rough seas near Cape Horn endangered.

_____

17. Ships can carry from one ocean to another in far less time.

_____

18. A Panama Canal pilot guides through the Canal.

_____

19. The United States paid to Panama for control of the Canal.

_____

Indirect Objects

An **indirect object** tells to whom or for whom the action of the verb is done.
Example:
> Jack showed the *dog* kindness.

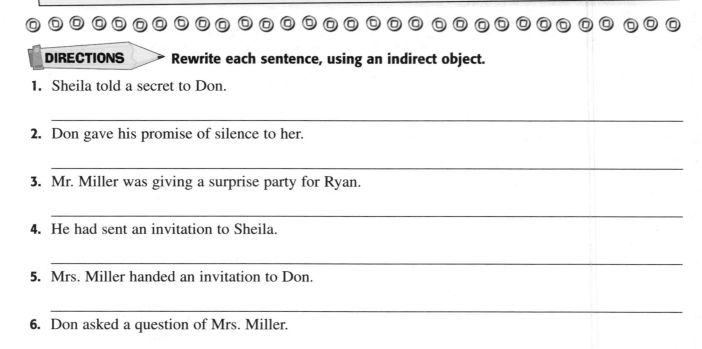

DIRECTIONS ▸ Rewrite each sentence, using an indirect object.

1. Sheila told a secret to Don.

_____

2. Don gave his promise of silence to her.

_____

3. Mr. Miller was giving a surprise party for Ryan.

_____

4. He had sent an invitation to Sheila.

_____

5. Mrs. Miller handed an invitation to Don.

_____

6. Don asked a question of Mrs. Miller.

_____

DIRECTIONS ▸ Underline the indirect object in each sentence.

7. The three pals gave their guests a hearty welcome.

8. I sent my friends holiday cards with pictures of the animals.

9. My friends asked me questions about the first meeting.

10. A TV talk show host gave us a spot on her program.

11. I told her the facts.

12. An animal-food company sent me boxes of free food.

13. A restaurant owner gave me a free meal.

14. The animals brought my family a lot of public attention.

15. My neighbors bought them new leashes.

16. The animals still gave everyone friendly greetings.

Predicate Nominatives

A **predicate nominative** is a noun or pronoun that follows a linking verb and renames the subject.
Example:
> Lassie has been a *celebrity* for decades.

DIRECTIONS ➤ **Write the predicate nominative from each sentence.**

1. Fred is an enthusiastic hiker. _____

2. He is a member of a hiking club. _____

3. Jill is his best friend. _____

4. She is the fastest walker in the club. _____

5. The president of the club is Michelle. _____

6. She is an energetic girl. _____

7. Her mother is a famous climber. _____

8. Mrs. Wu is the teacher of his art class now. _____

9. Oil painting is part of the class's training. _____

10. Enrique's first oil painting was a portrait of his mother. _____

11. Enrique will become a professional artist. _____

12. An obedience trial is a good test. _____

13. The person who observes your pet is the judge. _____

14. The pet show organizer was Estella. _____

15. The funniest entry in the show was a poodle. _____

DIRECTIONS ➤ **Complete each sentence, using a predicate nominative that fits the description in parentheses.**

16. It was _____.
(day of the week)

17. The group was _____.
(a club)

18. The leader of the hike was _____.
(a girl)

19. The group's destination was _____.
(a place)

Transitive and Intransitive Verbs

> A **transitive verb** is an action verb that is followed by a noun or a pronoun that receives the action.
> *Example:*
>   I *know* the story.
> An **intransitive verb** includes all linking verbs and any action verbs that do not take an object.
> *Example:*
>   My friends *cried*.

DIRECTIONS ▷ Underline the verb in each sentence. Label it *transitive* or *intransitive*.

1. The Mendozas went to the Grand Canyon.

2. They had never visited it before.

3. Mr. Mendoza drove the car most of the way.

4. He drove for miles through the desert.

5. The children rode in the back seat.

6. Luis saw the canyon first.

7. No one felt sadder than Roberto.

8. Roberto loved the shepherd!

9. The next day the caretaker did stop.

10. Bobby had found a home on the prairie.

11. The workers had built a sturdy metal fence.

12. I inherited a cat from the former tenants.

13. Smith, the cat, sat quietly on the sofa.

14. I drove to the kennel for my two dogs.

15. The dogs would see Smith soon.

16. I offered the dogs treats.

17. I gave each dog a warning about politeness.

18. Then I entered the house with the two canines.

19. The cat bristled.

20. I gave the cat a hug.

21. The poodle gave the cat a sniff.

22. Jones understood cats.

Adverbs

An **adverb** modifies a verb, an adjective, or another adverb.
An adverb tells *how, when, where,* or *to what extent.*
Examples:
Our skates moved *effortlessly*. (how)
The ice is glistening *now*. (when)
The canals are frozen *there*. (where)
The air was *very* dry. (to what extent)

◎ ◎

> **DIRECTIONS** Write the adverb from each sentence. Label the adverb *how, when, where,* or *to what extent.*

1. Kevin rose early and watched the sun rise. _____

2. He looked up and saw billowing clouds. _____

3. They were very beautiful in the soft light. _____

4. A large gray hawk circled lazily. _____

5. A gopher cautiously poked its nose out of its hole. _____

6. Hans dressed warmly. _____

7. He walked outside. _____

8. He waved happily to his friends. _____

9. The air was quite cold. _____

10. Many people skated tonight. _____

> **DIRECTIONS** Write each adverb and the word it modifies. Label the modified word *verb, adjective,* or *adverb.*

11. Kevin watched the gopher very quietly. _____

12. He remained quite still. _____

13. The world gradually awoke. _____

14. Singing birds sweetly greeted the morning. _____

15. Kevin heard his parents' voices and returned reluctantly. _____

16. He suddenly felt very hungry. _____

Placement of Adverbs in Sentences

Place most adverbs that modify adjectives or other adverbs just before the word they modify.

Examples:

Clouds scudded *very* swiftly across the sky.

The sky was *quite* beautiful.

Place most adverbs that modify verbs almost anywhere in the sentence.

Examples:

Lifeguards watched the swimmers *carefully*.

Lifeguards *carefully* watched the swimmers.

◎ ◎

DIRECTIONS ➤ **Write the adverbs from the sentences. Label each one *yes* if it can be moved or *no* if it cannot be moved.**

1. Very rough surf discouraged most of the sailors. _____

2. Bruce can be rather careless. _____

3. Recklessly, Bruce sailed out of the harbor. _____

4. Suddenly, the wind rose. _____

5. He struggled desperately with the sails. _____

6. The largest crowds appeared later. _____

7. A strong undertow could be quite dangerous. _____

8. Our lifeguard warned a swimmer sternly. _____

9. Smart swimmers always observe the rules. _____

10. The sand grew quite hot under the blazing sun. _____

DIRECTIONS ➤ **Add the adverb in parentheses to each sentence and write the sentence. Vary placement of the adverbs.**

11. A wave crashed over Bruce's boat. (heavily)

_____

12. The boat overturned in the water. (clumsily)

_____

13. Bruce floundered in the water. (helplessly)

_____

14. Another boat observed Bruce's struggle. (immediately)

_____

Comparison with Adverbs

To form the **comparative** or the **superlative** of most short adverbs, add *er* or *est*.
Example:
>   Bradley is *nicer* than his brother.

Use *more* or *less* and *most* or *least* instead of *er* and *est* with adverbs that end in *ly* or have two or more syllables.
Example:
>   Today is the *most enjoyable* day I have had all year.

DIRECTIONS ▸ Write the comparative form and the superlative form of each adverb.

1. low _____ _____

2. near _____ _____

3. slowly _____ _____

4. seriously _____ _____

5. eagerly _____ _____

6. fast _____ _____

7. frequently _____ _____

8. readily _____ _____

9. noticeably _____ _____

10. easy _____ _____

DIRECTIONS ▸ Complete each sentence. Use the correct form of the adverb in parentheses.

11. Leslie and Patrick practice archery _____ than Ron and Janet do.
(often)

12. Leslie scored _____ of all the students in the class.
(high)

13. She aimed _____ than the others.
(carefully)

14. Patrick was surprised when she shot _____ than he did.
(accurately)

15. He is strong, and his arrows always fly _____ than hers.
(far)

16. _____ than last time, he raised his bow.
(slowly)

Negatives

Negatives are words that mean "no." The words *no, not, never, nowhere, nothing, nobody, no one, neither, scarcely*, and *barely* are common negatives. Use only one negative in a sentence.
Example:

    CORRECT   No one should ever drive on ice.
    INCORRECT   No one should never drive on ice.

DIRECTIONS ▷ Write the word in parentheses that correctly completes each negative sentence.

1. On one side of the planet Mercury, the sun does not _____ set.
                                            (ever, never)

2. The other side of the planet gets _____ sun at all.
                                       (no, any)

3. _____ on this planet are the temperatures moderate.
    (Anywhere, Nowhere)

4. As far as we know, Mercury has _____ moons.
                                    (any, no)

5. There is not _____ who has been to Mercury.
                (anybody, nobody)

6. We do not know _____ about Mercury.
                (everything, nothing)

7. _____ of us can fly there.
   (Neither, Either)

DIRECTIONS ▷ Choose three statements from the activity above. Rewrite each negative statement using the word you did not choose from the parentheses. You will need to change other words to write the sentences correctly.

8. _____

_____

9. _____

_____

10. _____

_____

Adverb or Adjective?

Remember that most words ending in *ly* are adverbs.
Example:
> Weather changes *quickly*.

Use *good* only as an adjective.
Example:
> The play was *good*.

Use *well* as an adjective to mean "healthy" and as an adverb to tell how something is done.
Examples:
> Linda is doing *well* after her surgery.   The surgery went *well*.

DIRECTIONS **Write the word in parentheses that completes each sentence correctly.**

1. King Edward was _____ ill.
(serious, seriously)

2. He did not become _____ and finally he died.
(good, well)

3. His relative, William, was _____ determined to have the throne.
(real, really)

4. Edward had promised it to him _____ before he died.
(short, shortly)

5. The English nobles made Prince Harold king _____ after Edward's death.
(immediate, immediately)

6. William _____ refused to accept their decision.
(stubborn, stubbornly)

7. He _____ raised an army.
(quick, quickly)

8. The army attacked _____.
(fierce, fiercely)

9. Harold fought _____, but he was killed.
(brave, bravely)

10. William the Conqueror was a _____ fighter.
(good, well)

11. He was a _____ leader.
(powerful, powerfully)

12. His subjects were required to obey him _____.
(perfect, perfectly)

13. He punished disobedience _____.
(cruel, cruelly)

Prepositions and Prepositional Phrases

A **preposition** shows the relationship of a noun or a pronoun to another word in the sentence.
Example:
>   I walked *along* the beach.

The **object of the preposition** is the noun or the pronoun that follows the preposition.
Example:
>   The sands of the *beach* were white.

A **prepositional phrase** is made up of a preposition, the object of the preposition, and all the words in between.
Example:
>   Who lives *in that house*?

DIRECTIONS > Write the prepositional phrase from each sentence. Then underline the preposition. Circle the object of the preposition.

1. Marco Polo's family left Venice in 1271. _____

2. They took young Marco with them. _____

3. China lay far beyond the eastern mountains. _____

4. The Polos traveled all the way to China. _____

5. They stayed there for many years. _____

6. Marco returned from China twenty-five years later. _____

7. Marco Polo wrote a book about it. _____

8. He had traveled extensively through Asia. _____

9. The book described Marco's travels for his readers. _____

10. Europeans learned about Asia from Marco Polo's book. _____

DIRECTIONS > Underline the prepositional phrase or phrases in each sentence.

11. Many passengers leaned over the railing.

12. The ship was bound for England.

13. People waved to the passengers.

14. A few people walked down the gangplank.

15. The ship would soon be sailing into the Atlantic Ocean.

Prepositional Phrases Used as Adjectives

A prepositional phrase that modifies a noun or a pronoun is an **adjective phrase**.
Examples:

The killer whale is a species *of porpoise*. (tells what kind of species)
That whale *with the unusual markings* is our favorite. (tells which whale)
A pod *of twenty whales* was sighted recently. (tells how many in the pod)

DIRECTIONS ▷ Underline the adjective phrase or phrases in each sentence. Then write the word that the adjective phrase modifies.

1. Sheets of ice cover Antarctica.

_____

2. The land below the ice is always frozen.

_____

3. Explorers with dog sleds have crossed Antarctica.

_____

4. An admiral from the United States explored Antarctica.

_____

5. A camp on Ross Ice Shelf was where he lived.

_____

6. The view from the boat was spectacular.

_____

7. The whales blew huge spouts of water.

_____

8. The people in the boat cheered.

_____

9. Blue whales are the largest mammals in the world.

_____

10. The trainer of the porpoises waved her hand.

_____

11. Many people in the crowd laughed.

_____

12. The beginning of each show was the same.

_____

13. The porpoises' leaps into the air were unbelievable.

_____

14. A large pail held rewards for the performers.

_____

15. More than two percent of Earth's surface is frozen.

_____

16. Rivers and lakes contain one percent of that water.

_____

17. The oceans contain the rest of the water.

_____

18. The Pacific is the largest ocean on Earth.

_____

Prepositional Phrases Used as Adverbs

A prepositional phrase that modifies a verb, an adjective, or an adverb is an **adverb phrase**. An adverb phrase tells *how, when, where,* or *how often.*
Examples:
The porpoises performed *with ease.* (tells how)
Shows begin *on the hour.* (tells when)
The porpoises swim *in a large tank.* (tells where)
They are rewarded *after each trick.* (tells how often)

DIRECTIONS Underline the adverb phrase in each sentence. Then write the word modified by the adverb phrase. Label that word *verb, adjective,* or *adverb.*

1. Sam Adams supported the American Revolution with enthusiasm.

   _____

2. He spoke against the English king.

   _____

3. Sam would not ride a horse, so he traveled on foot.

   _____

4. He walked far from his home, giving speeches.

   _____

5. This revolutionary was enthusiastic about freedom.

   _____

6. Whales are the largest mammals that live on Earth.

   _____

7. Whales swim in the ocean.

   _____

8. Whales behave with great intelligence.

   _____

9. A whale must breathe air through its lungs.

   _____

10. Whales can dive for long periods.

    _____

11. Oceanographers work beneath the ocean's surface.

    _____

12. They descend in small diving ships.

    _____

13. Water pressure would crush some ships in a moment.

    _____

14. These vessels are designed for quick maneuvers.

    _____

15. Some of these ships carry scientists to the ocean floor.

    _____

Choosing the Correct Preposition

Use *in* to mean "already inside." Use *into* to tell about movement from the outside to the inside.

Examples:

The groceries are *in* the house.

He took the groceries *into* the house.

Use *between* for two and *among* for three or more.

Examples:

We divided the money *between* Ruthie and Daniel.

We divided the money *among* Ruthie, Daniel, and Luther.

Use *different from* to tell about differences.

Example:

The temperatures this summer are very *different from* the temperatures of last summer.

Do not use *of* in place of *have* when you write.

Example:

CORRECT: Joy *could have* become a teacher.

INCORRECT: Joy *could of* become a teacher.

◎ ◎

DIRECTIONS ▷ **Write the preposition in parentheses that correctly completes each sentence.**

1. Joe took a bus from the city _____ the desert.
(in, into)

2. The ride back to the city was _____ the ride to the desert.
(different from, different than)

3. The bus broke down _____ the desert and the city.
(between, among)

4. The driver of a car going _____ town called for help.
(in, into)

5. The passengers wandered _____ the many desert plants while the bus was
(between, among)
being repaired.

6. Joe had several juice drinks _____ his pack.
(in, into)

7. He _____ kept them all for himself.
(could of, could have)

8. Instead, he divided them _____ the thirsty passengers.
(between, among)

9. He and another passenger had brought ten drinks _____ them.
(between, among)

Recognizing Sentences

A **sentence** expresses a complete thought.
Examples:
> My father travels around the country.   The airplane has landed.

DIRECTIONS ▸ For each group of words, write *sentence* or *not a sentence*.

1. "The Fun They Had" is a story.

_____

2. Written by Isaac Asimov.

_____

3. It is about two students.

_____

4. Living in the year 2155.

_____

5. Their teachers are machines in their homes.

_____

6. A complicated computer.

_____

7. Ana has been telling Hakim an amazing story.

_____

8. It is *Fantastic Voyage*, a movie.

_____

9. To save a dying man.

_____

10. Scientists are shrunk to microscopic sizes.

_____

11. A tiny submarine.

_____

12. Into a world of unimagined complexity and beauty.

_____

13. Dangers await these brave voyagers.

_____

14. Through the valves of a beating heart.

_____

DIRECTIONS ▸ Write words to complete each sentence.

15. _____ study together.

16. Human teachers _____.

17. Today's students _____.

18. _____ would rather learn from machines.

19. _____ enjoys attending school with other students.

Four Kinds of Sentences

A **declarative sentence** makes a statement. Use a period at the end of a declarative sentence.

Example:

Janelle is painting a picture of an imaginary place.

An **interrogative sentence** asks a question. Use a question mark at the end of an interrogative sentence.

Example:

Who could ever create a more imaginative scene?

An **imperative sentence** gives a command or makes a request. Use a period at the end of an imperative sentence.

Example:

Think about all the uses for artwork.

An **exclamatory sentence** expresses strong feeling. Use an exclamation point at the end of an exclamatory sentence.

Example:

Who could ever create a more imaginative scene!

DIRECTIONS For each sentence, write *declarative, interrogative, imperative,* or *exclamatory*. Put the correct punctuation mark at the end of the sentence.

1. Look at the apes

2. How clever they are

3. They seem almost human

4. Do you notice anything about the biggest ape

5. That ape looks familiar

6. Doesn't it remind you of someone

7. Akiko has challenged me to a contest

8. Which one of us can create the most imaginative painting

DIRECTIONS Change each sentence into the kind of sentence identified in parentheses.

9. You should watch that ape. (imperative)

10. It is copying my movements. (interrogative)

Subjects and Predicates

Include a **subject** and a **predicate** in every sentence.
In the subject, tell whom or what the sentence is about.
Example:
> One person described her experience.

In the predicate, tell something about the subject.
Example:
> One person *described her experience*.

DIRECTIONS ▸ In each sentence, underline the subject once and the predicate twice.

1. Amelia Bloomer did not invent bloomers.
2. Bloomers were the first slacks for women.
3. These pants were very loose and comfortable.
4. Elizabeth Smith Miller became tired of long skirts and petticoats.
5. She first wore the pants in public.
6. The new outfit was described in Amelia Bloomer's newspaper.
7. People began to call the pants "bloomers."
8. Most people were shocked to see women in pants.

9. The circus began with a parade.
10. Every performer wore a glittery costume.
11. Lillie had been to the circus twice.
12. The acrobats flew through the air.
13. Our gym teacher has taught us to tumble.
14. The children bought refreshments.
15. The audience saw the animals perform.
16. Her aunt took her to the circus.
17. The work is dangerous.
18. Paolo tore his new red shirt.
19. The clowns threw candy into the crowd.
20. The family sat close to the top.

DIRECTIONS ▸ Think of a subject or a predicate to complete each sentence. Write *subject* or *predicate* to show what to add. Then write the sentence. Remember to begin each sentence with a capital letter and end it with a punctuation mark that shows what kind of sentence it is.

21. are awkward to wear for running _____

_____

22. different types of pants _____

_____

Complete and Simple Subjects

The **complete subject** is all the words in the subject.
Example:
My two older *brothers* stared at me silently.
The **simple subject** is the main word or words in the subject.
Example:
My two older *brothers* stared at me silently.
Sometimes the complete subject and the simple subject are the same.
Example:
Xavier stared at me silently.

DIRECTIONS ▶ Write the complete subject of each sentence. Underline the simple subject.

1. My best friend is afraid of snakes. _____

2. Some snakes are poisonous. _____

3. Glands in the snake's head produced the venom. _____

4. Special fangs inject the poison into the victim. _____

5. The deadly venom can kill a large man. _____

6. My brothers are acting suspiciously. _____

7. Jaime took a letter out of the mailbox yesterday. _____

8. The contents of that letter mystify me. _____

9. Two classmates of mine whispered behind my back. _____

10. This secret is fun for everyone except me. _____

11. Several members of the crew were sewing costumes. _____

12. Angelina was working in the costume room. _____

13. Many costumes were still unfinished. _____

14. Other outfits needed alterations. _____

15. Four students joined the costume crew. _____

DIRECTIONS ▶ Write a complete subject for each sentence. Underline the simple subject.

16. _____ is feared by desert travelers.

17. _____ watches for poisonous snakes.

18. _____ will avoid people if possible.

Complete and Simple Predicates

The **complete predicate** is all the words in the predicate.
Example:

Everyone in my house *is keeping a secret.*

The **simple predicate** is the main word or words in the predicate.
Example:

Everyone in my house *is keeping* a secret.

Sometimes the complete predicate and the simple predicate are the same.
Example:

Everyone *smiles.*

DIRECTIONS ▸ Write the complete predicate of each sentence. Underline the simple predicate.

1. Jeff carried his board toward the water. _____

2. He paddled out toward the large breakers. _____

3. A huge wave crashed over his head. _____

4. The surf tossed the board into the air. _____

5. Grandma López says nothing to me. _____

6. The secret was revealed on Saturday afternoon. _____

7. My relatives from near and far arrived on my birthday. _____

8. Even Aunt María came. _____

9. I had a wonderful, fantastic party. _____

10. The pink eraser bounced onto the floor. _____

11. Miles stared at the eraser for five minutes. _____

12. Every rubbery side stretched. _____

13. The enormous eraser bumped into the teacher's desk. _____

14. The entire class watched the eraser with amazement. _____

15. Mrs. Reyna quickly picked it up. _____

Finding Subjects of Sentences

To find the simple subject of an interrogative sentence, first make it declarative. Then, ask whom or what it is about.
Example:

Did *Sandra Cisneros* write that book?

Remember that the simple subject of an imperative sentence is usually not stated but is understood to be *you*.
Example:

(*You*) Read that book.

In a declarative sentence that begins with *here* or *there*, look for the simple subject after the predicate.
Example:

There are many *books* to read.

DIRECTIONS Write the simple subject of each sentence. Then write *declarative*, *interrogative*, *imperative*, or *exclamatory* to tell what kind of sentence it is.

1. Are the new neighbors home today?

_____

_____

2. There was a woman in the house an hour ago.

_____

_____

3. Where did she go?

_____

_____

4. Have you met them?

_____

_____

5. Here is a newspaper article about them.

_____

_____

6. Are there any children in the family?

_____

_____

7. There was a boy in the yard.

_____

_____

8. There is a puppy in the yard now.

_____

_____

9. How cute that puppy is!

_____

_____

10. Come to me.

_____

_____

Compound Subjects

Two or more simple subjects with the same predicate are called a **compound subject**. The simple subjects in a compound subject are usually joined by *and* or *or*.
Example:

Jon and Stacy congratulated the actress.

To save words, combine sentences with similar predicates into one sentence with a compound subject.
Example:

The *members* of the cast were nervous. The *director* was nervous.
The *members* of the cast and the *director* were nervous.

DIRECTIONS ▷ **Write the complete subject of each sentence. Then, underline each simple subject, and circle the connecting word.**

1. A tornado or a hurricane is very dangerous.

   _____

2. Lightning and the force of wind can destroy a town.

   _____

3. A person, a large animal, or an automobile may be hurled in the air.

   _____

4. My aunt, my uncle, and my younger cousin saw a tornado.

   _____

5. Dark clouds and powerful winds warned them of the approaching storm.

   _____

6. My aunt and uncle knew what to do.

   _____

7. The family, the cat, and the dog went to the cellar.

   _____

8. Their house and garage were left standing.

   _____

9. The school and the house across the street were badly damaged.

   _____

Compound Predicates

Two or more predicates with the same subject are called **compound predicates**. The simple predicates in a compound predicate are usually joined by *and* or *or*.
Example:
    We *will find* the card catalog or *will ask* the librarian for help.

DIRECTIONS ▶ Write the complete predicate of each sentence. Then, underline each simple predicate, and circle the connecting word.

1. The traffic light flashed for a few minutes and then turned red.

   _____

2. The cars slowed and finally stopped.

   _____

3. Candace reached over and adjusted the radio.

   _____

4. The announcer reported on traffic conditions and advised drivers.

   _____

5. Several drivers heard the report and chose a different route.

   _____

6. The three of us whispered, pointed, and made notes.

   _____

7. Twelve astronauts walked or drove across the dusty moonscape during the three and a half years of moon landings.

   _____

8. They took soil samples, measured temperatures, and tested the lunar gravity.

   _____

9. Back in orbit, the astronauts released the lunar module and measured the vibrations from its impact.

   _____

10. *Apollo 17*'s return to Earth brought the mission to a close and marked the end of manned moon landings.

   _____

Compound Sentences

Use a **simple sentence** to express one complete thought.
Example:
> Objects from space fall into the atmosphere.

Combine two or more simple sentences to make a **compound sentence**. The simple sentences can by joined by a comma and connecting words such as *and, or,* or *but,* or by a semicolon.
Example:
> A crater can be formed by a bomb, or it can be formed by a meteorite.

DIRECTIONS → For each sentence write *compound subject, compound predicate,* or *compound sentence.*

1. Jesse and Carroll watched a game show on television.

2. It was boring, and Carroll felt restless.

3. Carroll likes animals and prefers shows about wildlife.

4. Carroll called Jim, and he invited her over.

5. At Jim's house, Carroll and Jim enjoyed a film about dolphins.

6. Some meteors grow hot and burn up.

7. Metal or stone sometimes reaches the ground.

8. Friction makes meteors incredibly hot, and they burn up miles above Earth's surface.

9. Some large meteors do not burn up completely; they are called meteorites.

10. Have you or Becky seen the Meteor Crater in Arizona?

11. A meteorite exploded over Siberia and created more than 200 craters.

12. A meteorite crashed there perhaps 50,000 years ago, or it may have fallen earlier.

13. The Americans and the Russians have sent rockets into space.

14. My friends came, but they left early.

15. Robin or Kelly is on the telephone.

16. Elena chose the program Monday night; Ryan chose it Tuesday.

Conjunctions

Use a **conjunction** to join words or groups of words. A conjunction can be *and, or,* or *but.*
Example:
> Palak *or* Chris has a cell phone.

A conjunction can be used to combine sentences.
Example:
> Janet lives in Austin, *and* Elizabeth lives in New Braunfels.

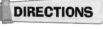 **DIRECTIONS** Circle the conjunction in each sentence. Then underline the words or groups of words it joins.

1. Florence Nightingale was the daughter of an English squire, but she was born in Florence, Italy.

2. She was raised and educated in Derbyshire, England.

3. Florence did not want to be idle or useless.

4. Nursing was not considered a proper occupation for ladies, but Florence was determined to be a nurse.

5. Florence went to Germany and studied nursing.

6. Llamas are quite gentle, and people often make pets of them.

7. Llamas climb easily over rocky terrain and make good pack animals in the mountains.

8. A llama is not carnivorous and prefers grass and leaves as food.

9. Sandra and Larry have a pet llama.

10. Llamas emit a humming sound, and you can hear it.

11. The llama lacks speech organs and is mute.

12. Sally talked to one expert, and he told her something interesting.

13. An angry llama will pull its ears back and spit.

14. Grasses and leaves are a llama's main source of food.

15. Llamas enjoy human company and are quite affectionate.

DIRECTIONS Rewrite each pair of sentences as one sentence. Use the conjunction in parentheses to join words or groups of words.

16. Florence returned to London. She became the supervisor of a hospital. (and)

_____

17. England entered the war. Florence joined the War Office as a nurse. (and)

_____

Interjections

An **interjection** is a word or a group of words that expresses strong feeling. You can separate an interjection from the rest of a sentence with either an exclamation point or a comma, depending on the strength of the feeling.

Examples:

    Whew!   That was close!   Oh, no!   That is the wrong answer!

DIRECTIONS > Write the interjection from each sentence. Label each one *strong* or *mild*.

1. Say, isn't Mary pitching today? _____

2. Hooray! We get to bat first. _____

3. Well, the team is in good shape. _____

4. Wow! Look at that pitch! _____

5. Hey! That should have been a strike! _____

DIRECTIONS > Add an interjection to each sentence. Write the new sentence. Add punctuation marks where they are needed.

6. That's the way to pitch.

_____

7. She missed that one.

_____

8. She'll hit it next time.

_____

9. What a hit she made!

_____

10. Look at her go!

_____

DIRECTIONS > Write sentences using the following interjections: *yikes, ugh, ssh,* and *bravo.*

_____

_____

_____

_____

Avoiding Sentence Fragments and Run-on Sentences

Avoid using a **sentence fragment**, which does not express a complete thought.
Example:

     Tells an interesting story.

Avoid using a **run-on sentence**, which strings together two or more sentences without clearly separating them.
Example:

     This picture is his it is not yours.

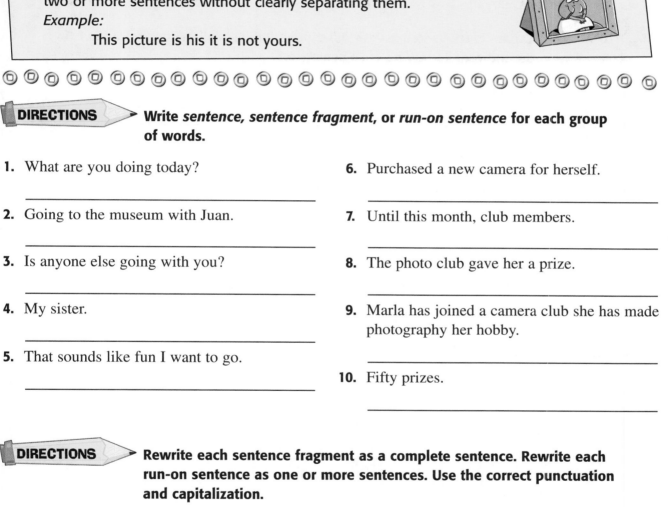

DIRECTIONS   Write *sentence, sentence fragment,* or *run-on sentence* for each group of words.

1. What are you doing today?

2. Going to the museum with Juan.

3. Is anyone else going with you?

4. My sister.

5. That sounds like fun I want to go.

6. Purchased a new camera for herself.

7. Until this month, club members.

8. The photo club gave her a prize.

9. Marla has joined a camera club she has made photography her hobby.

10. Fifty prizes.

DIRECTIONS   Rewrite each sentence fragment as a complete sentence. Rewrite each run-on sentence as one or more sentences. Use the correct punctuation and capitalization.

11. You have been to the museum before what do you want to see this time?

12. Some objects from the Egyptian pyramids.

13. I like ancient pottery I do not see it often.

Expanding Sentences

Sentences can be **expanded** by adding details to make them clearer and more interesting.

Example:

The waitress smiled.

The waitress in the red dress smiled happily to the customers.

ⓞ ⓞ

DIRECTIONS ▷ **Expand each sentence with descriptive details. Follow the instructions in parentheses to rewrite each sentence.**

1. A dog huddled in the shelter of the tunnel. (Add details about the subject.)

   _____

2. It shivered in the wind. (Add descriptive details about an item in the complete predicate.)

   _____

3. Finally, it left the shelter of the tunnel. (Add another predicate.)

   _____

4. Its shadow trailed behind it. (Add descriptive details about the subject.)

   _____

5. The dog trotted down the street. (Add another subject.)

   _____

6. The dog broke through the sheet of ice on the puddle. (Add descriptive details about an item in the complete predicate and add a second predicate.)

   _____

   _____

7. The curtain slowly opens. (Add details about the subject.)

   _____

8. I remember the drive. (Add descriptive details about an item in the complete predicate.)

   _____

9. We drove from Tucson to the Grand Canyon. (Add another predicate.)

   _____

10. The girl blew out the candles. (Add descriptive details about an item in the complete predicate and add a second predicate.)

    _____

    _____

Correcting Sentence Fragments and Run-on Sentences

Good writers correct sentence fragments and run-on sentences.

Example:

INCORRECT: The boys were hungry we made hot dogs.

CORRECT: The boys were hungry, so we made hot dogs.

DIRECTIONS ▷ **Rewrite the following paragraphs from a business letter. Correct any sentence fragments or run-on sentences.**

I should begin by telling you how long I have been a customer of Ronnie's. For five years. I have always been satisfied with your merchandise and your service.

I am happy to have an opportunity to tell you how much I have enjoyed shopping at Ronnie's. However, my letter has a different purpose. To ask you to carry my favorite line of sporting goods. Sporty's. I have begun shopping elsewhere for sporting goods. I would rather be shopping at Ronnie's it is my favorite store. Besides, your other customers would enjoy Sporty's top-quality goods. Available at Ronnie's low prices.

Please consider my suggestion let me know what you decide.

Phrases and Clauses

A **phrase** is a group of words that work together. A phrase does not have both a subject and a predicate.
Example:
    from the kitchen window
A **clause** is a group of words that has a subject and a predicate. Some clauses can stand alone as sentences; others cannot.
Example:
    Everyone should know about medical emergencies.

DIRECTIONS Write *phrase* or *clause* to identify each group of words.

1. we enjoy living in this town _____

2. near friendly, helpful neighbors _____

3. from the nearest ocean _____

4. since they moved to Ohio _____

5. between a rushing stream and a grassy slope _____

6. we built a cabin _____

7. from fragrant pine logs _____

8. in the huge stone fireplace _____

9. you can read first-aid manuals _____

10. although my aunt does not have a medical degree _____

11. while Eric played outside _____

12. in Joseph's construction site _____

13. she saved someone's life _____

DIRECTIONS Complete each sentence. Add the kind of word group named in parentheses.

14. When I grow up, _____.
    (clause)

15. I want to live _____.
    (phrase)

16. _____, who is my best friend.
    (clause)

17. After he examined Leah, the doctor said, "You have been bitten _____."
    (phrase)

Independent and Dependent Clauses

An **independent clause** expresses a complete thought and can stand alone as a simple sentence.
Examples:
> *Some pollution affects our homes and schools.*
> If their neighbors cooperate, *young people and adults can clean up their neighborhoods.*

A **dependent clause** contains a subject and a predicate, but it does not express a complete thought and it cannot stand alone.
Example:
> People became more sensitive to pollution problems *after they learned about toxic waste.*

DIRECTIONS In each sentence, underline the independent clause once. Underline the dependent clause twice. Write the word that begins each dependent clause.

1. Cleopatra lived in ancient Egypt, which she ruled. _____

2. She ruled with her brother until he seized the throne. _____

3. She regained her throne because Julius Caesar helped her.

_____

4. Mark Antony ruled Rome after Caesar died.

_____

5. Antony went to Egypt, where he lived for several years. _____

6. Antony and Cleopatra died when a Roman army attacked Egypt.

_____

7. If you go to New York City, consider a visit to Brooklyn. _____

8. Fifteen teenagers there gained some fame because they were pollution fighters.

_____

9. They called themselves the Toxic Avengers, a name borrowed from a pollution-fighting superhero. _____

10. Although it was located next to a school, the Radiac Research Corporation was storing large amounts of medical waste.

_____

11. When the Toxic Avengers heard about this, they planned a response.

_____

12. When a crowd gathered for a public rally, the teens told the people about Radiac.

_____

13. Public awareness grew after the rally was held. _____

14. Billy fell in the sewer on a neighborhood street as he was playing on a Saturday afternoon.

_____

Compound and Complex Sentences

A **compound sentence** consists of two or more independent clauses.
Example:

Fires are dangerous, and they cause great damage.

A **complex sentence** consists of an independent clause and at least one dependent clause. Dependent clauses often tell *why, when, where, what,* or *which one.*
A dependent clause that begins a sentence is usually followed by a comma.
Example:

Because someone had been careless with matches, a fire started at the Johnsons' home. (tells *why*)

A dependent clause that comes at the end of the sentence is usually not preceded by a comma.
Example:

Smoke filled the house *as firefighters arrived*. (tells *when*)

When a dependent clause comes in the middle of a sentence, it is usually set off by commas.
Example:

The fire, *which we saw spreading rapidly*, shot sparks into the sky.
(tells *which one*)

DIRECTIONS Write *compound* or *complex* to identify each sentence.

1. Aristotle lived in ancient Greece, and he became a great philosopher.

   _____

2. Since philosophers enjoy thinking about life, they also enjoy discussing it with others.

   _____

3. Because Plato was a famous philosopher, Aristotle attended his school.

   _____

4. Aristotle became famous himself, and many people studied his work.

   _____

5. Aristotle taught Alexander the Great before Alexander became king of Macedonia.

   _____

6. Aristotle started his own school when he received money from Alexander.

   _____

7. *Tsunami* is a Japanese word for tidal wave, but these waves occur around the world.

   _____

8. Some tidal waves begin after an earthquake occurs.

   _____

9. The worst recorded earthquake in history took place in 1201, and about one million people died.

   _____

10. Earthquakes are measured using a scale that was devised by Charles Richter and Beno Gutenberg.

    _____

Capitalization and End Punctuation

Begin every written sentence with a capital letter.
Example:

Let's go to the zoo.

End a declarative sentence with a period.
Example:

I can go, too.

End an interrogative sentence with a question mark.
Example:

Can Mark go with us?

End an exclamatory sentence with an exclamation point.
Example:

Of course you can go!

DIRECTIONS ▷ **Rewrite each sentence. Add a capital letter and the correct end punctuation.**

1. have you ever lost your voice

_____

2. what a strange feeling that is

_____

3. you try to talk, but you can only squeak

_____

4. no one can understand you

_____

5. the climbers left their base camp at six in the morning

_____

6. mr. Enami is a train engineer

_____

7. miles found his math problems to be very challenging

_____

8. does the community softball league meet every Friday

_____

9. pedro and I go to the museum in California

_____

10. he is such a conscientious student

_____

Commas and Semicolons

Use commas to separate words or phrases in a series.
Example:
> I studied for the test on *Monday, Tuesday*, and *Wednesday*.

Use commas to set off mild interjections.
Example:
> *Wow*, I did really well on the test!

Use commas and conjunctions, or use semicolons, to separate the clauses in compound sentences.
Examples:
> The book is entertaining, and interested people should read it.
> The book is entertaining; interested people should read it.

Use a comma after a dependent clause that begins a complex sentence.
Example:
> *After I studied for the test*, I passed it.

DIRECTIONS ➤ **Add commas or semicolons where they are needed in each sentence.**

1. As her plane touched down on the small runway Amanda felt excited.

2. Lucia made a dollhouse out of construction paper cardboard and fabric.

3. Her luggage was soon unloaded sorted and returned to her.

4. If you want to see her call her on the telephone.

5. Jon helped Amanda carry her gear and they walked out to the truck.

6. Ms. Rivera teaches Greek Latin and classical literature.

7. Hey did you decide to write a letter to the editor of the paper?

8. Although you may not agree I think people should join together to fight for a cause.

9. Do Noah Carrie and Katy still volunteer?

10. Many people were traveling to Dallas Phoenix and Los Angeles.

11. The weather is getting worse we should cancel the outdoor concert.

12. The pilot copilot and navigator flew us through the storm safely.

13. Oh I thought I'd surprise you!

14. Paula North is our team captain Shu Lee is her assistant.

15. Although the director thought the film was great the audiences walked out.

16. Even though the wind is low the boy tries to fly a kite.

Capitalization of Proper Nouns, Proper Adjectives, and *I*

Capitalize proper nouns and proper adjectives.
Examples:
> November, Chicago, Republican, American

Capitalize the pronoun *I*.
Examples:
> I am here.   Lynn and I are here.

DIRECTIONS Rewrite each item correctly.

1. beth ann drake _____

2. president lincoln _____

3. central Bookstore _____

4. waco, texas _____

5. logan, utah _____

6. italian marble _____

7. me, myself, and i _____

8. english accent _____

9. union army _____

10. american citizen _____

11. adams middle school _____

12. *beauty and the beast* _____

13. latin club _____

14. amelia earhart boulevard _____

15. declaration of independence _____

16. yellowstone national park _____

17. mexican pottery _____

18. new year's day _____

Abbreviations

Use a period after most **abbreviations**.
Examples:
      adj. (adjective)   Blvd. (Boulevard)
Capitalize abbreviations that stand for proper nouns.
Examples:
      Sat. (Saturday)   Oct. (October)
Do not use periods when writing postal abbreviations of the fifty states or the abbreviations of some large organizations.
Examples:
      NH (New Hampshire)   NATO (North Atlantic Treaty Organization)
Do not use periods for units of measure unless the abbreviation forms a word. (in., gal.)
Examples:
      cm (centimeter)   km (kilometer)

DIRECTIONS Write a correct abbreviation of each term. Use a dictionary, if necessary.

1. pound _____

2. ounce _____

3. foot _____

4. yard _____

5. Maine _____

6. milligram _____

7. liter _____

8. cubic centimeter _____

9. United States Postal Service _____

10. National Basketball Association _____

11. Rodeo Drive _____

12. Old Post Road _____

13. Fifth Avenue _____

14. National Collegiate Athletic Association

_____

15. medical doctor _____

16. miles per hour _____

17. revolutions per minute _____

18. Fahrenheit _____

19. Celsius _____

DIRECTIONS Rewrite each group of words, using abbreviations. Use initials for middle names.

20. Best Carpet Cleaners, Incorporated _____

21. The Farley Farragut Company _____

22. Doctor Thomas Francis Gorman _____

More Abbreviations

Use an abbreviation, or shortened form of a word, to save space when you write lists and addresses or fill out forms.

To write an initial, use the first letter of a name followed by a period.

DIRECTIONS Imagine that you are filling out an application for a job. Write the information in the chart below. Capitalize and punctuate each abbreviation and initial correctly.

JOE BOB'S RESTAURANT

Name: _____

Street address: _____

Birth date: _____

Date of application: _____

DIRECTIONS Use abbreviations whenever possible to complete the form with the following information: 120 Grant Avenue; The Parker School; Helena Moreno Ramírez; September 4, 2005; Ponca City, Oklahoma.

STUDENT INFORMATION CARD

School: _____

Address: _____

_____

Principal: _____

First Day of School: _____

Titles

Capitalize the first word, the last word, and all the important words in a title. Underline the titles of books, plays, magazines, newspapers, television shows, and movies. If you are using a computer, replace underlining with italics.
Examples:

> 60 Minutes, The Secret Garden, Los Angeles Times, Pinocchio

Place quotation marks around the titles of short works, such as poems, short stories, chapters, articles, and songs.
Examples:

> "Little Miss Muffet," "America the Beautiful"

DIRECTIONS ▸ Circle the words in each title that should be capitalized.

1. around the world in eighty days
2. the pirates of penzance
3. profiles in courage
4. stalking the wild asparagus
5. the cat ate my gymsuit

6. "shake, rattle, and roll"
7. "twist and shout"
8. "me and my shadow"
9. the red balloon
10. the wizard of oz

DIRECTIONS ▸ Write the title in each sentence correctly.

11. The movie stand by me is one of my favorites.

_____

12. Did you know it is based on a short story called the body?

_____

13. The story was written by Stephen King, who also wrote the novels cujo, christine, and carrie.

_____

14. The title of the movie comes from one of the best songs in it, stand by me.

_____

15. Where is last week's issue of time?

_____

16. Have you read John Steinbeck's book travels with charley?

_____

17. I just found that article, welcome to Pittsburgh.

_____

18. My family enjoys watching Monday night football.

_____

19. Did you see that movie about Dian Fossey called gorillas in the mist?

_____

Direct Quotations and Dialogue

Use quotation marks before and after a **direct quotation**.
Example:

   "The truth is powerful and will prevail," said Sojourner Truth.

If a quotation is interrupted by other words, place quotation marks around the quoted words only.
Example:

   "Give me liberty," Patrick Henry cried, "or give me death!"

Place a comma or a period inside closing quotation marks.
Example:

   "I have read those words before," said Ben.

Place a question mark or an exclamation point inside closing quotation marks if the quotation itself is a question or an exclamation.
Example:

   "Haven't you ever heard of Sojourner Truth or Patrick Henry?" asked Marcia.

DIRECTIONS Rewrite each sentence using correct punctuation and capitalization.

1. Leon dragged the huge crate through and shouted I'm home, Mom!

_____

2. She isn't back yet Leon's brother told him.

_____

3. Oh, Leon said his brother, staring at the box what is that?

_____

4. Queen Elizabeth I ruled a great empire, Marcia said.

_____

5. She told her critics, I have the heart and stomach of a king.

_____

6. Who else had a great impact on a country? asked Terri.

_____

7. Well, Ben remarked, Mohandas Gandhi inspired a nonviolent revolution in India.

_____

8. Gandhi inspired Martin Luther King! Terri added.

_____

9. New York has a new program, Nancy said, for student ticket buyers.

_____

Appositives

An **appositive** is a noun or a noun phrase that identifies or renames the word or words that precede it. Use commas to set off an appositive from the rest of the sentence.
Examples:

Our steward, *James Moreno*, speaks three languages.
His home is in Rome, *the capital of Italy*.

DIRECTIONS Rewrite each sentence correctly. Use commas where they are needed. Then underline the appositive. Circle the noun or pronoun it tells about.

1. The company High Flyers forgot to include instructions.

   _____

2. The Eagle our only car would not start.

   _____

3. Our neighbor Jim Delgado came to help.

   _____

4. Even Jim a good mechanic could not start it.

   _____

5. The starter an electric motor was not working.

   _____

6. The pilot Captain Songrossi said to fasten our seat belts.

   _____

7. A prairie a kind of grassland is home to many kinds of plants and animals.

   _____

8. Our teacher Ms. Pesek does not agree.

   _____

9. Our store Video Visions has many unusual movies.

   _____

10. The film an exciting dinosaur story is filed with other adventure films.

    _____

DIRECTIONS Rewrite the sentences, using appositives to add information.

11. Our school is open all year. _____

12. I would like to see my favorite film again.

    _____

Contractions

Form **contractions** by putting two words together and replacing one or more letters with an apostrophe.
Examples:
    is not = isn't, it is = it's, you will = you'll

DIRECTIONS ▸ Write the contraction in each sentence and the words from which it was formed.

1. I'd like to learn to ski. _____

2. I've asked Susan to teach me. _____

3. I know she's an excellent skier. _____

4. She says it isn't difficult. _____

5. We've asked Tom and Jack to come with us. _____

6. They've been skiing for years. _____

7. I'm working at a grocery store after school. _____

8. We aren't going to be able to sleep tonight. _____

9. Xavier didn't play football today. _____

10. They'd be here if they could. _____

11. Tiffany wasn't feeling well today. _____

12. Eloisa and Pete haven't been home all weekend. _____

13. You've signed up to take a weaving class. _____

14. Lina can't close the door. _____

15. Doesn't the mural look great? _____

DIRECTIONS ▸ Write a sentence using the contraction for each pair of words.

16. should not _____

17. will not _____

18. he would _____

19. let us _____

20. you are _____

Synonyms and Antonyms

Synonyms are two or more words that have the same or similar meanings.
Examples:
   bush—shrub, dogs—hounds, shoved—pushed
Antonyms are words that have opposite meanings.
Examples:
   old—new, young—old, awake—asleep

ⓞ ⓞ

DIRECTIONS Read the paragraphs. Write a synonym or an antonym for the underlined word in the space provided.

   Annette had been <u>ill (1)</u> for a week. The day she returned, class had already <u>begun (2)</u>.
She was <u>late (3)</u> because she had to stop at the office on her way to the classroom.
   Annette had missed an <u>examination (4)</u>. Mr. Castellanos sent her to a desk in the <u>rear (5)</u> of the room to make it up. There was <u>nobody (6)</u> at the desk to the right of Annette's, but Roland was sitting in the desk to the <u>right (7)</u>.
   The teacher told the students to be <u>quiet (8)</u> until Annette had finished the examination. When the class <u>left (9)</u> for recess, Annette stayed behind to <u>finish (10)</u> the examination. The examination was not <u>difficult (11)</u>. Annette was sure that all her answers were <u>correct (12)</u>.

1. (synonym) _____
2. (synonym) _____
3. (antonym) _____
4. (synonym) _____
5. (synonym) _____
6. (synonym) _____

7. (antonym) _____
8. (antonym) _____
9. (antonym) _____
10. (antonym) _____
11. (antonym) _____
12. (synonym) _____

DIRECTIONS Complete the chart by writing one synonym and one antonym for each word in the first column.

Word	Synonym	Antonym
13. wild		
14. bolder		
15. thick		
16. fortunate		
17. mend		
18. gather		

Homographs and Homonyms

> **Homographs** are words that are spelled alike but have different meanings.
> *Examples:*
>> The karate students *bow* to one another.
>> I made a red *bow* to put on top of the wrapped gift.

DIRECTIONS ▷ For each item, circle the correct meaning of the underlined word.

1. When Annemarie heard a <u>light</u> tapping at the door after curfew, she knew something was wrong.

   brightness   gentle

2. As her parents explained that the Rosens had gone into hiding, Annemarie could see that their faces were <u>drawn</u> with worry.

   sketched   pulled tight

3. Kristi believed that there had been fireworks for her birthday, but the truth was the bright light had come from the burning of the Danish <u>fleet</u>.

   a group of ships   swift

4. To disguise Ellen's identity, Annemarie pulled on her friend's necklace so hard that it <u>broke</u>, and then she hid it in her hand.

   cracked into pieces   without money

> **Homonyms** are words that sound alike but have different meanings and spellings.
> *Examples:*
>> write—right, flour—flower

DIRECTIONS ▷ Complete each sentence by writing the correct homonym.

5. (air, heir) Prince Chang wanted to reward Tang for the merry _____ he fiddled, and before Chang could stop himself, he let slip that he was _____ to the throne.

6. (rode, road) A group of enemy soldiers _____ their horses down the _____ to challenge Prince Chang as he traveled in disguise.

7. (throne, thrown) The prince was nearly _____ to the ground and killed, but he was saved by Lang the archer. Later, the fortunate prince took the _____ as the new king.

8. (sighed, side) Hostile soldiers gathered at the _____ of the river to attack Chang's kingdom, but they _____ with homesickness when they heard Tang play his fiddle.

Prefixes

A **prefix** is a letter or group of letters that can be added to the beginning of a base word to change its meaning.

Example:

    extra, meaning "outside of, beyond" + the base word *ordinary* = *extraordinary*, meaning "beyond ordinary"

Some prefixes have one meaning, and others have more than one meaning.

Examples:

Prefix	Meaning
im	not
in	not
over	too much, over
post	after
pre	before
re	back, again
un	not

DIRECTIONS ⟩ **Read each sentence. Write the word formed with a prefix and underline the prefix. Then write the meaning of the word.**

1. I have been inactive in the organization all year.

    _____

2. I thought the audience was impolite during the speeches.

    _____

3. They should not prejudge the candidates before hearing what they have to say.

    _____

4. It is unusual to have this many candidates.

    _____

5. I think Greg is overconfident.

    _____

6. He has already ordered food for his postelection celebration.

    _____

7. I hope it was inexpensive.

    _____

8. Last year the committee members had to recount the ballots.

    _____

Suffixes

A **suffix** is a letter or letters added to the end of a base word to change the meaning of a word.

Example:

      ful, meaning "full of" + the base word *wonder* = *wonderful*, meaning "full of wonder"

DIRECTIONS   Read each sentence. Write the word formed with a suffix. After each word, write the suffix.

1. "You look thoughtful," said Richard.

    _____

2. "I was just looking at those grayish clouds," replied Louise.

    _____

3. "I think it may be a rainy night."

    _____

4. "Yes," agreed Richard. "The cows sound restless."

    _____

5. "Do you think the rain will be harmful to the hay we have cut?" asked Louise.

    _____

DIRECTIONS   Match the suffixes with the base words to make 18 nouns. Write the nouns on the lines.

Suffixes									
ant	ent	er	or	ist	tion	ation	ance	ence	ment

Base Words								
attend	box	celebrate	contest	compete	cycle	determine	develop	
dominate	excel	organize	perfect	prominent	revere	salute	ski	

6. _____

7. _____

8. _____

9. _____

10. _____

11. _____

12. _____

13. _____

14. _____

15. _____

16. _____

17. _____

18. _____

19. _____

20. _____

21. _____

22. _____

23. _____

Compound Words

A **compound word** is a word that is made up of two or more words. The meaning of many compound words is related to the meaning of each individual word.
Example:
> rattle + snake = rattlesnake, meaning "snake that makes a rattling sound"

Compound words may be written as one word, as hyphenated words, or as two separate words.
Examples:
> shoelace, sister-in-law, orange juice

DIRECTIONS ▸ Underline the compound word in each sentence.

1. Ron and Diane went to visit their great-uncle.
2. He lives in a three-bedroom house on the beach.
3. The beach is at the foot of a mountain range.
4. Everyone wanted to go for a walk on the beach.
5. The cuckoo clock sounded when they left.
6. They had two hours before sunset.
7. Piles of seaweed had washed up on the sand.
8. Ron noticed a jellyfish on one of the piles.
9. Diane found a starfish farther down the beach.
10. They looked out across the blue-green water.
11. Diane spotted a sea lion on a distant rock.
12. The shadows of the palm trees were growing longer.
13. They walked back, watching the fast-sinking sun.
14. They were three-fourths of the way back when the sun set.
15. The beachfront was quiet.
16. Diane was spellbound by its beauty.
17. Ron found an old inner tube.
18. They sat down to read the newspaper.
19. Jess is a jack-of-all-trades.
20. Alicia lost her earring.

DIRECTIONS ▸ Answer the following questions.

21. A *rehearsal* is "a practice for a performance." What is a *dress rehearsal*?

_____

22. *Scare* means "to frighten." What is a *scarecrow*?

_____

23. A *date* is "a particular point or period of time." What is *up-to-date*?

_____

24. A *guide* is "something serving to indicate or direct." What is a *guideword*?

_____

Denotations and Connotations: Word Overtones

> The **denotation** of a word is its exact meaning as stated in a dictionary.
> *Example:*
> > The denotation of *skinny* is "very thin."
> The **connotation** of a word is an added meaning that suggests something positive or negative.
> *Examples:*
> > Negative: *Skinny* suggests "too thin." *Skinny* has a negative connotation.
> > Positive: *Slender* suggests "attractively thin." *Slender* has a positive connotation.

 **DIRECTIONS** ▷ **Read each of these statements about Ted's Restaurant. Underline the word in parentheses that has the more positive connotation.**

1. Ted's Restaurant is furnished with (old, antique) furniture.

2. The servers are all (young, immature).

3. You can sit at a table or in a (cozy, cramped) booth.

4. The service at Ted's is (slow, unhurried).

5. Ted's serves very (simple, plain) food.

6. One of the specialties is (rare, undercooked) steak.

7. (Blackened, Burned) prime rib is another.

8. Customers (sip, gulp) their cold drinks.

DIRECTIONS ▷ **Read each of these statements about Ted's Restaurant. Underline the word in parentheses that has the more negative connotation.**

9. The beef at Ted's Restaurant is (firm, tough) and juicy.

10. The pies are (rich, greasy) with butter.

11. The crust is so (crumbly, flaky), it falls apart.

12. A (moist, soggy) cake is also available for dessert.

13. A group of (loud, enthusiastic) regulars eats at Ted's every Saturday night.

14. The steaks at Ted's are cooked over a charbroiled (flame, inferno).

Idioms

An **idiom** is an expression that has a meaning different from the usual meanings of the individual words within it.
Example:
> *Pull my leg* means "to tease," not "to physically pull on my leg."

◎ ◎

DIRECTIONS ➤ **Read the dialogue and underline the idioms. Then rewrite the dialogue. Replace each idiom with a word or words that state the meaning of the idiom in the sentence.**

"What's the matter? Has the cat got your tongue?" demanded Randy. "Tell me where we're going tonight."

"Just hold your horses," said Lester. "I told you it's a surprise. It will knock your socks off when we get there. In the meantime, get off my back."

"I can't help it," said Joe. "I've been on pins and needles all day."

"I have to keep my nose to the grindstone until I finish my chores," said Lester. "Then we can take off."

"Well, get on the ball and finish," said Randy. "I'm about to burst with curiosity."

"Lend me a hand, then," said Joe.

_____

_____

_____

_____

_____

_____

_____

_____

_____

_____

_____

_____

_____

Subject-Verb Agreement

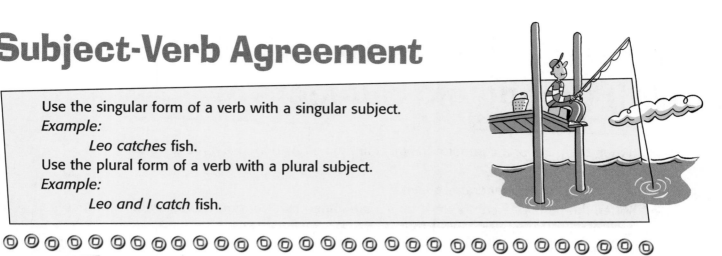

Use the singular form of a verb with a singular subject.
Example:
>   Leo *catches* fish.
Use the plural form of a verb with a plural subject.
Example:
>   Leo and I *catch* fish.

DIRECTIONS ▶ **Write the verb in parentheses that correctly completes each sentence.**

1. Our country _____ an election for president every four years.
   (holds, hold)

2. Each party _____ a candidate.
   (selects, select)

3. Every candidate _____ his or her ideas in speeches.
   (presents, present)

4. The candidates _____ all over the country.
   (travels, travel)

5. Groups of reporters _____ the candidates.
   (follows, follow)

6. We _____ about the candidates for months.
   (hears, hear)

7. Unfortunately, some people _____ the election.
   (ignores, ignore)

8. Only voters _____ the president.
   (elects, elect)

9. The president's decisions _____ the lives of all citizens.
   (affects, affect)

10. Not every citizen _____.
    (votes, vote)

11. Some people even _____ to register.
    (fails, fail)

12. Most candidates _____ their ideas with the voters.
    (shares, share)

13. Each voter _____ an opportunity to decide which candidate has the best ideas.
    (has, have)

14. Anna _____ her bowling ball down the lane.
    (hurls, hurl)

15. The ball _____ the target.
    (hits, hit)

Agreement of Verbs with Compound Subjects

When the parts of a compound subject are joined by *and*, use a plural verb.
Example:
> Pluto and Jupiter *are* planets.

When the parts of a compound subject are joined by *or* or *nor*, use the verb form that agrees with the subject closest to it.
Examples:
> Neither the cat nor the *puppies have* eaten yet.
> Neither the puppies nor the *cat has* eaten yet.

ⓓⓓⓓⓓⓓⓓⓓⓓⓓⓓⓓⓓⓓⓓⓓⓓⓓⓓⓓⓓⓓⓓⓓⓓⓓⓓⓓⓓⓓ

DIRECTIONS ▷ **Write the verb in parentheses that correctly completes each sentence.**

1. Jolene and her brother _____ to read about animal defenses.
   (likes, like)

2. An encyclopedia and a science book _____ good references.
   (is, are)

3. Fight or flight _____ an animal's usual response to danger.
   (is, are)

4. Shell and armor _____ good protection.
   (provides, provide)

5. Size and strength _____ some attackers.
   (discourages, discourage)

6. A snarl and a menacing look _____ others away.
   (frightens, frighten)

7. An antelope or a mustang _____ an attacker.
   (outruns, outrun)

8. Robins and bluebirds _____ away.
   (flies, fly)

9. A lion or a tiger _____ with teeth and claws.
   (fights, fight)

10 A chameleon or some fish _____ color to blend into surroundings.
   (changes, change)

11. A turtle or a tortoise _____ in its shell.
   (hides, hide)

12. Either the boys or their parents _____ driving to the game.
   (is, are)

13. Neither ivy nor moss _____ here.
   (grows, grow)

Personal Narrative

In a **personal narrative**, the writer tells about a personal experience. A personal narrative is autobiographical, but it typically focuses on a specific event.

A personal narrative
- is written in the first-person point of view.
- usually reveals the writer's feelings.
- has a beginning, a middle, and an end.

DIRECTIONS ➤ Read the personal narrative below. Then answer the questions that follow.

The family birthday party began as usual. First, my family gathered after dinner with my presents. I was excited, but I thought I knew what I was getting. My parents had never been able to surprise me.

After I had opened one gift, I heard a faint rustling noise. I paused for a moment, but I heard nothing more. A minute later, I noticed that a large box moved! It was creepy! I jumped to my feet in alarm.

Laughing, my father then picked up the moving present. The box had no bottom at all. A fluffy white kitten was curled up where the present had been. I was finally surprised—with the best birthday present I had ever received.

1. From what point of view is this narrative told?

   _____

   What words are clues to this point of view?

   _____

2. How did the writer feel at the beginning of the narrative?

   _____

3. How did the writer's feelings change by the end of the narrative?

   _____

4. List the events of the narrative in the order in which they happened. Write a signal word or phrase if one is given for each event.

   a. _____

   b. _____

   c. _____

   d. _____

   e. _____

Personal Narrative: Proofreading

To be a good proofreader, look for one type of error at a time. For example, proofread once for capitalization errors, once for punctuation errors, and once for spelling errors.

PROOFREADER'S MARKS

≡	Capitalize.	⋀̄	Replace something.
⊙	Add a period.	∿	Transpose.
∧	Add something.	○	Spell correctly.
∧,	Add a comma.	¶	Indent paragraph.
∨ ∨	Add quotation marks.	/	Make a lowercase letter.
⌐	Cut something.		

DIRECTIONS **Proofread the personal narrative, paying special attention to spelling. Use the Proofreader's Marks to correct at least eight errors.**

What an amazing experience my bothers and I had with the wind last autunm! We had driven with our parents to Point Reyes, north of San francisco. Point Reyes is known as one of the windyest spots in the cuontry, and on that day the winds were raging up to 50 miles an hour all along the California coast.

I had no way of determining the speed of the wind at Point reyes that afternoon. I can only tell you that when we jumped into the air, we were blown a full five feet before landing The wind picked us up and carried us with the force of rushhing water. we simpply could not fall backward. The wind was so strong that we could lean back against it and let it support us as firmly as a brick wall would. My brothers and I decided to take a short walk downwind along the beach. We allowed the wind to push us along at a rappid pace. For a while we stoped walking altogether. We simply jumped into the air, let ourselves be blown along like empty milk cartoons, and landed. Then we jumped into the air again. Borne by the wind, we progressed as quickly as if we had been walking

Personal Narrative: Graphic Organizer

DIRECTIONS Write a personal narrative about something you do well. Use the graphic organizer to plan your personal narrative.

What are you going to write about?

Tell what your skill is, how you learned it, and when you use it.

Tell how your skill makes your life more interesting.

Personal Narrative: Writing

Tips for Writing a Personal Narrative:
- Write from your point of view. Use the words *I* and *my* to show your readers that this is your story.
- Think about what you want to tell your readers.
- Organize your ideas into a beginning, a middle, and an end.
- Write an interesting introduction that "grabs" your readers.
- Write an ending for your story. Write it from your point of view.

DIRECTIONS Write a personal narrative about something you do well. Use the graphic organizer on page 477 as a guide for writing. Be sure to proofread your writing.

_____

_____

_____

_____

_____

_____

_____

_____

_____

_____

_____

_____

_____

_____

_____

_____

_____

_____

_____

_____

Descriptive Paragraph

DIRECTIONS ▷ **Read the paragraph. Underline the topic sentence. Then complete the items below.**

The room had clearly been ransacked. The drawers of the dresser next to the window were open and empty. A trail of assorted clothing led to the closet. The closet stood empty, its contents strewn across the bed and the floor. Glass from a broken perfume bottle crunched loudly underfoot, the fragrance of its contents mixing with the smell of garlic. The only item left undisturbed was a portrait on the wall over the bed. Its subject, a solemn young woman, stared thoughtfully into the room, like a silent witness to the recent crime.

1. List at least five words or phrases the writer used to appeal to your senses. After each word or phrase, tell which sense it is: *sight, hearing, smell,* or *touch.*

_____

_____

_____

_____

_____

_____

2. Is this paragraph written in space order or in time order?

_____

3. What words did the writer use that indicate this type of order?

_____

Descriptive Paragraph: Proofreading

To be a good proofreader, look for one type of error at a time. For example, proofread once for capitalization errors, once for punctuation errors, and once for spelling errors.

PROOFREADER'S MARKS

≡ Capitalize.
⊙ Add a period.
∧ Add something.
⋏ Add a comma.
ⱽⱽ Add quotation marks.
⤳ Cut something.

⋏ Replace something.
⤸ Transpose.
○ Spell correctly.
⩨ Indent paragraph.
／ Make a lowercase letter.

DIRECTIONS Proofread the description, paying special attention to the capitalization and end punctuation of sentences. Use the Proofreader's Marks to correct at least eight errors.

A set of smooth stone steps led up to a flat clearing in the forest Here the sun's rays filtered down through the branches of the towering pines, and the ground was covered with fragrant green pine needles. the carpet of needles felt thick and soft under Nina's feet.

a gentle breeze rustled the branches Nina inhaled the scent of the pines as it drifted on the breeze. mingled with the scent of pine was the smell of the pale green mosses growing on the north sides of the trees.

What was that in the middle of the clearing Nina saw a large stump, just under three feat tall and a full three feet in diameter. four smaller stumps were arranged around it Paul was already seated on one of the smaller stumps, and the large stump was clearly just the right hieght for a table.

On the large stump lay a basket of juicy blackberries, a canteen, and two shiny metal cups Paul looked up at Nina and asked, "Are you ready for a treat?"

Descriptive Paragraph: Graphic Organizer

DIRECTIONS To describe something, a writer tells what he or she sees, hears, feels, tastes, and smells. The writer uses interesting words. Describe a favorite relative. Use the graphic organizer to plan your descriptive paragraph. Which relative will you describe? Write his or her name in the circle. Then write words that describe this relative on the lines. Draw a picture of the person.

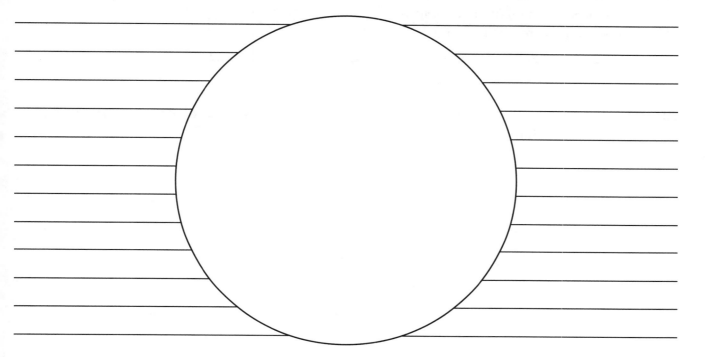

Descriptive Paragraph: Writing

Tips for Writing a Descriptive Paragraph:
- Use your voice when you write. That means you should use your special way of expressing yourself.
- Help readers see, smell, taste, feel, and hear what you are writing about.
- Use interesting words to help you describe.
- Use similes and metaphors to help your readers imagine the experience you are writing about.

DIRECTIONS ▷ Describe a favorite relative. Use the graphic organizer on page 481 as a guide for writing. Be sure to proofread your writing.

_____

_____

_____

_____

_____

_____

_____

_____

_____

_____

_____

_____

_____

_____

_____

_____

_____

_____

_____

_____

_____

How-to Paragraph

A **how-to paragraph**
- tells how to do something.
- has a topic sentence and detail sentences.
- tells what materials to use and what steps to follow.

DIRECTIONS > Use the following sentences to write a how-to paragraph. First, write the topic sentence that gives the purpose of the instructions. Next, write the sentence that lists the needed materials. Then write the steps in correct time order. Put in any special information where it is needed.

Boil the ginger, letting the water evaporate until only one cup of water remains.

You will need a fresh ginger root, three cups of water, a knife, and a glass pot or kettle.

If you ever need to warm your body when you are chilled, you should try making some ginger tea.

First, put three cups of water into the glass pot.

Next, cut six slices of ginger root. The slices should be $\frac{1}{8}$ to $\frac{1}{4}$ inch thick.

Strain the ginger tea into a cup. Drink it hot.

Add the ginger to the water in the pot.

___

How-to Paragraph: Proofreading

To be a good proofreader, look for one type of error at a time. For example, proofread once for capitalization errors, once for punctuation errors, and once for spelling errors.

PROOFREADER'S MARKS

≡ Capitalize.
⊙ Add a period.
∧ Add something.
⋏ Add a comma.
⌄⌄ Add quotation marks.
⚡ Cut something.

⌒ Replace something.
⁀ Transpose.
○ Spell correctly.
⊬ Indent paragraph.
/ Make a lowercase letter.

 **DIRECTIONS** > **Proofread the how-to paragraphs below, paying special attention to commas. Use the Proofreader's Marks to correct at least eight errors.**

With the help of a little tuna fish and some acting skill, you can easily get your dog Titan to take his pill. As you know, Titan often begs for tuna but you never give him any. If you suddenly offer Titan some tuna with the pill inside it, he will become suspicious and refuse eat it. Try this method instead.

Make a small ball of tuna around Titan's pill. Put the tuna ball on a plate. Then find sumthing you like to eat and put that on the plate, too. Take your plate and sit down at the kitchen table.

Titan will probably be watching you carefully but you should ignore him. He's a very smart dog and it will not be easy to fool him. your chances of success are best if you if just pretend you don't see him.

Titan will soon sit beside you, and start to beg. Eat your own food and continue to ignore Titan. Then, very casually, allow the ball of tuna to fall to the floor. You should make a quick grab for the tuna but you must be sure that Titan gets to it first. Titan will eagerly gulp the tuna—and the pill.

How-to Paragraph: Graphic Organizer

DIRECTIONS Think about your favorite park or restaurant. Write a how-to paragraph telling someone how to get there from your house. Use the graphic organizer to help you write.

Writing Plan

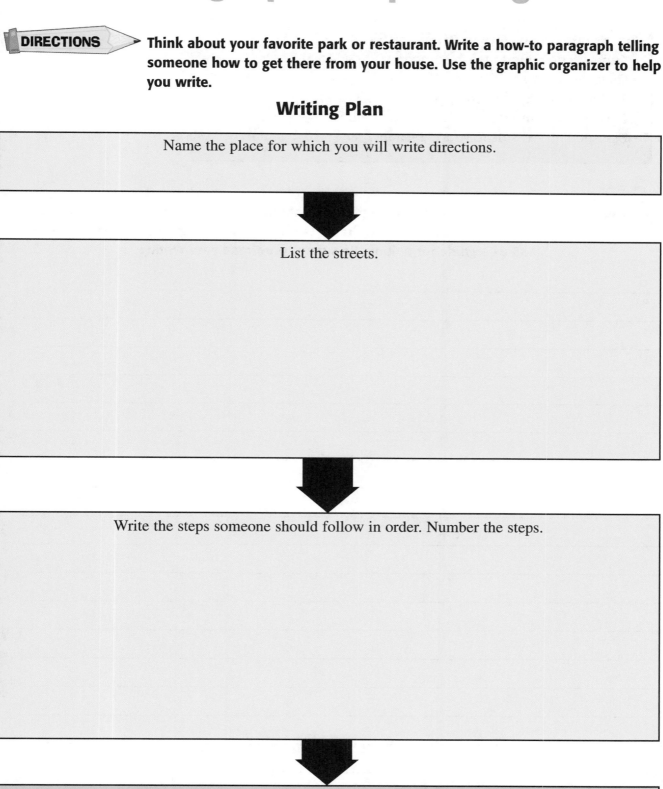

Name the place for which you will write directions.

List the streets.

Write the steps someone should follow in order. Number the steps.

Write some sequence words that help the reader know what to do.

How-to Paragraph: Writing

Tips for Writing a How-to Paragraph:
- Choose one thing to teach someone.
- Focus on a plan.
  1. Think of all the materials someone will need.
  2. Think of all the steps someone will follow.
- Use sequence words in your directions.

DIRECTIONS Think about your favorite park or restaurant. Write a how-to paragraph telling someone how to get there from your house. Use the graphic organizer on page 485 as a guide for writing. Be sure to proofread your writing.

_____

_____

_____

_____

_____

_____

_____

_____

_____

_____

_____

_____

_____

_____

_____

_____

_____

_____

_____

_____

_____

_____

Compare and Contrast Paragraph

A **compare and contrast paragraph**
• tells about the similarities and the differences of two or more items.
• answers the same questions about each item.

DIRECTIONS ▸ Read each paragraph. Label it *compare* or *contrast*. Circle the names of the two items being compared. Underline the key words that signal similarity or difference.

1. The new house was similar to the old house in some ways. Like the old house, it had three bedrooms. Both houses had two bathrooms. They both had fireplaces in the living room. The old house had a separate dining room, and so did the new house.

_____

2. The new house looked and felt different from the old house, and Janet did not know if she liked it as much. The old house was nearly one hundred years old. The new house had just been built. Unlike the old two-story house, the new house was all on one level. The hardwood floors at the old house could be seen beneath the old-fashioned rugs, while wall-to-wall carpet covered the floors of the new house.

_____

DIRECTIONS ▸ Use the information in the paragraphs above to complete the chart. Write the different characteristics of each house in the correct column. In the middle column, write the characteristics that both houses share.

Old House	Both	New House
_____	_____	_____
_____	_____	_____
_____	_____	_____
_____	_____	_____

Compare and Contrast Paragraph: Proofreading

To be a good proofreader, look for one type of error at a time. For example, proofread once for capitalization errors, once for punctuation errors, and once for spelling errors.

PROOFREADER'S MARKS

≡ Capitalize.
⊙ Add a period.
∧ Add something.
⩕ Add a comma.
ⱽⱽ Add quotation marks.
⤝ Cut something.

⌒ Replace something.
⤮ Transpose.
◯ Spell correctly.
Indent paragraph.
/ Make a lowercase letter.

DIRECTIONS ➤ Proofread the paragraphs of comparison and contrast, paying special attention to subject-verb agreement. Use the Proofreader's Marks to correct at least seven errors.

People sometimes asks me who my best friend is. Truthfully, I do not know. I have two close friends, and I like them both very much.

My friends judy and Margie is alike in many ways. Both are intelligent, loyal, and helpful Either can carry on a great conversation. Each has an excellent sense of humor, and we all enjoy many of the same activities.

However, my two friends are different in many ways. I has more arguments with Judy. She complains if she does not like something, and she argue if she disagrees with me. Margie rarely complains or argues, so we almost never fights.

On the other hand, Judy is a more honest friend. She always says exactly what she thinks or feels. In contrast, margie never say anything negative to me about things i have said or done. Instead, she may say something to someone else, and her comments often gets back to me. If Judy has a complaint, she discusses it with the person who has caused the problem.

Compare and Contrast Paragraph: Graphic Organizer

DIRECTIONS Compare and contrast two subjects you study at school. Use the Venn diagram to help you plan your writing. List what is true only about A in the A circle. List what is true only about B in the B circle. List what is true about both A and B where the circles overlap.

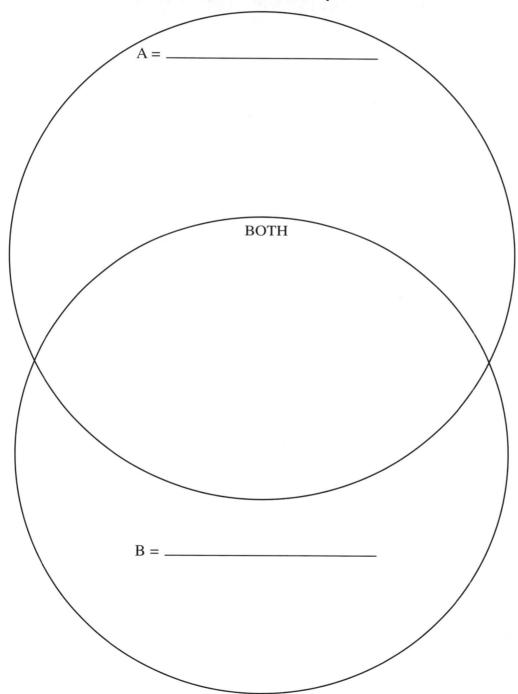

A = _____

BOTH

B = _____

Compare and Contrast Paragraph: Writing

Tips for Writing a Compare and Contrast Paragraph:
• Find information about your subjects.
• Organize the information you find into main ideas.
• Use details to explain each main idea.
• Explain how the subjects are alike.
• Explain how the subjects are different.
• Use your last paragraph to summarize your main ideas in a new way.

DIRECTIONS Compare and contrast two subjects you study at school. Use the Venn diagram on page 489 as a guide for writing. Be sure to proofread your writing.

Persuasive Letter

DIRECTIONS > Read this business letter. Then answer the questions that follow.

Kensington
London, England
December 21, 1846

Mr. Ebenezer Scrooge
Financial District
London, England

Dear Mr. Scrooge:
    One of your employees, Bob Cratchit, has applied for work with us. Mr. Cratchit is a fine man, and I think you should think carefully before letting him go. First of all, Bob is very quick with numbers—a valuable trait in your type of work. Second, he is a very loyal worker. If it were not for his son, Tiny Tim, he would never think of leaving your firm. Third, Mr. Cratchit is willing to work very long hours for very little pay. I feel I am certain that you should see to this immediately. For some reason, I sense that it may be of great importance.

Sincerely,

James Martin

1. What opinion is stated in this business letter?

_____

2. Write the topic sentence that states this opinion.

_____

3. How many reasons does the writer give to support his opinion?

_____

4. What warning does the writer give?

_____

Persuasive Letter: Proofreading

To be a good proofreader, look for one type of error at a time. For example, proofread once for capitalization errors, once for punctuation errors, and once for spelling errors.

PROOFREADER'S MARKS

≡ Capitalize.
⊙ Add a period.
∧ Add something.
⩘ Add a comma.
v̌v̌ Add quotation marks.
⤷ Cut something.

⌃ Replace something.
𝇇 Transpose.
○ Spell correctly.
⊬ Indent paragraph.
/ Make a lowercase letter.

DIRECTIONS ▷ **Proofread the business letter, paying special attention to capitalization and punctuation. Use the Proofreader's Marks to correct at least nine errors.**

> 431 palm Avenue
> Normand Massachusetts 02162
> june 26, 2005

Mr. glen Scrubb

Grime-Away cleaners

816 Ruby Street

Normand, massachusetts 02162

dear Mr. Scrubb

    My family has used your cleaners for seven years, and your service has always been satisfactory. however, last Thursday I picked up my favorite slacks from Grime-Away and discovered a tear in the cuff. I know that the tear was not there when I brought the slacks to Grime-Away. The clerk said she could not have the tear repaired without your authorization. Please send me a note stating that you will pay four the repair.

    Thank you for your help.

> sincerely,

> Donald Todd

Persuasive Letter: Graphic Organizer

In a persuasive letter, a writer tries to convince someone or a group of people to do something. The writer tries to make the reader feel a certain emotion about the topic he or she writes about.

DIRECTIONS Write a persuasive letter to the principal of your school asking him or her to change the homework policy of your school. Use this graphic organizer to help you write.

1. Write your address.

2. Write the date.

3. Write the principal's name and address.

4. Write a polite greeting, or salutation.

5. What will you say in the first paragraph to let your principal know why you are writing?

6. Complete the chart:

Main Points You Will Present	Supporting Details You Will Use

7. Use your last paragraph to write a conclusion. Summarize the important points you made.

8. Choose a friendly closing.

9. Sign your name.

Persuasive Letter: Writing

Tips for Writing a Persuasive Letter
• Use a strong beginning to grab your reader's attention.
• Make your purpose for writing clear to the reader.
• Use examples that will appeal to your reader's emotions.
• Organize your examples from least important to most important.
• Use a strong ending that leaves your reader convinced that you are right.

DIRECTIONS Write a persuasive letter to the principal of your school asking him or her to change the homework policy of your school. Use the graphic organizer on page 493 as a guide for writing. Be sure to proofread your writing.

Persuasive Essay

A **persuasive essay**
• gives an opinion about an issue.
• gives facts and reasons to back up the opinion.
• has an introductory paragraph, supporting paragraphs, and a conclusion.

DIRECTIONS ▷ **Read the following statements from a persuasive essay. Write the word or group of words from the box that best describes the techniques used in the statement.**

testimonial	emotional words	faulty generalization
begging the question	bandwagon technique	

1. We have to keep greedy builders from gobbling up our wilderness to make a buck.

   _____

2. Jack Tenor, the famous athlete, says that they passed a similar law in his town and everyone is happy with it.

   _____

3. Join the thousands of people all over the country who are demanding laws to restrict building in their area.

   _____

4. Since my neighbors like my idea, we're sure that this is what the community wants.

   _____

5. If you are a good citizen, of course you will support this law.

   _____

6. Do not trade the unspoiled beauty and the restful peace of our country for the crowded, smoggy rat race of the city.

   _____

7. María Gómez, a university professor, says that life in the city can be difficult.

   _____

Persuasive Essay: Proofreading

To be a good proofreader, look for one type of error at a time. For example, proofread once for capitalization errors, once for punctuation errors, and once for spelling errors.

PROOFREADER'S MARKS

≡ Capitalize.	⁄\‾ Replace something.
⊙ Add a period.	∿ Transpose.
∧ Add something.	○ Spell correctly.
∧, Add a comma.	¶ Indent paragraph.
∨∨ Add quotation marks.	/ Make a lowercase letter.
⌐ Cut something.	

DIRECTIONS **Proofread this persuasive essay, paying special attention to capitalization of proper nouns. Use the Proofreader's Marks to correct at least nine errors.**

The people of the World are faced with alarming environmental problems. I am convinced that we must all cooperate through international agencys to solve these problems. Working alone, one state or one nation cannot protect its land and people from environmental hazards. The problems faced by people in the united states are also problems for people in canada, Japan, and russia. Only by facing these problems together and trying to work out cooperative solutions can we protect ourselves and our Planet.

There are several reasons why international cooperation is needed. in the first place, some environmental dangers threaten the whole plant rather than local areas. Damage to the ozone layer is a good example. If someone in nebraska uses an aerosol spray, the chemicals do not stay in Nebraska. Those damaging chemicals travel to the ozone layer, where they affect the whole world. Therefore, a State or Country cannot protect itself against ozone damage simply by passing a law forbidding the local use of aerosols.

Persuasive Essay: Graphic Organizer

DIRECTIONS Should sodas and candy be sold in vending machines on school campuses? Write a persuasive essay expressing your opinion. Use the graphic organizer to help you write.

What will the topic of your essay be?
_____
_____

What is your opinion on this topic?
_____
_____

Reason 1
_____
_____
_____
_____

Why? Support your reason.
_____
_____
_____
_____
_____

Reason 2
_____
_____
_____
_____

Why? Support your reason.
_____
_____
_____
_____
_____

Reason 3
_____
_____
_____
_____

Why? Support your reason.
_____
_____
_____
_____
_____

Persuasive Essay: Writing

Tips for Writing a Persuasive Essay:
• Grab your reader's attention in the first paragraph.
• State your opinion clearly.
• Support your opinion with clear examples.
• Present your examples from least important to most important.
• Use the last paragraph to summarize your essay.
• Use your last paragraph to leave the reader convinced you are right.

> **DIRECTIONS** Should sodas and candy be sold in vending machines on school campuses? Write a persuasive essay expressing your opinion. Use the graphic organizer on page 497 as a guide for writing. Be sure to proofread your writing.

Poem

A **poem**
- expresses feelings, often through description.
- presents vivid images.
- may or may not rhyme.

DIRECTIONS ➤ Read each stanza of this poem. Answer the questions that follow.

The Sea That Joins the World

I stand at the blue, wave-ruffled border of the Pacific
And my eyes follow it to a distant meeting with the sky.
My mind tries to follow abroad to far-off continents
That Australians, Japanese, and Russians occupy.

My body sinks in the frothing salty ocean,
A bathtub shared with tribes in distant lands.
I feel my arms extend to unknown peoples
And, through the ocean, touch them with my hands.

1. What does the title suggest about the poem?

   _____

2. What picture is created in the first line?

   _____

   _____

3. Does this poem contain rhyme? If so, which words rhyme?

   _____

4. What metaphor does the second stanza contain?

   _____

5. What feeling is expressed in the second stanza?

   _____

Poem: Proofreading

To be a good proofreader, look for one type of error at a time. For example, proofread once for capitalization errors, once for punctuation errors, and once for spelling errors.

PROOFREADER'S MARKS

= Capitalize.
⊙ Add a period.
∧ Add something.
⋏ Add a comma.
ᵛᵛ Add quotation marks.
✁ Cut something.

⋏ Replace something.
𝒩 Transpose.
○ Spell correctly.
𝓗 Indent paragraph.
/ Make a lowercase letter.

DIRECTIONS ➤ **Proofread the poem, paying special attention to the correct use of pronouns. Use the Proofreader's Marks to correct at least seven errors.**

My Fair-Weather Friend

My greatest admirer is mine shadow.

He admires me so much that he mimics everything myse

He follows me everywhere.

I drag him threw puddles as i walk around.

His glides over their surface like a black film of oil.

I drag him over logs and stones.

He slithers over they like a snake.

I bump him into Boulders and Buildings.

He stays by me side, obedient as a slave, faithful as a fair-weather friend.

"What?" you ask. "I always thought a fair-weather friend was unfaithful."

Exactly. My shadow deserts me as soon as the son goes down or the sky turns gray.

He will not follow I into dark rooms or deep caves.

He is only a fair-weather friend.

Poem: Graphic Organizer

Poetry is usually written in rhythmic lines rather than in sentences. In a **rhymed** poem, syllable sounds are repeated at the ends of paired lines. For example, the following poem follows a rhyme scheme, or pattern. The first and third lines rhyme, and the second and fourth lines rhyme.

Example:

> A sleeping fawn,
> A single crow—
> Above, the dawn,
> Still night below.

In **unrhymed** poetry, rhythm, figurative language, and imagery express a mood.

Example:

> The quiet night
> Gentle breathing of branches.
> The sun creeps
> Glinting edges of hilltops.
> A crow calls
> Shrill salute to the morning.

DIRECTIONS ▷ **Think about your favorite holiday. Write colorful words that describe it on the graphic organizer. Then use the graphic organizer to help you write a poem about your favorite holiday.**

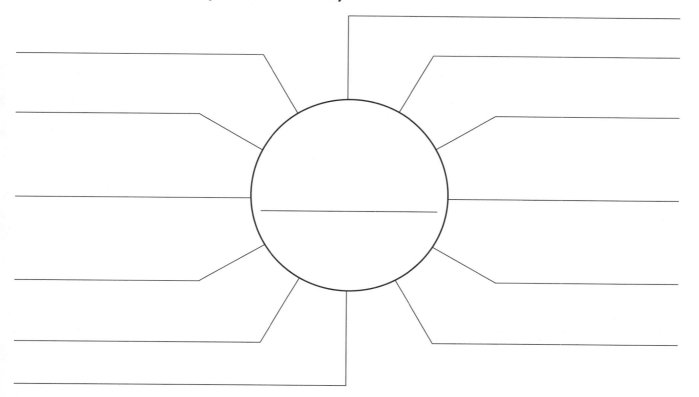

Poem: Writing

> **DIRECTIONS** Write a poem about your favorite holiday. Use the graphic organizer on page 501 as a guide to help you write. Be sure to proofread your writing.

Writing for a Test

Writing for a test requires special skills. Usually, the writer has no choice of topic; the topic is assigned. Often, there is a time limit during which all stages of the writing process must be carried out. Keeping in mind any such restrictions, you should build in the time to plan and revise your writing. Thinking about these questions may help:

PREWRITING

Choosing a Topic
- What questions must I answer?
- Am I being asked to compare, give an opinion, explain, analyze, or describe?
- What kind of writing will fulfill this assignment?

Gathering Information
- Am I allowed to refer to my textbook?
- Can I make a rough outline to help organize my thoughts?

DRAFTING
- What will I use as my topic sentence?
- How much time do I have to finish the draft? How many minutes should I allot to each question or essay?

RESPONDING AND REVISING
- Have I answered the question completely?
- Are there any additional facts I should include?

PROOFREADING
- Have I spelled every word correctly?
- Are my sentences grammatically correct?

FINAL DRAFT
- Do I have time to rewrite this neatly?

Essay Questions

Many tests include essay questions. The test taker must divide the given time into time to plan, time to draft, and time to revise each answer.

Example:

How did Native Americans adapt to their environment? Give two examples.

Inuit—igloos, travel for food 2
Iroquois—homes of wood and bark, hunted game 1

Freewrite facts and ideas
Organize by numbering facts in logical order

Topic sentence: Native Americans had to adapt their housing and eating habits to their environment.

Develop main idea for topic

Native Americans had to adapt their housing and eating habits to their environment. The Iroquois lived in the Eastern forests, where trees and game animals were plentiful. They built houses called longhouses out of wood and bark. An example of adaptation to extreme conditions is the Inuit way of life. In the Arctic, many Inuit built igloos for winter homes. They, too, traveled in search of food.

Write

Tips for Writing for a Test:
- Freewrite facts and ideas.
- Organize by numbering facts in logical order.
- Develop the main idea for a topic.
- Write.

Writing to Prompts

Many schools use tests to evaluate students' ability to write. One kind of test uses a **writing prompt**, which requires a written response to a statement, a question, or a picture. Careful reading of the prompt will help determine the writing form, the audience (if given), and the purpose for writing (to inform, to persuade, to entertain, or to describe). Often, students are supplied with enough paper to plan and write the response.

Example:

Prompt   **Some people say exercise not only keeps you fit but also can give you more energy and better concentration. Do you agree or disagree? Write an essay in which you state your opinion and support it with at least one example.**

Organizing notes

Does exercise keep me fit, boost my energy, and help me concentrate? Yes.
Example of this: my swimming
Reasons why (or how?) it helps:
1. the exercise gives me energy
2. easier to concentrate when I've exercised

Thesis statement

Frequent exercise can help improve your energy level and concentration.

 **DIRECTIONS**   Choose one of the writing prompts below. Follow the tips on pages 503 and 504 to prepare your written response to the prompt.

1. People take care of their teeth so they will stay healthy for a lifetime. Think about the steps in your daily dental-care routine. Then, write a how-to paper explaining this process.

2. Have you read a book that has been made into a movie or cartoon? How are they alike? How are they different? Write a paper that compares and contrasts the two versions of the story.

3. Are you allowed to stay up as late as you think you should? What would you like your bedtime to be? Write a letter to convince your parents that you should be able to stay up later.

Parts of a Book

The **title page** tells the name of a book and the author's name. It also tells the name of the company that published the book.

The **copyright page** is on the back of the title page. It tells when the book was published.

The **foreword/preface** contains introductory comments about the book. It can be written by the author or someone else.

The **contents page** lists the titles of the chapters or units in the book and the pages on which they begin.

The **glossary** contains definitions of difficult or unfamiliar words that appear in the book.

The **bibliography** is a list of books about a certain subject. It can also be a list of books the author used or referred to in the text.

The **index** is a list of all the topics in a book. It is in alphabetical order and lists the page or pages on which each topic appears.

DIRECTIONS > Identify in which part of a book the following information can be found. Choose from the list in the box below.

contents page	bibliography	index	title page
foreword/preface	copyright page	glossary	content or body

1. *All Wrapped Up in Mummies*
   By Sandy Desserte
   Impossible Press
   Cleveland, Ohio _____

2. The book you are about to read is the result of more than twenty years of research. To gather information about mummies, Miss Desserte made several trips to Egypt and actually took part in a number of archaeological digs.

   _____

3. Suggested Readings
   Aldred, Cyril. *The Egyptians*. Thames and Hudson, London, 1965.
   Barnes, James. *Land of the Pharaohs*. Jones Publishing Co., London, 1924.

   _____

4. Copyright © 1993 by Sandy Desserte _____

5. Foreword......................................8
   Looking for Mummies............................11
   Under the Desert Sky ....22 _____

Parts of a Book, page 2

DIRECTIONS In which book part would you find answers to these questions? Choose from the list in the box below.

title page	copyright page	contents page
AFRICA A Land of Empires by Dorothy J. Morgan LANDMARK PUBLICATIONS Chicago New York Toronto	Copyright © 1985 by Landmark Publications **Acknowledgments** *Millburn Publishing Company:* "Watusi Legends" from *African Literature*, ed. by R.R. Adams. Copyright © 1967. *Tifford, Inc.* "Sunset" from *Poetry Monthly*, October 1981. All rights reserved. Printed in the United States of America.	**CONTENTS** 1. The Africa of the Romans ... 1 2. The Sarakole Empire .... 25 3. The Mali Empire .... 53 4. The Ethiopian Empire ...... 75 5. The Baguirimi Empire ...... 153 Glossary .... 175 Index 187

contents page foreword/preface	bibliography copyright page	index glossary	title page content or body

1. What is the meaning of *papyrus*?

   _____

2. On what page does Chapter 2 begin?

   _____

3. When was the book published?

   _____

4. Who published the book?

   _____

5. What are some other books on the same topic?

   _____

6. Who wrote the book?

   _____

7. Who wrote the introductory remarks?

   _____

8. Which is the shortest chapter?

   _____

DIRECTIONS List at least one item of information that can be found in each of the following book parts.

9. copyright page _____

10. title page _____

11. foreword or preface _____

12. index _____

13. glossary _____

14. contents page _____

15. bibliography _____

Outlines

An **outline** organizes information into main topics, subtopics, and details. An outline follows certain rules of capitalization and punctuation.

DIRECTIONS Write *main topic, subtopic,* or *detail* to identify each item in this part of an outline.

I. Loch Ness monster _____

   A. Where it lives _____

      1. Northern Scotland _____

      2. Deep, narrow lake _____

   B. What it looks like _____

      1. Small head _____

      2. Long, thin neck _____

      3. Body 90 feet long _____

DIRECTIONS The lines in this part of the outline are in the correct order. Find the error or errors in each line, and write the line correctly. Remember to indent the lines properly.

II. the Yeti _____

   a. where it lives _____

      1 in Asia _____

      2 in the Himalayas _____

   b. what it looks like _____

      1. large ape or man _____

      2 covered with hair _____

DIRECTIONS Research famous monsters or other imaginary creatures. On your own paper, write an outline of the information you find. Revise and proofread your work, checking for correct outline form.

Using a Thesaurus

A **thesaurus** is a book that gives synonyms, words that have nearly the same meaning, and antonyms, words that mean the opposite of a word. Many thesauruses are like dictionaries. The entry words are listed in dark print in alphabetical order. Guide words at the top of the page tell which words can be found on the page. Use a thesaurus to enrich your vocabulary and make your writing more colorful.
Example:

buccaneer	budge

buccaneer *syn.* pirate, sea robber, desperado, outlaw, pillager, plunderer, ransacker, looter, raider

DIRECTIONS Rewrite each sentence. Use a thesaurus to replace the underlined word.

1. The Ross family left their <u>home</u> early.

   _____

2. The children climbed into the car <u>eagerly</u>.

   _____

3. Bill Ross was a <u>beginning</u> driver.

   _____

4. He had just finished a <u>class</u> in driving at school.

   _____

5. Bill and his father <u>changed</u> places before they reached the mountains.

   _____

   _____

6. The <u>smell</u> of pines was everywhere.

   _____

7. Bill and Susan immediately went for a <u>walk</u>.

   _____

8. They loved to spend time in the <u>woods</u>.

   _____

9. A cool <u>wind</u> blew through their hair.

   _____

10. They hiked until they were <u>tired</u>.

   _____

Using a Dictionary

A **dictionary** lists words in alphabetical order, giving their pronunciation, part of speech, and definition. There are two guide words at the top of every dictionary page. The word on the left is the first word on the page, and the word on the right is the last word. Each word in the dictionary is an entry word.

DIRECTIONS > **Read the dictionary entries and answer the questions that follow.**

---

nation   **nature**

na·tion [nā´shən] *n.* **1** A group of people who live in a particular area, have a distinctive way of life, and are organized under a central government. They usually speak the same language. **2** A tribe or federation: the Iroquois *nation.*

na·tion·al [nash´ən·əl] **1** *adj.* Of, belonging to, or having to do with a nation as a whole: A *national* law; a *national* crisis. **2** *n.* a citizen of a nation. **–na´tion·al·ly** *adv.*

na·tion·wide [nā´shən·wīd´] *adj.* Extending throughout or across a nation.

na·tive [nā´tiv] **1** *adj.* Born, grown, or living naturally in a particular area. **2** *n.* A person, plant, or animal native to an area. **3** *n.* One of the original inhabitants of a place; aborigine. **4** *adj.* Related or belonging to a person by birth or place of birth: one's *native* language.

Native American One of or a descendant of the peoples already living in the Western Hemisphere before the first Europeans came.

na·tive-born [nā´tiv·bôrn´] *adj.* Born in the area or country stated: a *native–born* Floridian.

---

1. What part of speech is *nation*? _____

2. What part of speech is *native-born*? _____

3. What is the meaning of *nationwide*? _____

4. What is the base word of *nationally*? _____

5. Which meaning of the word *nation* is used in the following sentence?

   Wilma Mankiller is the first woman to become chief of the Cherokee *nation.*

   _____

6. What is the entry word for *nationally*? _____

7. How many syllables does *nationwide* have? _____

8. Would *natural* be found on the page with the guide words shown above? _____

Using a Computerized Card Catalog

Libraries used to keep track of their inventory by having cards for each book. These cards were alphabetized and kept in "card catalogs." Most libraries now use **computerized card catalogs**. You can look up books by title, author, or subject. The computer can tell you whether the book is available or has been checked out. In public libraries in cities, you can find out which branches have the book if your location doesn't have it. Sometimes you can call another branch and have the book sent to the library closest to you.

DIRECTIONS ▸ Refer to the directions inside the box to answer the questions.

To look for a book by the author's last name:		To look for a book by title:	
STEP	**ACTION**	**STEP**	**ACTION**
1	Type: FA	1	Type: FT
2	Type: Author's last name	2	Type: Book title
3	Press: <RETURN> key	3	Press: <RETURN> key

1. Write the three steps you would follow to find a book by Thor Heyerdahl using a computerized book catalog.

_____

_____

_____

2. Write the three steps you would take to find a book called *Treasures of the Deep*.

_____

_____

_____

3. If you type FA to find a book by author's name, and you type FT to find a book by book title, what do you think you would type to find a book by subject? Explain your answer.

_____

_____

4. What three steps would you take to find books about whales?

_____

_____

_____

Taking Notes

Taking notes helps you organize information when you do research. Some facts are more important than others. Write down only the main ideas when you take notes.

ⓄⓄⓄⓄⓄⓄⓄⓄⓄⓄⓄⓄⓄⓄⓄⓄⓄⓄⓄⓄⓄⓄⓄⓄⓄⓄⓄⓄⓄⓄⓄ

DIRECTIONS ▷ **Read the following paragraphs and take notes about them on the note cards below.**

Among women in history, Queen Hatshepsut of Egypt holds a special place. She was the only woman ever to rule Egypt with the all-powerful title of pharaoh. Hatshepsut succeeded her husband Thutmose II to the throne about 1504 B.C. She enjoyed a relatively long reign, ruling as pharaoh for 21 years. During that time, Hatshepsut was remarkably productive. Egypt's trade improved under her leadership, and she embarked on a major building program.

NOTES

_____

_____

_____

_____

_____

_____

Meng T'ien, the general in charge of building the Great Wall, is also credited with another, smaller construction project. Sometime before 200 B.C., General T'ien is believed to have invented the *cheng*, a musical instrument of the zither family. Like other zithers of Asia, the *cheng* has a long, slightly curved sound box with strings that stretch the length of the instrument. Frets, or stops, are located on the sound box to help produce the melody. Although the *cheng* is no longer popular in China, its descendants are still popular in other Asian countries. In Vietnam the *tranh* is still used for courtly music, and the *koto* enjoys wide popularity in Japan.

NOTES

_____

_____

_____

_____

_____

_____

Analyzing a Textbook

A textbook gives much information. Use the table of contents to find the facts you need. The glossary defines difficult words in the text.

DIRECTIONS ▷ Read this table of contents for a science textbook about oceans. Answer the questions that follow.

CONTENTS

1. In which chapter would you find information about whales, dolphins, and sea otters? _____

   How do you know? _____

2. In which chapter would you expect to find pictures of the damage caused by an oil slick? _____

   What makes you think so? _____

3. Which is the longest chapter? _____

4. In which chapter might you find out how coral reefs are formed? _____

5. You're interested in finding out what kinds of seaweed grow near the coastlines. Where would you

   look? _____

6. You want to find out what the word *salinity* means. Where might you find it in this book?

   _____

7. In which chapter might you find information about pelicans? _____

8. You want to learn which creatures live in the deepest parts of the ocean. Which chapter would you

   read? _____

9. Which is the shortest chapter? _____

10. In which chapter would you find out what valuable things we can get from the oceans? _____

Using an Encyclopedia

An **encyclopedia** is a set of reference books, each of which is called a **volume**. Each volume contains many articles on various topics. The topics are arranged alphabetically. The spine of each volume indicates which articles are within. For example, a volume that says *N-O* has articles beginning with the letters *N* and *O*. At the end of most articles there is a list of related topics. These topics are called cross-references. Often you can find more pertinent information by reading these articles.

DIRECTIONS ▸ Find the entry for *armadillo* in an encyclopedia. Then answer the following questions.

1. Where do armadillos live? _____

2. What do they eat? _____

3. How do they protect themselves? _____

4. How much do they weigh? _____

5. Which encyclopedia did you use? _____

DIRECTIONS ▸ Find the entry for *Sir Edmund Hillary* in an encyclopedia. Then answer the following questions.

6. Why is Sir Edmund Hillary famous? _____

7. What country was he from? _____

8. When was he born? _____

9. What was his family's business? _____

10. How high is Mount Everest? _____

DIRECTIONS ▸ Find the entry for *Zimbabwe* in an encyclopedia. Then answer the following questions.

11. Where is Zimbabwe located? _____

12. Does it have a coast? _____

13. What is the capital and the largest city? _____

14. What is the former name of Zimbabwe? _____

15. What are the most important agricultural products? _____

Identifying Reference Sources

atlas – a book of maps
thesaurus – a book of synonyms and antonyms
dictionary – gives the pronunciation and the definitions of words
almanac – a book that is published each year and gives facts about various topics such as the tides, weather, time the sun rises, etc. Much of the information is presented in charts, tables, and graphs. An almanac also presents general information.
encyclopedia – a set of volumes that has articles about various topics
Books in Print – lists books that have been published about various subjects

 **DIRECTIONS** ➤ Write the reference source in which each item of information can be found. Choose from the list below. There may be more than one correct answer.

| atlas | almanac | thesaurus | encyclopedia | dictionary | *Books in Print* |

1. **Languages** – It is estimated that there are thousands of languages spoken in the world. Following is a list of the major languages spoken by the greatest number of people. They are ranked in order of usage.

   Name of Language
   Chinese (Mandarin)
   English (has the most words – 790,000)

   Major Areas Where Spoken
   China
   U.S., U.K, Canada, Ireland, Australia, New Zealand

2. **sincere** – honest, truthful, honorable, frank, open, aboveboard, unreserved, veracious, true, candid

3. **writing** – visible recording of language peculiar to the human species. Writing permits the transmission of ideas over vast distances of time and space and is essential to complex civilization. The first known writing dates from 6000 B.C. . . .

4. **language** [lang´ gwij] *n.* **1. a.** Spoken or written human speech. *Language* is used to communicate thoughts and feelings. **b.** A particular system of human speech that is shared by the people of a country or another group of people. **2.** Any system of signs, symbols, or gestures used for giving information.

5. Auberge, Tony, ed. *The Oxford Guide to Word Games.* LC83-25140. 240 p. 1984. 14.95 (ISBN 0-19-214144-9). Oxford U. Pr.

Using the Internet

You can use a computer to help you do research on the Internet. The World Wide Web allows you to access many websites that have pictures and sounds as well as written information. This makes it an interesting way to do research. Search engines are instruments that help you find the information you want.

DIRECTIONS > Connect to the Internet. Use the search engine www.yahooligans.com to search for the subject *elephant*. Then answer the questions.

1. How many category matches were listed? _____

2. How many site matches were listed? _____

3. Under which category do you find the most resources listed? _____

4. List the website addresses that have pictures of elephants. _____
_____

5. List the website addresses that have magazine articles listed. _____
_____
_____

DIRECTIONS > Use these different search engines to do a search for the subject *elephant*. Then answer the questions.

| www.yahooligans.com | www.ajkids.com | www.altavista.com |

1. Which search engine gave you the best results? _____

2. Which search engine gave you the most results? _____

3. Which search engine was the easiest to use? _____

4. If you were writing a report on elephants, which search engine would have helped you the most?
_____

5. Pick a topic that interests you, and search the Internet for information. Which search engine(s) did you use? Tell what you find out about your topic. _____
_____
_____
_____

Writing Skills

UNIT 1: Personal Narrative

HOW MUCH DO YOU KNOW?

Read the personal narrative below. Then answer the questions that follow.

My Uncle Mike is my hero. When he was seventeen, a fire broke out in his apartment building. As smoke billowed from the building, firefighters kept the neighbors at a safe distance. Suddenly, Uncle Mike heard the cries of a baby. He said that he didn't think, he just broke through the crowd and rushed into the burning building. Then he crawled up the stairs to try to stay below the smoke. He broke down the door of the apartment. Outside, the family stood in frightened silence. Finally, Mike appeared at the apartment window with the baby in his arms. He climbed out the window. Firefighters put up a ladder and helped Uncle Mike and the baby down. My mother hurried to them. She wept as she hugged both Mike and the baby, because that baby was me, her healthy son!

1. From what point of view is this narrative told?

   _____

2. List the event that happened at the beginning of the narrative.

   _____

Complete the chain diagram below as the writer might have done when planning to write this narrative.

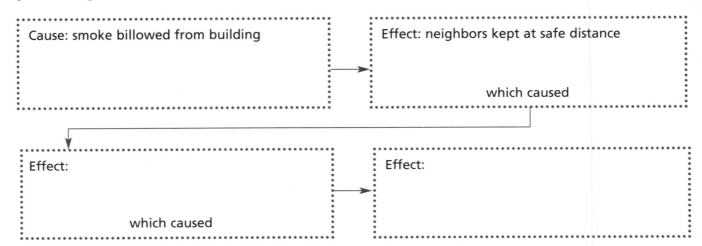

Cause: smoke billowed from building → Effect: neighbors kept at safe distance

which caused

Effect: ____ which caused → Effect: ____

Analyzing a Personal Narrative

A PERSONAL NARRATIVE
- is written in the first-person point of view
- usually reveals the writer's feelings
- has a beginning, a middle, and an end

Read the personal narrative below. Then answer the questions that follow.

The family birthday party began as usual. First, my family gathered with my presents after dinner. I was excited, but I thought I knew what I was getting. My parents had never been able to surprise me.

After I had opened one gift, I heard a faint rustling noise. I paused for a moment, but I heard nothing more. A minute later, I noticed that a large box moved! It was creepy! I jumped to my feet in alarm.

Laughing, my father then picked up the moving present. The box had no bottom at all. A fluffy white kitten was curled up where the present had been. I was finally surprised–with the best birthday present I had ever received.

1. From what point of view is this narrative told? _____

   What words are clues to this point of view? _____

2. How did the writer feel at the beginning of the narrative?

   _____

3. How did the writer's feelings change by the end of the narrative?

   _____

4. List the events of the narrative in the order in which they happened.
   Write a signal word or phrase if one is given for each event.

   a. _____

   b. _____

   c. _____

   d. _____

   e. _____

Connecting Cause and Effect

TO WRITE A PERSONAL NARRATIVE, GOOD WRITERS
- look for cause-and-effect connections among events
- build stories around cause-and-effect chains

Read the personal narrative below. Look for cause-and-effect relationships around which the writer built the story.

Hot winds from the desert had raised the temperature to 100 degrees. To escape the heat, thousands of people headed for the beach. The road to the beach was soon jammed with cars. The traffic slowed to a crawl. Stop-and-go driving in the heat caused many cars to overheat. Traffic was backed up for miles.

Luce's Juices is located at the side of the road that leads to the beach. People began to pull off the road and come into the juice bar. Hundreds of people decided they would rather wait in an air-conditioned juice bar than in the line of motionless cars. Some people liked the juices so well that they now stop every time they drive by. Because so many people discovered Luce's Juices that day, business has been great ever since.

Complete the chain diagram below as the writer might have done when planning to write this narrative. One example is done for you.

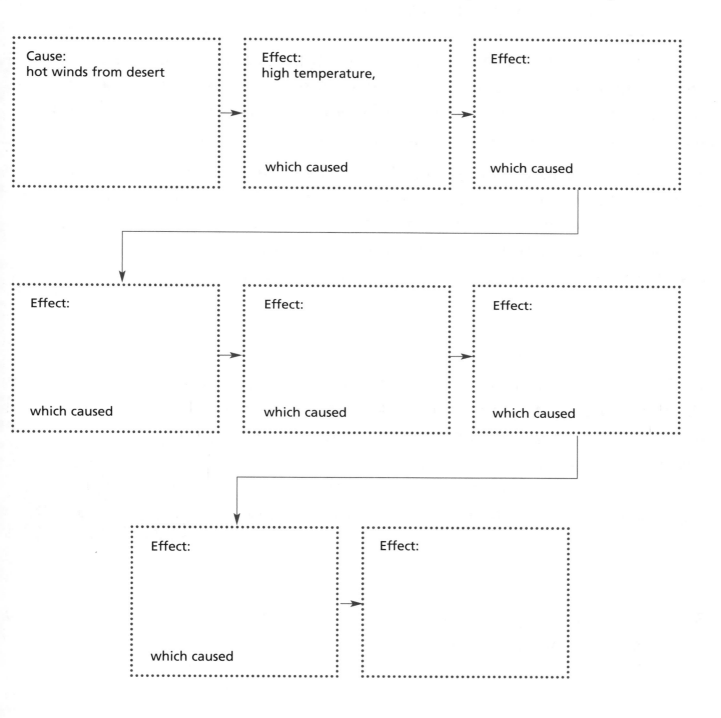

using Examples

> Good writers give a reader enough information by using
> - effective examples
> - the right number of examples

Read the following paragraphs. Label each paragraph as having the *right number* of examples, *too many*, or *too few*. If the paragraph has too few examples, write the examples you would add. If the paragraph has too many, write the examples that are not effective.

1. Wayne was a forgetful person. He was always leaving books on buses and benches. He often forgot to take his homework assignment home. When he did remember, he forgot to bring his completed assignment back to school. On those few occasions when he did bring a completed assignment back to school, Wayne usually forgot to turn it in.

_____

_____

2. That day everything went wrong for me. My breakfast was burned. My mother refused to buy me a horse. My hair would not go right. I had to iron my shirt. The dog chewed up my homework. I studied the wrong pages for my test. Joan won the spelling bee, and I only came in second. Worst of all, Wayne was assigned as my partner for the oral science report.

_____

_____

3. Working with Wayne, however, turned out better than I thought. He came up with some good ideas for our report.

_____

_____

Using a Thesaurus

Good writers sometimes use a thesaurus to find
the exact words they need.

Rewrite each sentence. Use a thesaurus to replace the underlined word.

1. The Ross family left their <u>home</u> early.

_____

_____

2. The children climbed into the car <u>eagerly</u>.

_____

_____

3. Bill Ross was the <u>driver</u> for the first thirty minutes.

_____

_____

4. He had just finished a <u>class</u> in driving at school.

_____

_____

5. Bill and his father <u>changed</u> places before they reached the mountains.

_____

_____

6. The <u>smell</u> of pines was everywhere.

_____

_____

7. Bill and Susan immediately went for a <u>walk</u>.

_____

_____

Proofreading a Personal Narrative

PROOFREADING MARKS	
⬭	spell correctly
⊙	add period
?	add question mark
≡	capitalize
ℐ	take out
∧	add
/	make lowercase
∽	switch
⋏	add comma
⋎ ⋎	add quotation marks
¶	indent paragraph

See the chart on page 637 to learn how to use these marks.

Proofread the beginning of the personal narrative, paying special attention to spelling. Use the Proofreading Marks to correct at least eight errors.

What an amazing experience my brothers and I had with the wind last autunm! We had driven with our parents to Point Reyes, north of San francisco. Point Reyes is known as one of the windyest spots in the cuontry, and on that day the winds were raging up to 50 miles an hour all along the California coast.

I had no way of determining the speed of the wind at Point reyes that afternoon. I can only tell you that when we jumped into the air, we were

blown a full five feet before landing The wind picked us up and carried us with the force of rushhing water. we simpply could not fall backward. The wind was so strong that we could lean back against it and let it support us as firmly as a brick wall would.

My brothers and I decided to take a short walk downwind along the beach. We allowed the wind to push us along at a rappid pace. For a while we stoped walking altogether. We simply jumped into the air, let ourselves be blown along like empty milk cartoons, and landed. Then we jumped into the air again. Borne by the wind, we progressed as quickly as if we had been walking

Make a Cause-and-Effect Chain

Write a series of causes and effects that tells a story about weather.
Write each sentence on a strip below.

Write a Letter

Write a letter describing a day in school. Include your feelings about the day's events. After you have revised your letter, proofread it. Show your letter to a friend.

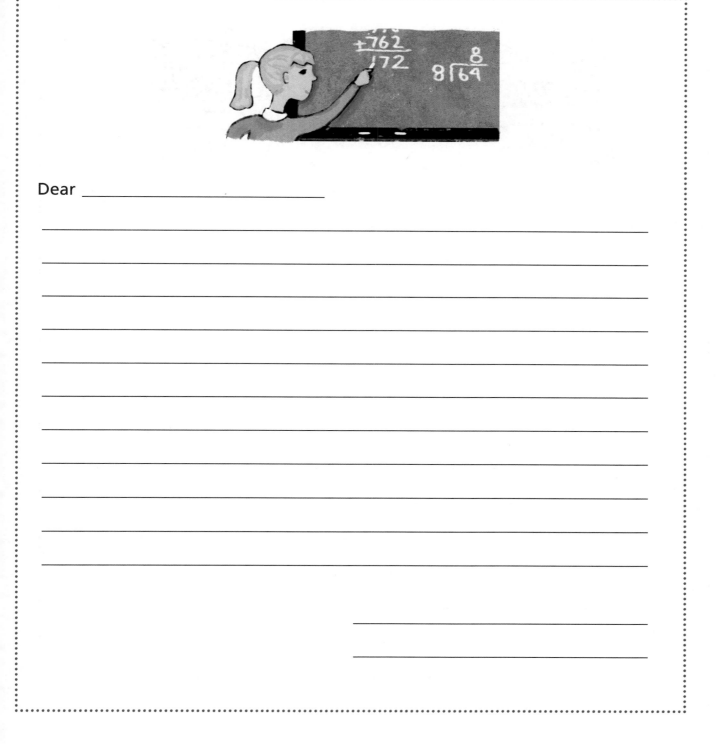

Dear _____

_____

_____

_____

_____

_____

_____

_____

_____

_____

_____

                                 _____

                                 _____

Write a Lifeguard's Report

Imagine that you are a lifeguard. You have rescued a surfer who was dragged out to sea. Write a personal narrative of the rescue. Be sure your narrative has a beginning, a middle, and an end.

_____

_____

_____

_____

_____

_____

_____

_____

_____

_____

_____

_____

_____

_____

Tell a Story about an Event in Your Life

Complete each of these sentences as a writing idea. Then, choose one writing idea and write a personal narrative on it.

The most exciting place I ever visited was

_____

_____

My most embarrassing moment was when

_____

_____

The most unusual person I ever met was

_____

_____

_____

_____

_____

_____

_____

_____

_____

A Practice Autobiographical Sketch

JULY THE FOURTH ON THE LLANO RIVER

We have family reunions every July 4th. I can't remember any of them but one. It was last year when we met at the Llano River. That's when I learned to swim.

We arrived at my aunt's house on Friday night. My cousin J.W. was already there. J.W. is in high school. He is loud and funny and a real pain. Every summer, he finds one of us younger kids and picks on us the whole time we are together. That year, it was my turn.

It started as soon as he saw me. "Hey, kid," he asked, "did you ever learn to swim? Are you going to do that doggy paddle thing again this year?" I hung my head down, embarrassed in front of my other cousins. My embarrassment didn't seem to bother J.W. He kept right on poking fun. "You know, kid, you remind me a lot of Aunt Betty's cocker spaniel when you're in the water. Pant, splash, pant, splash. Don't get me wrong. I love it. It's a scream and probably makes you popular with all of your friends back home. That's how everyone swims there, right?" I slipped away as quietly as I could.

The next morning, all the kids went down to the river right after breakfast. I sat around with the grown-ups. I couldn't bring myself to go down to the river. I kept talking to myself, building up my courage. It took until lunchtime for me to find it.

I grabbed a towel from the bathroom closet, put on my flip-flops, and marched down to the river. I may have looked like a cocker spaniel, but who cared? It was just J.W. talking, and I didn't need his opinion. Most of my cousins were in the water, splashing, tubing, and diving for pennies.

The afternoon sun was warm and made the water feel great. I dragged one of the inner tubes on the bank into the water and plopped inside it. I wasn't afraid to float down the rapids in a tube. It was fun, and I stayed on the surface of the water, even when the rapids were fast.

As I floated near the rapids, I saw my cousin Danny. He's a little guy and always funny to watch. He was too small for the tube and sat low. When the water shot him across the rocks, Danny bumped all the way down the river. He always got out at the end of the rapids rubbing his backside. He didn't seem to mind, though. Danny was always the first one to run back up the riverbank to get ahead of the rapids and start again.

Just below the rapids, the river had carved a deep swimming hole. I pulled my tube out of the water and watched my cousins playing from the bank. I really wanted to be out there with them, but what was the point? There was J.W., splashing, laughing, and dunking the little kids under the water. No way was I going out there.

About the time I was getting ready to leave, Donnie, my brother, swam over to the bank. He sat with me in a shallow place near some large rocks. The water was really warm there. We talked about the river, about swimming, and about J.W. Then Donnie did something surprising. He leaned over and whispered in my ear, "If you want to learn to swim, I'll help you." The idea sounded great to me.

"Can you teach me now?" I asked excitedly. I remember that made Donnie laugh.

"Hold on there, little spaniel, let's get in deeper water first," he said as he smiled.

We walked over to an area that was not too deep. Donnie showed me how to hold my face in the water and turn it to the side to breathe. I wasn't crazy about putting my face in the water at first. I had to practice for a while, but Donnie didn't seem to mind.

Next, he showed me how to move my arms in a big circle. Then we put breathing and circling together. When I could do both things at the same time, I thought I was ready. I didn't know what was coming next.

We moved into deeper water. I could still feel the river bottom squishing between my toes. Donnie told me to float on my back. That was easy. Then he told me to turn over and float on my stomach. That was hard. All of a sudden, water rushed into my nose. I couldn't breathe and I panicked. I started imitating a cocker spaniel again, a frightened one. So Donnie pulled my head up and helped me stand. I couldn't stop coughing and spitting out water. I think I spit out a tadpole, but Donnie told me I was imagining things.

When I looked up along the bank, I saw my mom and dad watching me. At first, my mom looked worried, but then I saw her smile. Her smile made me determined. I told Donnie I was ready to try again. We stayed in the water so long that my fingers shriveled like old raisins. At first, I swam circles around Donnie. Then the circles got bigger and bigger. I knew how to swim!

When I was too tired to move anymore, I swam back to where Donnie sat on the bank. By the time I got there, all of my cousins were there, too. Even J.W. was there. He helped me out of the water, slapped me on the back, and said, "Hey, little spaniel, you're not a puppy anymore." That was J.W.'s idea of a compliment, and I was glad to take it.

Respond to the Practice Paper

Write your answers to the following questions or directions.

1. In an autobiographical sketch, a writer talks about something important that happened to him or her. What important thing happened to this writer?

   _____

   _____

2. How would you describe the setting for this story?

   _____

   _____

3. What is the first clue the writer gives you to tell you what J.W. is like?

   _____

   _____

4. Based on the story, how would you describe the relationship between the writer and Donnie, his brother?

   _____

   _____

5. Write a paragraph to summarize the story. Think about the story's main ideas and what happens first, second, and so on. Also, think about how the story ends.

   _____

   _____

   _____

   _____

   _____

Analyze the Practice Paper

Read "July the Fourth on the Llano River" again. As you read, think about how the writer wrote the story. Answer the following questions or directions.

1. How does the writer add emotion, or strong feeling, to this story?

   _____

   _____

   _____

   _____

2. Read the third paragraph again. Why do you think the writer used dialogue in this paragraph?

   _____

   _____

   _____

   _____

3. How does the writer use humor to tell this story?

   _____

   _____

   _____

   _____

4. What does the writer do to help you "see" J.W. as he sees him?

   _____

   _____

   _____

   _____

Writing Assignment

Write an autobiographical sketch about something important that happened to you. Write about something you remember well. Use this writing plan to help you write a first draft on the next page.

What important thing happened to you?

What happened first? How will you describe it?

What happened second? How will you describe it?

What happened last? How will you describe it?

First Draft

TIPS FOR WRITING AN AUTOBIOGRAPHICAL SKETCH:

- Write about something important that happened to you.
- Write about something you remember well.
- Give details that help explain your experience.
- Describe events in the order that they happened.

Use your writing plan as a guide for writing your first draft of an autobiographical sketch. Include a catchy title.

_____

_____

_____

_____

_____

_____

_____

_____

_____

_____

(Continue on your own paper.)

Revise the Draft

Use the chart below to help you revise your draft. Check YES or NO to answer each question in the chart. If you answer NO, make notes to remind yourself how you can revise, or change, your writing to improve it.

Question	YES ✔	NO ✔	If the answer is NO, what will you do to improve your writing?
Does your autobiographical sketch describe something important that happened to you?			
Does your story have a clear setting?			
Do you include important characters in your story?			
Do you use specific details to help you tell your story?			
Do you describe events in the order they happened?			
Have you corrected mistakes in spelling, grammar, and punctuation?			

Use the notes in your chart and your writing plan to revise your draft.

Writing Report Card

Read your revised draft again or ask someone else to read it. Have the person who reads your paper complete the following Report Card. Revise your paper until you have no less than a Very Good Score for each item.

Title of paper: _____

Purpose of paper: _*This paper is an autobiographical sketch. It describes*_

*something important that happened in my life.*

Person who scores the paper: _____

Score	Writing Goals
	Is this story an example of an autobiographical sketch?
	Is the setting described in detail?
	Does the writer use important characters to help tell the story?
	Does the writer describe specific events?
	Does the writer use important details to help explain events?
	Does the writer describe events in the order they happen?
	Does the writer convince you that this experience was important to him or her?
	Are the story's grammar, spelling, and punctuation correct?

☺ Excellent Score   ☆ Very Good Score   + Good Score

✔ Acceptable Score   − Needs Improvement

UNIT 2: How-to Writing

HOW MUCH DO YOU KNOW?

Use the following sentences to write a how-to paragraph. First, write the topic sentence that gives the purpose of the instructions. Then write the steps in correct time order. Finally, answer the question that follows.

Finally, casually drop the ball of tuna on the floor.

First, make a small ball of tuna around the pill.

You will need the pill, a can of tuna, and a plate.

It's often not easy to give a dog a pill, but with the help of a little tuna fish, it can be done.

The dog will eat the tuna and never realize the pill was inside!

Next, put the tuna ball on a plate.

Sit at the kitchen table and pretend to eat the tuna ball.

_____

_____

_____

_____

_____

_____

What materials were needed in the instructions above?

_____

_____

Analyzing a How-to Paragraph

A HOW-TO PARAGRAPH

- tells how to do something
- has a topic sentence and detail sentences
- tells what materials to use and what steps to follow

Use the following sentences to write a how-to paragraph. First, write the topic sentence that gives the purpose of the instructions. Next, write the sentence that lists the needed materials. Then write the steps in correct time order. Put in any special information where it is needed.

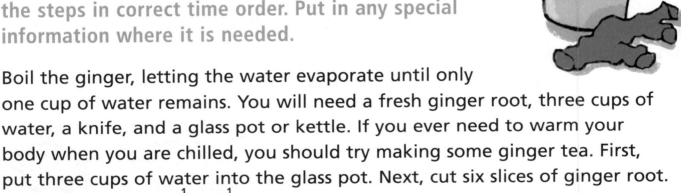

Boil the ginger, letting the water evaporate until only one cup of water remains. You will need a fresh ginger root, three cups of water, a knife, and a glass pot or kettle. If you ever need to warm your body when you are chilled, you should try making some ginger tea. First, put three cups of water into the glass pot. Next, cut six slices of ginger root. The slices should be $\frac{1}{8}$- to $\frac{1}{4}$- inch thick. Strain the ginger tea into a cup. Drink it hot. Add the ginger to the water in the pot.

_____

_____

_____

_____

_____

_____

Visualizing Steps in a Process

Read the following instructions. Answer the questions that follow.

Fooling Your Friends with Dishwater Punch

An April Fool's Day party can be fun. You can fool and surprise your friends by serving them this delicious punch. It looks like dishwater. Do not let your friends see you make the punch. You will need the following items:

- a bowl that holds at least three quarts
- a package of green drink mix
- one quart of orange juice
- one quart of lemon soda
- one pint of pineapple sherbet
- a large spoon

First, pour the orange juice into the bowl. Next, add the package of green drink mix. Stir it in. The juice should look grayish, like dishwater. Add the sherbet in small scoops. Stir the mixture briskly with a spoon until some of the sherbet is melted. Then, add the lemon soda. The punch should look like soapy dishwater.

Offer the punch to your friends and tell them it is dishwater. If none of them will try it, drink a glass yourself. When someone finally tries it, shout "April Fool!"

What steps might the writer of these directions have gone through before writing? Complete the chart below with notes the writer might have made while visualizing the steps. Include the steps in the right order, mentioning all the materials needed.

MATERIALS	STEPS
orange juice, bowl	1.
green drink mix, spoon	2.
pineapple sherbet	3.
spoon	4.
lemon soda	5.

Adjusting for Audience and Purpose

> Good writers adjust their writing for their audience and purpose.

Read the pair of how-to paragraphs below. Decide whether each paragraph has been written for a second-grader or for a sixth-grader. Circle your answer. Then write a sentence on the lines that gives at least two reasons for your answers.

A. Send secret messages to your friends! You will need a white crayon, white paper, and watery paint. First, write the message with the white crayon. Next, give the message to your friend. Say that you will do a little "magic." Paint over the message, and it will appear.

for a second-grader   for a sixth-grader

B. Write a secret message! You will need a white crayon, white paper, and watery paint. First, write the message on the white paper. Use the white crayon. Next, give the message to your friend. Say that you will do a little "magic." Paint over the message, and it will appear! The paint will not stick to the wax in the crayon. That is why you can see the message when you paint over it.

for a second-grader   for a sixth-grader

_____

_____

Avoiding Wordy Language

> Good writers revise their compositions to avoid wordy language.

Rewrite each sentence of this recipe to make it more concise.

1. If you are very thirsty on a hot day, you can make a refreshing yogurt shake to drink.

   _____

   _____

2. First, you get an eight-ounce carton of plain yogurt and measure two tablespoons of plain yogurt into a blender.

   _____

   _____

3. Next, you can add two tablespoons of apple juice, orange juice, pineapple juice, or your favorite fruit juice.

   _____

4. Get a jar of honey and take one-half teaspoon of the honey and add it.

   _____

5. Take a banana and cut off one-third of it and add it.

   _____

6. Find some nutmeg and add a pinch of it to the other ingredients.

   _____

7. Take two ice cubes and crush them and then add them to the mixture.

   _____

8. Turn on the blender and blend the ingredients until they are frothy.

   _____

Proofreading a How-to Paragraph

Proofread the beginning of the how-to paragraph below, paying special attention to commas. Use the Proofreading Marks to correct at least eight errors.

PROOFREADING MARKS	
⬭	spell correctly
⊙	add period
?	add question mark
＝	capitalize
ℒ	take out
∧	add
/	make lowercase
∿	switch
⋏	add comma
ⱽ ⱽ	add quotation marks
¶	indent paragraph

With the help of a little tuna fish and some acting skill, you can easily get your dog Titan to take his pill. As you know, Titan often begs for tuna but you never give him any. If you suddenly offer Titan some tuna with the pill inside it, he will become suspicious and refuse eat it. Try this method instead.

Make a small ball of tuna around Titan's pill. Put the tuna ball on a plate. Then find sumthing you like to eat and put that on the plate too. Take your plate and sit down at the kitchen table.

Titan will probably be watching you carefully but you should ignore him. He's a very smart dog and it will not be easy to fool him. your chances of success are best if you if just pretend you don't see him.

Titan will soon sit beside you, and start to beg. Eat your own food and continue to ignore Titan. Then, very casually, allow the ball of tuna to fall to the floor. You should make a quick grab for the tuna but you must be sure that Titan gets to it first. Titan will eagerly gulp the tuna–and the pill.

List Steps in a Process

With a friend, choose a recipe for a favorite snack. Visualize the steps for preparing the snack and list them. One person might want to illustrate each step. Share your recipes.

Materials	Steps	Illustrations
	1.	
	2.	
	3.	
	4.	
	5.	
	6.	

Write a Magazine Article

Pretend you are a writer for a gardening magazine. Work with a friend or two to plan and write a how-to paragraph on gardening. Revise and proofread your work.

_____

_____

_____

_____

_____

_____

_____

_____

_____

_____

_____

_____

_____

Making a Gift

Have you ever thought about making a gift for someone for a special holiday or birthday? Add two gift ideas to the list below. Then, choose one gift from the list and write a how-to paragraph on making one of these gifts.

picture frame

placemats

necklace

jewelry box

plant hanger

pencil holder

_____

_____

HOW TO MAKE _____

_____

_____

_____

_____

_____

_____

_____

Explain What You Are Doing

Check whether you have ever been in one or more of the situations described below. Add one other situation like these. Then, choose one and write a how-to paragraph explaining your answer to a family member, friend, or classmate.

	YES	NO
1. You are working on something in the garage, and a younger brother or sister asks, "What are you doing?"	❏	❏
2. You are playing a computer game, and a friend asks, "How do you play that game?"	❏	❏
3. You are working on a word problem for math, and a classmate asks, "How do you do those problems?"	❏	❏

4. _____

_____

_____

_____

_____

A Practice How-to Paper

BUILD A NEWTON'S CRADLE

Sir Isaac Newton was an English mathematician and scientist who lived in the 1600s and 1700s. He published his three laws of motion, which describe how forces affect the motion of an object, in 1687. You can demonstrate one of Newton's laws of motion with an apparatus called a Newton's cradle. The cradle will show that things at rest tend to stay at rest until acted on by an outside force. A Newton's cradle also demonstrates what scientists call the "Principle of Conservation of Energy." That means that energy is never created or destroyed. Energy can change from one form to another, but the total amount of energy stays the same.

It is easier to understand these scientific principles if you use your own Newton's cradle. You need only a few materials to build one. They are:

- 1 ruler marked in inches
- 1 pencil or dowel rod
- 5 eight-inch pieces of fishing line
- 5 paper clips
- scissors
- 5 wooden beads

Once you have your materials, you are ready to begin building. Here's how:

First, use your ruler to make five marks on the pencil or dowel rod. The marks should be exactly one inch apart. Be sure the third mark is in the center of the pencil or dowel rod.

Second, use the scissors to score, or cut, a ring around each mark on the pencil or dowel rod. The ring should go all the way around the pencil or rod. Handle the scissors carefully so that you don't cut your skin.

Next, tie a paper clip to one end of each piece of fishing line. Place each paper clip in exactly the same place on each line.

Then, thread one piece of fishing line through the hole in each bead. Each bead will rest on a paper clip.

Now, tie each piece of fishing line around the scored rings on the pencil or dowel rod. The beads must line up exactly and hang evenly.

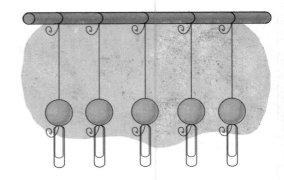

Use one hand to hold the pencil or rod horizontally. Pull the first bead on one end back. Then release it gently. Observe what happens. The bead you release exerts a force on the other beads.

Now consider the Principle of Conservation of Energy to examine what happens to the beads on your Newton's cradle. Before you released the bead, the bead had one kind of energy, called potential energy. When you let the bead fall, the potential energy changed into another kind of energy, called kinetic energy. Kinetic energy is the energy of motion.

Wait. There are still more changes in energy. When the first bead hit the second bead, what did you hear? You heard a click. A click is sound energy. Now think about what happens when two things rub together. For example, if you rub your hands together, can you feel your hands getting warmer? The kinetic energy in your hands changes to heat energy. The same thing happens with the beads on your Newton's cradle. As the first bead hits the second bead, energy moves through the beads to the bead at the other end. The bead lifts, swings back, and hits the line of beads. Each time a bead hits another bead, kinetic energy changes to sound and heat energy. Eventually, the kinetic energy changes completely to sound and heat, and the beads stop moving. But don't expect this to happen quickly. The changes of energy are small, so it takes some time for the beads to stop moving.

Now you know how to build a Newton's cradle. You also know how to use the cradle to demonstrate some interesting scientific principles. Try making other Newton's cradles. Use different sizes of dowel rods and string. Change the number of beads, or use metal beads. You might even want to demonstrate your super science skills for your class.

Respond to the Practice Paper

Write your answers to the following questions or directions.

1. What materials do you need to make a Newton's cradle?

   _____

   _____

2. Why is it important that the beads line up exactly and evenly?

   _____

   _____

3. Why do you need fishing line?

   _____

   _____

4. In the last paragraph, the writer suggests that you build different kinds of Newton's cradles. Write a paragraph to describe the materials you would use if you could build any kind of Newton's cradle you wanted. Draw a picture to go with your paragraph.

   _____

   _____

   _____

Analyze the Practice Paper

Read "Build a Newton's Cradle" again. As you read, think about why the writer wrote this paper. What did the writer do to help explain how to build a cradle? Write your answers to the following questions or directions.

1. Name at least two things that make this paper a good example of a how-to paper.

   _____

   _____

2. Read the first paragraph again. Why do you think the writer included this paragraph in a how-to paper?

   _____

   _____

3. Why does the writer list the materials you need to make a cradle before telling you how to do it?

   _____

   _____

4. Why does the writer use words like *first*, *next*, and *then*?

   _____

   _____

5. Read the next-to-the-last paragraph on page 552 again. Draw pictures to go with the words the writer uses to explain the Principle of Conservation of Energy.

Writing Assignment

Think about something you want to tell others how to do. Use this writing plan to help you write a first draft on the next page.

What will you tell others how to do?

▼

List the materials someone will need.

▼

Write the steps someone should follow in order. Number the steps.

▼

Write some sequence words that help the reader know what to do.

First Draft

Use your writing plan as a guide as you write your first draft of a how-to paper. Include a catchy title.

_____

(Continue on your own paper.)

Revise the Draft

Use the chart below to help you revise your draft. Check YES or NO to answer each question in the chart. If you answer NO, make notes to remind yourself how you can revise, or change, your writing to improve it.

Question	YES ✔	NO ✔	If the answer is NO, what will you do to improve your writing?
Does your paper teach someone how to do something?			
Do you use the first paragraph to introduce the project or task?			
Do you include all of the materials someone needs?			
Do you explain all of the steps someone must follow?			
Are the steps in order?			
Do you explain each step clearly so that it is easy to follow?			
Do you use sequence words to help guide your reader?			
Have you corrected mistakes in spelling, grammar, and punctuation?			

Use the notes in your chart and your writing plan to revise your draft.

Writing Report Card

Read your revised draft again or ask someone else to read it. Have the person who reads your paper complete the following Report Card. Revise your paper until you have no less than a Very Good Score for each item.

Title of paper: _____

Purpose of paper: _*This paper explains how to do something.*_____

Person who scores the paper: _____

Score	Writing Goals
	Does the writer introduce the topic in the first paragraph?
	Does the paper teach someone how to do something?
	Does the paper include the materials that someone needs?
	Does the paper explain each step that someone will follow?
	Are the steps in order?
	Is each step written clearly to make it easy to follow?
	Are there sequence words to help the reader understand?
	Are the paper's grammar, spelling, and punctuation correct?

☺ Excellent Score ☆ Very Good Score + Good Score
✔ Acceptable Score − Needs Improvement

UNIT 3: Descriptive Writing

HOW MUCH DO YOU KNOW?

Read the paragraph. Underline the topic sentence. Then fill in the chart below. List the details that the writer used to appeal to each sense. Write *none* if there are none.

Each summer Ron and Diane go to their favorite vacation spot—their great-aunt's beach house. The three-bedroom house has a view of the ocean in the front and a mountain range in the back.

As soon as they arrived this year, everyone headed out for a walk on the beach. The cuckoo clock sounded just before they left. They had two hours to explore before dinner. Piles of slippery seaweed had washed up on the sand. Ron noticed a jellyfish on one of the piles. Unfortunately, it smelled liked dead fish. They heard the bark of a sea lion in the distance. Looking out across the blue-green water, Diane spotted the sea lion on a distant rock.

As the shadows of the palm trees lengthened, the beachfront grew quiet. Soon, their walk would draw to a close. Diane picked up a large, smooth shell. They turned toward the house singing "The Twelve Days of Christmas" even though it was July.

sight	
hearing	
smell	
taste	
touch	

Analyzing a Descriptive Paragraph

> **A DESCRIPTIVE PARAGRAPH**
> - creates a picture with words
> - presents sensory details in a clear order
> - has a topic sentence and detail sentences

Read the paragraph. Underline the topic sentence. Then complete the items below.

The room had clearly been ransacked. The drawers of the dresser next to the window were open and empty. A trail of assorted clothing led to the closet. The closet stood empty, its contents strewn across the bed and the floor. Glass from a broken perfume bottle crunched loudly underfoot, the fragrance of its contents mixing with the smell of garlic. The only item left undisturbed was a portrait on the wall over the bed. Its subject, a solemn young woman, stared thoughtfully into the room, like a silent witness to the recent crime.

1. List at least five words or phrases the writer used to appeal to your senses. After each word or phrase, tell which sense it is: *sight, hearing, smell, taste,* or *touch.*

   _____

   _____

2. Is this paragraph written in space order or in time order? What words did the writer use that indicate this type of order?

   _____

   _____

Observing Details

> **TO WRITE A DESCRIPTIVE PARAGRAPH, GOOD WRITERS**
> - include specific details
> - arrange details in the way that makes the most sense for their purpose
> - use words that appeal to the reader's senses

Read the following paragraphs. Then fill in the chart below. List the details that the writer used to appeal to each sense.

After swimming for about a hundred yards, Marlene stopped and looked back at the island. From the top of the volcano, lush green vegetation grew down to meet the soft white sands of the beach. The white sands disappeared into the shimmering blue of the ocean.

Marlene rested for a moment. She enjoyed the contrast of the cool water on her body and the hot sun on her face. It was quiet except for the sound of the surf thundering on the shore.

Marlene tasted the salty water on her lips and thought about the luau that would begin very soon. The smoky smell of the roasting pig drifted out and mixed with the salty smells of the ocean. Marlene heard her stomach growl and began to swim to shore.

sight	
hearing	
smell	
taste	
touch	

Using Precise Words

> Good writers use precise words to create clear pictures for the reader.

Read each pair of sentences. Underline the sentence that is imprecise, or general. Then rewrite the sentence. Use precise words to create a clearer picture.

1. Bob heard a noise at the door.
   He could barely hear it over the wail of the siren outside.

   _____

2. Bob stood up quickly.
   He moved to the front door.

   _____

3. A person was there.
   A girl was beside him.

   _____

4. Sorrow was written all over the boy's face.
   The girl seemed unhappy.

   _____

5. "Have you seen any strange cats around?" asked the boy.
   "We have lost our tabby."

   _____

6. "Does your cat have spots?" asked Bob.
   "Yes, he also has black patches," answered the girl.

   _____

7. "I found him on the chair in my backyard," said Bob.
   "He is sleeping."

   _____

Expanding Sentences

Good writers add details as they revise, so their descriptions paint complete word pictures.

Expand each sentence with descriptive details. Follow the instructions in parentheses ( ) to rewrite each sentence.

1. A dog huddled in the shelter of the tunnel. (Add details about the subject.)

   _____

   _____

2. It shivered in the wind. (Add descriptive details about an item in the complete predicate.)

   _____

   _____

3. Finally, it left the shelter of the tunnel. (Add another predicate.)

   _____

   _____

4. Its shadow trailed behind it. (Add descriptive details about the subject.)

   _____

5. The dog trotted down the street. (Add another subject.)

   _____

6. The dog broke through the sheet of ice on the puddle. (Add descriptive details about an item in the complete predicate, and add a second predicate.)

   _____

   _____

Proofreading a Descriptive Paragraph

PROOFREADING MARKS

⬭	spell correctly
⊙	add period
?	add question mark
≡	capitalize
ℛ	take out
∧	add
/	make lowercase
∿	switch
⋏	add comma
⋎ ⋎	add quotation marks
¶	indent paragraph

Proofread the description, paying special attention to the capitalization and the end punctuation of sentences. Use the Proofreading Marks to correct at least eight errors.

A set of smooth stone steps led up to a flat clearing in the forest Here the sun's rays filtered down through the branches of the towering pines, and the ground was covered with fragrant green pine needles. the carpet of needles felt thick and soft under Nina's feet.

a gentle breeze rustled the branches Nina inhaled the scent of the

pines as it drifted on the breeze. mingled with the scent of pine was the smell of the pale green mosses growing on the north sides of the trees.

What was that in the middle of the clearing Nina saw a large stump, just under three feat tall and a full three feet in diameter. four smaller stumps were arranged around it Paul was already seated on one of the smaller stumps, and the large stump was clearly just the right hieght for a table.

On the large stump lay a basket of juicy blackberries, a canteen, and two shiny metal cups Paul looked up at Nina and asked, "Are you ready for a treat?"

Observe and Write Details

Work with a friend. In a book or a magazine, find a picture of a place you both would like to visit. Study the picture for a few minutes. Write the name of the place and some interesting details about it. Then write a descriptive paragraph about the place.

WE WOULD LIKE TO VISIT

_____

_____

_____

_____

Write a Visitor's Guide

Working with a friend or two, list places that visitors might like to visit in your community. Then, choose one place from the list and write a descriptive paragraph about that place.

Write an Action Paragraph

Find an action photograph in the sports section of a newspaper or magazine. Cut out the photograph and glue it to this page. Write a descriptive paragraph about the photograph. Be sure to use strong action verbs. Revise and proofread your work.

Rediscover Familiar Buildings

Have you ever looked closely at a familiar building? Use the following checklist to rediscover buildings in your area. You may add other buildings to the checklist. Choose one building from the list and write a descriptive paragraph about the building.

building	pillars	arches	tower	window	balcony	courtyard	stairway
school							
hotel							
pharmacy							
barn							

A Practice Descriptive Story

WEEKEND FRIENDS

Cole's dad was unusually late picking him up on Friday night. Cole didn't say anything to his mother, but he was a little worried. His dad was never late. Cole sat quietly, tracing the stitching in his overnight bag. Finally, the phone rang. Cole's mom rushed to the kitchen to answer it. "He's on his way," she announced with relief. "He got tied up at the office."

Soon Cole and his dad were in the car driving to his dad's apartment. "Sorry about that, Cole," his dad said. "Something came up at the office. I know it's too late to do much tonight. But," he added, "I have a special day planned tomorrow. I hope you don't mind."

"It's okay, Dad," Cole said quickly. Cole knew that their weekends together were as important to his dad as they were to him.

The next morning, golden rays spilled through Cole's bedroom window. Saturday had come. By the time his dad got up, Cole was already dressed and eating breakfast. "Wow," his dad said. "You're in a hurry this morning." His dad smiled. "Let me finish this cup of coffee, and we'll be on our way, okay?" Cole nodded.

The highway was a gray stripe through green countryside. On either side, wildflowers bounced in the wind. Their red and yellow heads moved up and down like fishing bobs on a lake. Cole's dad slowed the car and turned right onto a farm road. Then he turned again, this time onto a dirt road that sliced the pasture.

Cole's dad stopped the car. "Well, what do you think?" Cole looked puzzled. "What do you mean?" he asked.

His dad laughed softly. "This is our farm. This is why I was late last night. I had to sign the papers." Cole looked amazed. His eyes widened and his mouth fell open, but he couldn't speak a word.

Cole and his dad walked through the pasture to a row of graceful trees. The deep green live oaks and the giant cottonwoods bowed over a narrow creek. The creek babbled like a child. The sun's rays sparkled on the water. Cole and his dad sat on the bank. "What do you think, Cole?"

Cole turned slowly, forcing his eyes away from the creek. "I love it," he almost whispered.

His dad took him toward the old farmhouse beyond the creek. "I thought we could come here on the weekends, Cole. We could fix up the house together. I could use the help. Wait until you see it. It's been empty for more than forty years."

"Who lived here then, Dad?" Cole asked.

"I don't know," said his dad. "The agent said the last owner never used the house. He just let it fall down. He's the person who sold the farm."

They reached the farmhouse and, for the second time in one day, Cole didn't know what to say. This was the tallest, oldest, most run-down house he'd ever seen. He loved it. "Wow!" Cole yelled. "Cool house! This is great!" Cole started running.

His dad yelled, "Cole, slow down. You can't trust those steps. Wait." But Cole couldn't hear the last warning. It came just as his leg went through a rotten step. The bottom half of his body disappeared, swallowed by the steps. Cole's dad raced over. "Are you okay, Cole? Can you move?" he asked, with panic in his voice.

Cole groaned a little as his dad pulled him from the step. "I'm fine, really. I don't think anything's broken." While his dad checked his legs, Cole lay on the porch. His head turned toward the jagged hole. "Dad, I think there's something in there. Look." His dad ignored him and continued to ask what hurt.

"Dad, what is it?" Cole asked. He'd forgotten about his legs.

Cole's dad looked inside the hole. "I don't know, Cole, but you stay here. I'll go in this time." He squeezed through the hole, landing with a thud. When he came back up, he had a box caked in decades of dirt. He and Cole used a pocketknife to remove the dirt and pick the small, rusting lock that kept the box sealed.

"Wow," they said at the same time. Inside were a small leather box and a dirty envelope. The box contained a World War II Medal of Honor. Even now, the eagle shined and the ribbon looked fresh. Inside the envelope was a certificate and a single photograph. "Horace Mickel," Cole's dad said, reading the name on the certificate. "I'd say this medal and this house must have belonged to him."

"Who was Horace Mickel, Dad? Do you think he left anything else under those steps?" Cole asked. "Or in the house?" he added eagerly.

"I don't know," his dad chuckled. "Let's forget the steps for now. If you think you can get yourself up, we'll start looking for the answers to your questions inside." Cole's dad unlocked the front door and held Cole's elbow as Cole hobbled inside. The wind came with them, disturbing dust that had sat comfortably for forty years. Spider webs as fine as lace capped their heads.

"This is great, Dad. It looks like Mr. Mickel left everything behind. There are bound to be clues everywhere."

"I think you're right, Cole. But I have an idea. Let's not try to find all of our answers today. Let's make this last awhile. Let's make this our weekend project, and we'll come to know Mr. Mickel a little at a time, just like friends normally do." His dad hugged him hard.

"Good idea, Dad. I think I'll put this photograph above the fireplace. Then we'll know where to find Mr. Mickel when we come back."

Respond to the Practice Paper

Write your answers to the following questions or directions.

1. What makes this story an example of descriptive writing?

    _____

    _____

2. How does the writer let you know that Cole and his mom are nervous?

    _____

    _____

3. How does the writer let you know that Cole loves his dad, the farm, and the farmhouse?

    _____

    _____

4. Use a separate piece of paper to draw a picture of your favorite description in this story. Label your picture.

5. Write a paragraph to summarize the story. Use these questions to help you write your summary:
    • What are the main ideas of the story?
    • What happens first? Second? Third?
    • How does the story end?

    _____

    _____

    _____

    _____

    _____

Analyze the Practice Paper

Read "Weekend Friends" again. As you read, think about how the writer achieved his or her purpose for writing. Write your answers to the following questions or directions.

1. Read the fifth and eighth paragraphs again. What similes does the writer use? (A simile uses the word *like* or *as* to compare two things.)

    _____

    _____

2. What metaphor does the writer use in the fifth paragraph? (A metaphor does not use the word *like* or *as* to compare two things.)

    _____

    _____

3. List some interesting verbs the writer uses to describe the action in paragraphs 5, 8, 14, and 15.

    _____

    _____

4. Use a separate piece of paper to draw a picture of the description in paragraph 20.

5. Write a paragraph to describe what the farmhouse will look like when Cole and his dad finish fixing it up.

    _____

    _____

    _____

    _____

    _____

    _____

Writing Assignment

To describe something, a writer tells what he or she sees, hears, feels, tastes, and smells. The writer uses interesting words. The writer also compares things to other things, like a creek to a babbling child. Describe something that you and a relative or friend did together. Use this writing plan to help you write a first draft on the next page.

What experience would you like to describe? Write it in the circle. Then write words, similes, or metaphors that describe the experience on the lines.

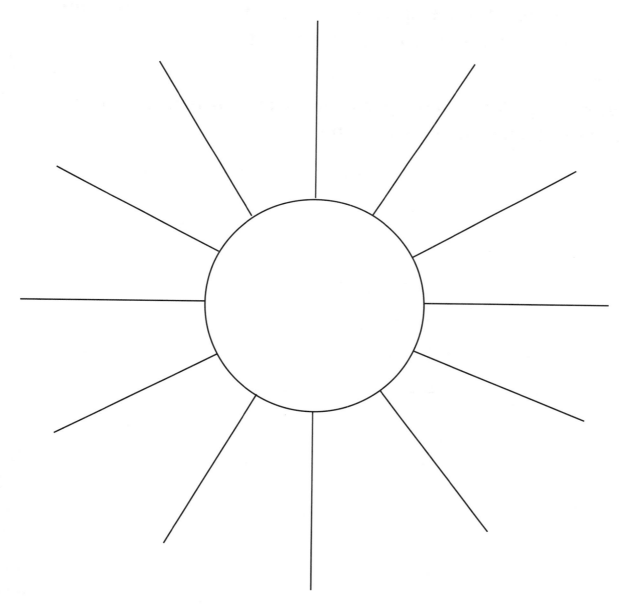

First Draft

TIPS FOR WRITING A DESCRIPTIVE STORY:

- **Use your voice when you write. That means you should use your special way of expressing yourself.**
- **Help readers see, smell, taste, feel, and hear what you are writing about.**
- **Use interesting words to help you describe.**
- **Use similes and metaphors to help your readers imagine the experience you are writing about.**

Use your writing plan as a guide as you write your first draft of a descriptive story. Include a catchy title.

____

____

____

____

____

____

____

____

____

____

____

____

(Continue on your own paper.)

Revise the Draft

Use the chart below to help you revise your draft. Check YES or NO to answer each question in the chart. If you answer NO, make notes to remind yourself how you can revise, or change, your writing to improve it.

Question	YES ✔	NO ✔	If the answer is NO, what will you do to improve your writing?
Do you describe something that happened to you and a relative or friend?			
Do you describe what you see, hear, smell, taste, and feel?			
Do you use action words to describe what happens?			
Do you use descriptive similes and metaphors?			
Do you describe events in the order they happen?			
Have you corrected mistakes in spelling, grammar, and punctuation?			

Use the notes in your chart and your writing plan to revise your draft.

Writing Report Card

Read your revised draft again or ask someone else to read it. Have the person who reads your paper complete the following Report Card. Revise your paper until you have no less than a Very Good Score for each item.

Title of paper: _____

Purpose of paper: ___*This paper is a descriptive story. It describes*___

___*something a friend or relative and I did together.*___

Person who scores the paper: _____

Score	Writing Goals
	Does this story tell about something that happened to the writer and a friend or relative?
	Are the events that happen in the story in order?
	Does the writer describe what he or she sees, hears, tastes, smells, and feels?
	Does the writer use interesting action words?
	Does the story include descriptive similes and metaphors?
	Are the story's grammar, spelling, and punctuation correct?

☺ Excellent Score   ☆ Very Good Score   + Good Score
✔ Acceptable Score   − Needs Improvement

UNIT 4: Comparative Writing

HOW MUCH DO YOU KNOW?

A. Read each paragraph. Label it *comparison* or *contrast*.

My friends Lena and Taylor are alike in many ways. Both are intelligent, loyal, and helpful. Either can carry on a great conversation. Each has an excellent sense of humor, and they enjoy many of the same activities.

1. _____

My two friends Lena and Taylor are different in many ways. Lena complains if she does not like something, and she argues if she disagrees with me. Taylor rarely complains or argues, so we almost never fight. But, Lena is a more honest friend. She says exactly what she thinks or feels. In contrast, Taylor never says anything negative to me about things I have said or done. Instead, she may say something to someone else, and her comments often get back to me.

2. _____

B. Use the paragraphs to answer the questions below.

3. In what one way are the two friends alike?

_____

_____

4. In what one way are the two friends different?

_____

_____

Analyzing Paragraphs of Comparison and Contrast

> ## A PARAGRAPH OF COMPARISON OR CONTRAST
> - tells about the similarities or the differences of two or more items
> - answers the same questions about each item

Read each paragraph. Label it *comparison* or *contrast*. Circle the names of the two items being compared. Underline the key words that signal similarity or difference.

1. The new house was similar to the old house in some ways. Like the old house, it had three bedrooms. Both houses had two bathrooms. They both had a fireplace in the living room. The old house had a separate dining room, and so did the new house.

   _____

2. The new house looked and felt different from the old house, and Janet did not know if she liked it as much. The old house was nearly one hundred years old. The new house had just been built. Unlike the old two-story house, the new house was all on one level. The hardwood floors at the old house could be seen beneath the old-fashioned rugs, while wall-to-wall carpet covered the floors of the new house.

   _____

Comparing and Contrasting

A. Imagine that you work for a toy company. You are deciding which of two stuffed rabbits your company should sell. One toy rabbit is tall and thin with long ears that stand up straight. Not fuzzy, this rabbit is wearing a sun hat and appears to be clever and shrewd. The other rabbit is cute and cuddly, with floppy ears. Wearing a fancy, flowered hat, this smiling rabbit is plump. Fill in the chart to describe the rabbits' similarities and differences.

Category	Rabbit A	Both	Rabbit B
1. type of animal			
2. shape			
3. clothes			
4. expression			
5. ears			

B. Use your chart to answer the questions below.

6. In what two ways are the stuffed animals alike?

_____

_____

_____

7. In what two ways are the stuffed animals different?

_____

_____

_____

Using Enough Details

Read each paragraph. If the paragraph needs more details, choose details from the box below and write them on the lines.

1. The lives of the Pueblo Indians and the Navajo Indians were similar in some ways. They both lived in the Southwest. They both lived in permanent homes.

   _____

   _____

2. Though the Pueblo Indians and the Navajo Indians both lived in the Southwest, their lives were different in some ways. The Pueblo Indians lived in villages called pueblos, with several families in one dwelling. The Navajo Indians lived in scattered hogans.

   _____

   _____

   _____

Pueblos and Navajos also both wove cloth.

The Navajos wove wool, while the Pueblos wove cotton and feathers together.

The Pueblos depended entirely on the crops and the livestock they raised. The Navajos hunted and gathered as well as raised food and livestock.

Both groups of Indians farmed and raised animals.

Using Effective Transitions

Good writers arrange their ideas carefully and use transition words to show how sentences are related.

Write paragraphs by arranging the sentences of each group in a smooth, logical order. Add any transition words that are needed.

1. Water-skiing is a sport for warm weather.
   The similarity ends there.
   Both water-skiing and snow skiing require skis.
   Snow skiing is a cold-weather sport.
   People snow ski on a mountain slope.
   Water-skiing is done on a large body of water.

   _____

   _____

   _____

   _____

   _____

2. In football, the whole team is in motion on every play.
   When a baseball team is at bat, most of the players are sitting and waiting.
   I like playing football better than playing baseball.
   I like to be moving throughout a game.

   _____

   _____

   _____

   _____

Proofreading Paragraphs of Comparison and Contrast

PROOFREADING MARKS

⬭	spell correctly
⊙	add period
?	add question mark
≡	capitalize
℘	take out
∧	add
/	make lowercase
∿	switch
⋏	add comma
⌄ ⌄	add quotation marks
¶	indent paragraph

Proofread the paragraphs of comparison and contrast, paying special attention to subject-verb agreement. Use the Proofreading Marks to correct at least seven errors.

People sometimes asks me who my best friend is. Truthfully, I do not know. I have two close friends, and I like them both very much.

My friends judy and Margie is alike in many ways. Both are intelligent, loyal, and helpful Either can carry on a great conversation. Each has an excellent sense of humor, and they enjoy many of the same activities.

However, my two friends are different in many ways. I has more arguments with Judy. She complains if she does not like something, and she argue if she disagrees with me. Margie rarely complains or argues, so we almost never fights.

On the other hand, Judy is a more honest friend. She always says exactly what she thinks or feels. In contrast, Margie never say anything negative to me about things i have said or done. Instead, she may say something to someone else, and her comments often gets back to me. If Judy has a complaint, she discusses it with the person who has caused the problem.

Write a Paragraph from Advertisements

Find advertisements for two competing products. Cut out the ads you find. Make a chart that compares the two products. Then, using the information from the chart, write a paragraph of comparison and contrast.

Four Out of Five Dogs Choose Beddie-By!

The Softest!
Odorless!
Why pay more?
Pet calming!

Product 1	Both	Product 2

_____

_____

_____

_____

_____

_____

_____

Create a Toy

With a friend, decide on a kind of toy you might design. On separate pieces of paper, each of you draw a picture of your version of the toy. Do not let the other person see it. When both of you are finished, write a paragraph to compare and contrast your drawings. Write at least three similarities and three differences.

_____

_____

_____

_____

_____

_____

_____

_____

_____

_____

_____

Compare Sports

Write a paragraph comparing or contrasting two sports. When you revise your paragraph, make sure your transitions are smooth.

_____

_____

_____

_____

_____

_____

_____

_____

_____

_____

_____

_____

_____

_____

_____

_____

_____

A Practice Compare-and-Contrast Paper

IN-LINE SKATES AND ICE SKATES

Two fast-moving sports popular with people of all ages are two kinds of skating. They are in-line skating and ice-skating. Whether skaters are on the sidewalk or on the ice, most of them can enjoy hours of fun. That is, of course, if they have the right equipment.

Skaters in both sports use equipment that is alike and different. Both kinds of skates are made for speed. Today's skates let a skater skate well all the time. Skaters can also use their skates in more than one sport. However, certain kinds of skates are made for different uses. They work best when a skater uses the right skate for the right sport. That means, for example, that a hockey player uses skates made for hockey. She can also use them to figure skate. However, in that case, she will probably skate better if she uses skates made for figure skating.

All in-line skates are made for land. So, they all have the same basic features. An in-line skate has a boot that is usually made from plastic. The boot is firm. It holds the skater's ankle comfortably. The boot's lining comes out so it can be washed. On the outside of the boot, there are laces, buckles, or both to fasten the boot.

An ice skate also has a boot, but this boot is made only for ice. The boot is usually made from leather. It provides support for the ankle. It is also designed to be comfortable and warm. The boot's lining is made from a material that helps air move. However, the longer the skater wears these boots, the more likely the skater's feet will perspire. Over time, this can cause the boots to deteriorate, or break down. That makes it important to wipe out the boots after each use.

Both kinds of skates have one or more objects that help the skater move. In-line skates use wheels, usually four. There are three things about the wheels that require the skater's attention. They are size, hardness, and

bearings. To check the size of the wheel, the skater measures the wheel's diameter in millimeters (mm). The size of the wheel is important, because the larger it is, the faster it rolls. Most ordinary in-line skates range from 72 mm to 76 mm. The size is marked on the side of the wheel.

The second important feature of the wheel is its hardness. Wheels are made from a kind of plastic. The hardness of the plastic varies and is measured in durometers. A zero durometer represents the softest plastic. One hundred durometers represent the hardest plastic. The harder the plastic, the faster the skater can go.

The last important feature of a wheel is its bearings. Ball bearings are inside the hubs of the wheels. These ball bearings let the wheels roll. So, the better the ball bearings, the faster the wheels roll.

Instead of wheels, ice skates use blades. Each blade is attached to the sole of the boot with a screw mount. This mount holds the blade tightly in place.

Blades are made of metal, usually stainless steel. Then they are coated with another metal, such as chrome, nickel, or aluminum. The blade is solid and has a toe pick at the front end. The toe pick lets the skater grip the ice. It also helps the skater take off. There is a ridge that runs along the bottom of the blade. This ridge is called the "hollow." The hollow cuts the ice as the skater glides over it.

Being able to stop is important to every skater. Only in-line skates have brakes. A brake pad is attached to the back of each boot. The skater stops by lifting his or her toes and pressing the brake pad to the ground.

For ice skaters, stopping is another matter. There are no brakes on ice skates. Instead, the skater uses his or her legs and feet to stop. The skater presses on the sides of his or her skates to stop.

In-line skating and ice-skating are alike in some ways and different in others. Their differences make both sports interesting to many skaters. The ways they are alike let skaters skate in both sports. For skaters with the right skates, skating is several sports in one.

Respond to the Practice Paper

Summarize the story by making a chart. Use the chart below to list ways in-line skates and ice skates are alike and different.

A COMPARE-AND-CONTRAST CHART FOR IN-LINE SKATES AND ICE SKATES

How In-Line Skates and Ice Skates Are Alike	How In-Line Skates and Ice Skates Are Different

Analyze the Practice Paper

Read "In-line Skates and Ice Skates" again. As you read, think about how the writer achieved his or her purpose for writing. Write your answers to the following questions or directions.

1. When does the writer tell you what this paper is going to be about?

   _____

   _____

   _____

2. Why do you think the writer talks about how in-line skates and ice skates are alike before explaining how they are different?

   _____

   _____

   _____

3. List three differences between in-line skates and ice skates. List them in the order the writer describes them. Explain why you think the writer used this order.

   _____

   _____

   _____

   _____

   _____

4. How are the first and last paragraphs related?

   _____

   _____

   _____

   _____

   _____

   _____

Writing Assignment

Think about two sports you would like to write about. Write about how they are alike and how they are different. Use this writing plan to help you write a first draft on page 595.

Choose two sports you want to write about. Call them A and B.

A = _____   B = _____

Use what you know, books, or the Internet to learn more about A and B. Learn about three main ideas: where the sports are played, what equipment players need, and the rules. Under each main idea, list what is true only about A in the A circle. List what is true only about B in the B circle. List what is true about both A and B where the two circles overlap.

MAIN IDEA:
Where are the sports played?

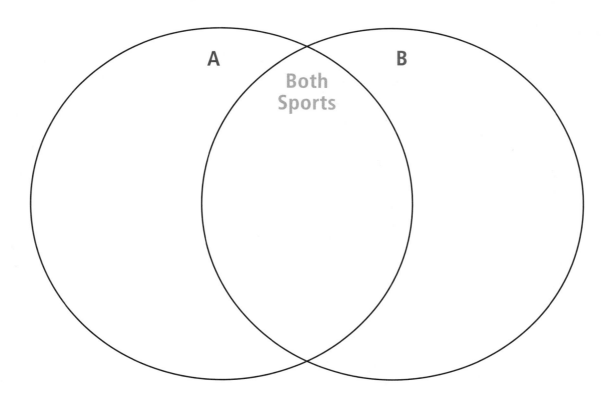

MAIN IDEA:
What equipment do players need?

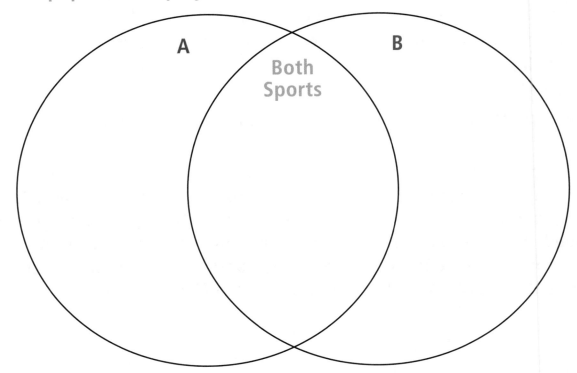

A Both Sports **B**

MAIN IDEA:
What are the rules?

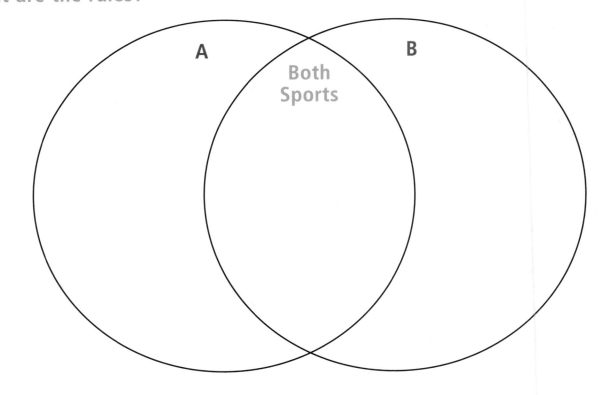

A Both Sports **B**

First Draft

> **TIPS FOR WRITING A COMPARE-AND-CONTRAST PAPER:**
> - Find information about your sports.
> - Organize the information you find into main ideas.
> - Use details to explain each main idea.
> - Explain how the sports are alike.
> - Explain how the sports are different.
> - Use your last paragraph to summarize your main ideas in a new way.

Use your writing plan as a guide as you write your first draft of a compare-and-contrast paper. Include a catchy title.

_____

_____

_____

_____

_____

_____

_____

_____

_____

_____

_____

(Continue on your own paper.)

Revise the Draft

Use the chart below to help you revise your draft. Check YES or NO to answer each question in the chart. If you answer NO, make notes to remind yourself how you can revise, or change, your writing to improve it.

Question	YES ✓	NO ✓	If the answer is NO, what will you do to improve your writing?
Do you introduce the sports you will write about in the first paragraph?			
Does your paper explain how the two sports are alike?			
Does your paper explain how the two sports are different?			
Do you have more than one main idea about each sport?			
Did you organize the main ideas into paragraphs?			
Do you use details to support each main idea?			
Do you summarize the main ideas of your paper in your conclusion?			
Have you corrected mistakes in spelling, grammar, and punctuation?			

Use the notes in your chart and your writing plan to revise your draft.

Writing Report Card

Read your revised draft again or ask someone else to read it. Have the person who reads your paper complete the following Report Card. Revise your paper until you have no less than a Very Good Score for each item.

Title of paper: _____

Purpose of paper: ____ *This paper compares and contrasts two sports.* ____

Person who scores the paper: _____

Score	Writing Goals
	Does the writer tell what the paper will be about in the first paragraph?
	Does the paper explain how two sports are alike?
	Does the paper explain how the two sports are different?
	Does the writer use more than one main idea to show the important ways the sports are alike and different?
	Does the writer organize the paragraphs in a way that makes sense?
	Does the writer use important details to support each main idea?
	Does the last paragraph summarize what the paper is about?
	Are the paper's grammar, spelling, and punctuation correct?

☺ Excellent Score ☆ Very Good Score + Good Score
✔ Acceptable Score − Needs Improvement

UNIT 5: Persuasive Writing

HOW MUCH DO YOU KNOW?

A. Read the following statements from a persuasive essay. Write the word or the group of words from the box that best describes the techniques used in the statement.

> testimonial
>
> faulty generalization
>
> emotional words
>
> bandwagon technique

1. Instead of mindless wasting of energy, energy-hogs must use less energy.

   _____

2. An expert from Nevada explained that when rivers are dammed for water power, it destroys beautiful valleys.

   _____

3. Nuclear power plants help solve energy problems, but the storage of huge amounts of radioactive wastes only makes the problem so much worse than anyone can imagine.

   _____

4. Fuels made from fossils pollute the air, so people should recycle more.

   _____

B. Read the following statements. After each sentence, write *fact* or *opinion*.

5. Even the manufacturing of equipment for other sources of energy uses energy and creates pollution in the process.

   _____

6. The best way to use less energy is to walk or ride a bike.

   _____

Analyzing a Persuasive Essay

A PERSUASIVE ESSAY

- gives an opinion about an issue
- gives facts and reasons to back up the opinion
- has an introductory paragraph, supporting paragraphs, and a conclusion

Read the following statements from a persuasive essay. Write the word or the group of words from the box on page 86 that best describes the techniques used in the statement.

1. We have to keep greedy builders from gobbling up our wilderness to make a buck.

   _____

2. Jack Tenor, the famous athlete, says that they passed a similar law in his town and everyone is happy with it.

   _____

3. Join the thousands of people all over the country who are demanding laws to restrict building in their area.

   _____

4. Since my neighbors like my idea, we're sure that this is what the community wants.

   _____

5. Do not trade the unspoiled beauty and the restful peace of the country for the crowded, smoggy rat race of the city.

   _____

6. Maria Gomez, a university professor, says that life in the city can be difficult.

   _____

Classifying Fact and Opinion

> **TO WRITE A PERSUASIVE ESSAY, GOOD WRITERS**
> - back up opinions with facts
> - keep opinions and facts separated

Read the following dialogue. Before each sentence, write *fact* if the speaker has expressed a fact. Write *opinion* if the speaker has expressed an opinion. If the speaker has used a signal word, underline that word in the sentence.

1. _____ "Quite a few people say they have seen the Loch Ness monster," said Rita.

2. _____ "That many people can't be wrong," said Richard.

3. _____ "Aw, they're all a bunch of cranks," said Craig.

4. _____ "Yes," said Bob. "They should be ignored."

5. _____ "It's people like you who ought to be ignored," responded Joe.

6. _____ "Nobody has proved that there is a monster," Bill pointed out.

7. _____ "Yes," agreed Nancy. "A hundred and fifty years ago, scientists didn't believe the giant squid existed."

8. _____ "Probably most people wouldn't believe in elephants if scientists hadn't seen them," commented Jill.

9. _____ "That's silly!" said Tracy. "I'm sure they would."

10. _____ "Loch Ness is deeper than other lakes in the area," said Ray.

11. _____ "It has not been completely explored," added David.

Using Vivid Words

> Good writers use vivid words and phrases.

Rewrite the following statements from a persuasive essay about the evils of slavery. Replace each word or phrase in parentheses ( ) with one from the box.

chained to their masters	demand	lashed
crush out	auctioned	disgraceful
track down	labor	mock

1. How can a planet such as Theron still tolerate the (wrong) laws that permit slavery in the year 3045?

   _____

2. The Theronites should (request) an end to that practice.

   _____

3. Thousands of Robots are (made slaves) by existing laws.

   _____

4. The Robots (work) from dawn until midnight without pay.

   _____

5. Robot catchers are hired to (find) escaping Robots.

   _____

6. To be a truly modern planet, Theron should (end) practices that deny freedom to all Theronites.

   _____

Varying Sentence Structure and Length

> Good writers make their compositions more interesting by varying the length and the structure of their sentences.

Rewrite each paragraph. Create sentence variety by combining sentences, adding words, and shifting the placement of words.

1. I think people should use less energy. It is important that they do this. Every kind of energy costs us something. Fuels made from fossils are in short supply. They also pollute the air.

   _____

   _____

   _____

2. Other sources of energy also have drawbacks. Water power requires damming rivers. This has destroyed many beautiful valleys. Even manufacturing the equipment for other sources of power uses energy. It creates pollution, too. We should cut our use of energy. We can avoid many harmful results of our present overuse of it.

   _____

   _____

   _____

   _____

   _____

Proofreading a Persuasive Essay

PROOFREADING HINT

To be a good proofreader, look for one type of error at a time. For example, proofread once for capitalization errors, once for punctuation errors, and once for spelling errors.

Proofread this beginning of a persuasive essay, paying special attention to the capitalization of proper nouns. Use the Proofreading Marks to correct at least eight errors.

PROOFREADING MARKS

◯	spell correctly
⊙	add period
?	add question mark
≡	capitalize
✌	take out
∧	add
/	make lowercase
∿	switch
⋏	add comma
✓ ✓	add quotation marks
¶	indent paragraph

The people of the World are faced with

alarming environmental problems. I am

convinced that we must all cooperate

through international agencys to solve these

problems. Working alone, one state or one

nation cannot protect its land and people

from environmental hazards. The problems faced by people in the united

states are also problems for people in canada, Japan, and russia. Only by

facing these problems together and trying to work out cooperative

solutions can we protect ourselves and our Planet.

There are several reasons why international cooperation is needed. in the first place, some environmental dangers threaten the whole plant rather than local areas. Damage to the ozone layer is a good example. If someone in nebraska uses an aerosol spray, the chemicals do not stay in Nebraska. Those damaging chemicals travel to the ozone layer, where they affect the whole world. Therefore, a State or Country cannot protect itself against ozone damage simply by passing a law forbidding the local use of aerosols.

List Steps to Save Energy

With a friend or two, list 10 specific steps to save energy. Use the ideas in your list to write a persuasive essay about energy conservation.

_____   _____

_____   _____

_____   _____

_____   _____

_____

_____

_____

_____

_____

_____

_____

_____

Vote for a Persuasive Essay Topic

Vote on each issue below. Then pick one issue that you feel strongly about. Write a persuasive essay on that issue. Read your essay to a friend.

BALLOT

YES	NO	Check one box.
☐	☐	All city parks should have an area for exercising dogs.
☐	☐	The school basketball courts should be open at night.
☐	☐	The school cafeteria should serve vegetarian lunches.
☐	☐	All students should wear uniforms to school.
☐	☐	Girls and boys should be allowed to play on the same school basketball teams.

Writing from a Picture

Look at each of the pictures below. Write a statement of opinion about each picture. Choose one of the opinions and write a persuasive essay to persuade your friends to accept your opinion.

Take Opposing Views

Think about some issues about which you haven't made up your mind, and then write down both sides of the issue. With a friend, find facts and reasons to support each side. Choose one side and write a persuasive essay on it. Read your essay to your friend. Here are examples of possible issues:

"All children should be in bed by 9:30 on school nights."

"Childen should be allowed to go to bed whenever they want."

ISSUE: _____

_____

SIDE 1:   SIDE 2:

_____   _____

_____   _____

_____   _____

_____

_____

_____

_____

_____

_____

_____

_____

_____

A Practice Persuasive Movie Review

BERNIE, THE LAUGHING OGRE

If a story needs one hero, one princess in distress, and one villain, or evil force, to be a fairy tale, then *Bernie, the Laughing Ogre* may be one of the funniest fairy tales you've ever seen. That's right, the word is *seen*, not *heard*. Because *Bernie, the Laughing Ogre* is a movie, and its characters are unlike any fairy tale characters you've ever met before.

Let's start with the hero, Bernie. Bernie is tall, but definitely not handsome. In fact, he's a chubby, purple giant with too much hair. Most of the time, too much hair on a giant isn't a problem. But Bernie's hair grows in all the wrong places. There's hair between his toes and fingers. There's even hair growing from his nose and ears, but there's no hair on his head. Bernie is bald.

There's something else that makes Bernie an uncommon hero. He's ticklish. A single scratch on his purple skin makes Bernie lose control. He falls to the ground, laughing and gasping for air. Bernie knows this is unacceptable behavior for a giant. In fact, his giant friends have threatened to kick Bernie out of their drama club if he can't be more serious. Bernie wants to act like other giants, but he can't help himself.

To be safe, Bernie never goes into the nearby village where he might rub up against the moles. That may not seem so funny, but you need to remember that moles are hairy and blind. They use their whiskers to see. Their short, stubby whiskers are always moving about. If you're a bald, ticklish giant like Bernie, you can see why moles might be a problem. In fact, Bernie avoids moles altogether. That includes princess moles.

The princess in this story is no ordinary fairy-tale princess. For one thing, she's a mole. For the second thing, she's not really in distress. She's used to the dull, dark castle where she lives. She's also used to the boring dragon that holds her captive. Princess Stella has learned to make herself laugh, but only when the dragon isn't around. Nothing makes the dragon angrier than laughter. The first time the princess laughed, the dragon shook and shivered. Steam came from its ears. Its skin turned from blue to red. This made the princess laugh, too. That made the dragon even more furious. The princess soon realized that of all the dragons in the world, she got the one without a sense of humor. That's when she decided to find a way out of the castle. Plus, she worried about the moles in her village. What was the villain Manco doing to them?

Manco is like most of the villains you read about in fairy tales. He never smiles unless he's being wicked. Nothing makes him happier than making someone else unhappy. That's why he let the dragon into the village to kidnap the princess. He knew that once the princess was gone, everyone in the village would be sad. That's where Bernie's problem begins.

Most of the time, no one comes near the dark, unfriendly forest where Bernie lives. Until the moles come, that is. You see, some of the moles decide they need a giant to help them rescue their princess and bring laughter back to the village. Their first stop is Bernie's forest.

Unless Bernie agrees to help, the moles tell him more moles will come. Bernie has no choice. He must say yes or risk becoming the laughingstock of giants everywhere. So, Bernie agrees to rescue the princess if the moles promise to return home. The moles promise, but that's not exactly what happens.

I could tell you more, but I don't want to spoil the surprises that fill this movie. Don't think about how Bernie helps all of those hairy, whiskered moles rescue the princess. Don't imagine what the dragon does the first time it hears Bernie laugh. You'll see how Bernie handles these problems when you see the movie. Right now, I'd like to talk about something else that's going to make you love this fairy tale.

Bernie, the Laughing Ogre, the movie, is an example of the best of computer technology. The people who brought these characters to life have done something extraordinary. Each character walks, talks, and looks like a real living thing. When Bernie smiles, you see wrinkles in his skin. When the wind blows, you see each mole whisker twitch. When the dragon breathes fire, you almost feel the flames. Characters look so real, you're sure they are.

There are hundreds of reasons why you should see *Bernie, the Laughing Ogre*. There's not a single reason not to see it. This story isn't like the fairy tales you read when you were a child. It will make you laugh. You'll also be amazed by the computer magic that made this movie. See the movie now. Then you can make plans to see it a second time because I'm sure you will.

Respond to the Practice Paper

Write your answers to the following questions or directions.

1. Why is the hero uncommon?

   _____

   _____

2. Besides the hero, who are the other important characters in this movie?

   _____

   _____

3. Describe the plot of the movie in one or two sentences.

   _____

   _____

   _____

4. Write a paragraph to summarize *Bernie, the Laughing Ogre*. Use these questions to help you write your summary:

   • What is the purpose of this paper?
   • What reasons does the writer give for seeing this movie?

   _____

   _____

   _____

   _____

   _____

   _____

   _____

Analyze the Practice Paper

Read *Bernie, the Laughing Ogre* again. As you read, think about the reasons the writer gives to convince readers to see this movie. Write your answers to the following questions.

1. How does the writer use the first paragraph to grab the reader's attention?

   _____

   _____

   _____

   _____

2. Read paragraph 9 again. Why do you think the writer included this paragraph?

   _____

   _____

   _____

   _____

3. The writer uses most of the review to talk about the characters and plot. Why do you think the writer includes paragraph 10?

   _____

   _____

   _____

   _____

4. What do the first and last paragraphs have in common?

   _____

   _____

   _____

   _____

Writing Assignment

In a persuasive movie review, writers try to convince readers to watch a movie. What's your favorite movie? Write a persuasive movie review to convince your friends to see this movie. Use this writing plan to help you write a first draft on the next page.

What is the name of the movie you will review?

Write reasons your friends should see this movie.
Write details to support each reason.

Reason #1

Details to support Reason #1

Reason #2

Details to support Reason #2

Reason #3

Details to support Reason #3

Reason #4

Details to support Reason #4

First Draft

TIPS FOR WRITING A PERSUASIVE MOVIE REVIEW:

- Make sure you have a strong opinion.
- Give good reasons to support your opinion.
- Give important details that support each reason.
- Grab your reader's attention in the first paragraph.
- Restate your opinion in the last paragraph.

Use your writing plan as a guide for writing your first draft of a persuasive movie review. Include a catchy title.

_____

_____

_____

_____

_____

_____

_____

_____

_____

_____

_____

_____

(Continue on your own paper.)

Revise the Draft

Use the chart below to help you revise your draft. Check YES or NO to answer each question in the chart. If you answer NO, make notes to remind yourself how you can revise, or change, your writing to improve it.

Question	YES ✔	NO ✔	If the answer is NO, what will you do to improve your writing?
Do you use your first paragraph to grab the reader's attention?			
Do you make it clear that you have a strong opinion?			
Do you give good reasons to support your opinion?			
Do you include details that help support each reason?			
Do you restate your opinion in the last paragraph?			
Does this review make your reader want to see the movie?			
Have you corrected mistakes in spelling, grammar, and punctuation?			

Use the notes in your chart and your writing plan to revise your draft.

Writing Report Card

Read your revised draft again or ask someone else to read it. Have the person who reads your paper complete the following Report Card. Revise your paper until you have no less than a Very Good Score for each item.

Title of paper: _____

Purpose of paper: _*This paper is a persuasive movie review.*_____

Person who scores the paper: _____

Score	Writing Goals
	Does the first paragraph grab the reader's attention?
	Is the writer's opinion clearly stated?
	Does the writer give good reasons for his or her opinion?
	Are there details to support each reason?
	Does the writer restate his or her opinion in the last paragraph?
	Does this review make you want to see the movie?
	Are the review's grammar, spelling, and punctuation correct?

☺ Excellent Score   ☆ Very Good Score   + Good Score
✔ Acceptable Score   − Needs Improvement

UNIT 6: Short Report

HOW MUCH DO YOU KNOW?

Read the following sentences. Mark where each would best fit in a research report about Marco Polo.

1. This is why Marco Polo became famous.
   - _____ a. introduction
   - _____ b. body
   - _____ c. conclusion

2. Shortly thereafter, Marco was captured and imprisoned for a short time.
   - _____ a. introduction
   - _____ b. body
   - _____ c. conclusion

3. Marco returned from China 25 years later.
   - _____ a. introduction
   - _____ b. body
   - _____ c. conclusion

4. For almost 300 years, *The Travels of Marco Polo* stood alone as the only Western description of Asia!
   - _____ a. introduction
   - _____ b. body
   - _____ c. conclusion

5. Marco Polo made his first trip to China when he was 17 years old – a trip that changed his life.
   - _____ a. introduction
   - _____ b. body
   - _____ c. conclusion

Analyzing a Short Report

> **A SHORT REPORT**
> - gives information about a topic
> - draws facts from various sources
> - has an introduction, a body, and a conclusion

Read the following sentences. Label each one *introduction, body,* or *conclusion* to identify where it would best fit in a short report about peanuts. Tell why you labeled each as you did.

1. George Washington Carver studied the peanut.

   _____

2. Many regions in the southern United States grow peanuts.

   _____

3. Did you know that peanuts are used in making dynamite?

   _____

4. Some farmers grow peanuts to put nitrogen into the soil.

   _____

5. Did you know that the peanut is not a nut?

   _____

6. A pound of peanuts has as much protein as a pound of beef.

   _____

7. As you can see, the peanut is a valuable product with many uses.

   _____

8. Some inks contain peanut products.

   _____

9. Peanut meal makes excellent feed for livestock.

   _____

10. Knowing all these uses, aren't you glad that people learned to cultivate peanuts?

   _____

Connecting Ideas in a Summary

> **TO WRITE A SUMMARY, GOOD WRITERS**
> - state the most important points about a subject
> - retell a story or an article briefly
> - use their own words without changing the meaning

A. Read the following report. Then read the numbered statements that follow. Underline each statement that should be included in a summary of the report.

It was 6:30 P.M. in Cottonville. The townspeople were going quietly about their business. The Johnsons were just sitting down to dinner. The Garcias were watching the news. Commuters all over the city were still on their way home from work. At 6:31, the earthquake hit. It measured 5.5 on the Richter scale. Some people rushed to stand in doorways or crawl under tables. After the earth had stopped shaking, people waited nervously to see if there would be more shocks. No deaths were reported, but a few people suffered minor injuries.

1. An earthquake occurred in Cottonville.
2. It happened at 6:31 A.M.
3. The Johnsons were sitting down to dinner.
4. The earthquake measured 5.5 on the Richter scale.
5. Some people stood in doorways.
6. There were no deaths.

B. Write a summary for the original source material below.

ORIGINAL SOURCE

SUMMARY

Young children learn through play. They may use blocks, toy vehicles, or costumes. Wise parents and teachers provide many opportunities for a variety of play experiences. These will include solitary play as well as play with friends.

_____

_____

_____

_____

_____

_____

_____

Catching the Reader's Interest

> **GOOD WRITERS**
> - begin with a striking sentence
> - use concrete details
> - use quotations

Read the following sentences from a short report. On the lines below, write the striking sentence that would make a good beginning. Then write the numbers of the concrete details and the quotation.

1. In the United States insects are sometimes sold in cans. Bees and ants may be roasted in oil. Caterpillars and other insects may be covered with chocolate.
2. Birds eat insects, too.
3. People eat all kinds of different foods.
4. My grandfather used to threaten to make grasshopper gravy, just as other people do around the world.
5. He was right. In some cultures people do eat locusts.
6. Termite grubs are eaten in many countries. They taste like pork skins when fried.
7. Although insects are a common food in some parts of the world, canned insects are rare and expensive in the United States and not very popular.
8. In areas where insects are a major food source, people do not cover them in chocolate.
9. Dr. Reiner, the famous anthropologist, says, "It makes sense to eat insects because they are far more plentiful than other animals."
10. Of course, these people eat other things, too.

Striking beginning: _____

_____

Concrete details: _____

Quotation: _____

Combining to Embed a Word or Phrase

Good writers sometimes embed a word or a phrase from one sentence in another sentence.

Combine the sentences in each pair by embedding a word or a phrase. The first one is done for you.

1. In the eighteenth and nineteenth centuries, the way people did their work changed. It changed dramatically.

   In the eighteenth and nineteenth centuries, the way people did

   their work changed dramatically.

2. During this period a new society was created. The period was the Industrial Revolution.

   _____

3. A spinner invented a new spinning machine. His name was James Hargreaves.

   _____

4. The new machine could spin eight threads at once. It was called the spinning jenny.

   _____

5. Edmund Cartwright invented a loom. It was operated by water power.

   _____

6. Eli Whitney invented a cotton gin. He invented it in 1793.

   _____

Proofreading a Short Report

Proofread the beginning of the short report, paying special attention to sentence fragments and run-on sentences. Use the Proofreading Marks to correct at least seven errors.

PROOFREADING MARKS

⬭	spell correctly
⊙	add period
?	add question mark
≡	capitalize
℘	take out
∧	add
/	make lowercase
∿	switch
⋏	add comma
⌄ ⌄	add quotation marks
¶	indent paragraph

Can you imagine an animal that seems

to be part mammal? Part reptile, and part

bird? If you succeed, you will probably

imagine an animal very much like the

duckbill, also called a platypus.

Animals that bear their young alive

and nurse their young are classified. As mammals. Duckbills nurse their

young as mammals do, but they lay eggs as birds do. Although scientists

classify the duckbill as a kind of mammmil, it has characteristics of other

animal groups.

In appearance, the duckbill most closely resembles a duck like a duck,

it has a large bill it also has webbed feet, fur, and a flat tail like a beaver's.

Most mammals are warm-blooded. Their body temperature remains

the same regardless of the temperature. Of their surroundings. A duckbill is

cold-blooded like a reptile its body temperature changes with the

temperature of its surroundings.

Duckbills die. In captivity, so they must be studied in their natural homes.

Write about Life in the 1700s

Imagine that you are a reporter in the 1700s. Write a research report about a day in the life of a weaver, a farmer, or a blacksmith. Make sure you have an introduction, a body, and a conclusion.

Write about History

Imagine that you are Florence Nightingale. You have arrived at a hospital for wounded soldiers. Research Florence Nightingale and nursing practices during the Crimean War. Write a report of conditions you found in the hospital.

_____

_____

_____

_____

_____

_____

_____

_____

_____

_____

_____

_____

_____

_____

_____

_____

_____

_____

_____

_____

Use a Picture for Writing Ideas

Look at the pictures below. List all the ideas you can think of in connection with each of these pictures. For example, a picture of a horse might make you think of farming, horse racing, and the constellation Pegasus. Then pick one topic and write a short report on it.

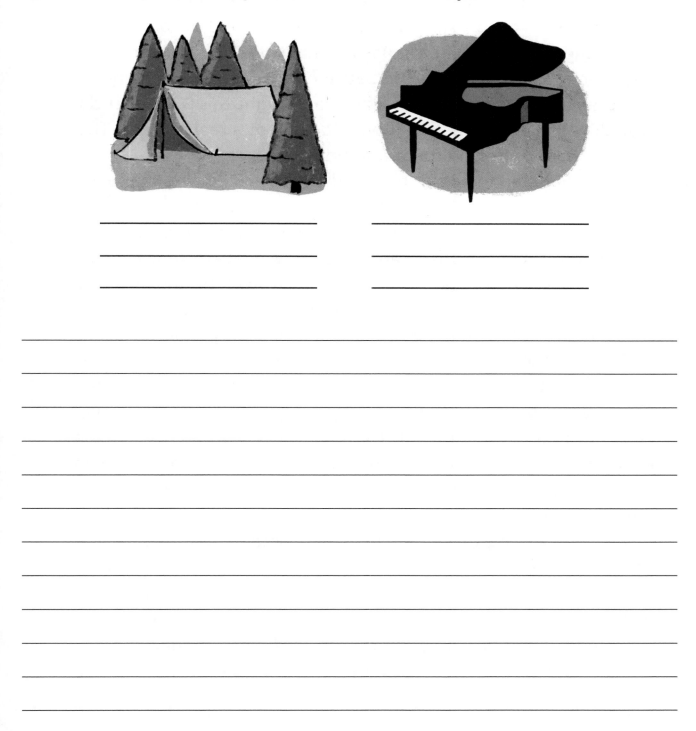

_____   _____

_____   _____

_____   _____

_____

_____

_____

_____

_____

_____

_____

_____

_____

_____

_____

A Practice Short Report

WHY DO BATS SING?

One day in December 1994, Barbara French began her daily routine. You might be surprised to learn what kind of routine she keeps. She takes care of bats. Barbara's bats are Mexican free-tailed bats (*Tadarida brasiliensis*). The bats she cares for have been hurt and cannot return to the wild. Barbara thought this December day would be like any other, but it wasn't. She got a real surprise. The surprise was the beginning of a scientific discovery.

As Barbara fed the bats, she heard an unfamiliar, bird-like song. She stopped to listen. She heard all of the normal sounds. She recognized Hannah's buzz. Hannah buzzes when she defends her favorite roosting spot. Then Barbara heard Wheatley's squeal. She could tell that another bat had chased him away from the mealworm tray. Barbara also heard the chirp Amy makes when she wants to be fed by hand. But she had never heard this new song before.

Barbara decided to solve the mystery. Whenever she heard the song, Barbara popped her head into the bat cage. As soon as her head was inside the cage, the singing stopped. It took Barbara two weeks to find the singing bat. The singer was Hank, an adult male. He seemed to be singing to a small group of females in his roosting pocket. A roosting pocket is a handmade fabric pouch, or bag, in the bats' cage.

In the following weeks, the male bats became unusually bold and ready to fight. They chased each other all the time. Free-tailed bats usually like the company of other bats, so Barbara thought this behavior was odd. Ordinarily, the bats like to roost together.

Barbara was worried by this change in the bats' behavior. Her familiar little bat colony was suddenly very different. The bats had been happy with each other for the past year. Of course, they sometimes squabbled, pushed, shoved, and swatted at each other. However, these were normal bat behaviors. Plus, the bats always settled their differences quickly. They didn't hurt each other. The bat that started a fight usually tried to end the fight. He or she would snuggle up with the other bats. It was as if the bat wanted to say it was sorry. The entire colony seemed to work together to keep the peace. However, Hank was different.

One day Barbara watched Hank attack Joshua, another bat. Hank darted from his pocket. He buzzed loudly and chased Joshua around the cage. Barbara decided Joshua had probably moved too near Hank's territory. Before Barbara could stop him, Hank caught Joshua and snagged his ear. Hank's anger bothered Barbara, but what followed really upset her. Moments after she had rescued Joshua, he squeezed out of her hand. Joshua zoomed back into Hank's territory. Joshua seemed ready to fight back.

Because she didn't understand the bats' new behaviors, Barbara decided to ask for help. She called Amanda Lollar. Amanda is a licensed expert in the care of captive Mexican free-tailed bats. Amanda told Barbara that Hank was probably "singing to his women." Amanda also told Barbara to watch for pups that would probably be born during the summer. Barbara was surprised that the explanation was so simple. The bats that Barbara cared for would never be wild again. Their problems made it impossible for them to care for themselves. Barbara didn't think that the bats were strong enough to have healthy pups.

The problems were not over. Barbara and the other bats found Hank's behavior too hard to manage. Hank fought with other males all the time. He bit Joshua's ear again. He even tried to attack Barbara as she fed a female.

Barbara noticed something new. Three females that had been

roosting with Hank suddenly began eating more. They ate everything Barbara fed them and wanted more.

Finally, Hank's singing stopped. The females left Hank and moved into Wheatley's roosting area. Eventually, Hank became himself again. The Hank problem was solved, but a Wheatley problem began. Wheatley began to guard the females that were expecting babies. Wheatley became as fierce as Hank had been.

In June, as Barbara was feeding the bats, she saw a little pink pup about the size of a walnut. Although the baby was very young, it was able to follow its mother around inside the roosting pocket. Twelve days later, Barbara saw the birth of a second pup. This baby was born with its eyes open. It was able to lick its tiny wings clean within minutes after birth.

Barbara learned a lot from her experience with her bats. So did scientists who study bats. Barbara was able to give scientists information they had never had before. Hank's music wasn't a mystery anymore. Neither was Wheatley's protective behavior. Thanks to Barbara and her bats, scientists now know much more about the mating behaviors of Mexican free-tailed bats.

Respond to the Practice Paper

Write your answers to the following questions or directions.

1. Why was Barbara surprised the first time she heard a bat sing?

   _____

   _____

2. Why was Barbara surprised when the male bats became more willing to fight?

   _____

   _____

3. Why did Barbara contact Amanda Lollar?

   _____

   _____

4. Write a paragraph to summarize the report. Use these questions to help you write your summary:

   • What are the main ideas in this report?
   • How did Amanda explain Hank's behavior?
   • What did scientists learn from Barbara's experience?

   _____

   _____

   _____

   _____

   _____

   _____

   _____

   _____

Analyze the Practice Paper

Read "Why Do Bats Sing?" again. As you read, think about the main ideas the writer tells about. Write your answers to the following questions.

1. Which paragraph did the writer use to tell you what this report was going to be about?

   _____

   _____

2. Read the second paragraph again. What details did the writer use to explain why the singing was unusual?

   _____

   _____

3. Read the fifth and sixth paragraphs again. How does the sixth paragraph support the fifth paragraph?

   _____

   _____

   _____

   _____

   _____

4. How is the first paragraph related to the last paragraph?

   _____

   _____

   _____

   _____

   _____

   _____

Writing Assignment

In a short report, writers write about one topic. They find information about the topic. Then they use the information to choose the main ideas for their report. They also choose details to help explain each main idea. Write a short report about a science topic that interests you. Your idea might even come from the report "Why Do Bats Sing?" Use this writing plan to help you write a first draft on the next page.

The topic of this paper is:

_____

Main Idea of Paragraph 1: _____

Detail: _____

Detail: _____

Detail: _____

Main Idea of Paragraph 2: _____

Detail: _____

Detail: _____

Detail: _____

Main Idea of Paragraph 3: _____

Detail: _____

Detail: _____

Detail: _____

First Draft

TIPS FOR WRITING A SHORT REPORT:

- Find information about your topic.
- Take notes about main ideas important to your topic.
- Take notes about important details for each main idea.
- Organize the main ideas and the details into paragraphs.
- Put paragraphs in a logical order.
- Use the last paragraph to summarize your report.

Use your writing plan as a guide as you write your first draft of a short report. Include a catchy title.

_____

(Continue on your own paper.)

Revise the Draft

Use the chart below to help you revise your draft. Check YES or NO to answer each question in the chart. If you answer NO, make notes to remind yourself how you can revise, or change, your writing to improve it.

Question	YES ✔	NO ✔	If the answer is NO, what will you do to improve your writing?
Does your report focus on one topic?			
Do you introduce your topic in the first paragraph?			
Do you have more than one main idea to explain your topic?			
Do you organize your main ideas into paragraphs?			
Do you include details to explain each main idea?			
Do you use your last paragraph to summarize your report?			
Have you corrected mistakes in spelling, grammar, and punctuation?			

Use the notes in your chart and your writing plan to revise your draft.

Writing Report Card

Read your revised draft again or ask someone else to read it. Have the person who reads your paper complete the following Report Card. Revise your paper until you have no less than a Very Good Score for each item.

Title of paper: _____

Purpose of paper: _*This paper is a short report.*_____

Person who scores the paper: _____

Score	Writing Goals
	Does this short report focus on one topic?
	Does the writer introduce the topic of this paper in the first paragraph?
	Does the writer use more than one main idea to explain the topic?
	Are main ideas organized into paragraphs?
	Are there details to explain each main idea?
	Does the report "stick" to the topic?
	Does the last paragraph summarize the report?
	Are the report's grammar, spelling, and punctuation correct?

☺ Excellent Score ☆ Very Good Score + Good Score
✔ Acceptable Score − Needs Improvement

Proofreading Marks

Use the following symbols to help make proofreading faster.

MARK	MEANING	EXAMPLE
◯	spell correctly	I ⟨liek⟩ dogs. _like_
⊙	add period	They are my favorite kind of pet⊙
?	add question mark	Are you lucky enough to have a dog
‗	capitalize	My dog's name is <u>s</u>cooter.
℈	take out	He is a great companion for me and my ~~my~~ family.
∧	add	We got Scooter when ∧ was eight weeks old. _he_
/	make lowercase	My U̸ncle came over to take a look at him.
∿	switch	He watched the puppy run ⌇in⌇ around⌇ circles.
∧̦	add comma	"Jack∧̦ that dog is a real scooter!" he told me.
⩔ ⩔	add quotation marks	⩔Scooter! That's the perfect name!⩔ I said.
¶	indent paragraph	¶Scooter is my best friend in the whole world. He is not only happy and loving but also the smartest dog in the world. Every morning at six o'clock, he jumps on my bed and wakes me with a bark. Then he brings me my toothbrush.

Test
Prep

GET READY FOR TESTS

WHAT ARE STANDARDIZED TESTS?

You will take many different tests while at school. A standardized test is a special test that your state gives to every student in your grade. These tests are designed to find out how much you know about subjects like reading and math. They may not be fun, but they do not have to be a nightmare. This workbook can help you prepare!

WHAT CAN YOU EXPECT ON A STANDARDIZED TEST?

All standardized tests are different, but they do have some things in common.

- **Multiple-Choice Questions**
  Most of these tests use multiple-choice questions. You have to pick the best answer from four or five choices. You usually indicate your choice on an answer sheet by filling in or darkening a circle next to the correct answer.

- **Time Limits**
  Standardized tests all have time limits. It is best to answer as many questions as possible before you run out of time. But do not let the time limit make you nervous. Use it to help you keep going at a good pace.

- **Short Answers and Essays**
  Some standardized tests have questions that require writing an answer. Sometimes the answer is a word or a sentence. Other times you will write a paragraph or an essay. Always read directions carefully to find out how much writing is required.

HOW CAN THIS BOOK HELP?

Everyone gets a little nervous when taking a test. This book can make test-taking easier by providing helpful tips and practice tests. You will learn strategies that will help you find the best answers. You will also review math, reading, and grammar skills that are commonly needed on standardized tests. Here are some hints for using this book.

- Work in a quiet place. When you take a test at school, the room is very quiet. Try to copy that feeling at home. Sit in a chair at a desk or table, just as you would in school.

- Finish one test at a time. Do not try to finish all of the tests in this book in one session. It is better to complete just one activity at a time. You will learn more if you stop at the end of a practice test to think about the completed questions.

- Ask questions. Talk with a family member or a friend if you find a question you do not understand. These practice tests give you the chance to check your own answers.

- Look for the Test Tips throughout this workbook. They provide hints and ideas to help you find the best answers.

A test-smart student knows what to do when it is test-taking time. You might not know all the answers, but you will feel relaxed and focused when you take tests. Your test scores will be accurate. They will provide a snapshot of what you have learned during the school year. Here is how you can become test-smart!

Things You Can Do All Year

The best way to get ready for tests is to pay attention in school every day. Do your homework. Be curious about the world around you. Learning takes place all the time, no matter where you are! When test day rolls around, you will be ready to show what you know. Here are some ways you can become a year-round learner.

- Do your schoolwork. Standardized tests measure how much you have learned. If you keep up with your schoolwork, your test scores will reflect all the things you have learned.

- Practice smart study habits. Most people study best when they work in a quiet, clean area. Keep your study area neat. Make sure you have a calculator, dictionary, paper, and pencils nearby.

- Read a wide variety of materials, including all sorts of fiction and nonfiction. Your school or local librarian can suggest books you might not have considered reading. Read newspapers and magazines to find out about current events.

- Practice. This book is a great start to help you get ready for test day. It provides practice for all the important skills on the tests.

How to Do Your Best on Test Day

Your teacher will announce a standardized test day in advance. Follow these tips to help you succeed on the big day.

- Plan a quiet night before a test. Trying to study or memorize facts at this point might make you nervous. Enjoy a relaxing evening instead.

- Go to bed on time. You need to be well rested before the test.

- Eat a balanced breakfast. Your body needs fuel to keep your energy high during a test. Eat foods that provide long-term energy, like eggs, yogurt, or fruit. Skip the sugary cereals—the energy they give does not last very long.

- Wear comfortable clothes. Choose a comfortable outfit that you like.

- Do not worry about the other students or your friends. Everyone works at different speeds. Pay attention to answering the questions in a steady fashion. It does not matter when someone else finishes the test.

- Relax. Take a few deep breaths to help you relax. Hold your pencil comfortably and do not squeeze it. Take a break every so often to wiggle your fingers and stretch your hand.

TEST-TAKING TIPS

Here are some hints and strategies to help you feel comfortable with any test. Remember these ideas while taking the tests in this book.

READ THE DIRECTIONS

This sounds obvious, but every year students lose points because they assume they know the right thing to do—and they are wrong! Make sure you read and understand the directions for every test. Always read the directions first. They will focus your attention on finding the right answers.

READ THE ANSWERS

Read the answers—ALL the answers—for a multiple-choice question, even if you think the first one is correct. Test writers sometimes include tricky answers that seem right when you first read them.

PREVIEW THE QUESTIONS

Scan each section. This will give you information about the questions. You also can see how many questions there are in the section. Do not spend too much time doing this. A quick glance will provide helpful information without making you nervous.

USE YOUR TIME WISELY

Always follow test rules. On most standardized tests, you can work on only one section at a time. Don't skip ahead or return to another section. If you finish early, go back and check your answers in that section.

- Before the test begins, find out if you can write in the test booklet. If so, add a small circle or star next to those questions that you find difficult. If time allows, come back to these questions before time is up for that section.

- Try not to spend too much time on one question. Skip a difficult question and try to answer it later. Be careful, though! You need to skip that question's number on your answer sheet. When you answer the next question, make sure you carefully fill in or darken the circle for the correct question.

- When finishing a section, look at your answer sheet. Did you answer every question for the section? Erase any extra marks on your answer sheet. Make sure you did not mark two answers for one question.

MAKE AN EDUCATED GUESS

Most standardized tests take away points for wrong answers. It might be wise to skip a question if you have no idea about the answer. Leave the answer blank and move on to the next question. But if you can eliminate one or more of the answers, guessing can be a great strategy. Remember, smart guessing can improve your test scores!

- Read every answer choice.

- Cross out every answer you know is wrong.

- Try rereading or restating the question to find the best answer.

THINK BEFORE YOU SWITCH

When you check your answers, you might be tempted to change one or more of them. In most cases, your first answer is probably the best choice. Ask yourself why you want to make a change. If you have a good reason, go ahead and pick a new answer. For example, you might have misread the question. If you cannot think of a specific reason, it is probably best to stick with your first answer.

FILL IN THE BLANKS

Many tests include fill-in-the-blank questions. The blank is usually in the middle or at the end of a sentence. Use these steps to answer a fill-in-the-blank question.

- Begin with the first answer choice. Read the sentence with that word or group of words in place of the blank. Ask yourself, "Does this answer make sense?"

- Then try filling in the blank with each of the other answer choices. Also, use the other words in the sentence as clues to help you decide the correct choice.

- Choose the best answer.

LOOK FOR CLUE WORDS

When you read test questions, watch for *clue words* that provide important information. Here are some words that make a difference.

- NOT: Many questions ask you to find the answer that is not true. These questions can be tricky. Slow down and think about the meaning of the question. Then pick the one answer that is not true.

- ALWAYS, NEVER, ALL, NONE, ONLY: These words limit a statement. They often make a generally true statement into a false one.

- SOMETIMES, SOME, MOST, MANY, OFTEN, GENERALLY: These words make a statement more believable. You will find them in many correct answers.

- BEST, MOST LIKELY, SAME, OPPOSITE, PROBABLY: These words change the meaning of a sentence. You often can use them to eliminate choices.

RESTATE THE QUESTION

Short answer or essay questions require writing an answer. Your response must answer the question. Restate the question to make sure your answer stays on target. For example, if the question is "What causes lightning?" your answer should begin with the words "Lightning is caused by . . ."

TEST TIP

Be sure to look for the Test Tips throughout this workbook. They will give you more test-taking strategies and specific help with certain subject areas.

SIX READING SKILLS

SKILL 1: DETERMINING WORD MEANINGS

Prefixes and suffixes are parts of some words. A *prefix* appears at the beginning of a word. A *suffix* appears at the end of a word. Both prefixes and suffixes affect the meaning of the word. Readers can use them to help figure out the meaning of a word.

Tom's grandfather came for the weekend. He played in the sandbox and on the swings, and his team won kickball in the park. Tom and his friends loved it, but Tom's mother thought her father was acting <u>childish</u>.

1 **In this paragraph, the word <u>childish</u> means —**

   A   like a child.

   B   in a cold, unfriendly manner.

   C   in the best interests of the children.

   D   like an invalid.

Hint: The suffix "-ish" means like.

Everyone in the class agreed that they should plant flowers around the flagpole. They wanted to <u>beautify</u> the school grounds.

2 **In this paragraph, the word <u>beautify</u> means —**

   F   to take something that is beautiful.

   G   to explain what beautiful means.

   H   to make something beautiful.

   J   the same thing as pretty.

Hint: The suffix "-fy" means to make.

Not only was the kitten inside a carrying case, but it was also inside the airliner with all the other cargo. The cat wanted its <u>freedom</u>!

3 **In this paragraph, the word <u>freedom</u> means —**

   A   ability to move without restraint.

   B   cat food.

   C   home.

   D   ability to choose actions.

Hint: The suffix "-dom" means state of.

GO ON

Answers
1 Ⓐ Ⓑ Ⓒ Ⓓ   **2** Ⓕ Ⓖ Ⓗ Ⓙ   **3** Ⓐ Ⓑ Ⓒ Ⓓ

Sometimes we can figure out the meaning of a new or difficult word by using the words around it as clues.

Someday, a computer in your car may tell you where you're going. An arrow will move across a map, showing where the car is. You won't see many of these computers in cars soon, however. Their cost is prohibitive.

4   In this paragraph, the word prohibitive means —

    F   lost all the time.

    G   too high.

    H   cheap.

    J   fast.

Hint: You get a clue about what the word prohibitive means by reading sentences 3 and 4.

Eli Whitney was ingenious. Not only did he invent the cotton gin, but he also produced the first working model of it in only ten days.

5   In this paragraph, the word ingenious means —

    A   unhappily married.

    B   a cloth maker.

    C   born in the South.

    D   very clever.

Hint: Check each choice to see which one fits best.

The king cobra is a very dangerous snake. Its bite can kill an elephant in three hours. Most animals attack only when threatened. But the king cobra will attack without being provoked.

6   What might happen if you provoked someone?

_____

_____

_____

_____

Hint: You get a clue about what the word provoked means by reading sentences 3 and 4.

TEST TIP

When you need to write a short answer, try restating the question to make sure your answer stays on target. To answer question 6, you might begin, "If I provoked someone, then . . ."

GO ON

Answers
4 Ⓕ Ⓖ Ⓗ Ⓙ   **5** Ⓐ Ⓑ Ⓒ Ⓓ

Specialized or technical words are words used in specific subjects, such as science and social studies. Readers can use all the other information in the text to help determine the meaning of these words.

The mummies of Egypt are very old. So people assume the Egyptians had special ways of embalming. Actually, it was the dry air that helped preserve their dead.

7 **In this paragraph, the word embalming means —**

F   making pyramids.

G   keeping the dead from decaying.

H   keeping things alive.

J   dealing with heat.

Hint: Embalming is a technical word. You get a clue about what it means by reading the entire paragraph.

Galileo was a famous scientist, but he did not invent the telescope. He did improve the device. He was the first person to use a telescope to look at the stars.

8 **In this paragraph, the word telescope means —**

A   a map of the sea.

B   an instrument to magnify.

C   a listening device.

D   a camera.

Hint: Telescope is a technical word. You get a clue about what it means by reading about what it was used for.

On the ocean, distance is measured in nautical miles. This kind of mile is about 800 feet longer than the mile used for measuring land.

9 **In this paragraph, the word nautical means —**

F   sea.

G   whale.

H   shorter.

J   probable.

Hint: The word nautical is a technical term. You get a clue about what it means by reading the entire paragraph.

Some owls have long, vicious talons. They use them to catch mice to eat. They also use them to defend their nests against enemies.

10 **What are talons?**

_____

_____

_____

_____

Hint: The word talons is a technical word. You get a clue about what it means by reading what they are used for.

TEST TIP

Technical words have special meanings. For example, you might have a lot of *work* to complete, but in science, *work* is the energy used when a force moves an object.

STOP

Answers

7 Ⓕ Ⓖ Ⓗ Ⓙ   **8** Ⓐ Ⓑ Ⓒ Ⓓ   **9** Ⓕ Ⓖ Ⓗ Ⓙ

Some facts and details are important. By noticing and remembering those that support the main idea or conclusion, you will better understand what the passage is about.

Toronto has the world's largest shopping mall under the ground. It has more than 1,000 shops and services. They are joined by miles of tunnels and sidewalks. These tunnels and sidewalks also join 35 high-rise buildings. To get to the underground mall, shoppers go in one of the buildings and ride the elevator down. People can also take the subway to other parts of the city. The city-under-the-city is always a pleasant place to walk. That's because the temperature is controlled. Outside, winter may be cold or summer may be hot. But deep down in the mall, the temperature stays the same all year round.

1 **In the shopping mall, there are more than 1,000 —**

    A tunnels and sidewalks.

    B shops and services.

    C business workers.

    D underground trains.

Hint: This fact is right in the passage.

2 **To get from one part of the mall to another, people take —**

    F tunnels.

    G skywalks.

    H subways.

    J elevators.

Hint: Look for the fact in the selection.

3 **Where is the largest underground mall located?**

_____

_____

_____

_____

Hint: Look at sentence 1.

TEST TIP

When you have to provide a short answer, choose your words carefully. Try to write an answer that gets right to the point. You do not need to impress people with fancy words. Simply give your answer as directly and completely as possible.

GO ON

Answers
1 Ⓐ Ⓑ Ⓒ Ⓓ   2 Ⓕ Ⓖ Ⓗ Ⓙ

Sometimes it is helpful to arrange events in the order they happened. This may help you to understand a passage better.

When Gregor Mendel was teaching high school students, he noticed that plants had different traits. For example, some pea plants were tall, while others were short. Mendel wondered why, so he decided to experiment.

Mendel collected the pollen from tall pea plants and put it on the stigmas of the flowers of the short pea plants. He gathered the seeds that were produced. He planted these new seeds and waited for the results. He wondered whether the new plants would be of medium height. Maybe the two traits would blend together. But all the plants that grew from the seeds were tall.

Mendel wanted to see what would happen to the next generation. He crossed the tall plants with each other in the same way he had experimented with the tall and short plants. When the new plants grew, three fourths of the plants were tall, and one fourth were short.

Mendel decided that a plant receives a message from each of its parents, and that message is carried by the plant's genes. For example, a pea plant gets a gene for tallness or shortness from one or both of its parents. Mendel also decided that some genes were stronger than others. The gene for tallness was stronger than the gene for shortness. So a plant would be tall if it had one gene for tallness and one gene for shortness. But if a plant had two genes for shortness, it would be short.

Mendel had made a great discovery, but few understood it at that time. Mendel became famous only after his death.

4   **What happened first?**

A   Mendel noticed that plants had different traits.

B   Mendel collected pollen from pea plants.

C   Mendel crossed tall plants with each other.

D   Mendel became famous.

Hint: Read the beginning to find out what happened first.

5   **Why did Mendel experiment with plants?**

_____

_____

_____

_____

Hint: Look at the first paragraph.

TEST TIP

When a question begins with *why*, look for a cause-and-effect relationship. Find information in the passage that gives exactly the reason why something happened. Look for the most logical answer.

GO ON ➤

Answers
4 Ⓐ Ⓑ Ⓒ Ⓓ

6 When did Mendel discover genes?

    F after he crossed the tall plants with each other

    G while he was working in the garden

    H before he taught high school students

    J before he collected the pollen from tall plants

Hint: Find the section where genes are first mentioned. See what comes before and after that discovery.

7 When did Mendel become famous?

    A after his death

    B when he made his great discovery

    C before he became a teacher

    D when he discovered genes

Hint: Look at the last paragraph.

8 What was one thing Mendel discovered as a result of his experiments?

_____

_____

_____

_____

Hint: Look at the second and third paragraphs.

TEST TIP

Questions that begin with *when* ask you to think about the order of events. Time order also is called *chronological order*. Pay close attention to dates and times, as well as signal words that tell about time, such as:

first	next
then	finally
before	after
since	lastly

You might circle these words in the test passage to help you decide the order of events.

GO ON

Written directions tell the reader how to do something. To follow them means to do them in the same order in which they are given.

Peter and his brother opened the box and began to construct the bookcase. They made sure all the parts were in the box by matching them up with the list of parts that also came in the box. The assembly involved different sizes and wooden pegs, screws, and washers; so they laid them out on the floor to make sure they used the right ones in each step. They attached the two sides of the bookcase to the base with the longest screws. The top required the wooden pegs so that the screws did not show through the surface. The shelf holders were metal, and they inserted them in the predrilled holes in each side of the bookcase. Then it was easy to slide the shelf in. The bookcase was complete.

9 **In this paragraph, before the brothers attached the two sides, they —**

F used the wooden pegs.

G inserted the metal shelf holders.

H slid the shelf in.

J laid the pegs and screws on the floor.

Hint: Read the sentence before the one describing how the sides were attached.

TEST TIP

Circle or underline key words in questions. This can prevent confusion about a question's intent.

• In question 9, you might circle the word *before* to remind you to find the event that should come before the step described in the question.

• In question 11, circle *last* to make sure that you identify the last thing in this series.

Richard was excited about the young tree he had just purchased at the nursery. He was told by the nursery salesperson that he should dig a hole larger than the root system. Then the hole should be watered. Fertilizer and peat moss should be mixed with the soil in the hole before the burlap is cut away from the roots of the tree. After placing the tree in the center of the hole, soil should be added to the hole in such a way that the tree remains upright. Richard should be careful not to allow too much of the tree trunk to be covered with soil. After planting the tree, Richard should water it thoroughly.

10 **Along with the tree, Richard needs to buy —**

A a root system.

B burlap.

C fertilizer and peat moss.

D a nursery.

Hint: Make a list of the supplies mentioned in the passage.

11 **What is the last thing Richard should do?**

_____

_____

_____

_____

Hint: Read the last sentence.

GO ON ➡

Answers
9 Ⓕ Ⓖ Ⓗ Ⓙ   **10** Ⓐ Ⓑ Ⓒ Ⓓ

The setting of a story lets the reader know when and where it is taking place.

In 1848, Joshua Norton went to San Francisco with money in his pocket. Gold had been discovered in California. Many people were making money. Joshua Norton was one of them.

At first, Norton was careful with his money. By 1853, he had saved more than $250,000. But then he invested in rice. Soon after, the price of rice went down. Norton was left without a penny. He vanished for six years.

12 Joshua Norton had saved $250,000 by the year —

    F 1853.

    G 1953.

    H 1848.

    J 1859.

    Hint: Read sentence 6.

13 Where does the story take place?

_____

_____

_____

_____

    Hint: What does the first sentence state?

The art of making perfumes was important in Asia. That was where English and French soldiers found the sweet scents in the 1200s. They returned to England and France with the perfumes. Some soldiers even wore perfume into war. They thought it brought them good luck. In the 1500s, perfume was very popular in Europe. In France, Queen Catherine de Medici told her chemist to produce a fragrance for each flower in France.
This was the start of a big business there. Even Napoleon had a perfumer. In the next centuries, many famous perfume companies were established.

14 When did the perfume industry begin in France?

    A at the time Catherine de Medici was queen

    B before the soldiers used it

    C at the same time that it was important in Asia

    D in the next century

    Hint: Read the entire passage to determine when the industry began.

15 According to the passage, perfumes were popular in Europe in —

    F the 1200s.

    G the 1500s.

    H the 1700s.

    J the 1900s.

    Hint: This fact is in the paragraph.

STOP

Answers
12 Ⓕ Ⓖ Ⓗ Ⓙ   **14** Ⓐ Ⓑ Ⓒ Ⓓ   **15** Ⓕ Ⓖ Ⓗ Ⓙ

The main idea is the overall meaning of a piece of writing. Often the main idea is written in the passage.

Bamboo is a giant grass. It grows very fast. One type of bamboo grows three feet in 24 hours! The bamboo is hollow and light but very strong. Bamboo is so strong that it can be made into fences, roofs, boats, and furniture. However, young bamboo is tender, and people eat its beautiful, green shoots.

1   The passage mainly tells that —

    A   bamboo can grow quickly.

    B   bamboo looks like giant grass.

    C   people eat bamboo plants.

    D   the bamboo plant is very useful.

Hint: What does the whole story talk about?

People once played football bareheaded. After many injuries, players began to wear plain leather caps. Plastic helmets and masks appeared later. Still, many players were getting hurt. To make the helmets better, designers studied woodpeckers! Their tough, spongy skulls became the model for modern football helmets.

2   What is the main idea of the story?

    F   Football helmets must be strong and light.

    G   Leather caps were used in football at one time.

    H   The woodpecker had a role in football helmet design.

    J   Many football players are injured.

Hint: What point does the story make?

Rescuers fought to free a man caught in a burning truck. The metal was so badly twisted that even a wrecker couldn't budge it. Then, suddenly a stranger ripped a door off the cab with his bare hands, twisted the steering wheel away, and braced his shoulders under the crushed top to lift it. Later, people found out that the stranger had once lost a child in a fire. His hatred of fire apparently gave him the enormous strength to save the trapped man.

3   What is the main idea of this story?

    A   A man got caught in a fire.

    B   A trapped man needed to be freed from a wrecked truck.

    C   The stranger was very strong.

    D   A man's emotions helped him save a life.

Hint: What is the point of the story?

North Carolina police may use germs to catch bank thieves. Important papers can be sprayed with harmless germs that will stick to the hands of anyone who touches the papers. If a dishonest employee steals the papers, anything that he or she touches will have the germs on it. A scientist can show that the person leaving the germs got them when stealing the treated papers.

4   What is this passage mainly about?

_____

_____

_____

_____

Hint: What does the whole story talk about?

GO ON

Answers

1 Ⓐ Ⓑ Ⓒ Ⓓ   2 Ⓕ Ⓖ Ⓗ Ⓙ   3 Ⓐ Ⓑ Ⓒ Ⓓ

Often the main idea is not given in the text. Sometimes the reader needs to draw his or her own conclusion by putting the facts together.

As a child, Jane Goodall loved to study animals and insects. She took notes on birds and bugs. She even opened a small museum for her friends. She hoped to travel to Africa when she grew up. At age 23, she got her wish and went to Kenya. She stayed in Africa and has become a famous scientist. Her field of study is the behavior of chimpanzees. Goodall has claimed her success is due to patience, courage, observation, and willpower.

5 **What is the implied main idea of this selection?**

F If you don't start a field of study as a child, you will never be a success.

G Jane Goodall went to Africa at the age of 23.

H Patience and courage will develop a person's love of animals.

J Jane Goodall developed her childhood love of animals and insects into a career as a famous scientist.

Hint: Read the entire passage to determine the implied main idea.

Allison was upset over a difficult homework problem. She had been working on it for a while, but she still couldn't get the answer. "Why don't we go outside for a walk?" her dad suggested. Allison looked up at the stars as they walked. Her dad pointed out the planet Venus. When they returned home, Allison felt ready to tackle the homework problem. "Thanks for the walk, Dad," she said.

6 **What is the main idea of this selection?**

_____

_____

_____

_____

Hint: Read the entire paragraph to determine the implied main idea.

Jessica had often seen people sleeping on the sidewalks downtown. Usually, she didn't think twice about them. But one day, she saw a young mother with two small children. They were getting food from a trash can behind a cafe. The sight made Jessica cry, and she promised herself she would do something to help. The next day, she began a food drive for the homeless.

7 **What is the main idea implied in this selection?**

A Jessica felt sorry for homeless people.

B The homeless people slept on sidewalks.

C A mother got food from a trash can.

D Jessica realized that the homeless need help.

Hint: Read the entire passage to determine the implied main idea.

TEST TIP

When you want to find the main idea of a test passage, ask yourself, "What is this passage mostly about?" The main idea should describe the big idea of a passage, not specific details.

Sometimes the main idea is stated in a topic sentence, often at the beginning of a paragraph. Other times, you need to figure out the main idea of a passage. In question 7, the word *implied* tells you that the main idea is not stated. You need to name the big idea that is supported by the paragraph's details.

GO ON

Answers

5 Ⓕ Ⓖ Ⓗ Ⓙ   **7** Ⓐ Ⓑ Ⓒ Ⓓ

A good summary contains the main idea of a passage. It is brief, yet it covers the most important points.

The Masai of East Africa raise cattle for a living. Very little grain is raised in the area, so the people depend on the cattle for food. Most people drink a gallon of milk a day, and beef is a popular meat. Cow's blood is also used as food. It doesn't spoil, it provides protein and minerals, and it can be taken from cows while traveling.

8   What is this passage mostly about?

    F   There is much grain raised in the world.

    G   People in different areas of the world eat odd foods.

    H   Cows provide food for the Masai.

    J   There are many different kinds of cattle raised by the Masai.

Hint: Which choice tells you about the whole passage?

Plant experts in Bolivia have found some odd potato plants. The potato leaves make a sticky glue. Insects that walk on the plant get caught and starve. Scientists want to breed more potatoes with these sticky leaves. Farmers would be able to grow potatoes and not have to spray their plants with chemicals to get rid of insects.

9   What is this passage mostly about?

    A   Insects are caught by potato plants.

    B   Potato plants grow in Bolivia.

    C   A special potato plant may be helpful to farmers.

    D   Chemical sprays help to kill insects.

Hint: Which choice tells you about the whole passage?

In colonial times, women were printers, whalers, and blacksmiths. Today, women are fighting hard to get some of these jobs. For years, men didn't deliver babies, but now there are many male doctors. Women's work used to be sewing, cooking, and raising children. But in 1960, the first female prime minister in the world was elected.

10   How have jobs changed over time?

    _____

    _____

    _____

    _____

Hint: Read the entire paragraph to find the answer.

TEST TIP

When you are looking for a main idea, many of the wrong answers will be details from the story. You might think they are the best answer because you remember reading the detail. Avoid this trap by staying focused on the question. Locate the main idea—what the passage is mostly about. Do not choose an answer that restates one detail. Look for the big idea that is supported by the paragraph's details.

GO ON

Answers
8 Ⓕ Ⓖ Ⓗ Ⓙ   **9** Ⓐ Ⓑ Ⓒ Ⓓ

One hundred viruses placed side by side would be no wider than a human hair. But these germs cause more than fifty diseases. Chicken pox, colds, and rabies are all caused by viruses. More than 21 million people have died from the flu caused by these germs. Scientists are seeking ways to get rid of these tiny killers.

11 **What is this passage mostly about?**

F Tiny viruses cause deadly diseases.

G Many people die from the flu.

H Chicken pox is caused by a virus.

J Many people have died from viruses.

Hint: Which sentence tells you about the whole passage?

The rare Chinese panda lives on tender, young bamboo shoots. But most bamboo plants die right after flowering. Without the bamboo, the pandas starve. Because some people fear that the rare pandas may die out, in some places food is given to the hungry animals. Some pandas are airlifted to places where bamboo is still plentiful.

12 **What is the best summary of this passage?**

A Chinese pandas usually eat bamboo.

B The flower of the bamboo plant is beautiful, but deadly.

C People are working to keep rare pandas alive.

D Pandas die without enough young bamboo shoots to eat.

Hint: Pick the choice that best covers the main point of the passage.

The spots on a fawn's coat let it hide in shady areas without being seen. The viceroy butterfly looks like the bad-tasting monarch, so birds avoid both. The hognose snake hisses and rolls on its back when it fears another animal. When the opossum is attacked, it plays dead. Distressed turtles hide in their shells until they're sure it's safe to come out again.

13 **What is the main idea of this story?**

_____

_____

_____

_____

Hint: All of the sentences together give you the main idea of this paragraph.

TEST TIP

Sometimes you can find the best answer by eliminating all of the other answers. In question 12, answer A is too general, answer B includes details that are not in the passage, and answer C focuses on only one detail. Check your reasoning by making sure that the remaining answer makes sense. Does answer D make sense as the main idea of the paragraph?

STOP

Answers
11 Ⓕ Ⓖ Ⓗ Ⓙ   **12** Ⓐ Ⓑ Ⓒ Ⓓ

Often when we read, we need to see cause-and-effect relationships. Knowing what caused a given event or a character's actions will help us to understand better what we read.

In the years before the American Civil War, there was a federal law that allowed slave owners to reclaim their escaped slaves. Anthony Burns was born a slave in Virginia. He escaped to Boston in 1854. He lived and worked there for a few months before his former owner appeared and had him arrested. The trial of Anthony Burns triggered angry mobs in Boston, a city where most people were against slavery. He was forced to go back to Virginia with his master, but he later gained his freedom.

1   Why was Anthony Burns arrested?

A   He was born a slave.

B   The angry mobs in Boston were against him.

C   His owner was allowed by law to reclaim him.

D   He was living and working in Boston.

Hint: Being arrested is the effect. What caused this to happen?

Joan was attending a concert with her parents. After the first few minutes, she noticed an odd smell. She whispered to her parents about it. Her parents realized that there was a gas leak in the building. They calmly alerted the ushers. Joan noticed a woman starting to faint as one of the ushers stepped up to the microphone to make an announcement.

2   What made Joan whisper?

F   She noticed an odd smell.

G   She didn't like the concert after the first few minutes.

H   She thought the usher was cute.

J   She noticed a woman starting to faint.

Hint: Whispering is the effect. What made this happen?

Matt was playing ball in the backyard when his sister burst from the house. "Chris has a piece of candy stuck in her throat and can't breathe!" she shouted. Matt quickly ran inside and found Chris lying on the floor. She was turning blue. Remembering some of his first-aid training, Matt picked up Chris and wrapped his arms just below her chest. He pushed in and up three times. Suddenly, Chris started to cry.

3   Why did Chris start to cry?

_____

_____

_____

_____

Hint: Making Chris cry is the effect. What made this happen?

TEST TIP

Remember that the word *why* asks you to find a cause-and-effect relationship. The effect is what happens; the cause is the reason why it happens. You can use the word *because* to answer a question that asks *why*. Begin your response to question 6 by writing, "Chris started to cry because . . ."

GO ON ➡

Answers
1 Ⓐ Ⓑ Ⓒ Ⓓ   2 Ⓕ Ⓖ Ⓗ Ⓙ

Often the reader can predict, or tell in advance, what is probably going to happen next. The reader must think about what would make sense if the story were to continue.

"I'll race you to my house!" Meg shouted. Jane struggled to catch up with her. She ran through the deep snow. Both girls dragged their sleds behind them. As soon as they reached the house, they pulled off their wet mittens, scarves, caps, boots, and coats. Meg made hot chocolate and offered some to Jane.

4   What might happen next?

A   Jane and Meg will drink hot chocolate.

B   The girls will clean Meg's room.

C   The girls will clean their clothes.

D   Jane will go back outside to play.

Hint: Which of the choices would most likely come next?

Pat couldn't get the awful conversation out of her mind. She had been so angry with Kate that she had said some things she didn't really mean. Now she wished she had put a big piece of tape over her mouth. Then she noticed the telephone on the kitchen wall. She grabbed the receiver and started to dial.

5   What will Pat probably do next?

F   call Kate and apologize

G   call to order take-out food

H   call her mother to ask her what she should do

J   call for the weather report

Hint: Think about how Pat feels.

Hope and Dave were playing a game of checkers. Their parents were out for the evening. The wind had been howling for several minutes. They heard the tornado siren go off. But before they could scramble down the basement stairs, the lights went out. The next thing Dave knew, his sister was screaming. In the dim light, Dave saw that a beam had fallen from the ceiling and trapped Hope.

6   What will probably happen next?

_____

_____

_____

_____

Hint: What would you most likely do next if you were Dave?

TEST TIP

When a test asks you to predict what will happen next, do not try to think of a creative or weird event that *could* happen. Your goal should be to answer with something that is likely to happen.

Look at question 6. What will probably happen next? Emphasize the word *probably* as you think of an answer. It is possible that a terrible earthquake might strike after the tornado. But this is not what the test writers think is the answer. They want to know what is the most likely thing to happen, not the most unusual or funniest event. Think about the clues in the paragraph. What do you think Dave will do when he sees his sister trapped under a beam?

STOP

Answers

4 Ⓐ Ⓑ Ⓒ Ⓓ   5 Ⓕ Ⓖ Ⓗ Ⓙ

Sometimes a passage will have a graph or diagram with it. These are there to help the reader better understand the passage.

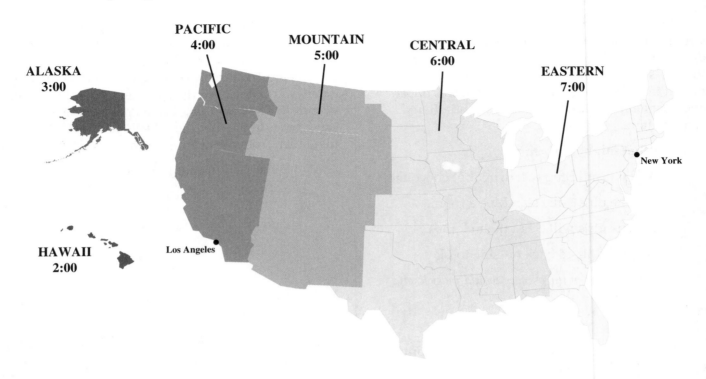

The United States is divided into six time zones. People on the West Coast are three hours behind people on the East Coast. Hawaiians are five hours behind Floridians. Rhode Islanders are four hours ahead of Alaskans.

1   If Tanya in New York wanted to call her friend in Los Angeles at noon Los Angeles time, at what time would Tanya have to make the call?

A   9:00 A.M.

B   noon

C   3:00 P.M.

D   9:00 P.M.

Hint: Look at New York and Los Angeles on the map to see which time zones they are in.

GO ON ▶

Answers
1 Ⓐ Ⓑ Ⓒ Ⓓ

IMMIGRATION TO THE UNITED STATES

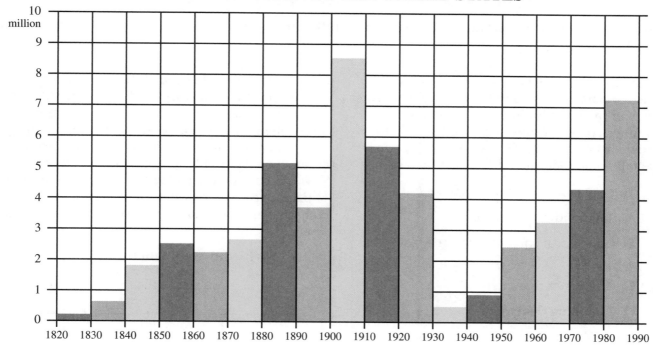

Many Americans are descendants of European immigrants. The number of European immigrants to the United States grew until a national quota system was set in 1921. The quota system was abolished in 1965. During the 1970s, 1.6 million people came from Asia alone to settle in the United States. Immigration today is more carefully controlled, and only about half a million people a year are allowed to settle in the United States.

2 **What is the largest amount of immigrants to come to the United States in a decade between 1820 and 1990?**

F about 7.5 million

G 10 million

H almost 9 million

J 6 million

Hint: Read the graph to find out the number of immigrants each decade.

TEST TIP

Sometimes you might not find an answer that exactly matches your own choice. For example, if you look at the graph to answer question 2 without looking at the answer choices, you might say the answer is 8.5 million. However, this is not one of the answer choices. You can look for the answer choice that is closest to your answer, or you can test each of the four answer choices for accuracy.

GO ON ▶

A logical conclusion is an ending that makes sense. Often it can be proved true by the information given in the paragraph.

Women, in general, have shorter vocal cords than men. Shorter cords vibrate faster, which makes the pitch of the voice higher. This causes women to have higher voices. Women also need less air to vibrate their vocal cords. That allows women to be able to talk longer and with less effort than men.

3   You can conclude that women —

A   talk louder than men.

B   have vocal cords that vibrate faster than men's.

C   talk faster than men.

D   talk more than men.

Hint: Pick the choice that can be proved true by what's in the passage.

Many people take aspirin for aches and pains. Aspirin was first sold around 1900 by the Bayer Company of Germany. It was sold under the trademark "Aspirin." Then World War I swept across the world, and Germany lost the war. Under its terms of surrender, Germany agreed to release the trademark. The name "Aspirin" could no longer be used to sell only Bayer's product. It became the common name of a drug for pain.

4   From the passage you can tell that —

F   Germany did not fight in World War I.

G   aspirin was first sold in Greenland.

H   an unusual term of surrender was met.

J   aspirin is no longer sold anywhere.

Hint: You must read the entire paragraph, especially the last three sentences.

Some people believe in the luck that charms can bring. This was the case of Mary Hopf. She was to compete in a race for the Junior Olympics in Nebraska. When Hopf discovered that she had forgotten her charms at home in Pennsylvania, she panicked. Suddenly, she remembered that her race would be shown on television. Hopf made a long-distance call to her sister. Her sister placed the charms on top of the television set. Hopf won the race.

5   Why did Mary win the race?

_____

_____

_____

_____

Hint: Think about what it takes for someone to win a race.

GO ON

Answers

3 Ⓐ Ⓑ Ⓒ Ⓓ   4 Ⓕ Ⓖ Ⓗ Ⓙ

Sometimes a reader needs to generalize. This means to come up with a general statement about something in the text.

Working at home sounds like fun. You can work in your pajamas. Or you can play the radio as loud as you want. You can even sleep an extra hour in the morning. But making money at home takes drive and dedication. To be successful you must use basic business practices. You must make yourself work rather than play.

6 **You can tell from the paragraph that to be successful you probably need to —**

A stock the refrigerator with plenty of food.

B make a schedule and stick to it.

C plan when to take naps.

D work as little as possible.

Hint: Read the last two sentences in the paragraph.

The Egyptian pyramids were built from stones weighing about two and one-half tons each. The structures are forty stories high. The number of stones used in each pyramid could build a wall around France. Yet the Egyptians used no animals. They had no cranes at that time. The wheel wasn't even in use.

7 **From this paragraph, you can make the generalization that —**

F the Egyptians built a wall around France.

G the pyramids must have been built by many people.

H the pyramids were two and one-half stories high.

J each pyramid weighed about two and one-half tons.

Hint: Eliminate the choices that can be proved untrue.

When the Tacoma Narrows Bridge was built in 1940, it was the third largest suspension bridge in the world. Large suspension bridges had been built before. But the builders didn't count on the winds near Tacoma, Washington. Four months after its opening, the bridge was blown down.

8 **Why didn't other earlier bridges have problems?**

_____

_____

_____

_____

Hint: Why did the Tacoma Narrows Bridge collapse?

TEST TIP

If you have trouble finding an answer, first cross off any answer choices you know are incorrect. Then keep the remaining answer choices in mind as you reread the paragraph. Look for clues in the paragraph to help you decide which answer makes the most sense.

GO ON ➡

Answers
6 Ⓐ Ⓑ Ⓒ Ⓓ   7 Ⓕ Ⓖ Ⓗ Ⓙ

A good reader will sum up what he or she reads and make his or her own judgment about the text. Often things are implied in a text, rather than stated directly.

Sleepwalking is most common among children 10 to 12 years of age. Experts think that it is linked to the growth and development of children. Most sleepwalkers just sit up in bed or stand near their bed. Some people, however, may walk around. Those who walk around can easily hurt themselves. It does not harm sleepwalkers to awaken them, but they may be so confused that they will strike out. After awakening, sleepwalkers don't remember what they did.

9   After reading the passage, you can assume that —

  A   sleepwalkers can be violent.

  B   sleepwalkers are really awake.

  C   sleepwalkers are aware of what they're doing.

  D   sleepwalkers are not aware of what they're doing.

  Hint: Read each of the choices carefully. Which one makes the most sense?

In an interview, world-renowned scientist Albert Einstein was once asked whether he got his great thoughts while in the bathtub, walking, or sitting in his office. Einstein replied, "I don't really know. I've only had one or maybe two."

10   From this story you might think that Einstein —

  F   was a modest man.

  G   did not think his ideas were good.

  H   took a lot of baths.

  J   did not really know much.

  Hint: Read the entire paragraph.

Harvey Gartley of Michigan did not really want to become a boxer. Maybe that's why he lost a fight without ever being hit. The boy was in a Golden Gloves match. As his opponent swung and jabbed, Gartley danced just out of reach. But he danced too much and soon fell down from exhaustion. The match was over in 47 seconds. When Gartley lost, his parents were disappointed.

11   What can you conclude about Gartley's parents?

  _____

  _____

  _____

  Hint: You need to read the entire paragraph and put together the facts before drawing a conclusion.

TEST TIP

Always read a question carefully. Notice that question 10 asks you to draw a conclusion about Gartley's parents. Think about the facts to draw your conclusion. You know that his parents were disappointed that he lost. You also know that Gartley did not want to be a boxer.

GO ON

Answers
  9 Ⓐ Ⓑ Ⓒ Ⓓ   **10** Ⓕ Ⓖ Ⓗ Ⓙ

The way a person in a story acts tells the reader about how the character feels. Other clues may be what is said to or about the character.

Once a poor student had to wander about the countryside. He had no money, and he had no home. One freezing night, the student knocked at the door of a farmer's house. The farmer was an agreeable person who said, "Come in! You look very tired and hungry." The farmer gave the student supper, and the two began talking. The farmer asked whether the student could answer a question he was wondering about. He asked, "What is it that the gods are doing up in the sky tonight?" The student pondered for a long time but confessed that he didn't know the answer. "Never mind," said the farmer. "Maybe there is no answer."

The farmer gave the student a cozy room in which to sleep and a big breakfast the next morning. "Now," said the student, "I'll be on my way. Thank you."

The student traveled on. He eventually found a good job as a teacher and purchased a home of his own. One day, the teacher saw a very old fellow limping up the path. His hair was white, and his clothes were ragged. The teacher invited the old man in. He fed the man, and they talked. The younger man recognized the stranger as the farmer who assisted him long ago.

The teacher said, "Now I know the answer to the question you asked me. The gods were constructing a wheel that turns very slowly. Someday the person at the top will be at the bottom, and the person at the bottom will be at the top. And since we are all on the same wheel, my friend, you may live in my house in comfort all the days of your life."

12 **How did the farmer feel when the student knocked on his door?**

A angry because he had to give him supper

B angry because the student could not answer his question

C pleased that he was able to help the student

D scared

Hint: Read the section to which the question refers.

13 **How did the teacher feel after he recognized the stranger?**

F angry that the old man had tricked him

G happy that he had learned a very important lesson in life

H determined to invest in Ferris wheels

J sure that the farmer would be a great handy man

Hint: Read the last four sentences.

14 **How was the student feeling when he knocked at the farmer's door?**

_____

_____

_____

_____

Hint: Read the first three sentences to determine how the student felt.

STOP

Answers
12 Ⓐ Ⓑ Ⓒ Ⓓ   13 Ⓕ Ⓖ Ⓗ Ⓙ

The author's point of view is what he or she thinks or feels about what he or she is writing. Opinions express points of view.

Ali Baba was a poor, hard-working man. He supported himself and his family by selling wood. He often journeyed high up into the mountains to cut down trees. By himself, he would load the wood he had cut onto his donkeys. Then he would take it into the village where he lived and sell it. He didn't make much money, but it was all he could do.

One day, after he had just finished cutting a load of wood, Ali Baba saw many men on their horses. The men were wearing armor and carrying weapons. Their horses were loaded with huge sacks. Ali Baba knew that the men were thieves. He was afraid that they would kill him, so he climbed up into a tree to hide from them. Ali Baba watched silently from his hiding place as forty thieves approached a huge rock. "Open, Sesame!" called their leader. A small door opened, and the thieves carried their stolen gold into the cave. After the thieves left, Ali Baba hastened to the rock and called, "Open, Sesame!" When the cave door opened, Ali Baba went inside, seized the gold, and took it home with him. He had a new home built for his family. He gave them the things they deserved.

Soon, the thieves found that their treasure was gone. They were furious. They rode into the village where Ali Baba lived. The leader asked villagers if anyone had recently become rich. A man mentioned Ali Baba. The leader of the thieves hid his men inside enormous oil jars. He asked if he might leave the jars at Ali Baba's house until it was time to go to market the next morning. Ali Baba welcomed the man, offering to help him out. He did not recognize him as the leader of the thieves. The thieves planned to sneak out of the jars during the night, take back the gold, and kill Ali Baba and his family. But Ali Baba's servant grew curious. She inspected the jars, saw the sleeping thieves, and tied them all up.

1   You can tell that the author thinks —

A   Ali Baba did not take good care of his family.

B   Ali Baba was a lazy man.

C   Ali Baba should not have taken all the gold.

D   Ali Baba deserves his good fortune.

Hint: Think about how Ali Baba is described throughout the passage.

2   How would the author probably describe Ali Baba's servant?

_____

_____

_____

_____

Hint: How does the author feel about the thieves? Does the author think they got the fate they deserved?

TEST TIP

Remember that the word *probably* is a clue for you to give a logical answer. When you answer question 2, think of the most logical or reasonable words that the author might use to describe Ali Baba's servant.

GO ON ➡

Answers
1 Ⓐ Ⓑ Ⓒ Ⓓ

When an author wants to convince the reader of something, her or she uses language that backs up his or her point of view. Often the language is very descriptive and emotional.

The word "natural" appears in large letters across many cans and boxes of food. But this word, and others like it, sometimes give shoppers false ideas about the food inside. Even though laws require that all food labels give truthful information, this does not always happen.

The word "natural" has not been defined by the FDA, the agency in charge of food labels. So any food maker can use the word on a package. Even the worst junk food is certain to have something natural in it. So the makers of these foods can use "natural" on their packages.

Consumers should read labels carefully and write letters of complaint to the FDA whenever they come across products that are not truly natural. Everyone in the marketplace can help to make truth in labeling work effectively.

3   What is the author trying to persuade the reader to do?

   F   help monitor the truth-in-labeling laws

   G   write better labels for consumer goods

   H   eat junk food because it is natural in part

   J   go shopping more often

   Hint: Read the first and last paragraphs.

4   The author states, "Even the worst junk food is certain to have something natural in it." What is the author trying to convince the reader of?

   _____

   _____

   _____

   _____

   Hint: Reread the sentence and the sentences before and after it.

TEST TIP

To answer question 4, ask yourself, "Why does the author include this detail?" Give your answer as directly as possible. Longer answers are not necessarily better ones. Try to use simple language and state your ideas as clearly as possible.

GO ON

Answers
3 (F) (G) (H) (J)

It is important to recognize the difference between fact and opinion. A fact is real and true. An opinion states a point of view. Words that describe feelings and beliefs are used to offer opinions.

A dozen small turtles slide off a rock and slip into a pond. These turtles look as if an artist had painted them. Pale-yellow stripes cross their upper shells, and a red border circles the edge. More red and yellow stripes are on the turtles' heads, and just behind each eye is another yellow spot.

These eastern painted turtles live in marshy areas, ponds, and slow-moving rivers. They like to be in places where rocks and fallen trees project from the water. The turtles like to climb out onto the rocks or dead trees to sleep in the warm sunlight. If something frightens them, they slide quickly into the water.

5 **Which of the following is an opinion?**

A Painted turtles are prettier than other kinds.

B Eastern painted turtles live in marshy ponds.

C The turtles like to sleep in the warm sunlight.

D Turtles go back into the water when something frightens them.

Hint: A fact is real and true. Look for words that are opinions.

Giant sequoia trees grow near the coast of northern California. Sequoia trees are also called redwoods. For many years, experts thought that these tall trees were the oldest living trees on Earth. In 1892, one of the trees was cut down. Scientists counted the growth rings in the tree to find out its age. They discovered that the tree was indeed old. It had lived for about 3,212 years. Today, experts know that the redwood trees average about 3,500 years in age.

Redwoods have straight trunks and branches that seem to brush against the sky. One redwood, named "General Sherman," is the largest living thing in the world. It is 272 feet tall.

In 1953, scientists became interested in another type of tree. They had discovered some very old bristlecone pines in Nevada. At heights of only twenty to sixty feet, these pines were not as grand as the redwoods. But the experts began to wonder if they were older.

In 1957, they found a pine over 4,000 years old. Their theory had been correct. Further study turned up even older trees. One of these trees, "Methuselah," is the oldest living tree in the world. It is 4,700 years old. But even though some pine trees may be older, most do not live as long as the redwoods. This is because the redwoods have a longer life span.

6 **Which of the following is an opinion?**

F Pine trees don't look as nice as giant sequoias.

G Pine trees are older than sequoias.

H The largest living redwood is 272 feet tall.

J Old bristlecone pines were discovered in Nevada.

Hint: Look for words that express a feeling, not a fact.

7 **Which of the following is an opinion?**

A Redwoods are also called sequoias.

B To find out the age of a tree, scientists count its rings.

C The straight trunk and branches of the redwood make it the most magnificent tree.

D The average age of a redwood tree is 3,500 years.

Hint: What is actually said in the passage? Which sentence is not always true?

GO ON

Answers

5 Ⓐ Ⓑ Ⓒ Ⓓ   6 Ⓕ Ⓖ Ⓗ Ⓙ   7 Ⓐ Ⓑ Ⓒ Ⓓ

"What an ugly boy!" many people whispered when they saw Hans Christian Andersen. His hands and feet were gigantic. His eyes were tiny, and his nose was too big for such a thin face. He seemed clumsy as he clattered to school in his wooden shoes. Young Hans lived a sad life. His father was a poor shoemaker, and his mother was often ill. So the lonely boy created a make-believe world of this own, designing toy theaters and carving tiny figures to act in them.

In 1819, when Hans was 14, he made a big decision. He left his home and traveled across Denmark to the city of Copenhagen. "Here," declared Hans, "I will make my dream come true. I will become a famous actor." But it soon became evident that the dream would not come true at all. For three years, Hans tried to find an acting job but had no luck. When he was 17, Hans sadly returned home.

Hans went back to school and worked hard at his lessons. He kept a journal, which he filled with his dreams, thoughts, and ideas for stories. In his journal, Hans told about an ugly bird that was laughed at by the ducklings in the farmyard. But the little bird was not a duck at all, and it grew into an elegant swan.

Hans graduated from school with a new dream of becoming a famous writer of novels and articles. He kept busy at his writing. But publishers would not buy his books or his news stories, and it seemed that this dream, too, would never come true. By the time he was thirty, Hans was very poor indeed. He decided to try writing stories for children. Adults and children loved these stories! People of all ages do. Andersen's best story is "The Ugly Duckling." In a way it is the story of Andersen himself.

8 **Which of the following is an opinion?**

F Hans tried to be an actor.

G Hans did not have a very happy childhood.

H Hans dreamed of becoming a famous writer.

J Han's best story is "The Ugly Duckling."

Hint: An opinion is someone's point of view, and not a fact.

9 **Write two facts you learned about Hans Christian Andersen from reading this story.**

_____

_____

_____

_____

Hint: A fact is something real and true. An opinion is what you think of something.

TEST TIP

Look for signal words that turn a statement into an opinion. Opinions often contain exaggerations, such as *most exciting* or *least interesting*. An opinion often names something as the *best* or *worst* or claims that one thing is *better* or *worse* than another.

STOP

Answers
8 Ⓕ Ⓖ Ⓗ Ⓙ

Directions: Read the selection carefully. Then read each question. Darken the circle for the correct answer, or write the answer in the space provided.

TRY THIS
More than one answer choice may sound correct. Choose the answer that goes best with the story.

Sample A   Sylvia's First Day

Sylvia's first day of school was difficult. She had just moved from another state. Sylvia felt lonely and scared as she tried to find her classrooms. Nothing seemed to go right that day at school.

Which word best describes Sylvia's feelings about the first day at her new school?

A   unhappy   C   confident

B   joyful   D   angry

THINK IT THROUGH
The correct answer is <u>A</u>. This was Sylvia's first day at a new school. The third sentence states that Sylvia was <u>lonely</u> and scared. The word <u>unhappy</u> best describes those feelings.

My Favorite Sport

Racing, Sweating
Bouncing, Jamming
Passing, Catching
Shooting, Dunking
Swishing, Jumping

All these actions make my body sore.
But I love to hear the crowd roar.
The noise lifts me out of my seat.
My ears hurt, though, when there's a defeat,
From the silence that bounces off the walls.
I go home reviewing the ref's calls.
I look forward to the next game.
They are always different, never the same.

1   Which of the following best describes the tone of the poem?

A   jealousy   C   liveliness

B   sadness   D   boredom

2   According to the poem, what makes the poet's ears hurt?

F   the roar of the crowd

G   the noise from bouncing

H   the jumping out of the seat

J   the silence that bounces off the walls

3   What sport does this poem describe?

_____

_____

_____

_____

GO ON ➡

Answers
SA Ⓐ Ⓑ Ⓒ Ⓓ   1 Ⓐ Ⓑ Ⓒ Ⓓ   2 Ⓕ Ⓖ Ⓗ Ⓙ

Outdoor Adventure

For weeks Jeff had been looking forward to the trip. He and his father were going snow camping in Yellowstone National Park. The two had been running several miles a day for *stamina*. They knew it wouldn't be easy to cross-country ski into the wilderness carrying heavy backpacks. They prepared for the trip by reading books about winter camping, and they carefully planned which gear they would take for the trip.

Finally the big day arrived. Jeff and his father rose early and drove to the entrance to the park. Mr. Cawley talked to the park rangers. He showed them the route they planned to take and where they would camp each night. The rangers said the weather and snow conditions were good for skiing and wished them a good trip. Jeff and his father strapped on their back packs and skied away from the car.

Jeff felt a little nervous at first. It was strange to be leaving the city behind and entering such a cold, empty land. The rangers said that Jeff and his father probably would not see anyone else on their excursion, although there was a chance they would see coyotes or bears. As Jeff's legs warmed up and he got into the rhythm of skiing, he felt less fearful. Rolling white hills stretched as far as he could see. The fir trees were dusted with snow, and a peaceful silence surrounded the two skiers. Jeff began to feel as if he were entering an enchanted land.

After a few hours, Jeff and his father rounded a bend and saw an elk standing a short distance away. Its head was down, and it made no effort to run. They stopped and watched it. "Something's wrong with it," Mr. Cawley commented. "It's probably old or sick. Maybe it's starving."

"It won't last long out here," Jeff said, remembering the coyotes and bears the rangers had told them about.

"You're right about that," his father replied.

A few miles later, the skiers entered a canyon formed by the Madison River. This was where they had decided to make their first campsite. "It feels great to take off this heavy pack," Jeff thought. Both he and his father had brought lightweight shovels. They began digging a pit in the snow. They chose a place in the open, away from the trees, where the morning sun would warm them. They used ski poles as center supports and slung the tarp over the pit. Then they piled snow on the edges of the tarp to form a snug, wind-proof shelter.

Jeff unpacked a cooking pot and walked to the river to get water. He watched huge trout swim by in the clear, icy river. Maybe he could catch some trout for breakfast, but just then he was too tired and hungry to think about fishing. He wanted something hot to drink and a quick, easy dinner. Jeff and his father crawled into their shelter and lit the camp stove. The freeze-dried dinners were simple to prepare. They simply had to pour boiling water into the pouches and stir the contents.

The temperature dropped quickly as soon as the sun set, so Jeff and his father decided to go to bed early. A few hours later, they were awakened by a loud, eerie baying. Coyotes! Jeff felt as if his heart froze. It sounded as if hundreds of coyotes were right outside the tarp. What would they do if they were surrounded by hungry coyotes?

Mr. Cawley lifted the tarp and looked out. "I can't see anything. I think they're up the canyon a mile or two," he said. "The howling is echoing off the canyon walls, making them sound nearer than they really are." Jeff and his father exchanged looks. Both of them were thinking about the elk they had passed that afternoon.

The next morning, they got out of their sleeping bags and were glad to see that the day was bright and beautiful. Jeff was surprised when he opened his contact lens case. The liquid they were soaking in had frozen! When he stepped outside, he saw vapor rising from the river like steam. It was so cold they decided not to fish, but to pack up and get moving right away.

"Why don't we leave our packs here, and ski back to where we saw the elk?" Jeff suggested.

Mr. Cawley agreed, and without the packs they skied easily. From a distance they could see that they had guessed right. The elk's skeleton lay in the valley surrounded by numerous coyote tracks. Jeff had read about animals in the wild, but had never before witnessed their struggle for survival. He shivered as he wondered what else they would see in the wilderness.

GO ON➧

4 Another good title for this story would be—

   A "Building a Wind-Proof Shelter."

   B "Falling Through Frozen Ice."

   C "Preparing Freeze-Dried Food."

   D "Witnessing the Frozen Wilderness."

5 Which words describe Jeff's reaction when he heard the coyotes howling?

   F "felt as if his heart froze"

   G "felt a little nervous"

   H "felt fearless"

   J "felt tired and hungry"

6 What time of year did Jeff and his father go camping?

   A during the summer

   B during late spring

   C during the winter

   D during the fall

7 In this story, *excursion* means—

   F a short journey.

   G a vacation.

   H a snowmobile.

   J a brief map.

8 This story mainly shows that Jeff and his father—

   A had been preparing for and looking forward to this trip for weeks.

   B were very tired after their first day of skiing.

   C went on a ski trip and experienced some of the realities of life in the wilderness.

   D camped beside the Madison River and were awakened by coyotes.

9 As Jeff and his father skied away from the car, Jeff can best be described as—

   F happy.

   G excited.

   H anxious.

   J tired.

10 If a person has *stamina,* it means that the person has—

   A wealth.

   B reasoning powers.

   C the ability to put up with strain and hardship.

   D the power to fast for several days.

11 Mr. Cawley probably showed the rangers the route they planned to take so the rangers—

   F could come and keep them company.

   G would know where to look for them if they did not return.

   H would know where to phone them.

   J could keep the wild animals away from them.

12 Why did Mr. Cawley think there was something wrong with the elk?

_____

_____

_____

GO ON

Daily Schedule
Fairfield Outdoor Education Center
Leonard Middle School

The following schedule shows a typical day at Fairfield Outdoor Education Center. Seating for meals is always at 8:00 A.M. for breakfast; 11:30 A.M. for lunch; and 5:00 P.M. for dinner. The rest of the program is quite flexible, depending on the needs of individual students, on the availability of teachers, and on the weather conditions.

Time	Activity
6:30–7:30 A.M.	Wake up. Make beds. Clean dorm rooms. Girls shower. Boys run laps around the lake.
7:30–8:00 A.M.	One group of students sets breakfast table. Another group of students prepares day packs for outdoor activities.
8:00–9:00 A.M.	Eat breakfast. Group that sets the table washes the dishes. Other group writes in journals.
9:00–11:30 A.M.	Instructional period. Students learn the proper techniques of hiking, skiing, and canoeing. Students learn about the plants and animals that live in Fairfield. Students use journals, sketch pads, binoculars, and cameras to help them record their sightings.
11:30 A.M.–12:30 P.M.	Lunch, dishwashing, and dorm break.
12:30–4:30 P.M.	Instructional period. Students explore a swamp area, a large granite quarry, and a dry creek bed. Students learn to hunt for fossils. Students use mallets, chiseling tools, journals, clipboards, sketch pads, and cameras to help them find and record ancient fossils.
4:30–5:00 P.M.	Silent reading time.
5:00–6:00 P.M.	Dinner, dishwashing, and dorm break.
6:00–9:00 P.M.	Students play a variety of games, such as volleyball. After dusk a campfire is started. Students identify constellations and nocturnal animals while on a night walk.
9:00–10:00 P.M.	Boys shower. Girls exercise. All students prepare for sleep.
10:00 P.M.	Lights out.

Final Night 6:00–9:00 P.M.	Families of all students are invited to a hot-dog roast. Students perform skits to show what they have learned.

GO ON

13 If a student's afternoon instructional period doesn't end until 5:00 P.M., the student will miss—

A dinner.

B a dorm break.

C silent reading time.

D dishwashing.

14 There is enough information in this schedule to show that—

F students are expected to do very little work in this program.

G students spend most of their day learning about outdoor activities.

H students will be at the Fairfield Outdoor Education Center for one week.

J boys and girls do not attend the education center at the same time.

15 Which activity do the students participate in after lunch?

A write in journals

B hunt for fossils

C canoe on the lake

D ski through woods

16 What does the group that is not setting the breakfast table do between 7:30 and 8:00 A.M.?

F prepares day packs

G makes beds

H runs laps

J washes the dishes

17 Who will participate in this outdoor education program?

A high school students from all over the state

B middle school students from Leonard

C middle school students in scout groups

D high school students from the county who study biology

18 Why will the students perform skits at the Final Night activities?

_____

_____

_____

_____

GO ON ➡

Helen Keller Remembers
by Helen Keller

The morning after my teacher came she led me into her room and gave me a doll. I had played with it a little while Miss Sullivan slowly spelled into my hand the word "d-o-l-l." I was at once interested in this finger play and tried to imitate it. When I finally succeeded in making the letters correctly I was flushed with childish pleasure and pride. Running downstairs to my mother I held up my hand and made the letters for doll. I did not know that I was spelling a word or even that words existed; I was simply making my fingers go in monkey-like imitation. In the days that followed I learned to spell in this uncomprehending way a great many words, among them *pin, hat, cup* and a few verbs like *sit, stand,* and *walk.* But my teacher had been with me several weeks before I understood that everything has a name.

One day, while I was playing with my new doll, Miss Sullivan put a rag doll into my lap, also spelled "d-o-l-l," and tried to make me understand that "d-o-l-l" applied to both. Earlier in the day we had a tussle over the words "m-u-g" and "w-a-t-e-r." Miss Sullivan had tried to impress it upon me that "m-u-g" is *mug* and "w-a-t-e-r" is *water,* but I persisted in confusing the two. In despair she had dropped the subject for the time, only to renew it at the first opportunity. I became impatient at her repeated attempts and, seizing the new doll, I dashed it upon the floor. I was keenly delighted when I felt the fragments of the broken doll at my feet. Neither sorrow nor regret followed my passionate outburst. I had not loved the doll. In the still, dark world in which I lived there was no strong sentiment of tenderness. I felt my teacher sweep the fragments to one side of the hearth, and I had a sense of satisfaction that the cause of my discomfort was removed. She brought me my hat, and I knew I was going out into the warm sunshine. This thought, if a wordless sensation may be called a thought, made me hop and skip with pleasure.

We walked down the path to the well-house, attracted by the fragrance of the honeysuckle with which it was covered. Someone was drawing water and my teacher placed my hand under the spout. As the cool stream gushed over one hand she spelled into the other the word *water,* first slowly, then rapidly. Suddenly I felt a misty consciousness as of something forgotten—a thrill of returning thought; and somehow the mystery of language was revealed to me. I knew then that "w-a-t-e-r" meant the wonderful cool something that was flowing over my hand. That living word awakened my soul, gave it light, hope, joy, set it free! There were barriers still, it is true, but barriers that could in time be swept away.

I left the well-house eager to learn. Everything had a name, and each name gave birth to a new thought. As we returned to the house, every object which I touched seemed to quiver with life. That was because I saw everything with the strange, new sight that had come to me. On entering the door I remembered the doll I had broken. I felt my way to the hearth and picked up the pieces. I tried vainly to put them together. Then my eyes filled with tears; for I realized what I had done, and for the first time I felt repentance and sorrow.

GO ON ➤

19 Another good name for this selection is—

    F "The Mystery of Language Revealed to Me."

    G "The Barriers Still Exist."

    H "I'll Never Learn to Communicate."

    J "How My Teacher Failed Me."

20 The word in quotation marks at the beginning of the selection was the first word—

    A Helen Keller spoke to Miss Sullivan.

    B Miss Sullivan spoke to Helen Keller.

    C Helen Keller spelled into Miss Sullivan's hand.

    D Miss Sullivan spelled into Helen Keller's hand.

21 There is enough information in this selection to show that—

    F it is very frustrating to be both blind and deaf.

    G children with bad manners are often punished.

    H people who take good care of their belongings keep them for a long time.

    J it is easier to learn new things when outside.

22 Which words did the author use to mean that language enabled her to understand the world around her?

    A "I flushed with childish pleasure."

    B "I persisted in confounding the two."

    C "My eyes filled with tears."

    D "I saw everything with the strange, new sight that had come to me."

23 Helen understood the true meaning of language when—

    F she walked into the well-house with Miss Sullivan.

    G she threw the doll down and broke it.

    H the word *water* was spelled into her hand.

    J she ran downstairs to her mother.

24 Why does Helen throw the doll on the floor and break it?

    A She doesn't like the doll anymore.

    B She is impatient with her lessons.

    C She wants to hurt her mother's feelings.

    D She wants to play outside.

25 If you wanted to know more about Helen Keller, you should—

    F look in the encyclopedia under "water."

    G read a book about famous people who are blind and deaf.

    H visit a doll museum.

    J ask a person with a well-house.

26 What is the first lesson Miss Sullivan tries to teach Helen Keller?

_____

_____

_____

_____

TEST TIP

Use the letter groups ABCD and FGHJ to make sure you are filling in the circle for the right question.

GO ON ➡

Answers

| 19 Ⓕ Ⓖ Ⓗ Ⓙ | 21 Ⓕ Ⓖ Ⓗ Ⓙ | 23 Ⓕ Ⓖ Ⓗ Ⓙ | 25 Ⓕ Ⓖ Ⓗ Ⓙ |
| 20 Ⓐ Ⓑ Ⓒ Ⓓ | 22 Ⓐ Ⓑ Ⓒ Ⓓ | 24 Ⓐ Ⓑ Ⓒ Ⓓ | |

Anyone Can Cook!

A cookbook of easy-to-make recipes that taste good and are good for you.

Just learning your way around the kitchen? Want some recipes that are easy to follow and quick to satisfy your sweet tooth? This cookbook is the one for you! And your parents will love it too! The recipes have been approved by the American Nutrition Association. The recipes are low-fat, high-taste.

Anyone Can Cook! comes with 200 recipes, full-color photographs of the finished products, and suggestions for setting the table for special occasions. The cookbook also helps you make grocery lists for the ingredients you will need for the recipes you want to try.

The cookbook has enough recipes and other ideas to help you prepare a completely balanced meal and surprise your family.

The cookbook will help you make and keep friends. Practice the recipes on your friends. They will be delighted! They'll want to help you with your creations.

For a limited time, we are offering *Anyone Can Cook!* for a fantastic price— $12.95 each or 2 for $20.95. And if you order within the next ten days, we will also send you *(FREE)* a complete set of measuring spoons and cups for each book ordered!!! Don't delay.

To order *Anyone Can Cook!*, just fill out the order form below. Please include a check.

Order Form

• Send me _____ copy(ies) of *Anyone Can Cook!*.
• Also send me _____ **FREE** set(s) of measuring spoons and cups.
• I have enclosed $___.___

Please send my cookbook(s) to:
Name_____
Address_____
City_____State_____Zip_____
Phone (including Area Code) _____

Cut out the order form and mail it to:
Anyone Can Cook!
1012 Cookie Dough Lane
Baking, PA 09876

Allow 4 to 5 weeks for delivery.

GO ON ➤

27 According to the advertisement, when you practice the recipes on your friends, they will—

    A want to help you make your creations.

    B not have room to eat dinner at home.

    C look for their favorite cookbook at home.

    D invite you over to try their favorite creations.

28 All of these are required on the order form except your—

    F identification number.

    G area code.

    H zip code.

    J address.

29 To get a free set of measuring spoons and cups you must—

    A pay for the cookbook with a check.

    B order within ten days.

    C fill out the order form.

    D buy two copies of the cookbook.

30 The ad tries to interest you in ordering the cookbook by—

    F making it sound like fun to make the recipes.

    G offering to send you a free copy.

    H showing you photographs from the book.

    J selling the book through the mail.

31 How long will it take to receive your cookbook?

    A 2 to 3 weeks

    B 3 to 4 weeks

    C 4 to 5 weeks

    D 5 to 6 weeks

32 Why would you buy the *Anyone Can Cook!* cookbook?

_____

_____

_____

_____

STOP

Answers

    27 Ⓐ Ⓑ Ⓒ Ⓓ   **28** Ⓕ Ⓖ Ⓗ Ⓙ   **29** Ⓐ Ⓑ Ⓒ Ⓓ   **30** Ⓕ Ⓖ Ⓗ Ⓙ   **31** Ⓐ Ⓑ Ⓒ Ⓓ

A sample question helps you to understand the type of question you will be asked in the test that follows.

Sample A

New From Old

Have you ever wondered what happens to the smashed-up cars you see in junkyards? Old plastic bumpers are recycled and used to make taillight housings for new cars. The metal from old cars are recycled and used for new parts on cars.

According to the selection, how are old plastic bumpers recycled?

A They are used to make trash cans.

B They are molded into milk cartons.

C They are used to make taillight housings for new cars.

D They are molded into playground equipment.

The Game of Water Polo

Do you like to swim and play basketball? Then water polo may be the game for you. Water polo originated in England in the 1870s. It is the oldest team sport played in the Olympics.

The object of water polo is to throw or push a ball into a goal that is about ten feet wide and three feet above the water level. The hollow rubber ball is similar to a volleyball. One point is awarded to the team scoring a goal. Water polo is played in pools about 65 feet wide and 98 feet long. The water depth is about 6 feet. As a result, players must be good swimmers.

A water polo team consists of seven players—a goalie and six field players. Both teams line up on opposite ends of a pool to start a game. A referee tosses the ball into the center of the pool and both teams race for the ball. The ball is moved by players passing it or swimming (also known as dribbling) with it. Field players can have only one hand on the ball at a time. The goalie is allowed to use both hands on the ball. Once a team has the ball, they must take a shot within 35 seconds or they lose possession of the ball.

1 **How is the ball moved in water polo?**

_____

_____

_____

_____

2 **You can conclude from the selection that —**

A few people play water polo.

B water polo is less dangerous than basketball.

C water polo is played in many countries in the world.

D fouls seldom occur in water polo.

GO ON

Answers

SA Ⓐ Ⓑ Ⓒ Ⓓ   2 Ⓐ Ⓑ Ⓒ Ⓓ

Soccer: From Past to Present

People have been playing soccer for hundreds of years. The ancient Chinese and Romans played a game similar to soccer. In London, children played a form of the game in the 1100s. The sport was introduced to the United States by immigrants in the early 1800s. Today soccer has become quite popular in the United States.

Soccer is played on a field just about the size of a football field. Goals, set at each end of the field, are the targets of the game. The players use a lightweight leather ball.

The rules of the game are fairly simple. Eleven players participate on each team. A team gains points each time a player kicks or hits the ball into the other team's goal. The only player on each team who is permitted to catch and throw the ball is the goalkeeper, who is assigned to protect the goal. The other players cannot catch the ball with their hands. They are allowed to kick it, bounce it off their heads, or block it with their bodies.

Soccer is one of the most popular games in the world. Many children begin playing soccer at an early age. High schools and colleges have soccer teams. Many countries have professional teams, whose players are paid for their full-time participation. They also have *semiprofessional* teams, whose members participate and are paid on a part-time basis.

One reason for the popularity of soccer is that it is relatively inexpensive to buy equipment for soccer teams. Perhaps the best thing about soccer is that players do not have to be a certain height, age, or weight. Soccer is a team sport that requires speed and cooperation. Soccer is a game for everyone.

3

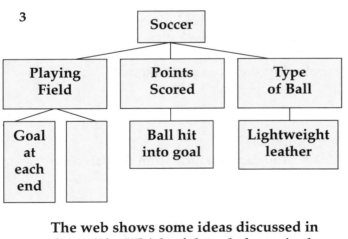

The web shows some ideas discussed in the article. Which of these belongs in the empty box?

F size of football field

G ancient Chinese and Roman

H bounce off heads

J certain height and age

4 **In this article, *semiprofessional* means—**

A paid on a full-time basis.

B not paid.

C not paid on a full-time basis.

D paid once a year.

5 **When was soccer first introduced to the United States?**

_____

_____

_____

GO ON

Answers

3 F G H J   4 A B C D

A Difficult Decision

Frieda and her mother lived in an apartment in New York City. Frieda had no brothers or sisters, and there were no children living nearby. Her best friend was a very old woman named Maria, who lived down the hall.

Maria's most prized possessions were a cat named Javier and an album of photographs from her family in Costa Rica. When she visited Maria, Frieda liked to study the album. Men in big mustaches and women in blouses *embroidered* with bright flowers, leaves, and native animals stared from the photographs. Maria would begin by talking about these long-dead relatives but would end by telling stories about the jaguars and parrots that lived in the rain forest near her family home. Frieda loved listening to these stories. She wanted to become a scientist to help save the rain forests from destruction.

One night as Frieda was doing her homework she heard sirens, and fire trucks suddenly appeared on the street below. The next thing she knew, a firefighter was pounding on their door. The top floors of the building were on fire. Frieda's mother shouted, "Grab your stereo and let's go!" Frieda had saved her money for a year to buy the stereo.

"Maria may need help," Frieda yelled as she raced down the hall to her friend's apartment. The door was standing open. The firefighters had already helped Maria and Javier downstairs. Frieda grabbed the heavy photo album from the shelf where Maria always kept it. Frieda hurried downstairs; smoke was filling the hallways.

Frieda's mother was anxiously waiting for her on the street. She saw that her daughter had saved only Maria's photo album. "I'm sorry about your stereo," Frieda's mother said.

"That's all right," Frieda said, "I made the right choice."

GO ON

6 According to the story, Frieda grabbed the photo album mainly because—

F she knew it meant a lot to Maria.

G she always wanted to own it.

H she did not see anything else to save.

J Maria told her to save it.

7 The story takes place in—

A Costa Rica.

B the country.

C a tropical rain forest.

D New York City.

8 Maria's most prized possessions were an album of photographs and a—

F collection of postcards.

G parrot from Brazil.

H a cat named Javier.

J a grandfather clock.

9 This selection is mostly about a girl who—

A fights a fire.

B saves her own favorite thing.

C knows how to save money.

D makes a difficult choice.

10 Why did Frieda want to become a scientist?

F to find a cure for cancer

G to become rich and famous

H to have a better life for herself and her mother

J to save the rain forests from destruction

11 Which statement is an opinion in the story?

A The top floors of the building were on fire.

B Frieda had no brothers or sisters.

C Frieda made the right choice.

D The firefighters helped Maria and Javier downstairs.

12 Which of these sentences would fit best at the end of this story?

F "My album cost more than the stereo."

G "I will give her a reward."

H "I am tired of my stereo."

J "I could never replace the album."

13 In order to answer question 12, the best thing to do is—

A reread the first sentence of each paragraph.

B think about the entire story.

C look for the words "stereo and album."

D analyze the picture that goes with the story.

14 In this story, *embroidered* means—

F decorated with fancy raised designs made with thread.

G dry-clean only.

H made in Costa Rica.

J smooth-textured, imported fabric.

15 Why did Frieda like to visit Maria?

_____

_____

_____

_____

GO ON ➡

Answers

6 Ⓕ Ⓖ Ⓗ Ⓙ   **8** Ⓕ Ⓖ Ⓗ Ⓙ   **10** Ⓕ Ⓖ Ⓗ Ⓙ   **12** Ⓕ Ⓖ Ⓗ Ⓙ   **14** Ⓕ Ⓖ Ⓗ Ⓙ

7 Ⓐ Ⓑ Ⓒ Ⓓ   **9** Ⓐ Ⓑ Ⓒ Ⓓ   **11** Ⓐ Ⓑ Ⓒ Ⓓ   **13** Ⓐ Ⓑ Ⓒ Ⓓ

DON'T BE LEFT IN THE DUST!

Make others eat *YOUR* dust.

Buy

DUST BUSTERS RUNNING SHOES.

Run faster! Run farther! Run forever!

Our shoes are the best running shoes on the market.
Chances are that 5 out of 6 runners wear our shoes.
You won't know for sure—those wearing our shoes can never be caught.

•**Dust Busters Running Shoes** come in more than 95 sizes—fit for ALL!

•Our shoes have all leather uppers and rubber soles.

•Our shoes offer extra support in the ankles and heels to prevent injury.

•Our shoes come with a money-back guarantee good for 5 years.

SO, WALK—NO, JOG—ON SECOND THOUGHT, RUN to your nearest shoe store.

You'll never eat dust again. We promise!

GO FOR THE GOLD!

No one wants to be second best.

Go for the GOLD! Buy *FINISH FIRST* running shoes.

■ We guarantee you will WIN EVERY RACE if you wear our shoes.

■ The design of our shoes is the LATEST SPORTS FASHION.
The shoes are streamlined to avoid any extra weight on your feet.
This lightens the load giving you the EDGE YOU NEED TO WIN!

■ The soles of the shoes have ridges that help your feet grip the track. NO MORE SLIPPING.

■ Air holes, scientifically positioned LET YOUR FEET BREATHE.

KEEP AHEAD OF THE PACK.

GO FOR THE GOLD!

GO ON ➤

16 You would most likely find these ads in a—

    A hardware store sales flyer.

    B sports magazine.

    C telephone book.

    D road atlas.

17 The Finish First ad stresses the shoes'—

    F streamlined design.

    G variety of sizes.

    H rubber soles.

    J leather uppers.

18 In the Finish First ad, the words "Go for the GOLD!" mean—

    A look for money.

    B race to win.

    C choose your color.

    D find a partner.

19 What material is used to make the upper part of the Dust Busters shoe?

    F rubber

    G leather

    H plastic

    J The ad does not say.

20 Which of these is an opinion in the Dust Busters shoe ad?

    A Dust Busters running shoes come in more than 95 sizes.

    B Our shoes come with a money-back guarantee good for 5 years.

    C Our shoes offer extra support in the ankles and heels.

    D Our shoes are the best running shoes on the market.

21 Why is there extra support in the ankles and heels?

_____

_____

_____

_____

TEST TIP

These questions ask you to find information in two different advertisements. Make sure that you look for information in the correct ad. For example, questions 17 and 18 focus on the ad at the bottom of the page. Questions 19, 20, and 21 focus on the ad at the top of the page.

GO ON ➡

Answers
16 Ⓐ Ⓑ Ⓒ Ⓓ   **17** Ⓕ Ⓖ Ⓗ Ⓙ   **18** Ⓐ Ⓑ Ⓒ Ⓓ   **19** Ⓕ Ⓖ Ⓗ Ⓙ   **20** Ⓐ Ⓑ Ⓒ Ⓓ

A Man of Many Talents

Thomas Jefferson was the third President of the United States. He is also well-known for many other achievements. He was a writer, an architect, an inventor, and a music lover.

Jefferson was involved in government for many years before he became President. He was the governor of Virginia, a U.S. congressman, the minister to France, and the Vice President of the United States. He helped to write the Declaration of Independence, the Constitution, and the Bill of Rights.

Jefferson served as President from 1801 to 1809. Many changes occurred during his time in office. He tried to keep government simple and began to reduce government spending and to cut taxes. In 1803, the United States bought the Louisiana Territory from France. This territory nearly doubled the size of the country. He asked two army officers and explorers, Lewis and Clark, to travel through the new land and find out all about it.

During and after his time as President, Jefferson followed his other interests. He designed Monticello, his Virginia home, and the Virginia Capitol building. He invented the swivel chair and the dumbwaiter.

Jefferson contributed greatly to the development of the University of Virginia. In addition to designing the university buildings, he planned the courses, hired the teachers, and selected the books. The university opened its doors in 1825.

Jefferson was a man of many talents, and he used his talents to improve life for many people in his country.

22 This article is most like—

F a folk tale.

G historical fiction.

H a biography.

J fantasy.

23 There is enough information in this article to show that Thomas Jefferson—

A was a good musician and a talented singer.

B paid too much money for the Louisiana Territory.

C greatly contributed to his country and its people.

D increased government spending and increased taxes.

24 To learn more about Thomas Jefferson you should—

F visit Louisiana.

G look in a book about Presidents of the United States.

H go to a university in France.

J look in the dictionary under "architect."

25 What are some of the things Thomas Jefferson is known for?

_____

_____

_____

_____

STOP

DETERMINING WORD MEANINGS

Directions: Darken the circle, or write the answer, for the word or group of words that has the same or almost the same meaning as the underlined word.

> **TRY THIS**
>
> Choose your answer carefully. The other choices may seem correct. Be sure to think about the meaning of the underlined word.

Sample A

Collapsed means—

A fell down   C sold out

B went up   D blew up

THINK IT THROUGH The correct answer is A. Collapsed means "fell down." Collapsed does not mean "went up," "sold out," or "blew up."

 STOP

---

1 To grieve is to—

A donate   C celebrate

B wonder   D mourn

2 To be vertical is to be—

F leaning

G straight up and down

H straight across

J broken

3 Something that is frequent is—

A occurring seldom

B a holiday

C happening often

D sad

4 To evaluate is to—

F judge   H destroy

G honor   J create

5 To capsize is to—

A load   C overturn

B get out of   D launch

6 An image is—

F an intention   H a subject

G a picture   J a fact

7 Final is the same as—

A last   C important

B first   D most exciting

8 What is another word that means the same as accused?

_____

_____

_____

_____

_____

STOP

Answers

SA Ⓐ Ⓑ Ⓒ Ⓓ   2 Ⓕ Ⓖ Ⓗ Ⓙ   4 Ⓕ Ⓖ Ⓗ Ⓙ   6 Ⓕ Ⓖ Ⓗ Ⓙ

1 Ⓐ Ⓑ Ⓒ Ⓓ   3 Ⓐ Ⓑ Ⓒ Ⓓ   5 Ⓐ Ⓑ Ⓒ Ⓓ   7 Ⓐ Ⓑ Ⓒ Ⓓ

Directions: Darken the circle, or write the answer, for the sentence that uses the underlined word in the same way as the sentence in the box.

TRY THIS Read the sentence in the box. Decide what the underlined word means. Then find the sentence in which the underlined word has the same meaning.

Sample A

> He cut his <u>head</u> when he fell.

In which sentence does <u>head</u> have the same meaning as it does in the sentence above?

A Stand at the <u>head</u> of the stairs.

B She laid her <u>head</u> on her arm.

C Did you buy a <u>head</u> of lettuce?

D She owns forty <u>head</u> of cattle.

THINK IT THROUGH The correct answer is <u>B</u>. In choice <u>B</u> and in the sentence in the box, <u>head</u> means "a part of your body."

STOP

1

> I wrote a <u>check</u> for the groceries.

In which sentence does <u>check</u> have the same meaning as it does in the sentence above?

A Melissa had to <u>check</u> her urge to laugh during the concert.

B The teacher will <u>check</u> the answers.

C Mom paid my fee with a <u>check</u>.

D You need to <u>check</u> your calculations.

2

> Ann trimmed the collar with <u>lace</u>.

In which sentence does <u>lace</u> have the same meaning as it does in the sentence above?

F The little boy tries to <u>lace</u> his shoes.

G Marissa bought a yard of <u>lace</u> for the dress she is making.

H They stopped the game while the girl tied her shoe <u>lace</u>.

J Dad will <u>lace</u> the drink with green food coloring.

3

> Each hall <u>monitor</u> is required to wear a name tag.

In which sentence does <u>monitor</u> have the same meaning as it does in the sentence above?

A Can you see the computer <u>monitor</u>?

B A <u>monitor</u> in the hospital room kept track of his heartbeats.

C The teacher will <u>monitor</u> the student's progress and report it to the parents.

D Is she the classroom <u>monitor</u> today?

4

> She used a <u>tissue</u> to dry her eyes.

Use <u>tissue</u> in a sentence where it has the same meaning as in the sentence above.

_____

_____

_____

_____

STOP

Answers

SA Ⓐ Ⓑ Ⓒ Ⓓ **1** Ⓐ Ⓑ Ⓒ Ⓓ **2** Ⓕ Ⓖ Ⓗ Ⓙ **3** Ⓐ Ⓑ Ⓒ Ⓓ

Directions: Darken the circle, or write the answer, for the word or words that give the meaning of the underlined word.

> **TRY THIS**
>
> Read the first sentence carefully. Look for clue words in the sentence. Then use each answer choice in place of the underlined word. Be sure that your answer and the underlined word have the same meaning.

Sample A

We were surprised by the principal's unexpected announcement. Unexpected means—

A long

B planned

C sudden

D last

> **THINK IT THROUGH**
>
> The correct answer is C. Unexpected means "sudden." The clue word is "surprised."

 STOP

---

1 There is some kind of obstacle blocking the highway. Obstacle means—

A a truck

B a traffic jam

C an accident

D a barrier

2 Events that are organized rarely have any last–minute problems. Organized means—

F in order

G dissolved

H exciting

J educational

3 Our food supplies were dwindling steadily. Dwindling means—

A increasing

B rotting

C shrinking

D improving

4 The people were eager for the opera to commence. Commence means—

F conclude

G begin

H continue

J close

5 When metal rusts it becomes tarnished. Tarnished means—

A brittle

B soft

C strengthened

D discolored

6 The reckless driver finally came to a stop when he crashed into the building. What does reckless mean?

_____

_____

_____

_____

STOP

Answers

SA Ⓐ Ⓑ Ⓒ Ⓓ   **2** Ⓕ Ⓖ Ⓗ Ⓙ   **4** Ⓕ Ⓖ Ⓗ Ⓙ

1 Ⓐ Ⓑ Ⓒ Ⓓ   **3** Ⓐ Ⓑ Ⓒ Ⓓ   **5** Ⓐ Ⓑ Ⓒ Ⓓ

Sample A

To astonish is to—

A decrease

B calm

C awaken

D amaze

STOP

For questions 1–8, darken the circle for the word or group of words that has the same or almost the same meaning as the underlined word.

1 **Abruptly means—**

A suddenly

B slowly

C tearfully

D angrily

2 **Sincerely means—**

F softly

G honestly

H angrily

J loudly

3 **To neglect is to—**

A ignore

B mold

C restrain

D behold

4 **To be incomplete is to be—**

F incorrect

G unfinished

H final

J difficult

5 **A conversation is a—**

A smile

B quality

C discussion

D solution

6 **To expand means to—**

F tumble

G divide

H assign

J swell

7 **Triple means—**

A three times

B double

C six times

D four times

8 **To be urgent is to be—**

F ideal

G simple

H important

J abundant

Write your answer for the following question:

9 **If something is fake, it's—**

_____

_____

_____

_____

GO ON

Answers

SA Ⓐ Ⓑ Ⓒ Ⓓ   **2** Ⓕ Ⓖ Ⓗ Ⓙ   **4** Ⓕ Ⓖ Ⓗ Ⓙ   **6** Ⓕ Ⓖ Ⓗ Ⓙ   **8** Ⓕ Ⓖ Ⓗ Ⓙ

1 Ⓐ Ⓑ Ⓒ Ⓓ   **3** Ⓐ Ⓑ Ⓒ Ⓓ   **5** Ⓐ Ⓑ Ⓒ Ⓓ   **7** Ⓐ Ⓑ Ⓒ Ⓓ

Sample B

> Don't try to <u>jam</u> the book into that little space on the shelf.

In which sentence does jam have the same meaning as it does in the sentence above?

A Aunt Harriet's homemade peach <u>jam</u> is delicious.

B We won't <u>jam</u> too many people into the elevator.

C He had to <u>jam</u> on the brakes to avoid a crash.

D Be careful not to <u>jam</u> your finger playing ball.

STOP

For questions 10–13, darken the circle for the sentence that uses the underlined word in the same way as the sentence in the box.

10

> Meredith operates a <u>crane</u> at the shipyard.

In which sentence does crane have the same meaning as it does in the sentence above?

A The <u>crane</u> lifted huge crates.

B The photographer approached the young <u>crane</u> at the water's edge.

C Don't <u>crane</u> your neck to see the film.

D We want to see the <u>crane</u> at the zoo.

11

> The <u>stock</u> market fell yesterday in light trading.

In which sentence does stock have the same meaning as it does in the sentence above?

F They will <u>stock</u> the river with trout.

G Chicken <u>stock</u> is the base for many soups.

H She bought some <u>stock</u> as an investment.

J You need to <u>stock</u> up on canned goods.

12

> Turn up the <u>volume</u> so we can hear the announcement.

In which sentence does volume have the same meaning as it does in the sentence above?

A The <u>volume</u> of the container was too small and the water spilled out.

B Which <u>volume</u> of the encyclopedia are you using?

C This is just one <u>volume</u> that the library owns.

D Play the CD player at full <u>volume</u>.

13

> Don't make a <u>rash</u> decision that you might regret later.

In which sentence does rash have the same meaning as it does in the sentence above?

F How did you get that <u>rash</u> on your arm?

G Mandy made a <u>rash</u> judgment about the new girl in her class.

H The store received a <u>rash</u> of complaints from the customers.

J A side effect of the medicine is a <u>rash</u>.

Write your answer for the following question:

14

> I thought her attitude was very <u>negative</u>.

Use <u>negative</u> in a sentence where it has a different meaning than in the sentence above.

_____

_____

_____

_____

GO ON →

Answers

SB ⒶⒷⒸⒹ   10 ⒶⒷⒸⒹ   11 ⒻⒼⒽⒿ   12 ⒶⒷⒸⒹ   13 ⒻⒼⒽⒿ

Sample C

Will you put your dirty clothes in the hamper? Hamper means—

A   room

B   bag

C   basket

D   washer

STOP

For questions 15–21, darken the circle for the word or words that give the meaning of the underlined word.

15   She bought fresh produce to use in her meal. Produce means—

A   yield

B   vegetables

C   make

D   show

16   It is customary for politicians running for office to make promises. Customary means—

F   unusual

G   unexpected

H   uncommon

J   usual

17   Ann's mother was excited about getting a job promotion. Promotion means—

A   demotion

B   description

C   advancement

D   notice

18   The triumphant team paraded around the field after the game. Triumphant means—

F   victorious

G   solemn

H   sad

J   defeated

19   Large-scale commerce is necessary for economic development. Commerce means—

A   conversation

B   buying

C   selling

D   business

20   They went to a health resort for the weekend. Resort means—

F   spa

G   chance

H   hope

J   store

21   A computer software company will occupy the top floor. Occupy means—

A   inhabit

B   lease

C   inherit

D   analyze

Write your answer for the following question:

22   You should trace the figure on your paper. What is another word that means figure?

_____

_____

_____

_____

STOP

Answers

SC (A) (B) (C) (D)   16 (F) (G) (H) (J)   18 (F) (G) (H) (J)   20 (F) (G) (H) (J)
15 (A) (B) (C) (D)   17 (A) (B) (C) (D)   19 (A) (B) (C) (D)   21 (A) (B) (C) (D)

MATH PROBLEM-SOLVING PLAN

THE PROBLEM-SOLVING PLAN

When solving math problems follow these steps:

STEP 1: WHAT IS THE QUESTION/GOAL?

Decide what must be found. This information is usually presented in the form of a question.

STEP 2: FIND THE FACTS

Locate the factual information in three different ways:
  A. KEY FACTS are the facts you need to solve the problem.
  B. FACTS YOU DON'T NEED are those facts that are not necessary for solving the problem.
  C. ARE MORE FACTS NEEDED? Decide if you have enough information to solve the problem.

STEP 3: SELECT A STRATEGY

Decide what strategies you might use, how you will use them, and then estimate what your answer will be. If one strategy doesn't help you to solve the problem, try another.

STEP 4: SOLVE

Apply the strategy according to your plan. Use an operation if necessary, and clearly indicate your answer.

STEP 5: DOES YOUR RESPONSE MAKE SENSE?

Check to make sure that your answer makes sense. Use estimation or approximation strategies.

Directions: Use the problem-solving plan to solve this math problem.

PROBLEM/QUESTION:

Joey worked at a camp for the summer. He worked 6 hours each day for 42 days and earned $12 each day. If Joey was paid $3.00 for each hour he worked instead of $12 per day, would he earn more or less money?

STEP 1: WHAT IS THE QUESTION/GOAL?

_____

_____

_____

STEP 2: FIND THE FACTS

_____

_____

_____

STEP 3: SELECT A STRATEGY

_____

_____

_____

STEP 4: SOLVE

_____

_____

_____

STEP 5: DOES YOUR RESPONSE MAKE SENSE?

_____

_____

_____

_____

_____

Directions: Use the problem-solving plan to solve this math problem.

PROBLEM/QUESTION:

Rosa walked to her friend's house, which was 12 blocks away. It took her 20 minutes. The return trip took an extra 10 minutes because she stopped for ice cream, which added 4 blocks to her trip. Draw a map that shows her trip and indicate the time it took.

STEP 1: WHAT IS THE QUESTION/GOAL?

_____

_____

_____

STEP 2: FIND THE FACTS

_____

_____

_____

STEP 3: SELECT A STRATEGY

_____

_____

_____

STEP 4: SOLVE

STEP 5: DOES YOUR RESPONSE MAKE SENSE?

_____

_____

_____

_____

MATH PROBLEM SOLVING

UNDERSTANDING NUMBER RELATIONSHIPS

Directions: Darken the circle for the correct answer, or write it in the space provided.

> **TRY THIS**
>
> Read each question carefully. Decide the best method to solve the problem. Make sure you understand the question that is being asked.

Sample A

Marla's most recent recorded times for the 100-meter dash were: 12.1 seconds, 12.08 seconds, 12.2 seconds, and 12.33 seconds. Which shows the times listed from fastest to slowest?

A   12.2, 12.1, 12.08, 12.33

B   12.33, 12.1, 12.08, 12.2

C   12.08, 12.1, 12.2, 12.33

D   12.08, 12.33, 12.2, 12.1

> **THINK IT THROUGH**
>
> The correct answer is <u>C</u>. First, look at the number in the tenths column. Next, look at the hundredths column.

STOP

---

1   Each square represents 0.01. What decimal number is shown below?

A   1.56   C   15.6

B   16.6   D   1.66

2   Which decimal shows the part of the figure that is shaded?

F   0.29

G   0.28

H   0.35

J   0.72

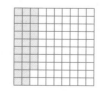

3   Write $\frac{38}{6}$ as a mixed number.

_____

_____

4

Trail mix (Makes six 8 oz. servings)	
2 cups raisins	$\frac{1}{2}$ cup walnuts
$2\frac{1}{2}$ cups peanuts	$1\frac{3}{4}$ cups dried fruit
$\frac{1}{2}$ cup sunflower seeds	$\frac{1}{4}$ cup shredded coconut

Which ingredient is used in the greatest quantity in the trail mix?

A   raisins   C   peanuts

B   coconut   D   dried fruit

5   How is 2,401,226,000 written in words?

F   two million, four hundred one thousand, two hundred twenty-six

G   two billion, four hundred one million, two hundred twenty-six thousand

H   two billion, four hundred ten million, two hundred twenty six thousand

J   twenty-four billion, one million, two hundred twenty-six thousand

STOP

Answers

SA Ⓐ Ⓑ Ⓒ Ⓓ   **2** Ⓕ Ⓖ Ⓗ Ⓙ   **5** Ⓕ Ⓖ Ⓗ Ⓙ

1 Ⓐ Ⓑ Ⓒ Ⓓ   **4** Ⓐ Ⓑ Ⓒ Ⓓ

Directions: Darken the circle for the correct answer, or write it in the space provided.

> **TRY THIS**
> Read each question carefully. Work the problem on scratch paper. Try each answer choice in the problem before you choose your answer.

Sample A

What number is shown here?

200,000 + 50,000 + 70 + 8

A 25,078

B 205,708

C 250,078

D 20,578

THINK IT THROUGH The correct answer is <u>C</u>. Add up the numbers as shown to get the answer.

$$\begin{array}{r} 200,000 \\ 50,000 \\ 70 \\ + \quad 8 \end{array}$$

 STOP

---

1 What is the value of the 6 in 45.261?

A 6 tenths

B 6 hundredths

C 6 thousandths

D 6 tens

2 What is the minimum number of cookies Margie would have to bake in order to divide the cookies equally among her 6 neighborhood friends with none left over or among her 24 classmates with none left over?

F 12

G 16

H 24

J 30

3 What is the greatest common factor of 40 and 24?

A 4

B 8

C 12

D 48

4 These beads represent the number 125,306,987. What place value is represented with three beads?

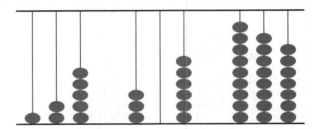

F thousands

G ten thousands

H hundred thousands

J millions

5 An airport runway measures 2,300 meters long. How long will the runway be if it is increased by 2,000 meters?

_____
_____
_____
_____

STOP

Answers
SA Ⓐ Ⓑ Ⓒ Ⓓ   1 Ⓐ Ⓑ Ⓒ Ⓓ   2 Ⓕ Ⓖ Ⓗ Ⓙ   3 Ⓐ Ⓑ Ⓒ Ⓓ   4 Ⓕ Ⓖ Ⓗ Ⓙ

Directions: Darken the circle for the correct answer, or write it in the space provided.

> **TRY THIS**
>
> Check your work by making sure both sides of an equation are equal values. Try using all the answer choices in the problem.

Sample A

If $y + 13 = 25$, what number replaces the y to make the sentence true?

A 6   C 15

B 12   D 38

> **THINK IT THROUGH**
>
> The correct answer is <u>B</u>. Change + 13 to − 13 and move it to the right side of the equation. Subtract from 25 to get the value of y.

STOP

---

1 If $x + 14 = 33$, what is the value of x?

A 11

B 15

C 19

D 47

2 Which of the following number sentences is related to $20 \div 4 = \square$?

F $4 \times \square = 20$

G $4 \times 20 = \square$

H $20 - 4 = \square$

J $4 \div \square = 20$

3 Which expression shows that 12 less than x equals 40?

A $x - 12 = 40$

B $12 - x = 40$

C $12 \div x = 40$

D $40 - 12 \leq x$

4 Which number sentence is related to $8 + 3 = 11$?

F $8 \times 3 = 24$ H $5 + 6 = 11$

G $11 - 3 = 8$ J $8 - 11 = 3$

5 There are 4 sixth-grade teachers at Emerson Middle School. Each teacher has 23 students. These teachers will give 2 worksheets to every student. Which number sentence would be used to find W, the total number of worksheets needed?

A $(23 \div 4) + 2 = W$

B $2 + (4 + 23) = W$

C $(4 \times 23) \times 2 = W$

D $23 + (2 \times 4) = W$

6 Each rack at the bowling alley holds 18 bowling balls. There are 6 racks on each of 3 walls. Write a number sentence to find B, the total number of bowling balls that the racks can hold.

_____

_____

_____

_____

STOP

Answers

SA Ⓐ Ⓑ Ⓒ Ⓓ   **2** Ⓕ Ⓖ Ⓗ Ⓙ   **4** Ⓕ Ⓖ Ⓗ Ⓙ

 1 Ⓐ Ⓑ Ⓒ Ⓓ   **3** Ⓐ Ⓑ Ⓒ Ⓓ   **5** Ⓐ Ⓑ Ⓒ Ⓓ

Directions: Darken the circle for the correct answer, or write it in the space provided.

> **TRY THIS**
>
> Read each problem carefully. Look for key words or numbers in the question that tell you what to look for in the graph or table.

Sample A

Each letter in the word *mathematics* is written on a card and placed in a box. If Keiko chooses a card without looking, what is the probability that she will choose the letter *t*.

A $\frac{1}{11}$ C $\frac{3}{11}$

B $\frac{2}{11}$ D $\frac{4}{11}$

> **THINK IT THROUGH**
>
> The correct answer is B. There are 2 Ts in the word mathematics, which contains 11 letters. The probability of choosing the letter T is expressed as $\frac{2}{11}$.

STOP

THEME TOPICS

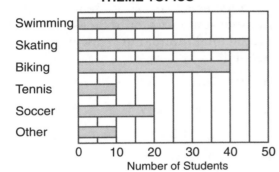

1. How many more students wrote about biking than about tennis?

    A   30 students   C   40 students

    B   50 students   D   10 students

2. The school cafeteria sells sandwiches on whole wheat or white bread, made with turkey, beef, chicken, or tuna fish. How many different sandwich combinations are possible?

    F   2   H   6

    G   4   J   8

3. Hal planned to buy a new shirt. The store had red, white, and blue shirts. Each color was available with or without a pocket, in short sleeves or long sleeves. How many different combinations did Hal have to choose from?

    A   7   C   12

    B   10   D   14

4. It is Tonya's turn in a board game she is playing with her family. Why is there a greater probability that Tonya will go back 2 spaces than move ahead 2 spaces?

    _____
    _____
    _____
    _____
    _____
    _____
    _____
    _____

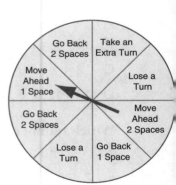

GO ON

Answers

SA Ⓐ Ⓑ Ⓒ Ⓓ   **1** Ⓐ Ⓑ Ⓒ Ⓓ   **2** Ⓕ Ⓖ Ⓗ Ⓙ   **3** Ⓐ Ⓑ Ⓒ Ⓓ

5 According to the graph, what was the average number of cars sold by the four dealerships in one year?

Number of Cars Sold in 1 Year

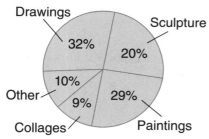

Car City	
Downtown Motors	
Smith's Car Emporium	
Carver Car Sales	

Each 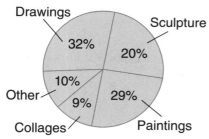=100 cars

F 445

G 475

H 525

J 1,900

The students in Mrs. O'Brien's art classes completed their projects last month. The graph shows the kinds of projects the students made. Use the graph to answer questions 6 and 7.

Drawings 32%
Sculpture 20%
Other 10%
Collages 9%
Paintings 29%

6 If 500 art projects were completed, how many were drawings?

A 32   **C** 468

B 160   **D** 532

7 What fraction of the projects was made up of sculpture?

F $\frac{1}{20}$ **H** $\frac{1}{10}$

G $\frac{1}{16}$ **J** $\frac{1}{5}$

8 According to the table shown here, which two cities together receive a total of 72 inches of rain per year?

Texas City	Rain Per Year
Austin	30 inches
Dallas	35 inches
El Paso	8 inches
Fort Worth	35 inches
Houston	42 inches

A Austin and Dallas

B Dallas and El Paso

C Fort Worth and Dallas

D Austin and Houston

9 This chart shows the number of days spent in each city by the Jones family on their vacation to Florida. In what cities did the Jones family spend 4 or more days?

City	Number of Days
Miami	|||
Ft. Lauderdale	||
Orlando	⊮⊮ |||
Tampa	||||
Naples	⊮⊮

_____
_____
_____
_____
_____
_____

STOP

Answers

5 Ⓕ Ⓖ Ⓗ Ⓙ   **6** Ⓐ Ⓑ Ⓒ Ⓓ   **7** Ⓕ Ⓖ Ⓗ Ⓙ   **8** Ⓐ Ⓑ Ⓒ Ⓓ

Directions: Darken the circle for the correct answer, or write the answer in the space provided.

TRY THIS	Read each question carefully. Use the objects shown to help you answer each question. Remember that perimeter is the measurement around the outside, while area is the measurement of the inside of a space.

Sample A

Which line segment is a radius of this circle?

A $\overline{AC}$

B $\overline{PB}$

C $\overline{AB}$

D $\overline{CA}$

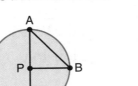

THINK IT THROUGH	The correct answer is <u>B</u>. A radius is a line segment that connects the center with the outside of the circle.

STOP

---

1 In the circle shown here, C is the center. How long is the diameter of the circle?

A 8 inches

B 16 inches

C 3.14 inches

D 4 inches

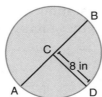

2 Name the coordinates of point B on the grid shown here.

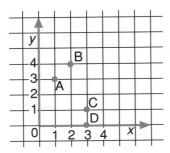

F (1, 3)

G (2, 4)

H (3, 1)

J (4, 2)

3 Which slice of pie forms a right angle?

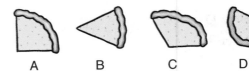

A A

B B

C C

D D

4 Which figure does <u>not</u> show a line of symmetry?

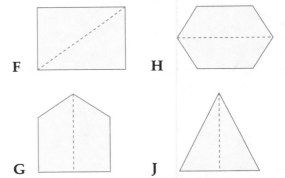

GO ON

Answers

SA (A) (B) (C) (D)　　**1** (A) (B) (C) (D)　　**2** (F) (G) (H) (J)　　**3** (A) (B) (C) (D)　　**4** (F) (G) (H) (J)

5 Use your inch ruler to help you answer this question. What is the perimeter of the triangle shown here?

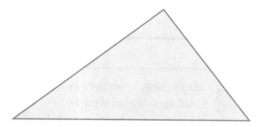

A $4\frac{1}{2}$ in.

B $5\frac{3}{4}$ in.

C 6 in.

D 7 in.

6 Use your centimeter ruler to help you answer this question. Which figure shown here has an area of 6 cm²?

F

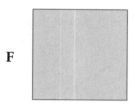

G

H

J

7 Which figure shows the result of rotating the tennis shoe 180°?

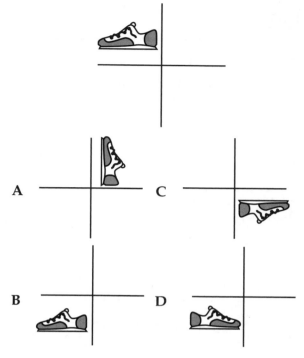

8 Which coordinates represent the location of Midtown University on the map?

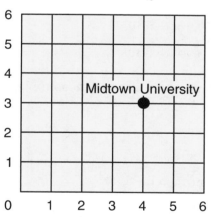

_____

_____

_____

_____

_____

_____

STOP

Directions: Darken the circle for the correct answer, or write the answer in the space provided.

> **TRY THIS**
>
> Read each question carefully. Use the objects shown or named to help you answer each question.

Sample A

Which unit of measurement is best to use to describe the weight of an egg?

A ounces   **C** inches

B liters   **D** yards

> **THINK IT THROUGH**
>
> The correct answer is <u>A</u>. Liters are used to measure capacity, and inches and yards are units of linear measurement.

---

1 What is the area of the shaded section of this figure?

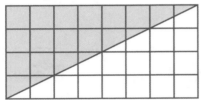

A 20 square units

B 16 square units

C 15 square units

D 12 square units

2 What units are used to measure length on a ruler?

F degrees

G kilograms

H centimeters

J liters

> ### TEST TIP
>
> Pay attention to units listed in answer choices. A choice is incorrect if it uses the wrong units.

3 Use your inch ruler and the map to help you answer the question. What is the actual distance between the two universities?

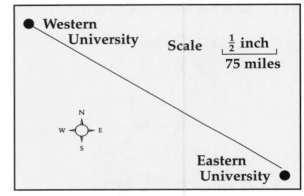

A 150 miles   **C** 450 miles

B 300 miles   **D** 600 miles

4 Lilly measured the driveway from the street to the garage. She measured 30 feet. How would you change that measurement to inches?

_____

_____

_____

_____

_____

_____

GO ON

Answers

SA Ⓐ Ⓑ Ⓒ Ⓓ   **1** Ⓐ Ⓑ Ⓒ Ⓓ   **2** Ⓕ Ⓖ Ⓗ Ⓙ   **3** Ⓐ Ⓑ Ⓒ Ⓓ

5 The Marsh family rode their bikes to the state park and back last Saturday. It took 1 hour 40 minutes to ride to the park and 1 hour 55 minutes to ride back home. How long was their trip altogether?

F   4 hours

G   3 hours 35 minutes

H   3 hours 25 minutes

J   2 hours 35 minutes

6 The parade began at 8:45 A.M. If it lasted 2 hours and 30 minutes, at what time did the parade end?

A   10:45 A.M.

B   10:30 A.M.

C   11:15 A.M.

D   11:45 A.M.

7 How many centimeters are there between the two trees?

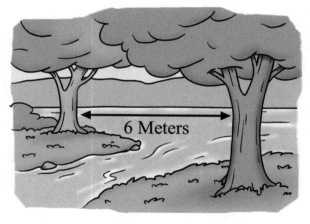

6 Meters

F   6,000 centimeters

G   600 centimeters

H   60 centimeters

J   0.06 centimeters

8 Which of these equals the least amount?

A   4 cups   C   2 quarts

B   3 pints   D   1 gallon

9 A football player kicked a football 45.5 feet. How long was the kick in yards and inches?

F   2 yards 13 inches

G   3 yards 9 inches

H   12 yards 3 inches

J   15 yards 6 inches

10 The testing session began at 8:45 A.M. The time limit on the first test was 35 minutes and the time limit on the second test was 40 minutes. There was a 10-minute break between the tests. At what time did the session end?

A   10:00 A.M.   C   10:25 A.M.

B   10:10 A.M.   D   11:05 A.M.

11 How would you compute the actual distance from the nautical museum to the lighthouse?

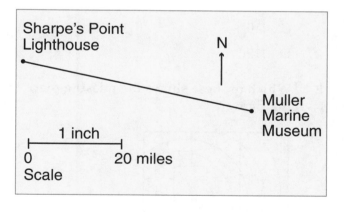

_____

_____

_____

_____

_____

_____

STOP

Answers

5 Ⓕ Ⓖ Ⓗ Ⓙ   **7** Ⓕ Ⓖ Ⓗ Ⓙ   **9** Ⓕ Ⓖ Ⓗ Ⓙ

6 Ⓐ Ⓑ Ⓒ Ⓓ   **8** Ⓐ Ⓑ Ⓒ Ⓓ   **10** Ⓐ Ⓑ Ⓒ Ⓓ

Directions: Darken the circle for the correct answer, or write the answer in the space provided.

TRY THIS

Read each problem carefully. Try to determine the nature of the pattern or the relationship in the problem. Try using all the answer choices in the problem. Then choose the answer that you think best answers the question.

Sample A

A special machine multiplies any number entered into it by a secret number. The table shows how numbers are changed. Which number is missing from the table?

Original number	6	4	10
New number		20	50

A 50   C 30

B 40   D 15

THINK IT THROUGH

The correct answer is <u>C</u>. Each original number is multiplied by 5 to get the new number.

STOP

---

1 Look at the pattern shown here. What number is missing from this number pattern?

101, 105, _____, 113, 117

A 107

B 109

C 110

D 112

2 Which of these shows the missing piece in the figure?

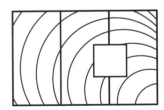

F   H

G   J

3 How many stars would be in the eleventh figure if this pattern continues?

A 25   C 35

B 28   D 42

4 How many dots will form the seventh figure in this pattern?

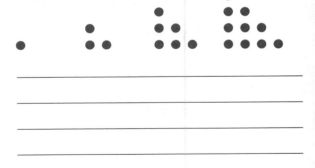

_____

_____

_____

_____

_____

_____

STOP

Answers

SA Ⓐ Ⓑ Ⓒ Ⓓ   **1** Ⓐ Ⓑ Ⓒ Ⓓ   **2** Ⓕ Ⓖ Ⓗ Ⓙ   **3** Ⓐ Ⓑ Ⓒ Ⓓ

Directions: Darken the circle for the correct answer, or write it in the space provided.

TRY THIS Round numbers when you estimate. For some problems, there are no exact answers. Then you should take your best guess. You can check your answer by using the numbers given in the problem.

Sample A

The closest estimate of the cost of 22 packs of gum is—

1 pack = 47¢

A $0.10

B $1.00

C $10.00

D $100.00

THINK IT THROUGH The correct answer is <u>C</u>. 22 is rounded to 20, and 47¢ is rounded to 50¢ × 20 = <u>$10.00</u>

STOP

1 During a recent census, the population in Valley View was 6,488. This is an increase of 843 since the last census. What is the best estimate of how many people were counted in the previous census?

A 5,700   C 7,300

B 6,800   D 7,500

2 Lila's restaurant bought 28 cases of canned tomatoes. There are 48 cans of tomatoes in each case. What is the best estimate of the total number of cans of tomatoes that the restaurant bought?

F 600   H 1,500

G 1,000   J 4,000

3 The distance from Chicago to Atlanta is 708 miles. The distance from Dallas to Atlanta is 822 miles. About how much farther is Dallas from Atlanta than Chicago is from Atlanta?

A 100 miles   C 800 miles

B 700 miles   D 1,500 miles

4 Mrs. McMurphy set up trust funds for her 4 children. If she had $22,000 to divide evenly, what is the best estimate of the amount of money in each of the 4 trust funds?

F $10,000   H $7,000

G $8,000   J $5,000

5 Mr. Petrovich has 11,200 coins in his collection. He plans to add another 1,600 to his collection this year. What is the best estimate of the number of coins Mr. Petrovich will have at the end of this year?

A 9,000 coins   C 11,000 coins

B 10,000 coins   D 13,000 coins

STOP

Answers

SA Ⓐ Ⓑ Ⓒ Ⓓ   2 Ⓕ Ⓖ Ⓗ Ⓙ   4 Ⓕ Ⓖ Ⓗ Ⓙ

1 Ⓐ Ⓑ Ⓒ Ⓓ   3 Ⓐ Ⓑ Ⓒ Ⓓ   5 Ⓐ Ⓑ Ⓒ Ⓓ

Directions: Darken the circle for the correct answer, or write the answer in the space provided.

TRY THIS

Study the words in each problem carefully. Think about what each problem is asking, then decide what you have to do to find the answer.

Sample A

Marie works in a bakery. She made 90 fewer bagels on Sunday than she did on Saturday. She made 70 more bagels on Monday than she did on Sunday. If she made 340 bagels on Monday, how many bagels did she make on Saturday?

A 160

B 320

C 360

D 380

THINK IT THROUGH

The correct answer is <u>C</u>. Marie made 340 bagels Monday, 270 Sunday, and <u>360</u> on Saturday.

STOP

---

1 Martha is training for a marathon. On Monday she ran 6 miles. On Tuesday she ran 8 miles. On Wednesday she ran 10 miles. On Thursday she ran 12 miles. If this pattern continues, how many miles will she run on Sunday?

A 14 miles   C 18 miles

B 16 miles   D 20 miles

2 If 1 prism weighs the same as 4 spheres, what do you need to add to Side B to balance the scale?

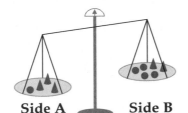

Side A   Side B

F 1 prism

G 1 sphere

H 3 spheres and 1 prism

J 2 spheres and 2 prisms

3 Ethan, Kenny, and Lance are brothers. Kenny is not the oldest, and Lance is not the youngest. Ethan is younger than Kenny. Which of these shows the birth order from oldest to youngest?

A Ethan, Kenny, Lance

B Kenny, Lance, Ethan

C Lance, Ethan, Kenny

D Lance, Kenny, Ethan

4 Elyse took some friends to the movies. The price of a child's ticket was $3.00, and the price of an adult's ticket was $6.00. What do you need to know to find out how much Elyse paid for all of her friends' tickets?

_____

_____

_____

_____

_____

STOP

Answers

SA Ⓐ Ⓑ Ⓒ Ⓓ   **1** Ⓐ Ⓑ Ⓒ Ⓓ   **2** Ⓕ Ⓖ Ⓗ Ⓙ   **3** Ⓐ Ⓑ Ⓒ Ⓓ

Sample A

What fraction means the same as $4\frac{3}{5}$?

A $\frac{7}{5}$ C $\frac{12}{5}$

B $\frac{7}{5}$ D $\frac{17}{5}$

STOP

For questions 1–42, darken the circle for the correct answer, or write the answer in the space provided.

1 Madelaine has a paperweight collection she wants to give away. How many paperweights would she have to give away if she was going to divide them equally among her 18 cousins with none left over or among her 12 classmates with none left over?

A 12

B 18

C 24

D 36

2 Attendance at the basketball game was 23,458 last night. This number included 1,000 promotional tickets that were given away. How many paid tickets were used?

F 22,458

G 23,358

H 23,658

J 24,458

3 In the number 52,658, the 2 means

A 20

B 200

C 2,000

D 20,000

4 Each square represents 0.05. What decimal number is shown below?

F 130.25

G 13.25

H 13.025

J 0.1325

5 What mixed number is shown by the shaded part of the circles?

A $1\frac{5}{6}$

B $1\frac{1}{5}$

C $\frac{4}{5}$

D $1\frac{4}{5}$

6 One week it snowed 6.05 inches. The next week it snowed 6.4 inches. The third week it snowed 6.21 inches. The fourth week it snowed 6.75 inches. How would these amounts of snow be listed in order from least to greatest?

F 6.05, 6.21, 6.4, 6.75

G 6.4, 6.75, 6.21, 6.05

H 6.75, 6.4, 6.05, 6.21

J 6.21, 6.4, 6.75, 6.05

7 Last year a company sold 3,421,095,804 assorted household gadgets. How is 3,421,095,804 written in words?

_____

_____

_____

_____

_____

GO ON

Answers

SA (A) (B) (C) (D) 2 (F) (G) (H) (J) 4 (F) (G) (H) (J) 6 (F) (G) (H) (J)

1 (A) (B) (C) (D) 3 (A) (B) (C) (D) 5 (A) (B) (C) (D)

8 If $x = 4$, $y = 16$, and $z = 5$, what would $x + y + z =$?

   A 29

   B 26

   C 25

   D 21

9 What number is shown here?
20,000 + 8,000 + 400 + 70

   F 2,847

   G 28,470

   H 28,000,470

   J 208,000,407

10 Michael bought 5 books. He bought 2 art books for $27.99 each. The rest were science-fiction books that cost $6.59 each. Which number sentence could be used to determine how much Michael paid altogether for the books?

   A $(5 - 2) \times \$6.59 = \square$

   B $\$27.99 - \$6.59 = \square$

   C $(2 \times \$27.99) + (3 \times \$6.59) = \square$

   D $(5 - 2) \times (\$27.99 + \$6.59) = \square$

11 Which of the following number sentences is related to $8 \times 7 = \square$?

   F $\square \div 8 = 7$

   G $8 - \square = 7$

   H $8 \div 7 = \square$

   J $8 + 7 = \square$

TEST TIP

Related facts share opposite operations. Addition and subtraction are related. Multiplication and division are related.

Julio has 10 letter cards. Use the picture of the cards to answer questions 12 and 13.

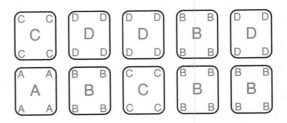

12 If the cards are shuffled and Julio draws 2 cards from the pack at the same time, which of these pairs would he most likely choose?

   A A, B

   B B, C

   C B, D

   D A, C

13 With his eyes closed, which card will Julio most likely pick and why?

_____

_____

_____

_____

14 Meili has 4 pairs of white socks, 2 pairs of yellow socks, and 6 pairs of black socks. If she reaches into her sock drawer without looking, what is the probability that she will pick a pair of white socks?

   F $\frac{1}{2}$

   G $\frac{1}{3}$

   H $\frac{1}{4}$

   J $\frac{1}{6}$

Answers

8 Ⓐ Ⓑ Ⓒ Ⓓ   **10** Ⓐ Ⓑ Ⓒ Ⓓ   **12** Ⓐ Ⓑ Ⓒ Ⓓ

9 Ⓕ Ⓖ Ⓗ Ⓙ   **11** Ⓕ Ⓖ Ⓗ Ⓙ   **14** Ⓕ Ⓖ Ⓗ Ⓙ

TEST PREP

The graph below shows the sources of each $100 collected by a local PTA. Use the graph to answer questions 15–17.

PTA Income Sources

The table below shows the rare coins collected by two boys over a four-month period. Use the table to answer questions 18–20.

Rare Coin Collection Record

Reggie	June	July	Aug.	Sept.
Pennies	28	93	86	43
Dimes	12	15	12	18
Len	**June**	**July**	**Aug.**	**Sept.**
Pennies	14	21	15	14
Dimes	35	24	24	44

15 Which two sources of income bring in about the same amount of money?

A Fall Fiesta and Market Day

B Spring Plant Sale and Pizza Lunches

C Book Fair and Spring Plant Sale

D Book Fair and Market Day

16 Which of these income sources is more than twice the Book Fair income?

F Market Day

G Fall Fiesta

H Pizza Lunches

J Spring Plant Sale

17 How much of each $100 comes from Market Day?

A $10

B $16

C $24

D $41

18 How many more dimes does Len have than Reggie?

F 184

G 80

H 70

J 65

19 What was the average number of dimes per month collected by both boys during the 4 months?

A 8

B 46

C 39

D 60

20 If the average value of the pennies collected by the two boys was $0.15 per coin, what was the value of their combined penny collections after 4 months?

_____

_____

_____

_____

_____

GO ON

Answers

15 Ⓐ Ⓑ Ⓒ Ⓓ   16 Ⓕ Ⓖ Ⓗ Ⓙ   17 Ⓐ Ⓑ Ⓒ Ⓓ   18 Ⓕ Ⓖ Ⓗ Ⓙ   19 Ⓐ Ⓑ Ⓒ Ⓓ

21 Which line segment names a diameter of the circle shown here?

F $\overline{AB}$

G $\overline{XA}$

H $\overline{AC}$

J $\overline{XC}$

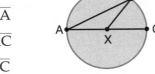

22 The angle formed by the hands of the clock is—

A less than 90°

B exactly 90°

C exactly 180°

D more than 90° and less than 180°

23 The graph shows Paul's savings over the last four months. How would the average monthly savings be computed?

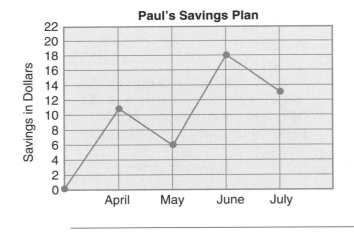

_____

_____

_____

_____

The tally chart below shows points scored by some local teams. Use the chart to answer question 24.

Team	Scores
Eagles	卌 I
Lasers	卌 卌 卌
Falcons	卌 卌 卌 III
Jets	III
Bulls	卌 卌 II

24 Which team scored 6 more points than the Bulls?

F Eagles

G Lasers

H Falcons

J Jets

25 Manuel is ordering pizza. His choices include thin or thick crust, each with a choice of cheese, sausage, or mushroom toppings. How many different combinations of crusts and toppings are possible?

A 2

B 3

C 5

D 6

GO ON ➡

Answers
21 Ⓕ Ⓖ Ⓗ Ⓙ   **22** Ⓐ Ⓑ Ⓒ Ⓓ   **24** Ⓕ Ⓖ Ⓗ Ⓙ   **25** Ⓐ Ⓑ Ⓒ Ⓓ

26 What is the area of the shaded section of this figure?

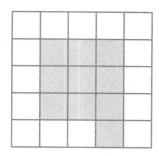

 = 1 square unit

F 10 square units

G 12 square units

H 15 square units

J 16 square units

27 Which figure shows a line of symmetry?

A

B

C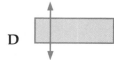

D

28 Which of the following metric units of measurement is best to use to measure the length of a room?

F meters

G liters

H centimeters

J kilograms

29 The dress rehearsal began at 2:20 P.M. If it lasted 1 hour and 25 minutes, at what time did the rehearsal end?

A 6:05 P.M.

B 5:05 P.M.

C 3:45 P.M.

D 2:25 P.M.

30 What are the coordinates of point C?

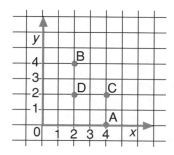

F (2, 4)

G (2, 2)

H (4, 1)

J (4, 2)

31 The local ice-skating rink is shown here. How would you find the area of the rink?

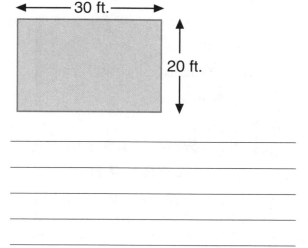

GO ON ➡

Answers

26 Ⓕ Ⓖ Ⓗ Ⓙ   **27** Ⓐ Ⓑ Ⓒ Ⓓ   **28** Ⓕ Ⓖ Ⓗ Ⓙ   **29** Ⓐ Ⓑ Ⓒ Ⓓ   **30** Ⓕ Ⓖ Ⓗ Ⓙ

32 If the pattern shown here continues, how many dots would there be in the seventh figure in the pattern?

A 20

B 28

C 30

D 32

33 Use your inch ruler and the map to help you answer the question. What is the actual distance between the two bridges?

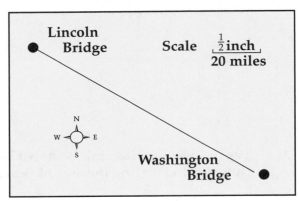

Lincoln Bridge

Scale $\frac{1}{2}$ inch / 20 miles

N W E S

Washington Bridge

F 120 miles

G 110 miles

H 100 miles

J 90 miles

TEST TIP

Solve multistep problems one step at a time. To answer question 33, first measure the line. Then use the map scale. Multiply the length in inches by 40 miles.

---

34 Jon has played soccer for 14 years, the longest of his 5 friends. Charles has played soccer for only 9 years, fewer years than his friends. What is the best estimate of the total number of years all 6 friends have played soccer?

A 209 years

B 125 years

C 90 years

D 70 years

35 A special machine multiplies any number entered into it by a secret number. The table shows how numbers are changed. Which number is missing from the table?

Original number	5	9	11
New number	25	45	

F 75

G 65

H 60

J 55

36 Chris is older than Sam. Ralph is older than Sam, but younger than Chris. Sam is younger than Ben. Chris is not the oldest. List the boys in order from youngest to oldest.

_____

_____

_____

_____

GO ON ➡

Answers

32 Ⓐ Ⓑ Ⓒ Ⓓ   **33** Ⓕ Ⓖ Ⓗ Ⓙ   **34** Ⓐ Ⓑ Ⓒ Ⓓ   **35** Ⓕ Ⓖ Ⓗ Ⓙ

37 To raise funds for a special project, the Girls' Athletic Association ordered 450 flowers from a nursery to sell at school. The nursery charged $0.35 each for the daisies and $0.45 each for the carnations. If the sales tax is 7.25%, what other information is needed to find the total cost of the flowers?

A the colors of the flowers

B how many flowers each member is required to sell

C the total number of members in the Girls' Athletic Association

D how many of each kind of flower was ordered

38 At the supermarket yesterday, Lucas bought 3 magazines at $2.85 each. About how much money did he spend altogether?

F $10.50

G $9.00

H $7.00

J $6.50

39 Carl has 36 fish in one aquarium and 52 fish in another aquarium. How many fish should he move from the second aquarium in order to have the same number of fish in both aquariums?

A 24

B 16

C 12

D 8

TEST TIP

You can solve a problem in several ways. You might draw a picture. You also can test each answer choice.

40 There were four cross-country team members running in an event. Robin finished after Earl. Nick finished after Robin. Neal finished ahead of Robin but after Earl. Which of the following shows the order in which the runners finished the event from first to last?

F Earl, Neal, Robin, Nick

G Neal, Earl, Robin, Nick

H Robin, Earl, Nick, Neal

J Nick, Robin, Neal, Earl

41 Maria went to the zoo with friends from school on Saturday. What do you *not* need to know to find out how much money Maria had left when she got home?

A how much money Maria spent on snacks

B how much money Maria's ticket to the zoo cost

C how much money Maria spent on souvenirs

D how long Maria stayed at the zoo

42 In 1790, the population of the United States was 3,929,000. What other information do you need to know to find how much the population has increased since then?

_____

_____

_____

_____

_____

_____

STOP

Answers

37 Ⓐ Ⓑ Ⓒ Ⓓ   **38** Ⓕ Ⓖ Ⓗ Ⓙ   **39** Ⓐ Ⓑ Ⓒ Ⓓ   **40** Ⓕ Ⓖ Ⓗ Ⓙ   **41** Ⓐ Ⓑ Ⓒ Ⓓ

Directions: Darken the circle for the correct answer, or write the answer in the space provided. Darken the circle for NH (Not Here) if the correct answer is not given.

| TRY THIS | Work the problem on scratch paper. Then check your answer before comparing it to the answer choices where given. Check the answer to a division problem by multiplying. |

Sample A

$526 \times 37 =$

A 19,462
B 19,252
C 18,264
D 563
E NH

| THINK IT THROUGH | The correct answer is A. When 526 is multiplied by 37, the answer is 19,462. |

STOP

1

$4563 \div 9 =$

A 590 R4
B 548
C 507
D 57
E NH

2

$0.6 \times 0.9 =$

F 5.4
G 0.54
H 0.054
J 0.0054
K NH

3

$\frac{1}{4}$
$+ \frac{1}{3}$

A $\frac{14}{32}$
B $\frac{1}{2}$
C $\frac{7}{12}$
D $\frac{8}{12}$
E NH

4

$0.762 - 0.471 =$

F 1.233
G 0.309
H 0.299
J 0.281
K NH

5

$7\frac{2}{3}$
$+10\frac{1}{4}$

A $17\frac{3}{7}$
B $17\frac{10}{12}$
C $17\frac{11}{12}$
D $18\frac{1}{12}$
E NH

6 $\frac{5}{8} \times \frac{2}{7} =$

_____
_____
_____
_____

STOP

Answers
SA Ⓐ Ⓑ Ⓒ Ⓓ Ⓔ
1 Ⓐ Ⓑ Ⓒ Ⓓ Ⓔ
2 Ⓕ Ⓖ Ⓗ Ⓙ Ⓚ
3 Ⓐ Ⓑ Ⓒ Ⓓ Ⓔ
4 Ⓕ Ⓖ Ⓗ Ⓙ Ⓚ
5 Ⓐ Ⓑ Ⓒ Ⓓ Ⓔ

Directions: Darken the circle for the correct answer, or write the answer in the space provided. Darken the circle for NH (Not Here) if the correct answer is not given.

TRY THIS

Read the word problem carefully. Then set up the word problem as a computation problem. Work the problem on scratch paper and compare the answer with the answer choices given.

Sample A

Sonia bought 80 plants from her garden supplier.

If the plants cost $22.75 each, what was the total cost of the plants before tax was added?

A $1,760

B $1,800

C $1,820

D $1,860

E NH

THINK IT THROUGH

The correct answer is <u>C</u>. To find the total cost multiply 80 x 22.75. The total cost is $1,820.

STOP

---

1 Miguel is buying a camera for $58.59. What is this amount rounded to the nearest dollar?

A $60.00

B $59.00

C $88.60

D $58.00

E NH

2 At an arts-and-crafts fair, $\frac{1}{3}$ of the vendors are selling wooden handicrafts and $\frac{1}{6}$ are selling paintings.

How many of the vendors at the arts-and-crafts fair are selling either wooden handicrafts or paintings?

F $\frac{2}{9}$

G $\frac{1}{3}$

H $\frac{1}{2}$

J $\frac{2}{3}$

K NH

3 Kyle collects models of all kinds. He has 14 model trucks, 12 model airplanes, and 23 model cars. How many models does Kyle have altogether?

A 28

B 31

C 37

D 49

E NH

4 Mr. Jackson bought 64 ounces of orange juice for his family. If each of the 8 family members received 8 ounces of juice, what percent of the total did each person receive?

_____

_____

_____

_____

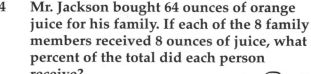

STOP

Answers

SA Ⓐ Ⓑ Ⓒ Ⓓ Ⓔ   **1** Ⓐ Ⓑ Ⓒ Ⓓ Ⓔ   **2** Ⓕ Ⓖ Ⓗ Ⓙ Ⓚ   **3** Ⓐ Ⓑ Ⓒ Ⓓ Ⓔ

Sample A

$$\frac{7}{9} \times \frac{3}{5} =$$

A $\frac{10}{45}$

B $\frac{7}{15}$

C $\frac{27}{35}$

D $\frac{10}{14}$

E NH

STOP

Sample B

$$344 \div 7 =$$

F 39

G 49 R1

H 49RS

J 50

K NH

STOP

Directions: Darken the circle for the correct answer. Darken the circle for NH, Not Here, if the correct answer is not given. If no choices are given, write in the answer.

1

$$0.4 \times 0.8 =$$

A 0.0032

B 0.032

C 0.32

D 3.2

E NH

2

$$\frac{3}{8}$$

$$+ \frac{6}{24}$$

F $\frac{9}{32}$

G $\frac{1}{2}$

H $\frac{5}{8}$

J $\frac{3}{4}$

K NH

3

$$0.7 \times 0.8 =$$

A 0.056

B 0.506

C 0.56

D 5.6

E NH

4 Rosa went on a fishing trip last weekend. On Saturday she caught 11 fish, and on Sunday she caught 16 fish.

How many fish did she catch altogether?

F 37

G 27

H 19

J 5

K NH

5

$$92 \times 54 =$$

A 5,298

B 5,008

C 4,978

D 4,968

E NH

6

$$1.908 - 0.564 =$$

F 1.344

G 1.244

H 1.094

J 0.986

K NH

7

$$14.357 - 11.269 =$$

A 3.080

B 3.112

C 3.808

D 3.880

E NH

8 What must you do first, before solving this problem?

$$\frac{1}{4}$$

$$- \frac{1}{6}$$

_____

_____

_____

_____

_____

_____

GO ON ➡

Answers

SA Ⓐ Ⓑ Ⓒ Ⓓ Ⓔ   2 Ⓕ Ⓖ Ⓗ Ⓙ Ⓚ   5 Ⓐ Ⓑ Ⓒ Ⓓ Ⓔ

SB Ⓕ Ⓖ Ⓗ Ⓙ Ⓚ   3 Ⓐ Ⓑ Ⓒ Ⓓ Ⓔ   6 Ⓕ Ⓖ Ⓗ Ⓙ Ⓚ

1 Ⓐ Ⓑ Ⓒ Ⓓ Ⓔ   4 Ⓕ Ⓖ Ⓗ Ⓙ Ⓚ   7 Ⓐ Ⓑ Ⓒ Ⓓ Ⓔ

9 Last year a store sold 1,657 radios. This year the store sold 423 radios.

How many radios did they sell in the two years altogether?

F   2,090

G   2,190

H   2,881

J   5,887

K   NH

1,657

423

10 Donna set a goal to swim 32 laps in the pool without stopping. After 24 laps she stopped to rest.

What percent of her goal did Donna complete?

A   125%

B   75%

C   60%

D   25%

E   NH

11 The Atlantic Ocean covers approximately 41,000,000 square miles.

What is that number rounded to the nearest million?

41,000,000

_____

_____

_____

_____

12 Every day Jenny and Lori ride their bicycles $1\frac{1}{2}$ kilometers to school. They ride $\frac{3}{4}$ kilometer to the park.

$1\frac{1}{2}$ km

How much farther is their ride to school than to the park?

F $\frac{1}{8}$ kilometer

G $\frac{1}{6}$ kilometer

H $\frac{3}{4}$ kilometer

J $\frac{4}{5}$ kilometer

K   NH

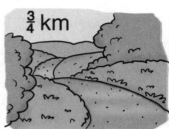

$\frac{3}{4}$ km

13 There are 300 summer campers at Camp Willow.

If $\frac{3}{5}$ of the campers are boys, how many boys are there at Camp Willow?

A   180

B   150

C   120

D   100

E   NH

STOP

Answers

9 F G H J K   12 F G H J K

10 A B C D E   13 A B C D E

PREWRITING, COMPOSING, AND EDITING

Directions: Read each sentence carefully. Then darken the circle for the correct answer to each question, or write the answer in the space provided.

> **TRY THIS**
>
> Pretend that you are writing each sentence. Use the rules you have learned for capitalization, punctuation, word usage, and sentence structure to choose the correct answer.

Delivering Mail by Pony Express

In his social studies class, Michael learned about the pony express, a mail delivery service in the Old West. He wanted to learn more details about the history of this mail service. Michael decided to use this as the subject of his research paper for social studies class.

Sample A

Michael is reading the book *The First Overland Mail* to help him with his research. Where should he look to find the name of the author of the book?

A   the bibliography

B   the title page

C   the index

D   the table of contents

> **THINK IT THROUGH**
>
> The correct answer is <u>B</u>. The author's name is found on the title page.

STOP

Traveling by Bicycle

Alyson wants to organize a bicycle tour for her scouting group. She is interested in traveling along one of the bicycle paths in the forest preserves located in her county. Alyson decides to write a letter to obtain information about bicycling in the county forest preserves.

Dear County Forest Preserve Director,

I am writing to ask you to send me a map of bicycle paths in our county forest preserves. I am organizing a bicycle tour for my scouting group. When you can send it. I need to make arrangements as soon as possible.

1   Which of these is <u>not</u> a complete sentence?

A   I am writing to ask you to send me a map of bicycle paths in our county forest preserves.

B   I am organizing a bicycle tour for my scouting group.

C   When you can send it.

D   I need to make arrangements as soon as possible.

GO ON

Answers
SA Ⓐ Ⓑ Ⓒ Ⓓ   1 Ⓐ Ⓑ Ⓒ Ⓓ

Michael used the dictionary to look up some words for his report.

2 Which definition of the word *switch* is used in the following sentence?

The pony express rider would *switch* to a fresh horse at each relay station.

   F beat with a stick

   G move suddenly

   H change

   J break an electrical circuit

3 The "a" in *dangerous* sounds most like the vowel sound in—

   A travel

   B locate

   C barometer

   D necklace

TEST TIP

Remember that many words have multiple meanings. For example:

- We warmed our hands by the cozy *fire*.
- The boss will *fire* her if she comes in late one more time.

Test questions often ask you to identify the precise meaning of a word. In question 2, all of the answer choices are possible definitions for the word *switch*. However, only one of these definitions describes how the word is used in the example sentence.

Michael used the information he found on the pony express to make a concept web. Use the concept web to answer questions 4 and 5.

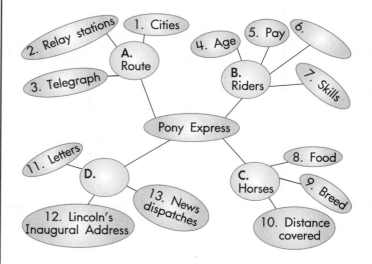

4 Which of these belongs in circle D?

   F Mail

   G Stagecoaches

   H Mining camps

   J Swing stations

5 Which of these belongs in number 6 next to circle B?

   A St. Joseph, Missouri

   B Weight

   C Mustangs

   D $5 a half-ounce

GO ON➡

Answers

  2 Ⓕ Ⓖ Ⓗ Ⓙ   **3** Ⓐ Ⓑ Ⓒ Ⓓ   **4** Ⓕ Ⓖ Ⓗ Ⓙ   **5** Ⓐ Ⓑ Ⓒ Ⓓ

Here is a rough draft of the first part of Michael's paper. Read the rough draft carefully. Then answer questions 6–10.

Delivering Mail by Pony Express

The gold rush in California in the 1840s and 1850s brought thousands of
(1)

people to the West. Most of them were seeking gold. They had left family
(2)   (3)

members in the eastern part of the United States. Families and friends in the
(4)

East waited to hear from their loved ones who had moved west.

In 1860, the fastest method of delivering mail was by stagecoach.
(5)

Unfortunately, this delivery system took 25 days in some cases, the wait
(6)

for mail was even longer. This was especially true in mining camps where
(7)

letters took three to four months to be delivered.

In 1860, a businessman named William Hepburn Russell devised a plan for
(8)

a faster mail delivery system. His mail service would take just ten days. The
(9)   (10)

Civil War lasted for four years. Russell spent $100,000 on the pony express
(11)

with the hope of making a fortune. He built 190 stations on the pony express
(12)

trail. It extended and stretched for 1,800 miles through the western frontier.
(13)

The eastern terminal was in St. Joseph, Missouri, and the western terminal
(14)

was in Sacramento, California.

GO ON ➡

6 Which is a run-on sentence?

F 5 H 7

G 6 J 8

7 Which of the following sentences could be added after sentence 7?

A St. Joseph, Missouri, was the western end of the United States railroad service.

B When the relay stationkeeper heard hoof beats, he would get a fresh horse ready.

C Therefore, miners hungered for a faster mail delivery service.

D As a result of this, few young men applied for the job as a pony express rider.

8 How can sentences 2 and 3 best be combined?

F Most of them were seeking gold and had left behind family members in the eastern United States.

G They had left family members in the eastern part of the United States most whom were seeking gold.

H Most of them were seeking gold and family members in the eastern part of the United States.

J They were seeking gold in the eastern part of the United States who had left behind family members.

9 What is the most colorful way to write sentence 4?

A Families and friends back East anxiously awaited word from their loved ones who had traveled west.

B Families and friends in the East waited to receive letters from their loved ones who had moved west.

C Families and friends waited for long periods of time to receive letters from their loved ones in the West.

D As it is written.

10 Which sentence does <u>not</u> belong in Michael's report and why?

_____

_____

_____

_____

_____

GO ON →

Answers

6 Ⓕ Ⓖ Ⓗ Ⓙ   7 Ⓐ Ⓑ Ⓒ Ⓓ   8 Ⓕ Ⓖ Ⓗ Ⓙ   9 Ⓐ Ⓑ Ⓒ Ⓓ

Here is the next part of Michael's rough draft for his research paper. This part has certain words and phrases underlined. Read the draft carefully. Then answer questions 11–16.

William Hepburn Russell bought 500 horses for his new business. The
(15)   (16)

horses were wild mustangs that <u>had been rounded up</u> on the plains. Each
(17)

horse <u>were broken</u> by a cowboy. Russell hired 80 men—usually
(18)

teen-agers—as pony express riders. <u>A riders' job</u> as a mail carrier on
(19)

the pony express trail was dangerous. These young men carried the mail
(20)

through deserts, over mountains, through rain, snow, extreme heat, and

unfriendly Native American territory. They risked their lives daily. As one
(21)   (22)

rider <u>explained "It is dangerous</u> work, but I know it's an important service."

When President Abraham Lincoln gave his first speech to Congress, a copy
(23)

of it was carried to Sacramento by the pony express.

    The pony express <u>riders are carrying</u> the mail for 75 miles a workday.
(24)

They stopped at relay stations every 5 to 10 miles to switch horses. A
(25)   (26)

rider's workday ended at a swing, or home station, <u>where hed eat and sleep</u>

between runs. Another rider at the station would take the mail and
(27)

continue the run. The pony express rider received from $100 to $150 a
(28)

month for this dangerous work.

GO ON

11 In sentence 16, <u>had been rounded up</u> is best written—

   F will be rounded up

   G have been rounded up

   H are going to be rounded up

   J As it is written.

12 In sentence 17, <u>were broken</u> is best written—

   A has broken

   B broken

   C was broken

   D As it is written.

13 In sentence 19, <u>A riders' job</u> is best written—

   F A riders jobs

   G A rider's job

   H A riders job

   J As it is written.

14 In sentence 22, <u>explained "It is dangerous</u> is best written—

   A explained, "It is dangerous

   B explained "It, is dangerous

   C explained, "it is dangerous

   D As it is written.

15 In sentence 24, <u>riders are carrying</u> is best written—

   F rider's are carrying

   G riders are known to carry

   H riders carried

   J As it is written.

16 In sentence 26, <u>where hed eat and sleep</u> is best written—

   A where he'd eat and sleep

   B where he'ld eat and sleep

   C where hew'd eat and sleep

   D As it is written.

STOP

Answers

11 Ⓕ Ⓖ Ⓗ Ⓙ   **13** Ⓕ Ⓖ Ⓗ Ⓙ   **15** Ⓕ Ⓖ Ⓗ Ⓙ

12 Ⓐ Ⓑ Ⓒ Ⓓ   **14** Ⓐ Ⓑ Ⓒ Ⓓ   **16** Ⓐ Ⓑ Ⓒ Ⓓ

Directions: Read each sentence carefully. If one of the words is misspelled, darken the circle for that word. If all the words are spelled correctly, darken the circle for *No mistake*.

| TRY THIS | Read each sentence carefully. If you are not sure of an answer, first decide which answer choices are spelled correctly. Then see if you can recognize the misspelled word from your reading experience. |

Sample A

Aunt Jane <u>remarked</u> that Tommy had <u>groan</u> three <u>inches</u>. <u>No mistake</u>
        A   **B**   **C**   **D**

| THINK IT THROUGH | The correct choice is <u>B</u>. When you increase in size, the word is spelled *grown*. <u>Groan</u> is the sound you might make when you are in pain. |

STOP

---

1 Bernard <u>kickt</u> the <u>soccer</u> ball <u>high</u> in the air. <u>No mistake</u>
          A   **B**   **C**   **D**

2 She <u>asked</u> us please to <u>reafrain</u> from <u>walking</u> on the grass. <u>No mistake</u>
       F   **G**   **H**   **J**

3 He <u>appealled</u> the jury's <u>decision</u> on the <u>case</u>. <u>No mistake</u>
      A   **B**   **C**   **D**

4 The crowd <u>reacted</u> <u>positively</u> to the speaker's <u>statements</u>. <u>No mistake</u>
        F   **G**   **H**   **J**

5 The <u>peel</u> of the <u>church</u> bells rang <u>throughout</u> the valley. <u>No mistake</u>
     A   **B**   **C**   **D**

6 Being on top of a <u>mountain</u> can give you the <u>lonelyest</u> <u>feeling</u>. <u>No mistake</u>
         F   **G**   **H**   **J**

7 We had a long <u>converseation</u> on Thursday <u>evening</u>. <u>No mistake</u>
         A   **B**   **C**   **D**

8 Guillermo was <u>agonizing</u> over his <u>difficult</u> decision. <u>No mistake</u>
        F   **G**   **H**   **J**

STOP

Answers

SA Ⓐ Ⓑ Ⓒ Ⓓ	**3** Ⓐ Ⓑ Ⓒ Ⓓ	**6** Ⓕ Ⓖ Ⓗ Ⓙ	
1 Ⓐ Ⓑ Ⓒ Ⓓ	**4** Ⓕ Ⓖ Ⓗ Ⓙ	**7** Ⓐ Ⓑ Ⓒ Ⓓ	
2 Ⓕ Ⓖ Ⓗ Ⓙ	**5** Ⓐ Ⓑ Ⓒ Ⓓ	**8** Ⓕ Ⓖ Ⓗ Ⓙ	

Sample B

Many of the Native Americans on the
(1)
Great Plains had migrated from the eastern

woodlands because of increasing populations

and the arrival of the Europeans. Many of
(2)
these Native Americans depended upon the

buffalo for food, clothing shelter and even fuel.

How is sentence 2 best written?

A Many of these Native Americans depended upon the buffalo for food clothing shelter and even fuel.

B Many of these Native Americans depended upon the buffalo for food, clothing, shelter, and even fuel.

C Many of these Native Americans depended upon the buffalo for: food, clothing, shelter, and even fuel.

D As it is written.

STOP

Keiko is reading the book *Everglades National Park*. Study the Table of Contents from that book. Then answer questions 1 and 2.

Table of Contents

1 Which chapter should Keiko read to find information about recreational activities in the Everglades?

A Chapter 1   **C** Chapter 3

B Chapter 2   **D** Chapter 4

2 Which chapter should Keiko read to learn about the habitat of alligators?

_____

_____

_____

_____

Keiko's Trip

Keiko is on a trip to the Florida Everglades with her family. Keiko is excited because the Everglades is such an unusual place to visit. She decides to write a letter to her friend Erin about the Everglades.

3 Keiko cannot remember the correct way to write a friendly letter. In which reference source could she find an example of one?

F an almanac

G a science textbook

H an atlas

J an English textbook

4 Why is Keiko writing a letter?

A to ask Erin for further information about the Everglades

B to tell Erin about her trip to the Everglades

C to invite Erin on a trip to the Everglades

D to ask Erin to send her a map of the Everglades

GO ON →

Answers
SB Ⓐ Ⓑ Ⓒ Ⓓ   **1** Ⓐ Ⓑ Ⓒ Ⓓ   **3** Ⓕ Ⓖ Ⓗ Ⓙ   **4** Ⓐ Ⓑ Ⓒ Ⓓ

Here is a rough draft of the first part of Keiko's letter. Read the rough draft carefully. Then answer questions 5–8.

April 27, 1998

Dear Erin,

My family and me a week ago arrived at Everglades National Park. I am
(1)   (2)

learning about the wildlife in the Everglades my family and I spend our

days canoeing along marked waterways called trails.

So far we have followed the easiest trails in the park. The West Lake
(3)   (4)

Trail is a seven-hour trip. Another trip is along the Bear Lake Trail. It
(5)   (6)

is a twelve-mile paddle. Next year we plan to go backpacking in the Ozarks.
(7)

It was on this trip I saw my first alligator! I thought I would be afraid of
(8)   (9)

alligators, but they are usually sunning themselves along the banks.

---

5 Which sentence does <u>not</u> belong in Keiko's letter?

F 4   **H** 7

G 6   **J** 9

6 Which of the following sentences could be added after sentence 1?

A I have become an expert at paddling a canoe.

B We are camping in our trailer at Long Pine Campground.

C We had shrimp for dinner last night.

D Dad tripped over the canoe and fell into the lake!

7 What is the best way to write sentence 1?

F My family and I arrived at Everglades National Park a week ago.

G A week ago I and my family arrived at Everglades National Park.

H Me and my family arrived a week ago at Everglades National Park.

J As it is written.

8 Which sentence is a run-on and how would you correct it?

_____

_____

_____

GO ON ➡

Here is the next part of Keiko's rough draft of her letter. This part has certain words and phrases underlined. Read the rough draft carefully. Then answer questions 9–14.

I've also seen hundreds of different species of birds. My favorite bird are
(10)   (11)

the white ibis. This bird has a long beak that curves down. It is all white
(12)   (13)

except for the ends of its wings which are tipped with black.

Another species of bird that is abundant in Everglades National Park is
(14)

the heron. There are many kinds of herons that live in the park.
(15)

Yesterday when we were canoeing in Bear Lake, my father whispered
(16)

"Look, bald eagles. Eagles are so graceful. What a large wingspan they have!"
(17)   (18)

Tomorrow we went on a bike hike. We expect to see several kinds of
(19)   (20)

trees along the bike path. One tree I am looking forward to seeing is the
(21)

gumbo limbo tree. This unusual tree has adapted to living in hurricane
(22)

country. If it is blown over, any part of it that touches the ground sends out
(23)

roots and goes on growing!

Your best friend

Keiko

GO ON

9 In sentence 10, <u>I've also seen</u> is best written—

    A You've also seen

    B Iv'e also seen

    C Ih've also seen

    D As it is written.

10 In sentence 11, <u>favorite bird are the white ibis</u> is best written—

    F favorite bird has been the white ibis

    G favorite bird will be the white ibis

    H favorite bird is the white ibis

    J As it is written.

11 In sentence 16, <u>whispered "Look, bald</u> is best written—

    A whispered, "Look, bald

    B whispered "look, bald

    C Whispered Look, bald

    D As it is written.

12 In sentence 18, <u>they have!"</u> is best written—

    F they have,"

    G they have!

    H they have.

    J As it is written.

13 In sentence 19, <u>we went</u> is best written—

    A we weren't

    B we was

    C we are going

    D As it is written.

14 At the end of Keiko's letter, <u>Your best friend</u> is best written—

    F your best friend

    G Your Best Friend,

    H Your best friend,

    J As it is written.

GO ON

Answers

  9 Ⓐ Ⓑ Ⓒ Ⓓ   **11** Ⓐ Ⓑ Ⓒ Ⓓ   **13** Ⓐ Ⓑ Ⓒ Ⓓ

 10 Ⓕ Ⓖ Ⓗ Ⓙ   **12** Ⓕ Ⓖ Ⓗ Ⓙ   **14** Ⓕ Ⓖ Ⓗ Ⓙ

For questions 15–26, read each sentence carefully. If one of the words is misspelled, darken the circle for that word. If all of the words are spelled correctly, darken the circle for *No mistake*.

15 Ralph received a <u>certificate</u> when he <u>finished</u> lifeguard <u>training</u>. <u>No mistake</u>
                    A   **B**   **C**   **D**

16 Marge <u>translatet</u> several journal <u>articles</u> for the <u>university</u>. <u>No mistake</u>
          F   **G**   **H**   **J**

17 Chameleons use <u>camouflage</u> to <u>avoid</u> becoming the <u>pray</u> of other animals. <u>No mistake</u>
               A   **B**   **C**   **D**

18 Rosa <u>receives</u> an <u>allowance</u> of ten dollars <u>every</u> week. <u>No mistake</u>
        F   **G**   **H**   **J**

19 Tom hit two <u>consecutive</u> <u>fowl</u> balls in the second <u>inning</u>. <u>No mistake</u>
             A   **B**   **C**   **D**

20 Michael has <u>always</u> had a very <u>vivid</u> <u>imagineation</u>. <u>No mistake</u>
            F   **G**   **H**   **J**

21 I hope to <u>reagain</u> <u>complete</u> use of my <u>hand</u> by next week. <u>No mistake</u>
           A   **B**   **C**   **D**

22 She is a <u>member</u> of several <u>charitable</u> <u>organizeations</u>. <u>No mistake</u>
           F   **G**   **H**   **J**

23 It is <u>difficult</u> to solve such a <u>complicatted</u> <u>problem</u>. <u>No mistake</u>
        A   **B**   **C**   **D**

24 Sara went to the <u>hospital</u> to <u>deliver</u> Joel's <u>simpathy</u> card. <u>No mistake</u>
               F   **G**   **H**   **J**

25 That was the <u>drearyest</u> <u>meeting</u> I have ever <u>attended</u>. <u>No mistake</u>
            A   **B**   **C**   **D**

26 She has <u>strong</u> <u>memories</u> of her early <u>childhood</u>. <u>No mistake</u>
          F   **G**   **H**   **J**

STOP

Answers

15 Ⓐ Ⓑ Ⓒ Ⓓ	**18** Ⓕ Ⓖ Ⓗ Ⓙ	**21** Ⓐ Ⓑ Ⓒ Ⓓ	**24** Ⓕ Ⓖ Ⓗ Ⓙ
16 Ⓕ Ⓖ Ⓗ Ⓙ	**19** Ⓐ Ⓑ Ⓒ Ⓓ	**22** Ⓕ Ⓖ Ⓗ Ⓙ	**25** Ⓐ Ⓑ Ⓒ Ⓓ
17 Ⓐ Ⓑ Ⓒ Ⓓ	**20** Ⓕ Ⓖ Ⓗ Ⓙ	**23** Ⓐ Ⓑ Ⓒ Ⓓ	**26** Ⓕ Ⓖ Ⓗ Ⓙ

Use the removable answer sheet on page 127 to record your answers for the practice tests.

Sample A

Polar Bears

Polar bears are sometimes called ice bears or snow bears. These huge bears live in the icy lands near the North Pole. They sometimes weigh more than 1,000 pounds. Polar bears live by themselves except when a mother has cubs. Their thick, white fur and layers of fat help them stay warm in freezing winters.

Why can polar bears live near the North Pole?

A   They build fires.

B   They huddle close together.

C   They stay in caves all winter.

D   They have thick fur and layers of fat.

For questions 1–30, carefully read each selection and the questions that follow. Then darken the circle for the correct answer to each question, or write in the answer.

Neon Lights

Have you seen brightly colored lights flashing in front of restaurants and other businesses? These brightly colored lights are most likely made from a gas called neon. Neon is one of many gases in the earth's atmosphere. About eighty years ago, Georges Claude, a French chemist, found a way to use neon to make lights. He took the air out of a glass tube and replaced it with neon. When electricity was passed through the neon, a colorful light was created.

You have probably seen neon lights in restaurant signs or on highways. Airports sometimes use neon lights to guide airplanes because neon can be seen through thick fog. Some people use neon signs in their businesses and offices. Some pieces of art are made of neon lights.

1   Why did the author begin with a question ?

A   to explain the meaning of "neon"

B   to outline and summarize the main ideas in the article

C   to show that the topic relates to the reader's experience

D   to identify the main character

2   Neon lights are used at airports because

_____

_____

3   This article was mainly written to—

F   describe the various kinds of neon signs.

G   describe the advantages of neon lights.

H   advertise neon lights.

J   inform us about neon.

4   What is neon?

A   a gas used to make signs

B   a brightly colored sign

C   a kind of electricity

D   a thick fog

GO ON➡

STATE SWIMMING FINALS
WESTMONT HIGH SCHOOL
JUNE 22

Welcome to the 100th Annual State Swimming Finals for the state of Iowa. We are happy to report that each high school in the state is represented in the meet this year. Swimmers who are participating have qualified for these events during school competitions. Good luck to one and all!

BOYS' EVENTS

9:00 A.M. 100-, 200-, 800-, 1,500-meter Freestyle	Swimmers may choose any stroke. Most use the front crawl, which is usually the fastest stroke.
10:00 A.M. 400-meter Freestyle Relay	Four swimmers make up a team. Each team member swims 100 meters. The team with the lowest combined time wins.
10:30 A.M. 800-meter Freestyle Medley	Four swimmers make up a team. Each team member swims a different stroke for 200 meters. The team with the lowest combined time wins.
11:00 A.M. 100-meter, 200-meter Butterfly	Come watch the most graceful stroke performed in swimming. The butterfly stroke, when performed correctly, looks like a butterfly in flight.
11:30 A.M. 100-meter, 200-meter Backstroke	The back crawl is another name for the backstroke. The stroke is somewhat similar to the front crawl, except it is performed as the swimmer lies on his back.

12:00 Food sold in the cafeteria.

GIRLS' EVENTS

1:00 P.M. 100-, 200-, 400-, 800-meter Freestyle	As in the boys' freestyle event, girls swim using the stroke of their choice.
2:00 P.M. 400-meter Freestyle Relay	Four swimmers make up a team. Each team member swims 100 meters. The team with the lowest combined time wins.
3:00 P.M. 100-meter, 200-meter Butterfly	This popular race looks easy because it is so graceful, but it takes a great deal of endurance.
4:00 P.M. 100-meter, 200-meter Backstroke	Although the backstroke is similar to the front crawl, the backstroke is performed more slowly than the front crawl.

5:00 P.M. Demonstration of Synchronized Swimming—All participating schools have a team of synchronized swimmers, who will demonstrate their graceful, acrobatic movements to music.

5:30 P.M. Medal presentation. The top three winners in each event will be presented with medals.

GO ON➡

5   If you leave at 3:30 P.M., you will miss—

   F   all the boys' events.

   G   the boys' 800-meter freestyle medley.

   H   the girls' 100-meter backstroke.

   J   all the girls' events.

6   Which of the events listed in the program probably requires the most endurance?

   A   100-meter freestyle

   B   400-meter freestyle relay

   C   200-meter butterfly

   D   200-meter backstroke

7   Which swimmers will take part in the demonstration of synchronized swimming ?

   F   teams from all participating schools

   G   the top three winners in each event

   H   the winners of the 800-meter freestyle

   J   the swim team from the host school

8   Who will participate in this swim meet and how did they qualify for it?

_____

_____

_____

_____

_____

_____

9   According to the swim meet program, which event will be performed by the girls, but not the boys?

   A   400-meter freestyle relay

   B   400-meter freestyle

   C   100-meter butterfly

   D   100-meter backstroke

10   There is enough information presented in this program of events to show that—

   F   more girls than boys will race in the swim meet.

   G   food can be bought in the cafeteria.

   H   you will miss a boys' event if you watch a girls' event.

   J   most people watch the girls' events.

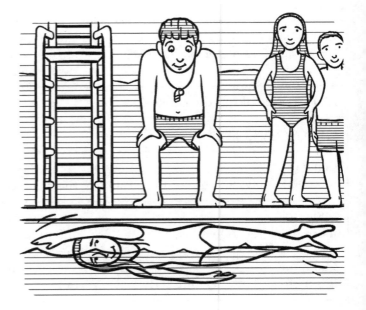

GO ON➡

Laura's Summer Project

It was the middle of summer, and Laura was bored. Her best friend was away on vacation, and her brother was at camp. She didn't have anyone to play with or talk to.

She decided to bicycle up the street to the bookstore. She liked to visit there. It had a lot of interesting toys, posters, and computer games, as well as books. She had become friends with Mr. Hoffman, the owner.

"How are you doing today, Laura?" Mr. Hoffman greeted her.

"Okay, I guess. I'm kind of bored," she confessed.

"Well, I have something exciting to show you," he said. "It's about one of your favorite authors." He led her to the notice board. She read the poster.

Laura was so excited she could hardly stand still. She had read all of Elizabeth Blalock's books. Laura thought Ms. Blalock was a wonderful writer. She couldn't think of anything more wonderful than meeting her—except maybe winning the contest and having a story of her own published! Suddenly Laura wasn't bored anymore. "Thanks, Mr. Hoffman!" she said as she hurried out the door.

MEET ELIZABETH BLALOCK

Well-known author Elizabeth Blalock will be at Treehouse Bookstore on Saturday, July 13, from 1:00 P.M. to *autograph* copies of her books.

STORY-WRITING CONTEST

Contest sponsored by Treehouse Bookstore and open to boys and girls ages 6–12.

Contest Rules

Stories must be:
1. Original fiction
2. Between 500 and 700 words in length
3. Neatly written or typed

Mail your story to:
Treehouse Bookstore
1204 Jefferson Avenue
Madison, Wisconsin 53047

We must receive your story by August 1.

Winners will be notified on August 15.

Contest Prizes

First place: $50 Treehouse Bookstore gift certificate
Second and Third places: $30 Treehouse Bookstore gift certificates

Ms. Blalock will judge our story-writing contest and hold a personal writing conference with the first-place winner. Then the winning story will be published in *Tom Thumb* magazine.

GO ON➡

11 In this selection, *autograph* means—

   A to illustrate a book.

   B to sign one's name.

   C to give away money.

   D to sell a book.

12 How did Laura feel after she read the poster?

   F She was worried.

   G She was excited and eager to start writing a story.

   H She was still bored.

   J She was sad.

13 Why did Laura like to visit the bookstore?

   A She needed a book for class.

   B It sold birthday cards and balloons.

   C She needed a poster for her bedroom.

   D It had interesting toys, posters, games, and books.

14 Besides the Treehouse Bookstore, where else would you most likely find this poster?

   F at camp

   G at the beach

   H at the library

   J at the post office

15 Why does Laura want to enter the contest?

_____

_____

_____

_____

16 For this contest, you may enter—

   A a story you made up.

   B a report on an animal.

   C a biography about a famous person.

   D a short poem.

17 Where does most of the selection take place?

   F in a bookstore

   G at a camp

   H in a shopping center

   J in a department store

18 Which of these is an *opinion* expressed in the selection?

   A Ms. Blalock writes books.

   B Laura and Mr. Hoffman are friends.

   C Ms. Blalock is a wonderful writer.

   D Laura often goes to the bookstore.

19 Which of these statements is the best summary of the story?

   F Laura was bored because her best friend was away on vacation and her brother was at camp.

   G Laura liked to go to the bookstore and was friends with Mr. Hoffman, the owner.

   H Ms. Blalock will judge a story-writing contest sponsored by Treehouse Bookstore.

   J Laura was bored until she learned that one of her favorite authors would be the judge in a story-writing contest.

GO ON ➡

Navajo Life

The Navajo make up one of the largest groups of Native Americans in the United States. Archaeologists believe that the Navajo used to live in Canada or Alaska. About five hundred years ago, they moved into the region where they now live: Arizona, New Mexico, and Utah.

Navajo spiritual beliefs were centered around their homeland. They believed that the four mountains that defined their territory were sacred. Often, members of the group made long, difficult journeys to the four mountains and collected soil from the top of each. The four bits of soil were wrapped in a small pouch. This became the individual's sacred bundle and was treasured throughout the person's life. Stories about the beginning of the world explained physical features in the region. For example, black lava near Grants, New Mexico, is thought to be the dried blood of a monster that was killed by a Navajo hero.

Traditionally the Navajo lived in hogans—dome-shaped shelters covered with earth. Doorways faced east to greet the sun. The Navajo did not live in villages, but sometimes they situated their hogans near those of relatives. A small settlement might include a few hogans, a herd of sheep, grazing land, and some fields where corn and other vegetables were grown. Marriages were often arranged between families. Girls were usually married at an early age, and the couple lived near the girl's mother. The girl's mother was the head of the household and ruled over the family group.

Every Navajo belongs to one of about sixty clans. Clans are groups of relatives who share a belief that they have a common ancestor. Salt People, Bitter Water, Many Goats, and Water Flowing Together are the names of a few clans. Two people from the same clan may not marry.

Since the late 1700s, sheep have played an important role in traditional Navajo life. The sheep are owned by individuals but graze in one big herd. Parents give lambs to their children so that they can learn to take care of them. Sheep are also an important source of meat. Both lamb and mutton are eaten. Mutton is often cooked with vegetables to make a stew.

Once a year the sheep are sheared. Women weave the wool into blankets with bold, colorful designs. The blankets are greatly admired by people outside the group and to this day continue to be sold or traded for other items. Navajo craft workers also have become well known for the turquoise jewelry they make.

Although a number of Navajo are sheep ranchers or farmers, many are technicians, teachers, miners, and engineers. The growth of industry on Navajo land makes these Native Americans one of the richest groups in the country. Each year the Navajo earn millions of dollars from mining operations. The Navajo also own a lumber mill and a manufacturing plant, which they lease to an electronics firm. In addition, the first college owned and operated by Native Americans, Navajo Community College, is located on Navajo land.

The Navajo gained fame during World War II. The Allies needed a secret code that the Japanese could not break. The son of a missionary, who had grown up on Navajo land, suggested that the Navajo language be used for the code. The Marines liked the idea and recruited hundreds of Navajo to train as Codetalkers. The Codetalkers were able to communicate rapidly, and the code was never broken by the Japanese.

GO ON➡

20 A sacred bundle contains—

   A turquoise and silver collected from the mines.

   B soil collected from the four holy mountains.

   C black lava and ash.

   D feathers and polished stones.

21 Which of these is a *fact* stated in this selection?

   F People from different clans do not associate.

   G The journeys to the four mountains were long and difficult.

   H Many Goats is the most unusual name of a Navajo clan.

   J Sheep play the most important role in Navajo life.

22 The growth of industry on Navajo land has probably—

   A brought increased poverty to the Navajo.

   B caused many Navajo to look for work away from Navajo land.

   C helped the Navajo become more self-sufficient.

   D led to a decline in the Navajo population.

23 How do the Navajo explain some of the physical features of their homeland?

   F They talk about geology.

   G They have stories about the beginning of the world to explain these features.

   H They believe that other Native Americans formed the land.

   J They accept the world and do not try to explain it.

24 According to the selection, where do most Navajo live?

_____

_____

_____

_____

_____

25 The web shows some ideas discussed in the selection.

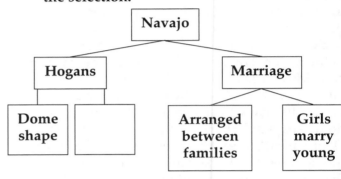

Which of these belongs in the empty box?

   A Difficult journeys

   B Electronics firm

   C Covered with earth

   D Weave into blankets

26 There is enough information in this article to show that—

   F the Navajo made an important contribution to the Allies in World War II.

   G Navajo crafts are greatly valued, but no longer handmade.

   H buffalo played an important role in traditional Navajo life.

   J today there are many Navajo in the United States Marines.

GO ON➡

Jerry's Plan

The other day, while my family and I were stuck in a traffic jam, my brother Jerry started to draw what he called the "future vehicle." It was the most unusual vehicle I had ever seen.

We had just heard a siren. It was an ambulance trying to make its way through the thick traffic jam on the highway. It had to zigzag through the slow-moving automobiles.

"You see, that's the problem with ambulances. They are too wide to navigate easily through heavy traffic. They should be *elongated* and narrower. Then they could fit between lanes of traffic. Look at my idea of an ambulance," said Jerry, pointing to his unearthly drawing.

As traffic began to flow smoothly, Jerry continued to explain how his version of an ambulance would work. It was beginning to make sense to me. Dad said it was a great idea. Mom suggested that Jerry get a patent for his invention to make sure his idea was not stolen.

Jerry was excited and decided to find out how to get a patent. He went to the library and read about patents. Jerry learned that before you try to obtain a patent for your idea, you must make sure that no one has a similar patent already. Some people hire an agent to check this for them. The agent checks with the U.S. Patent and Trademark Office, which has millions of patents registered. The agent must also check foreign patents. After the search, Jerry would have to fill out an application and include drawings and a description of his new vehicle. It could take as long as two years for the patent to be granted.

If Jerry receives his patent, he will be given a patent number, which tells the date of the invention. Jerry will have certain rights as an inventor. No one other than the inventor can make or sell the patented item for 17 years.

Learning about patents was an interesting experience. Jerry learned that he is not the only one with an unusual invention. I hope that his idea is successful and that it does not become just another number on the shelf in the U.S. Patent and Trademark Office in Arlington, Virginia.

27 The boxes below show events from the selection.

Jerry observed an ambulance stuck in a traffic jam.		Dad said Jerry's new ambulance was a great idea.
1	2	3

Which event belongs in the second box?

A Jerry went to the library.

B Jerry drew the "future vehicle."

C Jerry learned about the patent process.

D Mom suggested Jerry get a patent.

28 **Why does Jerry think ambulances should be narrower?**

F They could be seen more easily.

G They could fit between traffic lanes.

H They could move more quickly.

J They would prevent traffic jams.

29 **In this selection, *elongated* means—**

A broken into parts.

B lengthened.

C removed.

D trimmed.

30 **What conclusion can be drawn from the last sentence of the selection?**

_____

_____

_____

_____

_____

_____

_____

STOP

Sample A

To **adapt** is to—

A take   **C** adjust

B borrow   **D** run

STOP

For questions 1–9, darken the circle for the word or group of words that has the same or almost the same meaning as the underlined word.

1 **Frigid** means—

A warm

B tight

C stiff

D cold

2 Something that is **definite** is—

F certain

G sweet

H harmful

J important

3 **Gradual** means—

A back and forth

B one by one

C little by little

D over and over

4 Someone who is **courteous** is—

F polite   **H** stern

G rude   **J** happy

5 A person who is **valiant** is—

A meek

B wealthy

C weak

D courageous

6 A **petition** is a kind of—

F charity

G request

H poison

J conference

7 A **cunning** person is—

A popular

B sly

C educated

D well known

8 If you **dispose** of something, you—

F wash it

G paint it

H throw it away

J cover it

9 Another word that means the same thing as **reinforced** is—

A purchased

B strengthened

C burned

D emptied

GO ON

Sample B

| Those beams will <u>support</u> the roof. |

In which sentence does <u>support</u> have the same meaning as it does in the sentence above?

A That planet cannot <u>support</u> life.

B He thanked us for our <u>support</u> during the campaign.

C That table will not <u>support</u> this heavy lamp.

D The oldest child helped <u>support</u> the family.

For questions 10–14, darken the circle for the sentence in which the underlined word means the same as it does in the sentence in the box.

10 | She offered no <u>excuse</u> for her mistake. |

In which sentence does <u>excuse</u> have the same meaning as it does in the sentence above?

F The judge will <u>excuse</u> her from jury duty.

G We'll <u>excuse</u> the noise from outside.

H What is her <u>excuse</u> for missing class?

J Please <u>excuse</u> me for a moment.

11 | I lost my ring near the tennis <u>net</u>. |

In which sentence does <u>net</u> have the same meaning as it does in the sentence above?

A She will <u>net</u> the fish.

B The <u>net</u> weight of this box of cereal is 13 ounces.

C Grandmother Lucy always wears a hair <u>net</u> to bed.

D He hopes to <u>net</u> great profits from these investments.

12 | Mom is cleaning the window <u>frame</u>. |

In which sentence does <u>frame</u> have the same meaning as it does in the sentence above?

F My uncle has a very large <u>frame</u>.

G I bowled a strike in the first <u>frame</u> of the game.

H Please <u>frame</u> your questions carefully.

J I need a new <u>frame</u> for this picture.

13 | They <u>range</u> in size from small to extra large. |

In which sentence does <u>range</u> have the same meaning as it does in the sentence above?

A The plane flew out of radar <u>range</u>.

B The prices <u>range</u> from two dollars to ten dollars.

C My aunt camped in that mountain <u>range</u> during her vacation last year.

D A pot of soup simmered on the <u>range</u>.

14 | Don't <u>force</u> the child to eat. |

In which sentence does <u>force</u> have the same meaning as it does in the sentence above?

F Will the storm <u>force</u> us to cancel our plans to go camping?

G Is this school rule still in <u>force</u>?

H Electricity is a powerful <u>force</u>.

J The sales <u>force</u> was given a bonus for their outstanding work this year.

GO ON

Sample C

The king issued a proclamation stating that everyone in the kingdom had to pay the new tax. **Proclamation** means—

A   report.

B   law.

C   announcement.

D   letter.

🛑 STOP

For questions 15–21, darken the circle for the word or words that give the meaning of the underlined word, or write in the answer.

15   Please secure this rope to the dock. **Secure** means—

A   fasten.

B   paint.

C   measure.

D   throw.

16   Ling was very excited to get her favorite star's autograph. **Autograph** means—

F   photograph.

G   address.

H   telephone number.

J   signature.

17   Robin Hood is a famous fictitious character. **Fictitious** means—

A   heroic.

B   imaginary.

C   adventurous.

D   real.

18   This puppy is apparently lost. **Apparently** means—

F   always.

G   hardly.

H   slightly.

J   clearly.

19   The police assured her that it was merely a routine investigation. **Routine** means—

A   short.

B   serious.

C   regular.

D   private.

20   The guide told us to heed his instructions so we would not get lost in the forest. **Heed** means—

F   mind.

G   ignore.

H   read.

J   sing.

21   We had to walk seven miles from the plane to the remote mountain village. What is meant by **remote**?

_____

_____

_____

_____

🛑 STOP

PART 1: MATH PROBLEM SOLVING

Sample A

What number is shown here?

60,000 + 5,000 + 10 + 8

A   60,518   C   605,108

B   65,018   D   650,018

For questions 1–53, darken the circle for the correct answer, or write in the answer.

1   It is 38.459 meters from the reviewer's stand to the end of the parade route. What is the value of the 4 in this number?

A   4 hundred-thousandths

B   4 thousandths

C   4 hundredths

D   4 tenths

2   Jan is making a quilt. The pattern requires these fabrics and amounts.

Blue floral	$1\frac{7}{8}$ yds.
White solid	$2\frac{1}{8}$ yds.
Gold checked	$2\frac{2}{3}$ yds.
Navy calico	$2\frac{1}{4}$ yds.

Jan uses the *most* of which fabric?

F   Blue floral   H   Gold checked

G   White solid   J   Navy calico

3   What fraction means the same as $\frac{38}{6}$?

A $6\frac{1}{6}$ C $6\frac{3}{6}$

B $6\frac{1}{3}$ D $6\frac{7}{6}$

4   Each square represents 0.01. What decimal number is shown below?

F   0.239   H   2.39

G   2.0239   J   23.9

5   What mixed number is shown by the shaded part of the circles?

A $\frac{6}{8}$

B $1\frac{3}{4}$

C $1\frac{2}{6}$

D $1\frac{2}{6}$

6   There are 34,578 permanent seats at the outdoor concert arena. In addition, there are 1,000 temporary seats set up for the concert. How many seats are there altogether?

F   33,578   H   34,678

G   34,478   J   35,578

7   Mr. Campos raises turkeys. To measure their growth, he records their weights periodically. Yesterday he weighed a turkey at 4.63 kilograms, another at 4.7 kilograms, a third at 4.09 kilograms, and a fourth at 4.04 kilograms. List the weights of the turkeys in order from lightest to heaviest.

_____

_____

GO ON

8 If $\frac{9}{13} - x = \frac{9}{13}$, then $x =$

_____

_____

_____

_____

9 If $130 + x = 420$, what number replaces the x to make the sentence true?

A 550

B 390

C 290

D 210

10 Each section of the parking garage has 4 levels and each level has 45 parking spaces. Which number sentence shows how to find T, the total number of parking spaces in 6 sections of the garage?

F $(4 \times 6) \div T = 45$

G $(4 \times 45) \times 6 = T$

H $(4 \times T) \times 6 = 45$

J $(4 \times 45) \div 6 = T$

11 These beads represent the number 351,642,227. What place value is represented by the wire with 6 beads?

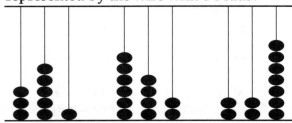

A hundred millions

B ten millions

C millions

D hundred thousands

12 What is the smallest number of raffle tickets that can be shared equally among 6 children with no tickets left over or among 18 children with no tickets left over?

F 36

G 24

H 18

J 8

13 Which of the these number sentences is related to $28 \div 4 = \square$?

A $4 \times \square = 28$

B $28 - 4 = \square$

C $4 + \square = 28$

D $28 + 4 = \square$

14 The Lakewood High School Chess Club held their annual fall bake sale last week to raise funds for new chess sets. They made a total of 173 items to sell. They sold 57 cakes and 103 cookies. What number sentence could be used to find L, the number of baked goods left unsold?

F $173 - (57 + 103) = L$

G $57 + L = 173 + 103$

H $173 + (103 - 57) = L$

J $L - (57 \times 103) = 173$

GO ON

15 Cassie has 24 cartoon videos, 4 family videos, and 12 movie videos. If she randomly selects 1 video off the shelf, what is the probability that it will be a cartoon?

A $\frac{1}{24}$

B $\frac{1}{6}$

C $\frac{1}{2}$

D $\frac{3}{5}$

16 It is Oliver's turn in a board game he is playing with his cousins. What is the probability that Oliver will have to go back 2 spaces on this spin?

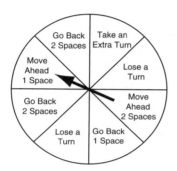

F $\frac{1}{4}$

G $\frac{1}{8}$

H $\frac{3}{8}$

J $\frac{5}{8}$

17 Which vowel (a, e, i, o, u) appears most frequently in the following sentence?
The elephants graze near the mountains.

A a

B e

C i

D u

18 Tomás has 6 nickels and 8 pennies in his backpack. What is the probability that Tomás will randomly pick a nickel out of his backpack?

F $\frac{1}{8}$

G $\frac{1}{6}$

H $\frac{3}{7}$

J $\frac{5}{3}$

19 Cards labeled with A, B, C, or D are placed on a table. What is the probability of choosing a card with the letter C?

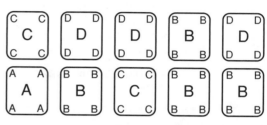

A $\frac{1}{10}$

B $\frac{1}{5}$

C $\frac{1}{4}$

D $\frac{1}{2}$

20 Nielson's Sporting Goods Store sells polo tops with short sleeves or long sleeves. They come in white, red, and black. They come in small, medium, and large. How many total choices of polo tops are there?

_____

_____

_____

_____

_____

_____

GO ON➡

This graph shows the results of a survey regarding trips people make. Use the graph to answer questions 21 and 22.

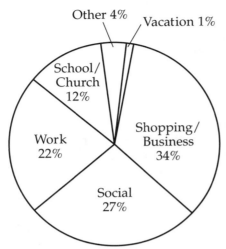

Trips People Make

21 Which two categories account for most of the trips people make?

F School/Church and Vacation

G Shopping/Business and Social

H Social and Work

J Work and Shopping/Business

22 Out of 100 trips, how many are made for shopping/business reasons?

A 4

B 12

C 22

D 34

23 Wanda is trying to decide what to wear to school. On this particular morning, she has 3 pairs of jeans, 4 tops, and 2 pairs of shoes to choose from. How many different clothing combinations does Wanda have?

F 24

G 14

H 12

J 9

24 A special machine multiplies any number entered into it by a secret number. The table below shows how the numbers are changed. Which numbers complete the table?

Original number	5	8	9
New number	35		

A 40 and 43

B 44 and 72

C 40 and 63

D 56 and 63

25 There are 4 red beads, 8 yellow beads, and 2 pink beads in a container. If 1 bead is picked at random from the container, what are the chances that it will be red?

_____

_____

_____

_____

GO ON➡

26 Which line segment names a radius of the circle shown here?

F $\overline{AC}$

G $\overline{AB}$

H $\overline{PB}$

J $\overline{CA}$

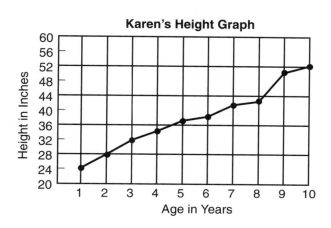

27 The graph shown here is a record of Karen's growth. Approximately how many inches did Karen grow between the ages of 6 and 9?

Karen's Height Graph

_____

_____

_____

_____

28 What kind of angle is formed by the hands of the clock?

A less than 90°

B exactly 90°

C exactly 180°

D more than 90° and less than 180°

This table shows the total reading time for Mr. Rivera's 8 honor students for each week of March. Use the table to answer questions 29 and 30.

Weekly Reading	
Week	**Hours**
1	14
2	18
3	16
4	12

29 What was the average number of hours per week in March that the students spent reading?

F 15 hours

G 14 hours

H 13 hours

J 12 hours

30 Which tally chart shows the information presented in the table?

A

Week 1	ℕℕ ℕℕ
Week 2	ℕℕ ℕℕ ℕℕ I
Week 3	ℕℕ ℕℕ III
Week 4	ℕℕ ℕℕ II

B

Week 1	ℕℕ ℕℕ IIII
Week 2	ℕℕ ℕℕ II
Week 3	ℕℕ ℕℕ ℕℕ III
Week 4	ℕℕ ℕℕ ℕℕ

C

Week 1	ℕℕ ℕℕ ℕℕ
Week 2	ℕℕ ℕℕ II
Week 3	ℕℕ ℕℕ ℕℕ I
Week 4	ℕℕ ℕℕ ℕℕ III

D

Week 1	ℕℕ ℕℕ IIII
Week 2	ℕℕ ℕℕ ℕℕ III
Week 3	ℕℕ ℕℕ ℕℕ I
Week 4	ℕℕ ℕℕ II

GO ON

31 What is the area of the shaded section of this figure?

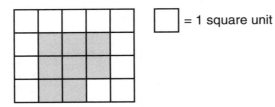

☐ = 1 square unit

    F 20 square units

    G 12 square units

    H 9 square units

    J 8 square units

32 Which figure shows a translation of the car?

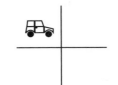

A

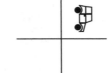

C

B

D

33 Which of the following metric units of measurement is best to use to measure the capacity of a bucket?

    F centimeter

    G liter

    H kilograms

    J milligram

34 Ray bought the toys shown below at the toy store. Which of the toys has a line of symmetry?

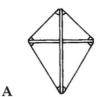

A

B

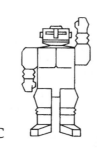

C

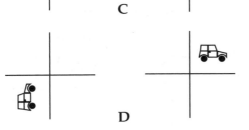

D

35 Name the coordinates of point B shown on the grid.

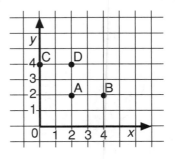

_____

_____

_____

_____

GO ON➡

36 A musical program began at 4:05 P.M. If it lasted 1 hour and 30 minutes, at what time did the program end?

F 5:35 P.M.   **H** 6:05 P.M.

G 5:50 P.M   **J** 6:40 P.M.

37 Use your inch ruler and the map to help you answer the question. What is the actual distance between the two farms?

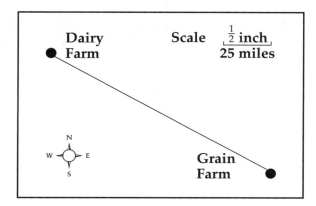

Dairy Farm   Scale $\frac{1}{2}$ inch, 25 miles

Grain Farm

A 200 miles   **C** 125 miles

B 175 miles   **D** 75 miles

38 Use your inch ruler to help you answer this question. How would you calculate the perimeter of this miniature magnetic frame?

_____

_____

_____

_____

_____

_____

39 Katie measured a piece of rope 18 feet long. How many yards is that?

F 648 yd   **H** 6 yd

G 54 yd   **J** $\frac{1}{2}$ yd

40 Which shaded shape shown here has an area of 11 square units?

□ = 1 square unit

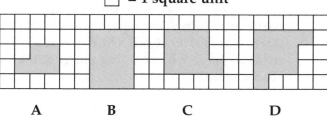

A   B   C   D

41 Use your centimeter ruler to help you answer this question. Which figure shown here has an area of 5cm^2 ?

F

G

H

J

GO ON➡

42 Lisa measured 8 gallons of water. How many quarts is that?

  A 128 quarts

  B 32 quarts

  C 16 quarts

  D 2 quarts

43 The school store sells paper with or without binder holes that is available in white or yellow. The paper comes in 3 sizes. How many choices of paper do students have when buying paper at the school store?

  F 12

  G 7

  H 6

  J 3

44 Which shows the piece that is missing from the figure?

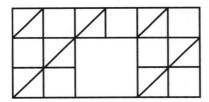

  A

  B

  C

  D

45 Kala is a photographer who sells her portraits for $46.95 each. Last week she sold 8 portraits. What is the best estimate for Kala's total earnings for the portraits?

  F $200

  G $300

  H $400

  J $500

46 Marco designed the rock wall around his garden by using 2 brown rocks, then 5 gray rocks, then 8 tan rocks, then 3 white rocks. If Marco continues this pattern, what will be the color of the thirty-fifth rock?

  A white

  B tan

  C gray

  D brown

47 Stephanie is 5 inches taller than her cousin. What other information is needed to find the height of Stephanie's cousin?

_____

_____

_____

_____

_____

_____

GO ON➡

48 The sum of the first two numerals in Max's apartment number is twice the sum of the last two numerals. Which of these could be Max's apartment number?

F 842

G 824

H 428

J 248

49 Each rectangular prism in the picture is equal in weight to 2 cylinders. What should be added to Side A in order to balance the scales?

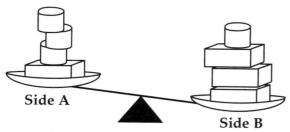

Side A

Side B

A 1 cylinder

B 2 cylinders

C 1 rectangular prism and 1 cylinder

D 2 rectangular prisms

50 Karen, Bill, and Mike turned in the most book reports during the first grading period. Mike did not read the most and Karen did not read the least. Bill had fewer book reports than Mike. Which of these shows the order from most to the least number of book reports?

F Karen, Bill, Mike

G Mike, Bill, Karen

H Karen, Mike, Bill

J Bill, Mike, Karen

51 David went shopping for school clothes. He bought 2 pairs of slacks, 3 shirts, and 1 sweater. What do you *not* need to know to find out how much money David had left after shopping?

A how many hours David shopped

B how much money David started with

C how much money each pair of slacks cost

D how much money the sweater cost

52 There are 13 dancers in one chorus line and 29 dancers in another chorus line. How many dancers need to move from the second line to the first line in order to have the same number of dancers in both chorus lines?

F 24

G 16

H 8

J 4

53 The Hernandez family raised 558 cattle. They sold 215 of them. What is the best estimate of the number of cattle they have left?

_____

_____

_____

_____

_____

Sample A

$8 \times 0.6 =$

A 0.0048
B 0.48
C 1.4
D 4.8
E NH

Sample B

Susan had $2\frac{5}{6}$ pizzas left from her party. What is that amount rounded to the nearest whole number?

F $2\frac{1}{2}$
G 3
H 4
J 5
K NH

STOP

Directions: For questions 1–13, darken the circle for the correct answer, or write in the answer. Darken the circle for NH (Not Here) if the correct answer is not given.

1

$58 \times 24 =$

A 348
B 1,126
C 1,262
D 1,392
E NH

2

$4\frac{5}{8}$
$-\frac{3}{8}$

F $\frac{2}{8}$
G $4\frac{1}{8}$
H $4\frac{1}{4}$
J $4\frac{1}{2}$
K NH

3

$0.543 + 0.791 =$

A 1.23
B 1.334
C 1.34
D 13.34
E NH

4

$\frac{6}{8}$
$-\frac{1}{2}$

F $\frac{1}{4}$
G $\frac{7}{16}$
H $\frac{3}{8}$
J $\frac{5}{6}$
K NH

5

$\frac{2}{3} \times \frac{4}{5} =$

A $\frac{3}{4}$
B $\frac{8}{15}$
C $\frac{6}{15}$
D $\frac{2}{15}$
E NH

6

$\frac{2}{3}$
$+\frac{3}{10}$

F $\frac{9}{20}$
G $\frac{6}{10}$
H $\frac{7}{10}$
J $\frac{3}{5}$
K NH

7

$675 \div 6 =$

A 110
B 110 R6
C 112
D 112 R3
E NH

GO ON

8 Find the product.

876 × 65 =

_____

_____

_____

_____

9 Elizabeth wrapped 15 gifts for a grab bag booth at the carnival.

She needs 5 feet of ribbon for each gift. How many feet of ribbon does she need altogether?

F 3

G 10

H 20

J 75

K NH

10 Each admission ticket to the amusement park costs $24.50. A family packet of 5 tickets cost $98.00.

How much can be saved on 5 tickets by buying the family packet?

A $3.75

B $5.50

C $19.25

D $24.50

E NH

11 Alice read 2 books last weekend. She read the first book in $4\frac{3}{4}$ hours and the second book in $3\frac{3}{4}$ hours.

How many hours did it take Alice to read both books?

F $8\frac{1}{2}$ hours

G $7\frac{1}{2}$ hours

H $6\frac{3}{4}$ hours

J 1 hour

K NH

GO ON ➡

12 Roberto needs to know the net weight of the package he is mailing in order to calculate the amount of postage he will pay.

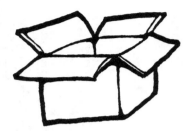

If the package contains 12 copies of a report that weighs 37.3 grams each, what is the total weight of the package?

A   447.6 grams

B   424.7 grams

C   398.7 grams

D   49.3 grams

E   NH

13 Brian bought 3 boxes of hamster food at the pet store.

Each box cost $ 0.75.

How much change will he get from a ten-dollar bill?

F $8.75

G $7.75

H $6.75

J $2.25

K   NH

STOP

Sample A

Nan would like to build a dog exercise pen in her back yard. She saw an exercise pen that she liked in a photograph in the newspaper. Nan decides to write a letter to the newspaper editor asking for information about the pen. Before Nan writes the letter, she needs to find the address of the newspaper. She should look in—

A a thesaurus.

C an atlas.

B a telephone book.

D a dictionary.

STOP

For questions 1–4, read the passage below. Then darken the circle for the correct answer to each question, or write in the answer.

Tropical Fish

Andrew has had an aquarium of tropical fish for as long as he can remember. He decided that the care of tropical fish would be an excellent subject for a science research report.

1 Andrew located the book *Tropical Fish: A Complete Pet Owner's Manual*. Where should he look to find the name of the author of the book?

A the table of contents

C the index

B the glossary

D the title page

2 What information would Andrew **not** want to include in his report?

F a list of the most popular species of tropical fish for aquariums

G a description of the feeding habits of tropical fish

H a discussion of the kinds of tropical fish that can coexist in an aquarium

J a chapter on raising turtles in aquariums

3 What should Andrew do before he writes his report?

_____

_____

_____

_____

4 Which of the following sources should Andrew use to locate a book about tropical fish?

A a telephone directory

B a library card catalog

C a science textbook

D an atlas

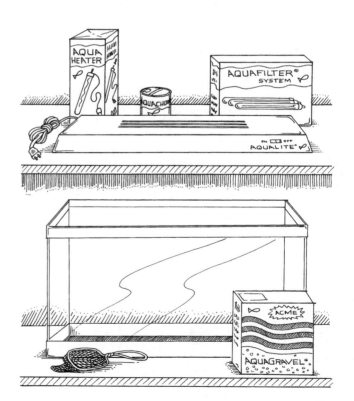

GO ON ➡

Andrew used the dictionary to check some words he wanted to use in his report.

5   Which guide words might mark the page where Andrew would find the word *degree*?

F   definition–degrade

G   delay–desert

H   defeat–defrost

J   deform–delicious

6   What is the correct way to divide thermostat into syllables?

A   ther mos tat

B   therm o stat

C   ther mo stat

D   the rmos tat

Here is the Table of Contents from *Tropical Fish: A Complete Pet Owner's Manual*. Study it carefully. Then answer questions 7 and 8.

Table of Contents	
Chapter . . . . **Page**	
1 **How To Choose an Aquarium**	5
2 **Equipment and Accessories**	11
3 **Preparing the Aquarium**	16
4 **Decorating the Aquarium**	24
5 **Choosing Plants**.	27
6 **Choosing Fish**	32
7 **Feeding and Caring for Fish**.	35

7   Which chapter should Andrew read to find information about the size of the aquarium to purchase?

F   Chapter 1

G   Chapter 2

H   Chapter 6

J   Chapter 7

8   Which chapter should Andrew read to find information about the best kind of lighting to use in an aquarium?

A   Chapter 1

B   Chapter 2

C   Chapter 3

D   Chapter 4

GO ON➡

Here is a rough draft of the first part of Andrew's report. Read the rough draft carefully. Then answer questions 9–12.

Raising Tropical Fish

If you want to raise tropical fish, you must decide how much money you
(1)

want to spend. Consider the kind of fish you want. You also need to know
(2)   (3)

how many fish you want to raise. Once you have decided these three things,
(4)

you are ready to buy an aquarium.

You will have many questions to ask, so you want to do business with
(5)

someone who knows about tropical fish. Be sure to get a tank that is made
(6)

and constructed of glass and can be used with salt water. The more fish you
(7)

plan to raise, the larger the tank must be. An aquarium cover is a must
(8)

because it keeps the fish in the tank and the dust out. A good cover has
(9)

openings that allow for feeding the fish, for a heater, and for a filter.

The equipment should include a heater, a thermostat, a filter, and a light
(10)

you need for your aquarium. Other recommended items include a fish net,
(11)

plant tongs, and a window washer. A heater is also necessary because tropical
(12)

fish need water that is constant in temperature.

GO ON➡

9 Which sentence could begin the second paragraph?

    F It is important to buy your aquarium at a well-respected pet store.

    G You should not add fish to the tank until the water has reached the correct temperature.

    H Some people add decorative rocks to their aquariums.

    J Your favorite fish will live a long healthy life.

10 What is the best way to write sentence 10?

    A The equipment should include, a heater, a thermostat, a filter, and a light for your aquarium.

    B The equipment for your aquarium, needed are a heater, thermostat, filter, and light.

    C The equipment for your aquarium should include a heater, a thermostat, a filter, and a light.

    D As it is written.

11 Which group of words needlessly repeats an idea?

    F …will have many questions to ask…

    G …aquarium cover is a must…

    H …many choices of sizes and shapes…

    J …that is made and constructed of glass…

12 How can sentences 2 and 3 best be combined?

_____

_____

_____

_____

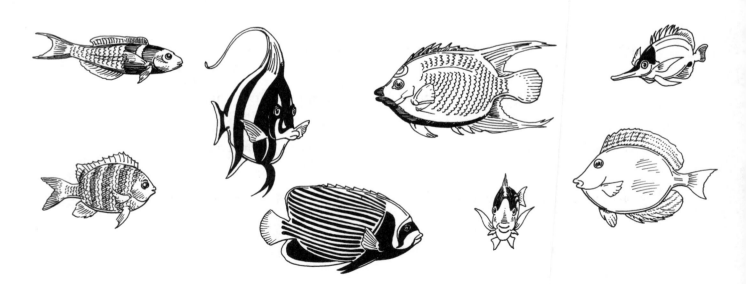

GO ON▶

Here is the next part of the rough draft of Andrew's report. This part has certain words and phrases underlined. Read the draft carefully. Then answer questions 13–19.

Once you have all <u>you're equipment</u> you are ready to set up the aquarium.
(13)

Place the tank on a level surface and install your filter and heating systems.
(14)

Next, add about 2 inches of gravel or sand to the bottom of the tank. Add
(15)   **(16)**

fertilizer for your plants. It <u>has been found</u> that fertilizer added to the gravel
                                        (17)

or sand helps the plants grow. Add your decorative rocks and driftwood.
                                        (18)

When you <u>are finishing decorating</u> your tank, fill it about one-third full
(19)

with water. Be careful not to stir up the gravel. The <u>pet store owner, Ms.</u>
            (20)   **(21)**

<u>Lauren Kirby</u> suggests that you place a large plate in the bottom of the tank.

Then slowly pour the water on the plate. Be sure to take the plate out when
(22)   **(23)**

you are finished.

Now you are ready to add your plants. Ms. Kirby <u>suggests, "Make a hole</u>
(24)   **(25)**

in the gravel and place the plant in it as deep as possible. Be sure the root tips
                                                            (26)

are pointing down. Arrange the plants so they will be <u>appealing to the eye</u>".
            (27)

<u>Waiting two days</u> before you add your fish to the aquarium. This gives
(28)   **(29)**

the plants a chance to take root.

GO ON➡

13 In sentence 13, <u>you're equipment</u> is best written—

   A you are equipment

   B your equipment

   C their equipment

   D As it is written.

14 In sentence 17, <u>has been found</u> is best written—

   F have found

   G has found

   H will find

   J As it is written.

15 In sentence 19, <u>are finishing decorating</u> is best written—

   A is finished decorating

   B will be finishing decorating

   C have finished decorating

   D As it is written.

16 In sentence 21, <u>pet store owner, Ms. Lauren Kirby</u> is best written—

   F pet store owner Ms. Lauren Kirby

   G pet store owner ms. Lauren Kirby

   H pet store owner, Ms. Lauren Kirby,

   J As it is written.

17 In sentence 25, <u>suggests, "Make a hole</u> is best written—

   A suggests "make a hole

   B suggests, "make a hole

   C suggests "Make a hole

   D As it is written.

18 In sentence 27, <u>appealing to the eye".</u> is best written—

   F appealing to the eye."

   G appealing to the eye"

   H appealing to the eye.

   J As it is written.

19 In sentence 28, <u>Waiting two days</u> is best written—

   A Waited two days

   B Wait two days

   C Have waited two days

   D As it is written.

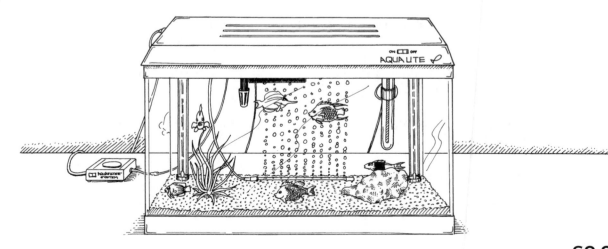

GO ON ➡

For questions 20–31, read each sentence carefully. If one of the words is misspelled, darken the circle for that word. If all of the words are spelled correctly, darken the circle for *No mistake*.

20 Peter's admireation for his father knows no bounds. No mistake
            F   G   H   J

21 I store my fishing tackle in the garage. No mistake
           A   B   C   D

22 The highway was obstructet by the fallen tree. No mistake
        F   G   H   J

23 Matilda was the stingyest of the three witches in the fable. No mistake
             A   B   C   D

24 The mechanic lubricated the bearings before he reaplaced them in the wheel. No mistake
        F   G   H   J

25 The Waltons are one of the wealthyest families in the United States. No mistake
           A   B   C   D

26 Marta addressed the inviteations yesterday. No mistake
        F   G   H   J

27 We always save our receipts for tax purposes. No mistake
        A   B   C   D

28 Xavier is working as a senator's aid during this legislative session. No mistake
                    F   G   H   J

29 Sammy smearred strawberry jam all over his new shirt. No mistake
          A   B   C   D

30 Mom's new cookware is made of stainless steal. No mistake
        F   G   H   J

31 Miriam honkt her horn at the squirrel in the street. No mistake
        A   B   C   D

STOP

Answer Sheet

STUDENT'S NAME		SCHOOL:

LAST **FIRST** **MI** TEACHER:

FEMALE ○   MALE ○

BIRTH DATE

MONTH	DAY	YEAR
Jan ○	⓪ ⓪	⓪ ⓪
Feb ○	① ①	① ①
Mar ○	② ②	② ②
Apr ○	③ ③	③ ③
May ○	④	④ ④
Jun ○	⑤	⑤ ⑤
Jul ○	⑥	⑥ ⑥
Aug ○	⑦	⑦ ⑦
Sep ○	⑧	⑧ ⑧
Oct ○	⑨	⑨ ⑨
Nov ○		
Dec ○		

GRADE ② ③④⑤⑥⑦⑧

(Name grid columns with bubbles A–Z)

Fill in the circle for each multiple-choice answer. Write the answers to the
open-ended questions on a separate sheet of paper.

TEST 1   Reading Comprehension

SA Ⓐ Ⓑ Ⓒ Ⓓ	6 Ⓐ Ⓑ Ⓒ Ⓓ	11 Ⓐ Ⓑ Ⓒ Ⓓ	16 Ⓐ Ⓑ Ⓒ Ⓓ	21 Ⓕ Ⓖ Ⓗ Ⓙ	26 Ⓕ Ⓖ Ⓗ Ⓙ
1 Ⓐ Ⓑ Ⓒ Ⓓ	7 Ⓕ Ⓖ Ⓗ Ⓙ	12 Ⓕ Ⓖ Ⓗ Ⓙ	17 Ⓕ Ⓖ Ⓗ Ⓙ	22 Ⓐ Ⓑ Ⓒ Ⓓ	27 Ⓐ Ⓑ Ⓒ Ⓓ
2 OPEN ENDED	8 OPEN ENDED	13 Ⓐ Ⓑ Ⓒ Ⓓ	18 Ⓐ Ⓑ Ⓒ Ⓓ	23 Ⓕ Ⓖ Ⓗ Ⓙ	28 Ⓕ Ⓖ Ⓗ Ⓙ
3 Ⓕ Ⓖ Ⓗ Ⓙ	9 Ⓐ Ⓑ Ⓒ Ⓓ	14 Ⓕ Ⓖ Ⓗ Ⓙ	19 Ⓕ Ⓖ Ⓗ Ⓙ	24 OPEN ENDED	29 Ⓐ Ⓑ Ⓒ Ⓓ
4 Ⓐ Ⓑ Ⓒ Ⓓ	10 Ⓕ Ⓖ Ⓗ Ⓙ	15 OPEN ENDED	20 Ⓐ Ⓑ Ⓒ Ⓓ	25 Ⓐ Ⓑ Ⓒ Ⓓ	30 OPEN ENDED
5 Ⓕ Ⓖ Ⓗ Ⓙ					

TEST 2   Reading Vocabulary

SA Ⓐ Ⓑ Ⓒ Ⓓ	4 Ⓕ Ⓖ Ⓗ Ⓙ	8 Ⓕ Ⓖ Ⓗ Ⓙ	11 Ⓐ Ⓑ Ⓒ Ⓓ	SC Ⓐ Ⓑ Ⓒ Ⓓ	18 Ⓕ Ⓖ Ⓗ Ⓙ
1 Ⓐ Ⓑ Ⓒ Ⓓ	5 Ⓐ Ⓑ Ⓒ Ⓓ	9 Ⓐ Ⓑ Ⓒ Ⓓ	12 Ⓕ Ⓖ Ⓗ Ⓙ	15 Ⓐ Ⓑ Ⓒ Ⓓ	19 Ⓐ Ⓑ Ⓒ Ⓓ
2 Ⓕ Ⓖ Ⓗ Ⓙ	6 Ⓕ Ⓖ Ⓗ Ⓙ	SB Ⓐ Ⓑ Ⓒ Ⓓ	13 Ⓐ Ⓑ Ⓒ Ⓓ	16 Ⓕ Ⓖ Ⓗ Ⓙ	20 Ⓕ Ⓖ Ⓗ Ⓙ
3 Ⓐ Ⓑ Ⓒ Ⓓ	7 Ⓐ Ⓑ Ⓒ Ⓓ	10 Ⓕ Ⓖ Ⓗ Ⓙ	14 Ⓕ Ⓖ Ⓗ Ⓙ	17 Ⓐ Ⓑ Ⓒ Ⓓ	21 OPEN ENDED

TEST 3   Part 1: Math Problem Solving

SA (A) (B) (C) (D)

1 (A) (B) (C) (D)
2 (F) (G) (H) (J)
3 (A) (B) (C) (D)
4 (F) (G) (H) (J)
5 (A) (B) (C) (D)
6 (F) (G) (H) (J)
7 OPEN ENDED
8 OPEN ENDED

9 (A) (B) (C) (D)
10 (F) (G) (H) (J)
11 (A) (B) (C) (D)
12 (F) (G) (H) (J)
13 (A) (B) (C) (D)
14 (F) (G) (H) (J)
15 (A) (B) (C) (D)
16 (F) (G) (H) (J)
17 (A) (B) (C) (D)

18 (F) (G) (H) (J)
19 (A) (B) (C) (D)
20 OPEN ENDED
21 (F) (G) (H) (J)
22 (A) (B) (C) (D)
23 (F) (G) (H) (J)
24 (A) (B) (C) (D)
25 OPEN ENDED
26 (F) (G) (H) (J)

27 OPEN ENDED
28 (A) (B) (C) (D)
29 (F) (G) (H) (J)
30 (A) (B) (C) (D)
31 (F) (G) (H) (J)
32 (A) (B) (C) (D)
33 (F) (G) (H) (J)
34 (A) (B) (C) (D)
35 OPEN ENDED

36 (F) (G) (H) (J)
37 (A) (B) (C) (D)
38 OPEN ENDED
39 (F) (G) (H) (J)
40 (A) (B) (C) (D)
41 (F) (G) (H) (J)
42 (A) (B) (C) (D)
43 (F) (G) (H) (J)
44 (A) (B) (C) (D)

45 (F) (G) (H) (J)
46 (A) (B) (C) (D)
47 OPEN ENDED
48 (F) (G) (H) (J)
49 (A) (B) (C) (D)
50 (F) (G) (H) (J)
51 (A) (B) (C) (D)
52 (F) (G) (H) (J)
53 OPEN ENDED

Part 2: Math Procedures

SA (A) (B) (C) (D) (E)
SB (F) (G) (H) (J) (K)
1 (A) (B) (C) (D) (E)

2 (F) (G) (H) (J) (K)
3 (A) (B) (C) (D) (E)
4 (F) (G) (H) (J) (K)

5 (A) (B) (C) (D) (E)
6 (F) (G) (H) (J) (K)
7 (A) (B) (C) (D) (E)

8 OPEN ENDED
9 (F) (G) (H) (J) (K)
10 (A) (B) (C) (D) (E)

11 (F) (G) (H) (J) (K)
12 (A) (B) (C) (D) (E)
13 (F) (G) (H) (J) (K)

TEST 4   Language

SA (A) (B) (C) (D)

1 (A) (B) (C) (D)
2 (F) (G) (H) (J)
3 OPEN ENDED
4 (A) (B) (C) (D)
5 (F) (G) (H) (J)

6 (A) (B) (C) (D)
7 (F) (G) (H) (J)
8 (A) (B) (C) (D)
9 (F) (G) (H) (J)
10 (A) (B) (C) (D)
11 (F) (G) (H) (J)

12 OPEN ENDED
13 (A) (B) (C) (D)
14 (F) (G) (H) (J)
15 (A) (B) (C) (D)
16 (F) (G) (H) (J)
17 (A) (B) (C) (D)

18 (F) (G) (H) (J)
19 (A) (B) (C) (D)
20 (F) (G) (H) (J)
21 (A) (B) (C) (D)
22 (F) (G) (H) (J)
23 (A) (B) (C) (D)

24 (F) (G) (H) (J)
25 (A) (B) (C) (D)
26 (F) (G) (H) (J)
27 (A) (B) (C) (D)
28 (F) (G) (H) (J)
29 (A) (B) (C) (D)

30 (F) (G) (H) (J)
31 (A) (B) (C) (D)

ANSWER KEY

READING SKILLS

P. 8
Fact: December 1903
Fact: Orville Wright

P. 9
3. B

P. 10-11
1. B
2. C
3. A
4. C
5. D
6. B
7. A
8. C
9. A
10. D

P. 12-13
1. D
2. B
3. D
4. A
5. C
6. D
7. B
8. C
9. B
10. A

P. 14-15
1. B
2. C
3. C
4. A
5. C
6. D
7. A
8. B
9. A
10. C

P. 16-17
1. C
2. A
3. B
4. A
5. B
6. D
7. A
8. C
9. A
10. B

P. 18-19
1. B
2. A
3. B
4. C
5. C
6. A
7. A
8. B
9. A
10. D

P. 20-21
1. A
2. A
3. B
4. D
5. D
6. B
7. A
8. C
9. C
10. C

P. 22-23
1. D
2. C
3. A
4. D
5. B
6. B
7. A
8. C
9. C
10. B

P. 24-25
1. A
2. C
3. D
4. B
5. C
6. B
7. A
8. C
9. D
10. B

P. 26
Possible answers include:
1. The Statue of Liberty is a figure of a robed woman holding a torch.
2. France gave the statue to the United States as a gift.
3. The statue is 151 feet tall.

P. 27
Check that you have four facts in your paragraph.

P. 28
2, 3, 1

P. 29
3. B

P. 30-31
1. 2, 3, 1
2. B
3. B
4. B
5. C

P. 32-33
1. 1, 2, 3
2. B
3. B
4. A
5. C

P. 34-35
1. 2, 3, 1
2. A
3. B
4. B
5. C

P. 36-37
1. 3, 1, 2
2. A
3. A
4. C
5. C

P. 38-39
1. 2, 3, 1
2. A
3. A
4. C
5. A

P. 40-41
1. 1, 3, 2
2. A
3. C
4. C
5. C

P. 42-43
1. 3, 1, 2
2. A
3. C
4. C
5. B

P. 44-45
1. 2, 1, 3
2. A
3. B
4. B
5. C

P. 46
Possible answers include:
1. The first thing Janet does is strap on spurs and loop a rope around a tree.
2. Janet ties herself to the tree when she reaches the nest.
3. Janet clamps the band on after she has slowly pulled the eagle close.
4. A baby eagle might jump from the nest if it has been frightened.

P. 47
Check that your paragraph is written in sequence.
Check that you have used time order words, such as first, next, and last.

P. 49
2. B
3. D

P. 50-51
1. B
2. D
3. A
4. B
5. D
6. C
7. D
8. A
9. B
10. B
11. D
12. D
13. B
14. C
15. C
16. B

P. 52-53
1. D
2. B
3. C
4. A
5. D
6. A
7. B
8. A
9. D
10. C
11. A
12. B
13. B
14. C
15. C
16. A

P. 54-55
1. C
2. C
3. C
4. A
5. A
6. B
7. C
8. D
9. C
10. D
11. B
12. A
13. C
14. A
15. B
16. D

1. C
2. B
3. C
4. B
5. D
6. C
7. A
8. C
9. D
10. C
11. A
12. B
13. A
14. C
15. A
16. D

p. 58-59
1. B
2. C
3. D
4. A
5. B
6. C
7. A
8. A

p. 60-61
1. B
2. D
3. B
4. D
5. B
6. C
7. B
8. B

p. 62-63
1. C
2. D
3. C
4. D
5. B
6. D
7. C
8. A

p. 64-65
1. B
2. C
3. B
4. C
5. C
6. A
7. D
8. B

p. 66
Possible answers include:
1. game or party
2. pizza or tacos
3. neighborhood or world
4. welcome or comfortable
5. clouds or city
6. toys or ants

p. 67
Possible answers include
1. It might be an elephant. It might be a lion.
2. A baby giraffe was eating leaves. Some chimps were eating bananas.
3. He shot a whole roll of film. He took many pictures.
4. They talked about making banners. They talked about getting old photos of the city.
5. They might do a play. They might have a band concert.
6. She suggested fireworks. She suggested a parade.

p. 69
The correct answer is C. The paragraph tells about the ways in which microchips are used in wristwatches, computers, robots, video games, and space shuttles.

p. 70-71
1. B
2. D
3. D
4. C
5. D

p. 72-73
1. D
2. A
3. C
4. C
5. B

p. 74-75
1. B
2. C
3. C
4. C
5. D

p. 76-77
1. B
2. D
3. B
4. A
5. A

p. 78-79
1. C
2. C
3. C
4. C
5. B

p. 80-81
1. C
2. C
3. A
4. D
5. A

p. 82-83
1. C
2. C
3. B
4. D
5. A

p. 84-85
1. B
2. C
3. C
4. C
5. A

p. 86
Possible answers include:
1. Pigs used to search for truffles in France.
2. Men used to wear masks and dance women's parts in ballets.
3. Matzeliger invented the shoe-shaping machine.

p. 87
Check that you have underlined your main idea.
Check that you have used four details in your story.

p. 89
1. at a job interview
2. at a car wash
3. at a traffic light
4. on a mountain

p. 90-91
1. C
2. B
3. A
4. C
5. D

p. 92-93
1. A
2. A
3. D
4. A
5. D

p. 94-95
1. A
2. B
3. C
4. C
5. B

p. 96-97
1. A
2. C
3. D
4. A
5. B

p. 98-99
1. D
2. A
3. C
4. B
5. D

p. 100-101
1. D
2. C
3. B
4. A
5. A

p. 102-103
1. B
2. D
3. A
4. C
5. B

p. 104-105
1. B
2. D
3. D
4. C
5. C

p. 106
Possible answers include:
1. You can't play polo if you can't ride a horse.
2. Phillis Wheatley was good with languages.
3. Alonso's weather station isn't finished yet.

p. 107
Possible answers include:
1. Juneteenth is not a holiday in all states. It is celebrated only by people in Texas and in some other states.
2. There was slavery in Texas. Union troops ended slavery there.
3. Texans did not know the Civil War had ended. The Union troops told them.
4. Californians did not coin the word *Juneteenth*. People in Texas created this word.

p. 109
2. A. F   B. I   C. I   D. F

p. 110-111
1. A. I   B. I   C. F   D. F
2. A. F   B. F   C. I   D. F
3. A. F   B. I   C. I   D. I
4. A. I   B. I   C. F   D. F
5. A. F   B. I   C. F   D. F

p. 112-113
1. A. F   B. I   C. F   D. I
2. A. F   B. I   C. I   D. I
3. A. F   B. I   C. F   D. I
4. A. I   B. F   C. I   D. F
5. A. F   B. F   C. I   D. F

p. 114-115
1. A. I   B. F   C. I   D. I
2. A. F   B. F   C. I   D. I
3. A. I   B. I   C. F   D. I
4. A. F   B. I   C. F   D. I
5. A. I   B. I   C. I   D. F

p. 116-117
1. A. F   B. I   C. F   D. I
2. A. I   B. I   C. F   D. I
3. A. I   B. F   C. F   D. I
4. A. F   B. F   C. F   D. I
5. A. F   B. I   C. I   D. F

p. 118-119
1. A. F   B. I   C. F   D. I
2. A. F   B. I   C. I   D. F
3. A. I   B. F   C. I   D. F
4. A. F   B. I   C. I   D. F
5. A. I   B. F   C. F   D. I

p. 120-121
1. A. F   B. F   C. I   D. I
2. A. I   B. I   C. I   D. F
3. A. F   B. I   C. F   D. F
4. A. F   B. I   C. F   D. I
5. A. I   B. F   C. F   D. F

p. 122-123
1. A. F   B. I   C. F   D. I
2. A. F   B. F   C. F   D. I
3. A. I   B. I   C. I   D. F
4. A. I   B. I   C. F   D. F
5. A. I   B. F   C. F   D. I

p. 124-125

1. A. F	B. F	C. I	D. F
2. A. F	B. F	C. I	D. I
3. A. I	B. F	C. F	D. I
4. A. F	B. I	C. I	D. F
5. A. I	B. F	C. I	D. I

p. 126

Possible answers include:
1. Juanita is batting in a baseball game.
2. Nicholas was changing his hearing aid because his new hearing aid wasn't working.
3. Keisha is in a grocery store or supermarket.

p. 127

Possible answers include:
1. Santiago was on a desert.
2. Santiago didn't know about the hardships on the desert. He didn't carry water with him.
3. The story probably happened in the 1800s in a time before people had cars for transportation.
4. Santiago is rugged, strong willed, and considerate.

SPELLING SKILLS

p. 132

1. salmon, attract, catalog, mammal, camera, balance, rapid, magnet, gravity, command, alphabet, graph, passed, accent, scramble, imagine, sandwich, paragraph, photograph
2. laughed

p. 133

1. balance
2. gravity
3. catalog
4. camera
5. magnet
6. graph
7. sandwich
8. paragraph
9. accent
10. salmon
11. mammal
12. passed
13. command
14. attract
15. scramble
16. photograph
17. rapid
18. laughed
19. imagine

p. 134

Spell correctly: catalog, photograph, balance, laughed, salmon
Capitalize: November, I, We
Take out: to (between "to" and "photograph"), he (between "he" and "will")

p. 135

1. accent, alphabet
2. catalog, camera
3. season, second
4. pass, people

p. 136

1. agent
2. mayor, disobey
3. trace, parade, escape, invade, misplace, safety, hesitate, congratulate
4. complain, stain, raincoat, remain, entertain, explain
5. neighborhood, straight, weighted

p. 137

1. safety
2. invade
3. disobey
4. straight
5. misplace
6. entertain
7. remain
8. hesitate
9. weighted
10. stain
11. escape
12. complain
13. neighborhood
14. raincoat
15. mayor
16. explain
17. trace
18. congratulate
19. parade

p. 138

Spell correctly: mayor, straight, safety, remain, entertain
Make lowercase: bands, road, parade
Add period: after "Main Street"; after "all traffic"

p. 139

1. May our dog Sunny march in the neighborhood parade with us?
2. Even Rhonda and Eric did not hesitate to jump in the river for a swim.
3. Watch out for that spider on the raincoat next to Taylor!
4. When Kelly leaves, Tiger and Fluffy complain with loud meows.

p. 140

1. length, tennis, envelope, energy, echo, excellent, insects, restaurant, metric, separate, success
2. instead, pleasant, headache, breakfast, measure, treasure
3. guessed, guest
4. against

p. 141

1. insects
2. tennis
3. length
4. headache
5. guest
6. envelope
7. breakfast
8. excellent
9. treasure
10. guessed
11. separate
12. instead
13. against
14. pleasant
15. energy
16. echo
17. metric
18. measure
19. success

p. 142

Spell correctly: length, excellent, headache, treasure, success
Add question mark: after "coming from"; after "a success"
Add: the (between "was" and "echo"), the (between "with" and "red"), to (between "tried" and "concentrate")

p. 143

1. Mother served our guest a pleasant breakfast of eggs, bacon, and toast.
2. We all played tennis, softball, and tag to use up our extra energy.
3. Extreme heat, biting insects, and pouring rain ruined our camping trip.
4. At the restaurant we talked about hitting a home run, scoring a touchdown, and catching a high fly.
5. Our guest left behind a sealed envelope, a metric converter, and a tape measure.

p. 144

1. darken, weaken, often, lessen, listen, quicken, strengthen, fasten, kitchen, soften
2. person, onion, prison, lemonade, seldom, lesson, ransom, custom
3. captain, mountains

p. 145

1. mountains
2. soften
3. darken
4. weaken
5. often
6. seldom
7. lessen
8. fasten
9. listen
10. strengthen
11. kitchen
12. ransom
13. prison
14. lesson
15. onion
16. person
17. custom
18. lemonade
19. quicken

p. 146

Spell correctly: often, mountains, listen, kitchen, lesson
Capitalize: Ramona, Paris, Please
Take out: in (between "in" and "Paris"), are (between "you" and "became")

p. 147

1. My (father) often watches movies on (television).
2. One (film) was about an (outlaw) in the old West.
3. He was hiding in a (canyon) in the (mountains).
4. He seldom had enough (food) to eat.
5. It was his (custom) to sleep with one (eye) open.
6. I never found out the (end) of the (story).
7. I went to the (kitchen) to make (lemonade).

p. 148

1. Caribbean Sea, North America, Indian Ocean, Atlantic Ocean, Pacific Ocean, Nile River, Rocky Mountains, Central America, Mediterranean Sea, Appalachian Mountains, Mississippi River, South America, Amazon River
2. Alps, Asia, Andes, Europe Australia, Africa, Himalayas

p. 149

1. Alps
2. Nile River
3. Mississippi River
4. Europe
5. Rocky Mountains
6. Andes
7. Himalayas
8. Indian Ocean
9. Central America
10. Caribbean Sea
11. Mediterranean Sea
12. Asia
13. Amazon River
14. South America
15. Africa
16. Appalachian Mountains
17. North America
18. Australia
19. Atlantic Ocean

p. 150

Spell correctly: North America, Appalachian Mountains, Mississippi River, Rocky Mountains, Pacific Ocean
Capitalize: Last, Alabama, California
Trade places: they/there, in/up

p. 151

1. Today my teacher, Mrs. Ward, talked about the climate in Europe and Asia.
2. Then Gayle pointed out the Atlantic Ocean, the Pacific Ocean, and the Indian Ocean.
3. Last month I did a report on the Nile River in Africa.
4. I hope Billy Spinney will tell us about his trip to the Andes.
5. Last year he actually traveled down the Amazon River in South America!

p. 152–153

1. imagine
2. accent
3. salmon
4. laughed
5. paragraph
6. disobey
7. weighted
8. congratulate
9. straight
10. agent
11. mayor
12. measure
13. separate
14. against
15. guessed
16. captain
17. person
18. strengthen
19. seldom
20. Central America
21. Europe
22. Appalachian Mountains
23. Pacific Ocean
24. Mississippi River
25. Mediterranean Sea

p. 154

1. meter, piano, memory, liter, library
2. breeze, brief, degrees, breathing, ceiling, succeed, piece, speaker, repeat, receive, increase
3. complete, scene
4. extremely
5. gasoline

p. 155

1. degrees
2. succeed
3. increase
4. repeat
5. brief
6. memory
7. complete
8. receive
9. extremely
10. speaker
11. breathing
12. piece
13. breeze
14. scene
15. liter
16. gasoline
17. meter
18. piano
19. library

p. 156

Spell correctly: extremely, memory, scene, complete, brief
Capitalize: Many, They, Other
Add period: after "they observed"; after "brief notes"

p. 157

1. laugh
2. trace
3. guess
4. touch
5. myth
6. appear
7. knowledge
8. hesitate
9. although
10. chose

p. 158

1. thumb, struggle, umbrella, justice, difficult, crumb, discuss, plumber, result
2. government, tongue, compass, among
3. touch, trouble, double, enough, cousin, tough
4. flood

p. 159

1. compass
2. umbrella
3. government
4. enough
5. cousin
6. difficult
7. discuss
8. result
9. crumb
10. justice
11. tongue
12. among
13. flood
14. double
15. struggle
16. thumb
17. tough
18. trouble
19. touch

p. 160

Spell correctly: cousin, difficult, trouble, enough, discuss
Add comma: after "Chicago"; after "June 10"; after "Captain Murphy"
Take out: in (between "in" and "trouble"), the (between "the" and "job")

p. 161

1. My favorite cousin lives in a small southern town.
2. A major flood badly damaged the area.
3. The federal government soon moved in to help the people.
4. The difficult struggle to survive was over.
5. My cousin's old compass was ruined in the flood.
6. His family had to hire a plumber to repair the damaged pipes.

p. 162

1. student, human, smooth, humor, ruin, cruel
2. refuse, glue, renew, rude, threw, clue, pollute
3. coupon, canoe, improvement, through
4. nuisance, beautiful, juice

p. 163

1. canoe
2. juice
3. humor
4. human
5. pollute
6. nuisance
7. beautiful
8. through
9. improvement
10. coupon
11. renew
12. smooth
13. glue
14. threw
15. rude
16. refuse
17. cruel
18. clue
19. ruin

p. 164

Spell correctly: nuisance, beautiful, refuse, ruin, smooth
Make lowercase: jackets, wearers, boat
Add period: after "is dangerous"; after "be safe"

p. 165

Answers for "Pronunciation I Use" will vary.
1. student
2. nuisance
3. tomato
4. coupon
5. fragile
6. renew
7. roommate
8. neutral

p. 166

1. canoes, holidays, voyages, pianos
2. tomatoes, mosquitoes, heroes, potatoes, echoes
3. knives, loaves, mysteries, memories, halves, industries, wolves, countries, bakeries, factories, libraries

p. 167

1. echoes
2. mysteries
3. heroes
4. countries
5. memories
6. loaves
7. industries
8. potatoes
9. halves
10. tomatoes
11. voyages
12. factories
13. pianos
14. mosquitoes
15. canoes
16. bakeries
17. libraries
18. knives
19. wolves

p. 168

Spell correctly: libraries, countries, voyages, wolves, bakeries
Capitalize: This, Instead, They're
Take out: or (between "or" and "wrestled"), the (between "the" and "real")

p. 169

1. One of my heroes is Julie, the main character in the book Julie of the Wolves.
2. I'm writing a poem called "Holidays of the Year."
3. I like the song "Whippoorwills" because of the echoes in it.
4. The movie The Red-Headed League is one of my favorite mysteries.
5. My father likes the book Where the Red Fern Grows because it brings back childhood memories.

p. 170

1. several, natural, hospital, carnival, general, principal, usually
2. nickel, novel, label, tunnel
3. wrestle, muscle, vegetable, grumble, castle, bicycle, example, whistle, principle

p. 171

1. carnival
2. example
3. label
4. nickel
5. grumble
6. general
7. several
8. usually
9. castle
10. vegetable
11. principal
12. natural
13. wrestle
14. novel
15. muscle
16. hospital
17. tunnel
18. bicycle
19. whistle

Spell correctly: usually, grumble, natural, principle, nickel
Capitalize: I, No, Pete
Add period: after "can't whistle"; after "I've tried"

p. 173
1. nickel
2. 2
3. 1
4. grumble, tunnel
5. noun, verb
6. Sentences will vary.
7. Sentences will vary.

p. 174–175
1. gasoline
2. piece
3. liter
4. library
5. succeed
6. breathing
7. meter
8. receive
9. extremely
10. government
11. flood
12. justice
13. enough
14. canoe
15. threw
16. human
17. nuisance
18. coupon
19. cruel
20. memories
21. knives
22. pianos
23. tomatoes
24. several
25. principal

p. 176
1. million, margarine, opinion, brilliant, definite, relative, scissors, liquid
2. rhythm, myth, system
3. select, experiment
4. business, electric, spinach, equipment, gymnastic, witness, detective

p. 177
1. scissors
2. million
3. liquid
4. spinach
5. margarine
6. select
7. relative
8. brilliant
9. rhythm
10. system
11. witness
12. myth
13. gymnastic
14. detective
15. business
16. experiment
17. opinion
18. definite
19. equipment

p. 178
Spell correctly: brilliant, detective, opinion, business, equipment
Add period: after "a phone"; after "let me know"
Take out: to (between "to" and "start"), and (between "to" and "open"), the (between "a" and "pen")

p. 179
1. At 5:45 A.M. on April Fool's Day, my electric alarm clock rang.
2. Then I decided to conduct a brilliant experiment.
3. I switched the margarine and the butter at 6:15.
4. "This isn't margarine," my sister said at 6:45.
5. She was a good detective and no April Fool!

p. 180
1. luggage, cabbage, private, percentage, sausage, advantage, beverage, passage, message, storage, desperate, courage, average, chocolate, pirate, accurate, language, fortunate
2. immediate, image

p. 181
1. luggage
2. beverage
3. fortunate
4. accurate
5. private
6. average
7. message
8. language
9. passage
10. storage
11. cabbage
12. image
13. immediate
14. pirate
15. advantage
16. chocolate
17. sausage
18. desperate
19. percentage

p. 182
Spell correctly: fortunate, pirate, passage, accurate, storage
Capitalize: Mexico, Friday, Pelican
Add period: after "in gold"; after "city library"

p. 183
1. choc-olate (or choco-late)
2. per-centage (or percent-age)
3. per-formances (or perform-ances)

p. 184
1. strike, surprise, survive, realize, appetite, describe, advertise, recognize
2. notify, deny, apply
3. science, violin, violet, choir, silence, design, assign
4. sigh
5. style

p. 185
1. violin
2. appetite
3. science
4. notify
5. violet
6. realize
7. silence
8. design
9. assign
10. surprise
11. survive
12. recognize
13. apply
14. strike
15. describe
16. choir
17. style
18. sigh
19. deny

p. 186
Spell correctly: surprise, violin, describe, choir, realize
Add period: after "a solo"; after "we are"
Trade places: play/to, my/made, she/and

p. 187
1. Here are some suggestions that we sent to a TV station.
2. Always notify us of future programs.
3. Realize that we are intelligent viewers.
4. You should recognize talent at all ages.
5. Advertise products that offer us good services.
6. Deny time to companies that have false advertising.
7. Remember that if you turn us off, we can turn you off!

p. 188
1. merge, square
2. dis-tort, ap-pear, spi-ral, back-ground, clock-wise, re-volve, e-qual, fore-ground, pro-files, slant-ing, ob-ject
3. il-lu-sion, in-cor-rect, par-al-lel, con-cen-trate, con-stant-ly, con-tin-ue
4. un-u-su-al

p. 189
1. unusual
2. appear
3. incorrect
4. merge
5. continue
6. equal
7. spiral
8. constantly
9. clockwise
10. square
11. illusion
12. parallel
13. foreground
14. revolve
15. background
16. profiles
17. object
18. slanting
19. concentrate

p. 190
Spell correctly: illusion, square, appear, foreground, concentrate
Add question mark: after "didn't it"; after "seeing things"
Add: to (between "had" and "be"), the (between "of" and "painting"), be (between "would" and "gone")

p. 191
1. Yes, the bright light looked unusual against the dark sky.
2. No, it didn't continue to shine past midnight.
3. Okay, it did seem to revolve around a smaller light.
4. Well, it could have been one airplane moving clockwise around another one.

p. 192
1. na-ture, wo-ven, cul-ture, frag-ile, reg-ion, cli-mate
2. in-flu-ence, re-sourc-es, be-hav-ior, skel-e-tons, art-i-facts, sci-en-tists, prim-i-tive, a-dapt-ed, ev-i-dence
3. so-ci-e-ty, ex-ca-va-tion, cer-e-mo-nies, i-den-ti-fy, en-vi-ron-ment

p. 193
1. artifacts
2. nature
3. resources
4. behavior
5. scientists
6. region
7. influence
8. society
9. primitive
10. environment
11. culture
12. skeletons
13. adapted
14. evidence
15. fragile
16. excavation
17. identify
18. ceremonies
19. woven

p. 194
Spell correctly: excavation, primitive, region, skeletons, scientists
Capitalize: Last, New, These
Add period: after "Mexico"; after "shell jewelry"

p. 195
1. "I read articles about scientists digging in excavation sites," said Matthew.
2. "I have pictures of beautiful Pueblo artifacts!" exclaimed Victoria.
3. Mr. Fine said, "We are going to discuss the behavior of the Pueblo people."
4. Mr. Fine asked, "How did the environment influence their society?"

1. definite
2. spinach
3. million
4. opinion
5. electric
6. rhythm
7. scissors
8. message
9. average
10. desperate
11. private
12. choir
13. style
14. surprise
15. sigh
16. design
17. describe
18. realize
19. deny
20. science
21. parallel
22. revolve
23. fragile
24. environment
25. climate

p. 198
1. closet, ecology, comic, probably, astonish, opposite, omelet, molecule, impossible, forgotten, moccasins, proper, honor, octopus, tonsils, operate, honesty, demolish
2. equality
3. knowledge

p. 199
1. knowledge
2. forgotton
3. honor
4. proper
5. impossible
6. equality
7. omelet
8. closet
9. octopus
10. honesty
11. ecology
12. tonsils
13. opposite
14. comic
15. demolish
16. molecule
17. astonish
18. probably
19. operate

p. 200
Spell correctly: honesty, knowledge, ecology, impossible, probably
Make lowercase: you, but, animals
Add period: afer "ecology"; after "homes, too"

p. 201
1. catalog
2. omelet
3. honor
4. practice

p. 202
1. noble, poetry, solar
2. throne, telescope, propose, lone, microphone, suppose, telephone
3. loan, approach, groan
4. grown, thrown, snowy, blown
5. plateau, bureau
6. although

p. 203
1. throne
2. loan
3. poetry
4. microphone
5. telescope
6. groan
7. snowy
8. solar
9. approach
10. bureau
11. blown
12. suppose
13. lone
14. noble
15. although
16. thrown
17. grown
18. propose
19. plateau

p. 204
Spell correctly: telescope, loan, grown, groan, propose
Add comma: after "January 25"; after "sixth graders"
Take out: it (between "it" and "around"), the (betwen "the" and "news"), to (between "to" and "the")

p. 205
1. /byŏŏ′r ō/
2. noun
3. bureaus, bureaux
4. Please telephone me tomorrow.
5. Sentences will vary.

p. 206
1. crawl, awful
2. laundry, audience, saucers, daughter, autumn, auditorium
3. sword, ordinary, support, perform, formal, chorus, forward, orchestra
4. chalk, wharf
5. course, coarse

p. 207
1. saucers
2. wharf
3. coarse
4. crawl
5. sword
6. chalk
7. forward
8. awful
9. autumn
10. course
11. perform
12. laundry
13. formal
14. orchestra
15. ordinary
16. support
17. daughter
18. chorus
19. auditorium

p. 208
Spell correctly: perform, orchestra, auditorium, formal, audience
Capitalize: Elmer, I, March
Add comma: after "Elmer"; after "March 1"

p. 209
1. She sewed a blue silk gown for her daughter.
2. The ancient wharf was covered with pink starfish.
3. The chorus sang our new school song.
4. The handsome knight carried a massive bronze sword.
5. I put my dirty green shirt in the laundry.
6. That tiny baby will soon learn to crawl.

p. 210
1. bathrobe, passport, weekday, farewell, backpack, waterproof, proofread, chessboard, thunderstorm, flashlight, roommate, tablecloth, throughout, weekend, eavesdrop, applesauce
2. brand-new, self-confidence, old-fashioned, cross-country

p. 211
1. chessboard
2. eavesdrop
3. tablecloth
4. passport
5. backpack
6. flashlight
7. waterproof
8. cross-country
9. self-confidence
10. weekend
11. old-fashioned
12. throughout
13. proofread
14. applesauce
15. weekday
16. thunderstorm
17. roommate
18. farewell
19. bathrobe

p. 212
Spell correctly: cross-country, roommate, self-confidence, brand-new, weekend
Capitalize: Brandon, Lincoln
Take out: the (between) "the" and "cross-country"), at (between "and" and "in"), an (between "have" and "my")

p. 213
1. I wore my bathrobe and slept deeply.
2. The thunderstorm started suddenly.
3. Our waterproof rain gear covered us completely.
4. My flashlight shone brightly.
5. We hungrily ate some applesauce.
6. Finally Dad and I said farewell to camping.

p. 214
1. breath, breathe, choose, chose, dairy, diary, lose, loose, quiet, quite, accept, except, desert, dessert, cloths, clothes
2. all ready, already, weather, whether

p. 215
1. clothes
2. breathe
3. desert
4. dessert
5. already
6. quiet
7. diary
8. weather
9. lose
10. cloths
11. breath
12. choose
13. loose
14. quite
15. accept
16. except
17. whether
18. all ready
19. chose

p. 216
Spell correctly: lose, accept, choose, Whether, already
Add comma: after "selfish"; after "lazy"
Take out: in (between "are" and "told"), on (between "in" and "fables"), deeds (between "as" and "words")

p. 217
1. Either Audrey is very shy, or she is just extremely quiet.
2. Her family chose to move here, for it's a good place to start a dairy business.
3. They used to live in the desert, and it was terribly hot.
4. Audrey told us that she wore loose clothes, but she was still quite uncomfortable.

p. 218-219
1. impossible
2. knowledge
3. probably
4. forgotten
5. honesty
6. equality
7. opposite
8. although
9. solar
10. telephone
11. plateau
12. groan
13. thrown
14. chalk
15. daughter
16. awful
17. coarse

18. course
19. ordinary
20. old-fashioned
21. roommate
22. loose
23. quite
24. quiet
25. lose

p. 220
1. blouse, doubt, couch, cloudy, mound, ouch, wound, surround, pronounce, proudly, scout, thousand
2. howl, crowded, prowl, eyebrow, allowance, coward, growled, snowplow

p. 221
1. snowplow
2. howl
3. growled
4. thousand
5. cloudy
6. crowded
7. eyebrow
8. pronounce
9. allowance
10. proudly
11. coward
12. doubt
13. Ouch
14. mound
15. scout
16. blouse
17. prowl
18. couch
19. wound

p. 222
Spell correctly: coward, doubt, prowl, howl, proudly
Capitalize: It, Wolves, The
Take out: a (between "is" and "little"), run (between "run" and "until")

p. 223
1. 2
2. 2
3. 1
4. 1

p. 224
1. refer, personal, merchant, emergency, observe, prefer, service
2. thirsty, squirrel
3. curly, purchase, furniture, disturb, current, curtains, murmur, urgent, occurred
4. worst, worry

p. 225
1. curly
2. purchase
3. urgent
4. occurred
5. disturb
6. murmur
7. worry
8. service
9. merchant
10. observe
11. refer
12. worst

13. curtains
14. thirsty
15. current
16. emergency
17. personal
18. prefer
19. furniture

p. 226
Spell correctly: purchase, observe, thirsty, furniture, disturb
Make lowercase: pet, strange, dog
Take out: the (between "new" and "pet"), to (between "to" and "purchase")

p. 227
1. adjective, noun
2. Sentences will vary.
3. Sentences will vary.
4. Sentences will vary.
5. Sentences will vary.

p. 228
1. carve, salami, barber, partner, armor, marvelous, argument, apartment, marble, marvel, scarlet, arch, harbor, regard, carpenter, guitar, departure, harmony, harmonica
2. guard

p. 229
1. arch
2. argument
3. harmonica
4. marvel
5. partner
6. marvelous
7. departure
8. regard
9. guard
10. carpenter
11. barber
12. carve
13. harmony
14. harbor
15. marble
16. apartment
17. salami
18. guitar
19. armor

p. 230
Spell correctly: marvelous, apartment, harbor, harmony, regard
Capitalize: Ginger, Here, Did
Add: the (between "near" and "harbor"), that (between "structure" and "is")

p. 231
1. guitar
2. harmonica
3. regard
4. Marvelous Music Company
5. Notes and Strings, Inc.
6. Consumer Complaint Bureau

p. 232
1. enjoyable, disagreeable, available, flammable, comfortable, breakable, usable, remarkable, valuable, reasonable, lovable, honorable, probable

2. terrible, responsible, invisible, divisible, flexible, possible, sensible

p. 233
1. breakable
2. reasonable
3. usable
4. honorable
5. sensible
6. divisible
7. enjoyable
8. responsible
9. probable
10. possible
11. lovable
12. remarkable
13. disagreeable
14. terrible
15. valuable
16. flexible
17. available
18. invisible
19. flammable

p. 234
Spell correctly: lovable, available, comfortable, responsible, valuable
Capitalize: We, Max, Can
Add period: after "a home"; after "of him"

p. 235
1. My puppy, Bongo, saved me from a ⟨terrible⟩ problem.
2. ⟨Flammable⟩ curtains were burning in the kitchen.
3. The pup knocked over a ⟨breakable⟩ lamp.
4. The crash of the ⟨valuable⟩ lamp awakened me.
5. I jumped out of my ⟨comfortable⟩ bed and got help.

p. 236
1. nimbus, flurries, ⟨windchill⟩, ⟨forecast⟩, ⟨long-range⟩, cirrus
2. atmosphere, pollution, Celsius, cumulus, Fahrenheit, prediction, ⟨thunderhead⟩, ⟨overcast⟩
3. humidity, temperature, velocity, thermometer
4. precipitation
5. meteorologist

p. 237
1. overcast
2. forecast
3. windchill
4. long-range
5. thunderhead
6. flurries
7. Celsius
8. pollution
9. atmosphere
10. temperature
11. humidity
12. meteorologist
13. cirrus
14. Fahrenheit
15. prediction
16. precipitation
17. nimbus
18. cumulus
19. velocity

p. 238
Spell correctly: forecast, prediction, precipitation, flurries, temperature
Make lowercase: winter, snow, spring
Add comma: after "January 12"; after "freezing winds"

p. 239
1. We had some snow flurries a few weeks ago on Thanksgiving.
2. The sky was overcast, and the temperature was only 30 degrees Fahrenheit.
3. The long-range prediction is that we will have a white New Year's Day.
4. The meteorologist on TV gave the temperature tonight as 0 degrees Celsius.
5. I don't care if we have precipitation on Memorial Day, the Fourth of July, or even Labor Day.

p. 240-241
1. pronounce
2. allowance
3. crowded
4. doubt
5. proudly
6. squirrel
7. worst
8. curtains
9. furniture
10. occurred
11. emergency
12. guard
13. guitar
14. argument
15. marvelous
16. departure
17. possible
18. comfortable
19. disagreeable
20. usable
21. terrible
22. precipitation
23. velocity
24. temperature
25. atmosphere

p. 242
1. pajamas, atlas, amount, balloon, husband
2. legend, item, celebrate
3. pencil, cabinet, multiply, engine
4. history, balcony, purpose
5. triumph, injury, fortune, circus, focus

p. 243
1. balcony
2. injury
3. celebrate
4. balloon
5. fortune
6. focus
7. engine
8. multiply
9. history
10. atlas
11. purpose

12. triumph
13. legend
14. item
15. cabinet
16. amount
17. pencil
18. circus
19. husband

p. 244
Spell correctly: engine, balcony, balloon, husband, triumph
Capitalize: Dear, I, They
Add period: after "woke me"; after "their faces"

p. 245
1. Henry and his brother went to the circus to celebrate Henry's birthday.
2. The boys' father wanted to take them up in a hot-air balloon.
3. Henry also received a set of colored pencils and a children's atlas.
4. Dad's plan was for Henry to draw what he saw.

p. 246
1. cellar, vinegar, calendar, similar, lunar
2. fever, cheeseburger, modern, soccer, hamburger, discover, customer, bother, computer, answer, consumer
3. director, favorite, governor, effort

p. 247
1. soccer
2. governor
3. calendar
4. modern
5. fever
6. director
7. cellar
8. lunar
9. bother
10. customer
11. hamburger
12. cheeseburger
13. computer
14. consumer
15. favorite
16. answer
17. effort
18. similar
19. discover

p. 248
Spell correctly: favorite, customer, hamburger, vinegar, effort
Add period: after "people"; after "vegetarian"
Trade places: watching/been, noticing/by, a/orders

p. 249
1. Soccer fever hit (Alleyville) (this year.)
2. My sister and I (rode a city bus to) (the stadium.)
3. (On the way) we (bought a) (hamburger and a cheeseburger.)

4. (With much effort) the Alleycats (won by three goals)
5. The governor of the state (congratulated the players)
6. Everyone in the town (marked the) (next game on their calendar.)

p. 250
1. courageous, jealous, serious, spacious, generous, delicious, mysterious, curious, various, nervous, tremendous, dangerous, conscious
2. special, social, commercial, official
3. efficient, ancient
4. genius

p. 251
1. official
2. curious
3. serious
4. ancient
5. mysterious
6. special
7. genius
8. commercial
9. tremendous
10. efficient
11. social
12. spacious
13. courageous
14. jealous
15. nervous
16. various
17. delicious
18. conscious
19. generous

p. 252
Spell correctly: official, social, courageous, tremendous, spacious
Capitalize: Rosa, They, Young
Take out: are (between "are" and "serious"); some (between "some" and "very")

p. 253
1. A mysterious woman visited me (yesterday.)
2. She drove up (slowly) in a spacious car.
3. I was (extremely) nervous and curious.
4. She (politely) said that she was a special official.
5. Then she (quickly) asked some serious questions.
6. She wanted to send me on a (highly) dangerous mission.

p. 254
1. attendance, performance, ignorance, distance, entrance
2. sentence, experience, difference
3. assistant, constant, vacant, instant, distant
4. incident, intelligent, different, apparent, absent
5. assignment, instrument

p. 255
1. entrance
2. intelligent
3. assistant
4. apparent
5. sentence
6. vacant
7. incident
8. different
9. performance
10. experience
11. instrument
12. ignorance
13. absent
14. distance
15. instant
16. attendance
17. difference
18. assignment
19. constant

p. 256
Spell correctly: apparent, assistant, instant, ignorance, absent
Make lowercase: instrument, scientists, inventor's
Add period: after "to develop"; after "our calls"

p. 257
1. in the distance; keep one's distance
2. Idiom will vary.
3. Idiom will vary.
4. Idiom will vary.

p. 258
1. collection, fraction, correction, attention, transportation, station, election, information, direction, education, population, conversation, invention, selection
2. fixture, future, agriculture, feature, signature, lecture

p. 259
1. invention
2. transportation
3. education
4. election
5. population
6. conversation
7. correction
8. attention
9. collection
10. lecture
11. feature
12. future
13. fixture
14. information
15. direction
16. agriculture
17. signature
18. station
19. selection

p. 260
Spell correctly: conversation, information, direction, election, future
Capitalize: I, Sojourner, She
Add period: after "hundred years"; after "to vote"

p. 261
1. mayor
2. pleasant
3. against
4. loaves
5. carnival
6. system
7. private
8. sigh
9. bureau
10. laundry
11. thirsty
12. invisible
13. balcony
14. different
15. lecture
16. correction

p. 262-263
1. pencil
2. injury
3. balloon
4. celebrate
5. purpose
6. answer
7. favorite
8. calendar
9. ancient
10. special
11. courageous
12. mysterious
13. conscious
14. efficient
15. sentence
16. different
17. assistant
18. distance
19. assignment
20. experience
21. future
22. collection
23. signature
24. attention
25. direction

Math Skills

p. 268

1.		4	6	8,	9	3	7,	5	7	4
2.	5,	9	1	0,	3	8	2,	6	5	4
3.			8,	3	4	2,	3	8	4
4.					7	6,	0	9	8

5. **a:** ten thousands, **b:** hundreds
6. **a:** ones, **b:** hundred thousands
7. **a:** tens, **b:** billions
8. **a:** thousands, **b:** hundred millions
9. one hundred thirty-two thousand, three hundred forty-two
10. seven million, six hundred forty-two thousand, three hundred fifty-three

p. 269

	a	b
1.	<	>
2.	<	<
3.	<	=
4.	<	<
5.	<	>
6.	<	<
7.	<	>

	a	b	c
8.	21	54	96
9.	468	487	532
10.	231	322	632
11.	45,875	67,956	94,234
12.	543,865	565,978	765,645
13.	13,764	16,576	432,877

p. 270
1. a: 1,011, b: 1,128, c: 1,080, d: 1,159
2. a: 14,867, b: 102,038, c: 82,385, d: 1,290,838
3. a: 1,110,178, b: 168,317, c: 1,251,129, d: 903,320
4. a: 12,299, b: 1,071
5. a: 307,877, b: 4,693

p. 271
1. a: 1,348, b: 1,611, c: 717, d: 1,225
2. a: 1,071, b: 1,292, c: 4,872, d: 11,705
3. a: 2,293,094, b: 162,442, c: 2,358,875, d: 2,809,623
4. b: 1,478, c: 1,709

p. 272

	a	b	c	d
1.	289	198	6	149
2.	354	154	4,101	2,735
3.	5,564	20,168	205,145	677,112
4.	511	177		
5.	10,968	2,467		

p. 273

	a	b	c	d
1.	7,200	5,100	53,800	539,000
2.	11,000	12,000	15,000	19,000
3.	300	500	200	100
4.	53,000	13,000	70,000	42,000

p. 275
1. Aaron is 11 years old. Laura is 12 years old.
2. *Titanic* won 11 awards. *Gone with the Wind* won 8 awards.
3. 16 legs
4. Yoga was 50 minutes. Aerobics was 20 minutes.
5. 6 dimes, 1 penny or 1 quarter, 2 dimes, 3 nickels, and 1 penny

p. 276
1. a: 360, b: 39, c: 216, d: 175
2. a: 870, b: 1,803, c: 5,348, d: 7,536
3. a: 19,278, b: 24,000, c: 31,824, d: 41,670
4. a: 81,779, b: 257,050, c: 70,028, d: 1,211,105
5. a: 1,719, b: 235,564, c: 1,698,429

p. 277

	a	b	c	d
1.	880	4,560	4,410	5,040
2.	1,200	4,200	17,400	200,300
3.	30,100	222,300	240,00	

p. 278
1. a: 112,993, b: 228,046, c: 194,181, d: 562,890
2. a: 572,850, b: 362,043, c: 731,620, d: 321,200
3. a: 267,786, b: 280,500, c: 431,844

p. 279

	a	b	c	d
1.	1,500	1,000	4,200	8,100
2.	1,400	1,500	2,400	4,800
3.	15,000	63,000	27,000	70,000
4.	1,400	4,500	21,000	

p. 280
1. a: 34 R1, b: 94 R4, c: 96 R1, d: 54 R4
2. a: 167 R12, b: 70 R54, c: 127 R12, d: 140 R14
3. a: 153 R2, b: 156 R4, c: 2724 R4

p. 281
1. a: 11 R39, b: 5 R30, c: 18 R8, d: 49 R7
2. a: 127 R10, b: 192 R16, c: 147 R20, d: 98 R10
3. a: 55 R25, b: 259 R3

p. 282

	a	b
1.	too large; 1	too small; 4
2.	too large; 3	too large; 2
3.	too large; 7	too large; 2

p. 283

	a	b	c	d
1.	304	107	205	209
2.	507	602	208	

p. 284

	a	b	c
1.	40	70	90
2.	700	300	600
3.	40	20	20
4.	20	15	8

p. 286
1. addition; 147,825 sq. mi.
2. subtraction; 13,600 people
3. division; 7 hours
4. division; $13 an hour
5. division; 15 feet

p. 287

	a	b
1.	millions	ten thousands
2.	1,050,045	
3.	2,007,006	

	a	b	c
4.	>	<	<
5.	702	720	722
6.	6,789	9,786	9,789
7.	563	387	23,826
8.	331,889	187,042	296,402
9.	610	200	1,000
10.	110,000	20,000	27,000

p. 288
11. a: 138, b: 188, c: 2,064, d: 4,984
12. a: 11,700, b: 47,775, c: 290,496, d: 1,743,200
13. a: 1,856,960, b: 386,078, c: 332,906, d: 450,000
14. a: 84 R3, b: 222 R2, c: 1,275 R3, d: 13,409
15. a: 22 R10, b: 9 R33, c: 219 R6, d: 120 R2
16. a: 2,543 R3, b: 782 R2, c: 704 R76, d: 1,509 R39
17. a: 4,800, b: 50, c: 1,600
18. a: 800, b: 35,000, c: 4

p. 289
19. Shawn made 48 cupcakes. Andy made 38 cupcakes
20. 1 nickel, 3 pennies, 3 quarters, 1 dime
21. addition; 802 cards
22. multiplication; 114,500 papers
23. subtraction; 1,153 cars

p. 290
1. a: $\frac{2}{3}$ or two-thirds, b: $\frac{5}{8}$ or five-eighths, c: $\frac{1}{5}$ or one-fifth
2. a: $\frac{2}{6}$ or two-sixths, b: $\frac{7}{10}$ or seven-tenths, c: $\frac{3}{7}$ or three-sevenths
3. a: $\frac{3}{8}$, b: $\frac{1}{4}$, c: $\frac{4}{5}$
4. a: five-sixths, b: two-sevenths, c: seven-eighths

p. 291

	a	b	c	d
1.	4.	3	7	8
2.	$3\frac{3}{4}$	$4\frac{1}{5}$	$3\frac{5}{6}$	$3\frac{1}{2}$
3.	$\frac{27}{10}$	$\frac{25}{3}$	$\frac{31}{6}$	$\frac{17}{5}$

p. 292

	a	b	c	d
1.	10	12	8	4
2.	15	6	20	14
3.	$\frac{2}{3}$, $\frac{6}{3}$	$\frac{5}{10}$, $\frac{6}{10}$	$\frac{14}{20}$, $\frac{15}{20}$	$\frac{14}{21}$, $\frac{15}{21}$

p. 293

	a	b	c	d
1.	$\frac{3}{7}$	$\frac{1}{5}$	$\frac{1}{3}$	$\frac{2}{5}$
2.	$\frac{2}{3}$	$\frac{1}{4}$	$\frac{4}{5}$	$\frac{3}{5}$
3.	1	$\frac{4}{5}$	$\frac{1}{6}$	$\frac{3}{4}$
4.	$\frac{3}{4}$	$\frac{1}{3}$	$\frac{1}{3}$	$\frac{2}{9}$
5.	$\frac{3}{7}$	$\frac{9}{10}$		

p. 294

	a	b	c	d	e
1.	$\frac{1}{2}$	$\frac{2}{5}$	$\frac{1}{2}$	$\frac{3}{8}$	$\frac{5}{8}$
2.	$1\frac{1}{6}$	$1\frac{1}{2}$	$1\frac{3}{10}$	$1\frac{2}{5}$	$1\frac{5}{12}$
3.	$\frac{1}{4}$	$\frac{2}{5}$	$\frac{1}{6}$	$\frac{1}{2}$	$\frac{3}{4}$

p. 295

	a	b	c	d
1.	$\frac{3}{10}$	$\frac{3}{4}$	$\frac{7}{8}$	$\frac{7}{8}$
2.	$\frac{5}{6}$	$\frac{4}{5}$	$\frac{8}{5}$	$\frac{5}{7}$
3.	$\frac{4}{16}$	$\frac{9}{2}$	$\frac{11}{5}$	$\frac{3}{7}$
4.	$\frac{5}{9}$	$\frac{7}{24}$	$\frac{11}{18}$	

p. 296

	a	b	c	d
1.	$1\frac{1}{6}$	$\frac{13}{14}$	$1\frac{5}{12}$	$1\frac{8}{45}$
2.	$1\frac{13}{24}$	$1\frac{5}{24}$	$1\frac{7}{15}$	$\frac{20}{21}$
3.	$1\frac{7}{12}$	$\frac{19}{30}$	$1\frac{13}{30}$	$1\frac{1}{18}$
4.	$\frac{19}{28}$	$1\frac{24}{55}$	$\frac{11}{28}$	

p. 297
1. JAMAL'S CD COLLECTION

2. FAVORITE ICE CREAM

3. LAURA'S WORKDAY
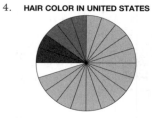

4. HAIR COLOR IN UNITED STATES

p. 299

	a	b	c	d
1.	$4\frac{3}{4}$	$8\frac{5}{8}$	$6\frac{3}{8}$	$9\frac{7}{8}$
2.	$21\frac{1}{2}$	$17\frac{3}{5}$	$19\frac{3}{10}$	$14\frac{4}{9}$
3.	$2\frac{7}{12}$	$3\frac{1}{12}$	$7\frac{5}{6}$	$1\frac{29}{56}$
4.	$11\frac{7}{24}$	$17\frac{7}{18}$	$11\frac{9}{10}$	$15\frac{4}{5}$

p. 300

	a	b	c	d
1.	$5\frac{1}{3}$	$10\frac{7}{30}$	$4\frac{5}{9}$	$7\frac{17}{56}$
2.	$10\frac{7}{12}$	$14\frac{1}{9}$	$18\frac{5}{77}$	$11\frac{5}{12}$
3.	$10\frac{5}{12}$	$7\frac{5}{6}$	$11\frac{3}{10}$	$9\frac{1}{6}$
4.	$13\frac{7}{12}$	$18\frac{3}{8}$	$19\frac{7}{10}$	$10\frac{1}{2}$

p. 301

	a	b	c	d
1.	4; $3\frac{1}{12}$	5; $4\frac{1}{20}$	6; $5\frac{1}{10}$	4; $3\frac{1}{6}$
2.	$\frac{7}{12}$	$\frac{13}{24}$	$\frac{3}{10}$	$\frac{3}{10}$
3.	$\frac{1}{2}$	$\frac{5}{18}$	$\frac{3}{8}$	$\frac{19}{36}$
4.	$\frac{3}{5}$	$\frac{7}{72}$	$\frac{13}{24}$	

p. 302

	a	b	c	d
1.	4; $\frac{7}{4}$	3; $\frac{11}{3}$	8; $17\frac{8}{8}$	12; $27\frac{12}{12}$
2.	$3\frac{1}{3}$	4; $1\frac{1}{4}$	8; $3\frac{3}{8}$	6; $4\frac{1}{6}$
3.	$2\frac{1}{2}$	$4\frac{3}{8}$	$3\frac{4}{5}$	$14\frac{7}{10}$
4.	$2\frac{5}{6}$	$15\frac{1}{2}$	$2\frac{4}{5}$	$8\frac{2}{5}$

P. 303

	a	b	c
1.	$5\frac{2}{5}$	$6\frac{1}{2}$	$3\frac{2}{3}$
2.	$8\frac{3}{8}$	$1\frac{2}{3}$	$2\frac{23}{40}$
3.	$6\frac{1}{6}$	$11\frac{9}{10}$	$8\frac{1}{8}$
4.	$1\frac{7}{10}$	$1\frac{23}{28}$	$14\frac{2}{3}$

P. 305
1. no
2. yes
3. no
4. about 6 inches
5. no

P. 306

	a	b	c
1.	$\frac{1}{3}$ or one-third	$\frac{4}{6}$ or four-sixths	$\frac{6}{7}$ or six-sevenths

	a	b	c	d
2.	7	$8\frac{2}{3}$	5	$3\frac{1}{2}$
3.	$\frac{13}{4}$	$\frac{23}{4}$	$\frac{23}{5}$	$\frac{17}{10}$
4.	12	5	16	15
5.	$\frac{3}{12}$ $\frac{4}{12}$	$\frac{4}{20}$ $\frac{15}{20}$	$\frac{9}{24}$ $\frac{16}{24}$	$\frac{11}{22}$ $\frac{8}{22}$
6.	$\frac{1}{6}$	$\frac{1}{3}$	$\frac{1}{15}$	$\frac{1}{3}$
7.	$\frac{1}{7}$	$\frac{3}{5}$	$\frac{1}{9}$	$\frac{1}{2}$

P. 307

	a	b	c	d
8.	$1\frac{1}{7}$	$\frac{7}{9}$	$3\frac{3}{11}$	$5\frac{23}{40}$
9.	$8\frac{8}{9}$	$7\frac{7}{24}$	$5\frac{7}{10}$	$\frac{19}{42}$
10.	$1\frac{7}{12}$	$15\frac{19}{21}$	$6\frac{4}{11}$	$4\frac{9}{16}$
11.	$6\frac{1}{2}$	$21\frac{7}{9}$	$28\frac{1}{12}$	$12\frac{27}{40}$
12.	$\frac{7}{24}$	$5\frac{3}{5}$	$2\frac{4}{7}$	$2\frac{3}{4}$
13.	$\frac{1}{2}$	$1\frac{1}{12}$	$\frac{1}{4}$	$\frac{7}{12}$
14.	$4\frac{25}{36}$	$\frac{3}{10}$	$6\frac{11}{24}$	$1\frac{1}{2}$
15.	$2\frac{7}{20}$	$3\frac{6}{7}$	$3\frac{13}{15}$	$\frac{8}{99}$

P. 308

	a	b
1.	$\frac{2}{15}$	$\frac{3}{50}$
2.	$\frac{12}{35}$	$\frac{35}{48}$
3.	$\frac{2}{7}$	$\frac{2}{11}$
4.	$\frac{1}{4}$	$\frac{3}{16}$
5.	$\frac{1}{8}$	$\frac{1}{12}$

P. 309

	a	b
1.	$\frac{1}{4}$	$\frac{7}{18}$
2.	$\frac{3}{14}$	$\frac{1}{16}$
3.	$\frac{1}{12}$	$\frac{1}{12}$
4.	$\frac{7}{12}$	$\frac{13}{20}$
5.	$\frac{1}{4}$	$\frac{1}{6}$
6.	$\frac{1}{2}$	$\frac{1}{2}$

P. 310

	a	b	c	d	e
1.	$\frac{7}{1}$	$\frac{18}{1}$	$\frac{20}{1}$	$\frac{4}{1}$	$\frac{12}{1}$
2.	2	4	$4\frac{1}{2}$		
3.	$1\frac{1}{2}$	9	$6\frac{2}{3}$		
4.	6	$7\frac{1}{2}$	20		
5.	24	$16\frac{1}{2}$	20		

P. 311

	a	b	c
1.	15	7	36
2.	10	14	14
3.	13	21	50
4.	$66\frac{2}{3}$	$11\frac{1}{2}$	$12\frac{4}{5}$
5.	$8\frac{1}{2}$	$10\frac{1}{3}$	79
6.	$41\frac{1}{3}$	$123\frac{1}{3}$	$4\frac{8}{9}$

P. 312

	a	b	c
1.	$\frac{3}{5}$	$\frac{3}{5}$	$\frac{5}{6}$
2.	$2\frac{1}{10}$	$\frac{3}{4}$	$\frac{17}{20}$
3.	$\frac{14}{15}$	$3\frac{11}{12}$	$5\frac{2}{5}$
4.	3	$3\frac{1}{2}$	$3\frac{1}{2}$
5.	10	$\frac{1}{2}$	3

P. 313

	a	b	c
1.	$7\frac{1}{5}$	$2\frac{1}{4}$	$2\frac{2}{3}$
2.	$8\frac{1}{3}$	$16\frac{1}{4}$	$7\frac{1}{3}$
3.	$18\frac{3}{8}$	$14\frac{4}{5}$	$56\frac{1}{4}$
4.	15	9	15
5.	12	8	9

P. 315
1. 4 inches
2. $102.00
3. $\frac{1}{4}$ hour
4. pink
5. $30\frac{5}{12}$ feet
6. $1\frac{3}{4}$ tablespoons

P. 316

	a	b	c	d	e
1.	$\frac{3}{2}$	6	$\frac{8}{5}$	$\frac{9}{5}$	$\frac{1}{8}$
2.	$\frac{5}{3}$	$\frac{13}{4}$	$\frac{4}{7}$	$\frac{5}{1}$	4
3.	$\frac{13}{3}$, 3	$\frac{14}{5}$, 5	$\frac{16}{9}$, 9	$\frac{21}{4}$, 4	
4.	$\frac{56}{11}$, 11	$\frac{21}{13}$, 13	$\frac{49}{8}$, 8	$\frac{23}{6}$, 6	
5.	$\frac{9}{7}$	$\frac{5}{1}$	$\frac{1}{9}$	$\frac{2}{7}$	

P. 317

	a	b
1.	$\frac{14}{15}$	$1\frac{1}{8}$
2.	$1\frac{1}{2}$	$1\frac{1}{2}$

	a	b	c
3.	8	$\frac{5}{9}$	4
4.	$\frac{9}{16}$	1	$\frac{5}{18}$
5.		$1\frac{5}{9}$	$1\frac{1}{10}$
6.	$1\frac{9}{16}$	$1\frac{5}{12}$	$5\frac{1}{2}$

P. 318

	a	b
1.	$\frac{1}{16}$	$\frac{1}{8}$
2.	$\frac{3}{8}$	$\frac{1}{15}$

	a	b	c
3.	$\frac{1}{21}$	$\frac{1}{30}$	$\frac{1}{48}$
4.	$\frac{1}{32}$	$\frac{1}{36}$	$\frac{1}{30}$
5.	$\frac{3}{16}$	$\frac{1}{60}$	$\frac{1}{65}$
6.	$\frac{1}{50}$	$\frac{1}{36}$	$\frac{3}{50}$

P. 319

	a	b
1.	$12\frac{1}{2}$	$7\frac{1}{2}$
2.	4	$3\frac{1}{2}$
3.	14	15
4.	$3\frac{1}{5}$	30
5.	8	9
6.	$32\frac{2}{3}$	12

P. 320

	a	b	c
1.	$\frac{2}{3}$	$\frac{1}{2}$	$2\frac{1}{2}$
2.	$\frac{2}{3}$	$1\frac{1}{2}$	$3\frac{3}{4}$
3.	$1\frac{1}{3}$	$\frac{5}{12}$	$2\frac{3}{4}$
4.	$1\frac{1}{5}$	$\frac{5}{36}$	$2\frac{2}{9}$
5.	$\frac{5}{14}$	$\frac{3}{8}$	$2\frac{2}{9}$

P. 321

	a	b	c
1.	7	9	14
2.	$8\frac{5}{6}$	$14\frac{1}{2}$	$1\frac{9}{10}$
3.	46	$15\frac{3}{7}$	$2\frac{5}{8}$
4.	$8\frac{9}{12}$	$2\frac{7}{9}$	$14\frac{2}{5}$
5.	$3\frac{3}{32}$	$5\frac{4}{7}$	$6\frac{4}{7}$

P. 322

	a	b
1.	$1\frac{1}{3}$	$6\frac{2}{3}$
2.	$1\frac{1}{15}$	$5\frac{1}{2}$
3.	$1\frac{1}{5}$	$\frac{36}{65}$
4.	$3\frac{7}{51}$	$\frac{3}{10}$
5.	$2\frac{3}{5}$	2
6.	$2\frac{5}{6}$	$\frac{5}{12}$

P. 324
1. $9\frac{1}{2}$ pieces
2. $\frac{5}{8}$ pound
3. 6 honeybees
4. 40 magnets
5. $6\frac{13}{15}$ inches
6. $3\frac{23}{99}$ feet

P. 325

	a	b	c	d	e
1.	$\frac{19}{1}$	$\frac{3}{1}$	$\frac{25}{1}$	$\frac{16}{1}$	$\frac{17}{1}$
2.	$\frac{4}{15}$	$\frac{12}{21}$	$\frac{5}{16}$		
3.	$\frac{3}{8}$	$\frac{5}{8}$	$\frac{1}{16}$		
4.	$3\frac{3}{4}$	9	$4\frac{1}{3}$		
5.	8	$16\frac{4}{5}$	10		
6.	$13\frac{1}{3}$	42	$40\frac{4}{5}$		
7.	$3\frac{3}{4}$	$14\frac{1}{5}$	$\frac{19}{48}$		
8.	18	$11\frac{6}{35}$	$13\frac{1}{8}$		
9.	$7\frac{1}{14}$	$11\frac{11}{15}$	$28\frac{1}{3}$		

P. 326

	a	b	c	d	e
10.	$\frac{7}{1}$	$\frac{12}{5}$	$\frac{9}{4}$	$\frac{7}{17}$	$\frac{15}{2}$

	a	b	c
11.	2	3	$1\frac{1}{20}$
12.	$1\frac{5}{9}$	$\frac{5}{36}$	$2\frac{10}{11}$
13.	$\frac{13}{144}$	$\frac{5}{162}$	$\frac{2}{25}$
14.	$\frac{1}{16}$	$\frac{1}{75}$	$\frac{1}{12}$
15.	35	24	$19\frac{1}{4}$
16.	$\frac{12}{25}$	$\frac{23}{48}$	$\frac{23}{160}$
17.	$4\frac{6}{11}$	$1\frac{1}{5}$	$1\frac{53}{150}$
18.	$\frac{152}{531}$	$5\frac{5}{24}$	$2\frac{9}{10}$

P. 327
19. $4\frac{1}{3}$ jars or 4 full jars
20. $62\frac{1}{2}$ cm
21. 28 times
22. $1\frac{1}{20}$ feet
23. 30 passes

P. 328

	a	b
1.	0.2	0.02
2.	0.002	6.02
3.	0.021	1.001

4. eight and seven hundredths
5. fifty-three and nine thousandths
6. seventy-six and twelve hundredths

	a	b	c
7.	$6.00	$0.60	$0.06
8.	$0.99	$0.12	$31.00
9.	$420.05		
10.	$3,000.98		

P. 329

	a	b	c
1.	<	<	<
2.	<	>	>
3.	=	<	>

	a	b
4.	0.2 0.4 0.42	0.031 0.13 0.31
5.	0.081 0.18 8.1	2.75 27.5 275

P. 330

	a	b	c	d
1.	$\frac{5}{10}$	$\frac{4}{10}$	$\frac{2}{10}$	$\frac{6}{10}$
2.	$\frac{5}{100}$	$\frac{4}{100}$	$\frac{2}{100}$	$\frac{6}{100}$
3.	$2\frac{1}{10}$	$45\frac{9}{10}$	$31\frac{6}{10}$	$99\frac{2}{10}$
4.	$3\frac{94}{100}$	$6\frac{25}{100}$	$12\frac{54}{100}$	$10\frac{1}{10}$
5.	0.9	0.3	0.1	0.8
6.	0.07	0.91	0.063	0.527
7.	6.7	4.2	8.7	7.6
8.	2.04	6.10	1.754	3.062

P. 331

	a	b	c
1.	0.4	0.25	0.5
2.	0.25	0.2	0.35
3.	4.25	3.5	2.6
4.	1.48	2.15	3.16
5.	6.2	10.75	
6.	3.2	4.28	
7.	13.5	7.4	

P. 333
1. Chile = 9.5
Russia = $9\frac{1}{10}$
Alaska = $9\frac{1}{5}$
2. hand = 16.42 ft.
face = $17\frac{1}{4}$ ft.
tablet = 25.58 ft.
3. Proxima Centauri

P. 334

	a	b	c	d
1.	4	4	3	8
2.	44	52	45	73
3.	6	9	5	10
4.	$4	$25	$8	$6
5.	$8	$3	$10	$62
6.	$1	$6	$3	$9
7.	0.6	0.9	0.6	0.8
8.	4.1	8.7	2.3	9.3
9.	40	25.8	72	21.6

P. 335

	a	b	c	d
1.	41.1	89.0	47.8	$17.87
2.	11.035	8.104	21.81	38.59
3.	$77.99	$39.93	3.248	3.629
4.	58.92	321.64	7.471	91.999

p. 336

	a	b	c
1.	8	$7	$22
2.	0	$3	$50
3.	7	13	67
4.	6.4	7.2	41.7
5.	116.5	36.4	2

p. 338

1. $289.73
2. 60 years old
3. 28 students
4. 54.38 cm
5. 10 people

p. 339

	a	b
1.	0.067	0.76

2. forty-two and six hundred fifteen thousandths
3. seventy-eight thousandths
4. $68.27
5. $405.03

	a	b	c
6.	>	>	<

	a			b		
7.	0.052	0.25	0.5	0.019	0.19	0.91

	a	b	c	d
8.	$\frac{3}{10}$	$\frac{25}{100}$ or $\frac{1}{4}$	$\frac{7}{100}$	$\frac{8}{10}$ or $\frac{4}{5}$
9.	$1\frac{75}{100}$ or $1\frac{3}{4}$	$5\frac{2}{10}$ or $5\frac{1}{5}$	$24\frac{6}{100}$ or $24\frac{3}{50}$	$16\frac{75}{100}$ or $16\frac{3}{4}$
10.	1.08	0.7	0.6	0.44
11.	2.75.6	10.25	8.75	

p. 340

	a	b	c	d
12.	8	2	4	1
13.	$8	$4	$9	$15
14.	0.4	0.2	5.1	72.1
15.	111.6	3.958	86.44	69.314
16.	$90.00	0.19	39.639	357.86
17.	14	11	79	3
18.	9.7	12.6	2.7	13.2

p. 341

19. Donovan Bailey
20. Douglas fir = 100.3 m
    redwood = 83.88 m
    giant sequoia = 95.4 m
21. 53.35 feet
22. $25.20

p. 342

	a	b	c
1.	5.8	58	0.58
2.	75	8.3	46
3.	280	70	7
4.	4,600	6,200	75
5.	31	310	3,150

p. 343

	a	b	c	d
1.	1.6	0.96	23.5	18.552
2.	1.28	1,139.6	10.857	0.874
3.	78.052	7.175	11.776	890.709
4.	631.4	68.8	50,232	

p. 344

	a	b	c	d
1.	0.40	0.54	3.64	3.84
2.	0.31	0.036	0.03	0.032
3.	3.336	33.06	5.1072	4.488
4.	0.00822	0.61632	2.34364	

p. 346

1. Earth ~~is 92.96 million miles from the sun.~~ It orbits the sun ~~in about 365.26 days, traveling~~ at an average speed of 18.51 miles per second. How far does Earth travel in 1 minute? (60 seconds) 1,110.6 miles
2. Fleas can jump up to 150 times the length of their bodies. ~~This is equivalent to a person jumping nearly 1,000 feet.~~ The average flea is about 0.2 inch long. How high can it jump? 30 inches
3. Fingernails grow about 0.004 inch a day. ~~After not cutting his nails for 44 years, a man in India has the world's longest nails. His thumbnail is 4.67 feet long.~~ How many inches do fingernails grow in 1 week? (7 days) 0.028 inch
4. ~~Every day, 274,000 carats of diamonds are mined.~~ One carat is 0.02 grams. The Cullinan Diamond is ~~the largest diamond ever discovered. It~~ is 3,106 carats. How many grams does the Cullinan Diamond weigh? 62.12 grams
5. The movie *Forrest Gump* earned a total of $679.7 million worldwide. $329.7 million of that total was made in the United States. ~~Forrest Gump was nominated for 13 Academy Awards and won 6.~~ How much of its total earnings were made outside the U.S.? $350 million
6. The "Rattler" ~~is one of the world's tallest wooden roller coasters. Each ride~~ is 2.25 minutes long. "Superman the Escape" is ~~one of the world's tallest steel roller coasters, at~~ 415 feet. Its ride lasts 0.467 minutes. How much longer is a ride on the "Rattler" than on "Superman"? 1.783 minutes

p. 347

	a	b	c
1.	0.689	0.07	0.056
2.	1.23	0.049	0.81
3.	0.1411	0.0003	0.0289
4.	0.037737	0.000991	0.1342
5.	0.0039	5.555	0.00715

p. 348

	a	b	c	d
1.	2.2	4.6	$0.64	1.6
2.	1.2	5.1	5.2	$0.26
3.	0.628	54.32	0.55	

p. 349

	a	b	c	d
1.	2.6	17	5.8	3.3
2.	5.4	7.6	12.6	78.1
3.	1.8	1.66	64.1	

p. 350

	a	b	c	d
1.	4	90	60	150
2.	600	2,700	3,500	1,830
3.	360	530	8,700	

p. 351

	a	b	c	d
1.	2.075	11.42	2.07	0.1095
2.	1.75	21.25	2.5	102.4

p. 352

	a	b	c
1.	6.3	7.33	0.8
2.	$0.33	$40.58	$21.00

p. 354

1. 3
   30
   300
   Answer = 300 days
2. 24
   2.4
   0.24
   Answer = 0.24 mi.
3. 2
   20
   200
   2,000
   Answer = 2,000 mL
4. 80
   8
   0.8
   0.08
   Answer = $0.08
5. 3
   30
   300
   Answer = 300 nickels
6. 45
   4.5
   0.45
   Answer = $0.45

p. 355

	a	b	c
1.	23.1	56	7,800
2.	8.3	640	380

	a	b	c	d
3.	14.46	30.084	$2.01	7.28
4.	3.4	2,123.8	69.825	$203.88
5.	0.45	2.52	13.44	80.01
6.	0.0854	0.0594	62.31	5.3998
7.	42.5	182.5	1,328	
8.	0.315	0.5336	4.8972	

p. 356

	a	b	c
9.	0.034	0.0092	0.00158
10.	0.005	0.019	0.006495

	a	b	c	d
11.	1.3	6.3	$7.60	2.1
12.	1.5	22	19	26.5
13.	300	20	1,128	470
14.	1.3	$2.15	0.35	

p. 357

15. Pluto ~~is the farthest planet from the sun, at 5.9 billion kilometers.~~ It takes Pluto ~~90,950 days to~~ orbit the sun at a speed of 4.74 kilometers per second. How far does Pluto travel in 30 seconds? 142.2 km
16. In 1996, ~~31.9% of students in the United States had access to a computer.~~ The average student that year used a computer 5.3 hours a week. How many hours did the average student use a computer each day in 1996? Round the answer to the nearest tenth. (1 week = 7 days) about 0.8 hour
17. ~~In-line skates were introduced to the United States in the late 1970s.~~ In 1998, the record for the highest speed on in-line skates was set at 64.02 miles per hour. How far could a person skate in 2 hours at this speed? 128.04 miles
18. ~~On December 17, 1903,~~ Orville Wright became the first man to fly an engine-powered airplane. His flight ~~took place near Kitty Hawk, North Carolina,~~ and covered 120 feet in 0.2 minutes. On average, how many feet per minute did the plane fly? 600 feet/minute
19. 9
    90
    900
    Answer = 900 cups
20. 24
    2.4
    0.24
    Answer = $0.24

p. 358

	a	b	c
1.	$15\frac{1}{2}$	7,920	88
2.	45	63	7,040
3.	$4\frac{1}{4}$	$12\frac{2}{5}$	5
4.	$2\frac{1}{2}$	$18\frac{1}{2}$	3
5.	<	>	
6.	=	>	

p. 359

	a	b	c
1.	52	5,000	96
2.	8,000	22	67
3.	$3\frac{5}{8}$	$3\frac{1}{2}$	5
4.	$4\frac{1}{2}$	$2\frac{1}{4}$	$1\frac{1}{5}$
5.	=	>	
6.	>	<	

p. 360

	a	b	c
1.	17	9	26
2.	33	36	24
3.	$1\frac{3}{4}$	$2\frac{5}{8}$	$5\frac{1}{2}$
4.	6	7	$3\frac{3}{8}$
5.	>	<	
6.	=	<	

p. 361

1. 8 gal 1 qt. 14 ft 2 in. 11 yd.
2. 1 yd. 2 ft. 1 gal. 3 qt. 73 lb. 8 oz.
3. 39 ft. 8 in. 1 lb. 5 oz. 1 yd. 1 ft.

p. 362

	a	b
1.	2 cm	300 km
2.	8 mm	5 m

	a	b	c
3.	14,500	725	180
4.	340	21,000	900
5.	4.8	0.796	0.061
6.	8.542	3.128	9.3

p. 363

	a	b
1.	27 kg	283 g
2.	70 g	45 kg

	a	b	c
3.	32,000	7	1,800
4.	490	825,000	6,783
5.	0.0128	0.009	0.137
6.	5.268	0.025	0.0049

p. 364

	a	b
1.	200 mL	450 mL
2.	50 L	2.84 L

	a	b	c
3.	27,000	5,300	7,450
4.	825	2,000	39,600
5.	3.096	6	0.4125
6.	0.058	0.798	0.0192

p. 365

1. **a:** 37 cm 1 mm, **b:** 8 kg 125 g, **c:** 11 L 775 mL
2. **a:** 1 kg 950 g, **b:** 3L 125 mL, **c:** 22 m 95 cm
3. **a:** 28 km 125 m, **b:** 35 kg 210 g, **c:** 46 L 500 mL
4. **a:** 1 kg 275 g, **b:** 3 L 840 mL, **c:** 2 km 250 m

p. 367

1. decimeter
hectometer
decigram
hectogram
2. 9 different ways
3. 6 different ways

p. 368

	a	b	c
1.	13	210	78
2.	2,400	4,500	40
3.	42	21,000	28
4.	300 km	2.5 m	
5.	2g	3 L	
6.	$10\frac{1}{2}$	2	1.123
7.	0.0059	2	2.102
8.	2.5	$3\frac{1}{2}$	0.0215
9.	<	<	
10.	<	>	

11. 3 gal 1 qt.
1 cm 9 mm
1 L 4 mL
99 gal. 6 pt.

p. 369

12. 1 half dollar, 1 quarter
1 half dollar, 2 dimes, 1 nickel
1 half dollar, 1 dime, 3 nickels
1 half dollar, 5 nickels
13. black, silver, black, blue
black, clear, blue, silver
blue, clear, silver, clear
14. 9 outfits

p. 370

1. plane PQR>
2. line PQ or line RS
3. line segment PR or line segment RS
4. ray PQ or ray SR
5. point P or point R
6. line PQ and line RS
7. line RS and line SQ
8. line PR and line RS

p. 371

	a	b	c	d
9.	line	ray	plane	line segment

10. $\overleftrightarrow{AB}$ or $\overleftrightarrow{BA}$ B $\overleftrightarrow{LM}$ $\overrightarrow{RS}$ or $\overrightarrow{SR}$
11. a: intersecting
b: parallel
c: perpendicular
d: intersecting

p. 372

1. **a:** ∠LMN or ∠NML, **b:** ∠QRS or ∠SRQ, **c:** ∠F, **d:** ∠ABC or ∠CBA
2. **a:** obtuse, **b:** acute, **c:** right, **d:** straight

p. 373

1. **a:** not congruent, **b:** not congruent
2. **a:** not congruent, **b:** congruent

p. 375

1. triangle
2. right angles or congruent angles
3. 22 feet

p. 376

	a	b	c
1.	16 units	14 units	10 units
2.	24 units	12 units	18 units
3.	16 units	20 units	22 units
4.	22 units	14 units	22 units

p. 377

	a	b	c
1.	54 in.	118 cm	9 m
2.	124 yd.	84 in.	$21\frac{1}{2}$ ft.
3.	45.8 m	200 mm	80 yd.
4.	334 cm	67.6 m	112 ft.

p. 378

1. **a:** 12 sq. units, **b:** 18 sq. units, **c:** 18 sq. units,
2. **a:** 8 sq. units, **b:** 30 sq. units, **c:** 10 sq. units
3. **a:** 28 sq. units, **b:** 6 sq. units, **c:** 24 sq. units
4. **a:** 15 sq. units, **b:** 32 sq. units, **c:** 20 sq. units

p. 379

1. **a:** 270 sq. cm, **b:** 3,276 sq. mm, **c:** $11\frac{1}{4}$ sq. ft.
2. **a:** 24.7 sq. m, **b:** 76 sq. yd., **c:** 160 sq. ft.
3. **a:** 3.145 sq. in., **b:** 3.96 sq. m, **c:** 75.25 sq. cm
4. **a:** $10\frac{1}{8}$ sq. yd., **b:** 117 sq. m, **c:** 28 sq. in.

p. 380

1. **a:** 24 cubic units, **b:** 60 cubic units, **c:** 84 cubic units
2. **a:** 18 cubic units, **b:** 90 cubic units, **c:** 80 cubic units
3. **a:** 280 cubic units, **b:** 200 cubic units, **c:** 180 cubic units

p. 381

1. **a:** 1,400 cu. ft., **b:** 6,000 cu. mm, **c:** 15,232 cu. in.
2. **a:** 15.6 cu. cm, **b:** 1,250 cu. in., **c:** 1,440 cu. ft.
3. **a:** 1,920 cu. yd., **b:** 281.6 cu. m, **c:** 990 cu. yd.

p. 383

1. 480 cubic in.
2. $5,333\frac{1}{3}$ sq. yd.
3. 6,807.6 cubic cm
4. 222 in.
5. 1,110 m
6. 8 cans

p. 384

1. point A or point B
2. line AC or line DF
3. ∠FBC
4. ray BE or ray DF
5. line DF and line AC
6. line segment AB or line segment BC
7. ∠ABE and ∠EBC
8. **a:** 18 units, **b:** 15 sq. units, **c:** 24 cu. units
9. **a:** 8.2 m, **b:** 340 cm, **c:** $34\frac{2}{3}$ yd.
10. **a:** 168 sq. mm, **b:** $1,296\frac{1}{4}$ sq. in., **c:** 6.63 sq. cm
11. **a:** 432 cu. yd., **b:** 170 cu. m, **c:** 225 cu. ft.

p. 385

12. rectangle
13. Anita and Tremont
14. $101\frac{3}{4}$ in
15. area = 175 sq. cm
volume = 175 cu. cm

Language Arts

p. 388

1. Carlos—person; week—idea or thing; aunt—person; uncle—person, 2. daughter—person; Mary—person; cousin—person, 3. children—person; discussions—thing; happiness—idea, 4. family—thing; ranch—place or thing; Montana—place, 5. Saturday—thing; neighbor—person; meal—thing, 6. Grandma—person; dishes—thing; table—thing, 7. Sam—person; kitchen—place or thing; dishes—thing, 8. month—idea or thing; memory—idea or thing; veterans—person; town—place, 9. Volunteers—person; mural—thing; school—place or thing, 10. Dr. García—person; mayor—person; parade—thing; bands—thing, 11. lifeguard—person; days—thing; week—idea or thing, 12. Lightning—thing; barn—thing or place

p. 389

1. Harriet Tubman was born as a <u>slave</u> in the <u>state</u> of Maryland., 2. Her <u>husband</u>, John Tubman, was free., 3. Harriet fled from the <u>plantation</u> of her <u>master</u>., 4. The former <u>slave</u> found <u>freedom</u> in Philadelphia., 5. Her <u>family</u> and <u>friends</u> were still enslaved., 6. This courageous <u>woman</u> returned for her <u>sister</u>, Mary Ann., 7. Her <u>brother</u> James, escaped later with his <u>family</u>., 8. During her <u>life</u>, Harriet led many other <u>escapes</u>.

p. 390

1. painter; school; painting, 2. name; style; painting, 3. movement, 4. artists, 5. painters; 6. exhibit; paintings; group, 7. canvas; eye; light, 8. painters; way; objects; light, 9. boat, 10. painter, 11. Children; world; hopscotch, 12. versions; game, 13. town; children; board; squares, 14. stone; coin; square; foot; square, 15. paragraph; sport, 16. Diego Rivera; Mexico, 17. Mexico, 18. Spanish; Mexico, 19. Zapotec Indians, 20. Rivera; Mexico City; United States, 21. Detroit Institute of Arts; Michigan; Diego Rivera, 22. Constitution; United States; Constitutional Convention, 23. Philadelphia; Pennsylvania, 24. Bill of Rights; James Madison, 25. April; George Washington

p. 391

Common nouns: generals, river, violin, tune, sorrow, song, melody, joy, place, songs, future, country, peace
Proper nouns: General Tang, General Wang, Tang, General Lang, General Mang
Webs: Nouns That Name People: generals, General Tang, General Wang, General Lang, General Mang
Nouns That Name Ideas: sorrow, joy, future, peace, The additional nouns will vary.

p. 392

1. horses, 2. donkeys, 3. patches, 4. days, 5. puppies, 6. porches, 7. ladies, 8. dresses, 9. hills, 10. trails

p. 393

1. women, 2. Cars, oxen; calves, 4. sheep, 5. Wolves, 6. teeth; knives, 7. potatoes, 8. tomatoes, 9. Deer; leaves

p. 394

1. brushes, 2. louse, 3. butterfly, 4. men, 5. suitcase, 6. turkeys, 7. watch, 8. melodies, 9. cheese, 10. gas, 11. cranberries, 12. scarves, 13. heroes, 14. axes, 15. blueberry, 16. goose, 17. mouths, 18. reefs, 19. canaries, 20. glitch, 21. umbrella, 22. well, 23. vases, 24. moss, 25. lances, 26. masses, 27. patches, 28. videos, 29. babies, 30. gulches, 31. cellos, 32. sashes

p. 395

1. Lewis Carroll's book, 2. the knife's edge, 3. the book's cover, 4. Mayor Sanita's speech, 5. the flowers' aroma, 6. the children's bicycle, 7. the sirens' roar, 8. the rainbow's colors, 9. Chris's shoes, 10. the women's purses, 11.–15. Answers will vary.

P. 396
1. sculptor's, 2. artist's, 3. hour's, 4. country's, 5. thief's, 6. Robert Frost's, 7. week's, 8. minute's, 9. weaver's, 10. Samuel Clemens's, 11. wolf's, 12. nurse's, 13. King Henry's, 14. moment's, 15. secretary's, 16. Mr. Jones's, 17. hostesses', 18. teachers', 19. women's, 20. masters', 21. workers', 22. hours', 23. oxen's, 24. spies', 25. buffaloes', 26. surgeons', 27. sheep's, 28. secretaries', 29. Britain's worst balloonist, 30. a colleague's help, 31. the balloon's ropes, 32. the flyers' calls for help

P. 397
1. Luis's—singular, 2. children's—plural, 3. parents'—plural, 4. sheep's—plural, 5. deer's—plural, 6. cousins'—plural, 7. person's—singular, 8. adults'—plural; children's—plural, 9. Wilsons'—plural, 10. Uncle Bernie's—singular, 11. neighbor's—singular, 12. families'—plural

P. 398
1. they—stories, 2. his—Aesop, 3. he—slave, 4. it—story, 5. its—donkey, 6. she—owner, 7. The owner gave the dog a soft bed and fed it well., 8. The donkey tried to make its owner treat it well. 9. The donkey learned that it should not try to be something else., 10. Can you write two fables and illustrate them?, 11. The chief engineer and her/his team watched., 12. Moses took a kite and attached a rope to it.

P. 399
1. his; Thurgood Marshall, 2. their; parents, 3. her; mother, 4. he; Marshall, 5. It; Howard University Law School, 6. her, 7. her, 8. his, 9. him, 10. they

P. 400
1. us—object pronoun, 2. me—object pronoun, 3. She—subject pronoun, 4. She—subject pronoun, 5. her—object pronoun, 6. we—subject pronoun, 7. He—subject pronoun, 8. us—object pronoun, 9. her—object pronoun, 10. me—object pronoun, 11. him—object pronoun, 12. you—subject pronoun, 13. I—subject pronoun, 14. They—subject pronoun, 15. him—object pronoun

P. 401
1. I, 2. We, 3. her, 4. They, 5. them, 6. him, 7. they, 8. them, 9. I, 10. We, 11. I, 12. They, 13. him, 14. her, 15. them, Sentences will vary. Be sure that two of the following pronouns are used correctly: me, us, she, he.

P. 402
1. Annie Oakley was famous for her shooting ability., 2. Mr. Oakley let her use his gun., 3. Buffalo Bill made Annie a star in his show., 4. Annie never missed her target., 5. Audiences could hardly believe their eyes., 6. Jeremy wants to use your stereo., 7. The dog devoured its food., 8. The Reynas had their couch reupholstered., 9. I want to change my schedule., 10. The animals ran for their lives.

P. 403
Answers may vary. Possible answers are given. 1. their, 2. our, 3. his, 4. our, 5. their, 6. its, 7. their, 8. theirs, 9. their, 10. their, 11. her, 12. its, 13. their, 14. his, 15. their, 16. their, 17. Its

P. 404
1. herself—Diane, 2. himself—Ben, 3. themselves—members, 4. ourselves—we, 5. myself—I, 6. yourself—you, 7. itself—dog, 8. themselves—Ed and Beverly, 9. myself—I, 10. ourselves—Estella and I, 11. herself, 12. itself, 13. himself, 14. yourself, 15. ourselves, 16. themselves, 17. myself, 18. ourselves, 19. yourself, 20. themselves

P. 405
1. Everyone—singular, 2. Some—plural, 3. Everything—singular, 4. anybody—singular, 5. many—plural, 6. have, 7. create, 8. helps, 9. needs, 10. want, 11. is

P. 406
1. Who, 2. Whom, 3. who, 4. whom, 5. Who, 6. whom, 7. who, 8. Who, 9. whom, 10. Who, 11. Who's, 12. Whose, 13. Who's, 14. Who's, 15. whose, 16. Whose, 17. Who's, 18. Who's, 19. whose, 20. Who's

P. 407
1. him; some; her, 2. him, 3. She; them, 4. few, 5. I; them, 6. her, 7. He; it. 8. I, 9. they; her, 10. him, 11. herself, 12. it, 13. them; herself; she; her, 14. her, 15. themselves, 16. they; her, 17. she; it, 18. their, 19. herself, 20. she, 21. their, 22. her; hers, 23. herself; she, 24. her, 25. he, 26. themselves, 27. it, 28. she, 29. she; herself, 30. she; it, 31. me; I; them, 32. I; he; it, 33. she, 34. I; her; I, 35. I; myself

P. 408
1. an—article; enormous—describing, 2. long—describing; cold—describing, 3. Rich—describing; the—article; black—describing; fertile—describing, 4. the—article; early—describing, 5. The—article; a—article; sociable—describing, 6. A—article; calm—describing; alert—describing; smallest—describing, 7. important—describing; an—article; early—describing, 8. Nightly—describing; rich—describing

P. 409
Answers will vary.

P. 410
1. African; Africa, 2. Hungarian; Hungary, 3. English; England, 4. Yugoslavian; Yugoslavia, 5. Italian; Italy, 6. Tibetan; Tibet, 7. Islamic; Islam, 8. Egyptian; Egypt, 9. Japanese; Japan, 10. Mexican; Mexico, 11.–15. Sentences will vary. Be sure that proper adjectives are used correctly.

P. 411
1. This—singular, 2. those—plural, 3. These—plural, 4. these—plural, 5. that—singular, 6. this—singular, 7.–14. Sentences will vary. 7. pronoun, 8. adjective, 9. pronoun, 10. adjective, 11. pronoun, 12. adjective, 13. pronoun, 14. adjective

P. 412
1. warm—air, 2. sweet—flowers, 3. High—sun, 4. peaceful—horses, 5. happy—Sharon, 6. eager—She, 7. ready—horse, 8. beautiful—day, 9. skillful—surgeon, 10. bitter—mango, 11. fast—horse, 12. gray—coat, 13. silver—it, 14. unusual—Horses, 15. well-trained—They, 16. brave—Rin Tin Tin/Lassie, 17. good—they, 18. fearless—Rin Tin Tin, 19.–20. Sentences will vary.

P. 413
1. colder; coldest, 2. safer; safest, 3. funnier; funniest, 4. flatter; flattest, 5. shinier; shiniest, 6. taller; tallest, 7. whiter; whitest, 8. sweeter; sweetest, 9. sadder; saddest, 10. younger; youngest, 11. larger, 12. smaller, 13. smallest

P. 414
Answers may also use *less* and *least*.
1. more energetic; most energetic, 2. more difficult; most difficult, 3. more generous; most generous, 4. more affectionate; most affectionate, 5. more active; most active, 6. worse; worst, 7. more; most, 8. more likely; most likely, 9. more expensive; most expensive, 10. more crowded; most crowded, 11. Ruffles is the most beautiful puppy of the litter., 12. Sport is more intelligent than Ruffles., 13. Of all the puppies, Tuffy is the most fun.

P. 415
1. stronger; more impressive, 2. most elaborate, 3. beautiful; greatest, 4. more aggressive; largest, 5. best, 6. bad, 7. better, 8. better; worse, 9. more, 10. best, 11. The;

fierce, 12. This; the; first; the, 13. Few; Union, 14. A; the; Confederate, 15. The; heavy, 16. That; an, 17. Many; both, 18. a; pivotal; American, 19. the; several, 20. a; memorable; the

P. 416
1. originated, 2. compete, 3. leaped, 4. stretched, 5. grabbed, 6. dribbled, 7. aimed, 8. flew, 9. bounced, 10. jumped, 11.–15. Sentences will vary.

P. 417
1. celebrated—action, 2. is—linking, 3. reaches—action, 4. cooked—action, 5. appeared—linking, 6. greeted—action, 7. smelled—linking, 8. became—linking, 9. looked—linking, 10. is—linking, 11. rises—action, 12. escapes—action, 13. are—linking, 14. were—linking, 15. was—linking, 16. study—action, 17. recycles—action, 18. was—linking, 19. opened—action, 20. were—linking

P. 418
Action verbs: compete, need, carries, defeated, ran, ran
Linking verbs: are, are, is, is, is, 1.–10. Answers will vary.

P. 419
1. are moving—moving, 2. have lived—lived, 3. am missing—missing, 4. has been—been, 5. had moved—moved, 6. do want—want, 7. has accepted—accepted, 8. is living—living, 9. was working—working, 10. did offer—offer, 11. Does like—like, 12. was complaining—complaining, 13. had lived—lived, 14. is enjoying—enjoying, 15. will find—find, 16. has entered—entered, 17. might meet—meet, 18. may visit—visit, 19. is living—living, 20. could give—give

P. 421
1. helping, 2. helping, 3. main, 4. main, 5. main, 6. helping, 7. main, 8. helping, 9. helping, 10. main, 11. main, 12. helping, 13. helping, 14. helping, 15. helping, 16.–20. Answers will vary. Suggested: 16. are blooming, 17. will be, 18. should visit, 19. does; need, 20. were; picked

P. 421
1. studies—present, 2. reading—present participle, 3. taught—past participle, 4. learned—past participle, 5. visited—past, 6. gone—past participle, 7. seen—past participle, 8. read—past participle, 9. planning—present participle, 10. talks—present, 11. learns—present, 12. watching—present participle

P. 422

2. trying; tried; tried, 3. showing; showed; shown. 4. talking; talked; talked, 5. bringing; brought; brought, 6. ringing; rang; rung, 7. creating; created; created, 8. flying; flew; flown, 9. drinking, drank; drunk, 10. witnessing; witnessed; witnessed, 11. wearing; wore; worn, 12. catching; caught; caught, 13. growing; grew; grown, 14. beginning; began; begun, 15. going; went; gone, 16. sitting; sat; sat, 17. thinking; thought; thought, 18. seeing; saw; seen, 19. teaching; taught; taught, 20. understanding; understood; understood, 21. forgetting; forgot; forgotten, 22. splashing; splashed; splashed, 23. eating; ate; eaten, 24. watching; watched; watched, 25. arriving; arrived; arrived

P. 423

1. works—present, 2. prepared—past, 3. will set—future, 4. planted—past, 5. will appear—future, 6. will pick—future, 7. pulls—present, 8. will be—future, 9. will bat—future, 10. bats—present, 11. played—past, 12. changes—present, 13. gives—present, 14.–17. Sentences will vary. 14. waters, 15. will dig, 16. will grow, 17. helped

P. 424

1. have started—present perfect, 2. will have discussed—future perfect, 3. had suggested—past perfect, 4. have enjoyed—present perfect, 5. will have finished—future perfect, 6. has written—present perfect, 7. had interviewed—past perfect, 8. have chosen—present perfect, 9. has enjoyed, 10. had met, 11. will have known, 12. have shared, had recommended

P. 425

1. am, 2. have, 3. Are, 4. Does, 5. were, 6. are, 7. was, 8. are, 9. do, 10. have, 11.–14. Answers may vary. Suggested: 11. was, 12. had, 13. is, 14. Does

P. 426

1. grown, 2. bought, 3. sold, 4. spent, 5. taken, 6. become, 7. seen, 8. given, 9. eaten, 10. froze, 11. made, 12. chosen, 13. told, 14. grew, 15. bought

P. 427

1. North America, 2. travel, 3. continents, 4. route, 5. canal, 6. rumble, 7. noise, 8. forests, 9. people, 10. homes, 11. tomatoes, 12. potatoes, 13. covers, 14. pillows, 15. nap, 16.–19. Sentences will vary. Suggested: 16. Rough seas near Cape Horn endangered the ships.,

17. Ships can carry passengers from one ocean to another in far less time., 18. A Panama Canal pilot guides ships through the Canal., 19. The United States paid money to Panama for control of the Canal.

P. 428

1. Sheila told Don a secret., 2. Don gave her his promise of silence., 3. Mr. Miller was giving Ryan a surprise party., 4. He had sent Sheila an invitation., 5. Mrs. Miller handed Don an invitation., 6. Don asked Mrs. Miller a question., 7. guests, 8. friends, 9. me, 10. us, 11. her, 12. me, 13. me, 14. family, 15. them, 16. everyone

P. 429

1. hiker, 2. member, 3. friend, 4. walker, 5. Michelle, 6. girl, 7. climber, 8. teacher, 9. part, 10. portrait, 11. artist, 12. test, 13. judge, 14. Estella, 15. poodle, 16.–19. Sentences will vary.

P. 430

1. went—intransitive, 2. had visited—transitive, 3. drove—transitive, 4. drove—intransitive, 5. rode—intransitive, 6. saw—transitive, 7. felt—intransitive, 8. loved—transitive, 9. did stop—intransitive, 10. had found—transitive, 11. had built—transitive, 12. inherited—transitive, 13. sat—intransitive, 14. drove—intransitive, 15. would see—transitive, 16. offered—transitive, 17. gave—transitive, 18. entered—transitive, 19. bristled—intransitive, 20. gave—transitive, 21. gave—transitive, 22. understood—transitive

P. 431

1. early—when, 2. up—where, 3. very—to what extent, 4. lazily—how, 5. cautiously—how, 6. warmly—how, 7. outside—where, 8. happily—how, 9. quite—to what extent, 10. tonight—when, 11. very—quietly: adverb; quietly—watched: verb, 12. quite—still: adjective, 13. gradually—awoke: verb, 14. sweetly—greeted: verb, 15. reluctantly—returned: verb, 16. suddenly—felt: verb; very—hungry: adjective

P. 432

1. Very—no, 2. rather—no, 3. Recklessly—yes, 4. Suddenly—yes, 5. desperately—yes, 6. later—yes, 7. quite—no, 8. sternly—yes, 9. always—yes, 10. quite—no, 11.–14. Sentences will vary. Be sure that each sentence includes the adverb and that the position of adverbs in sentences is varied.

P. 433

1. lower; lowest, 2. nearer; nearest, 3. more slowly; most slowly, 4. more seriously; most seriously, 5. more eagerly; most eagerly, 6. faster; fastest, 7. more frequently; most frequently, 8. more readily; most readily, 9. more noticeably; most noticeably, 10. easier; easiest, 11. more often, 12. highest, 13. more carefully, 14. more accurately, 15. farther, 16. More slowly

P. 434

1. ever, 2. no, 3. Nowhere, 4. no, 5. anybody, 6. everything, 7. Neither, 8.–10. Sentences will vary.

P. 435

1. seriously, 2. well, 3. really, 4. shortly, 5. immediately, 6. stubbornly, 7. quickly, 8. fiercely, 9. bravely, 10. good, 11. powerful, 12. perfectly, 13. cruelly

P. 436

The words in bold should be circled. 1. in **1271**, 2. with **them,** 3. beyond the eastern **mountains,** 4. to **China,** 5. for many **years,** 6. from **China,** 7. about **it,** 8. through **Asia,** 9. for his **readers,** 10. about **Asia;** from Marco Polo's **book,** 11. over the railing, 12. for England, 13. to the passengers, 14. down the gangplank, 15. into the Atlantic Ocean

P. 437

1. of ice; Sheets, 2. below the ice; land, 3. with dog sleds; Explorers, 4. from the United States; admiral, 5. on Ross Ice Shelf; camp, 6. from the boat; view, 7. of water; spouts, 8. in the boat; people, 9. in the world; mammals, 10. of the porpoises; trainer, 11. in the crowd; people, 12. of each show; beginning, 13. into the air; leaps, 14. for the performers; rewards, 15. of Earth's surface; percent, 16. of that water; percent, 17. of the water; rest, 18. on Earth; ocean

P. 438

1. with enthusiasm—supported: verb, 2. against the English king—spoke: verb, 3. on foot—traveled: verb, 4. from his home—far: adverb, 5. about freedom—enthusiastic: adjective, 6. on Earth—live: verb, 7. in the ocean—swim: verb, 8. with great intelligence—behave: verb, 9. through its lungs—breathe: verb, 10. for long periods—can dive: verb, 11. beneath the ocean's surface—work: verb, 12. in small diving ships—descend: verb, 13. in a moment—would crush: verb, 14. for quick maneuvers—are designed: verb, 15. to the ocean floor—carry: verb

P. 439

1. into, 2. different from, 3. between, 4. into, 5. among, 6. in, 7. could have, 8. among, 9. between

P. 440

1. sentence, 2. not a sentence, 3. sentence, 4. not a sentence, 5. sentence, 6. not a sentence, 7. sentence, 8. sentence, 9. not a sentence, 10. sentence, 11. not a sentence, 12. not a sentence, 13. sentence, 14. not a sentence, 15.–19. Answers will vary.

P. 441

1. imperative; period, 2. exclamatory; exclamation point, 3. declarative; period, 4. interrogative; question mark, 5. declarative; period, 6. interrogative; question mark, 7. declarative; period, 8. interrogative; question mark, 9.–10. Sentences may vary. Suggested: 9. Watch that ape., 10. Is it copying my movements?

P. 442

1. Amelia Bloomer did not invent bloomers., 2. Bloomers were the first slacks for women., 3. These pants were very loose and comfortable., 4. Elizabeth Smith Miller became tired of long skirts and petticoats., 5. She first wore the pants in public., 6. The new outfit was described in Amelia Bloomer's newspaper., 7. People began to call the pants "bloomers.", 8. Most people were shocked to see women in pants., 9. The circus began with a parade., 10. Every performer wore a glittery costume., 11. Lillie had been to the circus twice., 12. The acrobats flew through the air., 13. Our gym teacher has taught us to tumble., 14. The children bought refreshments., 15. The audience saw the animals perform., 16. Her aunt took her to the circus., 17. The work is dangerous., 18. Paolo tore his new red shirt., 19. The clowns threw candy into the crowd., 20. The family sat close to the top., 21.–22. Sentences will vary. 21. subject, 22. predicate

P. 443

1. My best friend, 2. Some snakes, 3. Glands in the snake's head, 4. Special fangs, 5. The deadly venom, 6. My brothers, 7. Jaime, 8. The contents of that letter, 9. Two classmates of mine, 10. This secret, 11. Several members of the crew, 12. Angelina, 13. Many costumes, 14. Other outfits, 15. Four students, 16.–18. Answers will vary.

P. 444

1. <u>carried</u> his board toward the water, 2. <u>paddled</u> out toward the large breakers, 3. <u>crashed</u> over his head, 4. <u>tossed</u> the board into the air, 5. <u>says</u> nothing to me, 6. <u>was revealed</u> on Saturday afternoon, 7. <u>arrived</u> on my birthday, 8. <u>came</u>, 9. <u>had</u> a wonderful, fantastic party, 10. <u>bounced</u> onto the floor, 11. <u>stared</u> at the eraser for five minutes, 12. <u>stretched</u>, 13. <u>bumped</u> into the teacher's desk, 14. <u>watched</u> the eraser with amazement, 15. quickly <u>picked</u> it up

P. 445

1. neighbors—interrogative, 2. woman—declarative, 3. she—interrogative, 4. you—interrogative, 5. article—declarative, 6. children—interrogative, 7. boy—declarative, 8. puppy—declarative, 9. puppy—exclamatory, 10. (You)—imperative

P. 446

The words in bold should be circled. 1. A <u>tornado</u> **or** a <u>hurricane</u>, 2. <u>Lightning</u> **and** the <u>force</u> of wind, 3. A <u>person</u>, a large <u>animal</u>, **or** an <u>automobile</u>, 4. My <u>aunt</u>, my <u>uncle</u>, **and** my younger <u>cousin</u>, 5. <u>Dark clouds</u> **and** powerful <u>winds</u>, 6. My <u>aunt</u> **and** <u>uncle</u>, 7. The <u>family</u>, the <u>cat</u>, **and** the <u>dog</u>, 8. Their <u>house</u> **and** <u>garage</u>, 9. The <u>school</u> **and** the <u>house</u> across the street

P. 447

The words in bold should be circled. 1. <u>flashed</u> for a few minutes **and** then <u>turned</u> red, 2. <u>slowed</u> **and** finally <u>stopped</u>, 3. <u>reached</u> over **and** <u>adjusted</u> the radio, 4. <u>reported</u> on traffic conditions **and** <u>advised</u> drivers, 5. <u>heard</u> the report **and** <u>chose</u> a different route, 6. <u>whispered</u>, <u>pointed</u>, **and** <u>made</u> notes, 7. <u>walked</u> **or** <u>drove</u> across the dusty moonscape during the three and a half years of moon landings, 8. <u>took</u> soil samples, <u>measured</u> temperatures, **and** <u>tested</u> the lunar gravity, 9. <u>released</u> the lunar module **and** <u>measured</u> the vibrations from its impact, 10. <u>brought</u> the mission to a close **and** <u>marked</u> the end of manned moon landings

P. 448

1. compound subject, 2. compound sentence, 3. compound predicate, 4. compound sentence, 5. compound subject, 6. compound predicate, 7. compound subject, 8. compound sentence, 9. compound sentence, 10. compound subject, 11. compound predicate, 12. compound sentence, 13. compound subject, 14. compound sentence, 15. compound subject, 16. compound sentence

P. 449

The words in bold should be circled. 1. <u>Florence Nightingale was the daughter of an English squire</u>, **but** <u>she was born in Florence, Italy.</u>, 2. She was <u>raised</u> **and** <u>educated</u> in Derbyshire, England., 3. Florence did not want to be <u>idle</u> **or** <u>useless.</u>, 4. <u>Nursing was not considered a proper occupation for ladies</u>, **but** <u>Florence was determined to be a nurse.</u>, 5. Florence <u>went to Germany</u> **and** <u>studied nursing.</u>, 6. <u>Llamas are quite gentle</u>, **and** <u>people often make pets of them.</u>, 7. Llamas <u>climb easily over rocky terrain</u> **and** <u>make good pack animals in the mountains.</u>, 8. A llama <u>is not carnivorous</u> **and** <u>prefers grass and leaves as food.</u>, 9. <u>Sandra</u> **and** <u>Larry</u> have a pet llama. 10. <u>Llamas emit a humming sound</u>, **and** <u>you can hear it.</u>, 11. The llama <u>lacks speech organs</u> **and** <u>is mute.</u>, 12. <u>Sally talked to one expert</u>, **and** <u>he told her something interesting.</u>, 13. An angry llama <u>will pull its ears back</u> **and** <u>spit.</u>, 14. <u>Grasses</u> **and** <u>leaves</u> are a llama's main source of food., 15. Llamas <u>enjoy human company</u> **and** <u>are quite affectionate.</u>, 16. Florence returned to London and became the supervisor of a hospital., 17. England entered the war, and Florence joined the War Office as a nurse.

P. 450

1. Say—mild, 2. Hooray—strong, 3. Well—mild, 4. Wow—strong, 5. Hey—strong, 6.–10. Sentences will vary. Suggested: 6. Aha! That's the way to pitch., 7. Oops! She missed that one. 8. Oh, she'll hit it next time., 9. Hooray! What a hit she made!, 10. Wow! Look at her go!, Sentences will vary.

P. 451

1. sentence, 2. sentence fragment, 3. sentence, 4. sentence fragment, 5. run-on sentence, 6. sentence fragment, 7. sentence fragment, 8. sentence, 9. run-on sentence, 10. sentence fragment, 11.–13. Sentences will vary.

P. 452

Sentences will vary.

P. 453

Paragraphs will vary. Suggested:

I should begin by telling you how long I have been a customer of Ronnie's. I have shopped at Ronnie's for five years. I have always been satisfied with your merchandise and your service.

I am happy to have an opportunity to tell you how much I have enjoyed shopping at Ronnie's. However, my letter has a different purpose. I want to ask you to carry my favorite line of sporting goods, Sporty's. I have begun shopping elsewhere for sporting goods. I

would rather be shopping at Ronnie's because it is my favorite store. Besides, your other customers would enjoy Sporty's top-quality goods available at Ronnie's low prices.

Please consider my suggestion. Let me know what you decide.

P. 454

1. clause, 2. phrase, 3. phrase, 4. clause, 5. phrase, 6. clause, 7. phrase, 8. phrase, 9. clause, 10. clause, 11. clause, 12. phrase, 13. clause, 14.–17. Sentences will vary.

P. 455

1. <u>Cleopatra lived in ancient Egypt</u>, <u>which she ruled.</u>; which, 2. <u>She ruled with her brother</u> <u>until he seized the throne.</u>; until, 3. <u>She regained her throne</u> <u>because Julius Caesar helped her.</u>; because, 4. <u>Mark Antony ruled Rome</u> <u>after Caesar died.</u>; after, 5. <u>Antony went to Egypt</u>, <u>where he lived for several years.</u>; where, 6. <u>Antony and Cleopatra died</u> <u>when a Roman army attacked Egypt.</u>; 7. <u>If you go to New York City</u>, <u>consider a visit to Brooklyn.</u>; If, 8. <u>Fifteen teenagers there gained some fame</u> <u>because they were pollution fighters.</u>; because, 9. <u>They called themselves the Toxic Avengers</u>, <u>a name borrowed from a pollution-fighting superhero.</u>; a, 10. <u>Although it was located next to a school</u>, <u>the Radiac Research Corporation was storing large amounts of medical waste.</u>; Although, 11. <u>When the Toxic Avengers heard about this</u>, <u>they planned a response.</u>; When, 12. <u>When a crowd gathered for a public rally</u>, <u>the teens told the people about Radiac.</u>; When 13. <u>Public awareness grew</u> <u>after the rally was held.</u>; after, 14. <u>Billy fell in the sewer on a neighborhood street</u> <u>as he was playing on a Saturday afternoon.</u>; as

P. 456

1. compound, 2. complex, 3. complex, 4. compound, 5. complex, 6. complex, 7. compound, 8. complex, 9. compound, 10. complex

P. 457

1. Have you ever lost your voice?, 2. What a strange feeling that is!, 3. You try to talk, but you can only squeak., 4. No one can understand you., 5. The climbers left their base camp at six in the morning., 6. Mr. Enami is a train engineer., 7. Miles found his math problems to be very challenging., 8. Does the community softball league meet every Friday?, 9. Pedro and I go to the museum in California., 10. He is such a conscientious student!

P. 458

Commas and semicolons should be placed after words as listed.
1. runway, 2. paper, cardboard, 3. unloaded, sorted, 4. her, 5. gear, 6. Greek, Latin, 7. Hey, 8. agree, 9. Noah, Carrie, 10. Dallas, Phoenix, 11. worse; 12. pilot, copilot, 13. Oh, 14. captain; 15. great, 16. low

P. 459

1. Beth Ann Drake, 2. President Lincoln, 3. Central Bookstore, 4. Waco, Texas, 5. Logan, Utah, 6. Italian marble, 7. me, myself, and I, 8. English accent, 9. Union army, 10. American citizen, 11. Adams Middle School, 12. *Beauty and the Beast*, 13. Latin Club, 14. Amelia Earhart Boulevard, 15. Declaration of Independence, 16. Yellowstone National Park, 17. Mexican pottery, 18. New Year's Day

P. 460

1. lb., 2. oz., 3. ft., 4. yd., 5. ME, 6. mg, 7. l, 8. cc, 9. USPS, 10. NBA, 11. Rodeo Dr., 12. Old Post Rd., 13. Fifth Ave., 14. NCAA, 15. M.D., 16. mph, 17. rpm, 18. F, 19. C, 20. Best Carpet Cleaners, Inc., 21. The Farley Farragut Co., 22. Dr. Thomas F. Gorman

P. 461

Joe Bob's Restaurant: Answers will vary.
Student Information Card: School: The Parker School, Address: 120 Grant Ave., Ponca City, OK, Principal;: Helena M. Ramírez, First Day of School: Sept. 4, 2005

P. 462

1. *Around the World in Eighty Days*, 2. *The Pirates of Penzance*, 3. *Profiles in Courage*, 4. *Stalking the Wild Asparagus*, 5. *The Cat Ate My Gymsuit*, 6. "Shake, Rattle, and Roll", 7. "Twist and Shout", 8. "Me and My Shadow", 9. *The Red Balloon*, 10. *The Wizard of Oz*, 11. *Stand by Me*, 12. "The Body", 13. *Cujo, Christine, Carrie*, 14. "Stand by Me", 15. *Time*, 16. *Travels with Charley*, 17. "Welcome to Pittsburgh," 18. *Monday Night Football*, 19. *Gorillas in the Mist*

P. 463

1. Leon dragged the huge crate through and shouted, "I'm home, Mom!", 2. "She isn't back yet," Leon's brother told him., 3. "Oh, Leon," said his brother, staring at the box, "what is that?", 4. "Queen Elizabeth I ruled a great empire," Marcia said., 5. She told her critics, "I have the heart and stomach of a king.", 6. "Who else had a great impact on a country?" asked Terri., 7. "Well," Ben remarked,

"Mohandas Gandhi inspired a nonviolent revolution in India.", 8. "Gandhi inspired Martin Luther King!" Terri added., 9. "New York has a new program," Nancy said, "for student ticket buyers."

P. 464
The words in bold should be circled. 1. The **company,** High Flyers, forgot to include instructions., 2. The **Eagle,** our only car, would not start. 3. Our **neighbor,** Jim Delgado, came to help. 4. Even **Jim,** a good mechanic, could not start it., 5. The **starter,** an electric motor, was not working., 6. The **pilot,** Captain Songrossi, said to fasten our seat belts., 7. A **prairie,** a kind of grassland, is home to many kinds of plants and animals., 8. Our **teacher,** Ms. Pesek, does not agree., 9. Our **store,** Video Visions, has many unusual movies., 10. The **film,** an exciting dinosaur story, is filed with other adventure films., 11.–12. Sentence will vary.

P. 465
1. I'd; I would, 2. I've; I have, 3. she's; she is, 4. isn't; is not, 5. We've; We have, 6. They've; They have, 7. I'm; I am, 8. aren't; are not, 9. didn't; did not, 10. They'd; They would, 11. wasn't; was not, 12. haven't; have not, 13. You've; You have, 14. can't; can not, 15. Doesn't; Does not, 16.–20. Sentences will vary. 16. shouldn't, 17. won't, 18. he'd, 19. let's, 20. you're

P. 466
Answers will vary. Suggested: 1. sick, 2. started, 3. early, 4. test, 5. back, 6. no one, 7. left, 8. noisy, 9. arrived, 10. begin, 11. easy, 12. right, 13.–18. Answers will vary. Suggested: 13. untamed; tame, 14. daring; timid, 15. bulky; thin, 16. lucky; unfortunate, 17. fix; break, 18. collect; scatter

P. 467
1. gentle, 2. pulled tight, 3. a group of ships, 4. cracked into pieces, 5. air; heir, 6. rode; road, 7. thrown; throne, 8. side; sighed

P. 468
1. inactive—not active, 2. impolite—not polite, 3. prejudge—judge before, 4. unusual—not usual, 5. overconfident—having too much confidence, 6. postelection—coming after an election, 7. inexpensive—not expensive, 8. recount—count again

P. 469
1. thoughtful; ful, 2. grayish; ish, 3. rainy; y. 4. restless; less, 5. harmful; ful, 6.–23. Answers will vary. Suggested: attendant, attendance, attention, boxer, celebrant, celebration, contestant, competitor, competition, cyclist, determinant, determination, developer, development, dominance, domination, excellence, organizer, organization, perfection, prominence, reverence, salutation, skier

P. 470
1. great-uncle, 2. three-bedroom, 3. mountain range, 4. Everyone, 5. cuckoo clock, 6. sunset, 7. seaweed, 8. jellyfish, 9. starfish, 10. blue-green, 11. sea lion, 12. palm trees, 13. fast-sinking, 14. three-fourths, 15. beachfront, 16. spellbound, 17. inner tube, 18. newspaper, 19. jack-of-all-trades, 20. earring, 21.–24. Answers will vary.

P. 471
1. antique, 2. young, 3. cozy, 4. unhurried, 5. simple, 6. rare, 7. Blackened, 8. sip, 9. tough, 10. greasy, 11. crumbly, 12. soggy, 13. loud, 14. inferno

P. 472
Dialogue will vary. Idioms: the cat got your tongue; hold your horses; knock your socks off; get off my back; on pins and needles; keep my nose to the grindstone; take off; get on the ball; about to burst; Lend me a hand

P. 473
1. holds, 2. selects, 3. presents, 4. travel, 5. follow, 6. hear, 7. ignore, 8. elect, 9. affect, 10. votes, 11. fail, 12. share, 13. has, 14. hurls, 15. hits

P. 474
1. like, 2. are, 3. is, 4. provide, 5. discourage, 6. frighten, 7. outruns, 8. fly, 9. fights, 10. change, 11. hides, 12. are, 13. grows

P. 475
1. first person; my, I, me, 2. excited, but not expecting to be surprised, 3. The writer became surprised., 4. a. The family gathered after dinner.—first, b. The writer heard a rustling noise.—after, c. The writer noticed that a box moved.—a minute later, d. Father picked up the present.—then, e. The writer was surprised.—finally

P. 476
Errors are corrected in bold type.
What an amazing experience my **brothers** and I had with the wind last **autumn!** We had driven with our parents to Point Reyes, north of San **Francisco.** Point Reyes is known as one of the **windiest** spots in the **country**, and on that day the winds were raging up to 50 miles an hour all along the California coast.

I had no way of determining the speed of the wind at Point **Reyes** that afternoon. I can only tell you that when we jumped into the air, we were blown a full five feet before landing. The wind picked us up and carried us with the force of **rushing** water. **We simply** could not fall backward. The wind was so strong that we could lean back against it and let it support us as firmly as a brick wall would.

[paragraph indent] My brothers and I decided to take a short walk downwind along the beach. We allowed the wind to push us along at a **rapid** pace. For a while we **stopped** walking altogether. We simply jumped into the air, let ourselves be blown along like empty milk **cartons**, and landed. Then we jumped into the air again. Borne by the wind, we progressed as quickly as if we had been walking.

P. 477–478
Graphic organizers and personal narratives will vary.

P. 479
Topic sentence: The room had clearly been ransacked., 1. Suggested answers: open and empty drawers, strewn clothes, empty closet, portrait of a solemn young woman—all sight; crunch of glass—hearing; fragrance of perfume, garlic smell—smell; broken glass underfoot—touch, 2. space order, 3. Suggested answers are "next to," "trail . . . led," "underfoot," "on the wall."

P. 480
Errors are corrected in bold type.
A set of smooth stone steps led up to a flat clearing in the forest. Here the sun's rays filtered down through the branches of the towering pines, and the ground was covered with fragrant green pine needles. **The** carpet of needles felt thick and soft under Nina's feet.

A gentle breeze rustled the branches. Nina inhaled the scent of the pines as it drifted on the breeze. **Mingled** with the scent of pine was the smell of the pale green mosses growing on the north sides of the trees.

[paragraph indent] What was that in the middle of the clearing? Nina saw a large stump, just under three **feet** tall and a full three feet in diameter. **Four** smaller stumps were arranged around it. Paul was already seated on one of the smaller stumps, and the large stump was clearly just the right **height** for a table.

On the large stump lay a basket of juicy blackberries, a canteen, and two shiny metal cups. Paul looked up at Nina and asked, "Are you ready for a treat?"

P. 481–482
Graphic organizers and descriptive paragraphs will vary.

P. 483
If you ever need to warm your body when you are chilled, you should try making some ginger tea. You will need a fresh ginger root, three cups of water, a knife, and a glass pot or kettle. First, put three cups of water into the glass pot. Next, cut six slices of ginger root. The slices should be $\frac{1}{8}$ to $\frac{1}{4}$ inch thick. Add the ginger to the water in the pot. Boil the ginger, letting the water evaporate until only one cup of water remains. Strain the ginger tea into a cup. Drink it hot.

P. 484
Errors are corrected in bold type.
With the help of a little tuna fish and some acting skill, you can easily get your dog Titan to take his pill. As you know, Titan often begs for tuna, but you never give him any. If you suddenly offer Titan some tuna with the pill inside it, he will become suspicious and refuse **to** eat it. Try this method instead.

Make a small ball of tuna around Titan's pill. Put the tuna ball on a plate. Then find **something** you like to eat and put that on the plate, too. Take your plate and sit down at the kitchen table.

Titan will probably be watching you carefully, but you should ignore him. He's a very smart dog, and it will not be easy to fool him. **Your** chances of success are best if you [delete extra if] just pretend you don't see him.

[paragraph indent] Titan will soon sit beside you [delete comma] and start to beg. Eat your own food and continue to ignore Titan. Then, very casually, allow the ball of tuna to fall to the floor. You should make a quick grab for the tuna, but you must be sure that Titan gets to it first. Titan will eagerly gulp the tuna—and the pill.

P. 485–486
Graphic organizers and how-to paragraphs will vary.

P. 487
1. Circle: new house, old house; Underline: similar to, Like, Both, both, and so did—compare, 2. Circle: new house, old house; Underline: different, Unlike, while—contrast. Old House: old, hardwood floor, rugs, two-story; Both: three bedrooms, two bathrooms, fireplace in living room, dining room; New House; brand new, wall-to-wall carpet, one-story

P. 488

Errors are corrected in bold type.

People sometimes **ask** me who my best friend is. Truthfully, I do not know. I have two close friends, and I like them both very much.

My friends **Judy** and Margie **are** alike in many ways. Both are intelligent, loyal, and helpful. Either can carry on a great conversation. Each has an excellent sense of humor, and we all enjoy many of the same activities.

However, my two friends are different in many ways. I **have** more arguments with Judy. She complains if she does not like something, and she **argues** if she disagrees with me. Margie rarely complains or argues, so we almost never **fight**.

On the other hand, Judy is a more honest friend. She always says exactly what she thinks or feels. In contrast, **Margie** never **says** anything negative to me about things **I** have said or done. Instead, she may say something to someone else, and her comments often **get** back to me. If Judy has a complaint, she discusses it with the person who has caused the problem.

P. 489–490

Venn diagrams and compare and contrast paragraphs will vary.

P. 491

1. that Bob Cratchit is a good worker, 2. Mr. Cratchit is a fine man, and I think you should think carefully before letting him go., 3. 3, 4. that it may be of great importance

P. 492

Errors are corrected in bold type.

431 Palm Avenue
Normand**,** Massachusetts 02162
June 26, 2005

Mr. **Glen** Scrubb
Grime-Away Cleaners
816 Ruby Street
Normand, **Massachusetts** 02162

Dear Mr. Scrubb**:**

My family has used your cleaners for seven years, and your service has always been satisfactory. **However,** last Thursday I picked up my favorite slacks from Grime-Away and discovered a tear in the cuff. I know that the tear was not there when I brought the slacks to Grime-Away. The clerk said she could not have the tear repaired without your authorization. Please send me a note stating that you will pay **for** the repair.

Thank you for your help.
Sincerely,
Donald Todd

P. 493–494

Graphic organizers and persuasive paragraphs will vary.

P. 495

1. emotional words, 2. testimonial, 3. bandwagon technique, 4. faulty generalization, 5. begging the question, 6. emotional words, 7. testimonial

P. 496

Errors are corrected in bold type.

The people of the **world** are faced with alarming environmental problems. I am convinced that we must all cooperate through international **agencies** to solve these problems. Working alone, one state or one nation cannot protect its land and people from environmental hazards. The problems faced by people in the **United States** are also problems for people in **Canada** Japan, and **Russia**. Only by facing these problems together and trying to work out cooperative solutions can we protect ourselves and our **planet**.

There are several reasons why international cooperation is needed. **In** the first place, some environmental dangers threaten the whole **planet** rather than local areas. Damage to the ozone layer is a good example. If someone in **Nebraska** uses an aerosol spray, the chemicals do not stay in Nebraska. Those damaging chemicals travel to the ozone layer, where they affect the whole world. Therefore, a **state** or **country** cannot protect itself against ozone damage simply by passing a law forbidding the local use of aerosols.

P. 497–498

Graphic organizers and persuasive essays will vary.

P. 499

Answers will vary. Suggested: 1. It will focus on the fact that the sea touches every continent., 2. a view of the coast as the ruffled border of something blue, perhaps fabric, 3. yes; sky, occupy; lands, hands, 4. The ocean is compared to a bathtub., 5. a sense of community formed by bathing in the same ocean

P. 500

Errors are corrected in bold type.

My Fair-Weather Friend
My greatest admirer is **my** shadow.
He admires me so much that he mimics everything **I** do.
He follows me everywhere.
I drag him **through** puddles as **I** walk around.
He glides over their surface like a black film of oil.

I drag him over logs and stones.
He slithers over **them** like a snake.
I bump him into **boulders** and **buildings**.
He stays by **my** side, obedient as a slave, faithful as a fair-weather friend.
"What?" you ask. "I always thought a fair-weather friend was unfaithful." Exactly. My shadow deserts me as soon as the **sun** goes down or the sky turns gray.
He will not follow **me** into dark rooms or deep caves.
He is only a fair-weather friend.

P. 501–502

Graphic organizers and poems will vary.

P. 505

Responses to prompts will vary.

P. 506

1. title page, 2. foreword/preface, 3. bibliography, 4. copyright page, 5. contents page

P. 507

1. glossary, 2. contents page, 3. copyright page, 4. title page, 5. bibliography, 6. title page, 7. foreword/preface, 8. contents page. 9.–15. Responses will vary: Suggested: 9. the date a book was published, 10. title and author of book; publisher, where published, 11. introductory comments about the book, 12. list of all the topics in the book and the page numbers where they appear in the book, 13. definitions of difficult or unfamiliar words that appear in the book, 14. chapter titles; page numbers on which chapters begin, 15. other books on the same topic

P. 508

I. main topic, A. subtopic, 1. detail, 2. detail, B. subtopic, 1. detail, 2. detail, 3. detail,
II. The Yeti
    A. Where it lives
        1. In Asia
        2. In the Himalayas
    B. What it looks like
        1. Large ape or man
        2. Covered with hair
Outlines will vary.

P. 509

Answers will vary.

P. 510

1. noun, 2. adjective, 3. Extending throughout or across a nation, 4. nation, 5. A tribe or federation, 6. national, 7. 3, 8. yes

P. 511

1. 1. Type: FA 2. Type: Heyerdahl 3. Press: <Return> key, 2. 1. Type: FT 2. Type: Treasures of the Deep 3. Press: <Return> key, 3. Type FS, because FA means Find Author, and FT means Find Title, so FS means Find Subject., 4. 1. Type: FS 2. Type: whales 3. Press: <Return> key

P. 512

Notes should include key ideas. Suggested responses: Queen Hatshepsut: Only woman pharaoh. Succeeded Thutmose II about 1504 B.C. Ruled 21 years. Productive: Trade improved. Major building program.
Cheng: Meng T'ien, inventor, before 200 B.C. Musical instrument, zither family. Long, curved sound box. Strings stretch length of box. Frets help produce melody. Descendants of *cheng: tranh* (Vietnam); *koto* (Japan)

P. 513

1. Chapter 4; These animals are mammals., 2. Chapter 7; "Our Oceans in Danger" suggests pollution., 3. Chapter 4, 4. Chapter 2, 5. Chapter 1, 6. Glossary, 7. Chapter 5, 8. Chapter 3, 9. Chapter 7, 10. Chapter 6

P. 514

Answers may vary depending on encyclopedia used. 1. From Argentina north to south central and south eastern parts of the United States, 2. snails, insects, spiders, and earthworms, 3. They hide in their burrows if these are close by; if not, they dig a hole. Sometimes they roll up in a ball., 4. Up to 15 pounds, 5. Answers will vary., 6. He and Tenzing Norkay were the first climbers to reach the summit of Mount Everest., 7. New Zealand, 8. July 29, 1919, 9. Beekeeping, 10. 29,028 ft., 11. Southern Africa, 12. No., 13. Harare, 14. Rhodesia, 15. Cattle, coffee, corn, cotton, sugar, tea, tobacco, and wheat

P. 515

1. almanac or encyclopedia, 2. thesaurus, 3. encyclopedia, 4. dictionary, 5. *Books in Print*

P. 516

Answers will vary.

WRITING SKILLS

Answers to the practice paper exercises questions may vary, but examples are provided here to give you an idea of how your child may respond.

P. 518

1. first person 2. A fire broke out in Uncle Mike's apartment building. Answers will vary but should show cause/effect from story.

P. 519

1. first person; my, I, me 2. excited, but not expecting to be surprised 3. The writer became surprised. 4. a. The family gathered after dinner.—first b. The writer opened the first gift. c. The writer heard a rustling noise.—after d. The writer noticed that a box moved.—a minute later e. Father picked up the present.—then

P. 520-521

people headed for the beach, which caused traffic to be jammed, which caused overheated cars, which caused people to become hot and thirsty, which caused people to stop at juice bar, which caused increased business

P. 522

1. right number 2. too many—Possible responses to cross out: My mother refused to buy me a horse. I had to iron my shirt. Joan won the spelling bee, and I only came in second. 3. too few—Accepted one or two examples of Wayne's ideas.

P. 523

Possible responses: 1. The Ross family left their apartment house early. 2. The children climbed into the car enthusiastically. 3. Bill Ross was the motorist for the first thirty minutes. 4. He had just finished a course in driving at school. 5. Bill and his father switched places before they reached the mountains. 6. The scent of pines was everywhere. 7. Bill and Susan immediately went for a hike.

P. 524-525

What an amazing experience my brothers and I had with the wind last ~~autunm!~~ *autumn* We had driven with our parents to Point Reyes, north of San ~~francisco~~. Point Reyes is known as one of the ~~windyest~~ *windiest* spots in the ~~cuontry~~ *country*, and on that day the winds were raging up to 50 miles an hour all along the California coast.

I had no way of determining the speed of the wind at Point ~~reyes~~ that afternoon. I can only tell you that when we jumped into the air, we were blown a full five feet before

landing The wind picked us up and carried us with the force of ~~rushhing~~ *rushing* water. ~~we~~ ~~simply~~ *simply* could not fall backward. The wind was so strong that we could lean back against it and let it support us as firmly as a brick wall would.

My brothers and I decided to take a short walk downwind along the beach. We allowed the wind to push us along at a ~~rapid~~ *rapid* pace. For a while we ~~stoped~~ *stopped* walking altogether. We simply jumped into the air, let ourselves be blown along like empty milk ~~cartoons~~ *cartons* and landed. Then we jumped into the air again. Borne by the wind, we progressed as quickly as if we had been walking⊙

P. 533

1. The writer learned how to swim. 2. The main setting for this story is the Llano River. The cool river has fast rapids, shallow places, and deep swimming holes that feel good when the hot sun is beating down. 3. In the second paragraph, the writer tells us that J. W. is loud, funny, and a real pain. 4. The writer is surprised when Donnie offers to teach him to swim, so they probably don't do a lot of things together. You can tell he cares about him, though, because he talks to him when he is sitting by herself and he is patient with him as he practices each step. I think the writer trusts Donnie and looks up to him. 5. Check to see that your child summarizes the significant events of the story. Summaries should be organized in a thoughtful way, with the main ideas and important details clearly presented.

P. 534

1. The writer uses dialogue and vivid descriptions to show emotion. 2. Reading exactly what J.W. says instead of a description helps us understand why the writer was so embarrassed. 3. The writer adds funny comments to help readers

picture what is going on and to help us understand her personality. Humor keeps the reader interested in the story. 4. For the most part, the writer uses dialogue to help the reader picture J.W. She gives examples of how he teased him and how he complimented him on learning to swim.

P. 539

It's often not easy to give a dog a pill, but with the help of a little tuna fish, it can be done. You will need the pill, a can of tuna, and a plate. First, make a small ball of tuna around the pill. Next, put the tuna ball on a plate. Sit at the kitchen table and pretend to eat the tuna ball. Finally, casually drop the ball of tuna on the floor. The dog will eat the tuna and never realize the pill was inside! Materials: the pill, a can of tuna, a plate

P. 540

If you ever need to warm your body when you are chilled, you should try making some ginger tea. You will need a fresh ginger root, three cups of water, a knife, and a glass pot or kettle. First, put three cups of water into the glass pot. Next, cut six slices of ginger root. The slices should be $\frac{1}{8}$ to $\frac{1}{4}$ inch thick. Add the ginger to the water in the pot. Boil the ginger, letting the water evaporate until only one cup of water remains. Strain the ginger tea into a cup. Drink it hot.

P. 541-542

Materials: orange juice, bowl, green drink mix, spoon, pineapple sherbet, lemon soda. Steps: 1. Pour orange juice into bowl. 2. Add green drink mix. 3. Add sherbet in small scoops. 4. Stir until some sherbet melts. 5. Add lemon soda.

P. 543

a. for a sixth-grader b. for a second-grader
The second paragraph used shorter sentences and explained how the trick works.

P. 544

Possible responses: 1. If you are thirsty, you can make a refreshing yogurt shake. 2. First, measure two tablespoons of plain yogurt into a blender. 3. Next, add two table-spoons of fruit juice. 4. Add one-half teaspoon of honey. 5. Add one-third of a banana. 6. Add a pinch of nutmeg to the other ingredients. 7. Crush two ice cubes and add them to the mixture. 8. Blend the ingredients until they are frothy.

P. 545-546

With the help of a little tuna fish and some acting skill, you can easily get your dog ∧ Titan to take his pill. As you know, Titan often begs for tuna but you never give him any. If you suddenly offer Titan some tuna with the pill inside it, he will become suspicious and refuse ^*to* eat it. Try this method instead.

Make a small ball of tuna around Titan's pill. Put the tuna ball on a plate. Then find ~~sumthing~~ *something* you like to eat and put that on the plate ∧ too. Take your plate and sit down at the kitchen table.

Titan will probably be watching you ∧ carefully but you should ignore him. He's a very smart dog ∧ and it will not be easy to fool him. your chances of success are best if you ~~it~~ just pretend you don't see him.

Titan will soon sit beside you⸮ and start to beg. Eat your own food and continue to ignore Titan. Then, very casually, allow the ball of tuna ∧ to fall to the floor. You should make a quick grab for the tuna but you must be sure that Titan gets to it first. Titan will eagerly gulp the tuna–and the pill.

p. 553
1. You will need the following materials to make a Newton's cradle: a ruler marked in inches, 1 pencil or dowel rod, a pair of scissors, 5 paper clips, 5 eight-inch pieces of fishing line, and 5 wooden beads. 2. The beads must line up exactly and evenly in order to hit each other and transfer energy. 3. The fishing line holds the beads and lets them swing freely. 4. Possible response: If I could, I would build a life-sized Newton's cradle. For the frame, I would use a backyard swing set with all the swings taken off. I would use four old bowling balls as the "beads." They would all need to be the same weight, but they could be different colors. I would ask my dad to help me drill 1-inch holes through the bowling balls with his electric drill. Then, I would find a long rope 1 inch thick. I would use a yardstick to measure the rope into four 5-foot-long pieces. Then, I'd ask my dad to help me cut it. I'd use the pieces of rope to hang the bowling balls on the frame.

p. 554
1. The writer states the purpose of the paper clearly, lists materials, and gives step-by-step instructions. 2. A Newton's cradle is used to demonstrate scientific principles. If the writer had not included the first paragraph, we might know how to make a Newton's cradle, but we wouldn't know what to do with it or why it is interesting. 3. Listing the materials before giving the directions helps readers make sure they have everything they need before they start building the cradle. 4. The writer uses sequence words such as *first, next,* and *then* to help you understand the order of the steps. These words also help you find your place in the process quickly. 5. Answers may vary. Pictures should illustrate moving beads. Pictures or labels should explain the change from kinetic energy to sound and heat energy.

p. 559
Your child underlines "Each summer Ron and Diane go to their favorite beach house—their great-aunt's beach house." Possible responses: sight: three-bedroom house, ocean in front, mountain range in back, piles of seaweed, jellyfish, blue-green water, sea lion, shadows lengthened. hearing: cuckoo clock, bark, singing. smell: dead fish. taste: none. touch: slippery, smooth shell

p. 560
Your child underlines "The room had clearly been ransacked."
1. Possible responses: open and empty drawers, strewn clothes, empty closet, portrait of a solemn young woman—all sight. crunch of glass—hearing. fragrance of perfume, garlic—smell. broken glass underfoot—touch 2. space order; Possible answers are "next to," "trail . . . led," "underfoot," "on the wall."

p. 561
Possible responses: sight: green vegetation, white sand, blue water. hearing: surf thundering, stomach growling. smell: salty smell of ocean, smoky smell of roasting pig. taste: salty water. touch: soft sands, cool water, hot sun

p. 562
Be sure that your child includes precise words. Possible responses: 1. underline first sentence. Bob heard a loud banging at the door. 2. underline second sentence. He ran to the front door. 3. underline first sentence. A young boy was standing on the front porch. 4. underline second sentence. The girl's tears clearly showed her grief. 5. underline second sentence. "We have lost our big cat." 6. underline first sentence. "Does your cat have brown rings?" asked Bob. 7. underline second sentence. "He is curled up asleep."

p. 563
Possible responses: 1. A small brown dog huddled in the shelter of the tunnel. 2. It shivered in the icy, penetrating wind. 3. Finally, it left the shelter of the tunnel and began to wander down the street. 4. Its dark shadow trailed behind it. 5. The dog and its shadow trotted down the street. 6. The dog broke through the thin sheet of ice on the puddle and wet its paw.

p. 564–565

A set of smooth stone steps led up to a flat clearing in the forest ⊙ Here the sun's rays filtered down through the branches of the towering pines, and the ground was covered with fragrant green pine needles. the carpet of needles felt thick and soft under Nina's feet.
=
a gentle breeze rustled the branches Nina inhaled the scent of the pines as it drifted on the breeze.
=

mingled with the scent of pine was the smell of the pale green mosses growing on the north sides of the trees.

What was that in the middle of the clearing? Nina saw a large stump, just under three (feat) tall and
feet

a full three feet in diameter. four smaller stumps were arranged around it ⊙ Paul was already seated on one of the smaller stumps, and the large stump was clearly just the right (hieght) for a table.
height

On the large stump lay a basket of juicy blackberries, a canteen, and two shiny metal cups ⊙ Paul looked up at Nina and asked, "Are you ready for a treat?"

p. 573
1. The writer uses interesting words, similes, and metaphors to describe what Cole and his dad saw, heard, felt, and did. 2. Cole traced the stitching on his bag. His mom was relieved when Cole's dad telephoned. 3. The writer tells us that Cole reassures his dad that he's not upset about the late start to the weekend. Cole tells his dad that he loves the farm and the house. 4. Answers will vary. Check drawings. 5. Guide your child in summarizing the significant events of the story.

p. 574
1. "Their red and yellow heads moved up and down like fishing bobs on a lake." "The creek babbled like a child." 2. "The highway was a gray stripe through green countryside." 3. Some interesting verbs included <u>sliced</u>, <u>bowed</u>, <u>babbled</u>, <u>sparkled</u>, <u>swallowed</u>, and <u>groaned</u>. 4. Drawings should show the interior of a farmhouse, covered with dust and spider webs. Cole should be in the room, with his dad holding his elbow. 5. Answers will vary. Look for descriptive language that expresses the five senses, comparisons, varied sentence length, and personal style, or voice.

p. 579
1. comparison 2. contrast 3. Possible responses: intelligent, loyal, helpful, good conversationalists, excellent sense of humor 4. Possible responses: Lena complains and argues. Taylor rarely complains or argues. Lena is more honest. Taylor talks behind someone's back.

p. 580
1. circle: new house, old house underline: similar to, like, both, both, and so did—comparison 2. circle: new house, old house underline: different, unlike, while—contrast

p. 581

Category	Rabbit A	Both rabbits	Rabbit B
1. type of animal			
2. shape	tall, thin		short plump
3. clothes	hats	hats	
4. expression	clever, shrewd		happy
5. ears	standing up		floppy

6. Both are rabbits; both are wearing hats. 7. Possible responses include differences in shape, expression, and ears.

p. 582
1. Both groups of Indians farmed and raised animals. Pueblos and Navajos also both wove cloth. 2. The Pueblos depended entirely on the crops and livestock they raised. The Navajos hunted and gathered as well as raised food and livestock. The Navajos wove wool, while the Pueblos wove cotton and feathers together.

p. 583
Possible responses: 1. Both water-skiing and snow skiing require skis. However, the similarity ends there. Snow skiing is a cold-weather sport. In contrast, water-skiing is a sport for warm weather. People snow ski on a mountain slope, while water-skiing is done on a large body of water. 2. I like to be moving throughout a game. Therefore, I like playing football better than playing baseball. Indeed, in football, the whole team is in motion on every play. In contrast, when a baseball team is at bat, most of the players are sitting and waiting.

p. 584-585

People sometimes ~~asks~~ *ask* me who my best friend is. Truthfully, I do not know. I have two close friends, and I like them both very much.

My friends judy and Margie ~~is~~ *are* alike in many ways. Both are intelligent, loyal, and helpful ⊙ Either can carry on a great conversation. Each has an excellent sense of humor, and they enjoy many of the same activities.

However, my two friends are different in many ways. I ~~has~~ *have* more arguments with Judy. She complains if she does not like something, and she ~~argue~~ *argues* if she disagrees with me. Margie rarely complains or argues, so we almost never ~~fights.~~ *fight*

On the other hand, Judy is a more honest friend. She always says exactly what she thinks or feels. In contrast, Margie never ~~say~~ *says* anything negative to me about things i have said or done. Instead, she may say something to someone else, and her comments often ~~gets~~ *get* back to me. If Judy has a complaint, she discusses it with the person who has caused the problem.

p. 591

Guide your child in organizing the information in a clear manner. How In-line Skates and Ice Skates Are Alike: Both in-line skates and ice skates are built for speed.; The way skates are made today lets skaters skate well all the time.; Skates can be used in more than one sport.; The boots of both in-line and ice skates support the ankles firmly and comfortably.; Both types of skates have devices that help them move. How In-line Skates and Ice Skates Are Different: In-line skates are used on land while ice skates are made for ice.; The boots of in-line skates are made of plastic, with a liner that can be removed and washed. Ice skates, however, have boots made of leather. The lining lets air move, but it must be wiped clean each time you use the skates because it cannot be taken out.; In-line skates have wheels, usually four, which make them move. The fastest in-line skates have wheels that are bigger (about 76 mm), harder (up to 100 durometers), and have good ball bearings. Ice skates, on the other hand, use blades to move. Blades are solid metal, usually stainless steel coated with chrome, nickel, or aluminum. Each blade has a toe pick to help the skater take off and a ridge called a "hollow" that cuts the ice.; Skaters using in-line skates have brakes at the back of each boot to help them stop, but ice-skaters have to use their legs and feet to press down on the sides of their skates to stop.

p. 592

1. The writer introduces the topic of the paper in the first paragraph. 2. The similarities are clear and easy to explain, so the writer describes those first. 3. The first difference is how the boots of in-line skates and ice skates are made. The boots of in-line skates are usually made of firm plastic, while ice skate boots are made of leather. Another difference is that in-line skates use wheels, but ice skates use blades. The third difference is related to stopping. In-line skates have brakes, but ice skates don't. I think the writer presented the differences in this order because he or she could talk about how the boots are made, then describe how they move when you're wearing them. When you're skating, the last thing you do is stop, so it makes sense to discuss that last. 4. The first paragraph introduces the topic of the paper. The last paragraph summarizes the paper's topic.

p. 598

1. emotional words 2. testimonial 3. emotional words 4. faulty generalization 5. fact 6. opinion

p. 599

1. emotional words 2. testimonial 3. bandwagon technique 4. faulty generalization 5. emotional words 6. testimonial

p. 600

1. fact 2. opinion 3. opinion 4. should; opinion 5. ought; opinion 6. fact 7. fact 8. probably; opinion 9. silly; opinion 10. fact 11. fact

p. 601

1. How can a planet such as Theron still tolerate the disgraceful laws that permit slavery in the year 3045? 2. The Theronites should demand an end to that practice. 3. Thousand of Robots are chained to their masters by existing laws. 4. The Robots labor from dawn until midnight without pay. 5. Robot catchers are hired to track down escaping Robots. 6. To be a truly modern planet, Theron should crush out practices that deny freedom to all Theronites.

p. 602

Possible responses: 1. I think it is important for people to use less energy. After all, every kind of energy costs us something. Fuels made from fossils pollute the air and are in short supply. 2. Other sources of energy also have drawbacks. For example, water power requires damming rivers, sometimes destroying beautiful valleys. Even manufacturing the equipment for other sources of energy uses energy and creates pollution in the process. When we cut our use of energy, we can avoid many harmful results of our present overuse of it.

p. 603-604

The people of the ~~W~~world are faced with alarming environmental problems. I am convinced that we must all cooperate through international ~~agencys~~ *agencies* to solve these problems. Working alone, one state or one nation cannot protect its land and people from environmental hazards. The problems faced by people in the united states are also problems for people in canada, Japan, and russia. Only by facing these problems together and trying to work out cooperative solutions can we protect ourselves and our ~~p~~Planet.

There are several reasons why international cooperation is needed. in the first place, some environmental dangers threaten the whole ~~plant~~ *planet* rather than local areas. Damage to the ozone layer is a good example. If someone in nebraska uses an aerosol spray, the chemicals do not stay in Nebraska. Those damaging chemicals travel to the ozone layer, where they affect the whole world. Therefore, a ~~S~~state or ~~C~~country cannot protect itself against ozone damage simply by passing a law forbidding the local use of aerosols.

p. 612

1. The Ogre is not your usual hero. He isn't handsome and he prefers to live alone. 2. Other important characters in the movie are Princess Stella, the moles, and Manco, the villain. 3. Bernie rescues the princess from a dragon so the moles will go back to their village and leave Bernie alone in the forest. 4. Check to see that your child identifies the purpose of the review and summarizes its significant points.

p. 613

1. The writer outlines the elements of a fairy tale, which are familiar to everyone. Then the writer tells the reader that the characters in this fairy tale are different, making this the funniest fairy tale ever. 2. The writer doesn't want to spoil the movie for the reader, but he or she wants to share a few exciting moments to convince the reader to see the movie. 3. Most movies have people or look like cartoons. It is amazing for a computer-animated movie to look so realistic that people will want to see it. 4. In the first paragraph, the writer presents the opinion that Bernie, the Laughing Ogre is one of the funniest fairy tales ever. In the last paragraph, the writer restates the opinion and summarizes the reasons the reader should see the movie.

p. 618

1. c 2. b 3. b. 4. c 5. a

p. 619

Possible responses; accept other supported responses:
1. body; gives a fact 2. body; gives a fact 3. introduction; gets attention 4. body; gives a fact 5. introduction; gets attention 6. body; gives a fact 7. conclusion; sums up 8. body; gives a fact 9. body; gives a fact 10. conclusion; sums up, leaves reader interested in topic

p. 620

A. Underline 1, 2, 4, 6 B. Possible response: Young children learn through play. Wise parents and teachers provide many opportunities for a variety of play experiences.

p. 621

Possible responses: Striking beginning: My grandfather used to threaten to make grasshopper gravy, just as other people do around the world. Concrete details: 1, 5, 6, 7, 8. Quotation: 9.

p. 622

Possible responses: 2. During this period, the Industrial Revolution, a new society was created. 3. A spinner, James Hargreaves, invented a new spinning machine. 4. The new machine, the spinning jenny, could spin eight threads at once. 5. Edmund Cartwright invented a water-powered loom. 6. Eli Whitney invented a cotton gin in 1793.

p. 623–624

Can you imagine an animal that seems to be part mammal, ⌃ part reptile, and part bird? If you succeed, you will probably imagine an animal very much like the duckbill, also called a platypus.

Animals that bear their young alive and nurse their young are classified, ⌃ as mammals. Duckbills nurse their young as mammals do, but they lay eggs as birds do. Although scientists classify the duckbill as a kind of (mammmil,) it has characteristics of other animal groups.

In appearance, the duckbill most closely resembles a duck ⊙ like a duck, it has a large bill ⊙ it also has webbed feet, fur, and a flat tail like a beaver's.

Most mammals are warm-blooded. Their body temperature remains the same regardless of the temperature ⌀ Øf their surroundings. A duckbill is cold-blooded like a reptile ⊙ its body temperature changes with the temperature of its surroundings.

Duckbills die ⌀ In captivity, so they must be studied in their natural homes.

p. 631

1. Barbara was surprised because she had heard the bats make lots of sounds, including buzzes, squeals, and chirps, but she had never heard them sing like a bird before.
2. Usually, the bats liked to roost together. Sometimes they had little fights, but they always got over them quickly and made up with each other. All this made Barbara curious about why the bats were fighting more often. 3. Amanda Lollar is a licensed expert in the care of Mexican free-tailed bats like the ones Barbara kept, which means she would probably be able to answer Barbara's questions. 4. Be sure that your child identifies the report's main ideas and includes significant details. Spelling, punctuation, capitalization, and grammar should be correct.

p. 632

1. The writer introduced the topic of the report, bats, in the first paragraph. 2. The writer lists all of the sounds that Barbara's bats usually make (chirps, buzzes, and squeals). Then the writer tells us that Barbara had never heard this song before. 3. The fifth paragraph explains how the bats usually act and tells the reader that Hank was different. In the next paragraph, the writer gives specific examples of how Hank's behavior was different from that of the other bats. 4. The first paragraph tells the reader that Barbara would make a scientific discovery. In the last paragraph, the writer explains that the behaviors Barbara observed helped scientists learn more about the bats' mating behaviors.

TEST PREP

p. 644–646

1. A 2. H 3. A 4. G 5. D 6. They might get angry. If you provoke someone you try to start a fight. 7. G 8. B 9. F 10. claws

p. 647–651

1. B 2. F 3. It is located in Toronto. 4. A 5. Mendel wanted to know why pea plants had different traits. 6. F 7. A 8. Mendel discovered a plant receives genes from its parents. 9. J 10. C 11. Richard should water the tree thoroughly 12. F 13. San Francisco, California 14. A 15. G

p. 652–655

1. D 2. H 3. D 4. The main idea is that police can use germs to solve crimes. 5. J 6. The main idea is that taking a break while working can help you think more clearly. 7. D 8. H 9. C 10. The jobs in which men and women work have changed over time. 11. F 12. C 13. The story is mostly about how animals protect themselves in different ways.

p. 656–657

1. C 2. F 3. Once Matt cleared the candy from her throat, Chris could breathe and make sounds. 4. A 5. F 6. Dave will try to lift the beam off Hope.

p. 658–663

1. C 2. H 3. B 4. H 5. She was faster than the other girls. 6. B 7. G 8. Earlier suspension bridges weren't in areas with high winds. 9. D 10. F 11. Gartley's parents were hoping he would win. 12. C 13. G 14. The student felt cold and hungry.

p. 664–667

1. D 2. brave and clever 3. F 4. The author is trying to convince the reader that "natural" does not always mean healthy. 5. A 6. F 7. C 8. J 9. Hans was very poor. He wrote the story "The Ugly Duckling."

p. 668–676

SA. A 1. C 2. J 3. basketball 4. D 5. F 6. C 7. F 8. C 9. H 10. C 11. G 12. It did not run away. 13. C 14. G 15. B 16. F 17. B 18. The students perform skits to show what they have learned. 19. F 20. D 21. F 22. D 23. H 24. B 25. G 26. Everything has a name. 27. A 28. F 29. A 30. F 31. C 32. I would buy the cookbooks so my friends and I can cook together.

p. 677–683

SA. C 1. The ball is moved by passing it or swimming with it. 2. C 3. F 4. C 5. Soccer was first introduced to the United States in the early 1800s. 6. F 7. D 8. H

9. D 10. J 11. C 12. J 13. B 14. F 15. They like to see the picture of Maria's relatives and listen to her stories. 16. B 17. F 18. B 19. G 20. D 21. to prevent injury 22. H 23. C 24. G 25. Thomas Jefferson was the third president of the United States. He was also a writer, an architect, an inventor, and a music lover

p. 684

SA. A 1. D 2. G 3. C 4. F 5. C 6. G 7. A 8. blamed

p. 685

SA. B 1. C 2. G 3. D 4. I used the tissue to wipe my nose

p. 686

SA. C 1. D 2. F 3. C 4. G 5. D 6. dangerously careless

p. 687–689

SA. D 1. A 2. G 3. A 4. G 5. C 6. J 7. A 8. H 9. false SB. B 10. A 11. H 12. D 13. G 14. I took the negative to be developed. SC. C 15. B 16. J 17. C 18. F 19. D 20. F 21. A 22. shape

p. 691

Step 1. If Joey was paid $3 for each hour instead of $12 a day, would he earn more or less? Step 2. Joey worked 6 hours a day. He worked 42 days. He earned $12 a day. Step 3. Compare the amounts Joey earned by the day or by the hour. Step 4. $12/day or 6 hours × $3 = $18 Joey would earn $18 a day if he earns $3 each hour, which is more than $12 each day. Step 5. Yes, the answer compares the day and hourly rates.

p. 692

Step 1. Create a map to show Rosa's trip and time Step 2. Rosa walked 12 blocks to her friend's house. It took 20 minutes. Return trip took an extra 10 minutes and was 4 blocks longer. Step 3. Create a map that includes each fact.
Step 4. ◄------16 blocks 30 minutes----------

Step 5. Yes, because the map shows two routes, one longer than the other.

p. 693

SA. C 1. D 2. G 3. 6 1/3 4. C 5. G

p. 694

SA. C 1. B 2. H 3. B 4. H 5. 4,300 meters

p. 695

SA. B 1. C 2. F 3. A 4. G 5. C 6. 18 × 6 × 3 = 324

p. 696-697

SA. B 1. A 2. J 3. C 4. Because there is a 2/8 probability of the spinner stopping on "Go Back 2 Spaces" and a 1/8 probability of the spinner stopping on "Move Ahead 2 Spaces." 5. G 6. B 7. J 8. D 9. Orlando, Tampa, and Naples

p. 698-699

SA. B 1. B 2. G 3. A 4. F 5. C 6. J 7. C 8. (4,3)

p. 700-701

SA. A 1. B 2. H 3. C 4. There are 12 inches in a foot. Multiply 30 feet by 12 inches. 30 × 12 = 360. The answer is 360 inches. 5. G 6. C 7. G 8. A 9. J 10. B 11. The line is about 2 1/2 inches long. This represents 50 miles, since each inch equals 20 miles.

p. 702

SA. C 1. B 2. H 3. C 4. 28

p. 703

SA. C 1. A 2. H 3. A 4. J 5. D

p. 704

SA. C 1. C 2. G 3. D 4. We need to know how many of Elyse's friends were children and how many were adults.

p. 705-711

SA. B 1. D 2. F 3. C 4. G 5. D 6. F 7. three billion, four hundred twenty-one million, ninety-five thousand, eight hundred four 8. C 9. G 10. C 11. F 12. C 13. B, because the probability of choosing a B card is 4/10, which is greater than the probability of choosing any other card. 14. G 15. B 16. G 17. C 18. H 19. B 20. $47.10 21. H 22. A 23. Add the approximate saving for each month. Divide by four. The answer is $12. 24. H 25. D 26. F 27. B 28. F 29. C 30. J 31. Multiply the width of the rink by the height: 30 feet × 20 feet = 600 square feet. 32. B 33. G 34. D 35. J 36. Sam, Ralph, Chris, Ben 37. D 38. G 39. D 40. F 41. D 42. the current population

p. 712

SA. A 1. C 2. G 3. C 4. K 5. C 6. 5/28

p. 713-715

SA. C 1. B 2. H 3. D 4. 12-1/2% SA. B SB. G 1. C 2. H 3. C 4. G 5. D 6. F 7. E 8. You must find the lowest common denominator, which is 12. The answer is 1/12. 9. K 10. B 11. 40,000,000 12. H 13. A

p. 716-721

SA. B 1. C 2. H 3. B 4. F 5. B 6. G 7. C 8. F 9. A 10. Sentence #10, because it does not talk about Russell's plan for a faster mail delivery system. 11. J 12. C 13. G 14. A 15. H 16. A

p. 722

SA. B 1. A 2. G 3. A 4. J 5. A 6. G 7. A 8. J

p. 723-727

SB. B 1. D 2. Chapter 2 3. J 4. B 5. H 6. B 7. F 8. Sentence 2. I am learning about the wildlife in the Everglades. My family and I spend our days canoeing along marked waterways called trails. 9. D 10. H 11. A 12. J 13. C 14. H 15. D 16. F 17. C 18. J 19. B 20. H 21. A 22. H 23. B 24. H 25. A 26. J

p. 728-735

SA. D 1. C 2. They can be seen through thick fog. 3. J 4. A 5. H 6. C 7. F 8. High school students who qualified for the various events during the past year will participate in this swim meet. 9. B 10. G 11. B 12. G 13. D 14. H 15. Laura wants to enter the contest so she can meet Ms. Blalock and submit a story. 16. A 17. F 18. C 19. J 20. B 21. G 22. C 23. G 24. Arizona, New Mexico, Utah 25. C 26. F 27. B 28. G 29. B 30. Not all inventions are successes.

p. 736-738

SA. C 1. D 2. F 3. C 4. F 5. D 6. G 7. B 8. H 9. B SB. C 10. H 11. C 12. J 13. B 14. F SC. C 15. A 16. J 17. B 18. J 19. C 20. F 21. distant

p. 739-747

SA. B 1. D 2. H 3. B 4. H 5. B 6. J 7. 4.04, 4.09, 4.63, 4.7 8.10 9. C 10. G 11. D 12. H 13. A 14. F 15. D 16. F 17. B 1 8. H 19. B 20. 18 21. G 22. D 23. F 24. D 25. 2/7 26. H 27. 12 inches 28. B 29. F 30. D 31. J 32. D 33. G 34. A 35. (4,2) 36. F 37. C 38. Add all four sides together. 8 inches 39. H 40. D 41. H 42. B 43. F 44. B 45. H 46. A 47. Stephanie's height 48. F 49. B 50. H 51. A 52. H 53. 400

p. 748-750

SA. D SB. G 1. D 2. H 3. B 4. F 5. B 6. K 7. D 8. 56,940 9. J 10. D 11. F 12. A 13. G

p. 751-757

SA. B 1. D 2. J 3. He should make an outline of ideas to include in his report. 4. B 5. J 6. C 7. F 8. B 9. F 10. C 11. J 12. Consider the kind of fish and how many fish you want to raise. 13. B 14. J 15. C 16. H 17. D 18. F 19. B 20. F 21. D 22. G 23. A 24. H 25. B 26. G 27. D 28. F 29. A 30. H 31. A